Lecture Notes of the Institute for Computer Sciences, Social Informatics and Telecommunications Engineering 299

More information about this series at http://www.springer.com/series/8197

Guanglu Sun · Jianhou Gan · Shuai Liu ·
Fei Lang · Zeguang Lu (Eds.)

e-Learning, e-Education, and Online Training

5th EAI International Conference, eLEOT 2019
Kunming, China, August 18–19, 2019
Proceedings

Springer

Editors
Guanglu Sun
Harbin University of Science
and Technology
Harbin, China

Shuai Liu
Hunan Normal University
Hunan, China

Zeguang Lu
Institute of Data Science
National Academy of Guo Ding
Harbin, China

Jianhou Gan
Yunnan Normal University
Kunming, China

Fei Lang
Harbin University
Harbin, China

ISSN 1867-8211 ISSN 1867-822X (electronic)
Lecture Notes of the Institute for Computer Sciences, Social Informatics
and Telecommunications Engineering
ISBN 978-3-030-35094-9 ISBN 978-3-030-35095-6 (eBook)
https://doi.org/10.1007/978-3-030-35095-6

This Springer imprint is published by the registered company Springer Nature Switzerland AG
The registered company address is: Gewerbestrasse 11, 6330 Cham, Switzerland

Preface

We are delighted to introduce the proceedings of the 5th edition of the 2019 European Alliance for Innovation (EAI) International Conference on e-Learning, e-Education, and Online Training (eLEOT 2019), held in the city of perpetual spring: Kunming, China. This conference has brought together researchers, developers, and practitioners from around the world who are leveraging and developing the research and applications of e-Learning, e-Education, and online training among the international scientific community. The main purpose of this conference series is to address the most recent and innovative trends in this broad area, ranging from distance education to collaborative learning, from interactive learning environments to the modeling of STEM (science, technology, mathematics, engineering) curricula. The program of this year's edition of eLEOT was especially interesting, as it covered the advancements in the ICT sector, the most effective educational paradigms, the most prominent learning strategies, and several other related topics, which were brought to the attention of our community by engaged authors who sent their contributions from all around the world.

This year, the technical program of eLEOT 2019 consisted of 99 full papers, including 5 invited papers in oral presentation sessions at the main conference tracks. At least three Technical Program Committee (TPC) members were assigned for each submitted paper during the rigorous, peer-review phase. At the end of the reviewing process, 46 papers (acceptance rate: 47%) were accepted as they met the requirements of scientific quality, novelty, and relevance set by the conference. The conference tracks were: Track 1 – Blended Learning and Social Network; Track 2 – Best Practices and Teaching/Educational Models; Track 3 – Assessment and Learning Analytics; Track 4 – Massive Open Online Course; and Track 5 – New Technology Applied in Education. Aside from the high-quality technical paper presentations, the technical program also featured two keynote speeches. The two keynote speeches were Prof. Zhijun Yang from Yunnan Institute of Educational Sciences, China, and Prof. Fei Lang from Harbin University of Science and Technology, China.

The coordination with the Steering Committee chairs, Prof. Imrich Chlamtac and Prof. Giovanni Vincenti, proved to be key to the success of this event, as well as the precious contribution of the general chair, Prof. Guanglu Sun, the general co-chair, Prof. Jian Liu, and the local chair, Prof. Tianwei Xu. We also wish to thank the publications chairs, Prof. Fei Lang, Prof. Suxia Zhu, and Zeguang Lu, the TPC chairs, Prof. Shuai Liu and Prof. Jianhou Gan, and all the other conference chairs for their valuable support during all phases leading to the hosting of this conference. Special thanks also to our EAI conference manager, Karolina Marcinova, and to our EAI proceedings editor, Lucia Sedlarova, for their constant dedication and help during all these months. We would also like to thank the city of Kunming for hosting the conference and all the authors who attended the event for their participation. We hope that the readers find several interesting research themes and insights into the topics in this volume and that they are encouraged to participate in the future editions of eLEOT!

Guanglu Sun
Jian Liu
Shuai Liu
Jianhou Gan

Organization

Steering Committee

Imrich Chlamtac	University of Trento, Italy

Organizing Committee

General Chair

Guanglu Sun	Harbin University of Science and Technology

General Co-chair

Jian Liu	Yunnan Normal University

TPC Chair and Co-chair

Shuai Liu	Inner Mogolia University
Jianhou Gan	Yunnan Normal University

Sponsorship and Exhibit Chair

Wei Zhong	Yunnan Normal University

Local Chairs

Tianwei Xu	Yunnan Normal University
Juxiang Zhou	Yunnan Normal University

Workshops Chair

Zhijun Yang	Scientific Research Institute of Education

Publicity and Social Media Chair

Ao Li	Harbin University of Science and Technology

Publications Chairs

Fei Lang	Harbin University of Science and Technology
Suxia Zhu	Harbin University of Science and Technology
Zeguang Lu	National Academy of Guo Ding Institute of Data Science

Web Chair

Jing Qiu	Harbin University of Science and Technology

Posters and PhD Track Chair

Bin Wen	Yunnan Normal University
Juxiang Zhou	Yunnan Normal University

Panels Chairs

Wenxing Hong	Xia Men University
Shuren Li	Chinese Academy of Sciences

Demos Chair

Lin Tang	Yunnan Normal University

Tutorials Chair

Mingjing Tang	Yunnan Normal University

Technical Program Committee

Guanglu Sun	Harbin University of Science and Technology
Juxiang Zhou	Yunnan Normal University
Mingjing Tang	Kunming University of Science and Technology
Nan Zhang	Yunnan Normal University
Suxia Zhu	Harbin University of Science and Technology
Wei Zhong	Yunnan University
Songling Tian	Tianjin University
Lingyun Yuan	Yunnan Normal University
Min Xie	Kunming University of Science and Technology
Fei Lang	Harbin University of Science and Technology
Hui Yao	Kunming University of Science and Technology
Hongyan Shi	Inner Mongolia University for the Nationalities
Wei Yan	Hebei University of Technology
Jing Qiu	Harbin University of Science and Technology
Xianming Yao	Yunnan Normal University
Chao Yang	Yunnan University
Jun Wang	Kunming University of Science and Technology
Deqiang Yang	Yunnan Normal University
Chengyan Li	Harbin University of Science and Technology
Lin Tang	Yunnan University
Xiaoqiang Wu	Inner Mongolia University for the Nationalities
Jianhou Gan	Yunnan Normal University
Yaming Zhang	Yunnan University
Zhiyong Luo	Harbin University of Science and Technology
Bo Zhao	Yunnan Normal University

Contents

Blended Learning and Social Network

Design and Implementation of Adaptive Push APP Based on Android for Fragmented English Reading Resources

Jianmin Zhang[1,2], Min Xie[1,2](✉), Bo Yuan[1,2], and Min Wang[1,2]

[1] Yunnan Normal University, Kunming 650500, China
294611018@qq.com
[2] Key Laboratory of Educational Information for Nationalities, Ministry of Education, Kunming 650500, China

Abstract. In the situation of mobile fragmentation learning, learning methods are becoming more and more mobile, and learning resources for English reading are becoming more and more abundant. It is difficult for learner to find the resources needed for his personalized learning quickly. This paper designs the five-dimensional characteristics of learner and the three-dimensional features of English reading resources in the fragmented learning environment. Combined with the ID3 algorithm, an auto-adaptive recommendation model for fragmented English reading resources is constructed. Based on this, and then according on the principles and methods of software engineering, an auto-adaptive recommendation APP for fragmented English reading resources based on Android is designed and implemented from three aspects: system analysis, system design and key technology implementation, to improve learner's English reading ability by pushing English reading resources that meet learner's individualized needs.

Keywords: Fragmentation learning · Adaptive push · Mobile learning APP · English reading · Design and implementation

1 Introduction

The revised edition of the College English Syllabus states: "The purpose of college English teaching is to train students to have a strong reading ability and a certain ability to listen, speak, read, write and translate, so that they can communicate in English." [1] Under the requirements, the reading comprehension in CET-4 (abbreviate for College English Test Band 4) test always has a high rating. This not only puts higher requirements on the reading ability of candidates, but also brings severe challenges to college English teaching of reading. It can be seen that English reading plays a central role in English learning and is the main goal of English learning. English reading is also a necessary content for various examinations or daily applications.

Fragmented English learning in mobile context has become more and more important. Whether in public or in school libraries, many college students choose mobile devices for English learning. Fragmented learning is based on digital learning and is effectively combined with mobile computing technology to enable students to

G. Sun et al. (Eds.): eLEOT 2019, LNICST 299, pp. 3–18, 2019.
https://doi.org/10.1007/978-3-030-35095-6_1

learn English at any time and any place. On the one hand, it can be a reasonable use of fragmentation time, which is a trend of learning at present; on the other hand, many English learning APPs have been designed some very good functions, such as punching sign, which can promote learner to develop good study habits.

English reading resources are rich, diverse in form, and highly shared. While bringing convenience to people, it also brings about the problem of information overload. In the face of massive information, learner cannot quickly get the information that is truly valuable to him. Reading is a complex cognitive process, but the existing English reading APPs only do the plans based on learning objectives and learning needs when resources are pushed, or push English reading resources to learner according to his learning preferences, but not fully considering the change of the learner in the dynamic learning process. So it is difficult to constantly adjust the resources of the next push according to the change of the learner. When the APP-based learning method is adopted by more and more people, the problem in learning adaptability of learner in this environment is becoming more and more prominent. It is difficult for learner to achieve real online self-learning, and it is more difficult to obtain adaptive learning resources [2]. How to help student find the learning resources quickly and accurately which are suitable for his needs in the process of mobile learning? So there is personalized recommendation. It enables information consumers to get information they need quickly, moreover it can also provide predicted information to users in a targeted manner, and strive to push the information that the target users want most. The e-commerce APP and the English word APP have made a good exploration in this respect, but there are almost few English reading APPs for auto-adaptive pushing in English reading resources. Therefore, how to combine fragmented English reading with auto-adaptive push in the fragmented learning of mobile context, construct an auto-adaptive resources push model based on Android, and develop an auto-adaptive resources push APP with fragmentation features? It has become one of the research topics in the mobilization of English reading.

According to the learner's learning model in the learning process (English reading ability, cognitive style, learning target, learning situation and learning result) and the characteristics of English reading resource model (question type, theme and difficulty), Jianmin, Min and Bin [3] used machine-learning algorithms, also known as ID3 algorithm to construct a learning recommendation model for learning resources in fragmented reading. In order to test the feasibility and results of auto-adaptive resources recommendation model in fragmented English reading, this paper uses the principles of software engineering to determine the learning needs of target learners. Through functional analysis, the relationship between the functional modules included in the platform and the relationships between modules were determined. After that, a database of fragmented English reading resources was built. Finally, using the C/S architecture system, Android studio, Visual Studio, and SQL Server development tools, the learning resource adaptive recommendation APP for fragmented English reading is designed and implemented.

2 Overview of Adaptive Recommendation of Mobile Learning Resources

2.1 Fragmented English Reading

Compared to "integrated" reading, incomplete, intermittent reading patterns through new media such as mobile phones and mobile networks are referred to as fragmented reading [4]. With the help of mobile terminals such as smart phones and mobile networks, learner can receive huge amounts of information anytime and anywhere. The information and knowledge in the learning process seem to be at your fingertips, and reading is easy and easy [5]. Fragmented English reading is to learn English by means of Fragmentation Reading in a mobile fragmented environment.

2.2 Adaptive Learning System

The Adaptive Learning System (ALS) is an active learning system that is based on the "learner-centered" educational philosophy and proposes individual differences for current learner, (such as age, professional background, interest preferences, cognitive level, etc.), and dynamically provide a system for personalized learning support services. The adaptive learning system was first introduced in the field of foreign intelligent teaching systems and adaptive hypermedia systems. In recent years, it has become a hot spot in the field of E-Learning distance education [6, 7]. With the help of the adaptive learning system, learner can monitor his own learning process and choose the learning content and learning strategy that suits him best according to their actual needs [8].

At present, the English learning APP on the mobile phone is becoming more and more popular in young people. It is more common to use the fragmented learning method for English reading and learning. The goal of these APPs is to provide learner with personalized learning, that is, according to learner's learning interests, behaviors in the learning process, learning history and learning level, and other characteristics, to push adaptive learning resources for learner through a certain algorithm. This provides a learning path that meets the learner's individual needs.

2.3 Adaptive Push Model of Learning Resources in English Fragmented Reading

Referring to Jianmin Zhang, Min Xie and Bin Wen, an *adaptive recommendation model for learning resources in fragmented English Reading* [3] was constructed in the article Adaptive Pushing of Learning Resources in Fragmented English Reading, as shown in Fig. 1.

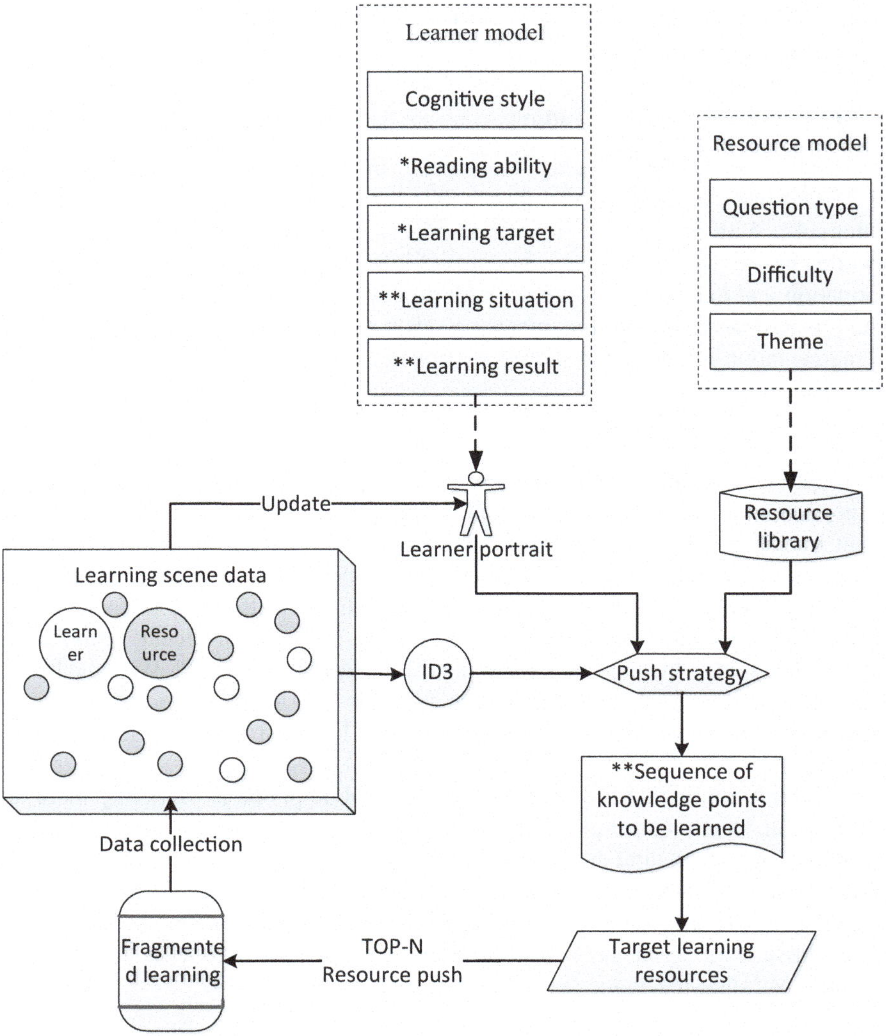

Fig. 1. Adaptive learning resources pushing model in English fragmented reading

Note: (1) In the learning scene, the white circle represents learners, and the gray circle represents the learning resources fragmented.
(2) "*" represents the relative stability of data. Items without "*" are more stable, items with "*" take a longer time to update, and items with "**" update the fastest.

On the basis of literature review, it is found that in fragmented learning environment, learner models can be established according to learner's reading ability, cognitive style, learning target, learning situations, learning result and other information in the four-level English reading. Then extract the feature information of English reading resources, and establish the connection between learner model and learning resources. Thereafter, based on the feature information of the learner, the sequence of knowledge points to be learned is generated. Based on this sequence, the push strategy is determined, the learning path is planned, and the learning resources are pushed.

The learner model shows that in order to realize the self-adaptive push of resources, the system needs to understand 4 aspects, that are what level the learner is at, what goals he want to achieve, where and how to learn, and how the effect is based on resource push learning. Among them, the assessment of learner's reading ability is based on CET-4 syllabus. It is mainly based on *the Chinese English Reading Ability Rating Scale* [10] and the seven factors mentioned in the article *A Study on the Structure and Development of College Students' English Reading Ability* [11]. And an assessment scale for English reading ability is developed. Cognitive styles are mainly field-dependent and field-independent. Students with different cognitive styles also have different interests in reading, thinking patterns, learning strategies and the impact of environment on them [9]. The vocabulary size and the accuracy of CET-4 are the main learning target. Learning situation mainly considers the decibels of the noise level of the current learner's geographical location in mobile debris learning environment. Learning result is mainly feedback through the correct rate of the problem of the learner in the complex learning situation.

The question types, theme, and difficulty of reading materials have a greater impact on learner. Different types of questions essentially examine different ways of thinking. Based on different growth environment, learners have different familiarity with reading materials on different subjects, and the results of the questions vary greatly. However, subjects with different degrees of difficulty require learners to be at different levels of learning. Understanding these differences in reading materials, the system can push resources more specifically for learner. This study extracts the feature information of English reading resources from the three-dimensional degree of topic type, subject matter and difficulty level of reading resources, and establishes a three-dimensional reading resource feature model. Question types are mainly considered from factual details, inference problem, semantic comprehension problem, main idea and the attitude of view problem. Theme is mainly considered from the humanities and social sciences and natural sciences. The difficulty mainly lies in people's experience of careful reading of Level 4 to decide which is difficult or easy.

On this basis, by collecting learner characteristics and resource characteristics information, the decision tree ID3 algorithm is used to establish the decision tree of resource push, from which the rules of resource push can be found. ID3 will be used to achieve the push of CET-4 careful reading resources in mobile fragmentation learning situation and meet the individual learning needs of learner.

3 Systems Analysis

3.1 Requirement Analysis

Faced with the rapid expansion and rapid renewal of knowledge, people are always eager to learn more knowledge to cope the rapidly changing times. Some developers have caught people's changes in this demand and developed a lot of learning APPs, but most of them lack in theory of teaching design, and just concentrate a large amount of resources. Seemingly very human, but it forced people to face with more multiple choices when using these APPs. It making them even more confused and do not knowing where to start. As a result, learning is like finding a needle in a haystack, and nothing is achieved.

Therefore, in the fragmented learning situation, it is urgent to solve the problem of auto-adaptive push of English reading resources. By collecting the learner's characteristics, resource characteristics, and the degree of influence of the environment (volume) on the learner in the process of the using of the APP, we can determine the learning demand based on the learning history data and adapt to push resources to help learner get the information he need quickly when the learner log in again [12]. On the other hand, the APP should also aim at the module of "Careful Reading" of CET-4, with the guide of relevant theories of fragmented learning in mobile context, and learner-centered, providing learner's needs for autonomous learning, and provides the possibility for learner to learn fragmented English reading in mobile environment. Therefore, the APP should include five core modules: login registration, context acquisition, learning resources recommendation, independent practice and learning process.

In addition to functional requirements, the APP should also have non-functional requirements. The APP should also be secure, simple to operate, and with appropriate openness to meet the future needs of users.

3.2 Target User Analysis

The main target users of App are undergraduates preparing for CET-4 and students who are willing to use App to improve their English read. Young students can quickly adapt to the popular new learning style of mobile fragmentation learning. This kind of learner has the following characteristics:

1. The frequency of using mobile devices and the willingness of mobile learning is higher. Mobile devices have become a necessity in people's daily life, and "carry-on" has become a habit of the youth. Because the purpose of this kind of learner is to obtain CET-4 certificate, most of them attach great importance to it. They often use the learning software in the intelligent terminal to study English. Therefore, they need a lot of mobile and fragmented English learning.
2. Limited learning time and easy to be interrupted. Most of these learners will make full and reasonable use of the fragmented and scattered time in their spare time for mobile fragmentation learning. Because of the short learning time and the complex

and diverse learning scenarios, it is easy to lead to the distraction of learner's learning attention. Therefore, in space-time of mobile fragmentation learning, English reading resources should be segmented reasonably and effectively.

3. Personalized demand is highly, and focuses on using experience. In the era of information explosion, it is difficult for the youth to find content that meets their personalized needs from mass information in a short time. Choosing an APP, the younger generation pays more attention to whether it can provide personalized learning services to help learner acquire learning resources quickly and accurately. In addition, there are so many learning APPs in the market, and the youth pays more attention to the UI design and user experience of APP.

3.3 Feasibility Analysis

Economic viability includes pre-investment, mid-maintenance and post-application and improvement. The pre-investment mainly includes the design, feasibility evaluation and cost of system development. In terms of software, based on the Windows operating system, with the client running on Android Studio 3.2.0, the server is deployed on IIS, and use ASP.NET WebAPI of Visual Studio 2013 to build framework. The database uses SQL Server 2008 R2. Therefore, these development tools can be easily obtained on the network. In terms of hardware, the server is deployed on personal computer through the network operation environment of the campus network (local area network), so there is no need to spend a lot of money to purchase server.

Mid-term maintenance requires only a simple back up the system regularly.

In terms of later application and harvest, for students, they only need to connect to the campus network WIFI to use this APP without logging in the account, thus saving the learning cost. Therefore, the system can bring great benefits in terms of economic feasibility.

In terms of technical feasibility, Android Studio is currently popular Android front-end development tool. Development based on Android is easier. ASP.NET has been recognized by many software manufacturers, and a large number of enterprises are using this technology for development. In addition, the SQL Server database uses the SQL language to manipulate data, which is easy to understand. ASP.NET+SQL Server as development platform on network has been quite mature, so it is feasible to use to build a Web Server. Combined with Android Studio front-end development, it is technically feasible to realize the development of an adaptive learning resource push APP for fragmented English reading.

In terms of application, more and more colleges and universities have used digital learning platforms to carry out education and teaching activities for many years, and mobile terminals are more favored by the younger generation. However, with the rapid growth of information, people's demand for personalization is getting higher and higher. At present, it is almost impossible to find resource recommendation function in mobile learning APP, in particular, there are few mobile terminals that push CET4 "carefully read" resources in the form of fragmented learning. Therefore, there is a great demand for the learning resource auto-adaptive push platform in fragmented English reading.

4 System Design

4.1 System Architecture Design

The purpose of system construction is to better help decision makers to formulate future recommendation strategies through effective data collection, so that the weak links in learning can be targeted and intensively trained. The general architecture of the adaptive push APP of English fragmented reading resources is shown in Fig. 2. The general framework of the system is divided into five levels, including the base layer, data layer, service layer, application layer and user layer.

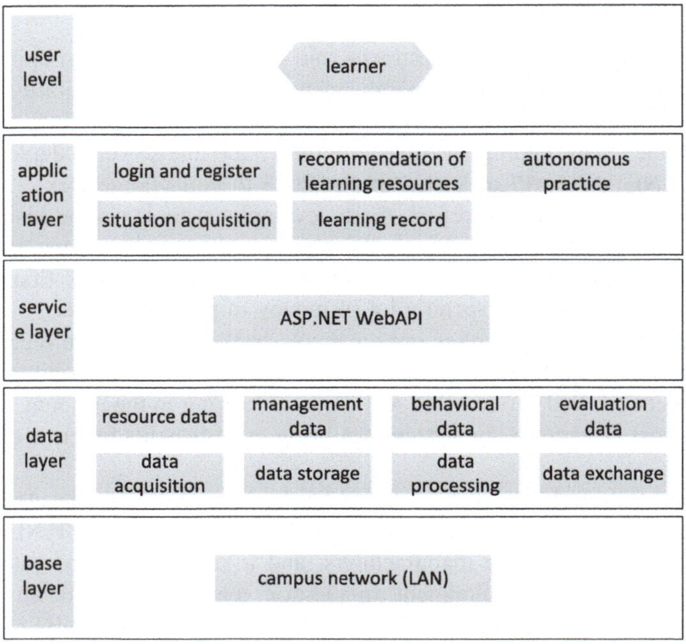

Fig. 2. General framework of system

1. Base layer
   The base layer is the lowest layer of the system architecture, mainly based on the campus network (local area network) to support the network service of the auto-auto-adaptive learning resource recommendation system to meet the requirements of network service of the system.

2. Data layer
   The data layer is the second layer of the system framework, which is mainly for operating and managing system data, including resource data, management data and behavioral data. The resource data includes English reading resources, cognitive style test resources and English reading ability scale test resources. Management data includes student personal information, software information, etc. Behavioral data includes learner's behavior data, self-designed learning plan and the semester test, etc. The evaluation data includes exercise results. The data layer is mainly for collecting, processing, exchanging and storing the above data.
3. Service layer
   The service layer is the middle layer of the general architecture of the system, which is used to connect the data layer and the service layer. The service layer is mainly used to support the system to provide application services for users at the application layer. The ASP.NET WebAPI framework is mainly used to quickly provide API for HTTP clients to create Web services.
4. Application layer
   The application layer presents an adaptive learning service that the auto-adaptive learning resource recommendation system ultimately provides for learner. It mainly embodies the functions of login and registration, learning resources recommendation, independent practice, situation acquisition, and learning record provided by the system. Among them, login and registration are used for authentication and reading ability, and cognitive style test. Learning resource recommendation is mainly used for the system to recommend learning resources for learner. Autonomous exercises are mainly used for learner to learn according to their own learning needs, selecting the learning module and autonomous setting plans to learn. The situational acquisition is mainly to obtain the environmental volume of the current user's geographical location, thereby judging the influence of the annoyance of the geographical volume on the learning. The learning record mainly records the current learner's basic information and learning behavior.
5. User layer
   The user layer is the mainly layer which the system directly contacts the users, and is the outermost layer of the system architecture. In the fragmented English reading, most of the user of the learning resources auto-adaptive push system is learners who are preparing for CET-4, and this system aims to provide learning services for them.

4.2 Function Module Design

The fragmented English reading resource auto-adaptive push APP has five main functional modules, including user center module (which include two modules of login registration and learning record), autonomous practice module, context acquisition module and auto-adaptive resource recommendation module, as shown in Fig. 3.

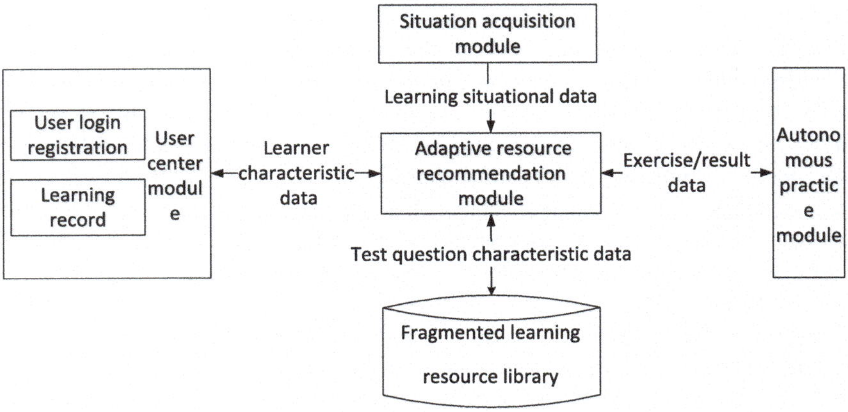

Fig. 3. System function model

The fragmented learning resource library is consisting with "carefully read" of CET-4, which is a fragmented reading resource that is reasonably segmented. In order to meet the characteristics of the fragmented learning situation, the reading materials are segmented according to the title and the dry information to meet the needs of fragmented learning when determines the length of reading resources.

The user center module includes user's registration (cognitive style test and reading ability test), learning record (viewing the wrong title set, reading history, reading progress, and setting the learning plan), managing the basic information that the current learner learns in the APP and records of learning behaviors.

The situation acquisition module dynamically acquires the volume decibel of the current environment during the learning process of the learner, so that the system can monitor the learning dynamics of the learner in real time, which is beneficial to the system to obtain the learner's learning data, and the recommendation strategy is more accurate and targeted.

The autonomous practice module is that the current learner chooses the learning content to train according to his needs. The APP has a selection of English reading learning resources classified according to different types, including five classification methods: test time, question type, subject matter, and by difficulty.

The auto-adaptive resource recommendation module is based on the learner model and resource model of the learner in the learning process, and comprehensively analysis the learning resources that conform to its personalized characteristics provide the possibility for learner to learn English reading in the mobile fragmentation situation [13].

5 Key Technology

In the fragmented English reading resources auto-adaptive push application, the Android-based C/S architecture system is adopted. Android Studio is used to implement the client's functional part. Written in java language, the server is deployed on IIS.

The framework is built by ASP.NET WebAPI of Visual Studio. SQL Server is used to store the database. The server and the database are connected through the corresponding interface. And the server is deployed on the computer through the specific IP address and port number in the campus network by using the convenience of the campus network. Communication principle: after the client sends a http request to the server, the server parses the data, and then indirectly accesses the database and returns the data from the server to the client. After the client obtains the data in the JSON format from the server, the program will parse these data quickly. After the analysis is completed, the results will be displayed to users through the interface of the mobile intelligent terminal, as shown in Fig. 4.

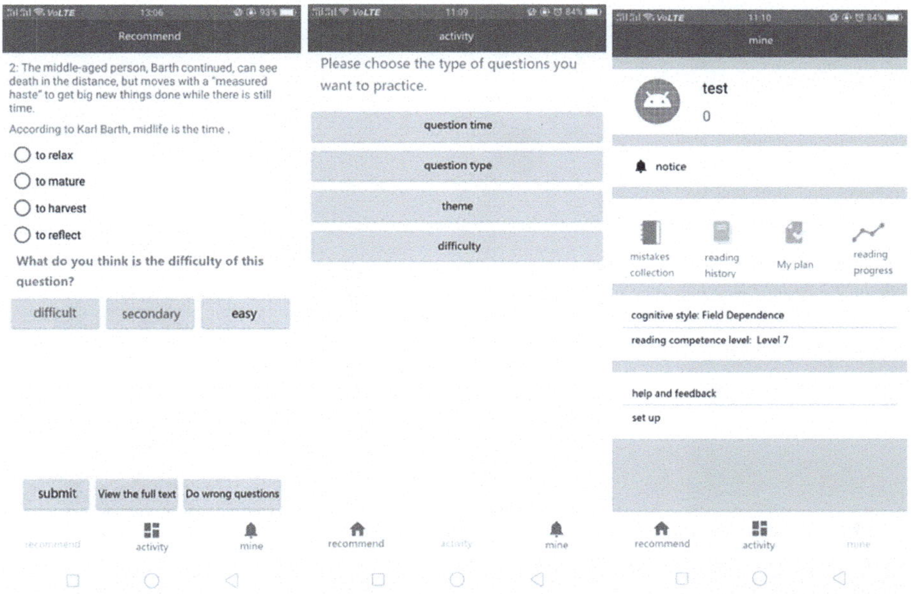

Fig. 4. Some of the system interface

5.1 Resource Push

In the process of mobile learning, it is difficult for learner to find the learning resources that are suitable for individual from massive resources quickly and accurately. This is the core problem that the auto-adaptive learning resource recommendation APP needs to solve in this paper, and is also the key technical point. By collecting the characteristic data of the learner in the learning process, and combining with the three-dimensional characteristics of the reading resources, the machine learning algorithm-ID3 decision tree algorithm is used to comprehensive analysis for auto-adaptive resource recommendation.

After the learner successfully logs in, the userId of the current learner is obtained, and the server API is accessed by GET() mode; the user information is obtained by the UserId. If the user is logged in for the first time, it is recommend based on the user's cognitive style test and English reading ability test during the registration process. If he is an old user, it will through the ID3 decision tree algorithm for comprehensive recommendation based on the learner's characteristics and learning behavior (cognitive style, reading ability, learning goal, learning plan, and learning result) to find matching questions in the database. Then encapsulate the relevant information of the title, options, corresponding articles, answers, etc. into an object PractisePackage, and use the JSON format to transfer to the front-end APP. The client uses the WebView control to display the returned data, which is equivalent to a browser is embedded in the client to load and display the web page. And the sliding answer effect answers of the selected questions, options, related articles which parsed by client, is achieved by ViewPager +fragment. The learning resources recommendation interface is shown in Fig. 5.

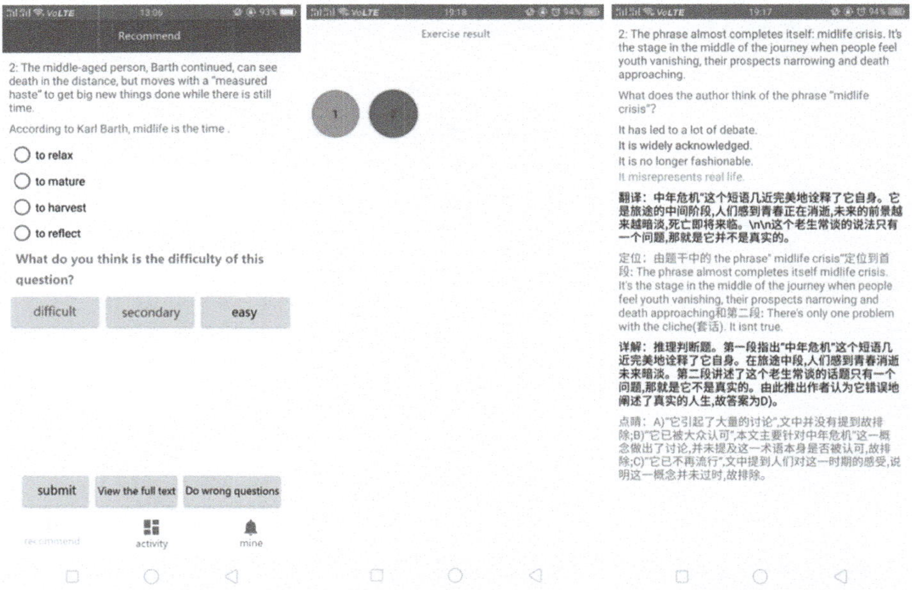

Fig. 5. Learning resource recommendation interface

The ID3 algorithm first acquires learner's characteristics, resources features and classification properties. Then stores them in a two-dimensional array, and preprocesses the discrete data to normalize it. According to ID3 algorithm, the information gain of each attribute is calculated by the formula. Compare the information gain of these attributes, and use the attribute with the largest information gain as the test attribute of the S set, that is, the root node of the decision tree [14]. The flow chart of the algorithm design is shown in Fig. 6.

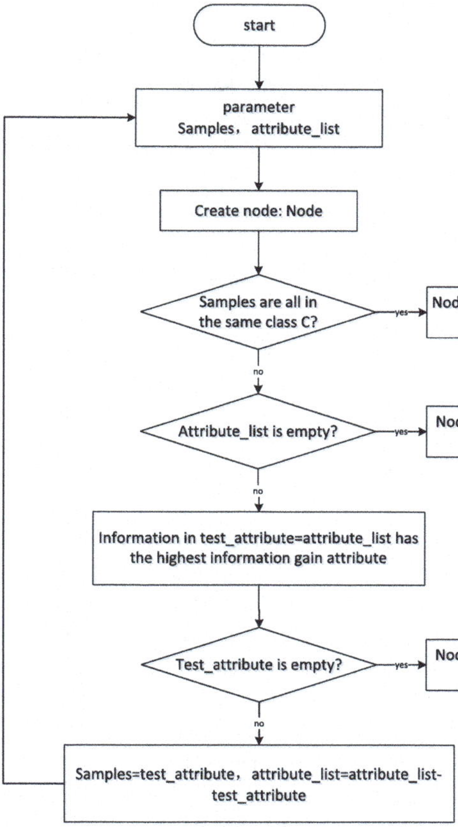

Fig. 6. Flow chart of decision tree algorithm

The algorithm is described in pseudocode as follows:

Input: training sample set; candidate attribute_list
Output: Decision Tree
Method:

```
Function ID3_Decision_Tree (samples, attribute-list)
{
      Create a node: Node;
         IF samples is in the same category C then
            return Node is a node with class C tags;
         IF attribute-list is Null then
            return Node is the leaf node and is labelled as the most common class
      in samples;
```

```
        select the highest gain attribute test-attribute from attribute-list;
          mark the attribute attribute-list as node: Node;
          known values for each test-attribute Ai;
          according to the condition test-attribute=a_i, the node Node is divided
    into a new branch;
          let Si be the set of test-attribute=a_i samples in samples;
          IF S_i is Null THEN
            add a leaf node and mark it as the most common class in samples;
       ELSE
            add a node returned by ID3_Decision_Tree (S_i, attribute-list);
}
```

5.2 Web API Based on ASP.NET

The back-end framework of web server uses ASP.NET WebAPI to provide a new framework for HTTP services, using GET, POST and other methods to request or respond to requests or return media types, providing Web services for mobile terminals. The APP client uses the HTTP protocol to access the network. The working principle is that the client wants the server to issue an HTTP request. After receiving the request, the server will return some data to the client, and then the client parses and processes the data. Fragmented English reading auto-adaptive resource push APP accesses the network by HttpURLConnection() method, and uses a computer in the campus network (LAN) as a server. Therefore, in the case of acquiring HttpURLConnection, we only need to create a new URL object based on our computer's IP and specific port number, and pass in the target's network address, then call openConnection () method to access the network. In the data interaction between the client and the server, generally we will transfer some formatted data on the network which have certain structure and semantics. When the other party receives the data message, it can parse by the same structural specifications, and get the part he wants. Therefore, this APP used the GSON open source library provided by Google to parse JSON data and implement the formatted data transmission on the network. The main advantage of JSON is its small size, which saves flow when transmitted over the network.

6 Conclusion

English reading is a complex process of cognition, and fragmented learning is characterized by fragmentation and dispersion of time and space, which inevitably leads to problems such as inattention of learner and fragmentation of knowledge construction in fragmented English reading. This study combines fragmented English reading with auto-adaptive resources push to provide learner with the possibility to learn English reading with mobile terminals in the context of fragmented learning. According to the learner characteristics and reading resources characteristics in the mobile fragmentation learning situation, combined with the machine learning algorithm ID3, the learning resources auto-adaptive push model in fragmented English reading based on Android is constructed. The APP pushes the resources close to the learner's personalized feature requirements auto-adaptively. In order to support fragmented English reading better, this paper use Android C/S architecture system, designed the architecture and functional modules of the auto-adaptive resources push APP for fragmented English reading. Through testing, it can provide users with real-time targeted learning resources push that meets individual needs, which enables learner to make rational use of fragmented time, and learn English reading anytime anywhere. Fragmented English reading as a new way of learning can effectively supplement the lack of traditional English reading learning. If learner can rational use of this APP with normal English learning, it will definitely improve the learning effect. Subsequent research can be carried out in the following areas:

- Improvement and optimization of ID3 algorithm in fragment English reading resources recommendation algorithm. Such as reduce the perspective consumption of the classifier, improve the accuracy of the recommendation and optimize the classification process, etc., to further improve the adaptability of the algorithm.
- Auxiliary recommendation for English vocabulary learning. A certain vocabulary is the basis of reading. In the subsequent work, four-level high frequency words in the English reading resources can be extracted for the learner to learn, and the vocabulary learner felling difficult may be mined according to the learner's learning behavior records, so as to meet the learner's need for mobile fragmented learning.
- Real-time access to learning situations. The fragmented learning situation in mobile learning may change at any time, and the noisy degree of the learning context in this APP is only acquired at first log in, which may lead to recommended learning resources not better adapted to changes in the learning environment.

Acknowledgments. The research is supported by a National Nature Science Fund Project (Nos. 61562093, 61661051), Key Project of Applied Basic Research Program of Yunnan Province (Nos. 2016FA024), Program for innovative research team (in Science and Technology) in University of Yunnan Province, Research Project of Undergraduate Education and Teaching Reform in Yunnan Normal University (Nos. YNJG201838) and Starting Foundation for Doctoral Research of Yunnan Normal University.

References

1. Hui, L.: Current situation analysis and promotion strategies of college English reading teaching. Occup. Time Space **6**(9), 122–123 (2010)
2. LuYan, Y.: Research on personalized knowledge recommendation technology in adaptive learning system. Chin. J. ICT Educ. **24**, 94–96 (2018)
3. Jianmin, Z., Min, X., Bin, W.: Auto-adaptive pushing of learning resources in fragmented English reading. Int. J. Perform. Eng. (IJPE) **15**(3), 884–894 (2019)
4. Chengbo, W., Xiaoping, L., Fengnian, Z., Lin, Z.: Fragmented learning research in big data era. Audiov. Educ. Res. **36**(10), 26–30 (2015)

5. Guangkuo, Y.: Fragmented reading cannot replace traditional reading. Yunnan Daily. Night Talk in the Book World (12) (2010)
6. Lianjia, M.: Research on the adaptability of networked learning system. Res. Audiov. Educ. (5), 50–54 (2009)
7. Xuekong, Z., Xiaodong, X., Shirong, L.: Research on personalized recommendation service of auto-adaptive learning system under B/S mode. China Distance Educ. (10), 71–78 (2015)
8. Xiuqin, L.: Research on the creation of domain ontology in self-auto-adaptive learning system based on semantic web. Northeast Normal University (2008)
9. The Chinese English Competence Scale was officially issued by the Ministry of Education and the State Language Commission, 15 May 2018. http://www.china-language.gov.cn/yw/gjywxx/201804/t20180418_29983.html
10. Peipei, B., Jufen, Z.: A study on the structure and development of college students' English reading ability. J. Shaoxing Univ. Arts Sci. **24**(2), 116–120 (2004)
11. Luyao, G.: Improved decision tree ID3 algorithm and application. Electron. Technol. Softw. Eng. **13**, 153–154 (2018)
12. Sun, G., Song, Z., Liu, J., et al.: Feature selection method based on maximum information coefficient and approximate Markov blanket. Zidonghua Xuebao/acta Automatica Sinica **43** (5), 795–805 (2009)
13. Sun, G., Lang, F., Xue, Y.: Chinese chunking method based on conditional random fields and semantic classes. J. Harbin Inst. Technol. **43**(7), 135–139 (2011)
14. Yuzi, L., Pengqi, Z.: Application of improved ID3 algorithm in students' comprehensive skills assessment. J. Jiamusi Univ. (Nat. Sci. Ed.) **4**, 575–578 (2013)

Research on Blended Teaching Mode Based on Internet Plus

Xiaofeng Li(✉) and Qiushi Wang

Heilongjiang International University, Harbin 150025, China
mberse@126.com

Abstract. With the development of Internet technology, teaching methods are also constantly innovating. As a form of innovation in the Internet plus, blended teaching has produced a relatively important influence in the field of teaching. This paper uses content analysis method to analyze the existing online courses of modern educational technology, understand the current status of modern educational technology courses, and focus on the mixed teaching needs of modern educational technology. Determine the learner's current level of knowledge and skill level, and find out the gap between the modern educational technology teaching goal and the current learner's situation, from the learner's online learning, offline learning, learner learning starting point, and learning expectation. Investigate to understand the needs of learners in the upcoming blended instruction and propose strategies to meet learner needs.

Keywords: Modern educational technology · Blended teaching · Learning needs

1 Introduction

The learning needs analysis is to find out the gap between the current level of the learner and the teaching objectives of the course [1–3]. The demand analysis of the blended teaching form is to find out the actual needs of learners for online and offline learning. Based on the characteristics of modern educational technology courses and the definition of blended teaching concepts, this study proposes a demand strategy that satisfies blended teaching [4]. According to previous research results and through the investigation and analysis of normal students' online learning, offline face-to-face teaching, the starting point of and learning expectation for modern education technology course, it is believed that learners' realistic demands should be met from the following four aspects in order to carry out blended teaching [5].

2 The Strategy of Constructing Learning Resources to Meet the Learning Needs

The online resource design of modern educational technology blended teaching is the main body of blended teaching. Therefore, it is necessary to explore strategies to meet the learning needs from the perspective of teaching resource design.

G. Sun et al. (Eds.): eLEOT 2019, LNICST 299, pp. 19–23, 2019.
https://doi.org/10.1007/978-3-030-35095-6_2

(1) In terms of teaching video duration, according to statistical analysis, more than 50% of learners hope that the length of the teaching video is less than 20 min. Therefore, when teaching video production, a single instructional video should be controlled within 10 min, preferably within 8 min. Too long a teaching video can easily cause learners to learn fatigue and aversion to the course, and this will affect the learner's online learning.
(2) In terms of video format, more than 50% of learners like studio recording, teacher image + slideshow, and field shooting. In the production of teaching videos, the above three forms should be used to avoid the direct use of classroom lectures as online learning resources. This form of online learning resources is meaningless for blended teaching.
(3) In terms of weekly hours, according to statistics, learners believe that the learning time under the class should be controlled within 2 h. Due to the characteristics of the modern educational technology curriculum itself, the teaching content is numerous, and the proportion of learning time between online and offline is an important issue that should be considered by designers of modern educational technology courses.

3 Strategies for Modern Educational Technology Course to Meet Learning Needs

(1) Make the teaching contents of modern educational technology course more targeted
The performance goal of modern educational technology courses is the teacher's information technology teaching ability, including the use of teaching to solve practical problems, and the use of modern teaching resources to support teaching. The current modern educational technology curriculum has many and complicated teaching contents and lacks basic pertinence. The professional characteristics of the learner will determine the different scenarios and conditions for the learner to apply modern educational technology in the future. Therefore, the teaching content can be differentiated according to the different professions of the learners. Moreover, the teaching content should be defined hierarchically according to the starting point of the learner, so as to avoid the phenomenon that the teaching content generated by the learner in the learning is too difficult or too easy.
(2) Adapt to learners' different levels of knowledge
Learners have different computer basic software skills. The science and engineering majors have a good level of mastery in computer basic software, while literature and history and art majors have relatively poor mastery. Therefore, in the teaching design, the basic level of literature and history and computer science in computer basic software should be fully considered. In Adobe Photoshop, art learners are far better than those in science, literature and history, and should consider the actual level of these three majors in teaching. For art learners, it is more difficult to improve the content of teaching. In terms of Flash software, art majors are far better than science and engineering and literature and history.

Therefore, when teaching in the art major, it is necessary to pay attention to the difficulty of the course and avoid invalid teaching. In terms of sound processing software and video processing software, art majors are far better than science and engineering and literature and history. Therefore, in the teaching of these software, we should pay attention to teaching differences and avoid invalid teaching and invalid courses.

(3) Consider the contextual differences in the application of modern educational technology by learners
In the teaching design, the software knowledge and skills of the modern educational technology course content should be different according to the major, and the teaching technology environment used by different majors is different such as hierarchical definition. For example, the use of unified teaching resources in the knowledge and skills of different majors. In the aspect of greater difference, the difficulty should be adapted to meet the learning objectives of the learners at different levels.

4 Tutors' Strategies to Meet the Needs of Blended Teaching

The teachers in blended teaching are not only the imparters of knowledge but also learner tutors. In the blended teaching, the tutor should strengthen the supervision and leadership of the learners, promptly feedback the questions raised by the learners, reasonably plan the teaching progress of the online and offline aspects and avoid the disconnection between online teaching and offline teaching. At the same time, the tutor should provide the learner with targeted learning resources, so that the learner has a good learning experience in the blended teaching.

(1) In the online learning process of blended teaching, the tutor should respond to the questions raised by the learners in a timely manner, and the time should not exceed half a day. According to the learner analysis, most of the questions that the learner hopes to raise should be answered within half a day.
(2) In the blended teaching, the tutor should establish an online and offline communication mechanism, and timely supervise the learners to conduct autonomous online learning according to the data of the learning platform so as to avoid the online teaching resources of the blended teaching become an advanced waste. If online learning progress is not guaranteed, blended teaching will not achieve the goal of promoting learning, which is counterproductive.
(3) In the offline face-to-face teaching in the blended teaching, the tutor should actively organize the learning to exchange and interact with the learning results and display the works. This can make the offline classroom a place for learning outcomes to collide, so that the learning outcomes of all learners can be sublimated again, and the offline classroom will not become a traditional teaching in which teachers teach and students listen to the teacher.

5 Learners' Own Strategies to Meet Learning Needs

The learner itself is an important factor affecting the learning effect, so the following strategies are proposed from the perspective of the learner.

(1) Strengthening the cultivation of learners' autonomous learning ability
In the process of blended teaching, teachers should effectively supervise learners' online learning. The learner's self-learning ability is related to the achievement of the blended teaching goal. In blended teaching, learners themselves should also focus on improving their self-learning ability. Online learning is different from traditional classrooms and lacks communication with teachers and peers. And there is a lot of information on the network, which is easy to cause the learners to distract attention. If the learner's self-learning ability is not strong, it is not conducive to the achievement of online learning results.

(2) Learners should master correct and reasonable learning strategies
Online learning requires learners to spend a certain amount of time after class. Therefore, learners should ensure that the weekly schedule, the consistency of each lesson, and the weekly study, avoid invalid learning, waste time, and ensure online learning content before online classroom teaching. Meanwhile, learners should promptly report the problems they encounter to the teachers and communicate and communicate with teachers and classmates in a timely manner.

(3) Learners should improve their learning expectations for the course
The learner's learning expectation is directly related to the learner's learning attitude and motivation. Learners should understand the function and role of modern educational technology and broaden their knowledge as the starting point for learning. It is necessary to find relevant books based on what you have learned in your online courses to further enrich your knowledge; Learners should reasonably arrange the progress of learning by virtue of the freedom of free time in online learning, and should not be able to cope with the learning of course content by evading the teacher's supervision mentality; Learners should not learn to use the utilitarian motivation to complete credits. It is necessary to understand and recognize the importance of modern educational technology courses as public courses for teachers and education majors.

6 Conclusions

In the online learning platform of the course, when carrying out the blended teaching, the tutor should ensure that the learner encounters a problem and gets a teacher response within half a day, so that the learning needs of most learners can be met. In terms of online video resources, it is necessary to mainly produce video recordings of studio recording video, field shooting video, slide + teacher image. When learning resources under the design line, the weekly learning time should be controlled within 2 h. According to the statistics, the length of the online teaching video of the blended teaching should be controlled within 10 min. It is necessary to avoid teaching videos from lasting too long, which affects learners' enthusiasm and interest in learning. Based on the conclusions of this study, in the design of my modern education technology course, the instructional designer should design offline and online teaching activities according to the major, focusing on the difference between teaching content and auxiliary learning resources. Therefore, it is close to the actual level of the learner to the greatest extent.

Acknowledgements. This work is supported by National Institute of Computer Basic Education in Colleges and Universities (2018-AFCEC-082).

References

1. Wen, Y.: Based on the "Internet + education" background, the construction of mixed teaching mode in Colleges and Universities. Mass Technol. **21**(01), 84–86 (2019)
2. Su, H.: Research on the online and offline mixed teaching mode under the background of "Internet plus" – taking the volume of reinforcement calculation as an example. J. Huainan Vocat. Tech. Coll. **17**(06), 93–95 (2017)
3. Wang, G.: Research on the effectiveness of the blended teaching mode to improve adult higher education in the context of "Internet plus" – taking Beihua University as an example. Chin. Adult Educ. **16**, 91–93 (2017)
4. Yu, Y.: Application of blended learning method in Vocational Education under the "Internet plus" environment. Mod. Econ. Inf. **16**, 392–393 (2017)
5. Zhou, C.: Blended teaching analysis based on "Internet plus". Yin Shan J. (Nat. Sci. Ed.) **31** (02), 130–132 (2017)

Engineering Ability Construction in Flipped Classroom Teaching Approach

Chengyan Li(✉), Jun Gao, Song Li, and Guanglu Sun

School of Computer Science and Technology,
Harbin University of Science and Technology, Harbin 150080, China
chengyan@hrbust.edu.cn

Abstract. Engineering ability is an important quality for college and university graduates majoring in engineering. Flipped classroom is an effective teaching mode, which has been widely used in colleges and universities. How to cultivating engineering ability in the process of flipped classroom teaching is an important problem. This paper considered the approach of engineering ability training, and discussed the requirements of flipped classroom in the aspects of curriculum goal, teaching process organization, teaching platform and evaluation system. The main major courses for undergraduates in specialties of Big Data is used to illustrate the approach. The results show that the proposed architecture and method are effective.

Keywords: Engineering ability · Flipped Classroom · Teaching process organization · Evaluation system

1 Introduction

Engineering ability is the foundation of human social progress to respect the natural law and social norms, the ability to use tools to carry out productive activities and create material wealth on the basis of understanding nature. For engineering college students, engineering ability is the ability to learn and apply professional knowledge, analyze and solve problems under the constraints of comprehensive consideration of laws and regulations, professional norms and social sustainable development, and having appropriate engineering ability is the most important training goal in the university stage [1]. Today, the accreditation represented by the *Washington Accords* is the most common international standard in engineering education. China became a regular member of the *Washington Accords* in 2016. Engineering accreditation emphasizes the whole process and the requirement of full coverage for all students' engineering ability training, and the school needs to review the working methods and results evaluation mechanism of each link, especially the teaching link [2]. In recent years, the research on the cultivation of engineering ability has been paid close attention to by many scholars, and more than 120 journal articles have been published during 2017 and 2018.

According to the *Engineering Education Accreditation Standard*, engineering graduates must have the ability to solve complex engineering problems [3]. This requires that students should be able to consider the solution of the problem in general,

G. Sun et al. (Eds.): eLEOT 2019, LNICST 299, pp. 24–35, 2019.
https://doi.org/10.1007/978-3-030-35095-6_3

including multi-disciplinary cross-cutting, as well as economic, social, sustainable development and other factors, not just the application of this professional technology [4]. How to cultivate students' ability to solve complex engineering problems in the course of teaching has become an important issue in the process of teaching organization, planning and implementation [5]. Reference [6] studies how to cultivate engineering ability in CDIO environment, Reference [7] discusses the reform of teaching methods oriented to the cultivation of engineering ability, and carries out the corresponding practice.

Based on the complexity of engineering ability cultivation, constructivist learning theory centered on learner individual provides scientific guidance to relevant teaching organizations [8]. Flipped Classroom is a teaching organization method based on Constructivism, which is a student-centered, through pre-class, in-class and after several stages of learning to complete the knowledge of the internal, its main purpose is to enhance students' self-learning ability, so as to better build the knowledge system [9]. The Teaching organization form of flipped classroom has been widely used in universities [10]. Many universities in the United States, especially higher engineering colleges, have begun to apply flipped classrooms for teaching organization, and have been recognized by teachers and students, which is considered to be a good way of teaching organization [11]. Domestic universities also began to apply flipped classroom, and combined with information technology to build a network teaching platform [12]. The teaching idea of student-centered, problem-oriented and encouraging practice in the process of flipped classroom teaching coincides with the requirements of the cultivation of engineering ability [13]. Therefore, it is an effective form to use Flipped classroom teaching method to cultivate students' engineering ability. However, in the practical application, the teaching organization method based on flipped classroom also exposes some problems in cultivating students' engineering ability, which needs to be further perfected in the aspects of teaching goal, teaching process organization, teaching platform and evaluation standard.

2 Current Problems

2.1 Lack of Quantitative Analysis of Engineering Capabilities, Take Knowledge Transfer Instead of Capacity Training Goals

The output standards set out here including 12 points: 1. Engineering knowledge, 2. Problem analysis, 3. Design and development solutions, 4. Research, 5. Using modern tools, 6. Engineering and social, 7. Environmental and sustainability, 8. Career norms, 9. Personal and team, 10. Communication, 11. Project management and 12. Lifelong learning. The cultivation of engineering ability objectively requires students to have more comprehensive ability, not only to have theoretical knowledge in professional field. This requires quantitative analysis of the content of the curriculum in the formulation of teaching objectives, and the identification of capacity development objectives, otherwise it will not be possible to adapt to this new environment. On the other hand, the cultivation of ability needs the support of the whole curriculum system, in the specific formulation of curriculum plan, it is necessary to design the curriculum and engineering ability Training target matrix, so that the curriculum and engineering ability requirements correspond, that is, with the training objectives of students, and then targeted curriculum content and teaching organization form design.

2.2 In the Teaching Process Organization Along the Traditional Teaching Habits, Flipped Classroom Effect Is not Fit

Although there have been many cases of flipped classroom application in China, it is not satisfactory in practical application, one of the important reasons is that traditional teaching habit has a strong psychological basis and practical feasibility among teachers and students, and this change of habit is not a slogan or a scheme can be completed. Flipped classroom education concept of *Student-centered* and *Active learning* in the actual operation process is very bony. Reference [14] analyzes the causes of this problem from the aspect of *field-habit* theory, and points out that because of the characteristics of students' and teachers' heterogeneity, The failure of flipped classroom has its internal reasons, it is necessary to construct a new form of teaching organization.

2.3 It Is Necessary to Combine Modern IT Technology to Build a Flipped Classroom Platform

Online learning platform, such as MOOC (massive open online courses), is a teaching aid that has been widely concerned in recent years, and has become an important carrier of the process of pre-class learning and after-school learning in the classroom. However, there are also problems in the application of the platform, such as passive acceptance, poor interactivity and inflexible feedback, many times the online learning platform is only a place for video playback tools and online operations, and does not provide better support for flipped classroom. With the advent of "Internet +" society, we should make full use of mobile computing technology to put forward new solutions, in order to achieve the teacher can lay the task on demand, check the completion of the situation, answer questions, organize student discussions, expand the limited classroom to unlimited space and time, to achieve all-weather.

2.4 It Is Necessary to Establish a Scientific Flipped Classroom Evaluation System, and Change the Knowledge Assessment to the Ability Assessment

According to the decomposition of curriculum engineering ability, improve the curriculum assessment mechanism, establish an objective flipped classroom evaluation system in line with the requirements of engineering accreditation, instead of the traditional examination form. The examination will run through the whole process of flipping the classroom, forming the evaluation system of the process assessment and final appraisal. Combining the training process of engineering ability with the result of students' assessment, it is directly linked with the student's grade, and the assessment of knowledge point is changed into the assessment of ability, which solves the problems existing in the traditional evaluation system. This kind of assessment will also transform the students' learning style, in order to promote the students to take the ability training as the focus of learning, improve the initiative and purpose of learning. Through the calculation of the degree of achievement, the various ability components are aggregated to form the comprehensive ability evaluation of students.

3 Curriculum Groups Setting and Analysis of Ability Indicator Point

3.1 Curriculum Groups Setting

The cultivation of engineering ability has a strong comprehensive, it is necessary to consider the correlation of relevant professional knowledge and ability requirements, not only the intersection between different disciplines, but also to consider the sequential relationship between courses and the integration of knowledge in the same subject, and the setting of curriculum group is based on this principle. Data science and big data program curriculum are professional courses, including Big Data Foundation, cloud computing Framework, Python, MapReduce Design Patterns, NoSql database, R language data mining, Spark programming and other theoretical courses and corresponding practical links. The teaching goal of the curriculum group is to adapt to the trend of technological development and the demand of information industry, to train Big Data engineer processing and Big Data analysis engineer, and the courses are interrelated and progressive, forming logical relations, causality, and composing knowledge system. The course group is offered in the field of computer science and technology, and the first courses include discrete mathematics, computational composition principle, operating system, computer network, data structure, programming Foundation, database and software engineering and other computer majors. Through the study of this kind of course, students can fully understand the basic knowledge of data science and big data, cultivate the ability of building and developing big data system and data processing and analysis, adapt to the needs of big data engineers at present and in the future, and have the ability of self-learning and renewal.

3.2 Quantitative Analysis of Competency Training Objectives

The E-learning environment in the learning system or architecture is based on an online learning platform, which is composed of co-operative learning and question-answer system.

Engineering accreditation determines the standard of personnel training by equivalence evaluation, which clearly requires students to have 12 engineering capabilities, including not only engineering knowledge, but also humanities, society, law and personal development. For the course teaching organization, we must first determine the ability requirement matrix of the course, and then can organize the corresponding teaching activities.

Through the research on the general standard of engineering accreditation and the supplementary standard of computer science and technology, combined with the specific contents of data science and big data program curriculum, the ability training target matrix of this curriculum group is developed within the framework of the overall training goal of computer specialty.

After intensive analysis, the engineering ability indicators corresponding to the data science and big data program curriculum are shown in Table 1.

Table 1. Engineering ability indicators for the major of data science and big data.

No.	Name	Sub-criteria	Description
1.	Engineering knowledge	1-1	It can carry out abstract thinking and apply knowledge of mathematics and natural sciences to the representation of computer engineering problems such as large data information processing
		1-4	Familiar to the process of analysis, design, development and implementation of large data information processing system, and can be properly applied in practice according to the problems
2.	Analysis	2-2	By means of literature search and data analysis, the nature and characteristics of complex large data engineering problems can be analyzed by combining the principles of mathematics, natural science and professional knowledge, and effective conclusions can be drawn
		2-3	It can model the solution, construct a prototype system based on computing principle, and analyze its rationality
3.	Design	3-1	It can carry out research on large data information processing engineering problems and clarify relevant constraints, and complete requirement analysis for computer hardware and software systems
		3-2	It can design and implement algorithms for specific large data information processing requirements, and test and verify the correctness of algorithms and programs
		3-3	It can take social, health, safety, legal, cultural and environmental factors into account in the design of large data information processing system, and make a comprehensive analysis of the above aspects, so as to improve the scheme
4.	Research	4-1	Guiding research by computational thinking can accomplish abstraction from practical problems to theoretical problems of computer science, or formalize theoretical problems of computer science by means of mathematical tools
		4-2	It can use mathematical and computer expertise and technical means to design and demonstrate the feasibility of the experimental scheme for the specific problems of large data information processing
		4-3	It can construct a large data information processing experimental system, carry out experiments, collect experimental data, and draw reasonable conclusions by analyzing the data
5.	Using modern tools	5-1	It can reasonably select, use or develop appropriate technologies, tools and resources in the field of large data information processing
		5-2	To meet the needs of analysis, design, development, operation and system maintenance of large data information processing system, we can choose appropriate methods and understand their scope of application or limitations

(*continued*)

Table 1. *(continued)*

No.	Name	Sub-criteria	Description
9.	Individual and team	9-2	Be able to integrate into the team and take on the corresponding roles in the work
10.	Communication	10-2	With an international perspective, understand the status and trends of data science and big data development, and can effectively communicate and communicate with peers and the public
12.	Self-learning	12-2	Master the method of self-learning and the way to expand knowledge and improve ability, and have the ability of self-improvement

In the process of teaching preparation of data science and big data program curriculum, a complete teaching file is developed, including syllabus, experiment outline, practice outline, teaching calendar, lesson plan, etc., these teaching files are the guiding documents to carry out teaching activities. Also prepared to assist students to learn a variety of teaching resources, including video, documentation, PPT, exercises, quizzes, etc., these resources through the online learning platform to provide students, to ensure that students in the flip class at all stages of learning.

4 The Teaching Process Organization of Flipped Classroom

4.1 Flipped Classroom Teaching Mode

The Flipped classroom teaching link is divided into three stages of pre-class study, in-class study and after-school study. The construction of engineering ability is a complex, comprehensive and gradual process, which completes different learning tasks through three stages of flipping the classroom, and satisfies the relevant requirements of engineering ability training.

The overall framework is shown in Fig. 1.

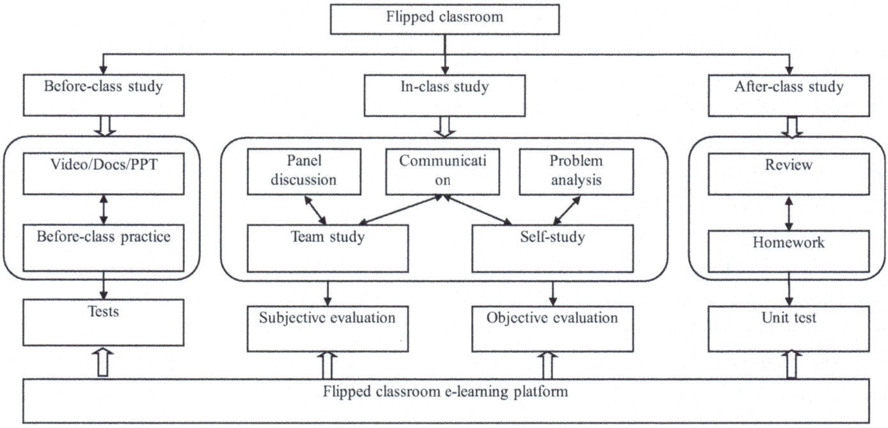

Fig. 1. Framework of flipped classroom

Pre-class tasks are mainly for students to watch video and other online resources, mainly self-learning, supplemented by appropriate pre-class exercises and quizzes, through self-study to complete the localization of knowledge. The ability of pre-class learning cultivation mainly includes 1. Engineering knowledge and 12. Lifelong learning, including 1-1, 1-4 and 12-2.

In-class tasks include classroom lectures, cases, discussions, exchanges, etc., and team collaboration training and evaluation. In order to complete the localization of classroom knowledge, the discussion and communication are carried out on the basis of studying engineering knowledge before class. The ability of learning and training in class mainly includes 2. Problem analysis, 4. Research, 9. Individuals and teams and 10. Communication, including 2-2, 2-3, 4-1, 4-2, 4-3, 9-2 and 10-2.

After-school tasks include after-school exercises, reviews, applications and quizzes, the main goal is to complete the localization of knowledge through application and practice. The ability to cultivate after-school learning mainly includes 3. Design/Development solutions, 5. Using modern tools, including 3-1, 3-2, 3-3, 5-1 and 5-2.

In this way, through three stages of learning, the use of pre-class learning, in-class discussion and after-school application of the model to complete the process of knowledge, the realization of student-centered, internal driving force as the leading learning mode. The evaluation results of all these stages are counted in the final general comment, and the final learning evaluation of the course is given.

4.2 Teaching Process Organization

Flipped classroom is a student-centered teaching model, but there are unsuitable situations both at the teacher's end and on the student side. Teachers send videos, documents and so on to students, and leave a large number of exercises for students to do, as a basis for students to self-study, that the realization of the main school supervisors from the teaching of the transformation; But students do not adapt to this way, no motivation to take the initiative to learn, leading to self-relaxation, the result is good students effect is good, poor students have poor effect, did not play the desired role.

In view of this problem, the following ways are adopted to solve.

First, on the basis of full research to consider the proportion of teachers and students to do, for the data science and big data program curriculum of the curriculum, to determine the overall proportion of the two is about 4:6, and there are differences between different content proportions. As the content of the introduction and concept appropriately increases the proportion of lectures, and the practical content increases the proportion of students.

The second is the use of task-driven Flipped classroom organization form. Task-driven is one of the constructivist learning methods, which realizes the transformation from knowledge to ability by completing tasks. The greatest benefit of task-driven is the integration of textbook abstract, fragmented knowledge in a unified form, encompassing both integration within the same course and integration between different courses. For example, in task design, students are required to use web crawler technology for a hit film in the domestic well-known video review site to obtain data, processing data, complete word frequency analysis. This task applies Hadoop cluster technology, Python program design, and MapReduce programming techniques, and involves three courses, such as *Big Data Basics*, *Python Language*, and *MapReduce Design Patterns*.

Third, adopt a team-based learning model. Team learning has two advantages, one is through the team's internal collaboration and mutual assistance, give full play to their respective advantages, complement each other, promote each other; Second, through the competition between the team, so that all participating students have upward learning driving force, change passive learning for active learning. In the specific implementation, first determine the number of groups, by a group of 4–6 people, thus ensuring that the organization can form an atmosphere of cooperation and discussion, as well as individual isolation due to the large number of persons. Secondly, the members in the group are determined, and the principle of combining stochastic allocation with voluntary team formation is adopted. According to the student's comprehensive achievement point ranking in the previous year, the number of groups ranked the top students as the team leader of each group, other students in a voluntary principle according to the way of choice to join one of the groups. Such grouping can avoid the psychological discomfort of completely random grouping and the *good students piling* phenomenon that may result from full voluntary grouping, and strike a balance to the learning ability of each group of members to the greatest extent.

In classroom teaching, two scoring strategies are adopted according to the different tasks, first, according to the number of students in the group completing the tasks to score; the second is to compete between the groups, according to the rankings to score. After each class in the teaching platform to publish the scores of each group, so that students timely understanding of the status of each group, enhance the sense of competition and promote learning. At the end of the semester, the scores of each group were counted, and the group with the highest scores was recorded as excellent (according to the current school regulations, excellent corresponding to the percentile of 95 points, other levels and so on), the scores of the other groups are calculated based on the relative ratio of the group with the highest score.

Practice shows that this kind of team classroom organization way has achieved good results. Students are active to answer questions, timely to submit homework, students in the group to help each other to solve problems, so that the classroom atmosphere unprecedented active, learning enthusiasm has been greatly improved, even students who do not do well can be integrated into the team to play a self-role, to meet the individual and team ability to develop the requirements.

5 Using Mobile Computing Technology to Build Flipped Classroom Learning Platform

In order to realize flipped classroom teaching and make use of Internet technology and multimedia technology, many schools have built an online teaching system based on MOOC. Such systems provide a wealth of teaching resources, while supporting teachers to set up their own courses on the platform, upload homemade courseware as needed, and provide student management, online assignments, exams, grade management, posting discussions, as well as students' learning behavior records and statistical analysis, which provide convenience for flipping classroom teaching. However, such systems also have poor communication, cannot send notifications in a timely manner and participate in discussions and other issues. Instant Messaging (IM), represented by QQ and WeChat, has spread across all corners of society, especially with the popularity of smartphones, IM has become a way of life. In the college student community, the penetration rate of smartphones has exceeded 100% (some students have more than one mobile phone). Therefore, leveraging the advantages of smartphones and IM, making full use of fragmentation time, combining system learning with fragmented learning will be an effective means of learning [15].

In the process of data science and big data program curriculum teaching, using online teaching system and IM complement each other to give full play to the advantages of the two, so that the flipped classroom teaching effect is better. Before the start of the course, the course is offered in the online teaching system that has been built in the school (currently selected as a company's cloud network teaching platform), the establishment of classes, the introduction of student rosters, and then the setting of knowledge points according to the requirements of the syllabus, the production of learning materials for each knowledge point, such as video, documentation, PPT, etc., students can log in to pre-class learning, and can record students' learning behavior, such as the number of times to watch the video, time duration, ruminant ratio, etc., so as to understand the input of students learning, but also the use of statistical functions to output student performance.

In IM (Instant Messaging), such as QQ, to establish a curriculum group, group name for semester + courses, such as *2017 Autumn 15 big data foundation*, the monitor will take all the students into the group, in the form of group announcements to issue a variety of notices. When learning in class, make full use of group functions, such as group files, discussions, voting, etc., to achieve instant information sharing, updates and feedback. The previous hands to speak, manual statistics and other work to be completed by the functions provided by IM, such as the form of group voting statistics of students on a certain issue or evaluation of a certain discussion, so as to achieve a combination of knowledge systematization and fragmentation of the new learning environment. At the same time, in this environment, teachers can be an organizer to mobilize students to participate.

In the after-school learning stage, the online teaching platform can publish assignments, conduct tests, and evaluate students' learning achievements. IM can be used for answering questions, discussing, or posting small questions, such as views on answers to a question, comments, and even single-choice and multi-choice forms in the form of a vote. It can make full use of fragmented time to arrange learning activities, the past can only fixed time, fixed location of teaching activities into anytime, anywhere, ubiquitous classroom, so as to complete the process of capacity construction after class.

6 Competency-Based Evaluation System

In traditional teaching process, the evaluation of students is mainly based on the mastery of knowledge, even if the assessment of the way of reform, essentially only increased the number of test examination, in most cases did not highlight the requirements of the ability assessment. The result is that the engineering knowledge part of the paper assessment is easy to evaluate when the achievement is calculated, while other abilities are not well measured. In order to solve this problem, the ability evaluation system is established in the teaching of data science and big data program curriculum.

The ability evaluation criteria are shown in Table 2.

Table 2. Ability evaluation criteria

Grade	Description
A	Ability to lead team; solid knowledge of data science and big data engineering; leading role in scheme design; core member of system development and implementation; strong research ability; proficiency in tool use; initiative to learn relevant knowledge, familiar with the development of big data information processing technology
B	Be a backbone member of the team; be familiar with data science and big data engineering knowledge; play a secondary role in scheme design; be an important member of system development and implementation; have strong research ability; be familiar with tool use; be able to learn relevant knowledge by oneself and understand the development of big data information processing technology
C	Be able to integrate into team; master data science and big data engineering knowledge; be able to complete responsible project design; be a member of system development and implementation; have research ability; be able to use tools; be able to learn relevant knowledge and understand the development of large data information processing technology as required

In the normal process examination, the evaluation criteria are used to evaluate the students. On the basis of the above team score, the team members are assessed in the form of mutual evaluation, and the assessment ratio is set to: A 20%, B 40%, and C 40%. The assessment level and the team score multiplication is the individual process ability assessment score, this part of the score and the final Test score added to get the personal total score. The evaluation mechanism in the group effectively promotes the benign competition among the students in the same group, embodies the value of learning and guarantees the fairness.

7 Conclusion

Aiming at the demand of engineering ability training for teaching organization form, this paper studies and practices the teaching organization mode of flipped classroom applied in engineering teaching. This paper discusses the curriculum goal of flipped classroom, the organization of teaching process, the construction of teaching platform and the evaluation system. In the teaching process of undergraduate data science and big data program curriculum, all aspects of flipped classroom are verified. The analysis shows that this kind of teaching organization satisfies the requirement of engineering ability cultivation, and the investigation feedback to students also shows that this way is effective to improve the ability.

Acknowledgments. This work was supported by grant No. 16G116 from the Research Program in 13th Five-Year the project of the Higher Education Society of Heilongjiang Province, and No. SJGZ20170056 from the Research Program of Education Department of Heilongjiang Province, China.

References

1. Blizzard, J., Klotz, L., Pradhan, A., et al.: Introducing whole-systems design to first-year engineering students with case studies. Int. J. Sustain. High. Educ. **13**(2), 177–196 (2012)
2. Gilliland, K.O.: The flipped classroom and learning analytics in histology. Med. Sci. Educ. **27**(1), 9–13 (2017)
3. Wang, A., Hou, C., Li, R.: The research of excellent talent training model reform and practice innovation aimed at computer specialty. In: Che, W., et al. (eds.) ICYCSEE 2016. CCIS, vol. 624, pp. 83–91. Springer, Singapore (2016). https://doi.org/10.1007/978-981-10-2098-8_12
4. Goggins, J.: Engineering in communities, learning by doing. Campus-Wide Inf. Syst. **29**(4), 453–508 (2012)
5. Zhelei, X., Binggang, X., Xiumin, W.: Reform and practice of talents training model of electronic information engineering majors. In: Wang, Y. (ed.) Education Management, Education Theory and Education Application. AINSC, vol. 109, pp. 451–455. Springer, Heidelberg (2011). https://doi.org/10.1007/978-3-642-24772-9_66
6. Rui, F., Shibin, Z.: The study and practice of training excellent network engineering based on CDIO mode. In: International Conference on Consumer Electronics. IEEE (2011)
7. Li, W., Zhang, C.: Reformation and exploration of higher engineering education based on CDIO syllabus. In: Zhang, L., Zhang, C. (eds.) Engineering Education and Management. LNEE, vol. 112, pp. 587–591. Springer, Heidelberg (2012). https://doi.org/10.1007/978-3-642-24820-7_94
8. Fu, H.: Applied research of integrated project teaching method in applied engineering management major teaching. In: Wang, J., Ding, Z., Zou, L., Zuo, J. (eds.) Proceedings of the 17th International Symposium on Advancement of Construction Management and Real Estate, pp. 1023–1028. Springer, Heidelberg (2014). https://doi.org/10.1007/978-3-642-35548-6_105
9. Hwang, G.J., Lai, C.L., Wang, S.Y.: Seamless flipped learning, a mobile technology-enhanced flipped classroom with effective learning strategies. J. Comput. Educ. **2**(4), 449–473 (2015)

10. Blair, E., Maharaj, C., Primus, S.: Performance and perception in the flipped classroom. Educ. Inf. Technol. **21**(6), 1465–1482 (2016)
11. Triantafyllou, E., Timcenko, O.: Out of classroom instruction in the flipped classroom: the tough task of engaging the students. In: Zaphiris, P., Ioannou, A. (eds.) LCT 2015. LNCS, vol. 9192, pp. 714–723. Springer, Cham (2015). https://doi.org/10.1007/978-3-319-20609-7_67
12. Chen, Y., Lang, F., Lu, Z., Shi, H.: Build up peer instruction based flipped classroom with social network. In: Liu, S., Glowatz, M., Zappatore, M., Gao, H., Jia, B., Bucciero, A. (eds.) eLEOT 2018. LNICST, vol. 243, pp. 298–304. Springer, Cham (2018). https://doi.org/10.1007/978-3-319-93719-9_41
13. Premlatha, K.R., Geetha, T.V.: Learning content design and learner adaptation for adaptive e-learning environment, a survey. Artif. Intell. Rev. **44**(4), 443–465 (2015)
14. Òscar, F., Del-Arco, I., Silva, P.: The flipped classroom model at the university: analysis based on professors' and students' assessment in the educational field. Int. J. Educ. Technol. High. Educ. **13**(1), 21 (2016)
15. Glahn, C., Gruber, M.R., Tartakovski, O.: Beyond delivery modes and apps: a case study on mobile blended learning in higher education. In: Conole, G., Klobučar, T., Rensing, C., Konert, J., Lavoué, E. (eds.) Design for Teaching and Learning in a Networked World. LNCS, vol. 9307, pp. 127–140. Springer, Cham (2015). https://doi.org/10.1007/978-3-319-24258-3_10

Research on Gamification Teaching of "Network Security Technology" Under Improved Flipping Classroom

Zhi-yong Luo(✉), Jing-yuan Wang, Guang-lu Sun, and Yi-dong Chen

Computer Science and Technology College, Harbin University of Science and Technology, Harbin 150080, Heilongjiang, China
luozhiyongemail@sina.com

Abstract. Network security technology is a professional course that must be offered by network engineering majors in colleges and universities. Then understanding the relevant principles and concepts that are difficult to understand is a fundamental reason that affects students' true mastery of network attack and defense technology. Based on the previous research, this paper designs an improved "flip classroom" gamification teaching model. The model optimizes the traditional "flip classroom" teaching process into four stages: pre-class, in-class, after-school and holiday review, which further deepens students' understanding of important knowledge points. At the same time, the new model also introduces the concept of gamification teaching, which further stimulates students' interest in learning. Practice has shown that the improved teaching model has certain advantages in improving the ability to solve practical problems, learning achievements and long-term grasp of relevant principles and concepts. In addition, the new model also provides a reference for the teaching methods of engineering courses in other colleges.

Keywords: Flipping classroom · Autonomous learning · Network security technology · Gamification teaching

1 Foreword

With the continuous emergence of new technologies such as "cloud computing" and "Internet +", education informatization has become more and more important to the attention of educators. The scientific application of emerging network technologies to current teaching activities not only enriches existing teaching methods to promote teaching reform, but also promotes the integration of China's teaching model with the world and towards a more favorable direction for students' learning. According to the spirit of the document "Development of Education Informationization Decade (2011–2020)" [1], domestic universities and colleges have applied modern information technology to their respective teaching activities, and basically established students to "self-study". The teaching system structure of the main and teacher-assisted, through the application of "micro-video", "flip classroom" and other new teaching models to achieve the purpose of improving teaching quality.

G. Sun et al. (Eds.): eLEOT 2019, LNICST 299, pp. 36–47, 2019.
https://doi.org/10.1007/978-3-030-35095-6_4

"Network Security Technology" is a theoretical and practical, professional-oriented course for engineering, and its practice links are more operational and engineering features [2]. Therefore, the teaching of this course not only allows students to verify the boring theoretical knowledge, but also allows students to design creative network security solutions, which seems to be incapable of achieving the ideal teaching objectives in the traditional teaching methods. Applying the improved "flip classroom" teaching mode to the teaching process of this course, not only can improve the existing teaching methods, but more importantly, it can also improve students' self-learning ability, and then introduce "gamification" teaching. Means can stimulate students' interest in learning, participate in the exchanges between teachers, students and students, improve their organizational ability and teamwork ability, so as to seamlessly realize the goal of training colleges and universities to train talents in the network security direction.

2 Improved Flip Classroom

2.1 The Connotation of Flipping Classroom and Its Research Status

The Flipped Classroom was first proposed in 2007 by American teachers Jonathan Bergmann and Aaron Sams, it is an emerging teaching mode, which divides the whole teaching process into three parts, namely, before, during and after class. The pre-school teaching mainly allows students to achieve self-study by watching micro-videos carefully prepared by teachers. The teaching in the class is mainly student-oriented, the teacher answers questions and explains the knowledge points; the after-school teaching is used for summarization, giving a scientific evaluation of the students' self-learning ability. Intel Global Education Director Brian Gonzalez [3] once pointed out: "Flip the classroom can give scholars more freedom of study, and put the teaching process in the spare time, so that scholars can accept knowledge points in the way that suits them best; The internalization of knowledge in the class is more convenient for teachers and students and students to communicate, and it is easier to master the knowledge". American education expert Stacey Roshan [4] used the flipping classroom in the teaching practice of the university pre-requisite course to further verify the effectiveness of the flip classroom.

China's research on flipping classrooms began in 2012 [5], and it is still a new thing. The most representative application is the flip classroom teaching experiment of Chongqing Jukui Middle School. In the following years, the domestic research on flipping classrooms has grown rapidly, and related research literature has gradually increased. Especially in 2014, the first national colleges and universities "flip classroom" micro-video teaching contest successfully held in 2014 will be "flip classroom". The teaching concept has been pushed to the top, which has greatly attracted the attention of domestic universities. According to the relevant statistics of the current statistics, the teaching mode of "flip classroom" is mainly applied in the basic education stage. The application of specialized courses in colleges and universities, especially engineering colleges, is mainly concentrated in the operating system [6], e-government [7], Chemistry [8] and modern educational technology [9–11] and other courses. With the construction of the shared curriculum platform in Shanghai universities, the MOOCs courses of multiple universities and colleges have been launched one after another, which provides convenience for the students of each college to select the excellent courses of the universities in the region, thus breaking the boundaries of learning between universities [12]. Through research, the implementation of flipping classroom teaching in the practical and practical professional course teaching can effectively stimulate students' interest in learning and improve their self-learning ability, organizational ability and practical ability Through research, the implementation of flipping classroom teaching in the practical and practical professional course teaching can effectively stimulate students' interest in learning and improve their self-learning ability, organizational ability and practical ability [13].

2.2 Traditional Flipping Classroom Problems

China's research literature on "flip classroom" began in 2012. The existing research found that the implementation of the traditional "flip classroom" has the following problems [14]:

1. Flipping the classroom requires a lot of spare time for the students, so the number of flipped classrooms opened in each school year is not too much. If there is no reasonable mechanism to stimulate students' interest in learning, it will be difficult to guarantee the preparation effect before class.
2. Flipping the classroom requires the use of a computer network teaching platform, which increases the workload of familiar software for students with low computer operation level, which affects their enthusiasm.
3. Flipping the classroom puts higher demands on the teaching ability of teachers and changes the organizational model of traditional teaching in the past. This is a new challenge for some old teachers or new teachers with insufficient experience.
4. Flipping the classroom requires a new teaching reform and evaluation mechanism, and the existing evaluation mechanism cannot meet the requirements in this regard. The reform of the evaluation mechanism includes two aspects, one is to evaluate the reform of teachers' teaching ability and rewards, and the other is to evaluate the reform of students' learning ability. The former will affect the ability and enthusiasm of teachers to control the classroom, and the latter will affect the enthusiasm of students to participate in teaching. If the evaluation mechanism of these two aspects is not perfect, it will directly affect the implementation effect of the flip classroom.

3 The Status Quo of Network Security Technology Teaching

3.1 Teaching Problems

The Network Security Technology course is one of the important means to train students to work on Internet of Things and Web security. However, through visits, research and years of teaching research, it is found that at present the teaching of this course has at least the following problems [2]:

(1) The teaching method is single and lacks the mechanism to stimulate students' interest in learning. At present, the network security technology of most colleges still adopts the traditional and single case demonstration teaching mode. The teacher gives the whole operation process of the case, the students only need to reproduce the case according to the process, and complete the knowledge point task assigned by the teacher. Therefore, this method can not stimulate the interest of students to learn independently, and students still complete the process of passive learning under the pressure of scores.
(2) Insufficient hours of study and complete case teaching. At present, more and more colleges have increased their investment in school hours. In our school, for example, the number of hours in the network security technology course has increased from 54 h to 64 h. However, due to the characteristics of this course, in order to complete the successful application of a network security case, students must complete security requirements analysis, program design, program code development or protection tool selection, debugging and installation and deployment, obviously 64 h Insufficient, and ultimately led to a serious decline in teaching effectiveness, making the case teaching model a "formal" project.
(3) The formulation of teaching content is too rigid and lacks the innovation of students' self-developed practice. At present, most of the cybersecurity technology courses are fixed, and students are not allowed to make their own questions. Students must also follow the teaching steps to achieve case recurrence. This limits the students' thinking, is not conducive to students' independent innovation, and designs content that is more suitable for their creativity.
(4) The teaching mode is old and lacks the teacher-student interaction mechanism. Due to the limitations of teaching conditions, a teacher often faces the teaching phenomenon of at least 30 students. This has made it difficult for teachers to fully guide each student, and the lack of mutual cooperation between the students has led to a lack of communication between the students. Therefore, when students are doing the case, the good students are busy reappearing, and the poor students simply do not, which ultimately affects the teaching effect.
(5) The assessment method is single and cannot reflect the true ability of students. Currently, most classroom computers have a recovery card installed. This has led to the students in the process of completing the case, the resulting works are difficult to save, and thus inconvenient for teachers to check. Over time, the student's grades are mainly based on their attendance, which does not reflect the true ability of the students.

3.2 Characteristics of Student Learning

The network security technology course is a professional direction course. The general colleges are usually opened in the fourth semester, so the subjects are often taught by lower grade students. Through years of practical teaching, low-level students have the following characteristics when conducting cybersecurity technology courses [2]:

(1) The level of network security operation technology is uneven. The junior students have just experienced public class learning, and most of their energy has not yet been put in the direction of cybersecurity, so students generally have huge differences in skill levels.
(2) The difference in learning interest is obvious. Due to the huge differences in students' awareness, employment direction, and personal preferences, students' interest in learning this course is different.

4 Improved Flipping Classroom Gamification Teaching Model

4.1 Improved Flipping Classroom Teaching Model Design

Traditional flipping classrooms use the teaching model shown in Fig. 1 [15]. Since the model has the problem described in 1.2 during the implementation, it has been improved in this paper.

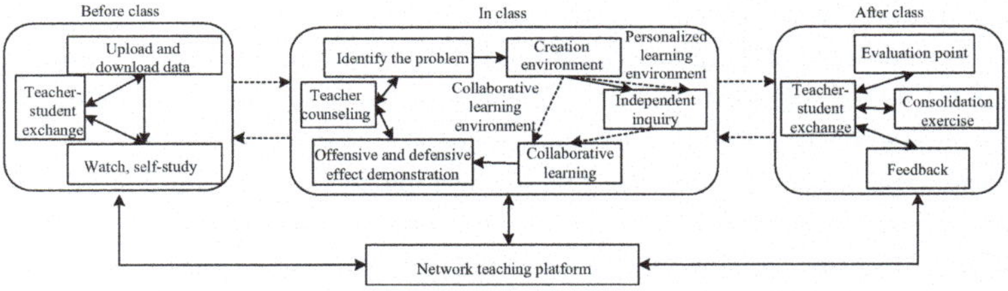

Fig. 1. Traditional flipping classroom teaching model

The new model will increase the game settings and student self-assessment and mutual evaluation modules to further stimulate learning interest; the model also increases the teacher evaluation and reward module, which inspires the enthusiasm of teaching. The improved model can effectively solve some of the problems described in 1.2. Other problems can only be solved through policy reform. For example, the total score of the course should be automatically generated by the system during the middle of the holiday, and the teacher only gives 90% of the total score at the end of the period. The remaining 10% should be automatically given by the system after the students return to important knowledge points twice and make reasonable suggestions at the end of the holiday. The improved flip-up gamification teaching model is shown in Fig. 2. The "Network Security Technology" course will use this model for teaching reform.

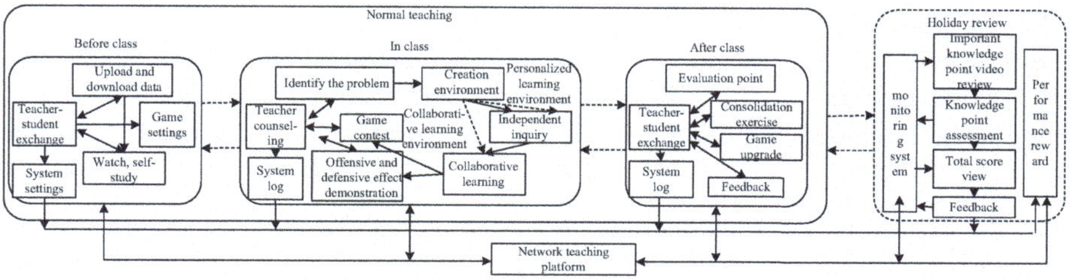

Fig. 2. Improved flipping classroom gamification teaching model

Figure 2 divides the entire teaching activity into two phases: normal teaching and holiday review. The normal teaching stage consists of three parts: before class, during class and after class. The improved new teaching model should be completed in addition to the pre-class, in-class and after-class tasks of the model in Fig. 1 (see the author's previous research results, the literature [15]), and should also provide the function of completing the new task. For example: before class, teachers and students can design game activities according to the characteristics of this data, give game rules and reward descriptions and update the game module; in the class, teachers and students can choose real-time confrontation of game competitions and record the whole process, giving the results of the game; After class, teachers and students can watch the game video in time, comment on the highlights to give mutual evaluation results, excellent game cases should be upgraded into a game library for future teaching use. During the holiday review period, the teacher sets the time period, the system automatically prompts the students to log in, and the students watch the video of the important knowledge of the course to review, and after the review, a simple test of the knowledge points is required. After the student submits the test results, the system automatically calculates the total score of the course for the students to view and ask for reasonable advice. At the same time, the system will also calculate the reward level of the teacher according to the log files of the course and the reasonable suggestions of the students, and give reward reference, pay attention to only reward without penalty.

4.2 Normal Teaching Case Design

Since the normal teaching stage of the "Network Security Technology" course uses the teaching model shown in Fig. 2, its teaching process design is divided into four aspects: pre-class design, in-class design, after-school design and game module design.

4.2.1 Pre-class Design

Pre-class design requires teachers to summarize the knowledge points of this course in advance, provide necessary courseware, previous students to learn the wonderful video, network security attack and defense tools and team division instructions, students download these materials through the network teaching platform Team analysis, preliminary understanding of these materials, design of competition cases or game content and rules, feedback from the group leader to teachers. After the teachers and students communicate, further design the game plan or the game case to upload to the system, so that the game can be compared in the class.

4.2.2 Class Design

The design of the class is the key to flipping the classroom. In the implementation process, we must actively implement the "student-led" thinking. Therefore, the design of this stage is divided into four parts. This article assumes that each course is 180 min or 4 h.

(1) The first 20 min of the course is the teacher's explanation part, focusing on the teaching tasks, important concept theorems, competition or game rules and reward methods of this course.
(2) The student prepares and starts the discussion according to the teacher's explanation. Teachers are required to participate in each group's discussion and task division activities, correcting the unreasonable part, which is expected to take 50 min. For example, taking the ARP attack defense in network security as an example, the natural class of 30 people is divided into 6 groups, among which 3 groups simulate network intrusion, 3 groups simulate network defense, each group independently designs its own attack and defense program, and each group of teachers tutors Go to the difficult issues and specify the offensive and defensive tools they can choose.
(3) Students are expected to take 90 min to showcase their work or play games. If the course selection program works, the students will complete the group work with the group to explain the wonderful ideas and the specific division of labor and tasks for each team member, other groups and teachers to ask questions; if you choose the game contest, then each The two groups are for a team to conduct offensive and defensive game competitions within a limited time, and the entire process requires recording screen records for easy post-evaluation.
(4) The teacher sums up this course and is expected to take 20 min. The teacher gives further explanations on the key and difficult issues of the course, gives comments on the performance of the students and the wonderful game works under the class and plans the contents of the next course.

4.2.3 After Class Design

After-school design is divided into four aspects: feedback, evaluation, consolidation exercises and game upgrades.

1. Feedback. The teacher collects the improvement suggestions in the course of the course through the online teaching platform, and completes the optimization of the course.
2. Evaluation points. The teacher gives the advantages and disadvantages of each student through the online teaching platform, and the students view their comments through the platform.
3. Consolidation exercises. According to the overall performance of the students, the teachers determine the problems of the students, and make relevant exercises for students to download exercises to further consolidate the knowledge points of this course.

4. Game upgrade. The game competitions used in this course are summarized, further optimized and saved as classic games, and the game library is updated for future reuse.

4.2.4 Game Module Design

Because the professional curriculum is different from the ordinary online game, the design of the module only uses the relevant title in the online game to complete the mapping with the teaching objectives of the network security technology course, as shown in Table 1.

Table 1. Game title and network security technology goal mapping relationship

Game appellation	Curriculum teaching goal	Game appellation	Curriculum teaching goal
An intruder	Network intruder	Guard the gate, BOSS	Network defender
Reporter	Classroom teacher	Game announcement	Classroom discipline norms
Novice's Guide	Introduction to case Operation Rule	Stage property	Network attack and defense tool
Empirical value	Score of the attack and defense task	Upgrade	Team Role
Clearance	End of case	Carbon	Team work
Game forum	Peer assessment	Hero list	Individual score ranking

Some of the game title functions in Table 1 are introduced as follows:

(1) Game announcements. It mainly introduces the classroom discipline of this lesson and the general content of the next lesson.
(2) Beginner's Guide. It mainly introduces the competition rules and evaluation criteria of this offensive and defensive game, and gives the precautions and knowledge points in the competition.
(3) Props. It mainly introduces the offensive and defensive tools that may be used in this course, and can exchange them with experience values.
(4) Empirical value. According to the performance of the player's offense and defense process, the score is given and the cumulative score is calculated. The high scorer will determine the role to play in the future competition tasks.
(5) Upgrade. When the experience value accumulates to a certain extent, the system automatically completes the role upgrade, and the high-level role plays a more important role in the subsequent tasks, and will give higher scores in the final results.
(6) Customs clearance. At the end of the game, if the player successfully defeats the BOSS, the network intruder team wins; if the player does not defeat the BOSS, the network defender team wins. No matter who wins, you will get the experience value, but the experience value is different.

(7) A copy. Sharing the solutions developed by the team facilitates teamwork, and the team can also collaborate in real time to complete the offensive and defensive tasks.
(8) Game forum. The exchange platform between students is convenient for recording the opinions or opinions of the team in the game in time for further discussion and analysis.
(9) Heroes list. Show the total experience value of each classmate who participates in the game competition. At the end of the period, the usual score will be given according to the hero list.

4.3 Holiday Review Design

The new teaching model will break the scoring standard of traditional teaching in the past, and arrange about 10% of the total score of this course in the winter and summer vacations, and be automatically calculated and generated by the network teaching platform. Since the holidays are the rest time of teachers and students, the design of this part should not be too cumbersome. Upload the video of the classic game competition and important knowledge points in the normal teaching activities to the system, and stipulate that the students can watch online before the start of the school, and answer some questions after watching. The system will give results based on the viewing and question answering, and automatically calculate the total score in conjunction with the final grade.

5 Implementation Effect Analysis

5.1 Experiment Procedure

The experiment compared the traditional and improved "flip classroom" students to learn, the target is a network engineering major sophomore, the number of students per class is 30. Questionnaires were surveyed before the lectures, and the results of the survey are shown in Table 2.

Table 2. Student network operation level statistics

Teaching object	Number of people	Male to female ratio	Computer-owned ratio	Net-to-net ratio	Programming experience ratio	Network security experience ratio
Traditional class	30	21:9	93.33%	93.3%	86.67%	16.67%
Improved class	30	20:10	96.67%	96.7%	83.33%	16.67%

The contents of Table 2 show that students in the traditional and improved flip-class classrooms are basically the same in terms of the relevant theories and skill levels of cybersecurity technology, and almost all have just come into contact with cyber-security. During the six months of normal teaching and holiday review, the author used the "flip classroom" teaching model shown in Fig. 1 for the traditional teaching class; the improved "flip classroom" shown in Fig. 2 for the improved teaching class. "The model is taught".

5.2 Comparative Analysis of Student Achievement

The total scores of the students in the traditional and improved classes are compared as shown in Fig. 3. After calculation, the average total score of the traditional class is 75.07, and the average total score of the improved class is 81.37. The average total score of the improved class is 6.3 points higher than the average total score of the traditional class.

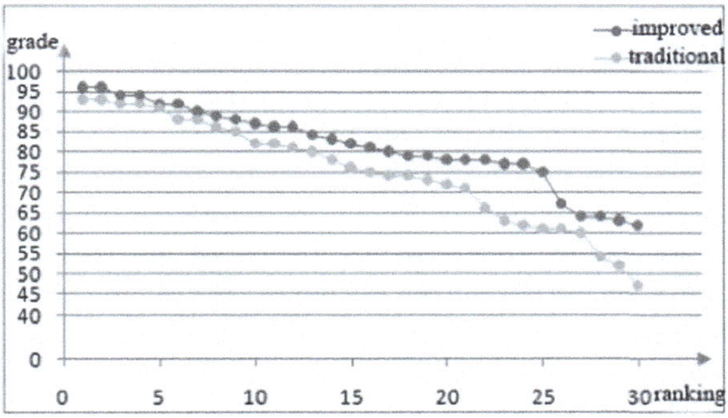

Fig. 3. Comparison of traditional teaching classes and improved teaching classes

If the final grades of the two classes are compared by the number of people in the score segment, the comparison is shown in Fig. 4. It can be seen from Fig. 4 that the ratio of the number of people in the traditional class is 16.66%, 26.67%, 26.67%, 20%, 10%; the ratio of the different segments of the improved class is 23.33%, 33.33%, 26.67%, 16.67%, 0%. The improvement rate of the improved class is higher than the traditional class of 6.67%, the good rate is higher than the traditional class of 6.66%, the medium rate is almost the same, and the pass rate is reduced by 3.33%. The overall performance of the improved class is obviously better than the traditional type. Classes are taught.

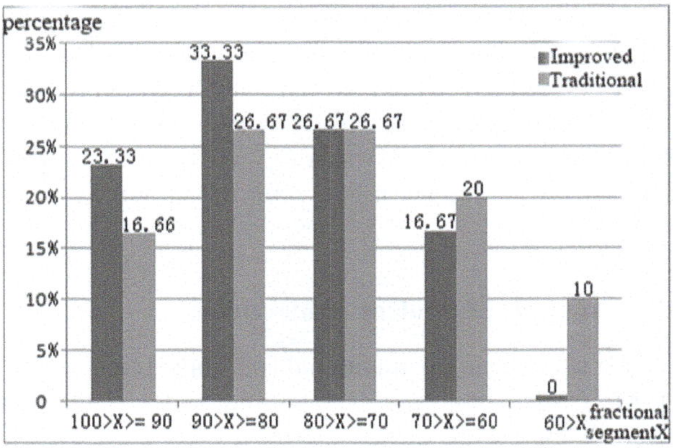

Fig. 4. Comparison of the number of people with different scores

5.3 Questionnaire Analysis

After the normal teaching activities, the author distributed 30 questionnaires to the traditional teaching class and the improved teaching class. The purpose is to understand the students' satisfaction with different teaching methods. According to the feedback from the questionnaire, the improved "flip classroom" teaching mode is very popular among students, which not only achieves the purpose of learning but also achieves interesting effects. In addition, the new teaching mode has also changed the short-comings of the past winter and summer vacations, so that students can not forget to review during the break, and achieve the purpose of consolidating the important knowledge points of network security technology for a long time without increasing the extra workload of teachers.

6 Conclusion

The "Network Security Technology" course can avoid the problems in the traditional "flip classroom" teaching while improving the "flip classroom" gamification teaching mode, and further increase the students' interest in learning, so that the students' learning activities run through the whole Semester and winter and summer vacations, to achieve work and relaxation to consolidate the purpose of learning. The reform of the gamification teaching method of "Network Security Technology" under the improved flipping classroom has changed the traditional concept of education and learning in the network engineering profession, and has raised new problems and challenges for teachers and students. At the same time, this learning model also provides a certain reference for the majority of educators.

References

1. Ministry of Education. Ten Years of Education Informationization Development Plan (2011–2020) [EB/OI.] [2012-05-06]. http://www.edu.cn/zong_he_870/20120330/t20120330_760603_3.Shtml
2. Zhiyong, L., Zhaowei, Q., Yidong, C.: Research on teaching methods of network security courses in engineering universities. Sci. Technol. Manag. **11**, 143–146 (2011)
3. Future classroom: upside down room. <http://www.jyb.cn/ad/news/201110/t20111010_456993.html>
4. Roshan, S.: Changing the Class Experience. <http://www.thedailyriff.com/articles/the-flipped-class-good-stuff-happens-715.php>
5. Yi, L.: An empirical study of "flip classroom" applied to information literacy education courses. J. Acad. Libr. **6**, 96–102 (2014)
6. Qiliang, Z., Yongsheng, C.: Application research of flip classroom in experimental teaching of operating system. Lab. Technol. Manag. **12**, 173–176 (2014)
7. Jianqiang, Z., Xiaozheng, W.: Research on the flipping classroom teaching mode and gamification experimental system. Comput. Educ. **12**, 43–47 (2014)
8. Wei, X., Shaochun, Z., Xiangchun, Ma.: Research on the teaching model and support system of chemistry experiment based on flipping classroom. J. Distance Educ. **5**, 107–112 (2013)
9. Jiumin, Y., Mingjie, S., Lei, H.: Application of flip classroom based on micro video resources in experimental teaching. Modern Educ. Technol. **10**, 36–40 (2013)
10. Qingsong, L.: Design of the "modern educational technology" experimental course based on flipping classroom. Lab. Res. Explor. **1**, 194–198 (2014)
11. Wei, H., Ling, J., Lei, H.: Application of flipping classroom in the experimental teaching of "Modern Educational Technology". China Electro-Educ. Educ. **4**, 110–115 (2014)
12. Shanghai University Curriculum Center, 18 July 2014. http://www.ucc.sh.edu.cn
13. Hailong, L., Minjie, D., Cunliang, L.: Design and application of task-based flip classroom teaching mode. Modern Educ. Technol. **9**, 46–51 (2013)
14. Baozhen, Q.: Application design of flipping classroom teaching mode in experimental teaching of colleges and universities. China Educ. Technol. Equipment **6**, 114–115 (2014)
15. Zhiyong, L., Yuanxin, T., Weicheng, Z., Hongzhuo, Q.: Research on the teaching model of network database system based on flipping classroom. Teach. Learn. **1**, 73–75 (2016)

Discussion on the Application of WeChat Mini Program in the Lifelong Education of Basic Computer Knowledge in the Age of Mobile Learning

Fang Wan(✉), Bo Xu, and Na Chang

Hainan Vocational University of Science and Technology,
Haikou, Hainan, China
1246303662@qq.com

Abstract. Since the beginning of the 21st century, with the rapid development of high technology, the application of computers has penetrated into the daily work and life. At the same time, mobile learning education, a style of education which is based on the development of smart phone mobile technology, has developed into the focus of education. As one of the representatives, WeChat mini program, by virtue of its convenience and ease of use, brings a "shock" to the education field.

How to use mobile technology to popularize computer basic knowledge among the people while bring people the opportunity to enjoy lifelong education? Based on the application of mobile technology in education and the theory of connected learning and lifelong education theory, this paper studies the impact of lifelong education development in the era of mobile technology, and uses the literature research method and literature analysis software "CiteSpaceII" to explore the domestic and international status on the combination of lifelong education and mobile technology.

Through the establishment of an open concept of lifelong education development, and enhance the WeChat mini program civilianizing application to narrow the "digital divide", and build a new model of Lifelong education development as well, this paper explores the popularization of computer basic knowledge and lifelong development of education.

Keywords: Mobile learning · WeChat mini program · Computer basic education · Life-long education · Development ideas

1 Introduction

The thoughts and behaviors of lifelong learning have a long history in Chinese history. For example, in the Spring and Autumn Period and the Warring States Period, which is more than 2,000 years ago, An ancient Chinese sage, the man named Kuang Shi said: "Young eager for knowledge, just like the sunshine at sunrise; adult eager for knowledge, just like the light of the sun at noon; Elderly eager for to learn knowledge, just like the light that lights up the candle. Illuminated by candles and exploring in the dark, which is better?" Another ancient Chinese sage ZiXun believes that "There is never an end to learning."

G. Sun et al. (Eds.): eLEOT 2019, LNICST 299, pp. 48–55, 2019.
https://doi.org/10.1007/978-3-030-35095-6_5

The idea of modern lifelong education was put forward by the French adult teaching scholar Paul Legrand, in 1965 It should abandon the "front-end" education model formed by traditional society, which separates the learning and work, and the education and labor as well. The modern lifelong education model is a new education model which supposes that education should be advocated throughout people's whole life, and realize the learning and life integration, as well as be participated by the whole society.

With the advancement of science and technology and the improvement of people's living standards, computers have affected the world's military, education, business and people's work and life in a wide range of fields. The information age has brought opportunities to China's development, but it has also brought challenges. The rapid development of computer technology and the relative lag of the people's computer level have brought many inconveniences to work and life. So how do you popularize computer knowledge and how to make people of all ages enjoy the benefits of education?

According to a report by the Pew Research Center on June 25, 2018, the penetration rate of smartphones in China has reached 68%, and the smart phone allocation rate is comparable to that in Western countries. According to a research report released by US agency Zenith, the number of smartphone users in China will rank first in the world by 2020, which is 1.3 billion, close to the average manpower level.

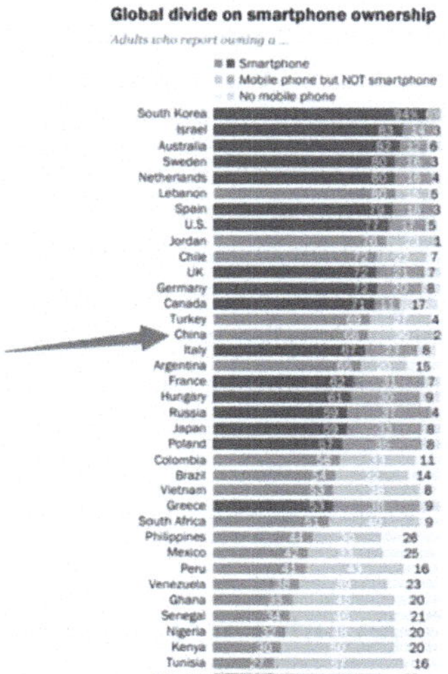

Fig. 1. Global divide on smartphone ownership

In the early morning of January 9, 2017, Zhang Xiaolong's 2017 WeChat Open Class Pro marked the official launch of WeChat's mini program. This is a revolution in mobile applications and a revolution in educational methods as well. The applet is an application that can be used without downloading.

It realizes the dream of the application "at your fingertips". Users can open the application by sweeping or searching, and also embody the concept of "run away". Users don't have to worry about installing too many apps, apps will be everywhere, ready to use, but no need to install and uninstall.

Due to the popularity of smartphone mobile Internet and WeChat and the fragmentation of user time, the Matthew effect of WeChat applet has gradually become apparent. WeChat applet is a kind of "light application". It relies on WeChat, a super APP, which solves the problem of long tail distribution and the connection between users and developers. The user also saves the trouble of downloading and installing the app. Since its launch, the mini program ecology has gradually been built into a huge ecology around the needs of clothing, food, housing, travel, entertainment, etc., which greatly facilitates people's lives and will undoubtedly produce patterns, channels and content for lifelong education. Great impact.

Since the age, occupation, study habits and learning time of the learners are not fixed, lifelong education in the new era should emphasize "where are the learners, where is the classrooms", creating an organic integration of space and time between the classroom and the learners. To provide "a ubiquitous classroom for learners." The WeChat applet also advocates the service to make the user "at your fingertips". Therefore, the concept of lifelong education has a perfect fit with the mini program, so that education can be "everywhere, at your fingertips".

Compared to APP and web applications, WeChat applets can be used across Android and iOS platforms, with a short development cycle and low cost. At the same time, we share more than 900 million user super traffic on WeChat platform, reducing the cost of acquisition and promotion costs. Moreover, the WeChat applet does not need to be downloaded and registered, and it will always exist when it is used up. It does not occupy memory and will make it easy to use. The mini program can be connected to the WeChat public account and the APP, and has a high level of experience similar to the native APP. Many educational resources are beyond the reach of more people. WeChat applets can enable more micro-courses, courseware, tutorials, handouts and other resources to have a wider market and more audiences.

2 Current Status of Relevant Theoretical Researches

By using the "WeChat mini program" and "lifelong education" as the key words, the author eliminates the unrelated literature by analyzing and comparing the search results. It is found that as of today, it is basically impossible to search the literature about the lifelong education applet. The related research that combines lifelong education with new things such as mini programs is still in the primary stage, and relevant theoretical research is not mature enough.

3 The Main Service Content of WeChat Mini Program About Lifelong Education

Construct standards for the integration of curriculum resources, and set up a curriculum system.

Integrate case materials, case resources, test resources, material resources, and training resources suitable for self-study. Based on WeChat applet, we design a platform that Includes student management, material library, online video course, problem test, and courseware download to realize online teaching resource sharing of "everywhere, at your fingertips". The user's personal center has a wide range of services, including user certification, my courses, my appointments, courses already taken, courses want to learn, my favorite lessons, personal information, and more.

4 Mini Program + QR Code Optimizing the Lifelong Education Model Offline Services

At present, most educational resources need to download a special APP to scan the code, which increases the difficulty of the reader's operation. After using the mini program, the user can directly use the WeChat scan code to obtain the service, which greatly reduces the difficulty for the scholar to obtain the teaching resources. The operation flow is shown in Fig. 1. It can be shown that the process of using the APP requires a total of six steps, and the user operation process using the applet only needs four steps. Each additional operation step increases the difficulty of the user operation. Some users may give up halfway, which using mini programs to optimize the two-dimensional code application scenarios for lifelong learning could shorten the service path. You can use the mini program to expand more application scenarios, such as the mini program sweeping the query course progress, sweeping the QR code through the mini program to complete the new scholar certification, sweeping the QR code to sign up for the course, sweeping the customer service Introduce the QR code to get the course consultation and more (Figs. 2, 3 and 4).

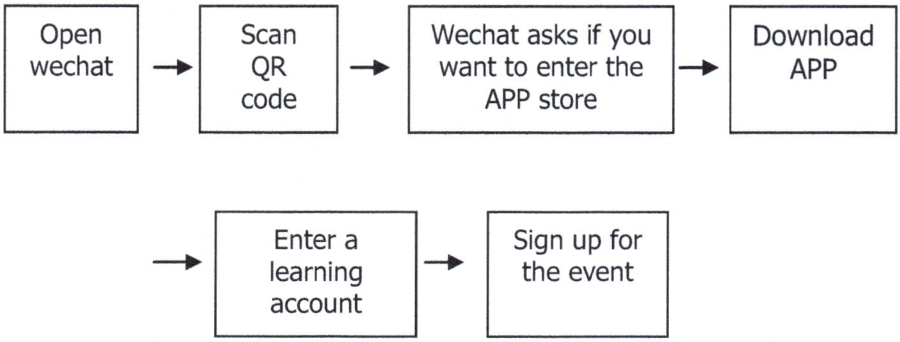

Fig. 2. App's Process

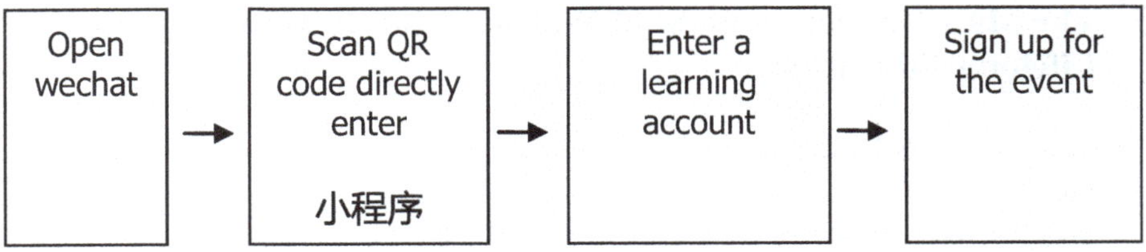

Fig. 3. The process of the mini program

Fig. 4. The QR code of this project

5 The Design Principles of Computer Basic Knowledge Popularizing Lifelong Education Mini Program

The design highlights the two principles of "light" and "smart" as much as possible. Light refers to ease of use, users can quickly enter the teaching Resources page anytime, anywhere, in the enjoyment of teaching resources without the limitation of time and space, there is no psychological burden, run out of the walk.

Coincidentally refers to the ingenious design, reflected in the interface value, process convenience, navigation clear and program abnormalities in the control, so that Let the user feel the lightness of learning with the small program.

(1) Interface value, pleasing to the eye: In order to improve the fun and convenience of learning, developers should pay attention to the uniformity and continuity of page color matching and page conversion, try to choose the uniform control and interaction mode, and have adapted to most of the use. The habit of the person.
(2) Clear navigation and smooth process: The navigation should be clear and clear, so that users can clearly understand their current location, how to go directly to the desired location, and save energy time.
(3) Reduce waits, highlight the point: If the page load waits longer, use a progress bar to let the user know what the program is doing. Minimize the waiting time of users, so the mathematical data uploaded should be short, mini, and precise, and focus on solving the difficult problems that may occur in learning.
(4) Reduce input, use interface: In order to avoid repeated input and time-consuming, you can make full use of the "memory" function, such as selecting in history or recent search, and using other methods of WeChat to quickly connect information resources.

(5) Abnormal prompt, solve the problem: When an exception occurs, the program should have a status indicating the possible cause of the exception, and inform the user how to solve the problem.

6 The Design of Users' Interfaces of This Project

See Fig. 5.

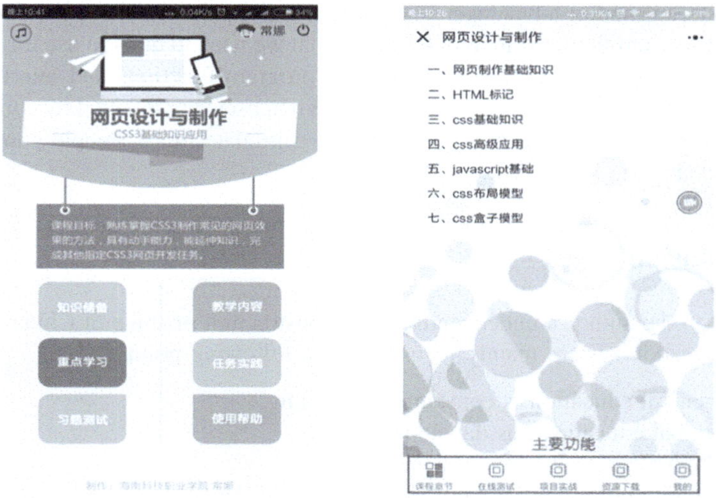

Fig. 5. Users' Interfaces

7 The Mini Program Further Empowers the Computer Basic Knowledge of Lifelong Learning

(1) Mini program with a variety of entrances may expand the service radius. If the public number menu can directly set the mini program entry, the user can press the identification and enter. The picture and text in the public number can be inserted into the mini program code to open the applet, applet message card, etc. through the picture or text, in addition to Nearly 50 entrances, such as mini programs, circle of friends, WeChat group, and mini program search, can realize more reach and expand service radius, which provides technical feasibility for the realization of this research.

(2) The mini program is comparable to the native APP experience, allowing the public to get more loyal users. Mini programs can get more system privileges through WeChat APP, such as network communication status, data caching ability, etc. Mini programs use the interaction between systems to make the mini program have the experience of the native APP, and the experience is not lost to the native APP and H5, and the delays, visual distortions, etc. that may occur in them will not appear in mini programs.

8 WeChat Applet + Social Sharing Helps the Popularity of Computer Basics and the Promotion of Lifelong Education

Compared with people's interactions such as "social islands", WeChat communication is a niche communication based on acquaintance networks, and its credibility and availability are unmatched by traditional media. After a period of development, WeChat mini program has accumulated an excellent "human relationship" and also reflects a strong market advantage. Users can share applets and friends with WeChat groups and forward them to circle of friends. What we need to do is to use the functions in WeChat to do the public content and mini program functions and interfaces, and create a scene based on active content sharing. When users are infected by content, they will be willing to share it actively, which may stimulate more. People come to participate in learning.

9 Conclusion

According to the author's understanding, the construction practice of China's existing lifelong education system mainly focuses on the following points:

(1) The general education is constantly expanding.
(2) Vocational education has developed rapidly.
(3) Adult education continues to advance.
(4) Community education is booming.
(5) Old-age education has sprung up everywhere.
(6) Enterprise education has gradually transformed.
(7) Social education is widely extended. 8. Open education prospered.

However, the current system construction practice of lifelong education is influenced and restricted by the time, space and occupation of the educated person, and the combination of WeChat mini program and lifelong education has solved this problem perfectly. Whether it is a young child or an old man, whether it is an unemployed or a social elite, as long as a smart phone has a WeChat app installed, you can use the WeChat learning program to learn the time at any time and anywhere.

All in all, from the above perspective, the construction of a new model for the development of lifelong education is conducive to the promotion of the WeChat mini program civilian platform to narrow the imbalances between the countries, regions, classes and individuals due to the rapid development of information technology and the imbalance of social and economic development. The problem of the "digital divide" brought about by the imbalance of information data between the social class and the social class and between people. To a certain extent, it guarantees people's rights and opportunities to participate in lifelong education, realizes the sharing of high quality resources on a global scale, and Optimizes the social atmosphere of public participation to ensure the fairness of education.

Acknowledgment. This research was supported by Hainan Higher Education Educational Reform Research Project (Hnjg2018-105).

References

Huifu, X.: China's learning-oriented society and the construction of lifelong education system; Reconsideration and re-exploration of "and" line. Res. Open Educ. (4), 23 (2017)

Changxue, Y.: WeChat Small program realizes the application of "at Your Fingertips" dream. Educ. Sci. Forum **2**, 12–15 (2017)

Zixue, G.: The multiple challenges and coping strategies of our lifelong education. Res. Continuing Educ. (7) (2018)

Youju, Q.: Probe into the construction of lifelong education system. Academic Forums (11) (2010)

Siyi, W.: Research on the development of WeChat small program. Wirel. Interconnection Technol. (7), 11 (2018)

Sun, G., Lang, F., Yang, M.: Traffic measurement system based on hybrid methods. Electric Mach. Control **15**(6), 91–96 (2011)

Sun, G., Li, X., Hou, X., et al.: GPU-accelerated support vector machines for traffic classification. Int. J. Performability Eng. **14**(5), 1088–1098 (2018)

Research and Design of College Courses Resources Sharing Platform Based on WeChat Mini Program

Na Chang, Qilang Liang, and Fang Wan(✉)

College of Information Engineering, Hainan Vocational University of Science and Technology, Haikou, Hainan, China
474263408@qq.com, 1246303662@qq.com

Abstract. The lightweight application development technology based on WeChat Mini Program is particularly popular at present. The framework of WeChat Mini Program is simple and easy to develop. Mini Programs can be used without deployment on the client and can easily call the camera, microphone and GPS, etc. Naturally, the development of college courses teaching resource sharing platform based on Mini Programs can facilitate teachers and students to share curriculum resources and enjoy online learning and communication.

The project follows the design principles of simple operation, clear interface layout, personalized learning mode, diversified communication means, scientific management methods, etc., adopting WeChat Mini Program, data acquisition and data analysis technologies to build a college courses teaching resource sharing platform, a teaching service system featuring university teaching resource sharing and students' individualized learning.

Keywords: WeChat Mini Program · College courses · Resource sharing · WeChat teaching · Online learning

1 Introduction

Tremendous desire of self-exploring study has emerged among the college student group, no longer is the traditional teaching mode with blackboard attractive to them. They prefer a variety of learning methods. According to statistics, almost every college student owns a mobile phone on which WeChat is one of the indispensable applications. This lays the foundation for promoting the use of WeChat Mini Programs to carry out the teaching and learning activities of college courses.

The current mobile Internet education and teaching platforms are mainly represented by WeChat official accounts classroom and educational applications. The former is easy to promote and attract a large number of customers, but its function is quite restricted due to system limitations. Also these educational applications involve downloading, installment, update, uninstall, etc., it is more difficult to promote and use. Whereas WeChat Mini Program combines the two advantages of them, providing developers with a solution that is both powerful and lightweight.

G. Sun et al. (Eds.): eLEOT 2019, LNICST 299, pp. 56–61, 2019.
https://doi.org/10.1007/978-3-030-35095-6_6

To begin with, this paper introduces the fundamental technology modules used, and then expounds on the main functions and user roles. In the last part, conclusions and prospects are given based on the analysis.

2 Research Objectives and Content

2.1 Research Objectives

The open online teaching resource sharing platform [1] is designed with the purpose of sharing services, with the completion of curriculum tasks as the guiding principle, emphasizing on the cultivation of students' self-learning ability [2], representing the characteristics of data sharing in the information era; This platform focuses on the integration of course objectives and teaching content to propel the transformation of teaching concepts; This platform also adopts diversified curriculum teaching methods [3] to promote teaching reform, thereby improving the quality of teaching.

2.2 Research Content

To fully utilize the ease of operation and accessibility of WeChat Mini Program [4] and meanwhile take into account of the characteristics of college courses, this open platform will include functions such as student management, material library, online course videos, quizzes, course documents downloading, online communication, etc. Finally, the goal of sharing teaching resources and cultivating students' self-learning ability will be realized.

3 The Introduction of Key Technology

3.1 WeChat Mini Program

WeChat Mini Program [5] is a kind of application that does not need to be downloaded or installed. Users can use WeChat to scan or search to open the program. Its outstanding properties include easy sharing, easy operation, convenient browsing of pictures, audio and video files.

3.2 Vue.js, Vue-resouse.js

Vue.js is a progressive framework for building data-driven web interfaces. The goal of Vue.js is to achieve a data binding and combined view component of the response through the simplest possible API, which uses Vue-resouse.js for data interaction [6, 7].

3.3 Data Collection and Data Analysis

The data collection [8] in this study refers to the extensive retrieval, downloading and categorization on the Internet by employing crawlers for teachers to integrate those data into appropriate teaching resources. Data analysis [9] refers to the system collecting the users' all operational behavior, analyzing their learning status according to users' behavior, and then giving constructive comments.

4 The Design of the Sharing Platform

4.1 Technical Solutions

This system adopts WeChat Mini Program [10] technology supplemented by HTML5 and vue.js [11] to build software interaction interface, using PHP to develop data response service and taking mysql [12] as data storage.

4.2 Overall Structural Design

See Figs. 1, 2, and 3.

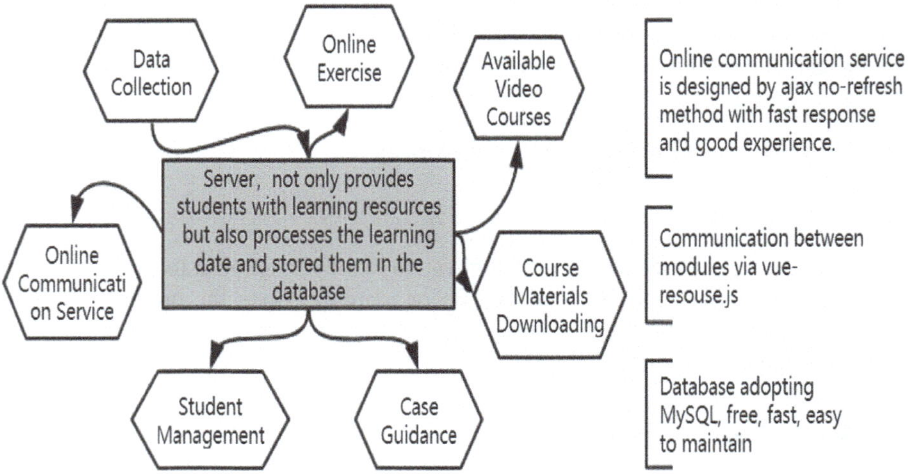

Fig. 1. Server design.

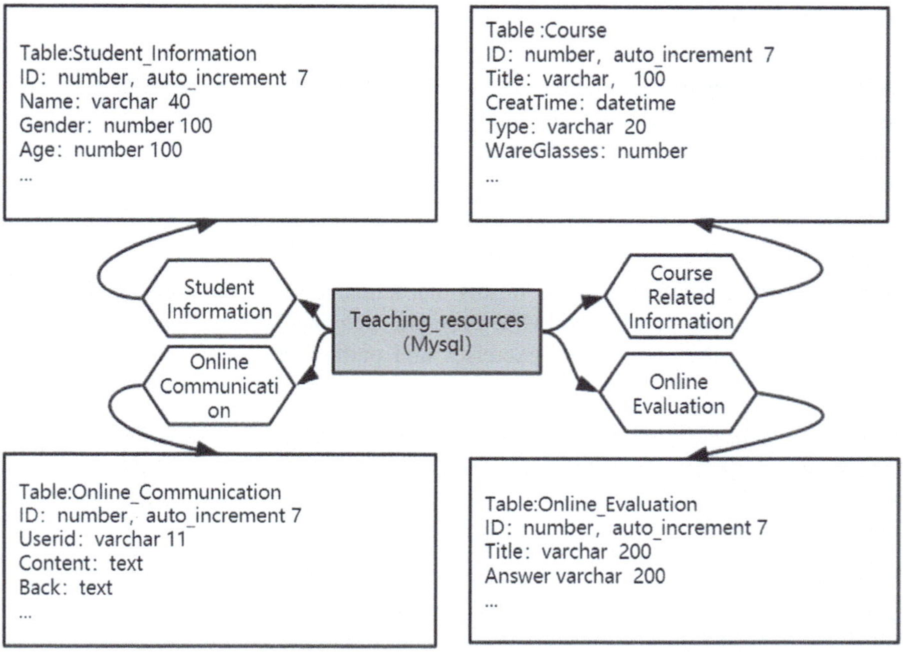

Fig. 2. Database design.

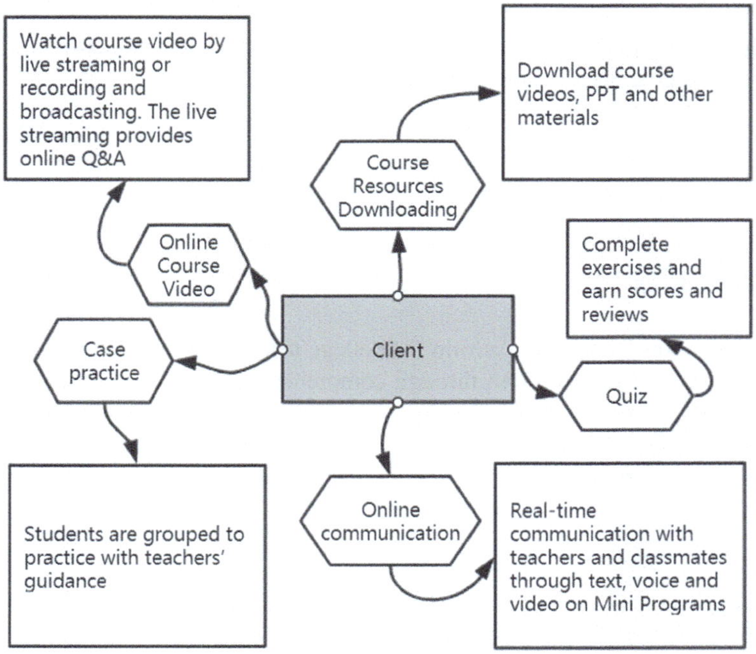

Fig. 3. Client design.

4.3 Main Functions

Course Management. Course management refers to teachers using the inherent models in the system, filling in the attributes of the course, creating courses, and then enriching the resources required for the course according to the teaching objectives and characteristics, such as PPT, audio and video, exercises, cases, experiments, etc., so that students can learn online. In the later stage, teachers can modify and maintain the resources of the course according to the feedback of students.

Online Learning. Online learning means that students study the courses created by the teachers through the WeChat Mini Program, acquire the basic knowledge of the course, complete the after-school exercises and participate in the case analysis and experiments.

Online Communication. Online communication refers to communication between teachers and students and among students. They can communicate through text, voice or video provided by WeChat Mini Program to solve the problems encountered in learning.

Online Evaluation. Online evaluation means that students can use the evaluation function after study and answer the teacher's preset questions to examine their own knowledge and then give corresponding comments and suggestions.

4.4 User Role Design

The system is designed with three roles: system administrator, teacher and student.

The System Administrator. The system administrator is responsible for the collection and classification of parameters and data of the system.

Teacher. The teacher is responsible for uploading course materials, guiding **Students.** Students to learn and practice, and communicating with students online.

Students use the system through the WeChat Mini Program.

5 Conclusions

This research aims to build a platform for college teaching resources sharing platform based on WeChat Mini Program through comprehensive use of information technology, ultimately to provide an effective way for students and people outside campus to learn online. This research will go on with long-term accumulation of curriculum resources through mutual cooperation between different universities, mutual recognition of college credits and other mechanisms to achieve regionalized curriculum sharing.

Acknowledgment. This research was supported by Hainan Higher Education Educational Reform Research Project (Hnjg2018-105).

References

1. Li, Z.: The construction of network teaching system in colleges and universities. Comput. Knowl. Technol. **11**(15), 108–110 (2015)
2. Li, Q.: Analysis of college students' self-directed learning in the era of the internet. Educ. Chin. After Sch. (Theory) (03): 90–91 (2019)
3. Wang, F.: Research on the diversified teaching models of college English courses. Mod. Commun. (15), 133 (2017)
4. Zhang, D., Huang, S., Zhu, W., Zhu, W.: Design of second class credit system based on small program. Comput. Knowl. Technol. **14**(36), 54–57, 71 (2018)
5. Jinyang, S.: Analysis of mini program technology and security issues. China New Commun. **20**(23), 137–138 (2018)
6. Sun, G., Song, Z., Liu, J., et al.: Feature selection method based on maximum information coefficient and approximate Markov blanket. Zidonghua Xuebao/Acta Automatica Sinica **43** (5), 795–805 (2009)
7. Sun, G., Li, X., Hou, X., et al.: GPU-accelerated support vector machines for traffic classification. Int. J. Perform. Eng. **14**(5), 1088–1098 (2018)
8. Pani, S.K., Mohapatra, D., Ratha, B.K.: Integration of web mining and web crawler: relevance and state of art. Int. J. Comput. Sci. Eng. **2**(3), 772–776 (2010)
9. Duan, Y., Edwards, J.S., Dwivedi, Y.K.: Artificial intelligence for decision making in the era of Big Data – evolution, challenges and research agenda. Int. J. Inf. Manag. **48**, 63–71 (2019)
10. Zhang, X., Pei, F.: Campus resource sharing based on WeChat platform in the background of informationization-development and use of mini programs. Comput. Prod. Circ. (01), 128 (2019)
11. Lu, P.: Design of shared space platform based on vue.js. Digit. Commun. World (03), 199, 280 (2018)
12. Fan, K., Chen, Y.: Research on MySQL database performance optimization. China New Telecommun. **21**(01), 57 (2019)

Design of PLC Technology Courses Based on Blended Learning in Colleges and Universities

Wei Yan(✉)

School of Physics and Electronic Information,
Inner Mongolia University for Nationalities, Tongliao, China
ms96590@163.com

Abstract. PLC technology course is a specialized course of electronic information engineering major of our school. It contains several programming languages such as sequential function chart, logic block diagram, statement list, ladder diagram, etc. It is important in cultivating and improving students' programming ability effect. Combining the characteristics of PLC technology course with the advantages of hybrid teaching method, this paper studies deeply from curriculum construction, instructional design to curriculum evaluation. Based on the Blended learning method, the "online" and "offline", The combination of theory and experiment teaching model, to optimize the teaching quality of PLC technology has a positive role in promoting.

Keywords: Blended learning · College teaching · Teaching process design

1 Introduction

With the advent of the information age, informationization has become a trend of higher education development. Mooc class, micro class, flip the classroom and other teaching methods appear in the daily teaching activities of various colleges and universities. The use of network resources and multimedia resources to optimize and assist the teaching of traditional classroom teaching, known as the hybrid teaching. As an important component of modern educational philosophy, hybrid teaching maximizes the advantages of traditional teaching and online teaching. But this advantage does not come naturally, it requires the careful design and implementation of the instructor.

PLC technology as a professional course of electronic information engineering, the course has a strong practicality, through the use of the PLC on the machine to understand its function; the same time, the course has a high degree of comprehensiveness, from the principle of the curriculum. It integrates basic knowledge of logic control, analog control, high-speed position control, pulse control and networking from an application point of view, combining knowledge of electrical control, analog electronics, digital electronics, computer programming, Communication control, etc.; In addition, the course is highly creative and requires creative instruction programming to solve practical production problems. In this context, how to use the hybrid teaching methods to optimize the teaching quality of PLC technology courses is of great significance.

G. Sun et al. (Eds.): eLEOT 2019, LNICST 299, pp. 62–68, 2019.
https://doi.org/10.1007/978-3-030-35095-6_7

2 Mixed Teaching Theory and Technical Basis

2.1 Mixed-Type Teaching Theory

Hybrid teaching is the traditional combination of face-to-face classroom learning and online learning (Fig. 1). The core idea is to solve it according to different problems and adopt different ways to solve them. Teaching involves different media and information transmission teaching. In the process of implementation, students should pay attention to the vital needs of knowledge according to the humanism and make them develop more. To some extent, the humanistic view of learning foreshadows the trend of instructional law. Rogers, the representative of humanistic thought, applies the humanistic psychology theory to teaching research and experiment, confirms the theory of "affective teaching" and "student-centered teaching mode". To overcome the traditional teaching emphasis on social function, neglect the development of personality development function, lack of initiative of students learning and other shortcomings, has a certain enlightenment and positive significance.

Jennifer Hofmann points out in the B-Learning Case Study that the idea behind hybrid learning is that instructional designers break up a learning process into many modules and then decide to use it to the best media present these modules to learners.

From this notion, it can be seen that Jennifer Hofmann and others agree that blended learning presents the best module (or combination of modules) for learner learning using the best media (or media mix) to achieve the best learning effect of teaching design ideas.

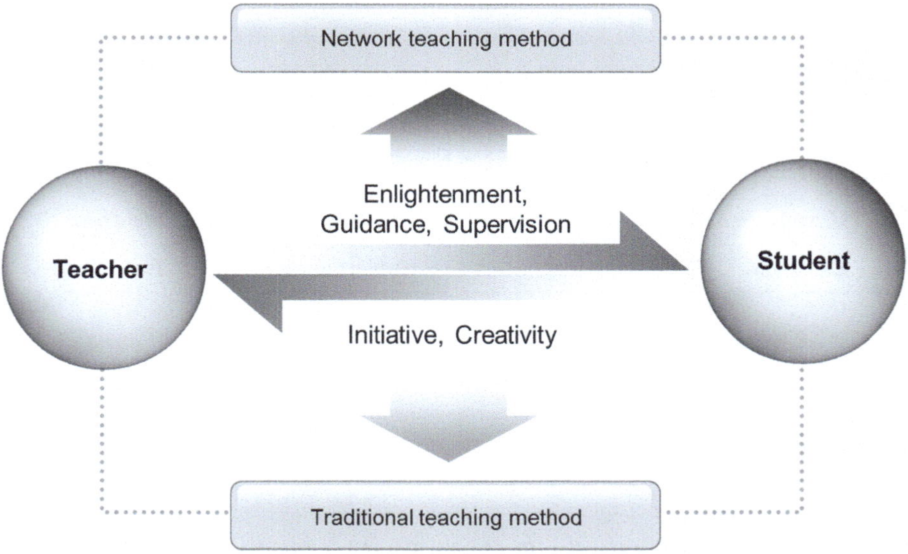

Fig. 1. A hybrid teaching

2.2 Hybrid Teaching Technology Base

Electronic performance support systems and knowledge management techniques provide the technical basis for blended instruction. E-Performance Support System is a work-support and learning support system that provides an integrated resource to facilitate efficient work or learning through the provision of templates, flexible help, expert systems, guides, flowcharts, and all other forms of media. Knowledge management techniques such as sociology, information management, psychology, education and other multidisciplinary and multi-disciplinary advanced concepts, in practical applications for educational technology reference and migration.

3 Course Construction

The PLC technology course is a specialized course for electronics professionals. This course teaches PLC technology widely used in modern control field based on the control technology (i.e., program control) based on the relay control circuit in the field of automatic control. As shown in Fig. 2, PLC technology courses teaching objectives specifically divided into knowledge goals, skills goals, process goals and values goals.

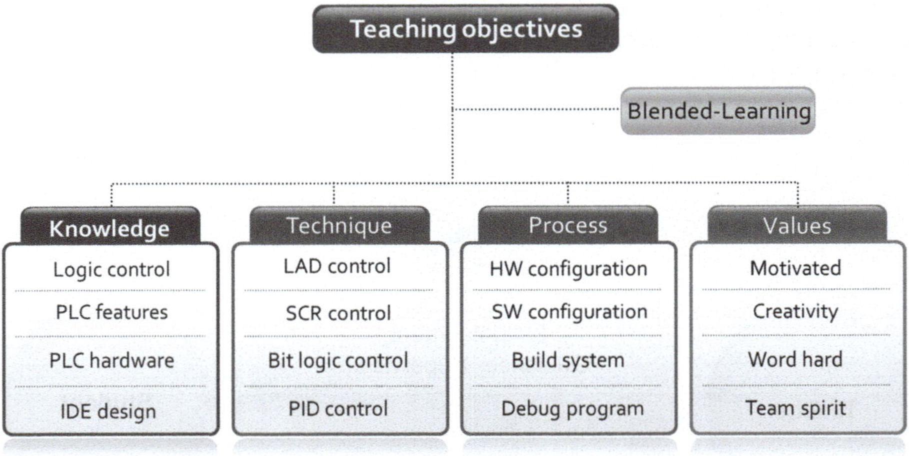

Fig. 2. PLC teaching objectives

4 Mixed Teaching Design

4.1 Design Principles

4.1.1 For Different Personality Students, Teaching Students According to Their Aptitude

Each student's learning abilities directly affect their learning efficiency. In the classroom, the teacher's knowledge is directed at most of the students in the class, often failing to cater to students with high scores and those with poor grades. Students who have scores above and below the class average can take a 1-on-1 online course to explain their knowledge. For students with excellent performance, teachers can interact deeply with students through online learning platform. For students with relatively poor grades, students can simplify the knowledge in the classroom and solve their problems.

Teachers through the online interaction to make up for offline teaching problems, answer students' questions, solve student problems, ensure that each student can really learn each knowledge point, and get more time to establish links with students to increase teachers and students' emotion.

4.1.2 Different Teaching Methods to Match Different Teaching Methods

Because of the limitation of time and space, the traditional teaching classroom unifies the process of "teaching" and "learning" in the classroom, resulting in fast paced classroom, low participation of students and inefficient teaching. Hybrid learning can adjust the teaching methods for these problems, and use video, audio, images and other forms to solve problems that are not solved in time online and communicate with students. "Teaching" and "learning" through online and offline organic combination, can make teachers in the limited class time will focus on difficult points to the students.

4.2 Mixed Teaching Content Design

Different from the traditional teaching mode, the hybrid teaching makes the students not only confined to the classroom when acquiring knowledge, but also exchanges with the teachers not only in the classroom. The entire teaching activities require the cooperation of teachers and students, teachers become the guide of the curriculum, the students become the main body of teaching, which greatly improves the learning initiative and improves and perfects the curriculum through the joint efforts of both parties. In this process of mutual learning and mutual promotion, the teacher is no longer just a simple communicator of knowledge. The teaching process is not merely the repetition of machinery. Instead, teachers and students cooperate with each other and think together. Teachers should understand that the students have Experience and foundation, and create a suitable situation and activities for students, so that students learn more in the learning process.

The teaching content mainly includes three aspects: one is teaching resources centered on micro-video and interactive exercises; the other is innovative experimental design; and the third is teaching activities aimed at teaching resources.

The construction of teaching resources is mainly based on the concept of "fragmentation", the teaching knowledge unit as short as possible, specific, so that students can digest and understand in a short time. Innovative experimental design is different from the previous confirmatory experiments. In the confirmatory experiment, the students are all mechanical input teachers to release the program. The output of the operation and the analysis results lead to the low enthusiasm of students and the too small expectation of the experimental results. Innovative experimental design is designed for a particular principle of a special task, grouping allows students to complete the process from program design, program debugging to run the entire process, and to sum up, and there should be exchanges between groups and groups, analysis and experience. The design of teaching activities is divided into before class, class, and after-school.

(1) Before class part
Develop a detailed before class learning tasks, summarize the knowledge of the previous section and send it to students. Students are required to preview the contents of this lesson, master the principles, write the program, and send it to the diagram of the students' knowledge points. During the preview process, students can communicate with teachers via online platforms, We Chat, email and other means of communication at any time. Teachers check through the hybrid teaching platform before the next class begins.

(2) Part of the lesson
In the hybrid teaching mode, classroom teaching is the most effective way of communication between teachers and students. The course is divided into two sections according to time. The first half of the section mainly explains and sorts out the knowledge points. The second section mainly focuses on question answering. At the end of the class, the teacher posts the learning tasks in the next section and informs the student about the resource link.

(3) After class part
In the hybrid teaching platform to modify homework, some of the typical problems that exist in students to organize, check each student's progress and learning status.

5 Course Evaluation

The traditional teaching model evaluates students' learning only in the final exams. As a result, many students do not usually study at the end of the exams. They take a comprehensive assault before the final exams, and their participation in learning is not high enough to deal with the exams. In a blended teaching model, evaluating a student's learning can actually achieve procedural evaluation. In the evaluation of the dimension is not limited to the final grade in the class and the final exam scores, but also the completion of each knowledge point in the teaching task, the completion of each experiment, the whole dimension of the students' learning evaluation. Evaluation of quantitative methods shown in Table 1, the assessment criteria shown in Table 2.

Table 1. Learning process evaluation method of quantification

Evaluation type	Evaluation object	Standard	Level
Process	Pre-mission record Platform practice scores	Duration Score	Understanding Analysis
Formative	Student discussion Online test Group activity	Knowledge points Score Theme tasks	Understanding Analysis
Summary	Experimental test Final exam	Score Score	Understanding Analysis

Table 2. PLC technical courses grade assessment standards.

Pre-mission record	10%	Usual grades 70%
Student discussion	30%	
Group activity		
Platform practice scores	10%	
Online test	20%	
Experimental test	10%	
	20%	

6 End

Based on the analysis of the hybrid teaching theory, combined with the characteristics of PLC technology courses, designed based on hybrid teaching of PLC technology courses teaching, to improve student learning participation, programming ability, ability to solve practical problems is very helpful. Under this mode, through the guidance of teachers and the active participation of students, the quality of teaching is greatly optimized, and there are also positive references for other courses.

7 Funding

This work was supported by Inner Mongolia University for Nationalities scientific research project grant No. NMDYB19066.

References

1. Helmer, S.M., Rogge, A.A.: Evaluation of a blended-learning training concept to train oncology physicians to advise their patients about complementary and integrative medicine (KOKON-KTO): study protocol for a prospective, multi-center, cluster-randomized trial. Trials **20**(1), 90 (2019)
2. Abraham, A., Corchado, E.: Hybrid learning machines. Neurocomputing **72**(13), 2729–2730 (2009)
3. Yeh, Y.C., Huang, L.Y.: Knowledge management in blended learning: effects on professional development in creativity instruction. Comput. Educ. **56**(1), 146–156 (2011)
4. Jia, J., Chen, Y.: Effects of a vocabulary acquisition and assessment system on students' performance in a blended learning class for English subject. Comput. Educ. **58**(1), 63–76 (2012)
5. Philipsen, B., Tondeur, J.: Improving teacher professional development for online and blended learning: a systematic meta-aggregative review. Educ. Technol. Res. Dev. (2019)
6. Roche, T., Harrington, M.: Recognition vocabulary knowledge as a predictor of academic performance in an English as a foreign language setting. Lang. Test. Asia **3**(1), 12 (2013)
7. Woltering, V., Herrler, A.: Blended learning positively affects students' satisfaction and the role of the tutor in the problem-based learning process: results of a mixed-method evaluation. Adv. Health Sci. Educ. Theory Pract. **14**(5), 725 (2009)

8. Derntl, M., Motschnig-Pitrik, R.: The role of structure, patterns, and people in blended learning. Internet High. Educ. **8**(2), 111–130 (2005)
9. Garrison, D.R., Kanuka, H.: Blended learning: uncovering its transformative potential in higher education. Internet High. Educ. **7**(2), 95–105 (2004)
10. Liu, S., Fu, W.: Distribution of primary additional errors in fractal encoding method. Multimed. Tools Appl. **76**(4), 5787–5802 (2017)
11. So, H.J., Brush, T.A.: Student perceptions of collaborative learning, social presence and satisfaction in a blended learning environment: relationships and critical factors. Comput. Educ. **51**(1), 318–336 (2008)
12. Bonk, C.J., Graham, C.R.: The handbook of blended learning: global perspectives, local designs. Turkish Online J. Dist. Educ. **10**(4), 181 (2009)
13. Meng, J.E., Deng, C.: Obstacle avoidance of a mobile robot using hybrid learning approach. IEEE Trans. Industr. Electron. **52**(3), 898–905 (2005)
14. Zhu, L., Bevilacqua, V.: Special issue on advanced intelligent computing methodologies and applications. Neurocomputing **188**(1), 1–2 (2016)
15. Pan, Z., Liu, S.: A review of visual moving target tracking. Multimed. Tools Appl. **76**, 16989–17018 (2016)
16. Liu, S., Pan, Z.: A novel fast fractal image compression method based on distance clustering in high dimensional sphere surface. Fractals Complex Geom. Patterns Scaling Nat. Soc. **25** (23), 1740004 (2017)
17. Crawford, R.: Rethinking teaching and learning pedagogy for education in the twenty-first century: blended learning in music education. Music Educ. Res. **19**(2), 1–19 (2017)
18. Sugiyanta, L., Sukardjo, M.: Adjusted framework of m-learning in blended learning system for mathematics study field of junior high school level VII. In: IOP Conference Series: Materials Science and Engineering, vol. 336, p. 012031 (2018)
19. Manwaring, K.C., Larsen, R., Graham, C., et al.: Investigating student engagement in blended learning settings using experience sampling and structural equation modeling. Internet High. Educ. **35**, 21–33 (2017)
20. Luo, L., Cheng, X., Wang, S., et al.: Blended learning with moodle in medical statistics: an assessment of knowledge, attitudes and practices relating to e-learning. BMC Med. Educ. **17** (1), 170 (2017)

Exploration on the Application of Blended Learning Model in Practical Training Teaching—Taking "Data Communication in Wireless Sensor Networks" as an Example

Heng Tang(✉) and Hongfang Cheng

Wuhu Institute of Technology, Wuhu, Anhui, China
195952801@qq.com, 403242688@qq.com

Abstract. As an important part of Higher Vocational Education, practical training teaching combines blended learning with online learning and traditional classroom teaching methods. Meanwhile, it uses various teaching resources such as online learning platform resources, online simulation system, experimental equipment and so on. Practical training teaching is divided into three stages: pre-class guidance, in-class learning and after-class expansion. It achieves good teaching effect and realizes the student-centered learning style.

Keywords: Blended learning · Practical training teaching

With the development of network and multimedia technology, new information-based education methods are constantly emerging, and the application of blended learning in higher education is becoming more and more popular. From the definition of blended learning, it can be seen that blended learning aims to combine the advantages of traditional teaching and online learning so as to reduce teaching costs and improve teaching benefits [1]. For different learning environments and activities, teachers should provide different learning resources [2]. On one hand, teacher can monitor the whole learning process; on the other hand, students, as the subject of learning, can show their independence, initiative and creativity [3]. During their learning process including self-consultation, observation, prediction, adjustment, and reflection, students become capable of accumulating knowledge, developing learning methods and abilities, resulting in the achievement the learning goals [4]. Blended learning in practical teaching can not only support teachers to play a leading role in the teaching process, but also give full play to students' initiative and enthusiasm, and derive the learning process steadily outside the classroom to achieve student-centered learning.

1 Instructional Design

The reason why teaching design of the blended learning of "Wireless Sensor Network Data Communication" begins with the analysis of the learner is that the level of students' previous knowledge is the key factor of predicting their performance [5].

G. Sun et al. (Eds.): eLEOT 2019, LNICST 299, pp. 69–73, 2019.
https://doi.org/10.1007/978-3-030-35095-6_8

1.1 Learner Analysis

The object of study of this content is the second-year students of Internet of Things application technology specialty. After one and a half years of professional study, the students at this stage have a certain understanding of network communication, sensors, programming languages and other professional knowledge, who can use professional tools such as microcontroller and computer, and can use information technology means to study independently.

1.2 Design of Training Objectives

The design of blended learning defines the teaching objectives of this course [6]. According to the professional training objectives, curriculum objectives and professional needs, the core objectives are abstracted: to train students' engineering application ability in the design, installation, networking and debugging of the Internet of Things; to clarify the focus of training is the installation, networking and debugging of ZigBee nodes, and to identify the difficulties in the process of debugging: fault detection and analysis debugging.

1.3 Design of Training Strategy

In practice, the mode of task-driven and blended learning is adopted to cultivate students' engineering application ability and professional quality. Taking "Home Internet of Things" as the content of the training project, students are required to simulated design and install a small Internet of Things system suitable for families according to this task. The whole training process is divided into three stages: pre-class guidance, in-class learning and after-class expansion. In these three stages, online learning runs through the whole process. The purpose of blended learning activity design is the integration of autonomy and interaction [7]. Teachers guide students to study by themselves, supervise learning progress, and answer students' questions through the network. Teachers derive their leadership outside the classroom, and students' consciousness and initiative are also enhanced. The content of online learning should be organized pertinently by teachers according to teaching objectives and students' cognitive process, and students should be the learning agent. The design of learning module arranges content around the training objectives, constructs a network knowledge structure framework, and enhances students' enthusiasm and sense of achievement by designing various interactive activities. At the same time, attention should be drawn to the fact that the learning distraction could be caused by poor teaching design, misguidance of course and improper interaction [8].

Online learning is implemented by means of online learning platform and online simulation system developed by Wuhu Institute of Technology. In the practical classroom teaching, relying on the integration of theory and practice in the wireless sensor network training room, students are guided to carry out standardized training operation steps through teachers' personal demonstration, students' mutual evaluation, fault evaluation and other ways.

1.4 Design of Training Evaluation

According to the purpose of the training and synthesizing learning process and learning results, the effect of mixed learning is evaluated: the process is evaluated according to the degree and performance of students' active participation, and the learning results are evaluated according to the completion of students' practical training, homework and so on. In the implementation of mixed training, by using online platform testing, teacher inspection, student mutual evaluation, platform homework, enterprise tutor scoring and other evaluation methods, teachers refine evaluation indicators according to actual work needs, cultivate students' professional quality, conduct multi-dimensional comprehensive evaluation of students, use a variety of teaching means and methods to consolidate teaching focus and break through teaching difficulties.

2 The Implementation Process of Hybrid Training

The teaching process is divided into three stages: pre-class guidance, in-class learning and after-class expansion, as shown in Fig. 1.

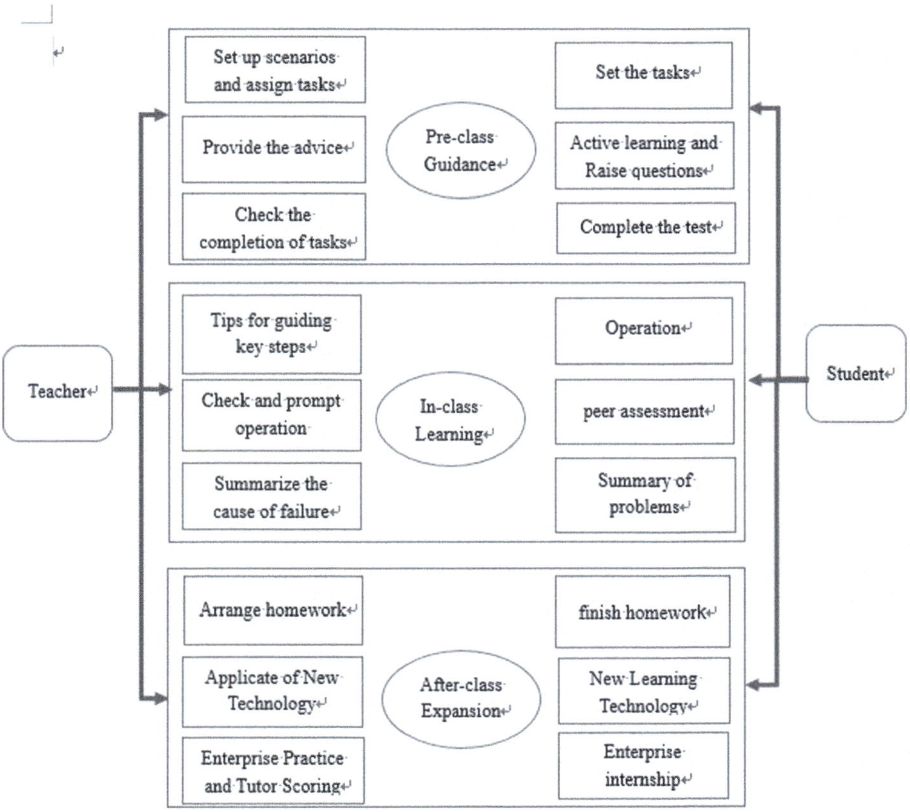

Fig. 1. The implementation process of hybrid training

2.1 Pre-class Guidance

Pre-class tasks are published by APP, so students can make clear their learning objectives and requirements according to pre-class tasks, then use the resources of online learning platform to learn autonomously, understand the layout of Zigbee nodes, wiring specifications and knowledge of electrical detection, as well as the role and difference of coordinator and terminal nodes. Through operating on-line simulation training system to simulate the real work task feeling workflow, students can understand the difficulty of fault detection, analysis and debugging in node communication. With the help of online learning platform, teachers can real-time view students' learning status, publish test tasks, and check students' learning performance.

2.2 In-class Learning

Teachers instruct students to arrange nodes, regulate wiring, check power on, use simulator to complete program burning, install ZigBee nodes, set up networks and debug by prompting key steps. Students can watch circuit wiring diagram and operation specification prompt in online simulation system repeatedly during operation. Teachers can guide students' operation process and specification on the spot through testing tools.

Fault detection, analysis and debugging are difficult problems in practical training. Because there are many kinds of faults and the forms of faults are similar, it is difficult for teachers to guide each group at the same time in traditional teaching. The problem that students' feedback is not clear or the problem of feedback can not be solved in time is more prominent. Mixed learning can solve this problem. In the pre-class tutorial, teachers make videos, pictures and animations to emphasize the common faults and solve them in advance, and check them through the test task. In class, students can also repeatedly check the online learning platform and the operation video and tips in the simulation training system to try to solve the problem by themselves. At the end of the training, teachers train students' ability of fault detection and analysis by organizing students' mutual evaluation. Finally, teachers use fault monitoring tools to collect students' fault content, and summarize the causes of the failure and analyze the solutions.

2.3 After-class Expansion

Teachers deliver homework after class according to the summary of the training content. Through providing rich resources on the online platform, students who have learning capability can be guided to learn the new technology of the Internet of Things and the application in the production process of enterprises, so as to stimulate students' enthusiasm for learning. Students' consciousness of career is inspired by their tutor for he or she has rich industry resources and working experience [9]. Students are organized to visit relevant enterprises for internship, compare real work scenes and processes, and enhance the ability of engineering application.

3 Conclusion

This paper takes "data communication in wireless sensor networks" as an example to discuss the design and practice of training activities under hybrid learning. Hybrid learning combines online learning with traditional practice through teacher's design, gives full play to their respective advantages, and solves the shortcoming of online learning testing students' consciousness through the comprehensive evaluation of learning process and learning results. The effectiveness of online learning activities is closely related to the participation of teachers [10]. In the part of warm-up, quality of topic discussion should be improved. Hybrid learning can be well applied to students at different levels in practical teaching. It can not only play the leading role of teachers, but also realize the student-centered learning mode.

Acknowledgment. This work was supported by the research on high school provincial quality engineering project of Anhui grant No. 2015mooc109 and No. 2016ckjh224, the excellent top talent cultivation project of Anhui high school grant No. gxyqZD2017141, Nature science research project of Anhui high school grant No. KJ2017A560, and school level scientific and technological innovation team grant No. Wzykj2018A02.

References

1. Dong, Y.: A study on the teaching design and curriculum practice of modern educational technology based on blended learning. J. Beijing City Univ. (03), 47–52 (2018)
2. Tian, L., Liao, H., Chen, C.: Research on mixed learning instructional design in information technology environment. Softw. Guide (06), 51–53 (2018)
3. Li, Y.: Research of SPOC supported blended learning in collaborative activity to solve problems. J. Zhengzhou Norm. Educ. (5), 29–33 (2018)
4. Lv, Q.: From MOOC to SPOC: advantage of blended learning in talent training. J. Nanjing Inst. Technol. (Soc. Sci. Ed.) **18**(3), 68–73 (2018)
5. Sun, Z., Song, J., Luo, L.: Research on dynamic design of blended courses. E-educ. Res. (7), 85–92 (2017)
6. Li, M.: Exploration of blended learning teaching practice based on Xuexitong platform. Henan Educ. (5), 74–76 (2018)
7. Zhou, Y., Han, Y.: Research on learners' engagement in blended learning activities. E-educ. Res. (11), 99–106 (2018)
8. Tian, Y., Du, J., Huang, R.: Research on learning and social synergy strategies for blended learning. China Educ. Technol. (8), 8–14 (2018)
9. Ma, J., Han, X., Zhou, Q.: The practical exploration of enterprise tutor system in the college students' career education. Educ. Teach. Forum (10), 45–46 (2018)
10. Ma, J., Han, X., Zhou, Q.: An empirical study on online teaching group behavior of teachers and students in universities based on learning analysis. E-educ. Res. (2), 13–18 (2014)

Research and Thinking on Diversified Teaching Methods of Mechanical Theory

Rui-can Hao(✉), Zhi-xin Feng, Xue-lei Wang, and Hui Yu

Beijing Polytechnic, No. 9 Liangshuihe First Street, Yizhuang, Beijing, China
haoruican@163.com

Abstract. The common problems in the teaching process of mechanical theory are found by analyzing the nature of this course. As for improving the enthusiasm of students, the project-driven teaching method, the method of introducing mechanical innovation design into the teaching case, mastery teaching method, the introduction of computer simulation software, and flipped classroom teaching model are studied respectively in order to ensure that students can improve their ability and level of personal knowledge application in the process of active participation and learning practice. It is concluded that these teaching methods can be combined in teaching different chapters of mechanical theory in line with students and situations. It is advocated to strengthen teachers' researches on the course, develop more innovative design cases, software analogue simulation, flipped classroom and other teaching resources so as to obtain better teaching results.

Keywords: Mechanical theory · Teaching methods · Diversity

1 Teaching Characteristics and Problems of Mechanical Theory

1.1 Teaching Characteristics of Mechanical Theory

Mechanical theory is an important professional foundation course which is compulsory in mechanical disciplines of China's universities and colleges to study the principles of mechanical composition, working, design and methods. It is not only a "bridge" course which is closely related to the actual production but also an important stage course for students to learn the innovative ideas and methods of mechanical design. In addition, it has relatively stronger applicability, practicality and engineering. In the process of learning this course, students need to understand the theoretical knowledge of mechanical structure analysis, structural kinematics analysis and kinetic analysis so as to improve their ability of theoretical analysis during learning and practice. If it is analyzed from microscopic perspective, mechanical theory is mainly intended to cultivate the students' ability to design the motion scheme of innovative mechanisms, analyze and study different design purposes and tasks in depth, consider actively different operational coordination and diversified structural operation schemes, and select the best scheme through comprehensive comparison and evaluation. Therefore, it has relatively stronger practicality [1, 2].

G. Sun et al. (Eds.): eLEOT 2019, LNICST 299, pp. 74–81, 2019.
https://doi.org/10.1007/978-3-030-35095-6_9

1.2 Common Problems in Teaching Process of Mechanical Theory

At present, the traditional teaching of mechanical theory has the following problems [3].

Firstly, theories are stressed, while practice is neglected. The classroom instruction limits students' understanding of mechanisms to bars, gears, cams or their combination. Take link mechanism as an example. Students see in books only a schematic diagram of the mechanism consisting of straight lines and circles. It is difficult for them to have a good perceptual understanding of real-life mechanical products. Mechanical innovative design, mechanical system transmission, basic scheme conception and design method evaluation, which closely relate subject frontiers to engineering application, should be supplemented and strengthened. And the new achievements, methods and concepts of science and technology related to mechanisms should be closely combined. Attention should be paid to strengthening the ability cultivation in practical application.

Secondly, each chapter is independent individually with few comprehensive theoretical chapters and practical teaching links, and the practice of global design ability of mechanical systems is lacked. It is found in the analysis of students' comprehensive innovation ability that many students face great difficulties and obstacles in the design stage when establishing the motion scheme of mechanical systems. It is difficult to ensure a close connection between theoretical study and practical research and they may even feel overwhelmed.

Thirdly, mechanical theory has little connection with other courses and mechanism analysis is usually made just for mechanism analysis. More comprehensive tasks may be proposed to combine mechanical theory with engineering mechanics and machine design for comprehensive analysis. Or design competition may be used together for connection.

Forthly, the design scheme of mechanical structure proposed in experiments or practice is too simple and students need a large amount of time and energy to complete relevant assignments, so the final teaching quality and results are not guaranteed. In addition, a class is usually assigned the same task, which does not reflect students' difference in personal ability and interest. The link is programmed, which restricts students' innovation ability.

Because of the questions above, the teaching of mechanical theory, which essentially has high innovation, divergent and flexible thinking as well as passionate creation, may become a cramming education with disconnected theory and practice, insipid teaching process, blind learning target, decreased learning enthusiasm and declined teaching quality.

2 Exploration and Thinking on Teaching Methods

In allusion to the teaching problems, teachers of mechanical theory should improve students' enthusiasm and explore diversified teaching methods to ensure that students can improve their ability and level of personal knowledge application in the process of active participation and learning practice, so that students can master the contents and essence of mechanical theory.

2.1 Exploration and Practice of Project-Driven Teaching Method

CDIO project-driven teaching method, led by engineering practice, fully reflects modern educational ideas. It is widely used in western countries with notable results. Practical teaching activities are exercised in this teaching method through a complete "project" task. The knowledge and skills involved in the course are assigned through a specific "project task" to students, who adopt the method of "team learning" and utilize their brains, hands, exchange and cooperation as well as their knowledge and skills according to the task requirements, through five stages of "determining projects, preparing work plans, organizing project implementation, inspection, examine and assessment, summary, appraisal and filing", to complete the project task and present their achievements. In allusion to present educational objectives of engineering education in China, it is recommended to adopt CDIO project-driven teaching method, which is led by problems and projects with "conceive, design, implement, operate" as the key link.

It is the most effective for students to learn in the process of experience and creation. Through project implementation and combination between theory with practice, students will study with questions, which can greatly improve their interest in mechanical theory and manufacturing of mechanical products of science and technology. In the process of manufacturing the product, students will have a clear learning objective, and the fun in the manufacturing process in turn will promote their interest in learning.

2.2 Introducing the Task of Mechanical Innovation Design into Teaching Case [3]

Innovation is the soul of a country. At present, a large number of high-quality all-round talents are needed, especially those with high innovation ability. Innovation points are important indicators in measuring a good mechanical product. The innovation ability of students majoring in mechanisms is often reflected in the innovation point of realizing mechanism functions and structures. Therefore, it not only promotes classroom teaching but also cultivates students' comprehensive ability to introduce mechanical innovative design into the teaching of mechanical theory and create an innovative and pioneering scientific and technological innovation environment.

As for the teaching of mechanical theory, teachers may require students to utilize their extra-curricular time to complete a large assignment implemented as mechanical innovative design project. The large assignment should be scheduled in the first class with specific requirements. For example, a thesis of analyzing and calculating the design scheme of a complete mechanical product must be finished, including function analysis and argumentation, mechanical innovative design and realization, kinetic analysis and calculation, and computer simulation.

The introduction of a multifunctional relief knapsack in the mechanical innovation competition is an example. Figure 1 shows a multifunctional relief knapsack. A detachable four-fold frame structure is proposed in the task. With folded canvas and tent matched tactfully, a knapsack is manufactured, which can not only transport materials but also turn into stretcher and tent. The introduction of this case not only expands students' innovative thinking but also provides them with knowledge of mechanism design, verifying calculation and computer software modeling [4].

Fig. 1. Teaching case of multifunctional relief knapsack

By introducing mechanical innovative design projects into the teaching of mechanical theory, students become gradually interested in participating in innovative designs, which greatly promotes their learning enthusiasm for mechanical theory and improves their global ability of scientific and technological manufacturing.

An excellent mechanical innovation product is also a favorable material for mechanical theory. The introduction of mechanical innovative design projects into the teaching of mechanical theory is beneficial for improving the teaching results of mechanical theory and students' mechanical innovative design ability. It is worth promoting by teachers of mechanical theory.

2.3 Mastery Teaching Method

Introduction to Mastery Teaching Method. As for mastery teaching method, students need to make full sense of previous concepts before the learning phase of greater difficulty. The opinion is held in this method that all students can master the knowledge without lagging behind or poor performance as long as teaching conditions meet students' demands. This teaching method was proposed more than 100 years ago and its advantages have been verified in the process of teaching. However, it is difficult to implement this method because it needs a large number of hardware resources. Nowadays, the development of cloud computing, Internet of things and big data technology is changing the social ecology and educational ecology. Tremendous changes will take place to education in future Internet plus environment. It will certainly become an important topic concerned and researched by the educational world to take advantage of mastery teaching method by Internet plus so as to meet the impact of Internet plus on education [5].

Practice Method of Internet Plus Mastery Teaching Method. Learning and perception are usually realized by perception—analysis—integration. At first, a comprehensive and global perception of the teaching content of mechanical theory should be obtained. Then the overall diagram of mechanical theory should be drawn by mind mapping, through which the course is perceived and cognized to know every knowledge point of the course most intuitively and analyze their connection. Finally the whole course system is understood better by course learning.

Mechanical theory studies common issues of the whole mechanical system. It expounds three parts of mechanical motion design, mechanical power design and mechanical system design and introduces other common mechanisms and motion principles. The grammar used in lots of conception description of mechanisms in present textbooks tends to be abstract and theoretical. It is usually difficult for undergraduates with less practical experiences to understand many concepts. And it is harder to connect the object to problems in engineering practice, which results in poor teaching results. Students may have a comprehensive understanding of knowledge points in the course of mechanical theory by mind mapping (e.g. Fig. 2).

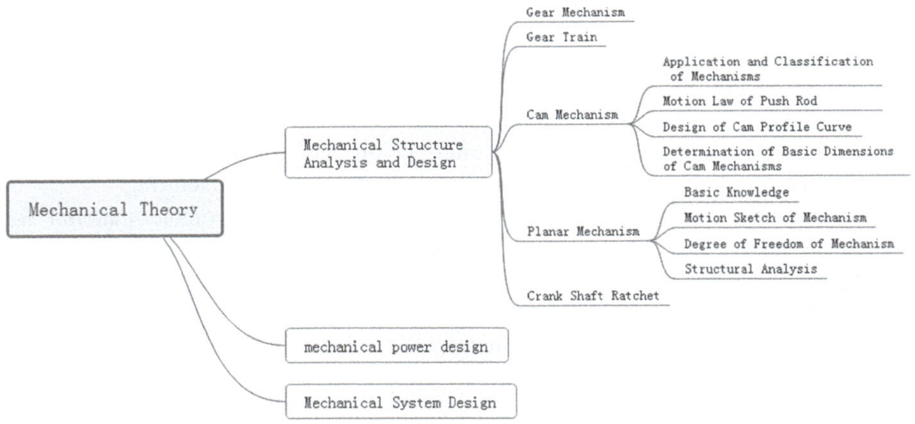

Fig. 2. Mind mapping for the course of mechanical theory

The diagram of knowledge point is about knowledge points derived from the knowledge and concepts of mechanical theory by mind mapping, which embodies radiant thinking. Radiant thinking is a natural way of thinking for human brain. The radiant thinking derived from mind mapping not only accelerates the accumulation of materials but also manages data by hierarchy and category according to their relevancy. Therefore, the storage, management and application of materials are systematized, which greatly improves the efficiency of brain.

As a result, it will improve students' comprehension on the learning of mechanical theory to arrange the knowledge and concepts of mechanical theory by mind mapping and generate a diagram of knowledge point distributed in 3D form.

2.4 Introduction of Computer Simulation Software

With the development of computer technology, CAD and CAE technologies also develop rapidly. Computer-aided instruction (CAI), which uses CAE software, has been widely promoted in various disciplines. Well-known CAE software includes Pro/E, UG and ADAMS, which can all meet the requirements of mechanical theory for aided teaching. For example, ADAMS software can realize D modeling and dynamic simulation for mechanisms in mechanical theory, which eliminates the defects of tedious and difficult operation of graphical method, analytical method and experimental method. In addition, it can not only improve students' learning interest and class performance but also help them with a better understanding and mastery of mechanism motion characteristics [6].

Virtual prototype technology is introduced into the motion analysis and design of mechanisms. Mechanism models are established by ADAMS software. Then motion simulation is used for dynamic display of the motion process of mechanisms. And the results of velocity, acceleration, angular velocity and angular acceleration are output in curves or charts.

Computer simulation technologies can improve students' learning interest. ADAMS software will be learned in the chapter of kinematics analysis, so students can use this software to complete after-class assignments. For example, Fig. 3 shows the model of slider-crank mechanism established by the software. The mechanism has a 200 mm long crank, 400 mm long connecting rod. The slider is a cube whose side is 80 mm. The offset distance is 40 mm and the angular velocity of crank is 10 rad/s. The crank rotates anticlockwise. Figure 4 shows the curves of angular velocity and angular acceleration derived from ADAMS software for the connecting rod.

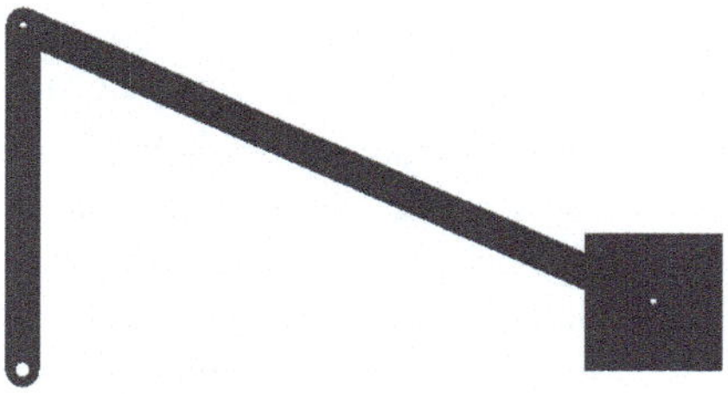

Fig. 3. Model of slider-crank mechanism

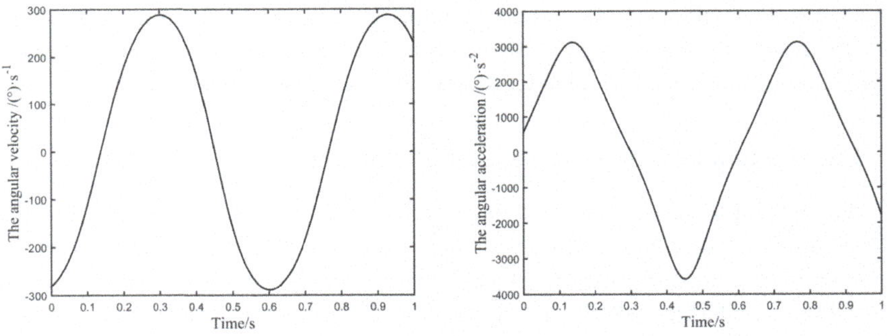

Fig. 4. Curves of angular velocity and angular acceleration of the connecting rod

2.5 Flipped Classroom Teaching Mode [7–9]

Flipped classroom fully reverses the traditional teaching mode of teaching in class and assignment after class. Flipped classroom is a new teaching mode, where teachers provide teaching materials, mainly including micro-videos of teaching, in the information environment and students complete the learning of teaching materials before class. Then teachers and students jointly complete problem solving, cooperation, exploration, interaction and other activities. It fully reverses the traditional teaching mode of teaching in class and assignment after class. Students, receivers listening to teachers passively in the past, become researchers posing problems actively and solving problems with others.

In flipped classroom teaching mode, students complete the learning of course contents independently in advance after class and they participate in learning, discussion and research with prepared questions. Therefore, they will pay attention and their brains will actively deal with problems of themselves and their classmates. And they will try their best to draw their own conclusion. This teaching mode can not only arouse the full enthusiasm of students for learning but also extricate teachers from repeated explanation and demonstration. This teaching mode is particularly appropriate for teaching of applied universities where theory courses are declining.

Flipped classroom teaching mode does not apply to all chapters of mechanical theory. Flipped classroom teaching mode is generally used jointly with traditional teaching modes. For example, it is applicable to the research and practice of "calculation of degree of freedom of plane mechanisms and cautions", "fundamentals of hinged four-bar linkage" and "design of cam profile curve". Relevant teaching process can be implemented by teachers' micro-videos, students' independent learning and questions, problem solving and posing new problems in class, new problem solving by group discussion, summary and evaluation by teachers and other steps.

3 Summary

It is found in the analysis of nature of mechanical theory and characteristics of teaching methods that diversified teaching methods can be combined to realize diversity of courses, arouse the enthusiasm of students, motivate the interest of students in class, and improve teaching quality and learning outcomes. Therefore, it is advocated to teaching courses in line with students and situations, strengthen teachers' researches on and development of the course, adopt diversified teaching modes so as to design more teaching methods and means and development more teaching materials for relevant chapters, such as design cases, software simulation and flipped classroom, to obtain better teaching results.

Acknowledgement. Thanks to the fund and support from the general program of Beijing Municipal Education Commission (KM201910858005).

References

1. Yang, Y., Jiang, J., Wang, D.: Exploration and practice of "Five in One" teaching system of mechanical principles course oriented to ability cultivation and process assessment. High. Educ. Forum **4**, 45–50 (2017)
2. Yin, G., Fang, T., He, C.: Thoughts and practice on improving the teaching quality of mechanical principle course. Exch. Field **9**, 210–227 (2018)
3. Sun, L., Kong, J., Huang, M., Gui, H.: Research on and practice of the machine innovate design project in mechanisms and machine theory teaching. Des. Res. **37**(12), 21–33 (2010)
4. Yang, K., Xu, C., Zhang, E., et al.: Multifunctional disaster relief backpack (2010). https://wenku.baidu.com/view/0abb6ea70722192e4436f628.html
5. Liu, Q., Zhu, Y., Hui, J., et al.: Research on the reform of teaching mode of "internet" mechanical principle course. Educ. Teach. Forum **19**, 102–104 (2018)
6. Chen, H., Chen, S.: Application of CAI in mechanical principle. J. Zhejiang Univ. Wat. Res. Electric. Pow. **29**(3), 76–79 (2017)
7. Ding, R.: Teaching reform and practice of mechanisms and machine theory under applied talents training mode. Mech. Manag. Dev. **8**, 76–85 (2017)
8. Ding, R.: Research and practice of flipping classroom teaching model in the course of mechanical principles. Explor. Educ. Reform **6**, 82–84 (2017). Higher Education Edition (Middle), Henan Education
9. Qiu, B., Zheng, T.: Discussion on the flipped classroom teaching model for "Mechanisms and Machine Theory" **48**, 143–144 (2018)

Massive Open Online Course

Design and Evaluation of Micro-class Based on WeChat Public Platform

Nan Zhang[1], Tianwei Xu[2(✉)], Juxiang Zhou[3], and Min Xie[1]

[1] School of Information, Yunnan Normal University, Kunming 650500, China
516230040@qq.com, 294611018@qq.com

[2] Graduate Faculty, Yunnan Normal University, Kunming 650500, China
335047699@qq.com

[3] Key Laboratory of Education Informatization for Nationalities, Ministry of Education, Yunnan Normal University, Kunming 650500, China
zjuxiang@126.com

Abstract. Vocational education, as an important part of Chinese education system, possesses great demands for informatization in teaching, learning and creative exploring, which meanwhile enjoys great prospects. How to develop informatization in vocational education has become one of the issues that must be solved in current Chinese education system. Taking the course of Mother and Baby Caregiver in vocational education and training as an example, this paper analyzes and summarizes characteristics of adult learners and learners who participate in vocational training based on the adult learning theory from the aspects of learners' background and their psychology. Modular teaching and participatory teaching methods are adopted to prepare for the content and resources for these micro-courses, of which recording, editing, releasing and testing are operated. Finally, this paper explores the learning effects of micro-learning courses from three aspects with the method of comparative analysis: micro-teaching design, micro-class learning effects and micro-teaching experience. Feedback on micro-courses from questionnaires and interviews of students and teachers are well collected to improve the study.

Keywords: Micro-course · Curriculum design · Vocational education · Course evaluation

1 Introduction

Accompanied by the rapid development of information technology in the field of education, education informatization has been widely used in the field of higher education and compulsory education in China and good results have been achieved [1]. Vocational education has always been an important part of China's education field. General Secretary Xi Jinping in the 19th National Party Report proposed the new orientation of vocational education with special characteristics in China [2] "Building a vocational education system with Chinese characteristics, improving vocational education and training systems, deepening the integration of production and education, as well the school-enterprise cooperation". China plans to modernize vocational education in 2035, making vocational education an important support for the country's

G. Sun et al. (Eds.): eLEOT 2019, LNICST 299, pp. 85–95, 2019.
https://doi.org/10.1007/978-3-030-35095-6_10

implementation of the innovation-driven strategy, making the strategy of rejuvenating the country through science and education, and the strategy of strengthening the country through talents, and further improving the basic quality and skills of workers. In 2018, a report entitled "2018 China Vocational Education Technology Outlook: Horizon Project Report" was published in the "Horizon Project Report" which was jointly researched by the New Media Alliance of the United States and the Institute of Wisdom Learning of Beijing Normal University. This article pointed out that educational technology has great needs and development prospects in the fields of teaching, learning and creative inquiry in the field of vocational education [3].

Micro-course is one of the more popular online courses. The earliest use case of micro-class is the organic chemistry 60s teaching method which was proposed by Professor LeRoy A. McGrew in the United States in 1933 [4]. The main purpose of the English Center in the United States is to help learners to learn English and to guide learners in English reading, writing, listening, speaking, and grammar [5]. The development and application of micro-curricular resources abroad relies on the government's education policy. With the wider field of micro-courses, academic institutions and related experts have gradually become the main institutions and groups for the development and application of micro-curricular resources, forming a large-scale, all-round micro-course curriculum system [6]. The micro-class firstly entered China in 2010, and the micro-courses only began to be constructed and used in Foshan, Shenzhen, Inner Mongolia and other regions of China. In 2012, micro-classes achieved spurt development in China [7]. Therefore, this article combines the "Newborn Touch" course in the "Mother and Baby Care" course in vocational training education to design and produce micro-courses, and develop a micro-course learning system for teachers and students to communicate and learn better. And finally the effectiveness of the micro-course teaching was analyzed and evaluated to assist the traditional teaching activities of the course.

1.1 A Micro-learning System Design

Teaching Content Design. The teaching content and teaching objects of vocational training are different from those of traditional teaching. Therefore, the design of micro-classes is also different from that of the traditional education [8]. This paper draws on the design of the vocational training courses in Peking University's civilian schools, combined with the teaching content of the "Newborn Touch" course, using modular and participatory methods for teaching design [9].

Modular Instructional Design. For the adult learners, especially the older learners with low academic qualifications, it is difficult to fully and systematically study the contents of the course [10]. Even through the detailed explanation of the teacher, it is difficult to fully grasp the contents of the course. In this paper, based on the characteristics of adult learners, the course is divided into eight modules in accordance with the characteristics of the "Newborn Touch" course.

Participatory Instructional Design. The "Newborn Touch" course is aimed at the middle-aged women who have children, who have more or less knowledge of maternal and child care. Therefore, the teaching design of the "Newborn Touch" course should allow learners to actively participate in the course learning in combination with their own experience. This kind of teaching method can enhance the interest of adult learners, and let adult learners be quickly integrated into the teaching. Students can improve their learning by the means of combining their own experiences. The subjective consciousness makes the students' sense of participation stronger and makes the students better understand the contents of the course [11].

Micro-learning System Design. He micro-course learning system based on WeChat public platform is mainly to meet the curriculum requirements of teachers and learners. The micro-class learning system mainly includes three modules, which is namely, personal center, curriculum resources and contact us. The overall functional design of the micro-learning system is shown in Fig. 1.

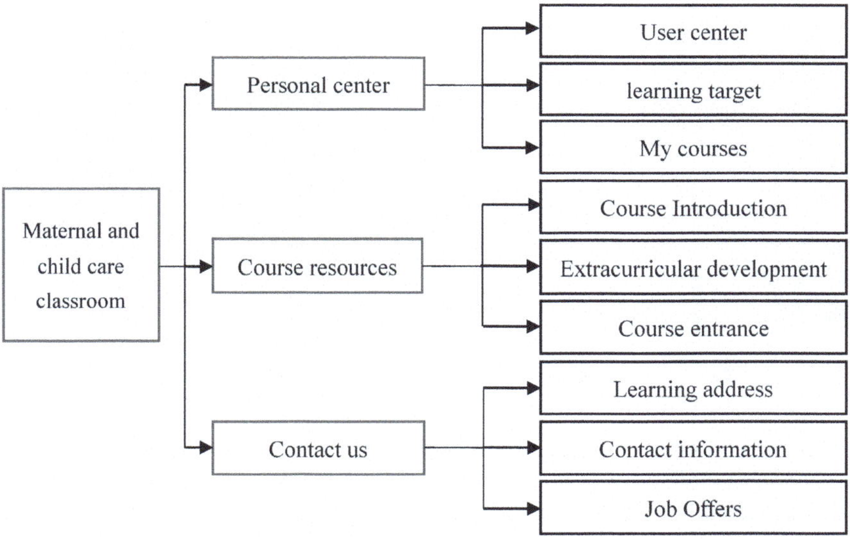

Fig. 1. System function architecture diagram

1.2 Implementation of Micro-learning System

Micro-course Recording. Mainly through the recording software of Screen Flash to complete the recording of theoretical knowledge, the realization of the micro-course of the theoretical course of this research is made. After the course recording is completed, the course will be produced through the Premiere software, theoretical course micro-class rendering effect is shown in Fig. 2.

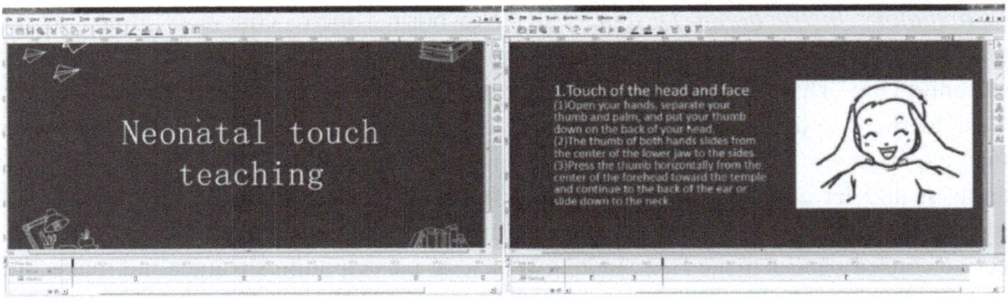

Fig. 2. Recording process of the micro-course theory knowledge

The implementation of this research practice course is mainly by the means of the completion of the recording of the practical operation part in the classroom, and the production of the course through the Premiere software after the completion of the course recording. The theoretical course micro-class presentation effect is shown in Fig. 3.

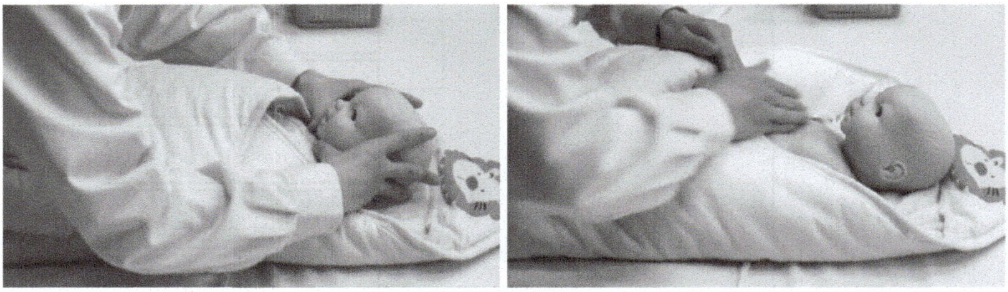

Fig. 3. Recording process of micro-curricular practical knowledge

Implementation of Micro-learning System. The micro-course learning system is a learning system for learners to learn independently through the WeChat public platform. The screenshot effect of the micro-course system is shown in Fig. 4.

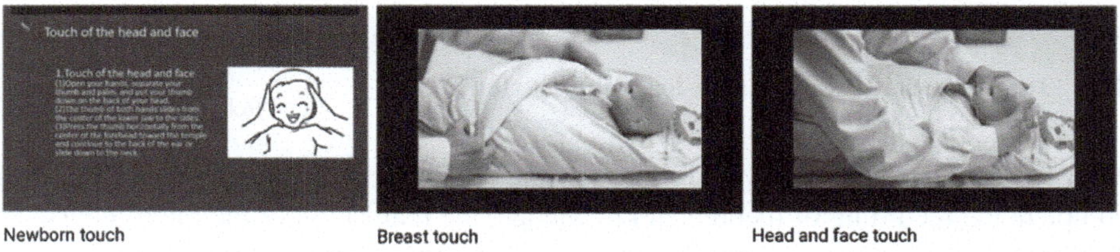

Fig. 4. Micro-course learning system course screenshot

2 Evaluation and Feedback of Micro-teaching Teaching Effect

2.1 Analysis of the Effect of Micro-class Learning

The analysis and evaluation of the learning effect of micro-class mainly includes the analysis of the effect design of micro-teaching and the analysis and evaluation of the learning effect of micro-class. The analysis of the design of micro-teaching is mainly through the questionnaire to analyze the teaching design of micro-class, the analysis of the learning effect of micro-class and the evaluation mainly analyzes and evaluates the learning effect of the students through the test scores of the students.

In this study, the comparative study method was used to classify learners into "Traditional classes" and "Micro-classes". The "Traditional classes" included two classes, and 50 students per class, with a total of 100 students. The "Micro-class" included two classes, each class consisting of 50 students, with a total of 100 students. The questionnaire on the design of micro-teaching was only distributed to 100 students in two "Micro-classes". The score distribution of the "Questionnaire for the evaluation of the teaching design of the "Newborn Touch" micro-teaching" is shown in Table 1.

Table 1. Questionnaire for "Newborn Touching" micro-course teaching design evaluation

Variable	Index	Theoretical course	Practical operation	Score
Teaching needs	Teaching objectives (10 point)	9 point	9 point	9 point
	Teaching content (10 point)	9 point	8.3 point	8.65 point
	Knowledge needs (15 point)	12.5 point	13 point	12.75 point
	Course equirements (15 point)	12 point	13.5 point	12.75 point
Teaching strategy	Micro-teaching order (5 point)	3.5 point	4.5 point	4 point
	Micro lesson video (20 point)	18 point	19 point	18.5 point
	Teaching session (20 point)	19 point	18 point	18.5 point
	Teaching method (5 point)	4.6 point	4.5 point	4.55 point
Grade	Total score (100 point)	87.6 point	89.8 point	88.7 point

From the analysis results of the eight variables of the micro-teaching design in Table 1, we can find that the design of the micro-course teaching of the "Newborn Touch" course is reasonable and can help the learners to better complete the learning tasks. It is a good supplement to traditional teaching.

2.2 Analysis and Evaluation of the Learning Effect of Micro Lessons

The evaluation object of the "Newborn Touch" micro-class learning effect is the two training classes which are the "Traditional class" and "Micro-class class". These two classes are taught by the same teacher, and the quality of the students of the two classes basis the same. The "Traditional class" is used with the traditional classroom teaching method. The "Micro-class class" uses the micro-course teaching method in this study to assist the teaching. There are 100 students in the two classes. After one week of training, the students in the two classes were tested with the same test papers. The results of the theoretical course are shown in Table 2:

Table 2. The results of the "traditional class" and "micro-class" theory courses

"Traditional class" test scores	Score distribution	Fractional segment	90–100	80–89	70–79	60–69	Below 60	
		100 people	0 people	0 people	12 people	78 people	10 people	
		Proportion	0%	0%	12%	78%	10%	
	Highest score	77 point	Lowest score	54 point	average score	65.17 point	Passing rate	90%
"Micro-class" test scores	Score distribution	Fractional segment	90–100	80–89	70–79	60–69	Below 60	
		100 people	0 people	2 people	54 people	44 people	0 people	
		Proportion	0%	2%	54%	44%	0%	
	Highest score	81 point	Lowest score	61 point	average score	70.855 point	Passing rate	100%

The test results show that the average score of the theoretical course of "Traditional class" is 65.17 points, and the average score of the theoretical course of "Micro class" is 70.855 points. From the average scores of the two classes, we can see that the average score of the "Micro-class" theory course is 5.685 points higher than the average score of the "traditional class" theory course. After two classes are made one week of training similarly. The learning scores of the "Micro-class classes" have been improved compared with the "traditional classes", indicating that learning with micro-classes can improve the learning effect of learners to a certain extent.

The results of the courses that pass the test of the course are shown in Table 3:

Table 3. The results of the "traditional class" and "micro-class" operation courses

"Traditional class" test scores	Score distribution	Fractional segment	90–100	80–89	70–79	60–69	Below 60	
		100 people	0 people	0 people	5 people	85 people	10 people	
		Proportion	0%	0%	5%	85%	10%	
	Highest score	72 point	Lowest score	52 point	average score	63.29 point	Passing rate	90%

(*continued*)

Table 3. (*continued*)

"Micro-class" test scores	Score distribution	Fractional segment	90–100	80–89	70–79	60–69	Below 60	
		100 people	0 people	4 people	47 people	49 people	0 people	
		Proportion	0%	4%	47%	49%	0%	
	Highest score	81 point	Lowest score	64 point	average score	70.78 point	Passing rate	100%

The test results show that the average score of the "traditional class" operation course is 63.29 points, and the average course of the "micro-class class" is 70.78 points. From the test results, the average score of the "micro-class" is "traditional". And the average score of the class is 7.49 points. From the analysis results, it can be seen that in the course of operation, the use of micro-teaching has significantly improved the learner's performance.

It can be seen from the analysis results that in the course of the theoretical course and the operation course, the "micro-class class" has a more obvious improvement than the "traditional class", especially in the process of teaching the course, the efficiency of the "micro-class class" is improved. And the effect is more obvious. In the 7-day training process, the average score increased by 7.49 points. The theoretical course improvement effect is also obvious, and the average score is also increased by 5.685 points. Therefore, we can see that the micro-course teaching has achieved good results as a kind of auxiliary teaching form into the classroom teaching, which has improved the learner's performance, reduced the teacher's teaching pressure, and completed the traditional classroom well. The supplement and improvement of teaching have made the training and teaching achieve better results.

2.3 Micro-teaching Effect Feedback

In this study, the students conducted a questionnaire survey on the effect of micro-class learning in the later stage of the "Micro-class" course training. The research and analysis were carried out from the aspects of the micro-teaching mode and teaching effects. 100 questionnaires were distributed, of which 93 were valid, including 12 electronic documents and 81 paper documents. The study obtained relevant results by statistical analysis of the questionnaire, and presented the analysis results in the form of a graph.

Students' Evaluation of Micro-teaching Teaching Mode. The evaluation of the micro-teaching mode is mainly to investigate whether the learners adapt to the new teaching mode of micro-teaching. The statistical results of the questionnaire are shown in Fig. 5.

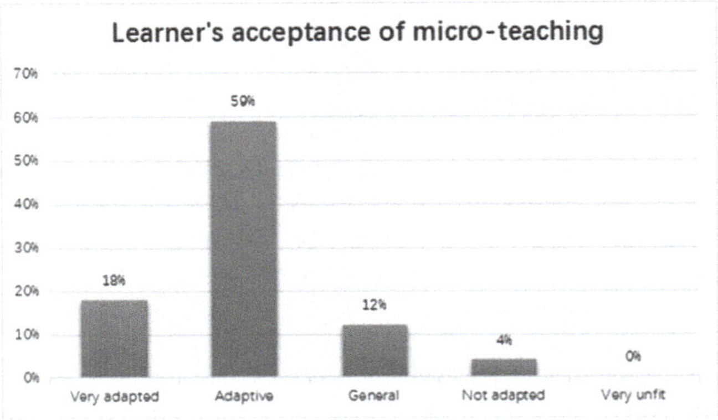

Fig. 5. Whether the learner adapts to the micro-teaching

From Fig. 5, we can see that after the micro-class study, 18% of the "micro-class" learners think that they are very suitable for this learning style, and 59% of the learners think that they are more suitable for this learning style. 12% of learners think that in general, and only 4% of learners do not adapt to this micro-teaching method. From the overall data, we can know that most learners are more suitable for the learning method of micro-teaching, which indicates that the teaching method is recognized by most people.

Students' Evaluation of the Effect of Micro-teaching. The evaluation of the teaching effect of micro-teaching mainly refers to whether the micro-courses have helped the students to learn after the micro-courses are studied, which reflects the teaching effect of the micro-courses. The results of the specific questionnaire survey are shown in Fig. 6.

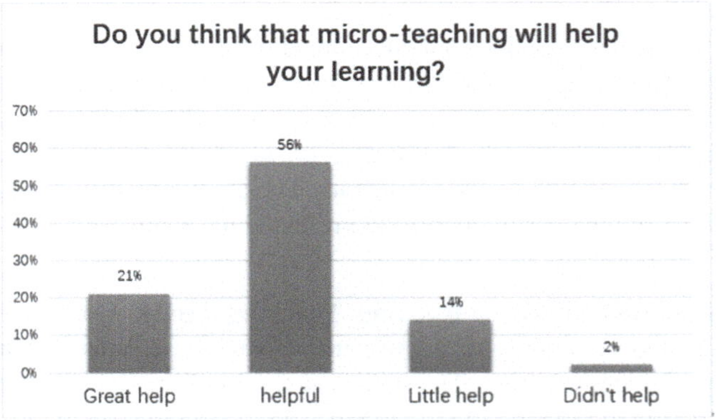

Fig. 6. Evaluation of the teaching effect of micro-teaching

From Fig. 6, we can see that after a week of micro-learning, 21% of the "micro-class" students believe that micro-teaching provides a lot of help for their own learning, and 56% of the learners think that micro-teaching is given to my own learning, which is helpful, and only 2% of learners believe that micro-teaching is not helpful for their own learning. It can be seen from the survey results that the learning method of the micro-teaching provides some support and help for most learners, so that the learners can achieve better learning results. The feedback of the micro-course teaching experience mainly includes two parts, the feedback of the students and the feedback of the teachers. The feedback of the students refers to the feedback of the micro-courses after the learners learn through the micro-courses. The feedback of the teachers refers to the teachers' feedback on micro-teaching after teaching assistance through the use of micro-courses.

Feedback on Student Micro-teaching Experience. From the results of the micro-class evaluation, it can be seen that after a week of micro-course learning, the micro-teaching course provides some help for the learners in the training process. After the micro-course assisted teaching, the learner's academic performance has been improved. As well that the earning efficiency has also been improved. In the process of learning, learners also put forward some feedbacks and suggestions for the micro-teaching of this study, including the following two aspects:

Micro-teaching Content is not Enough. After a week of micro-learning, some learners believe that the teaching content of micro-teaching is not sufficient compared with that of the traditional classroom teaching. The teaching of micro-teaching only introduces and teaches the knowledge points of the course. Some of the contents expanded by teachers in the traditional classroom are not reflected in the micro-courses. For the study of practical knowledge, micro-teaching is undoubtedly more suitable. The micro-teaching teaching reveals the operation steps to the learner more clearly and accurately, so that the learner can better complete the mastery of the knowledge point, thereby improving the learning efficiency of the learner.

Micro-teaching Knowledge is Too Fragmented. For the teaching of micro-courses, some learners also reported that the knowledge of micro-classes is too scattered. For the students who graduated from high school, it is difficult for them to link the knowledge point system. The fragmentation of micro-teaching is the characteristic of micro-teaching. However, for the junior high school graduates, too much fragmentation makes it difficult for learners to master all the knowledge. Therefore, in the process of micro-teaching, teachers need to communicate more with the learners to help learners to connect the knowledge points in tandem to achieve better learning outcomes.

Feedback From Teachers' Micro-teaching Experience. In this study, we also interviewed the teachers of this course who are in the course of using micro-teaching. We interviewed three teachers who have been engaged in training for many years and learned about the teaching experience after using micro-teaching. Through interviews, we found that the three teachers are still very willing to accept this teaching method. First, they believe that using micro-course assisted teaching in the training process can alleviate much of their teaching pressure, especially in the actual teaching process, because there are too many people. Even if the teacher repeatedly performs the demonstration exercises, the effect is not very good. After using the micro-course assisted teaching, the learner can learn independently by watching the video of the micro-course, which reduces the teaching burden of the teacher. Secondly, the teacher believes that after using the micro-course assisted teaching, the students can more easily understand the teaching contents in the traditional classroom training process, and the students have a stronger grasp of the knowledge points, thus improving the quality of the school's training and teaching.

Finally, all three teachers believe that micro-teaching can improve learners' self-learning ability. Micro-teaching provided a good learning platform, which is the micro-learning, the communication between learners and teachers is increasing. When students encountering problems in their studies, they can directly communicate with the teachers through WeChat, which promotes the interaction between teachers and students. Communication improves the relationship between teachers and students, and also improves the learning efficiency of learners.

3 Conclusion

Although this paper completed the micro-course design and implementation of the "Newborn Touch" course, through comparative analysis, it also verified that the micro-courses can really help the learners who participate in vocational training, but the amount of the experimental data, the richness of the course content and some shortcomings in analyzing learner characteristics, also need to be further improved. It is believed that with the further development of the education informatization in the field of the vocational education, there will be more micro-courses on vocational training and education in the future, so as to better promote the informatization of vocational training and education, and to provide more rich and diverse professional and technical talents, as well as the learning resources to promote the development of vocational education information.

References

1. Xi, D.: The New Era of Vocational Education: new goals leading the new role——a summary of the national vocational education and continuing education work promotion conference. Chinese Vocat. Tech. Educ. **1**, 9–15 (2018)
2. Gao, Y., Chen, X.: China vocational education technology outlook: horizon project report interpretation and enlightenment. Educ. Res. **39**(4), 101–108 (2018)
3. Mcgrew, L.R.A.: A 60-second course in organic chemistry. J. Chem. Educ. **70**(7), 543 (1993)
4. Chin, D.B., Dohmen, I.M., Cheng, B.H., et al.: Preparing students for future learning with Teachable Agents. Educ. Technol. Res. Dev. **58**(6), 649–669 (2010)
5. Chen, M., Sun, Y., Manqian, C.: The application practice and prospect of the development of english micro-curriculum resources in higher vocational colleges. J. Harbin Vocat. Techn. College **3**, 53–55 (2016)

6. Shiqing, H., Wen, C.: Analysis of the status quo and trend of micro-curricular research in China. Distance Educ. China **8**, 46–53 (2016)
7. Liang, X., Luo, J.: Micro-lesson design: a typical learning activity to develop pre-service mathematics teachers' TPACK framework. In: Educational Innovation Through Technology (2016)
8. Beatriz, G., Margarita, R., Eva, I., et al.: Evaluation of participatory teaching methods in undergraduate medical students' learning along the first academic courses. PLoS ONE **13**(1), e0190173 (2018)
9. Karthikeyan, K., Kumar, A.: Integrated modular teaching in dermatology for undergraduate students: a novel approach. Indian Dermatol. Online J. **5**(3), 266 (2014)
10. Sun, G., Lang, F., Xue, Y.: Chinese chunking method based on conditional random fields and semantic classes. J. Harbin Inst. Technol. **43**(7), 135–139 (2011)
11. Thai, N.T.T., De Wever, B., Valcke, M.: The impact of a flipped classroom design on learning performance in higher education: looking for the best "blend" of lectures and guiding questions with feedback. Comput. Educ. **107**, 113–126 (2017)

Research on the Construction of Teaching Evaluation System of Mathematics Courses at Applied Undergraduate Colleges in the Context of New Engineering

Yanxia Lu[1(✉)], Dongli Liu[1], and Zeguang Lu[2]

[1] Department of Information Engineering, Heilongjiang International University, Harbin 150025, China
Luyanxia0308@126.com
[2] National Academy of Guo Ding Institute of Data Sciences, Beijing 100190, China

Abstract. The proposition of "New Engineering" has guided the new direction of talent training at colleges and universities and also put forward new requirements for the teaching of college mathematics. According to the cultivation characteristics of applied undergraduate colleges and the requirements of new engineering training, this paper constructs a teaching evaluation system with mathematics literacy and practical ability as the training objectives. It is pointed out that in the context of "new engineering" and in the teaching process of mathematics courses in applied undergraduate colleges, teachers should be guided to focus on teaching content reform, strengthen practical teaching, highlight ability training, and pay attention to teaching assessment, so as to promote the development of students.

Keywords: New engineering · College mathematics, teaching evaluation system · Layered analysis method

1 Proposition of Problems

In recent years, the new industrial revolution has accelerated, the globalization process has deepened, the new economy has accelerated, and the modernity situation has become more complicated. China's engineering education has responded in a timely manner. The proposition of "new engineering" is an inevitable outcome of the development of science and technology.

According to the statistics of the "Manufacturing Talent Development Planning Guide" jointly issued by the Ministry of Education, the Ministry of Human Resources and Social Security, and the Ministry of Industry and Information Technology, by 2020, a new generation of information technology industry, power equipment, high-end CNC machine tools and robots, new materials will become the largest professional gap. Nowadays, only the next-generation information technology industry represented by big data, artificial intelligence, and cloud computing has a talent gap of 1.5 million. By 2050, the talent gap will reach 9.5 million. Training "new engineering" is a top priority for university education.

G. Sun et al. (Eds.): eLEOT 2019, LNICST 299, pp. 96–104, 2019.
https://doi.org/10.1007/978-3-030-35095-6_11

In the core competence of new engineering students, mathematics is the core of knowledge. The ability to apply math, science, and engineering knowledge to solve problems is a key skill for new engineering students [1]. However, there are many difficult factors in the reform and development of university mathematics. For example, the teaching ideas are old, only the basic teaching and the lack of mathematics practice; the teaching content is difficult to understand, the teaching results are more important in the teaching, and the cultivation of mathematical thinking is lighter; the mathematical structure of the mathematics is unchanged, and there is very little integration with the profession; the practical ability of the teacher engineering is weakened, and the mathematics teachers lack professional background. The mathematical structure of the mathematics is unchanged, and there is very little integration with the profession; the practical ability of the teacher engineering is weakened, and the mathematics teachers lack professional background.

Therefore, in the context of informationization, digitization, intelligent new situation and the construction of "new engineering", college mathematics as a basic discipline of engineering education must also make timely changes to meet the needs of professionals and the cultivation of talents. Timely and in-depth study of the undergraduate students' changes in mathematics knowledge and ability, exploring the reconstruction of the university mathematics curriculum system and the reform of teaching content has become the cornerstone of the "new engineering" talent training.

Under the requirements of the "New Engineering", the application of undergraduate mathematics teaching reform is imminent. The school should combine the application-oriented talent training orientation and the professional training requirements to study and formulate the university mathematics teaching evaluation system, so as to guide the teaching activities of teachers and students, cultivate students' mathematical literacy and improve students' mathematics practice ability. Moreover, this can promote student development to meet the needs of employment and social talent.

2 Research Process and Method

2.1 Principles for Evaluating the Construction of Indicator Systems

First, the principle of being scientific.

Through investigation and analysis, the evaluation indicators are basically in line with the objective reality, and can objectively and truly reflect the teaching characteristics and current situation of mathematics in applied undergraduate colleges. Therefore, it is necessary to avoid random, contingent, and subjective evaluations.

Second, the principle of being systematic.

There is a certain logical relationship between the indicators. They reflect the role and connection of university mathematics teaching in the quality training and practical ability of students from different aspects. The indicators are independent of each other, and they are connected with each other. The level is clear. From top to bottom, from macro to micro, an indivisible evaluation system is formed to form a true and systematic evaluation of college mathematics teaching.

Third, the principle of being classic.

This evaluation system has a certain typical representativeness. It reflects the characteristics of "new engineering" and "applied undergraduate" as much as possible. The setting of the evaluation indicators and the formation of the judgment matrix in the system all reflect the above two characteristics.

Fourth, the principle of being operative and quantified.

The selection of each indicator is consistent within the overall scope, which is convenient for decomposition, assessment and evaluation, and is convenient for practical operation. The indicators are consistent in terms of calculation metrics and calculation methods.

Fifth, the principle of being dynamic.

The selection of each indicator can be reflected by a certain time scale, and the research method of the problem facilitates the replacement of indicators and data, thus facilitating the sustainability study of the teaching evaluation system.

2.2 Layered Analysis of the Establishment of Evaluation Indicators

(1) Constructing Teaching Evaluation Indicator System

The layered analysis method was proposed by T.L. Saaty, an American operations research expert and professor at the University of Pittsburgh. This method can be used to determine the weight of each indicator and to prioritize the rated objects.

Combined with the research results of mathematics curriculum construction in relevant applied colleges [2–4], considering the requirements of "new engineering" and the characteristics of training talents in applied undergraduate colleges [5–8]. It is necessary to follow the principles of science, system, typicality, operability and quantifiability, and dynamics, aiming at cultivating students' literacy and practical ability. From the four aspects of teaching team, classroom teaching, class activities, teaching evaluation and feedback, the indicators are refined, and the indicators of the teaching evaluation system of mathematics courses in applied undergraduate colleges under the background of "new engineering" are analyzed as follows. The structure of the teaching evaluation index is shown in Table 1 below:

Table 1. Teaching evaluation indicators and their codes and descriptions

Primary indicators	Secondary indicators	Evaluation contents
Teaching team A_1	Education and title B_{11}	Teachers' teaching level, academic level, classroom organization and management ability
	Double-teacher B_{12}	"Double-teacher" teacher ratio, teacher enterprise and industry practice experience

(*continued*)

Table 1. (*continued*)

Primary indicators	Secondary indicators	Evaluation contents
Classroom teaching A_2	Teaching preparation B_{21}	Pre-testing, instructional design, and teaching resource preparation
	Teaching contents B_{22}	The depth, breadth, and degree of integration of the content of the teaching
	Teaching methods and means B_{23}	Teaching methods are diverse and teaching methods serve the purpose of teaching
	Teaching activities B_{24}	Students' subjectivity
Extracurricular activities A_3	Independent learning B_{31}	MOOC and other independent learning
	Mathematical activity B_{32}	The situation of mathematics activities involved under the guidance of teachers, such as mathematical modeling, mathematics competition, etc.
Teaching evaluation and feedback A_4	Evaluation of teachers B_{41}	Evaluation of the teaching content, design, assessment and organization of the teacher's activities
	Evaluation of students B_{42}	The degree of completion of the process assessment and final assessment

(2) Construct the judgment matrix:

Layered analysis is used to determine the weight of indicators at all levels. In this paper, the level of the same level index relative to the upper level index is assessed by a pairwise comparison [9]. The role of the judgment matrix is to compare the order of the same level indicators under the constraints of an indicator of the previous layer. Generally, the indicators of the pairwise comparison are assigned by referring to the table of the relative importance level of Table 2, and a judgment matrix (i.e., an importance level table) is formed.

Table 2. Star relative importance rating table

Relative importance	Equally important	Slightly important	Obviously important	Strongly important	Extremely important	Between the two extremes
Grade	1	3	5	7	9	2,4,6,8
Relative importance	Equally non-important	Slightly non-important	Obviously non-important	Strongly non-important	Extremely non-important	Between the two extremes
Grade	1	1/3	1/5	1/7	1/9	1/2,1/4,1/6,1/8

Based on the interviews and questionnaire surveys of teachers and students in applied undergraduate colleges, the paper obtains the judgment matrix of the first-level indicators and the second-level indicators in Table 1, which are as follows:

Table 3. Primary indicator judgment matrix

	A_1	A_2	A_3	A_4
A_1	1	1/8	1/4	1/3
A_2	8	1	3	4
A_3	4	1/3	1	1
A_4	3	1/4	1	1

Table 4. Secondary indicator judgment matrix

	B_{11}	B_{12}
B_{11}	1	1/3
B_{12}	3	1

	B_{21}	B_{22}	B_{23}	B_{23}
B_{21}	1	1/6	1	1
B_{22}	6	1	5	4
B_{23}	1	1/5	1	1/5
B_{23}	1	1/4	2	1

	B_{31}	B_{32}
B_{31}	1	1/5
B_{32}	5	1

	B_{41}	B_{42}
B_{41}	1	3
B_{41}	1/3	1

Record the above judgment matrix in turn as A, B_1, B_2, B_3 and B_4.

(3) Calculation of Weights

Step 1: Normalize elements of the judgment matrix $A = \det(a_{ij})$ to get the matrix $B = \det(b_{ij})$, in which

$$b_{ij} = \frac{a_{ij}}{\sum_{i=1}^{n} a_{ij}} (i,j = 1, 2, \cdots, n)$$

Step 2: Cumulate elements in matrix B to get the vector $C = (c_1, c_2, \cdots, c_n)^T$, in which

$$c_i = \sum_{j=1}^{n} b_{ij} (i,j = 1, 2, \cdots, n)$$

Step 3: Normalize vector C to get the featured vector $W = (w_1, w_2, \cdots, w_n)^T$, in which

$$w_i = \frac{c_i}{\sum_{k=1}^{n} c_k} (i,j = 1, 2, \cdots, n)$$

It is the weight of each indicators at this layer.
Step: Get the maximum featured root $\lambda_{\max}$:

$$\lambda_{\max} = \frac{1}{n} \sum_{i=1}^{n} \frac{(AW)}{w_i} (i,j = 1, 2, \cdots, n)$$

After calculation, the featured vectors of the judgment matrixes A, B_1, B_2, B_3 and B_4 can be obtained as follows:

Besides, according to the judgment matrix provided in Tables 3 and 4, and after calculation, the maximum featured roots of the judgment matrixes A, B_1, B_2, B_3 and B_4 can be obtained as follows:

(4) Consistency test

Due to differences in people's understanding, the above judgment matrix may not be consistent. To this end, we use a random consistency ratio to test the degree of deviation, and introduce the calculation formula and random consistency indicators here:

$$CR = \frac{CI}{RI},$$

In which, CI is the consistency index,
$CI = \frac{\lambda_{\max} - n}{n-1}$ (the larger CI is, the more inconsistent it is);
RI is the average random consistence indicator as shown in the following Table 5:

Table 5. Random consistency indicator RI

n	1	2	3	4	5	6	7	8	9	10	11
RI	0	0	0.58	0.9	1.12	1.24	1.32	1.41	1.45	1.49	1.51

Define the consistency ratio: when $CR \leq 0.1$, it can be considered that the judgment matrix has consistency, that is, the weight is valid; when $CR > 0.1$, it can be considered that the judgment matrix deviation is too large, and the score needs to be revised again until there is consistency.

With the maximum eigenvalue of each judgment matrix obtained in (3), the random consistency indicators CR of A, B_1, B_2, B_3 and B_4 are 0.0038, 0, 0.0215, 0 and 0. Each value is less than 0.1, which means that the degree of inconsistency of the above judgment matrix is within the allowable range, that is, the weight distribution of each level of indicators is very reasonable.

(5) Overall ranking calculation of secondary indicators

The ranking method of the secondary indicators is: the product of the weight of each indicator in the layer and the weight of the corresponding upper layer indicator. For example, the ranking weight of B_{11} (education and title) is the sum of the first dimensional vector $W_1 = (0.25, 0.75)$ in $W = (0.0579, 0.5465, 0.2163, 0.1793)$, i.e., 0.0579×0.25.

Applying the above calculation method, the overall ranking of teaching evaluation indicators can be obtained, as shown in Table 6.

Table 6. Overall ranking of secondary indicators

Secondary Indicators	Primary indicators				Overall ranking of secondary indicators	Rank
	A_1	A_2	A_3	A_4		
	0.0579	0.5465	0.2163	0.1793		
B_{11}	0.25				0.0145	10
B_{12}	0.75				0.0434	8
B_{21}		0.1213			0.0663	5
B_{22}		0.6126			0.3348	1
B_{23}		0.1034			0.0565	6
B_{24}		0.1627			0.0889	4
B_{31}			0.1667		0.0361	9
B_{32}			0.8333		0.1803	2
B_{41}				0.25	0.0448	7
B_{42}				0.75	0.1345	3
$\sum$	1.00	1.00	1.00	1.00	1.00	

2.3 Result Analysis

According to Table 6, from the evaluation results of the overall ranking of the secondary indicators, the weight indicator of (teaching contents) ranks the first. And the weight value is much higher than other indicators. This shows that in the context of "new engineering", the mathematics teaching of applied undergraduate colleges should pay special attention to the arrangement of teaching content. The weight indicator of (mathematical activity) ranks the second, which indicates that it is urgently needed for students to carry out relevant mathematical modeling and mathematics competitions under the class. This will greatly help to improve students' mathematics practice ability. The weight indicator of (evaluation of students) ranks the third. This shows that in the teaching process, the process evaluation and the final evaluation are very important components of teaching, and it plays an important role in promoting the evaluation of teaching [10].

In addition, it can be seen from Table 6 that the weight indicator of (double teacher) is higher than that of (education and title). This shows that at applied undergraduate colleges, teachers' business and industry experience are more important than academic qualifications and titles.

3 Conclusion

Faced with the new requirements of "New Engineering" for mathematics teaching in applied undergraduate colleges, teachers should actively update their understanding of the mathematics teaching evaluation system. In addition, teachers should pay attention to the adjustment of teaching content, to meet the cultivation of applied talents, and to pay attention to the combination of knowledge and professionalism. It is necessary to pay attention to the practical teaching of university mathematics, improve the cognitive ability of students' mathematical knowledge, use mathematics to conduct mathematical experiments, and solve practical professional problems. It is necessary to pay attention to the assessment of students' ability, enrich the assessment methods and assessment content, and the learning attitude, hands-on ability and innovative spirit are all important basis for evaluation. At the same time, teachers should pay attention to their own development. While upgrading their academic qualifications and professional titles, they will consciously enter relevant enterprises, understand the application of mathematics in the industry, and guide students to study mathematics in college.

With the advancement of science and technology and the development of professionalism, the evaluation system of mathematics teaching in universities is constantly changing and changing. Teachers should adjust the evaluation system in a timely manner according to the development requirements of students, so as to better complete the training of students.

Acknowledgments. This work was supported by National Education Innovation Science Research Planning Project (CMAS180506).

References

1. Zhoukaifa, Z.: Exploration on the core competence and teaching mode of new engineering education. Chongqing Higher Educ. Res. **5**(3), 22–35 (2017)
2. Fang, Q., Zhao, J., Zhang, B.: Study on the practical teaching mode of mathematics and applied mathematics specialty based on applied talents cultivation. **39**(1), 51–54 (2019)
3. Jiao, L.: On the Mathematical Knowledge, Skills and Related Information Technology of the Professional Development of Students in Higher Vocational Education—The Case Study of the Transportation Major at a Civil Aviation college, East China Normal University, Shanghai (2014)
4. Xinrui, Z., Yuqing, Z.: The construction of MOOC teaching quality evaluation index system in college physics based on analytic hierarchy process. Phys. Eng. **4**(4), 45–56 (2018)
5. Luodan, L.: Research on Quality Evaluation System of Applied Mathematics Professional Training in Applied Technological Universities. DangDaiJiaoYuLunCong, February 2017
6. Sun, G., Song, Z., Liu, J., et al.: Feature selection method based on maximum information coefficient and approximate markov blanket. Zidonghua Xuebao/acta Automatica Sinica **43**(5), 795–805 (2009)
7. Xuxiaofei, D.: Exploration on the reform of talents training model for new subjects facing sustainable competitiveness. China Univ. Teach. **6**, 6–10 (2017)
8. Zili, X., Jin, L., Yinhu, Q., Chunyu, Z., Kaibao, Z., Cheng, Z.: Path of talent cultivation of application -oriented colleges under the background of the new engineering department. J. Heilongjiang Univ. Technol. **18**(9), 19–23 (2018)
9. Cao, A., Zhou, X., Du, Y.: Research on the training mode of innovative talents for applied undergraduate colleges and universities under the view of new engineering. Educ. Teach. Forum **45**, 216–217 (2018)
10. Sun, G., Lang, F., Yang, M.: Traffic measurement system based on hybrid methods. Electr. Mach. Control **15**(6), 91–96 (2011)

Research on College Teaching Management Reform Under the Background of MOOC

Lei Li, Jinlong Liu(✉), Shu Lin, Siyang Yuan, and Yanyuan Fu

School of Electronics and Information Engineering,
Harbin Institute of Technology, Harbin 150006, China
{lileisunny, yq20, linshu}@hit.edu.cn,
yuansiyang_hit@163.com, 1150520404@stu.hit.edu.cn

Abstract. As an important form of Internet education, MOOC has been constructed and applied rapidly in recent years, which brings opportunities and challenges to the reform and development of higher education, especially to the college teaching management. Under the new situation, it has great significance to research characteristics of MOOC, influence of MOOC to teaching management, and reform strategy of teaching management mode, thereby taking advantages of MOOC and serving the cultivation target.

Keywords: MOOC · Teaching management · Reform research

1 Introduction

With the rapid development of Internet and information technology, MOOC has become a global trend and received more and more attention. In the year of 2013, Tsinghua University and Peking University joined edX, which marked the introduction of MOOC into China. By the end of 2017, there are more than 3200 MOOCs were constructed in China with more than 55 million learners [1]. The influence of MOOC to college teaching management is extensive and profound, including teaching concept, teaching quality and teaching management. Under the background of MOOC, it has great significance to explore and optimize teaching management mode to improve teaching level and promote education reform.

2 Concept and Characteristics of MOOC

2.1 Concept of MOOC

The Massive Open Online Course (MOOC) is a new approach for teaching online. In 2008, Dave Cormier and Bryan Alexander, two scholars of Canada, created the MOOC expression [2]. The definition currently displayed on Wikipedia is that "MOOC is an online course aimed at unlimited participation and open access via the web…… MOOCs provide interactive courses with user forums to support community interactions among students, professors, and teaching assistants (TAs), as well as immediate feedback to quick quizzes and assignments [3]". At present, relatively mature MOOC business platforms include Coursera, Udacity, edX, etc.

G. Sun et al. (Eds.): eLEOT 2019, LNICST 299, pp. 105–110, 2019.
https://doi.org/10.1007/978-3-030-35095-6_12

2.2 Characteristics of MOOC

The scale, openness and sharing of MOOC make it rich in teaching resources. The massive scale of MOOC is not only reflected in number of courses but also number of learners. By 2018 March, more than 800 universities globally joined MOOC, with 9400 courses and 81 million learners [4]. According to the statistics, the number of learners registered every minute has been reached to 50, which is increasing exponentially. The openness of MOOC teaching resources makes MOOC break through the limitation of time and space, which makes it possible for the excellent teaching resources to be shared among universities worldwide. The teaching resources of MOOC are thereby greatly enriched.

The informationized and networked MOOC makes it easy to be obtained and well-accepted. MOOC takes Internet information technology and computer technology as main media, which breaks constraints of traditional teaching form in time and space. Learners with deferent ages, education background, profession and areas can easily get rich teaching resources through various network tools such as mobile phones, computers and so on. Moreover, with the development of informationized, networked and intelligent devices, the teaching effect of MOOC is continuously improved, easily to be accepted with better teaching effect.

The flexibility of MOOC teaching methods makes it possible to realize self-directed and individualized learning. Learners with different knowledge background, learning targets and learning ability can independently choose teaching resources on different MOOC platforms, based on their needs, interests and hobbies. They can also independently finished the course of register, courses choosing, learning, evaluating, and effect analysis. Among the characteristics of MOOC, individuation is the most innovative and attractive one, which is also the most effective mode to meet learning needs of learners with different background.

3 Influence of MOOC to College Teaching Management

College teaching management refers to an important process that colleges and their managers take the talent training plan as a basic criterion, and utilize management means and methods to make the teaching activities and related academic activities achieve their talent training objectives, aiming at guaranteeing the normal teaching order [5]. There are huge differences between MOOC and the traditional teaching in teaching content, learners, management, operating mechanism, teaching methods and so on. Therefore, MOOC has huge and deep influence on college teaching management and it is shown in Fig. 1.

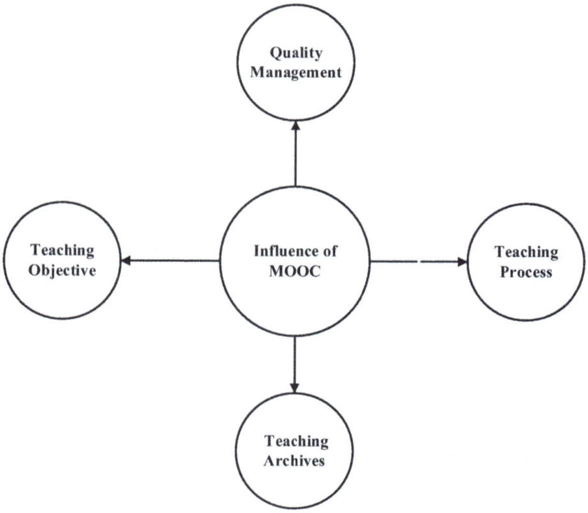

Fig. 1. Influence of MOOC to college teaching management

3.1 Teaching Objective

In the traditional ideas, "teaching" is understood as "knowledge imparting". The acquisition of knowledge by students is widely accepted as the teaching objective, and all the management activities are taken around the achievement of this goal. Students' knowledge acquisition is the fundamental starting point for teachers to carry out teaching work, as well as an important indicator to judge whether the traditional teaching management gets its effective success. However, MOOC changes the traditional teaching objective. At the same time that MOOC transfers knowledge to learners, it pays more attention to the cultivation of students' independent learning ability and innovative consciousness. The changes in teaching objectives promote college teaching managers to make the best use of the circumstances, change the teaching management philosophy, and improve every aspect of teaching activities.

3.2 Teaching Process

In the process of traditional teaching activities, on one hand the teachers are in a dominant position, imparting knowledge to the students by face-to-face teaching; on the other hand, the students are in a position of passive acceptance, lack of initiative. Therefore, in the traditional teaching activities, the teaching management pays more attention on the teachers, as well as the teaching content, teaching mode, teaching design and so on, lake of enough attention on students. In the process of MOOC teaching, interaction between teachers and students gets more attention. The teachers play a role of guiding and collaborating to guide the students to independently learn and research. The changes in teaching process make college teaching managers to actively promote combination of research style and participative innovative teaching modes, thereby changing the traditional management modes.

3.3 Quality Management

Teaching quality management is an important part of college teaching management and an important means to guarantee the quality of talents training in colleges and universities, which is related to realization of teaching objectives. The traditional cumulative assessment stresses students' attendance, classroom quizzes, midterm homework, and final exam and so on, based on which to evaluate students' learning outcomes. MOOC evaluates teaching quality based on not only the results but also the whole process of learning. The attendance, interaction and test of learners is recorded and analyzed by big data, thereby realizing a comprehensive evaluation of learning outcomes. The changes of teaching quality evaluation methods make college teaching managers to actively explore and improve management and supervision mechanism, and further make the teaching quality evaluation more scientific and rational.

3.4 Management and Application of Teaching Archives

Formation of teaching archives is an important part of the teaching process. The traditional teaching archives consist of examination papers, reports and materials for all the links of cumulative assessment. The teaching archives are the important support for teaching research, as well as important evidence for teaching evaluation and certification. The appearance of MOOC changes the teaching mode from physical to network. The teaching archives are changed from paper version to electronic version, and data size becomes richer. Therefore, higher requirements are put forward for the management of teaching archives. The development of computer information technology realized the information and intelligence of teaching archives management under the background of MOOC. Besides teaching archives formed after the teaching activities, students' questions and thoughts in the teaching process are also recorded by information technology, thereby forming a kind of evaluation for the teaching based on knowledge pointes, which multiplies the teaching archives. Moreover, the increase in the number of students produces big data of teaching archives. It's obviously that the data cannot be analyzed by the traditional means. Computer technology including multimedia and database management technology needs to be mastered. Teaching research based on the data will be deeper and more detailed.

4 Reform Strategy of College Teaching Management Mode

MOOC brings great influence to college teaching management, which on one hand challenges the college teaching management and on the other hand brings new ideas to the reform of college teaching management. It's beneficial for promoting the healthy development of MOOC to explore the reform strategies of college teaching management mode under the background of MOOC, thereby serving the target of college teaching management.

4.1 Strengthen the Construction of Information Platform, and Improve the Information Management Awareness of Managers

MOOC is a typical example of educational informatization, and the teaching process of MOOC depends on information service platform and network. The learning platforms of MOOC are mainly provided by main operators, but the teaching resources are mainly provided by colleges, universities and other various educational institutions. In order to provide more courses with high quality, the colleges need to provide professional guidance and service to teachers in the course of video production, including directing, copywriting, producing, editing, shooting and other aspects. In order to serve the students' study, the colleges need to integrate network, equipment, campus resources to build efficient information service platform with high quality, thereby improving the clarity and flexibility of information interaction applications and building an intelligent and digital campus management system. Meanwhile, the college teaching managers need to establish the concept of the Internet management and improve information working capability. The teaching managers need to fully realize the fact that the popularization of the Internet is the main feature of the current era, and apply Internet technology to all aspects of college teaching management. It's necessary for the teaching managers to change the traditional teaching management concept, improve their own information technology level, and innovate the inherent mode of teaching management, aiming at promoting the deep integration of college teaching management and Internet technology and better servicing the teaching activities.

4.2 Strengthen the Construction of Teaching Resources, and Ensure the Quality of MOOC

The quality of MOOC teaching resources is particularly important because of richness and openness of MOOC teaching resources, as well as students' learning autonomy. Colleges should take effective measures to provide or select excellent teaching resources for students. On one hand, colleges can encourage their own excellent course teaching teams to actively develop and provide courses with advantages and characteristics from the management mechanism, combined with the talent cultivation target. During this process, their own MOOC brands are created, thereby meeting the college teaching requirements and expanding the colleges' social influence. On the other hand, as for the off-campus MOOC teaching resources, comprehensive selecting and recognizing rules should be established, including teaching teams, teaching content, teaching design and so on. During this process, excellent teaching resources can be selected and recognized, and the students can be guided to choose suitable courses according to the cultivation program.

4.3 Establish the Teaching Quality Control System

It's necessary for the colleges to establish teaching quality control system, in order to reasonably evaluate and feedback the construction and application effects of MOOC, through which a working closed loop can be formed to improve the quality of teaching activities. Firstly, the responsibilities of different levels of teaching quality control personnel should be clarified to control and evaluate the teaching process and effects. Secondly, it's very important to evaluate the learners, including their learning experience, professional knowledge level, self-satisfaction evaluation and so on. Teaching presentation, questionnaire survey, teacher-student seminar and other means can be utilized for enhancing the communication information feedback between teachers and students as well as the teaching management department, thereby promoting the colleges and MOOC operators to continuously improve MOOC teaching service.

5 Conclusion

In the era of rapid development of the Internet, the rapid development of MOOC leads to the reform of teaching mode, which brings challenges and opportunities for the reform of teaching management in colleges. College teaching management departments should pay attention to the development of MOOC, reasonably utilize MOOC to improve teaching quality, continuously think about ways to improve the teaching management of colleges in the application of MOOC, thereby promoting the healthy development of higher education.

References

1. Hegyesi, F., Kartyas, G.: Experiments for real practice of the Óbuda University. In: International Conference on Intelligent Engineering Systems IEEE (2014)
2. Wikipedia [EB/OL]. https://en.wikipedia.org/wiki/Massive_open_online_course
3. By The Numbers: MOOCS in 2017 [DB/OL]. https://www.class-central.com/report/mooc-stats-2017/
4. Hood, N., Littlejohn, A., Milligan, C.: Context counts: how learners' contexts influence learning in a MOOC. Comput. Educ. **91**, 83–91 (2015)
5. Tieman, J., Miller-Lewis, L., Rawlings, D., et al.: The contribution of a MOOC to community discussions around death and dying. BMC Palliat. Care **17**(1), 31 (2018)

MOOC-Based Mixed Teaching Research on Microcomputer Principle Courses in Colleges and Universities

Wei Yan(✉)

School of Physics and Electronic Information,
Inner Mongolia University for Nationalities, Tongliao, China
ms96590@163.com

Abstract. With the rise of MOOC teaching mode, the hybrid teaching mode which combines online teaching and traditional teaching has drawn extensive attention. Based on the analysis of MOOC teaching mode, this paper synthetically compares the advantages and disadvantages of MOOC teaching mode with traditional teaching mode. Taking the microcomputer principle course set up by our electronic information engineering specialty as an example, this paper constructs a teaching platform based on MOOC and solves the problems of traditional teaching Middle school students lack of learning initiative, learning resources can not be fully utilized and other issues, have some referencet to reform of mixed teaching in colleges and universities.

Keywords: MOOC · Microcomputer principle teaching · Mixed teaching reform

1 Preface

The rise of the Massive Open Online Course (MOOC) in 2012 set off a digital tsunami in education that provides new teaching methods through platforms such as the Internet and WeChat, including micro classes, short videos, online work, Online testing and other content, with large-scale and open features promote the reform of the traditional teaching mode.

Microcomputer Principle is a professional basic course for electronic information engineering in our school. Through this course, students can understand the basic principle, basic composition, interface technology, hardware connection and assembly language programming method from the application point of view, and establish the microcomputer work the overall concept of training students with the software and hardware design and development of the basic ability to develop students' ability to think independently, analyze and solve problems. Due to the limitation of course hours combined with the difficulty of course learning, students generally have low interest in learning and can not make full use of learning resources. Through the construction of MOOC teaching platform, the hybrid teaching mode is used to solve the above problems while providing mixed teaching reform for other courses Some ideas and methods.

G. Sun et al. (Eds.): eLEOT 2019, LNICST 299, pp. 111–118, 2019.
https://doi.org/10.1007/978-3-030-35095-6_13

2 Elements of MOOC and Classification

According to Kop et al., The MOOC consists of five main elements: teachers, learners, topics, learning materials, and situations. Li Qing et al. (2012) observed and analyzed ten MOOC courses and summarized the general operation mode of MOOC, extracting elements of MOOC from the following: elements of things (platform and tools, course information, learning activities) and human factors (Teacher, learner, course coordinator).

MOOC includes both CMOOC, a large-scale open online course of communicative education, and xMOOC, which was developed by behavioral schools in well-known American universities. Both of them have great differences in teaching philosophy and are commonly known as xMOOC in the general media. The differences include: The cMOOC model emphasizes creativity, creativity, autonomy and social network learning; the xMOOC model emphasizes traditional learning methods such as video presentations, quizzes, and tests. In other words, cMOOC focuses on knowledge creation and generation, while xMOOC focuses on knowledge duplication. Specifically, from a practical point of view, cMOOC is a single course, which is organized and implemented by individual teachers and does not participate in the official institutions of the university. The xMOOC mode open course basically runs as an open course project website, with tens to several Hundreds of courses. In terms of organizational structure, xMOOC takes the form of corporatization of operations, with external funding, commercialization potential and cooperation with many well-known universities. These larger MOOC course websites provide more learners with open learning resources and learning tools that are well organized and process disciplined, far beyond cMOOC, regardless of size, benefit or social impact.

3 Advantages and Disadvantages of MOOC and Traditional Teaching Model

3.1 The Advantages and Disadvantages of MOOC

(1) The advantages of MOOC

Large-scale, online, open is a notable feature of MOOC. As a new learning and teaching method, MOOC is easy to use; it is low in cost; most MOOCs are free; it covers a large population; learns independently; and learning resources are abundant. As a new form of remote on-line teaching, MOOC is a characteristic of time and space separation. MOOC is conducive to individualized learning at low cost, coupled with its rich and open learning resources, as learners will undoubtedly be willing to embrace Join them.

(2) The disadvantage of MOOC

MOOC learning is done online, in the network environment, a lot of temptation, students are not easy to focus attention, learning efficiency is easy to lower, which is MOOC course completion rate and the main reason is not high adoption rate.

In addition, there are problems with MOOC in terms of integrity, course quality assurance, evaluation mechanisms and standards.

3.2 The Advantages and Disadvantages of the Traditional Teaching Model

(1) The advantages of the traditional teaching model

Compared with the MOOC, the school, as a special organization, has its own unique cultural characteristics in addition to having the characteristics of a general organizational structure and is manifested in a material, institutional and spiritual form. Campus culture can imperceptibly give students cultural infiltration, culture, which is unmatched by MOOC.

(2) Disadvantages of traditional teaching methods

The traditional teaching model is mainly teacher-centered, textbook-centered, and teachers' main functions are to teach courses and to convey the learning materials as ready-made conclusive knowledge, without repeating the process of human discovery and formation of relevant knowledge. The main function of students is "passive learning", that is, memory recitation plus mechanical repetitive training. This traditional teaching model greatly suppresses students 'learning initiative, initiative, enthusiasm and independence, and restrains students' reading and thinking, making students lack of innovative ability.

4 MOOC-Based Hybrid Instructional Design

Through the above analysis, MOOC teaching mode and the traditional teaching mode are relationship of mutual support and mutual supplement, rather than mutually exclusive, mutually incompatible relationship. According to the respective advantages of the two, combined with the characteristics of our microcomputer theory course, a MOOC-based hybrid teaching mode is constructed and an MOOC-based teaching interactive platform is set up to improve the actual teaching quality.

4.1 Design Ideas and Frameworks

In the stage of higher education, students not only master the discipline, the basic theory and basic knowledge of the discipline, but also master the basic skills, methods and relevant knowledge necessary for the major and have the initial ability to engage in practical and research work of the major. So design top-level from the knowledge and ability of two dimensions MOOC-based hybrid teaching model, the specific framework is shown in Fig. 1.

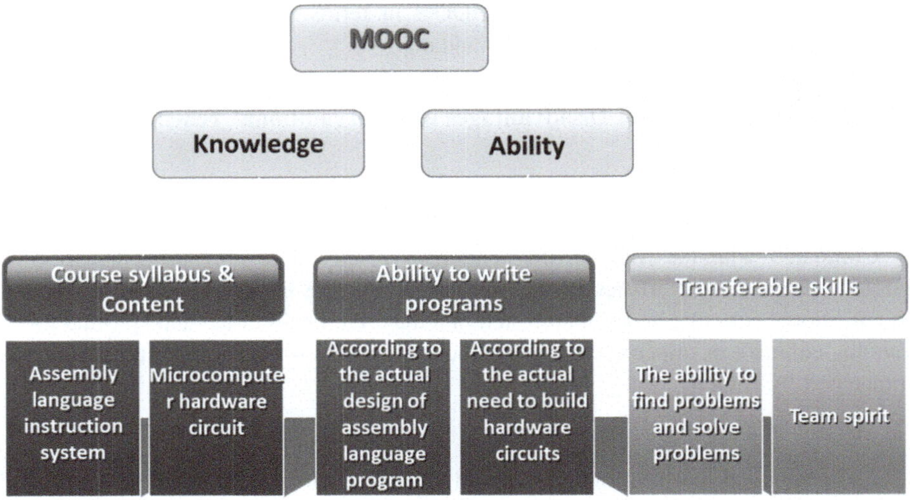

Fig. 1. Top-level design framework

4.2 MOOC-Based Hybrid Teaching Process Implementation

Organize students to carry out teaching based on the open teaching content in MOOC platform. The teaching process mainly includes online learning and offline learning. Specific teaching processes are shown in Fig. 2.

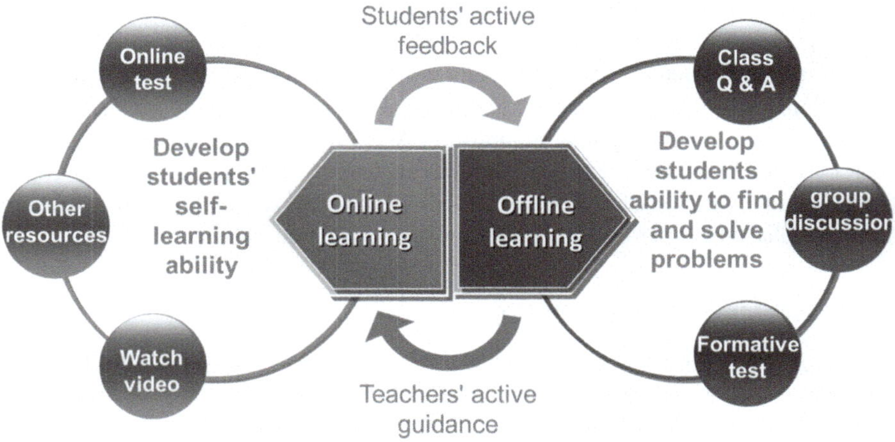

Fig. 2. Teaching process diagram

It can be seen from the figure above that the MOOC-based hybrid teaching mainly includes two parts: online learning and offline learning, which can be divided into five parts: teaching preparation, teaching process, teaching feedback, teaching replenishment and teaching improvement. The following sections address the way in computer theory courses as an example to illustrate the implementation of hybrid teaching on the MOOC platform.

(1) Teaching preparation

Teaching preparation phase includes teaching objectives and teaching plan. When setting teaching objectives, teachers should fully consider the diversity of audiences and set a multi-level goal so that students with different curriculum learning plans can enjoy a relatively complete learning experience.

Teachers should have a clear plan for the structure and development of the course and develop a detailed syllabus. Syllabus does not contain specific teaching content, but it is an important teaching tool from beginning to end. A science-based, clear, detailed syllabus will be a guide and contract for teachers and students throughout the course.

Teachers emphasize the teaching tasks, knowledge structure, schedule and assessment scope of this chapter so that students can clarify the contents of the next week in order to establish a learning plan.

(2) Teaching process

Online video, PPT and other teaching resources should try to be specific to each problem, short, in order to allow students to understand their principles within a limited time to master the part of knowledge. Such as the addressing mode should be immediately addressing, register addressing, direct addressing, register indirect addressing, indexing addressing, base address addressing, base address indexing addressing, etc. which way to facilitate the students to understand a short time grasp.

Learn online can add embedded tests to test your knowledge of what you have learned. For students, this function can be found in time to learn the doubts and difficulties in order to more smoothly the next chapter of learning. For teachers, this feature can significantly increase the interaction between teachers and students to improve the quality of teaching, you can also analyze the test results to assess this chapter teaching..

(3) Teaching feedback

The actual teaching can use verbal feedback, written feedback, body posture feedback, activity feedback, group feedback, personal feedback, collective feedback and other feedback. Oral feedback is an efficient and effective way of feedback in MOOC's blended instructional model. For example, what are the differences between immediate addressing and direct addressing that can be raised by asking students questions, what is the connection? The statu of the students grasp of knowledge can be known according to the student's verbal response.

(4) Teaching supplement

Teaching supplements mainly for some of the extension of knowledge points. For example, the address mode mainly explains assembly language operation registers and memory address method, as an extension of reading and according to the actual use of the process can explain the use of C language registers and memory address related instructions and differences, pay attention to the distinction between the two languages And contact to expand students' knowledge.

(5) Teaching improvement

Teaching improvement mainly aims at some problems found in the teaching process, summarizes, analyzes the causes and finds ways to improve. For example, most students are prone to confusion between direct addressing and immediate addressing. These two addressing modes are easily confused in testing and practical use. After careful analysis of the reason, the concept of student immediate versus immediate is not fully understood. The next phase of improvement requires the addition of the concept of immediate data.

5 Course Evaluation

In traditional teaching, general teachers are the main subjects of evaluation and students are the objects of evaluation. The evaluation methods usually adopt a single paper test and the final evaluation is the main one. The scores are the only criterion for evaluating students. Different from traditional teaching, MOOC shows its diversity with the support of big data technology.

(1) Multiple evaluation subjects

MOOC learning platform, through the analysis and processing of big data in the background, combined with the evaluation of learners by different subjects, helps teachers learn about students' learning from different channels in order to further improve teaching. At the same time, students can also recognize the advantages and disadvantages of their own existence and contribute to the overall development of students.

(2) Multiple evaluation targets

The diversified evaluation subject of MOOC determines its diversified evaluation objects and can evaluate hybrid teaching from multiple perspectives. MOOC through the background of big data to understand the specific circumstances of students in the learning process. Teachers can also be inspected from the aspects of the organization of teaching activities, the provision of learning resources and the guidance of the students' learning process.

(3) Multiple evaluation methods

MOOC provides a variety of evaluation methods, such as peer evaluation, student self-assessment, mutual peer review, machine evaluation, alumni evaluation, teaching evaluation. According to different disciplines, different courses choose different evaluation methods. Computer-based courses such as computer-based assessment of the main online learning evaluation, offline learning using paper-based assessment and the combination of mutual assessment. The use of a variety of evaluation methods can complement each other, help teachers improve teaching quality, improve the quality of students.

6 End

In view of the difficulty of computer theory course leading to students 'lack of initiative in learning and students' comprehensive utilization of learning resources effectively, this paper proposes a hybrid teaching reform mode based on MOOC, which combines the advantages of MOOC and traditional teaching mode, Strengthen the student's dominant position, improve the students' learning initiative, integrate rich teaching resources, expand students' knowledge and improve students' migratory learning ability. In this mode, it is conducive to cultivating students' autonomous learning ability, improving the ability of combining theory with practice, and finally achieving the purpose of using computer to control in practical work.

Funding. This work was supported by Inner Mongolia University for Nationalities scientific research project grant No. NMDYB19066.

References

1. Eberlein, E., Keller, U.: Hyperbolic distributions in finance. Bernoulli **1**(3), 281–299 (1995)
2. Hao, D.: Literature analysis of the current MOOC research. China Distance Educ. (21), 42–50 (2013)
3. Watted, A., Barak, M.: Motivating factors of MOOC completers: Comparing between university-affiliated students and general participants. Internet Higher Educ. **37**, 11–20 (2018)
4. Chen, X., Wang, D.M.: MOOC development history and main characteristics analysis. Modern Educ. Technol. **23**(11), 5–10 (2013)
5. Zhang, Y.Y.: The impact of MOOCs on higher education in China and countermeasures. J. Hebei Normal Univ. (Educ. Sci. Ed.) (2), 116–121 (2014)
6. Hu, J.H., Wu, Z.J.: MOOC-based college English flip classroom teaching model. Foreign Lang. Teach. (6), 40–45 (2014
7. Sneddon, J., Barlow, G., Bradley, S., et al.: Development and impact of a massive open online course (MOOC) for antimicrobial stewardship. J. Antimicrob. Chemother. **73**(4), 1091 (2018)
8. Deng, H.Z., Li, M.G.: Discussion on the problems in the development of mu'mu. Sci. Technol. Innov. Herald (19), 212–213 (2013). Application. Open Education Research, 11 (b08), 46–49 (2005)
9. Xu, Y., Jia, Y.Z.: MOOC to SPOC - an academic dialogue based on MOOC practice at UC berkeley and tsinghua university. Modern Distance Educ. Res. (4), 13–21 (2014)
10. Fu, T.Z., Zheng, J.P.: Strategies of university libraries in coping with MOOC challenges. Acad. Libr. Trib. **32**(1), 20–24 (2014)
11. Zhou, J.X., Zhou, Y.R.: Mixed teaching model in MOOC era. Educ. Sci. China (15), 71–74 (2017)
12. Wang, R., Yu, H.M.: MOOC based C programming language teaching ideas. Softw. Eng. (3), 60–61 (2015)
13. Nagano, Y., Yamaguchi, S., Fujita, Y., et al.: A differentiable gaussian-like distribution on hyperbolic space for gradient-based learning (2019)

14. Volkovicha, V.A., Griffiths, T.R., Thied, R.C., et al.: Behavior of molybdenum in pyrochemical reprocessing: a spectroscopic study of the chlorination of molybdenum and its oxides in chloride melts. J. Nucl. Mater. **323**(1), 93–100 (2003)
15. Schweizer, B.: Confessions of an unreconstructed MOOC(h)er. Thought Action, 29 (2013)
16. Brita-Paja, J.L., Gregorio, C., Llana, L., et al.: Introducing MOOC-like methodologies in a face-to-face undergraduate course: a detailed case study. Interact. Learn. Environ. (8), 1–18 (2018)
17. Davis, D., Kizilcec, R.F., Hauff, C., et al.: The half-life of MOOC knowledge: a randomized trial evaluating knowledge retention and retrieval practice in MOOCs. In: The 8th International Conference (2018)
18. Shapiro, H.B., Lee, C.H., Roth, N.E.W., et al.: Understanding the massive open online course (MOOC) student experience: an examination of attitudes, motivations, and barriers. Comput. Educ. **110**(C), 35–50 (2017)
19. Swinnerton, B.J., Morris, N.P., Hotchkiss, S., et al.: The integration of an anatomy massive open online course (MOOC) into a medical anatomy curriculum. Anat. Sci. Educ. **10**(1), 53–67 (2017)
20. Zhao, Y., Davis, D., Chen, G., et al.: Certificate achievement unlocked: how does MOOC learners' behaviour change? In: Adjunct Publication of the Conference (2017)

Discussion on the Reform of the Course "Data Structure" of Higher Vocational Education Based on MOOC Background

Tingting Wang(✉), Xiang Wu, and Wanshun Chen

Wuhu Institute of Technology, Wuhu, Anhui, China
792781716@qq.com, 280165198@qq.com, 858708130@qq.com

Abstract. Higher vocational education in China has nurtured a number of talents with certain qualifications and skills and made its own contribution to the society. MOOC is a product of the era of new technologies such as wireless networks, smart phones, adaptive technologies, cloud computing, and WeChat that are widely used in education. MOOC is a short video produced by teachers, its content is concise and its knowledge integration is strong, it can help students to find the key points of learning quickly. Students can learn online through the internet, and the process is completely free and learning freedom, without the limitations of time and space. In the background of Internet + vocational education, MOOC will bring huge influence and challenges to higher vocational education. The student and educational purpose of higher vocational colleges are different from those of undergraduate courses. A large part of the existing prestigious MOOC courses is not suitable for the learning needs of higher vocational students. Therefore, it is of great importance both in theory and practice to combine MOOC with traditional teaching and develop suitable subjects.

Keywords: Internet + vocational education · MOOC · Influence · Challenges

1 Introduction

MOOC is the short term of Massive Online Open Courses. 'Massive' describes the number of students; 'Open' means everyone can get free access to the online learning platform after a quick registration with an email account; 'online' means the whole learning process is conducted online, not like the traditional school education which study should be limited with certain time and place; 'course' is been defined as 10–15 min micro-course. The learning process of each step consists of a number of micro clips. Most online courses have their own period ranging from 1–3 months.

In January 1986, the pioneer of online teaching, professor of School of Communication of Simon Fraser University Dr. Linda Harasim unveiled the first online course the application of women and computer in education. Ten years later, University of British Columbia in Canada has provided the first group of online courses based on World Wide Web. 22 years later, massive online courses began to emerge. From 2012, Stanford University set up Udacity and Coursera, MIT co-founded edX with Harvard

G. Sun et al. (Eds.): eLEOT 2019, LNICST 299, pp. 119–124, 2019.
https://doi.org/10.1007/978-3-030-35095-6_14

University. MOOC, a brand new internet teaching mode has gained popularity around the world and triggered the new reform of online education.

In April 2013, Hong Kong University of Science and Technology offered The Science, Technology and Society of China, the first MOOC course in Asia on Coursera. Subsequently, Chinese universities such as Peking University, Tshinghua University and Shanghai Jiao Tong University established their own MOOC platforms. A bunch of Internet companies also developed similar platforms such as xuetangx, chinesemooc, icourse163, zhihuishu and topu.

2 Advantages of MOOC

2.1 Students

Student is the main accepter and plays a major part in course evaluation. There are two advantages of online courses for students.

1. The flexibility of time and place.
In traditional classroom teaching, students with poor comprehension ability can't fully grasp the knowledge within the limited class time, teacher fails to meet all demand of students. In contrary, online teaching allows a student to download the video and watch repeatedly when he encounters a difficult point. This helps students to better understand the knowledge and improve the study.

2. Breaking the area boundary and realizing the goal of sharing resources.
Currently, the regional disparities of teaching resources and faculties and the traditional teaching concept still exist, however, with plenty of resources and large quantity of courses, online learning allows students to choose courses at their own will, besides, all resources and information are fully open and can be broadcasted through the internet and without limitation of place, time and the number of students, so students can acquire more and better materials.

2.2 Teachers

TO students, teachers are intellectual development and personality shaping. Online courses serve as a medium to highlight the role of teachers in the following ways:

1. Setting up multi-dimensional educational concept and enhancing informational quality and teaching techniques
MOOC are often displayed on professional online websites. With the growing expansion of the websites, there are new requirements to the teaching concepts in accordance to the high quality of courses. When designing and developing MOOC on mature platforms, teachers should uphold a panoramic and systematic view and combine with multi-dimensional educational concepts such as synergetic development and cognitive recognition. Simultaneously, teachers should combine relevant teaching strategies and concepts such as sharing, cooperation and interaction with the courses and build study groups in order to let students learning from each other.

MOOC era requires teachers to be skillful developers, with the mastery of IT, a thorough analysis and exploitation of online resources, more multi-dimensional view and a more comprehensive knowledge system to better educate students. Teaching skills, a reflection of professional ability of teachers, include the integration of teaching materials, the innovation of teaching methodology and the combination of MOOC with traditional courses.

2. The transformation of teacher's role
MOOC not only becomes an important way for students to acquire educational recourses, but also set a higher standard for teachers in terms of education concept and methodology. It requires teachers reset themselves with a digital and internet oriented perspective and transform their roles. First, MOOC shifts teacher role from the only source of knowledge to serve students with cooperation of internet. Its authority in the teaching process is diminishing. Second, MOOC transform teacher role from knowledge provider to organizer of knowledge source; from lecturers and broadcaster to usher and question-solver. One advantage of MOOC is that teachers not only set suitable goal for students but also make tailored plans for individuals to help students acquire knowledge systematically. In short, there has been a dramatic change in teachers' qualifications and role recognition.

3 The Application of MOOC in Data Structure

3.1 Data Structure

Data Structure is a fundamental core course in computer-related majors and also an elementary one in some other majors. The goal of the course is enable students to grasp the knowledge of logic structure, storage structure, calculation, time analysis, spatial analysis, program and algorithm design. Through the study of the course, students can improve their abilities of innovation, comprehensive analysis and problem solving and also facilitate their job promise and improve their competitiveness. The traditional course is teacher-centered and fails to stimulate students' interest. As a result, the performance of students isn't satisfied. MOOC provides students with an alternative and can help them better grasp the course.

3.2 Content Fragmentation

In the traditional 45-min class, teachers usually spend 30 min analyzing abstract and difficult points, whereas the most effective attentive period for a human being lasts 6–10 min. Then the focus level will shrink with the result of the downfall of receiving information. The fragmented knowledge can be better absorbed and one of the most important content of designing MOOC is to transform the general knowledge to fragmented one. The traditional 45-min class period will be divided into several 10-min video clips so students could choose the clips according to their different goals. Besides, students could watch the clips at their convenience and in their most attentive time (Table 1).

Table 1. The concrete content

Course Title	Data structure and algorithm			Number of lectures	43 units
Expected total class hours	70 videos		Estimated total time	720 min	
Each lecture	Number	Title	Time	Key word	Note
	1	Course Introduction	5 min		
	2	What is a data structure?	5 min		
	3	Logical structure of data	10 min		
	4	Description of the algorithm	2 sections 20 min in total	Time and space efficiency	
	5	Basic concept of linear tables	10 min		
	6	Linear storage structure and its algorithm	3 sections 30 min in total	Insert, delete	
	7	Chain storage structure of linear table and its operation	3 sections 30 min in total	Insert, delete	
	8	Linear table application example	2 sections 20 min in total		
	9	Stack	3 sections 30 min in total	Push, pop	
	10	Queue	3 sections 30 min in total	Push, pop	
	11	Stack and queue application examples	2 sections 20 min in total		
	12	Basic concept of string	10 min	String	
	13	String storage structure	2 sections 20 min in total		
	14	Basic operation of the string	2 sections 20 min in total		
	15	String application example	2 sections 20 min in total		
	16	Array	3 sections 15 min in total		
	17	Basic concept of the tree	5 min		
	18	Binary tree	2 sections 20 min in total		
	19	Binary tree storage structure	2 sections 20 min in total		
	20	Traversal of binary tree	2 sections 20 min in total	Preorder, medium order	
	21	Clue binary tree	2 sections 20 min in total	Clue	
	22	Binary sort tree and balanced binary tree	2 sections 20 min in total		
	23	Conversion between tree, forest and binary tree	2 sections 20 min in total		
	24	Huffman Tree	2 sections 20 min in total		
	25	B tree	10 min		
	26	Basic terminology	5 min	Degree	
	27	Map storage structure	2 sections 20 min in total		

(*continued*)

Table 1. *(continued)*

Course Title	Data structure and algorithm			Number of lectures	43 units
	28	Traversal of graphs	2 sections 20 min in total	Depth, Breadth	
	29	Minimum spanning tree	2 sections 20 min in total	Prim algorithm	
	30	Shortest path	2 sections 20 min in total		
	31	Topological sorting	2 sections 20 min in total	Topology	
	32	Critical Path	10 min		
	33	Basic concept of finding	15 min		
	34	Sequential search	10 min		
	35	Dichotomy search	10 min		
	36	Block search	10 min		
	37	Hash table and its lookup	10 min		
	38	Basic concept of sorting	10 min		
	39	Insert sort	2 sections 20 min in total		
	40	Select sort	10 min		
	41	Exchange sort	2 sections 20 min in total		
	42	Merge sort	2 sections 20 min in total		
	43	Cardinality sort	10 min		
	44	Comparison of several sorting methods	10 min	Time complexity	

3.3 The Interaction of Teaching and Learning

Traditionally, teacher interacts with students through asking questions. In MOOC class, questions can be used in the video and quizzes can be arranged at the interval of video clips. Like the traditional way, asking questions can raise students' attention. In traditional class, when teacher raise a question, the lazy students tend to wait for peers to answer it without thinking about the question. However, each student must give answer to the inserted question before moving on to the next clip. When a clip finishes, student take the quiz and the system will automatically grade it. Students who don't get full scores will be required to watch the video again till they answer all questions correctly. The traditional classroom quiz will delay the study process and don't get a full feedback of students' performance. MOOC is better than the traditional one in interaction with teaching and learning. In addition to teacher-student interaction, the interactions between students are diversified. Students can share their homework and discuss with each other. They can also grade others' work. These enhance their learning motive and shape their attitude toward study.

4 Conclusion

With the introduction of MOOC, teachers should transform educational concept, upgrade relevant knowledge and improve informational skills.

MOOC is an inevitable outcome of web technology and a brand-new teaching mode. MOOC gradually makes universities more accessible and brings new opportunities to higher vocational education. The traditional functions of universities will change dramatically. MOOC will enhance the sharing of fine educational resources and equality. Education will exceed its original range to become an important carrier of national culture and soft power. Undoubtedly, the rising of MOOC will have a profound impact on the educational concept and teaching methodology to higher vocational education.

Acknowledgment. This work was supported by the research on high school provincial quality engineering project of Anhui grant No. 2017mooc368, No. 2017sjjd041, No. 2018jyxm0184 and University-level key projects grant No. Wzyzrzd201703.

References

1. Yongfen, W.: Discussion on MOOC teaching mode of data structure course. China Educ. Technol. Equip. (1), 37–38 (2017)
2. Jing, T.: Research on teacher professional development based on online courses. Sci. Technol. Chin. Univ. **8**, 92–94 (2018)
3. Li, X.: Advantages and disadvantages of online open course—taking MOOC teaching method as an example. Contemp. Educ. Pract. Teach. Res. (9), 12–14 (2018)
4. Mo, Z.: The influence of mu-class on higher vocational education and controversy. Guangxi Educ. (4), 109–110 (2016)
5. Xing, L.: Application research of flip class mode in computer basic courses. Comput. CD Softw. Appl. (24), 231–232 (2014)
6. Liu, H.: Discussion on the teaching mode of "flipping classroom": taking the teaching of data structure as an example. J. Guangdong Teach. Coll. Technol. (5), 70–72 (2016)
7. Zhang, X.: Exploration on the practice teaching of the "data structure" course under the CDIO concept. J. ChiFeng Coll. Nat. Sci. Ed. (10), 20–21 (2016)
8. Liang, L.: Online education in American universities: status, obstacle, motivation and. Open Educ. Res. (1), 27–36 (2016)
9. Liao, J.: Exploring the online collaborative learning experience of the moss learners-taking the teacher professional development class as an example. Open Educ. Res. **23**(6), 80–86 (2017)
10. Zhu, J.: The challenge and innovation of higher vocational teaching thinking in the era of big data-an effective teaching theory based on the perspective of "curtain course" in online courses. Shanghai City Manag. (1) (2014)

The Research of Combining MOOC and Classroom Teaching in Virtual Instruments Course

Xian-fei Zhou(✉)

Wuhu Institute of Technology, Wuhu, Anhui, China
664518164@qq.com

Abstract. Based on the analysis of the advantages and disadvantages of using MOOC in learning courses in Higher Vocational colleges, this paper proposes a teaching mode that combines MOOC resources with classroom teaching methods, and designs a "MOOC + classroom" teaching mode of virtual instrument courses to make full use of MOOC resources and give full play to classroom advantages in order to stimulate students' learning enthusiasm and help them master professional knowledge content.

Keywords: MOOC resources · Higher vocational education · Teaching mode

1 Introduction

MOOC, an acronym for Massive Open Online Courses, is a large-scale open online classroom specially designed for the masses through which people can learn without going to the regular classroom [1]. The core of this kind of course is to realize teaching, learning, evaluation, testing, training, certification, group and social interaction.

MOOC curriculum was proposed by the United States in 2012, and in 2013, MOOC was introduced to China. The development of large-scale online courses has a great impact on curriculum teaching, and it is one of the important forms of curriculum informatization teaching and network development [2]. Network resources can provide free online courses to expand the scope, effect and impact of curriculum teaching, accordingly some network learning platforms have been established which provides more students with the possibility of systematic learning.

Nowadays, universities attach much importance to classroom teaching and classroom teaching pays attention to theoretical knowledge learning and inculcation teaching. However, in the process of professional course learning, the theoretical content of classroom teaching can not meet the students' needs.

Helpfully, the powerful resources of MOOC can be combined with classroom teaching in higher vocational school to establish the teaching mode of "MOOC + classroom", and it can be used to improve the teaching effect and help the higher vocational education.

G. Sun et al. (Eds.): eLEOT 2019, LNICST 299, pp. 125–131, 2019.
https://doi.org/10.1007/978-3-030-35095-6_15

Virtual Instrument is a professional course with strong practicality. It is difficult to teach students in accordance with their aptitude in teacher-centered and interaction-inadequate teaching mode. So there is necessity that a new teaching mechanism should be established with the combination of MOOC and classroom teaching.

2 Advantages and Disadvantages of MOOC and Classroom Teaching

MOOC course is a course based on information and network [4], and it is a reflection of technological development. The advantages of MOOC include:

(1) MOOC courses provide teaching videos with the corresponding real-time online testing to carry out the course teaching;
MOOC is a complete curriculum system. With the help of many large MOOC platforms, such as www.xuetangx.com, students can easily start a course of study.
(2) The lecturers of MOOC course are all experts and scholars. The practical teaching of MOOC course lays more emphasis on the connotation. Teachers' perspective, critical thinking and overall design can be demonstrated through MOOC.
(3) High-quality resources can be shared without regional restrictions to promote comprehensive learning and lifelong learning.
With the combination of information technology and Internet technology, MOOC courses can be viewed and learned at any place via computers and mobile terminals, and the content is constantly updated.
(4) The results of learning analysis technology based on big data promote teachers to improve teaching content and help students self-adjust learning plans and learning methods;
(5) Learners can choose any course that be interested in to improve their interest in learning and the quality in learning. Now there are many MOOC platforms, where many teachers teach the same courses and students can choose as will.

Despite of the advantages discussed above, undeniably MOOC has some weaknesses:

(1) Because of long-distance network teaching, MOOC lacks the cheerful, mutual infection and timely interactive atmosphere compared with traditional classroom.
(2) Due to the lack of supervision mechanism, many students will give up learning in the course of MOOC course, and only less than 10% of the students can insist on completing the course.
(3) The form of teaching organization is mainly structured knowledge imparting, which is not entirely suitable for the training of distributed cognition and advanced thinking ability.
(4) The teaching mode is single and the teaching design is simple. There is neither the analysis of classified and stratified teaching objectives nor the demand of various students. It is difficult to meet the specific requirements of many disciplines and different types of courses in higher education.

The Advantages of current classroom teaching are listed as follows:

(1) It can target clearly and moderately according to the students' situation and teaching content. Teaching process can arrange teaching according to students' cognitive law and new teaching ideas.
(2) The teaching process is clear, the classroom structure is rigorous, the teaching density is reasonable, and the key to deal with the difficulties is clear, so it can control the complexity simply. Attention should be paid to the design and arrangement of exercises so that students can consolidate their knowledge immediately in learning.
(3) The teaching attitude is friendly, natural, dignified and generous, the teaching language is standard and concise, the blackboard writing is neat, and the teaching experiment is real; the random adjustment and adaptability in teaching are strong. It involves Teaching democracy, equality and harmony between teachers and students, harmonious classroom atmosphere, respect for underachievers, objective analysis of the situation of underachievers in learning, and targeted individual counseling.
(4) Teachers constantly renew their teaching theory of multiple intelligence in the process of teaching, and focus on the development of all aspects of students' abilities.

The shortcomings in classroom teaching:

(1) The synchronization of students' starting point of thinking and teaching presupposition should be valued. In teaching, teachers should not only pay attention to the starting point of students' thinking, but also pay close attention to the synchronization of learning and teaching presupposition. Basically, teachers should fully understand the individual students and presuppose the teaching methods of knowledge points according to different students.
(2) Effective cooperative learning should be implemented. In the past, although teaching by various means was emphasized in class, some of them were only in form, but they were not implemented in practice. For example, group cooperative learning, sometimes the problem is too simple, sometimes teachers have timely grasp the students' ideas. Sometimes in order to catch up with the progress, students have less time to discuss and communicate, so they can not grasp their real ideas.
(3) Operations should be carried out purposefully and systematically, not under any circumstances. Operational activities should be arranged according to the purpose, content and place of teaching. Generally, new concepts and rules of teaching, students lack perceptual experience or are difficult to understand, it is appropriate to start from the operation. New knowledge that is familiar or can be deduced from what has been learned does not necessarily begin with operation.

3 MOOC + Classroom Teaching Model

From the above analysis, we can combine the advantages of the two to form a "MOOC + classroom" teaching model [5], which is divided into three parts, MOOC resources, students and teachers, and finally analyzes and summarizes through learning effect evaluation. Figure 1 demonstrates the model of MOOC + classroom teaching.

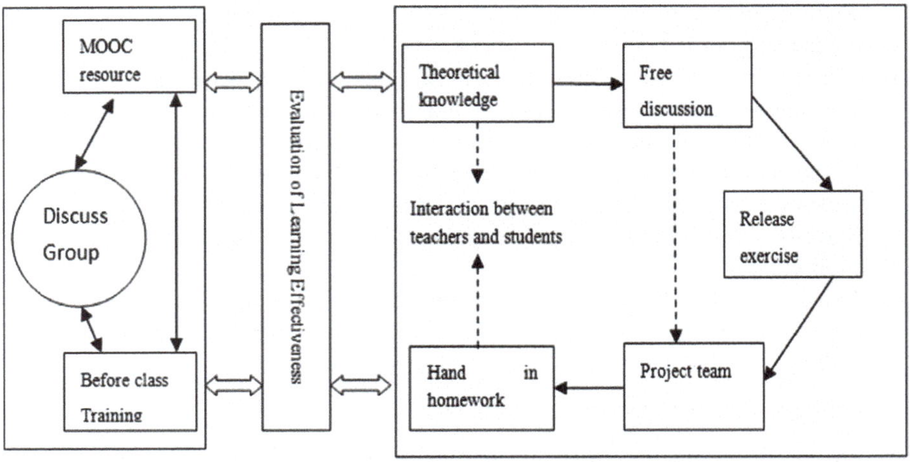

Fig. 1. MOOC + Classroom Teaching Model

(1) Students learn by themselves through the platform. The self-study part comprises pre-class preparation and after-class review, making use of MOOC's rich teaching resources.

And the online video open course resources are employed for self-study.

If there are incomprehensible content in the learning process, it can be timely communicated through the platform section, and can carry out online consultation on the handing in of teaching assignments and questions.

MOOC's teaching philosophy emphasizes the idea of returning learning to its origin. Through online and offline teacher's teaching, assistant's guidance, other learners' cooperation and self-participation in learning, learning interest can be stimulated to the greatest extent, and the pressure of passive learning can be transformed into the desire to acquire knowledge actively, which can be further implemented into specific learning behavior. Universities should make use of it to achieve fragmentation and personalized learning in MOOC, and gradually realize the change from teacher-centered teaching to student-centered teaching.

(2) Teachers Improve Teaching and Scientific Research Ability with MOOC

One of the aims of college reform is to improve the quality of higher education in an all-round way and the comprehensive quality of College graduates. To achieve this goal, teachers play a decisive role. MOOC has a large number of courses offered by famous teachers both in China and abroad. Learning their advanced educational and teaching concepts and methods, we can fully and profoundly understand the connotation and extension of the relevant courses. In addition, famous teachers' teaching experience contributes to our rational use of MOOC in our own courses. By learning some professional elective courses, our colleague teachers can understand the latest research fields and methods timely, and broaden their professional horizon to improve their own scientific research ability. Although MOOC can not make everyone become a famous teacher, it provides an effective way for teachers to further improve their teaching and scientific research ability through MOOC learning.

(3) Students are the main body of learning, thus the beneficiaries of all the teaching reforms must be students in order that students can acquire more knowledge. The students' academic assessment consists of the following four parts. The self-study on the platform mainly focuses on investigating the time of self-study and completing the tasks on the platform.

In the third part of the class, 15% of the students were assessed in class and 55% of the students were assessed in the final exam. The proportion of the final exam will be further reduced when the model is mature.

The advantages of this teaching mode lie not only in making full use of the advantages described in the first chapter of this paper, but also in avoiding the lack of students' systematic understanding of knowledge through the guidance and summary of teachers in classroom. The discussion in classroom aims to examine the learning effect of the platform and promote the learning on MOOC platform. In-class exercises and final examinations serve to solve the problem of impartiality that may arise from network assessment.

4 Analysis of Learning Effect

In this paper, a questionnaire is designed to investigate the"MOOC and classroom teaching methods effort". In order to understand the learning psychology and behavior of students in "MOOC +classroom" teaching mode.

Through the online testing platform, 85 students participated in the survey, with a recovery rate of 100%. Through the survey, it was found that the majority of students believed that it was necessary for them to learn autonomously by video before class. At the same time, they believed that completing the tutorial plan could improve the learning efficiency, as shown in Table 1.

Table 1. The analyses of students willingness for Moocs.

Question	Strong need	Need	Neutral	Reject
It is necessary to learn independently through MOOCs	60.9%	25.1%	11.7%	2.3%
Improve learning efficiency through cases	64.7%	23.5	8.2%	2.3%

In classroom teaching, students should compare, supplement and revise the knowledge they have learned according to what the teachers have said in class. Teachers attach more importance to students'learning outcomes, the more they can mobilize students' learning enthusiasm. Due to the introduction of cases in MOOC curriculum, in classroom teaching, case presentation is the most popular among students, and it is also one of the best ways to combine MOOC + Classroom teaching (Table 2).

Table 2. The effort for "MOOC + classroom teaching"

Question	Strong need	Need	Neutral	Reject
Show the case in classroom teaching	70.59%	17.65%	9.41%	2.35%
MOOC + Course Teaching Can Stimulate Learning Interest	76.47%	11.76%	9.41%	2.35%

5 Conclusion

The rise and rapid development of MOOC has brought a new era of online education. It is a new challenge to the traditional teaching mode. MOOC teaching has become one of the latest teaching methods and a trend of teaching reform in the context of globalization and information age. Undeniably, MOOC will not end traditional colleges. If we can make proper use of MOOC resources and design more advanced teaching models according to the characteristics of each course, the quality of teaching in universities can be improved greatly and students will get better academic achievements. It is advisable that higher vocational colleges make full use of the advantages of the MOOC curriculum resources, introduce them into the classroom and integrate them with traditional teaching.

Acknowledgement. This work was supported by the teaching researches on High-quality Resource Sharing Course at School Level and Pilot Major of Comprehensive Reform at School Level, Nature Science research project of Anhui high school grant No. KJ2018A0699.2019 Anhui Provincial Supporting Program for Excellent Young Talents in Colleges and Universities (Design and Implementation of Multiplexing Sensor Data Acquisition System Based on Virtual Instrument and ELVIS). 2016 Wuhu Vocational and Technical College Quality Engineering Project (Surveying and Instrument Resources Sharing Course).

References

1. Luoren, L.: MOOC platform and classroom teaching mode of combining exploration. J. Electron. world 429–4301 (2018)
2. Adams Becker, S., Cummins, M., Davis, A., Freeman, A., Hall Giesinger, C., Ananthanarayanan,V.: NMC Horizon Report: 2017 Higher Education Edition. The NewMedia Consortium, Austin, Texas (2017)

3. Mao, H., Yuan, H.: Exploration on the teaching mode of selective embedding MOOC. J. Ninbo Univ. Educ. Sic. Ed. (6), 99–104 (2018)
4. Ma, J.: The construction of a hybrid teaching model based on the idea of MOOCs. J. Shandong Agric. Eng. Coll. (10), 187–188 (2018)
5. Dong, H-b., Jian, G.E.: Exploration of flipped class model for "virtual instruments. Educ. Teach. Forum (51), 145–146 (2018)
6. McEvoy, C.S., Cantore, K.M., Denlinger, L.A.N., et al.: Use of medical students in a flipped classroom programme in nutrition education for fourth-grade school students. Health Educ. J. **75**(1), 38–46 (2016)
7. Fang, Z.: MOOC's innovative drive and teaching practice for the construction of quality courses in colleges and universities. Sci. Educ. Artic. Collects (B), 4–6 (2019)
8. Chen, W.: The influence of classroom teaching in regular college in the MOOC era. Educ. Teach. Forum (4), 237–239 (2019)

The Reform of Data Structure Course of MOOC + SPOC Diversified Practice Method

Wan-shun Chen(✉), Hong-fang Cheng, and Fei Hu

Wuhu Institute of Technology, Wuhu, China
858708130@qq.com, 403242688@qq.com, 540999537@qq.com

Abstract. In view of the existing phenomenon in the teaching of data structure in higher vocational colleges, this paper introduces the mixed teaching mode based on MOOC + SPOC. MOOC is an online network classroom, and SPOC method has achieved online MOOC support, which is the effective supplement of offline teachers. This paper expounds the nature and tasks of data structure course, applies this method for practical teaching, explores the effective role of diversified MOOC + SPOC methods in the course, and promotes the improvement of teaching quality effectively.

Keywords: MOOC · SPOC · Data Structure · Teaching mode

1 Introduction

Data Structure is a basic course of computer, which is an important theoretical and technical basis for subsequent courses such as Database and Operating System. Data Structure mainly aims at the implementation of non-numerical calculation, involving the representation, organization and processing of data in the computer during the non-numerical calculation. Due to the course status, the basis of data structure course affects students' learning many subsequent content during development and learning, both for further learning other courses in computer field, competition and practices, or in the future work and study to the student. Therefore, how to improve the teaching and learning quality of "Data Structure" course effectively is an important subject that needs our in-depth research, and it is also a difficult challenge that we have been facing all the time.

The rest of the paper is organized as the following: The teaching situation is discussed in the following section. The related work is discussed in Sect. 3. The proposed teaching model and method is presented in Sect. 4. The construction of Data Structure course under MOOC + SPOC mode is introduced in Sect. 5. Finally, the paper is concluded in Sect. 6.

G. Sun et al. (Eds.): eLEOT 2019, LNICST 299, pp. 132–139, 2019.
https://doi.org/10.1007/978-3-030-35095-6_16

2 Teaching Situation

At present, there are some problems in the teaching process of Data Structure course in higher vocational colleges:

(1) Lackage of theoretical knowledge of advanced courses

C language program "is one of the main leading course of Data Structure. Due to vocational students' weak foundation of C language knowledge, most of the students feel theoretical knowledge can understand, but they don't know where to start to realize the algorithm, and find it difficult to grasp, so they lose their interest in learning and confidence, to affect the teaching process directly.'

(2) Little teaching hours

Data Structure is rich in knowledge points and contents, but the current class hour is difficult to support the development of some new teaching models. The teaching method in higher vocational colleges is mainly "theory + experiment", which is mainly taught by classroom, and students complete experimental courses. How to let the students participate in the teaching, it is particularly important to arrange the reasonable use of different teaching modes [1].

In view of the above question in the teaching process, the new teaching methods have become an essential topic. "MOOC + SPOC" teaching mode is a good way to solve the current problem, combining information with traditional mode, so that the teaching mode becomes more perfect. This paper conducts preliminary design and research on the construction of Data Structure under the current new teaching mode "MOOC + SPOC".

3 Literature Review

In the teaching of Data Structure, many domestic scholars are exploring new teaching methods constantly. In this section, we review some of the previous works on Data Structure teaching. In view of the importance of data structure, many teaching methods have been proposed in the course of teaching. Starting from the teaching practice, aiming at the problems in the teaching of "data structure" course, Qiu Jin et al. proposed the teaching reform and practice research program of "Data Structure" course, which includes "reasonable organization of teaching content, reform of traditional teaching mode, optimization of teaching means, strengthening of engineering practice and establishment of scientific evaluation mechanism" [2]. Based on the analysis of the teaching mode, Li proposed a teaching mode with the problem driven as the core [3]. Yang et al. applied the combination of micro class and flipped class to the teaching process of "Data Structure" course, which brought new ideas to the classroom teaching [4]. Wu et al. discussed the application prospect of flipped classroom in the course based on the analysis of the current teaching situation of "Data Structure" under the current teaching mode. Taking the teaching content of "minimum spanning tree" as an example, they studied the feasibility of flipped classroom teaching [5]. Zhao proposed to introduce flipped classroom teaching experiment mode on the basis of cloud computing teaching platform, and designed the experimental teaching process. Practice shows that this method plays a role in promoting "teaching" and "learning" [6]. From the analysis situation and flip the concept of classroom teaching, Xiao Jingliu et al. explored how to turn effective classroom teaching mode in the classroom teaching in colleges and universities, and put forward the concrete implementation plan, finally proposed to solve the key problems in the implementation plan application analyzed [7]. Zhang yan used the WeChat public platform to assist the teaching and research of university data structure [8]. Zhang Shaowu et al. made a study of "data structure" teaching mode, studied the theory and teaching practice based on the desire platform flip of the classroom teaching, made every effort to make students learn by course, to be able to understand the logic of the master data structure, storage structure and algorithm design and analysis of the basic ideas, thus laid the foundation for study and research in the field of all kinds of computing [9].

4 SPOC + MOOC Teaching Mode

(1) MOOC

MOOC (Massive Of Open Course) is a significant reform of teaching through open online classroom. MOOC is free, self-directed learning that allows students to choose courses they are interested in. MOOC courses are rich in resources. But with the development of MOOC, some of their disadvantages have been highlighted. Firstly, MOOC learning emphasizes "autonomy", while it is difficult for students to stick to it until the end without supervision. Secondly, although resources in MOOC are classified, they are not systematic and can only be used to select courses based on personal interests. It cannot meet the university's talent training program. While MOOC are online teaching methods, the number of students from all over the world is so large that it is difficult to answer questions in real time.

(2) SPOC

SPOC (small private online course) is a small-scale limited flipped classroom method, which also uses network resources to take video resources in MOOC as auxiliary teaching content, and combines with actual classroom teaching method. First of all, teachers cut the existing MOOC video according to the requirements of the syllabus, and students learned online in advance. Then, they discussed the course content in class, arranged corresponding practice links according to the learning content, and finally assessed students according to the examination results and the usual experimental results. SPOC method enables students to solve problems in class through online learning. Teachers' understanding of students' understanding of MOOC through classroom teaching can effectively supplement and supervise students' learning status. Teachers in the evaluation of results, can be assessed through multiple aspects of students, the results of the authenticity, objectivity of the better effect. SPOC flipped classroom not only inherits the advantages of MOOC, but also makes up for the shortcomings of traditional education. It fully integrates the Internet and traditional classroom to help students complete the learning content faster.

5 Construction of Data Structure Course Under MOOC + SPOC Mode

"Data Structure" is a computer professional foundation course. Taking information engineering department of Wuhu Institute of Technology as an example, the course of the period is 64 class hours, four classes per weeks and 16-week course. The course of the training goal is to pass this course teaching, make students understand each data structure in the field of computer science knowledge, and the relevant application software to use various data structure knowledge, understand the commonly used data structure and the internal logic relationship, knowledge of computer software in the design of algorithm, familiar with the software design and programming skills, to create a preliminary comparison of different storage structure and corresponding algorithm, Have certain algorithm improvement ability, and lay a foundation for students to engage in software development and programmers in the future. At the same time, it is the theoretical basis of compiler, operating system, database system courses, but also for students to follow the successful study of courses to provide conditions. This course takes the "Data Structure" of Wuhu Institute of Technology under the MOOC platform of Anhui e-learning MOOC as the MOOC resource, takes the MOOC resource as the explanation of basic knowledge, and gives priority to teachers' guidance and comprehensive practice in class.

SPOC + MOOC mode is an online and offline teaching mode, which can be divided into "online independent learning", "online collaborative learning", "offline classroom learning", "offline practical experiment learning" and other parts. In addition, SPOC platform of course teaching should analyze the course learning needs and practical needs, make clear the professional requirements and skills, and summarize the whole teaching content and the required knowledge.

The specific steps are as follows:

Firstly, teachers download curriculum resources on MOOC platform, tailor video content appropriately according to syllabus requirements and training plan, and arrange MOOC resources as shown in Table 1. The teacher recorded 5 to 15 min of micro-lessons. Publish MOOC resources and knowledge outline to QQ group. Students study carefully after class. Teachers publish learning task content every week. Students are required to submit learning notes before class, record learning content outline and questions about videos, and take notes as homework, and give results according to the completion situation. Students can communicate and discuss online in QQ group, and teachers can answer questions online to achieve better learning effect.

Secondly, Online collaborative learning. Discussion area is very important in the course teaching. After watching the online teaching video, students will discuss their problems with their classmates through the discussion area function of the online course platform. Building a discussion community, students and teaching assistants and teachers help to answer questions. Meanwhile, the online collaboration section provides a space for students to exchange information and share resources, so they won't feel lonely in study. In the discussion area, a special person should be set up to answer questions. There should be not only a group among students, but also a special person to answer questions, so as to help students solve problems in the first time and move

Table 1. MOOC course content schedule

Course	Data Structure		Number	41units
	Num.	Chapter	Time	
	1	Introduce	5'	
	2	What is data structure	5'	
	3	The logical structure of the data	10'	
	4	Description of algorithm	20' (2 sections)	
	5	The basic concept of Linear table	10'	
	6	Sequential storage structure and algorithm of Linear table	30'(3 sections)	
	7	The chain storage structure of Linear table and its operation	30' (3 sections)	
	8	Examples of Linear table	16' (2 sections)	
	9	Stack	50'(5 sections)	
	10	Queue	50'(5 sections)	
	11	The basic concept of String	10'	
	12	The storage structure of String	20'(2 sections)	
	13	The basic operation of String	20'(2 sections)	
	14	Examples of applications	15'(3 sections)	
	15	Array	15'(3 sections)	
	16	The basic concept of Tree	5'	
	17	Binary tree	20'(2 sections)	
	18	The storage structure of Binary tree	25'(3 sections)	
	19	The traversal of Binary tree	15'(3 sections)	
	20	Binary sort tree	40'(4 sections)	
	21	Conversion between tree, forest, and binary tree	25'(3 sections)	
	22	Huffman tree	20'(2 sections)	
	23	Basic terms of Graph	5'	
	24	The storage structure of Graph	20'(2 sections)	
	25	The traversal of Graph	20'(2 sections)	
	26	Minimum spanning tree	30' (3 sections)	
	27	Shortest Path	10' (2 sections)	
	28	Topological sorting	30' (3 sections)	
	29	critical path method	10'	
	30	The basic concept of Search	15'	
	31	Sequential Search	10'	
	32	Binary search	10'	
	33	block search	10'	
	34	Hash table	10'	
	35	The basic concept of Sort	8'	
	36	Insertion sort	20'(2 sections)	
	37	Selection sort	10'	
	38	Exchange sort	20'(2 sections)	
	39	Merge sort	20'(2 sections)	
	40	Radix sort	10'	
	41	Comparison of sorting methods	10'	

forward smoothly. At the same time, questions related to the unit should also be set, so that students can participate in thinking and discussion and share information with each other.

Thirdly, guiding in class. "Data Structure" theory is strong, so how to do a good job in the classroom guidance, has become important particularly. In this study, MOOC and SPOC methods were used for classroom teaching of Data Structure. In the course teaching guidance, the teaching time and content are arranged as shown in Table 1. Due to the limited curriculum resources of MOOCS and the different levels of students, teachers should use MOOCS to supplement effectively and revise the teaching content. Through the teaching reform in this way, students pay more attention in class and improve their interest in this course. Through combining of MOOC and SPOC mode, students' analytical ability in the practice of Data Structure is cultivated.

Fourth, experimental arrangement. In order to enable students to better master the knowledge of "data structure", the corresponding experimental teaching contents are arranged, and the corresponding knowledge points are verified and enriched through experiments. According to the teaching objectives and requirements of "data structure" of the college, 16 experimental contents are arranged in this course to verify the key teaching knowledge in each stage. Meanwhile, the sequential experiment also carries on the review of previous experimental knowledge. In the experimental process, MOOC-related knowledge is interspersed to carry out effective experimental process. Through practice, our students' interest in experiment has been greatly improved, and students' independent learning ability and problem-solving ability have been cultivated.

Fifth, Comprehensive training. Experimental and practical training is the training stage of comprehensive ability of "Data Structure" course teaching and the integration stage of comprehensive practical ability of important knowledge points. Teachers should set practical training questions according to the characteristics of the courses. Practical training questions should contain important knowledge points in the "Data Structure" as far as possible. MOOC should be introduced to deepen students' grasp and understanding of knowledge points in practical training questions. At the end of the semester, the data structure will arrange the course design. Through this way of practical training, students have mastered the knowledge, completed the "Data Structure" teaching objectives and teaching objectives.

Sixth, performance evaluation. In the process of teaching and experimental training, MOOC and classroom teaching mode are adopted. The final score cannot be determined by one examination paper and students' usual scores. Based on the actual situation of our school, the independent study of MOOC students and the students' performance in SPOC teaching. The student performance evaluation of our school is effectively divided. In the process of score division, the weight of MOOC and SPOC will be added to effectively decompose the weight of the final examination paper. Through this way of reform to change the original test results, it can increase the students' learning initiative and improve the students' interest and ability of independent learning.

6 Conclusion

The MOOC mode allows students to learn the basic knowledge before class, and the teacher gives the initiative to the students in class. In this way, the MOOC content can be effectively reviewed, and the remaining time can be used for practical application and reasonable experiments, so as to achieve the goal of cultivating application-oriented talents. The diversified practical methods of MOOC + SPOC were applied in the course of data structure, which improved the practical ability of students and provided great help to the learning of subsequent courses.

The construction and implementation of Data Structure class teaching under MOOC + SPOC mode is a more effective reform in the information age. its establishment and the actual classroom mutual fusion, not only to release the classroom teaching of classroom space, but also to broaden the students' autonomous learning. So that it can greatly promote students' learning ability, improve the efficiency of the students' learning, let the students can put this to use. And the knowledge can better applied to the practice, at the same time it also lets teachers liberation the durance of pattern, realizes self teaching thoughts fly. It can use modern technology to optimize their teaching level and classroom teaching quality.

Acknowledgment. This work was supported by the research on high school provincial quality engineering project of Anhui grant No. 2015zdjy171, No. 2015mooc109, No. 2016ckjh224, No. 2017mooc368 and No. 2017sjjd041, the excellent top talent cultivation project of Anhui high school grant No. gxyqZD2017141, Nature science research project of Anhui high school grant No. KJ2017A560, school level scientific and technological innovation team grant No. Wzykj2018A02, and University-level key projects grant No. Wzyzrzd201702.

References

1. Tang, J., Tan, P.: The research of data structure and algorithm design training course teaching. Softw. Guide **15**(1), 193–194 (2016)
2. Qiu, J., Wang, P., Xu, Z.: On teaching reform and practice on the course of Data Structure. J. Southwest China Normal Univ. (Nat. Sci. Edn.) **38**(1), 139–142 (2013)
3. Li, Z., Liao, M., Zhang, Y.: Discussion on the teaching mode of data structure and algorithm course design. Comput. Educ. (2), 54–56 (2006)
4. Yang, F., Li, J., Wang, W.: Research on flipped classroom teaching model based on micro class: taking data Structure course as an example. Educ. Forum, (3), 8–9 (2016)
5. Wu, Y., Zhang, L., Zhao, W.: Application of flipped classroom in data structure course. Comput. Educ. (2), 55–57 (2016)
6. Zhao, Q.: Research on experimental teaching model of data structure course based on flipped classroom. Univ. Educ. (2), 9–10 (2016)
7. Liu, X., Zhong, Q., Zhang, J.: Research on the application of flipped classroom model in the teaching of Data Structure course. Chin. Educ. Technol. (8), 105–110 (2014)
8. Zhang, Y.: The teaching and research of Data Structure in colleges and universities on the WeChat public platform. Course Educ. Res. (2), 247–248 (2016)

9. Zhang, S., Lin, X., Li, D.: Exploration on the teaching mode of data structure and algorithm flipped classroom for postgraduates based on MOOC courses. Fujian Comput. (7), 44–45 (2015)
10. Cao, Y., Chen, Y., Ying, Y.: Research on innovative teaching mode of data structure course. Educ. Forum (4), 125–126 (2016)

An Empirical Study on the Integration of MOOCs Resources and College English Education

Yuanbing Duan[1(✉)], Jingzheng Wang[2], and Wei Zhong[1]

[1] Yunnan Normal University, 768 Juxian Road, Kunming 650500, People's Republic of China
yuanbingduan@qq.com
[2] Yunnan Open University, No. 113, Xuefu Road, Kunming 650223, People's Republic of China

Abstract. Massive Open Online Courses (MOOCs) have been rapidly increasing globally. In recent years, MOOCs and flipped classroom have drawn great attention from educators around the world. In China, these new learning models are being practiced by more and more college English teachers and students in their teaching and learning. To better understand the impact of MOOCs on current and future e-education globally, this paper reports an empirical study of Yunnan Open University (YNOU). In this study there are totally 32 teachers and 145 students answered the questionnaires, meanwhile 10 teachers randomly chosen were asked to take part in the in-depth interviews which were recorded and analyzed. The survey results demonstrate that there are some strengths and some limitations as well in using MOOCs. Five suggestions have been put forward for college English teachers and faculty members. Taking the impact of MOOCs on college English education into consideration, three stages are initiated for the construction of efficient integration of MOOCs and college English education. Furthermore, opportunities and challenges of MOOCs for traditional classroom practices and adult program management are discussed.

Keywords: MOOCs · College English education · Integration

1 Introduction

Modern open and distance education is characterized by web-based instruction, web-based assessment and research. Web-based learning support services are considered as the most essential inputs for learners which offer ground for them to produce considerable outputs so as to achieve better learning outcomes. From the year of 2011, Massive Open Online Courses (MOOCs), as a new network education mode, have been rapidly developed around the world. Cousera, edX and Udacity are regarded as "three carriages" of global MOOCs platforms, which attracted many universities to join, including some famous home universities like Peking University, Tsinghua University and so on. In recent years, MOOCs and flipped classroom have drawn lots of attention from educators around the world due to its great impact on e-learning and life-long learning.

G. Sun et al. (Eds.): eLEOT 2019, LNICST 299, pp. 140–150, 2019.
https://doi.org/10.1007/978-3-030-35095-6_17

To better understand the impact of MOOCs on current and future e-education globally, this paper reports an empirical study of Yunnan Open University (YNOU for short). Totally, there are 32 college English teachers and 145 students answered the survey questionnaires, meanwhile 10 teachers randomly chosen were asked to take part in the in-depth interviews which were recorded and analyzed.

In order to have a successful integration of MOOCs resources and college English courses, this paper examines the strengths of how MOOCs impact college English education with special focus on improving college English teaching quality at first. Secondly, limitations are summarized so as to assist the feasibility and effectiveness of conducting online MOOCs. Thirdly, suggestions together with corresponding possible solutions have been put forward for college English teachers and faculty members at YNOU. Based on challenges and opportunities, future integration of MOOCs resources into college English teaching will be discussed in the last part.

2 Literature Review

2.1 The Definition of MOOCs

The term MOOCs is shortened for Massive Open Online Courses, the integration of information technology and multiple intelligence. More importantly, they are mostly free online courses to the public. Therefore, it is very crucial to make a clear explanation about its connotative meaning.

According to Wikipedia, the first letter 'M' stands for Massive, referring to large scale of audience, massive numbers can be hundreds, thousands or millions. The second letter 'O' represents Open, its resources open to every student who is willing to learn. The third letter 'O' is a short for Online, providing online courses 24 h with automatic online evaluation system, to break through the traditional learning mode of time and space restrictions. The last letter 'C' abbreviates for Courses, the learning material is a complete course system, including curriculum objectives, curriculum requirements, curriculum tasks, curriculum evaluation and so on [1].

Based on the theory of open and e-learning, the global spread of high quality education resources can be realized through MOOCs. There are five main characteristics in the whole [2]. (1) Great: education for large scale of learners; (2) Open: anybody can learn, anywhere can learn, no constrains of time and space; (3) Free: most of the courses are free of charge, especially some first level courses offered by famous universities; (4) Personalized: different levels of learners can choose what they need to learn according to his/her own learning speed/background; (5) Blended: face-to-face learning and online learning modes are mixed together so as to achieve better learning outcomes.

2.2 Studies of MOOCs Abroad

The study of MOOCs resources can be dated back to the year of 2008 abroad; it was not popular until 2012, the first international year of MOOCs. Andrew Ng and Daphne Koller created Coursera collaboratively in November 2011, Sebastian Thrun and another two colleagues set up Udacity in February 2012, Edx online free courses platform was founded by MIT and Harvard University in April 2012. So far, Coursera, Udacity and Edx became three tycoons in MOOC era, leading the future of free university education by offering the world-top courses.

Since then many of the related platforms had been formed in Europe following North America. For example, Futurelearn of Britain joined MOOCs in 2012 and Iversity of Germany engaged with MOOCs in 2013 by offering their first online courses. Asia had explored its local platform based on Coursera, Udacity and Edx, too. Japan, India and China had done a lot in exploiting courses as well as building MOOCs schools. Other areas like Pakistan and Australia had developed MOOCs actively. Therefore, MOOCs start from the foreign countries, they are the products of informationized development to post-traditional era, attributed to the successful application of scientific technologies [3].

2.3 Studies of MOOCs at Home

In China, the development of MOOCs lags far behind from the west. In 2013, East-west Universities' Course Sharing Alliance was established, thus the year of 2013 has been regarded as the first year of China MOOCs [4], and that year was also the beginning year of MOOCs and college English teaching research. To sum up, there are four features in the process of MOOCs' development at home [5]. (1) Brand name universities pay special attention to MOOCs than other ordinary universities; (2) Developed areas, such as Beijing, Guangdong, Zhejiang provinces focus most on MOOCs; (3) Mass media concerns highly on MOOCs than other media; (4) Male audiences surpass female ones a lot, especially university students between 20 to 29 years old.

In a word, MOOCs-assisted teaching and learning is widely acknowledged as a new learning model to promote students' learning by all kinds of means. It is assumed that this new mode of service will play a greater role in stimulating and facilitating students' learning. They are being practiced by more and more college English teachers and students in their teaching and learning. The following is an empirical study of practicing MOOCs in YNOU.

3 Research Method

3.1 Research Questions

The study aims to answer the following three questions:

(1) What are the strengths and limitations of the integration of MOOCs resources into college English course in YNOU?
(2) What are the suggestions to improve the integration of MOOCs resources into college English course in YNOU?
(3) How can we conduct effective integration of MOOCs resources into college English course in YNOU?

3.2 Participants

There are totally 32 teachers and 145 students answered the questionnaires, meanwhile 10 teachers randomly chosen were asked to take part in the in-depth interviews. The subjects involved in the study are all the students registered at YNOU during the 2017 Autumn Semester. YNOU is the only Open University approved by the State Council in the Midwest region of China, and it aims to provide high quality distance education, with no exception of the utility of MOOCs resources for students from all walks of life in the area.

In the case of distance education in YNOU, it provides a complete and multi-functional system of assuring equal education opportunities in the Midwest, serving as an educational supply depot for all learning needs. Learners can be anyone who loves to study; they can study anywhere, at anytime, through YNOU learning platform and system. Among total more than 100,000 open and distant learning students, the majority are adult students whose College English is the toughest course. That is why the study has specific significance in improving learners' English education quality.

3.3 Instruments

The research instrument adopted in the study is composed of two, one is the questionnaire and another is the outline of the interview. The former contains a personal information sheet and a five point Likert scale of test in which the informants are asked to choose a response from strongly agree to strongly disagree. This is designed to explore the strengths and limitations of the integration of MOOCs. The latter contains a personal information sheet with six questions. It is designed to gain the suggestions. Both of them were based on works of Jonassen and Land [6], Wang and Zhang [7] and Linlin Huang, and distributed to the subjects after some modifications. A pilot study was conducted to further confirm its reliability and validity [8].

3.4 Procedures

The study was carried out in the Autumn Semester of 2017, lasting from November 2017 to April 2018. In the study, both quantitative and qualitative methods are applied, 32 teachers' and 145 students' questionnaires were collected by hard paper and 10 semi-structured interviews were conducted by the means of phone, We-chat and QQ Forum, when possible, face-to-face as well. The data of students' questionnaire performance was analyzed by descriptive method and the interview data by key words extraction method. Findings and discussion will be followed in the next part.

4 Findings and Discussion

4.1 Strengths of the Integration of MOOCs Recourses into College English Teaching

With the ever-increasing number of computers and the declining cost of using them, it becomes possible to take the advantages of MOOCs in students' learning process, so does College English course. According to the study, YNOU offers MOOCs-based learning for both teachers and students with a lot of advantages.

Factors Concerning Tutors. First of all, teacher's information literacy is improved. It can provide teachers with knowledge about how to make a mini video, how to use the network platform, how well MOOCs are conducted and how to be a qualified teacher in an information age. 86.5% of teachers questioned agree that the study raises their consciousness of being a modern teacher.

Secondly, teacher's working efficiency is achieved. Open and distance education in YNOU, where tutors and students meet for tutorials only once every week or every month or even once a semester in some remote areas, it is more difficult to collect information by using the traditional means, online learning of MOOCs will completely fill this gap. 80.2% of teachers agree that the study achieves the goal of working by MOOCs. In addition, 4V specialties of MOOCs in big data era brings many advantages, to be specific, Volume, Variety, Velocity and Value, indicating that MOOCs are also high capacity, great variety, fast speed, time-saving, high efficiency, time and space free features [9].

Thirdly, teachers' curriculum design and classroom management ability is improved. To have a better control in online and face-to-face classroom, teachers can benefit a lot from the roles in the process of e-teaching. 65% of teachers agree that their roles have been changed in classroom management. They should master some management strategies of classroom activities, such as problem based learning, game based learning, group learning and so on.

Factors Concerning Students. Firstly, students' information literacy is improved. Students must equip themselves with the knowledge of how to study with the help of MOOCs, how to do homework online, how to download learning materials and how to submit pre-course exercises. 90% of students agree that their information knowledge is improved during the study.

Secondly, students' autonomous learning abilities are promoted. MOOCs-based teaching offer different level of learning materials for various needs, so as to deal with the specific difficulties, thus learning interests are greatly motivated. It also can offer opportunities for students' self-study at their own pace through MOOCs. 78.5% of students agree that their roles have been changed in autonomous learning. They are the key characters in the process, their former knowledge consumers have been changed to knowledge generators, assimilating the knowledge by forms of group learning and collaborative learning [10].

Thirdly, the students' listening and speaking ability are improved under this new mode of learning. The flipped class videos are first created for the students who cannot go to school on time [11]; they can watch the videos whenever they are free. The class requires learners to listen and watch the relevant videos before class, then to finish the cooperative assignments involving students' listening and speaking. 79.3% of students agree that their listening and speaking abilities are improving.

Fourthly, learners' critical thinking abilities are helped. Flipped classroom, as a form of MOOCs-based teaching, was advocated by Baker, teachers used network tools in teaching after class while doing cooperative discussion and problem-solving in class [12]. Students often have more hands-on activities both outside and inside the classroom, more chances for communication and to help each other with the assigned tasks. 69% of students agree that their critical thinking abilities have been developed.

Lastly, students' learning environments are created. It provides a platform for building up a networked learning environment by integrating offline classrooms and cyber space, and is to change the traditional learning environment into a new, multiple and ecological one. 71% of students agree that their learning environment have been created.

4.2 Limitations of the Integration of MOOCs Recourses into College English Teaching

Based on the investigation, there are some potential problems for the utility of MOOCs in college English as far as modern technologies are concerned intensively. As a new learning method of MOOCs, the survey results demonstrate that it has limitations on college English for both teachers and students from the following aspects.

Factors Concerning Tutors. *Difficulty in Preparing Learning Materials.* MOOCs-based teaching requires lots of preparation before class. Teachers should face and realize that information technology is an inseparable part of today's world; they need work more to choose appropriate video materials to activate learners' motivation, to make the specific teaching resources for the learning difficulties. Then the most important and the toughest job is how to prepare the appropriate materials. Half of teachers do not know the principles of organizing text and multimedia; 60% of them have difficulties in allocating teaching tasks before and in the class; the others have confusions about how to evaluate learners' outcome.

Time-Consuming Course Design. Two thirds of college English learners in using MOOCs reach the consensus of that learning through service system is a very time-consuming process if they are not so familiar with computer skills and not easy to get access to computers or internet. In addition, it took college English teachers too much time for class preparation and video recordings, and many teachers complain about having increased burdens at the beginning of the reform.

During the evaluation process, teachers should check the learners' assignment online, answering the questions both online and offline, and offering feedback at anytime. In comparison with the traditional teaching mode, this complex course design is really time-consuming. Tutors have many new responsibilities added to their old ones required by traditional ways of teaching; all the extra time and efforts invested by the staff members involved in the application of the design should be taken into consideration in terms of the new type of workload.

Factors Concerning Students. *Poor Command of Computer Skills.* Some of the students understand the value of MOOCs as a means to improve their second language learning skills gradually. However, others might see their poor command of computer skills as the biggest obstacle to learn to use MOOCs as part of the supporting system, especially for those who are not familiar with this new learning mode. Most of the YNOU learners are not skilled in computer, such as taking part in the online activities, downloading the learning materials, participating in the online discussions and so on.

Besides, 79.2% of students have difficulties in learning the recorded videos on their own pace before tutorials. Nearly 80% of the students think the major difficulty they have with the system is that they do not have enough time for self-study, which lead to more troubles among students in the classroom.

Due to various reasons, 64% of students have unsuccessful experience in uploading their learning record and assignments. The main cause for this situation is that all the students are required to upload their learning records and assignments to the platform of OUC or YNOU. This makes the learning path very crowded, things are even worse if internet access has problems.

Difficult Access to Computers. Due to the lack of computers, more than half of the learners interviewed do not have easy access to computers. Since the number of computers at YNOU is limited, WIFI devices and the Internet speed is not very accessible sometimes, and the Learning Management System is still in the process of development. Over half of the learners do not have easy access to the internet; they complain that they are not given enough time online. Although WIFI devices are very common in most places in Yunnan, most students are working far from the study centers so that it is really not easy for them to get access to computers, and they might not necessarily have the internet anywhere meeting the requirements of the courses.

All in all, teachers should be encouraged to exploit MOOCs resources as a means to developing language skills and English classroom teaching quality. To this end, MOOCs materials can be introduced not only as a new dimension in college English teaching but also as a potential and possible solution to the above problems often mentioned by YNOU English teachers as a conundrum.

4.3 Suggestions on the Integration of MOOCs Recourses into College English Teaching

As far as our study concerned, teachers try to engage MOOCs in their courses, especially in the field of College English studies, but the results are not satisfied. Taking the impact of MOOCs on college English education into consideration [13, 14], especially opportunities and challenges of MOOCs bringing about for traditional classroom practices and undergraduate/graduate program management, five suggestions will be put forward to improve the English course learning outcomes for YNOU distance learners.

At first, attitudes toward the integration of MOOCs in college English should be changed. As Dowens [15] points out, the utility of MOOCs in college English, modern learners cannot learn by online MOOCs resources individually not only because of their ages but because of their attitudes towards modern technology. Reluctant learners are not willing to study through this system to some extend. Only enthusiastic learners can achieve the aim to meet the requirements of distance learning with web-based learning support services, to study online autonomously and freely.

Secondly, teachers' teaching mode should be changed. Since the utility of MOOCs in college English, the traditional mode of learning is being challenged; 'One Chalk One Blackboard' situation cannot be found anymore. i.e., sitting in the classroom and listening to lectures, distance learners do not feel safe and comfortable with the new through the web-based multimedia learning system. Vast volume and fast speed computers can deal with lots of the target culture information. Teachers can integrate the target teaching content by using some multi-dimensional signals such as multi-media graphs, images, authentic and auto-kinetic effects so as to increase learners' sense of freshness, to enlarge learners' knowledge capacity, and to promote learners to understand the teaching content at a further step [16].

In addition, the advantages of MOOCs can offer the ground of extending the perception of some specific knowledge points, deepening the degree of learners' cognitive competence. The 'sea' (vast) resources online can promote education informatization in terms of resources integration and optimization. For instance, the world-class open courses like "Happiness" and "Justice" provided by Harvard University have great help on building western cultural value. Courses from British BBC world service and TED may show the real English accent, motivating the multi-dimensional English output.

Thirdly, more efforts should be put into improving learning surroundings. Adequate training should be provided to the participants who are poor at using a computer before the learning system is introduced. Multi-media classrooms with Internet access should be set up extensively. The use of smart phones, emails, facebook, Skype, Wechat, QQ forum and offering students online help should be intensified to keep their pace of learning. In addition, possible solutions, which include improving teacher's professional development and providing technical support for learning such as the use of computers and WIFI, should be made to improve the effectiveness of MOOCs method. Gradually, the college English teaching, management and evaluation system will be promoted.

Fourthly, formulating related management policies might be a key countermeasure to improve the perceived job relevance and encourage college English teachers' practice of applying MOOCs in teaching; external control includes supports in funds, technology and the latest learning support services for MOOCs as well as to improve the perceived output quality. Poor computer skills, difficult access to Internet and computers, unsuccessful upload experience will torture the utility of MOOCs in college English study by the new mode. Given students support concerning technical support, learning process management, learning strategies, emotional factors and learning cooperation are promoted and well-served; all the above mentioned problems can be solved gradually. Combining study on the computers with study through various MOOCs resources for the course, such as the course books, videos, multimedia courseware etc., from easy to complex, avoiding upload materials at rush hours, all these will definitely help to achieve the purpose of MOOCs-based learning and save time for utility of MOOCs in college English eventually.

Lastly, tutor's workload should be reduced from a long term practices. Because "adults prefer face-to-face learning rather than learning through the use of video or audio communications" [17], it is not surprising that most of the tutors think the use of MOOCs has increased their workloads and they are really troublesome. Only few of the tutors are able to provide frequent and synchronous online help to students as this is a very time-consuming and demanding job. In addition, tutors have to get online to check students' learning process and mark students' written assignments uploaded as well.

From a long term point of view, once tutors are accustomed to the new mode of using MOOCs in college English, tutor's workload will be reduced.

5 The Construction of Efficient MOOCs-Based College English Teaching

With the increasing use of Internet in distance education, the possibility of conducting learning support services online is becoming greater. Teaching English with MOOCs by EFL teachers should be an essential part of teacher professional development programmes because it is more concerned with how language can affect personal and social change than it is with how to teach language more effectively.

From the stance of EFL teacher in Chinese context, a number of means are tried to improve second language learners' abilities, and College English, in contrast to other courses. It remains a kind of "being stuck", therefore it is very important to improve language ability via the application of MOOCs. The following three stages, namely pre-class, online class and post-class, are proposed to construct MOOCs-based College English teaching in this paper.

5.1 Pre-class Construction

In this process, the key point for teaching is getting familiar with videos of micro lectures, multimedia courseware, and videos online, and then to integrate these MOOCs resources' into learning objectives. As for teachers, choosing the most appropriate resources is a tough job. At first, make sense of the right materials to meet the exact teaching objectives and teaching content, so as to pave the way of good material preparation before class. Secondly, get to know learners' difficulties to make a targeted video clips to solve the major difficult teaching problems. Thirdly, make high quality videos to attract students' attention for different level of learners to help them prepare the class work in advance with great pleasure and relaxed feelings.

5.2 Online Class Construction

In this process, the key point for teaching is to change students into autonomous learners. Learning through the new mode is unprecedented and unstoppable; students have to learn on their own pace most of the time. The critical role of MOOCs-based college English teaching is to break through the traditional mode into an interactive and autonomous one, which activates learners' motivation at the most. This is undesirable as [18] argues that two key attitudes underlie learner autonomy: the first is learners' attitudes towards their own role in learning. The second is their attitudes towards their ability to learn and take responsibility for learning.

Firstly, teachers should pay more attention to the explanation of MOOCs resources, understanding learners' attitude to MOOCs at a further step, in order to construct a complete teaching mode of "Explore-Acquire-Answer-Feedback" in college English classrooms. Then teachers should try this pedagogy in the hope of diversifying their teaching methods, and enhancing classroom dynamics and interactivity for optimal instructional outcomes.

Secondly, teachers should conclude the problems rapidly, participating and conducting classroom discussions in order to solve pre-class problems. In the process, teachers can assign students into different groups, and guide them to follow the questions for cooperative learning designed by MOOCs materials. Cooperative works among students are encouraged.

Lastly, teachers can strengthen the content understanding by making good use of the flipped class and fragmental resources, leading students into some targeted questions, to form an automatic learner via autonomous learning, group discussion and communicative interaction.

5.3 Post-class Construction

During this process, the key point for the construction is the evaluation of MOOCs resources into College English teaching. The teachers should make a sound evaluation on students' learning outcomes and learning plan through MOOCs materials.

First, personalized learning environment is created to obtain a free and open evaluation so as to get an effective and fair appraisal system. Second, teachers should know the learning situation of every student at the post-class stage, carrying on a timely reflection and filling the gap between learning outcomes and teaching objectives. Third, teachers should take the advantage of the evaluation of MOOCs resources and teaching problems, in order to initiate a reasonable and scientific learning plan for the coming new stage.

6 Conclusion

This paper is devoted to the discussion of the employment of MOOCs in the target foreign language class by putting forward some feasible approaches and suggestions. Despite numerous studies done in supporting services, there has no research dealing with the integration of MOOCs with college English at YNOU. Therefore, it is worth and feasible trying to use and perfect them in the real situation. This paper ended by discussing some wider implications of MOOCs application in college English teaching.

MOOCs resources have many advantages by bringing the free and open idea of networked learning into College English course. For constructing a successful practice of MOOCs into English teaching, five corresponding possible solutions are summarized and three potential stages proposed so as to assist the feasibility and effectiveness of conducting MOOCs-based teaching. Within the three stages' integration of MOOCs and English course construction, the learners' outcomes will be greatly improved, increasing practical value in class and proving the integration with MOOCs is a good approach in modern e-education.

References

1. Marques, J.: A short history of MOOCs and distance learning. http://moocnewsandreviews.com/a-short-history-of-moocs-and-distance-learning. Accessed 07 Apr 2013

2. Sandeen, C.: Integrating MOOCs into traditional higher education: the emerging "MOOCs 3.0" era. Change: Mag. High. Learn. **45**(6), 34–39 (2013)
3. Chen, J.: Foreign language teaching in big data era. An opening remark on "PHD Salon of Shanghai International Studies University" (2015)
4. Ma, W., Hu, J.: Impact and reconstruct of international MOOCs on college English curriculum. Technol. Enhanced Foreign Lang. Educ. **36**(5), 48–54 (2014)
5. Huang, L.: Practical Exploration on MOOCs-based College English Teaching. Shanghai International Studies University, Shanghai (2015)
6. Jonassen, D.H., Land, S.M.: Theoretical Foundations of Learning Environment, vol. 2(21), pp. 128–143. Lawrence Ernaum Associates Inc., Mahwah (2012)
7. Wang, S., Zhang, L.: An investigation on acceptability about the filliped classroom of college English learner. Mordern Educ. Technol. **3**, 71–78 (2014)
8. Sun, G., Song, Z., Liu, J., et al.: Feature selection method based on maximum information coefficient and approximate markov blanket. Zidonghua Xuebao/Acta Automatica Sinica **43** (5), 795–805 (2009)
9. Ma, W., Li, X.: Enlightenment of International MOOCs on College English Follow-up Curriculum Construction. Modern Educ. Technol. **23**(11), 85–88 (2013)
10. Sun, G., Lang, F., Yang, M.: Traffic measurement system based on hybrid methods. Electr. Mach. Control **15**(6), 91–96 (2011)
11. Jonassen, D.H.: Handbook of Research for Educational Communication and Technology. Prentice Hall, New Jersey (2013)
12. Baker, W.J.: The classroom flip: using web course management tools to become the guide by the side. In: Chambers, J.A. (ed.) Selected papers from the 11th International Conference on College Teaching and Learning, pp. 33–42. Jacksonville, Florida (2000)
13. Bates, T.: What's right and what's wrong about Coursera-style MOOCs. http://www.tonybates.ca/whats-right-and-whats-wrong-about-coursera-style-moocs/. Accessed 04 Feb 2015
14. Daniel, J.: Making sense of MOOCs: musings in a maze of myth, paradox and possibility. http://jime.open.ac.uk/article/view/2012-18/466. Accessed 25 Nov 2012
15. Dowens, S.: MOOCs and Mookies: the connectivism & connective knowledge online courses. http://www.downes.ca/presentation/197. Accessed 16 Apr 2016
16. Chen, J.: The integration of computer and networks into foreign language curriculum-a research based on college English reform. Shanghai Foreign Language Education press, Shanghai (2010)
17. Stroot, S.: Peer Assistance and Review Guidebook. Ohio Department of Education. Ohio, Columbus (1998)
18. Wenden, A.: Learner Strategies for Learner Autonomy. Prentice Hall, New York (1991)

New Technology Applied in Education

Self-correction's Effects on EFL Writing on Web-Based Automatic Writing Evaluation Platform

Fei Lang(✉) and Xinfei Yan

School of Foreign Languages, Harbin University of Science and Technology, Harbin 150080, China
langfei@hrbust.edu.cn, 260069083@qq.com

Abstract. Recently, automatic writing evaluation (AWE) platform has been widely used in teaching English as a foreign language (EFL). It is popular in teaching of college EFL writing for its convenience and efficiency. "Pigai.org" is such an AWE platform with functions of automatic ranking, analyzing and giving advice on users' English writing. This study aims to explore the influence of students' writing behaviors based on "Pigai.org" on their writing scores. Firstly, a comparative analysis was conducted between times of submitting writing assignments for self-correction and the increases on scores. The analytical result show a positive correlation between times of self-correction and grade improvement. However, with submitting times increasing, phenomenon of language fossilization in self-correction appeared, which may result from metalinguistic awareness limitation. The result show that instant feedback and self-correction function on "Pigai.org" motivate the students to correct their compositions and improve their metalinguistic awareness.

Keywords: English writing · Self-correction · Pigai.org · Automated writing evaluation

1 Introduction

With the era of big data, traditional English writing teaching model has been innovated. The new online writing model can effectively evaluate students' compositions through the written corrective feedback, which is obviously advanced and scientific. AWE is based on corpus and cloud computing technology. The online automated writing evaluation system is to assist in the teaching of English writing and to promote students to learn and practice language knowledge independently and effectively. The well-known AWE system abroad has three main parts, including Project Essay Grade (PEG), Intelligent Essay Assessor (IEA), and E – rater. Most of them are used in native English writing, and less are applied to Chinese students' writing. "Pigai.org" is an intelligent teaching tool for teaching independently developed by China. It has been used by most universities in English teaching since its appearance on the market in 2010. Just like AES (Automated Essay Scoring), these advanced technologies have been successfully integrated into the writing standard [1]. "Pigai.org" is not about a teaching model of traditional English teaching class, but a cloud-based online service

G. Sun et al. (Eds.): eLEOT 2019, LNICST 299, pp. 153–169, 2019.
https://doi.org/10.1007/978-3-030-35095-6_18

for students to correct a great proportion of errors of English composition with confidence [2]. Is operating principle is to calculate the distance between the student's composition and the standard language in corpus. And then, the score of the student's composition, the evaluation of every sentence and content analysis are generated in the immediate time, which facilitates the students' effective learning and self-correction. "Pigai.org" aims to stimulate students' interest and enthusiasm in learning foreign language and help students to cultivate their good metalinguistic awareness.

The English composition correction processes of "Pigai.org" are as follows: (1). The teacher assigns the new composition on the website, and sets the writing requirements, the submission time and scoring requirements; (2) Students obtain the composition writing information and finish the assignment according to the composition search number after registering accounts; (3) After receiving the submitted composition, the system will automatically give the score and a comprehensive analysis of students' language ability from four aspects of vocabulary, sentence, structure and content, which aims to test the comprehensive English ability of students' writing; (4) The system will point out some language problems sentence by sentence. Students resubmit the composition after modifications until there is no language problems or get a satisfying score. Based on "Pigai.org", students can consciously think over the language mistakes they made and the reasons for making such mistakes. Through the repeated practice, this consciousness in mind to find the language errors will become unconscious. In other words, students may learn something valuable from the mistakes in the potential learning growth and the students' meta-consciousness will be improved in the subtle. Thus, this kind of self-correction will reduce the probability of making the same or similar kind of the mistakes in language output. At present, many domestic researchers study on AWE system, such as the impact of AWE on students' writing ability, the analysis of validity and reliability based on AWE, the research on the self-efficacy of college students' writing, and so on. However, studies on the students' self-correction ability of English writing based on "Pigai.org" is rare. Therefore, from the perspective of metalinguistic awareness, this study investigates the effect of "Pigai.org" on the self-correction of college students' English writing ability in the interaction between human and computer so as to make the online correction network better serve domestic writing teaching and improve college students' English writing level and ability.

2 Literature Review

As an online automatic evaluation system, "Pigai.org" is widely applied into English teaching in China, so it has high research value. In recent years, many scholars have explored this online system both at home and abroad. This kind of online automated feedback belongs to the direct feedback, which means the learning software offers the explicit correction and evaluation rather than the implicit correction with underlining or circling an error [3–5]. The direct feedback can provide enough suggestions for the students' self-correction so that they can correct the easier errors in a short time firstly and then under the help of some learning tools according to the key point for the language errors. In this way, the written feedback is effective in helping students to form good metalinguistic awareness and it is meaningful for teachers to apply it into the education of SLA (second language acquisition) [6]. Metalinguistic awareness is the potential awareness of monitoring the language errors. Similarly, it is inseparable from critical thinking, which makes use of categorization, decode, and clarify meaning to solve the problem [7]. Moreover, the students will benefit a lot from the metalinguistic awareness and the critical thinking in English writing.

Self-correction can be defined as the procedures of the learners themselves evaluating their language skills and knowledge from the perspective of some foreign researchers. In "Pigai.org", students can modify their compositions according to the online suggestions, which can also effectively reduce the burden on teachers. According to a research, students generally have a good experience of using "Pigai.org", and they believe that the warning hints and recommendation expressions provided by automated writing evaluation can help them correct the most basic mistakes in their compositions [8]. Liao's [9] study has conveyed that AWE tool can help students to enhance their grammatical performance. As for AWE, some researchers rethink the role of automated writing evaluation in ESL (English as a Second Language) writing, which reveals the effect of AWE corrective feedback on the students' writing accuracy by analyzing the number of submission [10]. There are also some researches about multiple feedback mechanism. Yu [11] explores the students' reflection on online self-correction and peer review, which verifies the self-correction can help them to correct lexical and grammatical mistakes and the peer review offers the interactive learning so as to revise the composition in a not mechanized way. However, there are some different views recently. Some scholars have conducted a survey on the richness and complexity of students' vocabulary after students using "Pigai.org", and the results show that the lexical richness of EFL (English as a Foreign Language) students' composition has not been well improved, which means that AWE makes little contribution to the modification of the words in compositions [12]. Correspondingly, it cannot deny the automated writing evaluation has improved students' self-correction ability of English writing. Yang [11], through an empirical study, finds that college students can benefit from their self-correction based on "Pigai.org", especially in the aspects of language accuracy and complexity. The study also reveals the feedback of the online system is not very helpful for students to revise the content or the structure of the essay. From this point of view, the "Pigai.org" has certain advantages for students to self-correct their writings, but it still has some limitations. The author suggests that teachers should give more opinions on the content and structure of writings rather than just let students modify the language errors of writings in the process of English writing teaching. Moreover, 76% of the students in another survey hold that the revision by the "Pigai.org" cannot totally replace teachers' feedback because the evaluation of "Pigai.org" is not as flexible and effective as the teacher's evaluation [13].

From the perspective of the current research, the research on the self-correction of college students' English writing based on the "Pigai.org" is still worthy of in-depth discussion. This study aims to analyze the improvement of college students' personal self-correcting composition ability with the instruction of AWE system, the reasons and factors of their constant revision and the relationship between the times of the revision and the final score, and the effect of "Pigai.org" on students' metalinguistic awareness. Through this study, the author hopes it can offer some reference meaning for helping instructors to make "Pigai.org" have better effect and guidance in English teaching and serving the students, and finally making the students have a steady and constant progress in the language output.

3 The Theory of Metalinguistic Awareness

Metalinguistic awareness which belongs to a type of metacognition refers to the conscious understanding and manipulation of language rules. The language system is a regularized system, which includes such regular systems as phonology, lexicology, syntax, semantics and pragmatics, etc. The systematic understanding and the mastery of these rules is called metalinguistic awareness. The platform of automated writing evaluation just offers the metalinguistic awareness a helpful and effective monitoring system. The function of metalinguistic awareness is mainly to detect and remedy language defects or errors. The mechanism of language operation inside the brain benefits from the constant practice of the automated writing evaluation. The immediate feedback of "Pigai.org" can make student quickly detect the language errors so as to help students to consciously learn the inner rules of language. It is generally that the continuous conscious learning will make the knowledge potential in the mind, which will contribute to the writing or speech. A study on the metalinguistic contribution to writing competence finds that the three components of metalinguistic awareness (phonological awareness, morphological awareness and syntactic awareness) have different contribution to writing competence, as well as two groups of children (monolingual and bilingual children) [14]. In Shintani and Ellis's [15] research, they find that this kind of direct corrective feedback is effective in helping some learners to correct certain language errors. And it may promote the development of implicit knowledge by the more intensive corrective feedback and repeated revisions. They conclude that only when learners concentrate on the understanding of language rules can the feedback have great effect on the accuracy and recreation of the new writing. This monitoring system of language rules is associated with the metalinguistic awareness.

The main contents of metalinguistic awareness include: 1. It has a deeper understanding of the language itself. 2. It is a kind of ability to distinguish between language and its referents. 3. The metalinguistic awareness can be aware of the existence of certain structures in language, and it can consciously manipulate these structures. It seems that the learning feedback from the automated correction network is beneficial to the construction of metalinguistic awareness. The self-correction of English writing in a long term can be a subtle influence on students' metalinguistic awareness, which will make a certain contribution to the second language learning. There is no denying that cultivating students' language metalinguistic awareness is a higher pursuing goal in the language teaching. Therefore, using the theory of metalinguistic awareness to explain the self-correction of students' English writing is valuable and necessary. Under the guidance of this theory, this paper empirically verifies the research questions.

4 Research Design

4.1 Research Questions

English writing, as an important kind of language output, plays an indispensible role in college teaching. This new and convenient way of correcting mistakes arouse more students' interest in writing, so they revise their English compositions repeatedly until get the satisfied scores. The immediate feedback of "Pigai.org" can form an effective cognition for students to revise the mistakes. And the score is one of the factors to verify their writing performance. In order to examine whether "Pigai.org" can have a good influence on the improvement of college students' self-correction and metalinguistic awareness, this paper aims to solve the following two questions: 1. Is the times of revision positively correlated with the score? 2. How does "Pigai.org" affect the metalinguistic awareness?

4.2 Participants

The participants in this research consist of 41 students from a non-English major class in Harbin University of Science and Technology. The students were freshmen, and they got similar English scores in the entrance examination for college. Moreover, the students have the same English course and the same English instructor. And, it can be guaranteed that the instructor of the experimental class would not be replaced during the experimental time. The research time is from March to May in 2019. Before the experiment, the students should have been instructed how to use www.pigai.org at the same time, like registering the account, finding the assignment, writing the compositions online, and so on. During the period of the experiment, the students submitted the composition online in time and revised the composition repeatedly according to the feedback given by the automated writing evaluation system. They were required to finish the assignment with the given topic by the teacher at "Pigai.org", and revised their compositions until get a satisfying score. To ensure the validity of the research, students are not told to act as the research participants to participate in the writing training.

4.3 Research Method

Sample

This study adopts the method of sample comparative analysis to discuss the self-correction of the students' English writing based on "Pigai.org" in college teaching with the combination of qualitative and quantitative methods, and selects 41 students from the class of software school. In the spring semester (March 2019–May 2019), the author selected compositions of four times as the study's data. The sample data analysis included statistics on the times of revisions on the "Pigai.org", the relationship between the frequency of students' revisions and scores, the correlation of online time of self-correction, the frequency of revisions and the increasing score, and the trend of average scores.

Questionnaire

The questionnaire includes four parts. One part is the survey about the overall students' English level and their self-evaluation. One part is the investigation of the basic situation of students' self-correction on the "Pigai.org", such as the reasons for the constant revising compositions, the aspects of significant improvement in English proficiency. The next part aims to find some regular rules about students' metalinguistic awareness. The last part is to ask about students' thought about the advantages and disadvantages of the use of the automated writing evaluation based on "Pigai.org", as well as the expectations and prospects of the online system for learning English.

4.4 The Results and Analysis

Sample

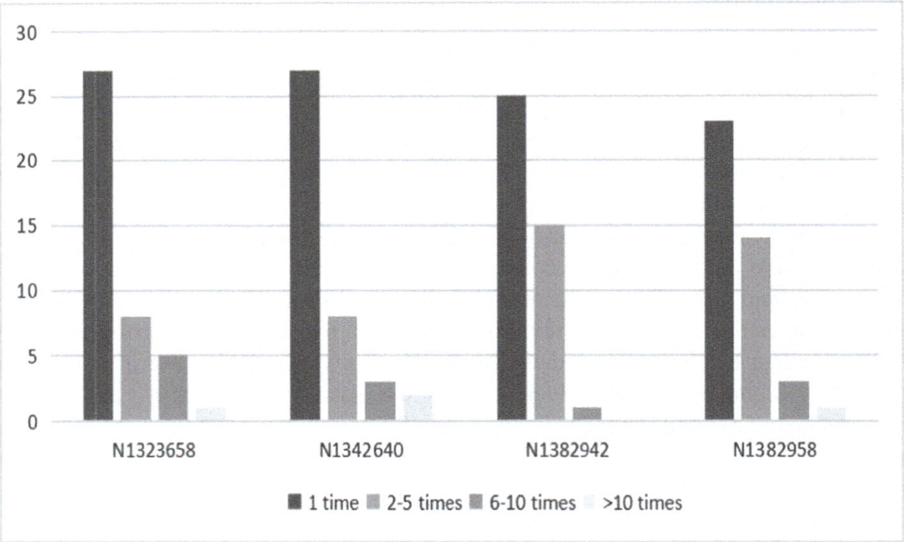

Fig. 1. Statistics of the relation between the submission times and the number of students in 4 tests

From the Fig. 1, the result reflects that the number of people which is about more than half of the whole class for submitting the composition only 1 time is the most, and the number of the students for submitting 2–5 times is the second. The students of submitting composition for more than 10 times is the least. This sample data shows that not all the students have the consciousness or motivation to revise the composition for multiple times. This means that the students don't make full use of the learning mode of "Pigai.org" for self-correction. If students try to self-correct the composition for multiple times according to the feedback given by "Pigai.org", they will master more new knowledge and improve their metalinguistic awareness by the repeated practice.

Therefore, how to make students more interested in self-correcting their compositions on "Pigai.org" is the key point of English writing teaching. In order to take advantage of the automated system, the students need to train it well (Figs. 2, 4 and 5).

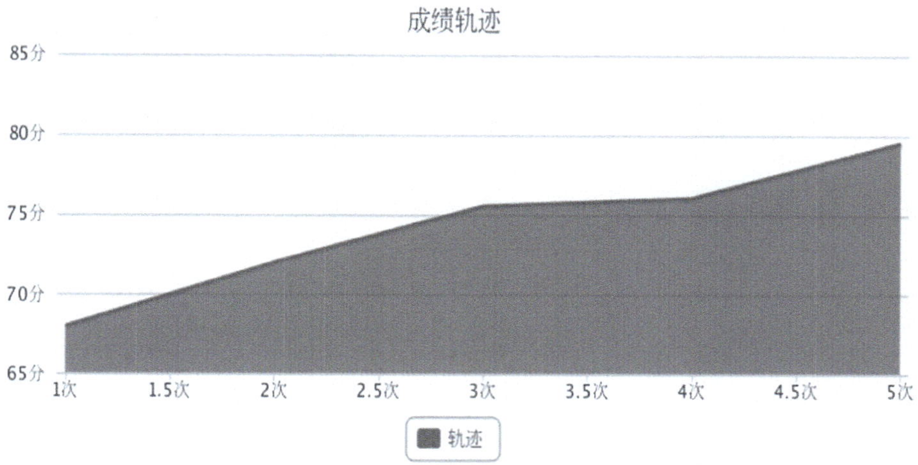

Fig. 2. .

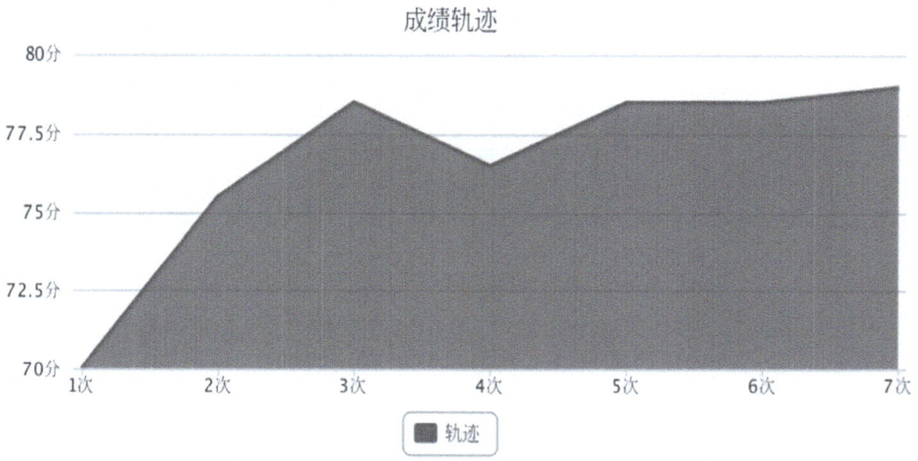

Fig. 3. .

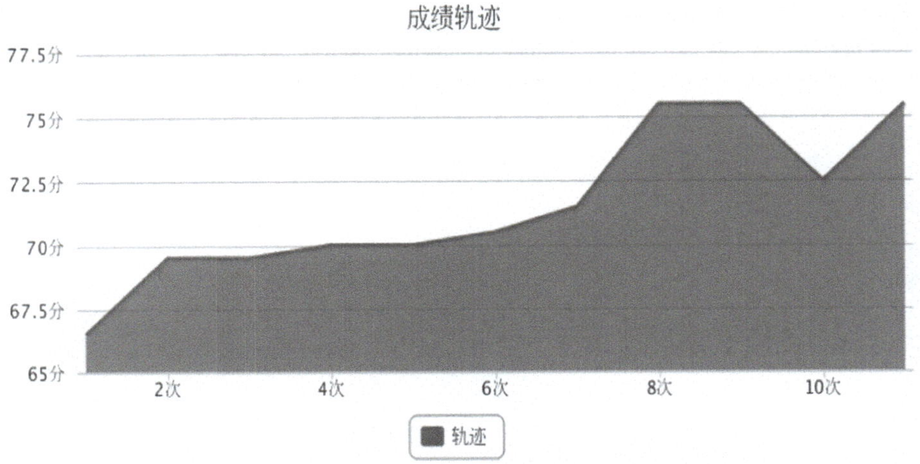

Fig. 4. .

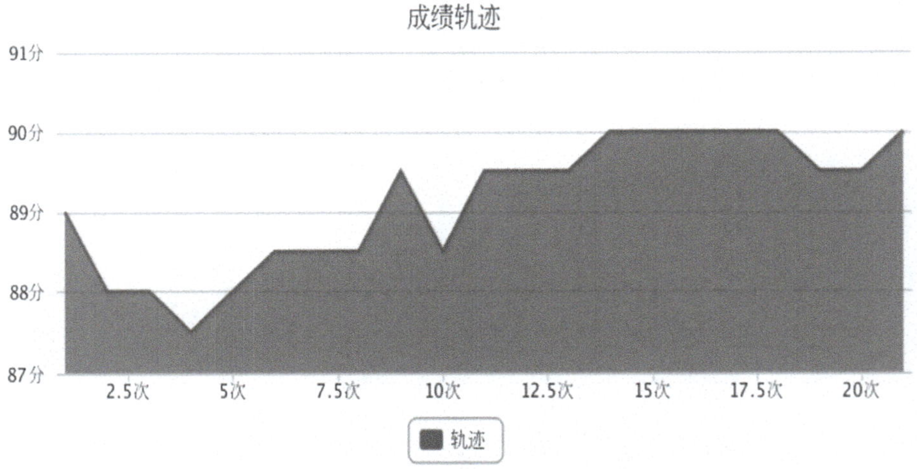

Fig. 5. The track of the grade growth

From the growth trajectories of the four groups of students, it is not difficult to find that the score of students' compositions is positively correlated with the times of revisions to some extent, which means the score of compositions increases as the times of self-corrections increase. The research objects selected in this study are typical representatives of the four groups in sample 1. From the track of student 1's scores, it can be seen that the student' scores in the first three revisions show a steady upward trend. The fourth revision shows a slow growth, and the fifth revision shows a significant improvement. From the track of student 2's score, it can be seen that the score of student 2 increases from 70 to 78 in the first three modifications. But after the fourth modification, the score decreases, and then changes back to 78 in the fifth modification. And, the score remains almost unchanged in the last two revisions. From the track of the scores of student 3, it shows that the scores of student 3 increase from 65 to 75.5 after several self-corrections. The scores of the first two self-corrections increase significantly, the scores from the second revision to the seventh revision increase slowly, the scores of the eighth self-correction increase strikingly, but the scores of the tenth revision decrease again. From the score track of student 4, it is found that the scores of the student in the first four revisions shows a downward trend. In the subsequent revisions, the score keeps changing in twists and turns, and then tends to be stable. Finally, the sores rise from 89 to 90.

From the analysis of the results of the four typical student representatives above, it can be preliminary concluded that students' scores are positively correlated with the times of revisions in most cases, especially in the first three self-corrections. This is because of explicit online teaching, where students can modify their compositions based on online writing corrective feedback. The learning model of "Pigai.org" is a kind of purposeful learning, providing accurate feedback for learners to study grammar rules and analyze sentence elements effectively. After such repeated practice, learners' metalinguistic awareness will also be improved. The fossilization in writing occurs when the score barely changes as the times of subsequent revisions increases. The so-called phenomenon of fossilization refers to that learners have no significant improvement in language rules or language systems during the learning of the second language. In other words, students' English writing level has reached its limit, and metalinguistic awareness cannot help them subconsciously analyze the grammar or semantic knowledge. The main reasons for the fossilization are as follows: 1. Striking language transfer occurs in English writing. Because of the interference of the mother tongue, the grammar rules of the target language are unclear and students often make errors of Chinglish. 2. Students' language input ability is insufficient. Due to the lack of students' own language ability, it is hard for them to carry out some difficult tasks of writing revision. 3. Less feedback in writing. In traditional English writing teaching, teachers are unable to give students comprehensive writing feedback, so it is difficult for students to timely recognize the shortcomings in writing. It can be explained that metalinguistic awareness cannot be developed in time. From the four trajectories, it is not difficult to find that students' scores may drop sometimes, which means they do not have enough language ability to correct the errors. In other words, the mistake is beyond the level of students' metalinguistic awareness, or the original language system has problems. Some relevant rules of grammar itself is wrong in mind. While students don't realize it in their daily writing, the drop in scores helps them recognize the loopholes in the language system. When writing becomes fossilized and regressive, instructors are called upon to help. The explicit teaching of instructors can directly point out the problems of learners in the writing process and give accurate and effective feedback to promote the students' written language output ability. Through students' self-correction on "Pigai.org" and the reference of scores' changes, it shows that appropriate explicit teaching can help students to strengthen language knowledge and improve metalinguistic awareness. To sum up, the times of correction are positively correlated with the scores, but not the more, the better. Therefore, it is suggested that students should pay more attention to the quality of self-correction not the times of revisions.

Table 1. The statistics analysis of 4 compositions

Descriptive statistic

	N	Minimum	Maximum	Mean	Standard Deviation
Revision frequency	62	2	32	4.98	4.921
Online time	62	1	50	11.11	11.604
Increasing score	62	-1.0	22.5	3.556	4.5782

Correlation 1

		Revision frequency	increasing score
Revision frequency	Pearson Correlation	1	.220
	Sig		.086
	N	62	62
Increasing score	Pearson Correlation	.220	1
	Sig	.086	
	N	62	62

Correlation 2

		Revision frequency	Online time
Revision frequency	Pearson Correlation	1	.428**
	Sig		.001
	N	62	62
Online time	Pearson Correlation	.428**	1
	Sig	.001	
	N	62	62

Correlation 3

		Online time	increasing score
Online time	Pearson Correlation	1	.389**
	Sig		.002
	N	62	62
increasing score	Pearson Correlation	.389**	1
	Sig	.002	
	N	62	62

The above four groups of data are based on SPSS20.0. The data are from students who have corrected their English compositions more than once for four compositions in the experimental class. In this group of data, descriptive statistic reflects the basic information, Correlation 1 is the correlation data of the revision frequency and the increasing score, Correlation 2 is the correlation data of the revision frequency and online time of self-correction, and Correlation 3 is about the correlation data of the online time of revision and the increasing score. It can be seen that there are total 62 compositions in data analysis. The average of the revision frequency is 4.98, with a minimum 2 and a maximum 32. The online time of self-correction ranges from 1 min to 50 min, with an average of 11 min. The students' average increasing score is 3.556, but score drops by one point because of the wrong correction. And, the highest increasing score is still as high as 22.5 points. In Correlation 1, Sig = 0.086 > 0.05, which indicates that there is no correlation between the revision frequency and increasing score, which means there is no statistical significance. In Correlation 2, Sig = 0.001 < 0.05, indicating that there is a striking correlation between the revision frequency and increasing score, and the two are positively correlated according to the statistics. In Table 1, Sig = 0.002 < 0.05, which points out that there is also a striking correlation between online time of revision and increasing score. According to the data, there is a positive correlation between the two either.

The results of sample 3 exactly confirms the conclusion drawn in sample 2, that is, the times of revisions are not positively correlated with the increasing score. This does not mean the more times students submit compositions online, the better. After all, multiple revisions do not mean high-quality revisions. However, from another perspective, the times of revisions can reflect students' attitude towards learning. Submitting a composition repeatedly represents that the student constantly tries to correct mistakes, which is also a process of constantly finding mistakes and making progress. Due to the limited language ability of students, it is normal to see language fossilization or regression. That is also the main reason why the times of revisions are not

Table 2. The statistics of 1382942 composition's score

People of revision for multiple times	The mean score of the final composition	The mean increasing score	The maximum of the increasing score
16	93.06	3.07	22.5

People of submitting the composition for once	The mean score of the composition	The mean increasing score
25	90.39	0

proportional to the score. However, in sample 3, Correlation 2 and Correlation 3 show that the online time of revision can promote the growth of scores. And, the more times of revisions, the longer the online time of revision will be. In other words, the student takes more time to revise a composition, their score will increase more, and the times of revisions may increase. This suggests that if students take enough time to revise their compositions, their written output ability of language will be greatly improved. And metalinguistic awareness is also developed in the continuous self-learning.

Table 2 reflects the statistics of 1382942 composition's score. The results show there are 16 students self-correcting their compositions for multiple times. And their mean score of the final composition is 93.06, which is higher than those who do not self-correct their compositions. The mean increasing score of 16 students is 3.07 and the maximum of the increasing score is 22.5. Obviously, the mean increasing score is 0 for those who submit for only once.

It can be concluded that the final composition's score is increasing of those who revise their compositions for multiple times. It shows that the students' self-correction has a certain influence on the final score. On the contrary, for those students who only submit their composition for only 1 time, their mean score is lower than that of those who revise the composition for multiple times. They do not have the process of self-correction, which makes them have no increasing score. It also indicates that they do not have the process of rethinking the internal rules of grammar. In such a way, their language skill or metalinguistic awareness can not be improved in a long term. Instead, the repeated self-correction is a good means for students to improve their language output ability, including grammar judgment, language analysis, sentence correction, and the rules of interpretation. Correspondingly, through the repeated self-correction, the metalinguistic awareness of students will also be enhanced, which is directly related to the writing ability (Fig. 6).

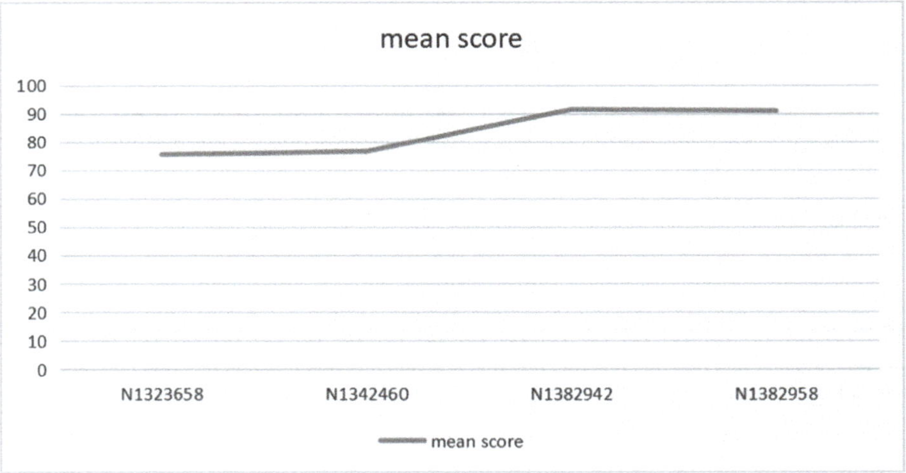

Fig. 6. The mean score of 4 compositions

As can be seen from Fig. 3, the average score of students shows an upward trend during the practice of 4 times on "Pigai.org", which indicates that students' self-correcting ability is gradually improved. It can be implied that the corrective writing feedback have a good effect on students' learning, whether they make many self-corrections online or not. All the four compositions belong to CET4, and CET has its own scoring standards with requirements on vocabulary, grammar, content, etc. Therefore, the increase of students' overall scores also shows that their metalinguistic awareness is improving.

According to the author's observation and analysis, students do well in the correction of vocabulary and some language grammar. But, the writing structure and the writing content have less relation with self-correction. That is where the "Pigai.org" needs to improve and develop. Since feedback of these two aspects of the structure and content is not direct, it is difficult for students to understand and modify the new composition. And that is one of the reasons of some students to choose to give up revising, and thus, they will make the same mistakes on semantics when facing a new composition. Because of technical problems of the automated writing evaluation, "Pigai.org" can not mark some difficult grammar and some fixed collocations. So, the author suggests the students should use more reference books and listen to the advice of the peer and instructor rather than rely on the feedback online too much when students self-correct their compositions. Moreover, students should think the central idea and the structure of the composition carefully. It is beneficial for them to exercise logical thinking so that they will have a good understanding of any topics.

Questionnaire

The questionnaire consists of 10 multiple-choice questions, which are used to investigate the basic information of students' self-correction of using "Pigai.org", which can also help us to well analyze the sample from a more comprehensive perspective. 41 questionnaires were issued, and 41 questionnaires were recovered. The valid rate is 100%.

According to the results of the questionnaire, 64.2% of the students think their current level of English writing is general and 31.6% of the students believe that their English writing is not good. From the result, it can be concluded that most students do not have a very high level in English writing. For the next question, 97.2% of the students choose "No", which means that most college students do not have some habits to learn some extracurricular knowledge of English. Moreover, 96.9% of the students didn't participate in any other English tutoring classes. Above the results of these three questions and the requirement of only one teacher, it can be easily verified that the students of the experimental class almost have the same level before the research, which excludes the effect of other variable factors. From this point of view, this study is reasonable and accurate. As for the forth question, 44% of the students would like to constantly revise the composition is because of the desire for a satisfying score. 56% of the students hold that they can learn something from the process of revising, which can help them to improve their writing ability. And none of the students choose it because of the teacher's request. It can be understood that the online writing is totally a kind of self-leaning and self-correction mode. 86% of the students agree that they have made great progress in the vocabulary, such spelling or words' collocation. 90% of the students think "Pigai.org" offers them a lot of help in the grammar. 8% of the students choose the online feedback can help them with the structure and none of them choose the content. It can be seen that the automated feedback can give students great help in terms of vocabulary and grammar, and the system still need to be strengthened in content and structure. To some extent, the learning mode of self-correction is not completely effective, so the teacher's teaching can not be totally replaced by the automated writing evaluation at present. 92% of the students agree that it is helpful for them to revise the composition. Therefore, the application of "Pigai.org" is effective and meaningful for students' self-correction of their English writing. For the seventh question, 30% of the students will pay attention to the learning of vocabulary and grammar, and 50% of the students will remember some of them. And 20% of the students choose ignorance. What's more, as for the next question, most of the students choose B. That means students won't make the same mistake through the repeated practice. In other words, the results of Question 7 and Question 8 show the learning mode on "Pigai.org" promotes students' metalinguistic awareness. As for the limitations for the online self-correction based on "Pigai.org", 78.9% of the students think the evaluation criteria are too mechanized, 58.6% of the students think the suggestions are not detailed, 39% of the students agree that some grammar mistakes are not recognized, and 70.5% of the students agree that the system has little help for the writing's structure and content. So, the students should pay more attention to get teacher's feedback or the peer feedback about the overall logic content and structure when self-correcting the composition. For the last question, most students hold the view that it would be better to have the combination of the teacher's feedback and "Pigai.org". Some students hope that the online system will update the language corpus so as to make the evaluation more detailed and accurate. And others hope the system will share the wonderful composition for students to learn after they finishing the writing self-correction of their writings.

5 Conclusion

This paper mainly focuses on the self-correction process of students based on feedback from "Pigai.org". The feedback at the language level of AWE system is very referential for the learning of self-correction. The analysis of the sample and questionnaire show that the automated writing evaluation is an effective and helpful tool for college students to study English writing. The online mode of self-correction in language promotes the construction of metalinguistic awareness. This kind of enhancement of metalinguistic awareness is of great help to English language learning. With the help of the online feedback, students' ability of language output can be improved constantly, especially in vocabulary and grammar. At the online writing platform, it is convenient for students to self-correct their writings. In that way, students can have a good understanding of language points, which is positively associated with the metalinguistic awareness. As for the relationship between the number of revisions and the scores, the study finds the accuracy rate of correcting errors is relatively high in the students' first several self-corrections. In the later revision process, different phenomena will appear according to the differences of students' language ability or metalinguistic consciousness. But the real purpose of students' self-correction is refinement, not quantity. Students will also benefit a lot from the combination of explicit learning and implicit learning. For the college teachers, the platform of "Pigai.org" provides them more extensive ideas of English teaching and it helps them lessen the burden of correcting the similar mistakes to some extent.

However, the research points out that the application of "Pigai.org" still exists some limitations. The feedback of "Pigai.org" does a little contribution on students' writing structure and content. Therefore, the combination of the instructor's teaching and the writing mode of "Pigai.org" is very necessary. As the rapid development of artificial intelligent, it is worth waiting for making up for the lack of comprehensive feedback. AWE system is of great significance for the improvement of students' self-correcting writing ability and English teaching study. The number of samples adopted in this study research is not very enough and the research scope is limited. Undoubtedly, the research on AWE of more extensive aspects still has a long way to go. From the perspective of metalinguistic awareness, a more flexible evaluation mode like the combination of automated evaluation and artificial evaluation will become a popular trend.

Appendix

Questionnaire

Thank you so much for taking the time to participate in this survey. All the results of the questionnaire are only for the research and they are strictly confidential, so please fill it in the truth.

1. What do you think about the current English writing level?
   A. Good B. General C. Not good
2. Do you usually read some English magazines or English news to study English?
   A. Yes B. No
3. Have you participated in other English tutoring classes besides the English class of college in 2019?
   A. Yes B. No
4. What are the reasons for constantly revising the composition?
   A. The desire for a satisfying score
   B. The desire for the improvement of English writing
   C. The instructor's request
5. Which aspect do you think that you've made great progress after using "Pigai.org"?
   A. Vocabulary B. Grammar C. Structure D. Content
6. Do you think it is helpful for you to revise your writing for multiple times?
   A. Yes B. No
7. When you revise a composition based on feedback, do you consciously memorize vocabulary or grammar knowledge?
   A. Yes B. A little C. No

8. Will you make the same mistakes in writing after your repeated self-corrections on "Pigai.org"?
   A. Always will
   B. Will make the same mistakes for a few times, and then won't
   C. Always won't
9. What limitations for the self-correction online on "Pigai.org"?
   A. The evaluation criteria are too mechanized
   B. Suggestions are not detailed
   C. Some grammar mistakes are not recognized
   D. Little help for the structure and content
10. What are your expectations for the future of "Pigai.org"?

References

1. Shermis, M.D., Burstein, J., Higgins, D., Zechner, K.: Automated essay scoring: writing assessment and instruction. In: International Encyclopedia of Education, 3rd edn., pp. 20–26 (2010)
2. Rubén, C.B.: Free-form writing: computerized feedback for self-correction. ELT J. Adv. **71** (2), 141–149 (2016)
3. Bitchener, J.: Evidence in support of written corrective feedback. J. Second Lang. Writ. **17**, 102–118 (2008)
4. Bitchener, J., Knoch, U.: The contribution of written corrective feedback to language development: a ten month investigation. Appl. Linguist. **31**(2), 193–214 (2009)
5. Bitchener, J., Knoch, U.: Raising the linguistic accuracy level of advanced L2 writers with written corrective feedback. J. Second Lang. Writ. **19**, 207–217 (2010)
6. Bitchener, J.: A reflection on 'the language learning potential' of written CF. J. Second Lang. Writ. **21**, 348–363 (2012)
7. Ismail, St. Suwarsono, Lukito, A.: Critical thinking skills of junior high school female students with high mathematical skills in solving contextual and formal mathematical problems. In: The 2nd International Joint Conference on Science and Technology (IJCST) (2017)
8. Yuan, X.: On automated online essay scoring in Chinese EFL writing evaluation. In: 2014 International Conference on Artificial Intelligence and Software Engineering (AISE 2014) (2014)
9. Liao, H.C.: Enhancing the grammatical accuracy of EFL writing by using an AWE-assisted process approach. J. Syst. (2016). https://doi.org/10.1016/j.system.2016.02.007
10. Li, J.R., Link, S., Hegelheimer, V.: Review of research on technologies for language learning and teaching. J. Second Lang. Writ. **27**, 1–18 (2015)
11. Yang, Y.: An empirical study on the effects of self-correction based on the "Pigai.org" on college EFL students' writing proficiency. In: Proceedings of the Sixth Northeast Asia International Symposium on Language, Literature and Translation (2017)
12. Liu, X., Wang, Y.: An investigation on lexical richness developed by automatic essay scoring-based self-revision. In: Proceedings of the 2018 Northeast Asia International Symposium on Linguistics, Literature and Teaching (2018 NALLTS) (2018)
13. Li, H.: A study of college English writing based on "Pigai.org"—exemplified by Anshan Normal University. In: Proceedings of the 2018 Northeast Asia International Symposium on Linguistics, Literature and Teaching (2018 NALLTS) (2018)

14. Sun, B.Q., Hu, G.w., Curdt-Christiansen, X.L.: Metalinguistic contribution to writing competence: a study of monolingual children in China and bilingual children in Singapore. Read. Writ. **31**(7), 1499–1523 (2018)
15. Shintani, N., Ellis, R.: The comparative effect of direct written corrective feedback and metalinguistic explanation on learners' explicit and implicit knowledge of the English indefinite article. J. Second Lang. Writ. (2013). https://doi.org/10.1016/j.jslw.2013.03.011

Exploration of Mechanical Principle Combined Curriculum Reform Based on Network Assisted Platform

Hongyan Shi(✉), Xiaoqiang Wu, and Lihua Wang

College of Mechanical Engineering, Inner Mongolia University for the Nationalities, Tongliao, Inner Mongolia, China
shy2160@163.com

Abstract. The course of Mechanical Principle combined with the network aided platform has carried out the reform of mixed curriculum, that is, the combination of network and classroom, forming an Online (before class) - offline (class) - online (after class) the new form of teaching, this form has broken the traditional method of teaching, by the students to decide the content of the lectures in the classroom, give full play to students' subjective initiative, and enhance students' interest in learning. After several rounds of teaching practice, has made gratifying teaching effect.

Keywords: *Mechanical principle* · Network auxiliary platform · Curriculum reform

1 Background of the Study

With the promotion of the bottom-up teaching reform, the students who entered the university in 2017 basically are the new generation experience all kinds of teaching reform. This requires that all colleges and universities should make corresponding changes to the traditional teaching methods that have been adopted for many years. At present, there are a variety of ways to reform such as MOOC and turnover of classrooms. However, because different schools accept students at different levels and can not adopt a one-size-fits-all or one-stop teaching method, and teaching reform should be flexible according to the acceptability of students and teaching conditions [1]. The hybrid teaching reform introduced by our school since 2016 is a teaching method that combines online teaching and classroom teaching. It fully takes into account the characteristics of our students and the current hardware facilities in schools. After two years of practice, we achieved gratifying results.

2 *Mechanical Principle* Course Profile

The course of *Mechanical principle* is a specialized basic course for students in the Institute of Mechanical Engineering. To study this course, courses such as advanced mathematics, engineering drawing, physics, theoretical mechanics and basic mechanics

G. Sun et al. (Eds.): eLEOT 2019, LNICST 299, pp. 170–176, 2019.
https://doi.org/10.1007/978-3-030-35095-6_19

are first completed. This course is offered in the fifth semester with a total of 56 academic hours, of which 42 are theoretical hours, 14 for experimental hours, and 2 weeks for the end of the semester. The *Mechanical principle* course is characterized by relatively loose knowledge, a relatively wide coverage, most of the content needs to be combined with the practical application of understanding. In order to enhance students' ability to connect with reality, the experimental class hours have been increased, the theoretical class hours decreased correspondingly, and the time for students to receive knowledge in class has been even more limited [2]. These questions all require "mechanics principle" instructor for teaching adaptability reform. Before the teaching reform, this course always adopts the traditional teaching mode. The students reflect that it is hard to learn the course, the knowledge is relatively large, the time is relatively tight, and their knowledge can not be well understood. We also conduct exploratory reforms on a small scale, but the results are not very good. After two years and three classes of mixed teaching reform, we have initially formed a hybrid teaching mode suitable for our students. We have a complete teaching plan and flexible PPT courseware, and also purchased and adapted to modify the test database.

3 *Mechanical Principle* Curriculum Reform Ideas

Based on the previous teaching experience and understanding of blended teaching methods, we conceived a set of teaching ideas for this course. Because *Mechanical principle* is a course that has close connection with practical application, we pay attention to the construction of machine and mechanism's movement and working principle. Our teaching idea is to combine the problem preview - the students ask the questions - the teachers combine the students' problems Focus on teaching - after school student feedback - online communication [3]. Knowledge guidance is through the network in the "before-class" completed. Knowledge internalization is accomplished through discussion and exchange in "Lesson", but after "after class" students are still more focused on completing higher level "knowledge inquiry".

Teachers combined with the content of each lesson to students with the practical application or the current research frontier related to guide the problem, so that students focus on the problem before class knowledge, and then through the network will not understand or want to learn more about the learning results to the teacher. Teachers in the class to focus on the above content, for students with a lesser learning effect combined with the effect of class counseling, after-school teachers and students can exchange lessons through the network learning, at the same time we can also guide students to learn through innovative content exploration, while homework is also completed through the Internet. Because we do not have the experience of network-assisted teaching, some aspects of the above model can not be modified in the learning process if it is not suitable, and improvement and enrichment can also be made in the teaching process. Due to the course after class a lot of knowledge needs to be done to consolidate the problem, not timely use of face-to-face communication can guide students practice through the network, if the effect is not very prominent, you can also explain by adding exercises, and the specific methods and methods to be based on the circumstances of specific students change.

4 *Mechanical Principle* Course Teaching Design

4.1 Teaching Reform Model

The curriculum reform of *Principles of Machinery* has gone through three stages and has been gradually improved. The current curriculum reform adopts the mode Before class (online) - class (offline) - after class (online) model, shown in Fig. 1. This model is conducive to students to complete all tasks more efficiently. In order to understand the learning purpose of each student in each class, students are asked to conduct a questionnaire on the purpose of learning before the commencement of classes so that they can be better targeted. After the end of the questionnaire is mainly on the current round of study of the effectiveness of learning from students get more advice and suggestions.

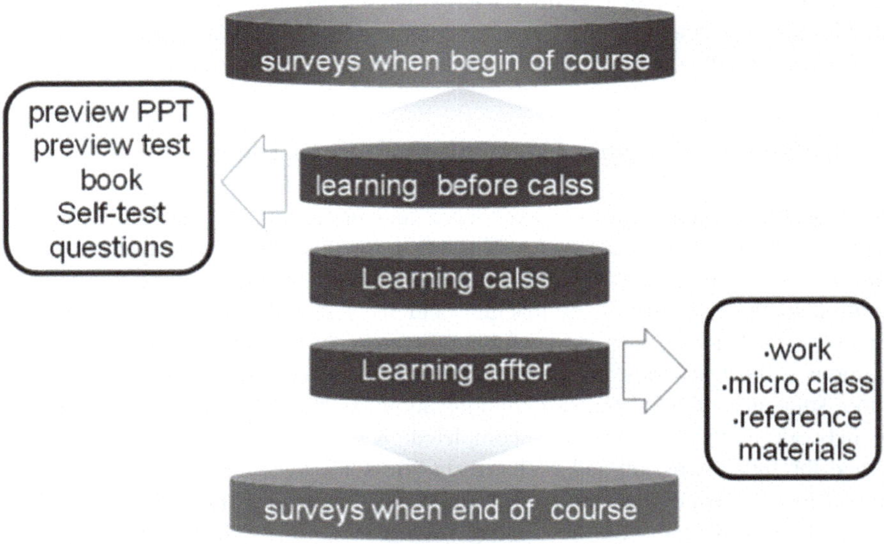

Fig. 1. Principles of Mechanics curriculum reform model

4.2 The Specific Implementation Process

(1) As this course is a combination of theory and practical application of relatively tight courses, is a thorough understanding of the theoretical basis of the premise, we apply the actual design or analysis of practical applications to find its theoretical basis. The former teaching method is that teachers fully explain the theoretical foundation in the classroom, and the combination of practical and practical part of the time without too much energy to start, the students for the boring theoretical knowledge has been passive acceptance, and failed to understand the characteristics of knowledge from the practical application. The focus of this reform is to enable students to increase interest in the learning of the course to find the starting point for learning theoretical knowledge, so that students become the guide of classroom teaching.

Before-Class (Online) Task. The advantages of using the network platform, before-class learning task is to enable students to understand the learning content of this lesson, heavy and difficult knowledge, the purpose of teaching teachers. There are three main work to be completed, simplified version of PPT, task book and test questions. PPT as a before-guide on the platform as a guide tool, according to the characteristics of student self-learning, PPT pages per lesson is best not more than 10 pages, so that students can not only see the focus but also to see. The content of the task book is divided into two parts, as shown in Table 1, part of the basic knowledge, this part of the knowledge to students can easily grasp the main requirements of students must do,

Table 1. Pre-class task book.

Mechanical Principle The fourth lesson test book

name: student number: calss: 14

content of courses: chapter three The motion analysis of plane mechanism §3-1 §3-2

emphasis: Vector equation (Velocity and acceleration analysis of the same component at two points)、velocity instant center method

difficulty: The drawing of the velocity and acceleration image、Velocity analysis with velocity instantaneous method

knowledge point	require						
	recite	understand	can do	understand the process	understand the sample	flexible use	your performance
basic knowledge (must complete)							
The purpose of motion analysis		√					
analytical method		√					
Vector equation		√					
instantaneous center	√	√					
Number of instantaneous center	√	√					
distinction between relative instantaneous center and absolute instantaneous center		√					
improve knowledge (choose)							
Dynamic vector equations f		√	√	√			
velocity and acceleration image		√	√	√			
Position ofinstantaneous center	√	√	√	√		√	
theorem of three centros	√	√			√		

if you can not explain why you can not do so. If 90% of the students have no problem, this part of the content can be taken by the time of class, which also saves a lot of time. Let students know what content belongs to a little knowledge before class, but also before the class via micro-channel means will be slightly about the content feedback to the students, let the students a definite target. High knowledge part is the difficult content of this class, students choose according to their ability to do, the process of class can make the ability of students to explain this part of the content. At the same time, students can also be the task book will want to in-depth understanding of the textbooks and textbooks outside the content feedback to teachers, teachers can also be targeted to prepare lessons.

The Self-test questions on the platform all come from the test bank, in addition to the usual static test questions, but also use the advantages of the network to add a dynamic test questions, dynamic test questions can come from online video or teacher shot video. This test questions allows students to intuitively understand the combination of theoretical knowledge and practical application, the corresponding knowledge will be more solid grasp. Teachers can also learn about the mastery of knowledge points through the self-test questions before class and reasonably introduce self-test questions during lecture so that students can understand why they made mistakes. Students through their self-test unit to measure their own learning, for their lack of directed listening, teachers can also find the focus of this lesson to be taught according to the students. Complete by the students to guide the classroom content to focus on the transformation of learning styles.

Class (Offline) Task. Specific to the class will be based on different classes using different forms. For small class teaching must take into account the feelings of each student, each student knowledge of the situation to take notes, during the class can use the discussion, questions, flip and other forms of teaching. For large classes of teaching can not be exhaustive, each class before the teacher randomly selected part of the students to take notes, during the class selection of different equivalent learning results feedback, try to simplify the problem, taking into account the majority of students' feeling. Because students have done a certain amount of preview work in advance, the classroom requires teachers to use some means to activate the classroom atmosphere. Since the *Principles of Mechanics* course is a very practical course, we have used a number of channels to find a large amount of news materials on the subject of video and scientific research, so that students can better understand the knowledge of fatten.

After Class (Online) Task. Another advantage of network-assisted platform is that teachers and students can narrow the distance, fully play the problem can be solved in time. At the same time, you can also make the stereotyped work rich and colorful. You can make use of a large number of animations on the Internet, or create 3D maps by yourself or research cutting-edge technologies as homework titles, and students can also make their own animated cartoon of the answer, the learned knowledge to learn and use. For those who can not keep up with the progress of lectures in class, they can also do self-study after class through the lectures recorded by teachers. For those who master the better students, you can learn more through reference materials. Many students in our college are participating in science and technology competitions of various scales. In this process, we need to use the knowledge of *Mechanical principle*, which is not fully taught in the textbook, and will be supplemented from time to time in the reference materials. Part of the discussion of this course is done after the class platform, the setting of the part requires the teacher to seriously arrange the topic, to discuss the results of divergent features, but also practical application value. For example, "finding a kind of organization from life and production reality, making a video and drawing a sketch of the movement of its organization" combined the knowledge point of "the mechanism sketch" with the practical application. The concept of this course is "before-class preview, class for learning, after-school in-depth review."

5 *Mechanical Principle* Course Teaching Facilities

The main teaching facilities of Mechanical principle are the network aided platform and PPT courseware. The platform includes a guided version of PPT, test questions bank and test repertoire for students' before-class preview, as well as the teacher's own mini-video recorded by the teacher. The main course is mainly PPT courseware professor, part of the need to use the board to complete the courseware most of the content for the picture or animation. At the same time, the lab also provides the models or parts needed in some chapters as an aid to the lesson.

6 *Mechanical Principle* Course Teaching Facilities

After the curriculum reform of different scales, most of the students are acceptable for the curriculum reform. After the class, the questionnaire for this course was released on the platform after class. The vast majority of students reflect the curriculum reform will help students learn this course, for the understanding and mastery of the curriculum played a significant role, but also many students give pertinent comments. From the exam results can also be found in the class after the mixed class curriculum performance is much higher than the other classes, which remove the normal differences between classes, you will find that there is still much to improve performance. 14 mechanism experimental class and 15 mechanism experimental class comparison results shown in Table 2.

Table 2. 15 and 14 mechanism experimental class Mechanical principle comparative results

Course title	Class	Student number	Final exam average score	Comprehensive score average score	Final exam pass rate	Comprehensive results pass rate
Mechanical principle	15 mechanism experiment class (reform class)	17	59.82	73.82	59.41%	94.12%
	14 mechanism experiment class (reform class)	22	69.82	80.73	86.36%	100%

14 mechanism experimental class is the first mixed-class classes, from the results point of view than the 15 mechanism experimental class is much higher, in part because the latter is caused by the difficulty of the test questions, and the passing rate of the two classes is much higher than that of the non-mixed classes. However, we can see that the obvious effect of the combined curriculum reform is the mechanism of 14 classes, the parallel class performance is shown in Table 3. From Table 3, we can find that the average score of the final exam of the reform class is much higher than the other two classes. Given that the usual grade scores given on the online platform are calculated based on the students' daily accumulation, the students' learning situation is reasonably reflected. The average grade score of this class is not much higher than that of the other two classes. However, the passing rate of the final exam will be able to fully reflect the effectiveness of the reform.

Table 3. 14 class "mechanical principle" comparative results

Course title	Class	Student number	Final exam average score	Comprehensive score average score	Final exam pass rate	Comprehensive results pass rate
Mechanical principle	14 mechanism (reform class)	73	52.09	66.64	31.51%	86.30%
	14 material (control class)	54	36.00	63.43	18.36%	85.19%
	14 farm machinery (control class)	42	37.86	62.52	14.76%	66.67%

After two years of mixed curriculum reform, the reform of the *Principles of Machinery* curriculum is being gradually promoted. During the course of the reform, many difficulties have been encountered as well as a lot of experience. Although the results are both sad and pessimistic, the overall result is remarkable.

References

1. Zhang, J., Guo, H., Hou, L.: Teaching reform and exploration of mechanical principle course. J. Yangtze Univ. (Nat. Sci. Edn.) **12**(05), 23–26 (2011)
2. Guo, W., Liu, R., Li, J., Gao, Z., Zhan, Q.: Reform and practice of the series and content of the course of theory of machines and mechanisms. J. Taiyuan Univ. Technol. (Soc. Sci. Edn.) **20**(06), 54–56 (2008)
3. Yang, J., Liu, J., Guo, D.: Exploration of hybrid teaching mode based on rain classroom platform. Ind. Sci. Trib. **24**(10), 67–69 (2017)
4. Chen, X.: Teaching reform for control engineering basis of mechanical engineering. J. Inner Mong. Univ. Natl. (Nat. Sci.) **12**(07), 34–36 (2015)

A Design for Experimental Program of Artificial Intelligence and Machine Vision Based on Online Learning

Sihan Gao(✉), Wanshun Chen, and Shuxiang Ma

Wuhu Institute of Technology, Wuhu, China
285819317@qq.com, 858708130@qq.com, 565498298@qq.com

Abstract. Aiming at the design for experimental program of Machine Vision in the course of artificial intelligence, this paper puts forward a concrete plan of experiment of Machine Vision in AI course as well as a concrete implementation of online learning. Through two aspects of basic knowledge and frontier technology, the design progressively demonstrates the concrete way of combining theories with practice, which enables polytechnic college students to obtain basic AI knowledge and technology quickly.

Keywords: AI course · Machine Vision · Experiments · Online learning

1 Introduction

As a multidisciplinary course, AI has made breakthroughs in machine learning, natural language understanding and some other fields. AI is not only an important branch of computer science, but also one of the core professional courses of computer science, software engineering, Internet engineering and so on. At present, AI is developing rapidly in China, but it is also facing a huge shortage of talents. Many colleges and universities in China have already set up courses related to AI. It is urgent for polytechnic colleges to cultivate practical talents of AI. However, most of the AI courses in polytechnic colleges lack a plan for practical links of AI courses, and there is no concrete design for experimental program.

2 Problems in the Teaching Practice of AI

In polytechnic colleges, there are various types of students, whose foundations are uneven. They are more willing to "do" than "use their brains". It seems that the AI technology, in comparison with abstract theory, arouses more initiative of polytechnic college students. AI involves so many subjects, abstract contents and so much knowledge that it is widely-involved and high-theoretical. Thus, it needs a good mathematical foundation and strong logical thinking to understand it well, which makes it difficult for teachers and students to communicate effectively in class. The teaching process should be more vivid, combined with words, images and videos.

G. Sun et al. (Eds.): eLEOT 2019, LNICST 299, pp. 177–181, 2019.
https://doi.org/10.1007/978-3-030-35095-6_20

At present, there are many kinds of experimental platforms for AI courses and programming languages such as C++, Python and MATLAB, can not be unified. As a result, students can't concentrate on AI-related algorithms while spending too much time on programming languages. At the same time, the traditional experimental cases are mostly abstract problems, and the content of experiment is biased towards theories, so it is difficult to see the intuitive results of the problems. With the rapid development of AI, Machine Vision has become a hot issue currently, and students are eager to master this latest technology.

Because of their weak foundation, it is difficult for students of polytechnic schools to settle down to preview and review. As the Internet develops, the platform for online learning plays an important role. First of all, teachers upload relevant videos which is required in the next lesson on the platforms for online learning such as Blue Ink Cloud, to attract students' attention. It's a good beginning for students to actively search the information related to the subject. Then basic knowledge points and principles are explained in the class for further mastery of related technologies. After demonstrating the experiment in class, if the students do not consolidate it in time, they will easily forget the knowledge points. Students can also use the platform to consolidate the knowledge they have learned in their spare time.

3 Design for Experimental Program of Machine Vision in the AI Course

Now Machine Vision is one of the researching hotspots in the field of AI. Machine Vision, in short, is a visual system simulated by machines instead of human beings. At present, combining the theories of AI with Machine Vision can effectively stimulate students' interest and initiative. The purpose of experiment is not only to consolidate knowledge points taught in theoretical courses, but also to cultivate students' programming habits.

3.1 Platform for Machine Vision Experiment

OpenCV, an open source computer Vision library, is used in the process of teaching. It supports many functions which can efficiently implement common algorithms of Machine Vision. OpenCV is developed by C/C++ and it has Python, Java, MATLAB and other interfaces. Students only need to master the basic principles of the algorithm and the specific parameters of the functions provided by OpenCV. Then we can invoke a function directly and see the intuitive result of it.

3.2 A Concrete Plan of Experimental Program

The courses of AI in polytechnic colleges should focus on practice. Machine Vision is an attractive breakthrough in AI. Machine Vision has a lot of application just as one of so many AI courses. It is reasonable that layering what will be taught not only can enhance students' understanding of knowledge points in an orderly and in-depth way, but also can provide knowledge for the introduction of follow-up experimental cases.

This paper divides contents of the experiment into three levels: basic knowledge points, frontier technologies and online learning.

(1) **Basic Knowledge Points**

The basic knowledge points of Machine Vision refer to the theories and basic methods in the field of vision, which have been developed relatively well so far. These widely-used knowledge points in the field of Machine Vision, can lay a foundation for further learning. In the process of teaching them, it is necessary for students to have a certain foundation of advanced mathematics, linear algebra, theory of probability, etc. Polytechnic school students have a weak foundation in this aspect, so we have to simplify knowledge points, weaken the process of formula derivation and use modern teaching methods and multimedia facilities to enable students to understand the basic knowledge points more deeply.

(2) **Frontier Technologies**

Frontier technologies refer to the theories and methods of Machine Vision, which are still being explored and developed. For example, deep learning attracts the most concern in the field of AI, as well as target detection, image recognition, automatic driving and other issues. All of those involve advanced technologies such as OpenCV and Tensorflow. These advanced technologies can provide polytechnic college students with a rapid access to AI, making up for the inadequacies of some professional knowledge and mathematics. From the aspect of practical problems and the application of technology, we can see the intuitive experimental results efficiently and quickly.

(3) **Online Learning**

Students preview before class through the platform of online learning, mainly by watching related videos and the direct results of algorithm experiments. Firstly, students should have a deeper understanding of knowledge points, and then go to class with the doubts. After the teacher's demonstration of the experiment in class, students can also review and consolidate the experiment through platform online learning after class, in order to strengthen the relevant knowledge points they have learned. Besides, they can also use the platform to ask questions. Teachers can know the situation of students' preview before class, and then focus on the knowledge points in class. After class, teachers can rethink and improve the teaching effects according to students' completion of the experiment.

3.3 A Concrete Design for Experimental Program

This paper takes the experimental case of Hough Circle Detection based on Machine Vision as an example. Before class, some examples of Hough Circle Detection will be shown on the platform of online learning, in order to have a preliminary understanding of Hough Circle Detection. The general equation of the induced circle is drawn forth as $(x-a)^2+(y-b)^2=r^2$. Therefore, a circle has three variables, the center coordinates (a, b) and the radius r, which means more computation. The function "cvHoughCircle ()" provided in OpenCV can set the range of radius r, which is equivalent to a priori setting. For each r, it can reduce the amount of calculation to find each a and b in two-dimensional space. Firstly, the image input is edge-detected to obtain its boundary points called the foreground point. If there is a circle in the image, the outline must belong to the foreground point. Then we express the general equation of a circle in another way, through coordinate transformation. It means that we transform the equation from X-Y coordinate system to A-B coordinate system. The circle will be written in the form of $(a-x)^2+(b-y)^2=r^2$. Therefore, a point on a circular boundary in the X-Y coordinate system corresponds to a circle in the A-B coordinate system. And many points on a circular boundary in the X-Y coordinate system, corresponds to many circles in the A-B coordinate system. Since these points in the original image are all on the same circle, the transformed a and b must also satisfy all the circular equations in A-B coordinate system. The intuitive phenomenon is that these circles corresponding to these points intersect at one point. The intersection may be the center of the circle. By counting the number of circles at the local intersection and taking each local maximum, the coordinates of the center of the circle corresponding to the original image can be obtained. Once a circle is detected under a certain r, the value of r is determined accordingly

The above is the basic principle of Hough Circle Detection, which is the basic knowledge point. It is a little difficult for polytechnic college students to implement the algorithm of this principle directly. Therefore, the introduction of the Hough Circle Detection function in the open computer visual, which is the cutting-edge technology, is necessary and helpful. The parameters in the cvHoughCircle() function provided in OpenCV are given to the students in detail, and students are required to call the program by themselves. Then, the students need to test the given image. If they get a circle, it proves the experiment is successful. After the experimental course, the basic knowledge points and the experimental related demonstrations will be combined and sent to the experimental teaching video platform. By this means, the students can use the platform for online learning to review and consolidate the knowledge points. In the end, the students summarize the experimental content and write an experiment report.

4 Conclusion

In this paper, the author deeply studies the design for experimental program of Machine Vision, and puts forward the concrete planning and implement scheme of experiment in AI courses. It includes the use of the platform for online learning, which is popular in recent years. The design of the experimental scheme demonstrates the specific way of linking theory with practice. AI has come into people's lives. As a cradle for cultivating applied talents, polytechnic colleges are urgently needed to explore the teaching methods of AI courses, which are suitable for the characteristics of students in polytechnic colleges.

Acknowledgment. This work was supported by the research on high school provincial quality engineering project of Anhui grant No. 2015jyxm477, No. 2017mooc368 and No. 2017sjjd041, and University-level key projects grant No. Wzyzrzd201702 and No. Wzyzr201816.

References

1. Cai, Z., Xu, G.: Principles and Applications, 3rd edn, pp. 9–10. Tsinghua University Press, Beijing (2017)
2. Chen, A.: Teaching exploration and practice of "artificial intelligence" course. J. Zhuzhou Inst. Technol. **20**(6), 137–139 (2006)
3. Zhu, F.: Research on the teaching methods of artificial intelligence course in high vocational education. Chin. J. Multimedia Netw. Educ. **9**(4), 9–10 (2007)
4. Wang, L., Wu, C., Guo, X.: Construction of intelligent visual experiment platform for artificial intelligence curriculum group. Comput. Educ. **10** (2018)
5. Song, C.: An empirical study on the effect of online open courses for polytechnic school students. Shanxi Educ. (High. Educ.) **55** (2018)

Construction of Online Platform Based on the Model of Honesty and Morality Education

Xu Zhang, Yunan Wang(✉), Jinlong Liu, and Xinyu Yang

Harbin Institute of Technology, Harbin 150006, China
{zhangxu, wangyunan, yq20}@hit.edu.cn,
18S105110@stu.hit.edu.cn

Abstract. Integrity and morality are the cornerstones of a person's foothold in society and career. Nowadays, frequent events of lack of integrity in society have affected the normal life and study of every one of us. As the source of social development, whether college students can abide by the integrity will be related to the development and fate of the society. Therefore, colleges and universities have listed the issue of honesty education as the core issue of students' moral education. In the process of the education of integrity and morality of college students, this subject combines the information system of the school itself and the technical advantages of relevant enterprises, universities and research institutes to plan and construct the model of the online platform for the integrity and moral education of students. This subject uses a quantitative assessment indicator system to assist teachers in strengthening the integrity and moral education of students.

Keywords: Integrity education · Cloud platform · Electronic signature · Bigdata

1 Introduction

Integrity, that is, sincerity and credibility, is the cornerstone of a person's foothold in society and career. And it's a person's basic principles of life. It requires us to be honest, trustworthy, and seek truth from facts. And it also requires us not to deceive, pretend to be fake, or falsify. Character education and integrity as a set of procedures or tools designed to help young people think about moral issues [1]. In recent years, frequent exposure of safety of food, academic fraud and other lack of integrity, which has seriously affected the normal life and study of every one of us, and also seriously hindered the development of an honest society. Reducing the scientific power of misconduct is a daunting challenge that emerging countries simply cannot ignore [2]. As the source of social development, whether college students can abide by the integrity will be related to the stabilization of the society. Colleges and universities have listed the issue of honesty education as the core issue of students' moral education. And many colleges and universities have introduced many policies to strengthen the integrity education of college students, and use online education information technology to help optimize the integrity education of colleges and universities.

G. Sun et al. (Eds.): eLEOT 2019, LNICST 299, pp. 182–190, 2019.
https://doi.org/10.1007/978-3-030-35095-6_21

Breaches in academic integrity are a pervasive and enduring international concern to the overall quality of higher education [3]. On the issue of college students' integrity education, colleges and universities have already included students' integrity education as the primary task of college students' moral education. Advances in technology brought changes to many sectors [4]. In cloud computing era, establishing a unified, open, and flexible education informatization platform has significant influence in realizing resource sharing and narrowing education informatization gap [5]. The security, full-covered characteristic of the cloud platform and the flexibility of desktop's virtualization technology, sharing, of thin clients, individuation and other advantages help to solve the traditional problem [6]. As educational industry has revolutionized along with advancement in technology, so is the growth of big data, which is doubling every year [7]. It is no surprise big data has found its place in education and is predicted to be extensively implemented in institutions of higher education in two to three years [8]. Using the advanced technology of the current computer industry and combining the mature technological advantages of relevant industry, academia and research units, they set out to build the information platform for students' integrity education, create an online platform for student credit, and establish a student electronic file and student integrity file for each student to record the learning situation, life situation and scientific research of each student during school, which includes basic files of information for students, study attendance, academic performance, rewards and punishments, awards and credits, and credit history. They use these to manage the basic information and integrity of students electronically. They use the data to electronically manage student basic information and integrity. When the students graduate, the employer company can use the integrity education platform of student to check the real learning status, life situation and personal credit report of each student during the school. Using the online platform of integrity and moral education, we can establish a credit evaluation mechanism for college students, quantitatively manage students' integrity records, and provide corresponding risk warnings. With the help of quantitative credit assessment indicators, we can help students establish good habits of observing integrity, strengthen students' awareness of risk of integrity, and reduce the occurrence of fraud. With the quantitative integrity assessment indicators, we can carry out targeted moral education activities for students. The student integrity education platform realizes the basic information and integrity information sharing of students and provides services for various business systems and the public by opening the information of electronic diplomas, student electronic files and student integrity files of anti-counterfeiting students.

2 Construction Methods of Online Platform for Integrity Education

2.1 Establish a Management System of Student Electronic File

The establishment of a student electronic file management system can help schools to aggregate and organize the results of the college and major teaching and educational process. In the process of real teaching, the data in the teaching and educational process of each major and college is relatively scattered. The information is distributed among multiple systems such as the educational management system and the educational support system of school. Relevant data on student study and life at school is also decentralized management. It is difficult to trace the teaching and educational process of students, which is not conducive to the management of information process in major and college. At the same time, some details of the ideological activity, social relations, rewards and punishments, awards and loans, training, counseling records, etc. that students have to experience in their daily lives are not managed well. Therefore, it is absolutely necessary to strengthen the management of relatively weak links in the management of student and simultaneously integrate data already existing in multiple systems. For information with a large amount of data, it is necessary to properly organize, extract and mine. The establishment of each student's information file is convenient for scientific analysis of students' learning and life, early detection of problems, avoiding risks, and thus strengthening the management of students' study and life.

2.2 Establish a File on Student Integrity

In order to effectively carry out integrity and moral education for students, on the basis of the student electronic file management system, continuously improve the students' integrity education management system, and according to the performance of students' study, life and other activities, such as whether the test is cheating, whether to take classes on time, whether academic copying, tuition and fees, book borrowing, reward and punishment, breach of contract, bank credit card records, resumes are fraudulent, etc., establish a quantitative model of students' integrity assessment indicators. Through the quantitative evaluation index system, we can quantitatively analyze and count the students' integrity in a timely manner, and establish a risk warning mechanism for students' integrity risks. For students who reach the critical value of integrity, the integrity platform will automatically issue a warning. At the same time, through the quantitative evaluation index system, teachers and managers can also provide targeted counseling on the integrity of students.

Through a comprehensive analysis of a series of activities related to the integrity of students' daily life, and with reference to the opinions of other education experts and scholars, this paper constructs a system of integrity assessment indicators as shown in Table 1. Using the entropy weight method to determine the relative weight of each factor, the final integrity assessment indicators and their weight distribution are shown in Table 2.

With the data recorded in the electronic file management system for student and integrity indicator maintenance, the online platform will automatically calculate the integrity data of each student. If the calculation result is less than 0.6, the platform will automatically send the integrity data to the students through the integrity warning mechanism for student. At the same time, with the evaluation value of each item in the evaluation index system, it can also provide detailed education assistance data for managers and teachers to help teachers and administrators with targeted education on students' integrity and morality. Quantitative credit assessment data can also help students to self-discipline, self-education, self-management and self-evaluation in daily life. This can also help students to establish a good habit of abide by integrity. At the same time, in the process of students' moral education, the importance of students' integrity files can be warned. Once the integrity files are established, they will be disclosed to the society, employers and financial institutions. Students with bad credit assessment will affect their follow-up life conditions such as employment.

Table 1. Student integrity assessment index system

Primary indicator	Secondary indicators	P(h|e)	CF(ei, e)	Wi	CFi(h, e)
Record of exam cheating	Never	0.8667	0.5305	0.9792	0.5195
	Occasionally	0.7111	−0.0172		0.0169
	Frequently	0.4000	−0.4413		0.4322
Record of absenteeism at school	Occasionally	0.7778	0.2175	0.2821	0.0614
	Frequently	0.7333	0.0610		0.0172
Academic plagiarism	Never	0.8667	0.5305	0.9565	0.5074
	Occasionally	0.8000	0.2958		0.2829
	Frequently	0.5333	−0.2551		0.2440
Delay in payment of tuition and fees	Never	0.8222	0.3740	0.6408	0.2262
	Occasionally	0.7556	0.1393		0.0842
	Frequently	0.4667	−0.3482		0.2106
Deferred return of the book	Occasionally	0.8667	0.5305	0.4931	0.2616
	Frequently	0.7778	0.2175		0.1073
Record of penalized	Yes	0.3111	−0.5655	0.4700	0.2658
	Not	0.8000	0.2958		0.1390
Record of random breach of contract	Yes	0.8222	0.3740	0.3521	0.1317
	Not	0.7111	−0.0068		0.0024
Record of credit card loss of trust	Never	0.8444	0.4523	1.000	0.4523
	Occasionally	0.8000	0.1173		0.1173
	Frequently	0.3778	−0.4724		0.4724
False resume	Never	0.8444	0.4523	1.000	0.4523
	Occasionally	0.8000	0.1173		0.1173
	Frequently	0.3778	−0.4724		0.4724

P(h|e) of them indicates the conditional probability of each evaluation indicator in the presence of different secondary indicators. CF(eie) indicates the certainty factor of each secondary indicator. Wi indicates the relative weight of each of Primary indicators in the evaluation index system. CFi(h, e) indicates the credibility of each secondary assessment indicator without default.

Table 2. Credit evaluation indicators and their weight distribution

Assessment index	Weight distribution
Record of exam cheating	0.1682
Record of absenteeism at school	0.0485
Academic plagiarism	0.1643
Delay in payment of tuition and fees	0.1039
Deferred return of the book	0.0847
Record of penalized	0.0807
Record of random breach of contract	0.0605
Record of credit card loss of trust	0.1718
False resume	0.1175

In the online education platform of integrity and morality, through the sharing of information on students' integrity, it can provide personalized services to all sectors of society and the public, establish a communication mechanism between the public and the school, and use feedback information to optimize the school's education system of integrity and morality.

2.3 Providing Interfaces and Service Interfaces for Graduates

Open student integrity platform, provide a series of service interface and interface, provide personal integrity information for graduates, which helps to accelerate the employment of students.

The Integrity Platform for student will provide a series of interfaces to provide some functions for graduate students, such as transcript printing, statistics on student life in school, inquiries on student integrity data, verification of student diplomas, which can help students avoid the phenomenon of lack of credibility such as resume counterfeiting, graduation certificate fraud.

3 Key Technologies for the Construction of Integrity Education Platform

3.1 Cloud Platform Technology

Cloud platform technology is the inevitable development trend of computer big data processing. Now many companies have started cloud platform technology to build their own business systems. The construction of the student integrity education platform is also based on the cloud platform technology, which establish the electronic file system and student integrity system for students in colleges and majors, and it can be a supplement to the school information system construction.

As a server-side data storage and processing center, the cloud platform is highly scalable, large-scale, high-availability, and low-cost. The school has completed the basic work of the cloud platform. Considering the popular services provided by the future integrity education platform, the characteristics of huge information throughput, and the need for support of big data modeling analysis and decision making, cloud platform is the cornerstone of building a platform for integrity education. It is also conducive to the integration of information resources such as teaching and moral education throughout the school.

3.2 Adopt Electronic Signature Technology and Network Security Authentication Technology

In this information times, the security of various networks and information systems is the primary task that needs to be solved in the construction of information technology, and it is an effective guarantee to ensure the safe operation of information systems. In the construction of information platform for college students' integrity education, the system will adopt technologies such as electronic signature and network security authentication to ensure the security and reliability of information recording.

Electronic signature technology is a PKI-based information security technology to ensure the security and reliability of the system. The electronic signature is stored in the database in the form of encrypted data, and the important log records are digitally signed in the data table to prevent modification. The electronic signature is also imported into the security device in encrypted storage. Electronic signature technology can ensure the security of data transmission between the seal server and the signature system by setting multiple protection methods. First, the data is compressed and encoded for transmission, and only the signature system with compression coding rules can identify it. Secondly, the server and the signature system use asymmetric encryption and decryption technology to encrypt important data, effectively ensuring that the designated user can securely obtain the original data.

3.3 Data Mining

In the process of education and teaching management in schools, a large amount of educational data and student education information have been accumulated, and a large amount of similar data is generated every year. Through informatization research, we found that these huge data are distributed in various management systems for management, and the data lacks relevance and cannot be effectively captured, managed and processed.

In the construction of the student integrity platform, we will use the relevant technology of big data to effectively extract and manage the data in the school's many decentralized systems, analyze the effective data in teaching affairs, teaching and student education, and establish a complete student electronic file, which will help improve the quality of teaching and morality education in major and college.

In the online platform of student integrity education, we will collect a large amount of data related to teaching and moral education through the student's electronic file, the student's credit file, and the feedback from the employer company. On the basis of the cloud platform, the problem domain model is established through big data technology, and through the analysis and mining of data, it provides decision-making basis for the education and teaching of the college and the moral education of the students.

4 Framework of the Integrity Education Platform

Based on the student integrity education management platform, we carry out detailed finishing and planning according to the user groups it faces and the different needs of these groups. According to the specific needs of each participants and the functions that the platform can provide, the following structural division was carried out. The structure of the platform is shown in Fig. 1.

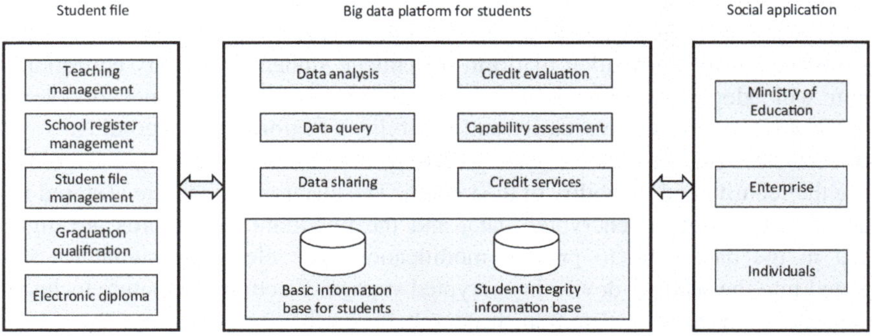

Fig. 1. Structure of the integrity education platform

The construction of the student integrity education management platform mainly includes the following three parts.

4.1 Student File

The student file section is mainly used internally by the school. The user group is mainly for teachers and individual students in the school. The module mainly completes the following functions, including school teaching management, student status management, establishing student electronic files, review of student graduation qualification, and management of students' electronic diploma. Through the construction of the student electronic file management system, we will extract and analyze the data of all the information systems of the school, and complete the construction of the student basic information database and the student integrity information database. Through the management of the student's electronic diploma, we use the electronic signature and digital signature encryption technology to complete the production and issuance of the student's electronic diploma, in order to prevent the occurrence of graduation certificate fraud.

4.2 Big Data Platform for Students

Based on the student basic information database and the student integrity information database, the student big data platform will refer to the relevant quantitative student integrity assessment indicators for data analysis and modeling. The system will automatically calculate the student's integrity data and complete the student's integrity assessment. It will also provide functions such as data sharing and data query for social employers and individuals to realize the sharing of integrity information among college students and provide services for the business systems of each company and the public.

4.3 Social Application

In the process of graduates working in the company, if the company needs to investigate the integrity of the graduates, it can enter the student integrity education platform through the credit service interface provided by the student big data platform to investigate the students' integrity. The contents of the survey mainly include the integrity report of the school, the status of the diploma, and so on.

Based on the student basic information database and the student integrity information database, the student integrity platform will provide functions such as honest data query, data statistics, and integrity evaluation of students. It will also provide companies and individual students with the necessary functions such as a public credit service interface. By using a mobile device such as a web browser or mobile phone, the company or individual student can access the open integrity service interface in the student integrity platform. In this interface, you can query the basic situation of the student, the school integrity record and the integrity analysis report. And through the feedback interface in the integrity interface, the system can provide timely feedback on the actual work situation and integrity of the students employed in the company. The graduated student himself can also use the similar interface to query the basic file data, integrity record and integrity statistics at school. The Student Integrity Service Interface provides flexible query and statistical conditions for the company and the student, which is facilitate query and operation.

5 Conclusion

Whether college students can develop good integrity and morality will, in a big respect, is related to the prosperity and strength of the country and the healthy development of society. For schools and individual students, it is related to the healthy development of colleges and universities and the future and destiny of the students. The construction of student integrity platform is an important part of the university's wisdom education system, and it is also an important part of academic integrity and the integrity education of school. Using the Student Integrity Platform can help students build good habits of integrity. The establishment and opening of the public service interface can establish a bridge between the school and the employer company, and if can also help the school to improve the integrity and morality education of the students.

Acknowledgement. This work was supported by the China Heilongjiang Province Philosophy and Society Project Planning (Grant No. 18EDC217), HIT Teaching Methods and Examination Methods Reform Project (Grant No. XJKGG2018006), China Minis-try of Education Industry-University Cooperation around Teaching Project (Grant No. 201801145015, 201801244004, 201801005002).

References

1. Chang'ach, J.K.: The centrality of character and integrity education in Kenya's Institutions of Higher Learning. Asia Pac. J. Multidiscip. Res. **2**(1), 47–56 (2014)
2. Hu, G., Yang, Y., Tang, L.: Retraction and research integrity education in China. Sci. Eng. Ethics **25**(1), 325–326 (2018)
3. Luo, Y., Zhang, X.Q.: Cloud-based platform building research of teaching resources. Appl. Mech. Mater. **347–350**, 3347–3350 (2013)
4. Kusen, E., Hoic-Bozic, N.: Use of new technology in higher education: a migration to a cloud-based learning platform. In: Uden, L., Tao, Y.H., Yang, H.C., Ting, I.H. (eds.) The 2nd International Workshop on Learning Technology for Education in Cloud. Springer, Dordrecht (2014). https://doi.org/10.1007/978-94-007-7308-0_19
5. Richards, D., Saddiqui, S., White, F., et al.: A theory of change for student-led academic integrity. Qual. High. Educ. **22**(3), 242–259 (2016)
6. Xu, Z., Yang, L., Lei, J.: Conception and design of desktop virtualization cloud platform for primary education: based on the citrix technology. In: 2015 International Conference of Educational Innovation through Technology (EITT), pp. 226–230. IEEE Computer Society (2015)
7. Pratiba, D., Shobha, G.: Educational bigdata mining approach in cloud: reviewing the trend. Int. J. Comput. Appl. **92**(13), 43–50 (2014)
8. Reyes, J.A.: The skinny on big data in education: learning analytics simplified. TechTrends **59**(2), 75–80 (2015)

Research on Digital Teaching Materials Under the Mode of "Educational Cloud Service + Cloud Terminal"

Jinlong Liu, Zhutian Yang(✉), Zhilu Wu, Zhendong Yin, and Yanyuan Fu

School of Electronics and Information Engineering, Harbin Institute of Technology, Harbin 150006, China
{yq20, yangzhutian, wuzhilu, yinzhendong}@hit.edu.cn, 1150520404@shit.edu.cn

Abstract. With the popularization and development of cloud computing technology and intelligent terminal, the "Educational Cloud Service + Cloud Terminal" (referred to as the "cloud + terminal" mode) mode, which is composed of educational cloud service and intelligent learning terminal has opened up a new teaching scene and learning situation for digital teaching materials. First of all, this paper introduces the educational cloud service system and the "cloud + terminal" model; Then, on the basis of deeply analyzing the elements and characteristics of personal learning environment, this paper constructs a model of personal learning environment oriented to digital teaching materials under the mode of "cloud + terminal", at the same time, the paper also introduces its main functions; Finally, the paper designs a learning system for the digital teaching materials under the mode of "cloud + terminal" from four aspects, that is, the terminal equipment, the tool software, the contents of digital teaching materials and the educational cloud service platform. The research contents of this paper have reference value and guiding significance for the design, development of digital educational materials and the construction of learning environment.

Keywords: Digital educational materials · Personal learning environment · Educational cloud service · Cloud terminal

1 Introduction

Under the background of "Internet+", digital teaching materials, as a kind of new teaching resource, are the key links and core elements in carrying out the educational reform, starting the wisdom education and improving the teaching quality [1–3]. Digital teaching materials have been popularized and applied in the field of education. However, due to the lack of effective supporting environment and service system in the applying process of digital teaching materials, some problems have been caused, such as the insufficient support for individualized learning, monotonous learning activities and singleness in interactive mode. The combination of cloud computing technology and intelligent cloud terminal device opens a brand new mode of Internet application,

G. Sun et al. (Eds.): eLEOT 2019, LNICST 299, pp. 191–201, 2019.
https://doi.org/10.1007/978-3-030-35095-6_22

that is, the "cloud + terminal" mode [4–7]. As a newly emerging IT service mode, the application of "cloud + terminal" mode in the field of education accords with the current concepts of universal learning and lifelong learning, which changes the way used by learners in acquiring and integrating knowledge [8]. In the "cloud + terminal" mode, the function, form and application mode of digital teaching materials have been greatly expanded and changed, so as to become an important approach in building the new digital learning environment.

2 The New Development of Digital Teaching Materials Under the Mode of "Cloud + Terminal"

2.1 Educational Cloud Service System

The migration and application of cloud computing in the field of education gave birth to the educational cloud service [9–11]. Cloud computing has large scale of users and massive data supporting ability, which are able to integrate the distributed educational resources effectively and provide the related resources to users through the virtualized educational service from bottom to top [12]. According to the characteristics of construction, management [13], distribution and application of educational resources, this research constructs an educational cloud service system including general service, educational service and the subject service, as shown in Fig. 1.

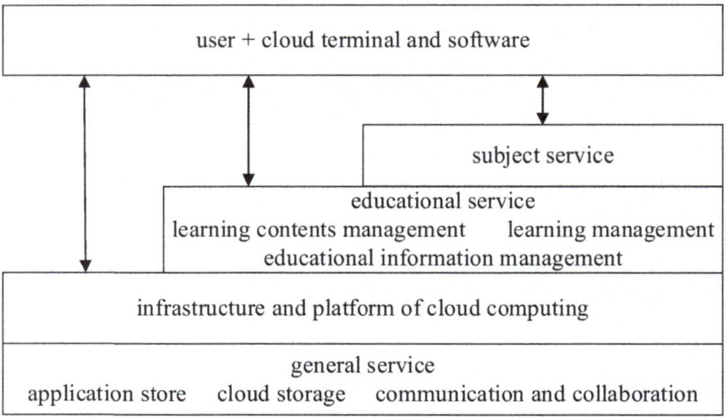

Fig. 1. Educational cloud service system

The educational cloud service system is supported by the infrastructure and platform of cloud computing, which effectively correlates and integrates the educational resources and the basic application software, so as to provide educational information services to teachers, students, parents and administrators through intelligent cloud terminal devices.

In the general service layer, the cloud storage service realizes the secure synchronization, backup and share out of local data and data in the cloud; the application store provides users with the application programs and content resources running on the terminal; communication and collaboration services support multiple forms of interpersonal interaction, including multimedia communication, unified communication, coordination of joint activities as well as the collaborative learning based on common objects.

Educational service layer mainly provides three major services: learning contents management, learning management and educational information management, among which the learning contents management service takes the learning objects as the basic unit, then, creating, storing, assembling and delivering the personalized learning contents; Learning management mainly provides the learning activities and curriculum management for learners, which includes the course registration and arrangement, student registration and attendance, learning progress tracking, homework and evaluation, data analysis and report generation. However, the processed objects of educational information management service are all kinds of data and information related to educational management.

The top-level subject service is directly related to the teaching of various kinds of subjects, such as speech recognition, automatic evaluation composition, mathematical calculation engine and visual learning environment and so on.

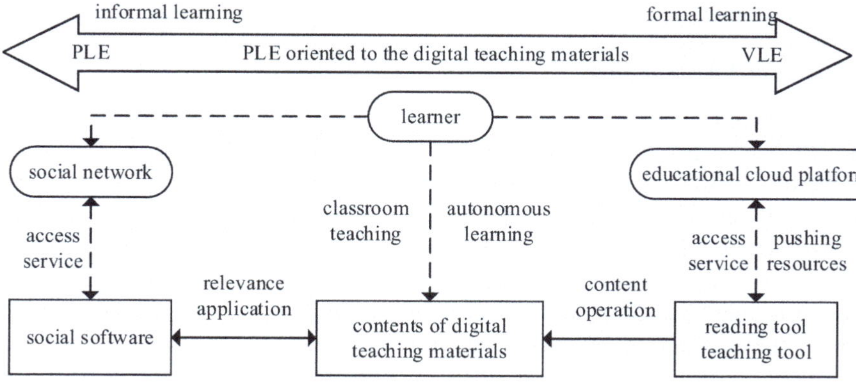

Fig. 2. PLE model for digital teaching materials under the mode of "Cloud + Terminal"

In different learning situations, users obtain the corresponding support from educational cloud service through the cloud terminal and related software.

2.2 "Cloud + Terminal" Mode

The "cloud" in "Cloud + Terminal" mode represents the connection and the educational cloud service; the "terminal" also can be called the client-end or the user-end, representing the cloud terminal and the terminal users. On the one hand, educational cloud service provides all kinds of resources to users dynamically and flexibly according to their demand by virtual service; On the other hand, the computing and storage functions of Internet software at client-end are migrated from local part to the server-side.

The "Cloud + Terminal" mode is shown with the following several characteristics: the cloud terminal has various means of information and communication, which can access to the educational cloud service efficiently and quickly; supporting the seamless connection between application data synchronization and educational cloud service from multiple terminals and different platform; the educational cloud service platform can actively push resources to terminal users, track users' behavior and enhance users' stickiness.

2.3 The New Development of Digital Teaching Materials Under the Mode of "Cloud + Terminal"

Digital teaching materials are also called electronic teaching materials or electronic textbooks, which are not only the product of textbook digitization, but also the product when e-book is applied to the field of education. The "Cloud + Terminal" mode effectively aggregates all kinds of educational resources and services, in order to provide new functional characteristics, individualized support services and diversified application situations for digital teaching materials, in addition, this mode profoundly changes the generation and application of digital teaching materials. Specifically speaking, the new development of digital teaching materials under the mode of "Cloud + Terminal" is mainly reflected in the following two aspects:

New Function-Two Supports

Providing Support for Ubiquitous Learning and Online Collaboration. Under the mode of "Cloud + Terminal", as the main carrier of digital teaching materials contents, the portability of mobile intelligent terminal directly affects the happening frequency and range of learning behavior. At the same time, the resources of digital teaching materials' contents that are stored on the "cloud" are always synchronized with the local resources, which are downloaded to the terminal devices, in this way, it can realize the fast and real-time updating of the contents, thus effectively supporting the ubiquitous learning and online collaboration.

Providing Support for Context-Awareness and Adaptive Learning. Under the mode of "Cloud + Terminal", the intelligent terminal can perceive biological characteristics of learners, spatial environment, equipment parameter and other dominant situation information, and conducting the adaptive adjust on the contents layout and display as well as the shown parameters of digital teaching materials. At the same time, only through the analysis of hidden situation information, such as learning style, interest preference, affective tendency and cognitive state, the digital teaching materials can recommend the dynamic learning path for learners.

New Characteristics—Two Characteristics

Rich Media Characteristic. Under the mode of "Cloud + Terminal", digital teaching materials are no longer just taken as the multimedia content resources, but gradually developing into the Rich Internet Applications (RIA) that can be read or presented on demand. The rich media characteristic of digital teaching materials is mainly manifested in rich presenting forms by the media and dynamic behaviors based on time or user interaction. However, the man-machine interaction mode of multi-sensory channel and powerful media processing ability of terminal devices are the important foundation to realize this characteristic.

Strong Interactive Characteristic. Based on the technologies of multi-touch, natural language recognition, etc. of intelligent terminal, digital teaching materials can realize the man-machine interaction mode in a more abundant form. At the same time, through the work of sensors in light, gravity, acceleration and so on, the intelligent terminal can perceive the external environment information and users' behavior data in real time, thus providing a more realistic and natural man-machine interaction experience, so that enhancing learners' immersion, participation degree and the adhesion of resources.

3 Personal Learning Environment Oriented to Digital Teaching Materials Under the Mode of "Cloud + Terminal"

Constructing the personal learning environment (PLE) oriented to digital teaching materials on the basis of "Cloud + Terminal" can effectively link up and integrate formal as well as the informal learning, which is an effective way to promote the popularization and application of digital teaching materials.

3.1 PLE Elements Oriented to Digital Teaching Materials Under the Mode of "Cloud + Terminal"

The construction of PLE is not limited to one particular technology or tool, but through the interrelation and interaction of various elements, so as to provide learners with an environment in which they can solve practical problems. It reflects the learner's initiative and creativity to act on the environment.

Under the mode of "Cloud + Terminal", PLE, which is oriented to digital teaching materials, has completely overturned the way of information aggregation and data processing existing in the traditional Internet era, and it has created a completely new learning environment in which educational information is liberalized and learners are diversified. Therefore, its main elements should include:

Learner, which is the main body in developing learning activities and the core element of PLE. Learners construct and manage their own learning environment according to individual learning needs, at the same time, they acquire, create and share knowledge.

The content resource, which is not only the carrier of knowledge information, but also contains abundant teaching design ideas. Through the learning activities in PLE, learners not only can acquire content resources, but also can participate in the creation of content resources.

Tool refers to the collection of various kinds of tools that are required during the process of carrying out learning activities. According to the PLE under the mode of

"Cloud + Terminal", the tool includes two parts, that is, the hardware terminal and the software tool. Hardware terminal mainly refers to the terminal devices that can obtain educational cloud service, including PC, smart phone, tablet computer and so on; Software tools include reading tools, teaching tools, cognitive tools, communication tools, etc.

Services include the general services provided by educational cloud service platform, such as resource storage, automatic evaluation, learning management and analysis, etc., and it also includes personalized services for learners, such as personalized resource push, online guide and answer questions, etc.

The social network refers to the relatively stable relationship system between learners and learning community, which is formed because of the interaction. Under the mode of "Cloud + Terminal", the communication and cooperation between learners and partners become more efficient and smooth, which is helpful to broaden the learners' vision, strengthen their construction of knowledge and promote their acquisition of knowledge as well as the ability.

3.2 PLE Features Oriented to Digital Teaching Material Under the "Cloud + Terminal" Mode

The "Cloud + Terminal" mode provides a new model for construction of PLE, reflecting a higher socialization, openness, autonomy and sharing, which is conducive for learners to actively construct, create and share knowledge when they fully enjoy the autonomy. The PLE of the digital materials under the "Cloud + Terminal" mode, with the learner as the center, the resource as the core, the learning task as the goal, and the collaboration as the form, supports the teacher's mixed teaching and student individualized learning, shows the following characteristics:

Promote the Integration, Co-construction and Sharing of Learning Resources. There are various educational resources in the Internet, but it also exists problems such as high dispersion and low aggregation. It is difficult for learners to quickly locate the required content from a large number of network resources. Under the support of "Cloud + Terminal" mode, the basic elements of PLE such as learning content resources, tools, services, etc. can achieve "on-demand, ready-to-use, fast aggregation", which is conducive to the effective integration, co-construction and sharing of learning resources.

Personal Learning Environment with Efficient Access. Under the "Cloud + Terminal" mode, each learner can create an individual PLE on the cloud platform and access it anytime and anywhere using any terminal device, thus greatly reducing the cost and difficulty of using internet learning resources and services. It is conducive to the seamless integration of learning in a ubiquitous situation, which enhanced the continuity and stability of teaching and learning.

Diversified Collaborative Learning Methods. Compared with traditional network collaborative learning, the "Cloud + Terminal" mode supports more diversified collaborative learning methods. The collaborative communication between learners is not only the synchronous or asynchronous information exchange based on the network platform, but also the collaborative editing of shared resources, such as collaborative editing of documents or collaborative programming, which greatly stimulates the creativity of learners.

Active Push Notification of Learning Resources. In order to locate the required learning resources quickly and efficiently in the Internet massive data environment, learners need to use search engines to achieve personal search and aggregation of information, which is an application mode for actively acquiring resources. Under the "Cloud + Terminal" Internet application mode, the cloud platform and the user have a closer relationship and stickiness. The educational cloud service platform can actively push personal learning resources and customized learning services in real-time according to the characteristics and needs of learners.

3.3 PLE Mode Oriented to Digital Teaching Materials Under the "Cloud + Terminal" Mode

Since the rise of online learning, the construction of Virtual Learning Environment (VLE) has been regarded as the dominant design idea of the network learning environment. VLE, with curriculum as its center, provides a top-down organization and management for the learning process, primarily for formal learning situations within educational institutions. When VLE is playing its role, at the same time, it also shows the disadvantages, such as insufficient personal support and limited initiative of learners. Unlike VLE, PLE follows an open, personal learner-centered construction idea that emphasizes learners' choice of learning tools, content resources as well as collaborative objects, manages learning activities by learners, and integrates different learning situations (including formal learning situations and informal learning situations). However, when PLE gives learners autonomy and openness, at the same time, it also brings many problems. For example, learners have difficulty in planning a clear and efficient learning path in a large and complex knowledge network, in lacking management and monitoring of learning processes and activities.

In response to the above problems, the PLE of the digital teaching materials under the "Cloud + Terminal" mode shows a new concept. It is different from the traditional PLE in which the learner chooses the learning resources and tools, is fully responsible for themselves and manages their own self-learning process. Nor does it completely follow VLE's top-down design idea, which is to dominate learners' learning activities through pre-designed resources or monitoring by teachers or educational management institutions. From learners' individual learning demands, this concept is organically combined traditional PLE with VLE. On the basis of ensuring learners' autonomy, taking digital teaching materials as learning objectives and teaching design as its carriers, the PLE of the digital teaching materials under the "Cloud + Terminal" mode provides necessary learning framework and support. Based on that, this study constructs the PLE mode of the digital teaching materials under the "Cloud + Terminal" mode, as shown in Fig. 2. The PLE of this model combines the advantages of traditional PLE and VLE, and its functions mainly include:

Connecting Formal Learning and Informal Learning. The PLE of the digital teaching materials under the "Cloud + Terminal" mode supports the formal and informal learning situations at the same time. In the formal learning situation, the "Cloud + Terminal" model has created a smart class-teaching environment. Teachers and students can independently choose various learning resources, tools and services on the "cloud" to support the teaching activities in the classes, thus the traditional form of classes have been broken through and the teaching result and efficiency have been greatly improved. In the informal learning situation, the learning objectives and paths as well as assessment services in the digital teaching materials can provide learners with systematic learning path planning and method guidance to prevent learners from "losing themselves" in the network environment where information overloaded.

Collaboration and Innovation Based on Content Resources. In the process of learning with digital teaching materials, learners will have a large amount of generative resources (such as note information, test answers, etc.). These generative resources are not only stored in the Internet, but are closely related to specific knowledge content in digital teaching materials. Relying on the communication platform and collaboration mechanism provided by PLE, any learner of digital teaching materials can access these relevant generative resources simultaneously, and can modify, update and iterate to carry out collaborative learning about specific knowledge content, problems or projects, and can promote the sharing and creation of knowledge.

Create a Personal Learning Environment Oriented To Digital Teaching Materials. In the process of learning using digital teaching materials, the reading environment settings, note-taking records, highlighting and other related information of the learners are simultaneously stored in the educational cloud service platform, which ensure that learners can obtain personal learning content and interface when they use digital teaching materials on any terminal device. At the same time, through the analysis of learners- content browsing, information retrieval, activity evaluation and other learning behaviors, the educational cloud service platform can actively push personal learning resources for learners.

4 The Learning System of Digital Teaching Materials Under the Mode of "Cloud + Terminal"

Under the "Cloud + Terminal" mode, the concept and function of digital teaching materials have been greatly enriched and extended. It not only represents digital teaching content, but also a digital learning system that effectively integrates content, terminals, teaching tools and services. Based on the PLE model of digital teaching materials under the "Cloud + Terminal" mode, this study comprehensively examines the functional requirements of digital teaching materials from a systematic perspective, and designs a learning system of digital teaching materials under the "Cloud + Terminal" mode, as shown in Fig. 3.

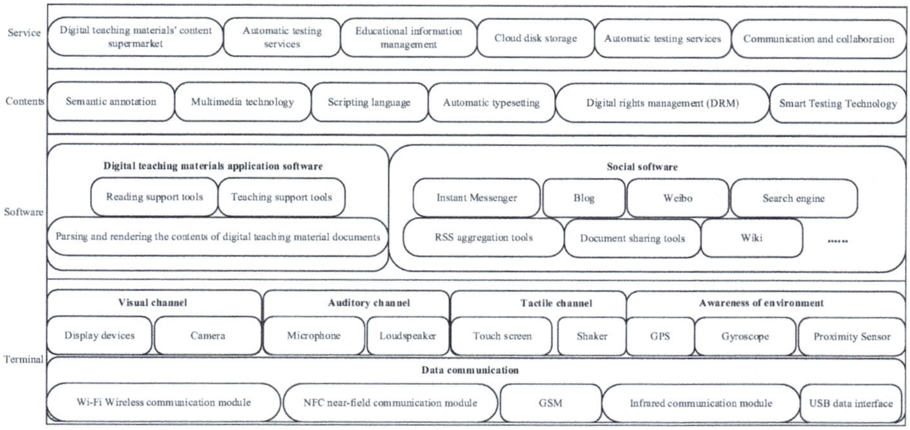

Fig. 3. The learning system of digital teaching materials under the mode of "Cloud + Terminal"

4.1 Terminal Devices

Terminal device is the physical basis and key elements of digital teaching materials' function realization. Its main function is media information processing and communication, which can be summarized into three aspects: 1. Communication between devices. In order to ensure data communication between different devices, the terminal should integrate a variety of data communication function modules. 2. Human-machine communication. In order to create a more natural, real and efficient learning situation, the terminal device needs to have powerful multimedia information processing capabilities, and supports a variety of natural human-computer interaction modes of the sensory channel; at the same time, along with the maturity and application of biometric identification technologies such as iris recognition and fingerprint recognition, virtual reality technology and augmented reality technology, the human-computer interaction mode of digital teaching materials will be further enriched and expanded, and presentation and organization mode of the content will be changed again; 3. Physical context-awareness. Terminal devices should also have the ability to perceive the natural environment and physical context.

4.2 The Tool Software

The tool software includes two categories of digital teaching materials application software and social software. Among them, the digital teaching material application software can parse and render the contents of digital teaching material documents, and provide relevant reading and teaching support tools - the reading support tool mainly sets the reading environment, such as font, color, brightness, etc.; Teaching support tools are used for activities related to teaching and learning, including labeling, sharing, and dictionaries. In addition, as an open learning system, besides digital teaching materials application software, related social software can also provide teaching support and services.

4.3 Content of Digital Teaching Materials

The content of digital teaching materials can be regarded as a fine-grained multimedia knowledge base based on semantic annotation. Through presetting a variety of content presentation templates, it can dynamically perform content layout, and provide various interaction activities that related to learning and recordable learning processes. Software of digital teaching materials uses semantic annotation, multimedia technology, scripting language, etc., combining with a rich knowledge base of subject areas to present content of digital teaching materials in a comprehensive, three-dimensional, intelligent way, providing funny, intelligent, interactive and efficient learning activities and methods.

4.4 Educational Cloud Service Platform

The Educational Cloud Service platform provides a series of general cloud services and educational cloud service functions such as digital teaching materials' content supermarket, learning management, cloud disk storage, communication and collaboration. The Educational Cloud Service Platform provides services to students, teachers, parents, educational administrators and resource providers, which provides a personal learning environment for learners and supports teachers to build virtual interactive teaching environments. It can support educational administrators to evaluate, supervise and manage the process of teaching and learning, and can also support exchanges and interactions between home-schools and schools-companies.

5 Conclusion

The learning system of digital teaching materials under the "Cloud + Terminal" mode is no longer just a simple organization and presentation of multimedia teaching resources, but a learning system that with learning content resource as its core, supported by hardware terminal devices, learning tool software and educational cloud service. With the support of "Cloud + Terminal" mode, new technologies such as big data analysis, virtual reality and augmented reality will further strengthen the personalized and contextualized features of digital teaching materials. There will be a more efficient, intelligent and open learning environment for digital teaching materials.

Acknowledgements. This work was supported by the China Heilongjiang Province Philosophy and Society Project Planning (Grant No. 18EDC217), HIT Teaching Methods and Examination Methods Reform Project (Grant No. XJKGG2018006), China Ministry of Education Industry-University Cooperation around Teaching Project (Grant No. 201801145015, 201801244004, 201801005002).

References

1. Balzotti, J.M., Mccool, L.B.: Using digital learning platforms to extend the flipped classroom. Bus. Profess. Commun. Q. **79**(1), 68–80 (2016)
2. Instefjord, E.J., Munthe, E.: Educating digitally competent teachers: a study of integration of professional digital competence in teacher education. Teach. Teach. Educ. **67**, 37–45 (2017)
3. Nganji, J.T.: Towards learner-constructed e-learning environments for effective personal learning experiences. Behav. Inf. Technol. **37**, 647–657 (2018)
4. García-Solórzano, D., Santamaría, E., Morán, J.A., et al.: Personal informatics systems for supporting self-regulation in online learning environments. Comput. Appl. Eng. Educ. (2018)
5. Belichenko, M., Davidovitch, N., Kravchenko, Y.: Digital learning characteristics and principles of information resources knowledge structuring. Eur. J. Educ. Res. **6**(3), 261–267 (2017)
6. Yuda, M.: Effectiveness of digital educational materials for developing spatial thinking of elementary school students. Procedia – Soc. Behav. Sci. **21**(2), 116–119 (2011)
7. Vermeulen, M., Kreijns, K., Van Buuren, H., et al.: The role of transformative leadership, ICT-infrastructure and learning climate in teachers use of digital learning materials during their classes. Br. J. Educ. Technol. **48**, 1427–1440 (2016)
8. Cramer, J., Quigley, E., Hutchins, T., et al.: Educational material for 3D visualization of spine procedures: methods for creation and dissemination. J. Digit. Imaging **30**(3), 296–300 (2017)
9. Cubero, S.N., Billingsley, J.: The use of games software to enhance educational material. In: Billingsley, J., Brett, P. (eds.) Mechatronics and Machine Vision in Practice 3, pp. 171–180. Springer, Cham (2018). https://doi.org/10.1007/978-3-319-76947-9_12
10. Johnson, M., Liber, O.: The personal learning environment and the human condition: from theory to teaching practice. Interact. Learn. Environ. **16**(1), 3–15 (2008)
11. Kuhn, C.: Are students ready to (re)-design their personal learning environment? The case of the e-dynamic space. J. New Approaches Educ. Res. **6**, 11–19 (2017)
12. Martínez, J.D.G., Rigo, E., Rafael, J.: Multimedia and textual reading comprehension: multimedia as personal learning environment's enriching format. J. New Approaches Educ. Res. **6**(1), 3–10 (2017)
13. Baldassarre, M.T., Caivano, D., Dimauro, G., et al.: Cloud computing for education: a systematic mapping study. IEEE Trans. Educ. **99**, 1–11 (2018)

A Study on the Application of EDA Technology in the Design of Virtual Digital Electronic Experiment

Jinlong Liu, Zhendong Yin(✉), Zhilu Wu, Zhutian Yang, and Yi Hui

School of Electronics and Information Engineering,
Harbin Institute of Technology, Harbin 150006, China
{yq20, yinzhendong, wuzhilu, yangzhutian}@hit.edu.cn,
1150540120@stu.hit.edu.cn

Abstract. Along with the rapid development of computer technology and electronic technology, the traditional digital electronic technology for experiment teaching can hardly meet the development requirements of the times. Therefore, it is essential to introduce Electronic Design Automation (EDA) into digital electronic experiments. From the perspective of EDA technology, the influences of EDA application to digital electronic experiments are analyzed intensively and the design frame and main functional modules for virtual experiment system are put forward, which can provide reference for digital electronic experiment teaching in universities.

Keywords: Electronic Design Automation (EDA) · Digital Electronic Experiment · Virtual experiment system · Functional modules

1 Introduction

As an important course for the major of Electronic Information in universities, Digital Electronic Experiment features both theoretical and practical significance [1]. Its main task is training talents for electronic application. With the development of computer and related technology, the environment for digital electronic experiment teaching in universities is changing continuously so that the teachers and students are faced with new opportunities and challenges [2–4]. Currently, traditional digital electronic experiment teaching can not cater for the development of modern education and even restrain the modernization of education. Therefore, it is essential to reform the traditional teaching methods and contents [5–7]. Electronic Design Automation (EDA) is a new emerging tool of electronic design automation [8]. It is good for changing traditional teaching mode and improving teaching quality of digital electronic experiment to meet the requirement of training innovative talents. Thus, it is an important tool for digital electronic experiment design [9]. This research introduces EDA technology and design procedures in detail and analyzes the merits of bringing EDA technology into digital electronic experiment system in hope of improving teaching effects and develop practical abilities of students.

G. Sun et al. (Eds.): eLEOT 2019, LNICST 299, pp. 202–209, 2019.
https://doi.org/10.1007/978-3-030-35095-6_23

2 EDA Technology and Its Design Procedures

2.1 The Concept of EDA Technology

EDA technology has its narrow definition and a broader understanding. Broadly speaking, EDA technology is modern electronic design, while EDA in narrow definition refers to the automatic hardware design which takes computer as the platform and large-scale programmable logic devices as the base and uses EDA software development tool. Dedicated chips ASIC or IES are integrated by the automated design [10]. EDA technology represents the new development trend of electronic design in the new era. Its main characteristic is that designers use computer as the tool to complete the whole design by following top-down design method. Meanwhile, advanced development tools are used to do segmentation, optimization and simulation automatically. This method is called high-level design method of digital logic circuits. This design scheme is convenient for designers to modify corresponding software, forecast design results, improve system design efficiency greatly, shorten product development cycle and reduce system development cost.

2.2 Characteristics of Different EDA Software

Currently, EDA software widely used in China includes EWB, Protel, Multisim, and Matlab etc. EWB was developed by NI in Canada and it was used for electronic circuit simulation. Later, it was updated as Multisim. Multisim provides all kinds of database simulation systems in line with actual electronic equipment and related electronic products for users. It can integrate circuit diagram establishment, simulation analysis and its results as a real experiment platform. It can also print experiment data and schematic diagrams. Multisim is excellent EDA software for circuit design. Protel is a circuit design system with strong functions. It gains a high popularity rate in China. Its function covers drawing circuit schematic diagrams, designing programmable logic devices and generating corresponding charts etc. Learning circuit layout and welding procedures with the software is good for students to improve their abilities of comprehensive designing and practical operation. As an effective engineering computing language, Matlab can be used to do conceptual design and modelling simulation etc. Dynamic modeling simulation tool is a sub-product based on Matlab. It relies on the strong computing function of Matlab, combines the interactive simulation interface and functions, and takes use of virtual equipment to demonstrate simulated dynamic results visually. Thus, it has become one of widely used software package in dynamic modeling and simulation experiments. However, the functions of the software mentioned above are similar but different with their advantages respectively. Multisim has convenient operation interface with which functions for creating circuits and choosing components can be selected directly from the shapes displayed on the screen. On the one hand, it can solve the problems, such as the shortage of components and unqualified specification etc. On the other hand, it can help students know the contents quickly and enhance their understanding on the concepts and principles they learn by various analysis methods included in the software so that it can enhance the innovation ability of the students. Meanwhile, the tool can expand the component database as much as possible, especially the component models in line with real components, to improve the practicability of the simulated circuits. As an advanced matrix/array language, Matlab has strong functions for design and dynamic modeling. Protel is good for students to make circuit independently and it can enhance hand-on abilities of the students. Therefore, students can select different EDA softwares to do designing.

2.3 Designing Procedures with EDA Technology

From the perspective of designing methods, EDA technology goes through the procedures like hardware designing, debugging, and welding for traditional circuits automatically on computers and it brings fundamental changes to digital electronic design. The process is shown as Fig. 1.

Input: One experiment item is composed of a single source file or several source files and these files can be schematic files or mixed input files etc.

Synthesizing: With EDA software synthesizer, VHDL software is synthesized with the hardware. It is the key point for turning software into hardware circuit. The synthesizer handles the source files in a comprehensive way for a certain product of the supplier FPGA/CPLD. EDA technology can provide good functions for optimization and logic synthesis. It can convert the logic circuit diagram made by the designer into gate level circuits and generate corresponding time series analysis documents or various reports.

Reasonable layout: After the synthesizing, FPGA/CPLD layout/wiring adapter is used to do logical mapping of netlist files to a certain target component, including logical segmentation, optimization and distribution etc. It shall be noticed that the adapted objects after processing shall be in line with the structural details of the components.

Simulation processing: Before downloading the programming, EDA tool is used to make simulation test on the adapted results, i.e. make simulation processing. EDA tool can be used to do simulation tests for different time series and functions. Among these, time series simulation is the simulation processing based on the adapted netlist files and it is the closest one to real object operation. During the simulation procedures, the hardware features of the components shall be taken full consideration. Therefore, the precision of simulation processing with EDA technology is much higher than other methods. Function simulation refers to test simulation on logic functions related to description and it is used to know if the functions meet the requirements of original design.

When the design passes the simulation tests and meets the standards, files generated by adaptation are downloaded through Byteblaster cable to FPGA/CPLD device for real-time hardware debugging and verification. After the above procedures are done, a comprehensive test is done for the whole FPGA or CPLD hardware system to check the operation of the design item in the system. Problems in the design are detected in time for the improvements of the entire experiment.

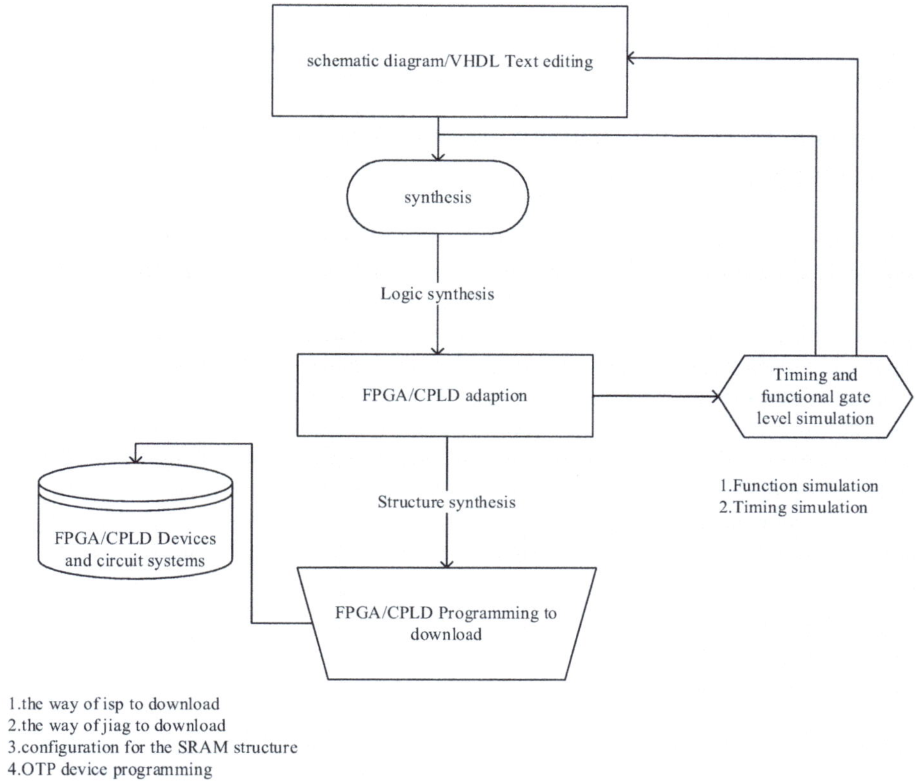

Fig. 1. EDA development and design process

3 Advantages of Using EDA Technology

3.1 It Is Good for Improving Teaching Effects

Using EDA technology in experiment teaching relies mainly on the computer for various operations. Even there are no experiment studies done, related designs can be done smoothly. In addition, all data and files of the experiment can be preserved after the design is done. Using EDA technology in digital electronic experiment can help teachers to solve the problems in traditional experiment teaching. It can not only improve experiment teaching effects, but also enhance the reliability of the experiment. Meanwhile, students can ask questions on the parts they do not understand, or design according to their own thinking without worrying about the device may be damaged. Thus, the experiment teaching effects are improved.

3.2 It Is Good for Improving Develop Practical Abilities of Students

Using EDA technology in digital electronic experiment can facilitate circuit debugging and the development time is shortened. With its advantages, students can understand the key of electronic design intensively. At the same time, students can get better experiment results by taking advantage of this platform. Therefore, it has a positive impact on stimulating students' interest and enthusiasm in learning, facilitating students to master experimental methods and knowledge, and expanding students' thinking.

4 Design Virtual Experiment System Based on EDA Technology

Traditional digital electronic experiment uses small and medium scale integrated circuits to do experiments and it completes the experiments with wire lapping or test box. However, a lot of problems like poor electrical contact performance, high loss and low efficiency often happen in these experiments. Meanwhile, if such problems happen in experiment teaching, teachers shall waste a lot of time helping students to check errors in wire connection and to remove bugs in techniques or processes. It is a waste of teaching time and it also has a negative influence on students' enthusiasm. Therefore, more and more universities start to develop virtual experiment systems voluntarily to facilitate digital electronic teaching. To analyze from the perspective of experiment content, it can make experiment courses more flexible and teaching tasks to be fulfilled more easily. Besides, the system allows every student to try different ways to do the design so that it is good for students to expand their thinking and their creativity and imagination can be inspired.

4.1 General System Frame

In traditional digital electronic experiment teaching, one device is assigned to one certain student. In fact, preparation for an experiment usually takes a lot of time, while the time for the student to use the equipment for the experiment is limited. To some extent, it is a waste of the experiment resource. Therefore, traditional experiment teaching cannot cater for university development and the reform on digital electronic experiment is an urgent issue which needs solutions. This virtual digital electronic

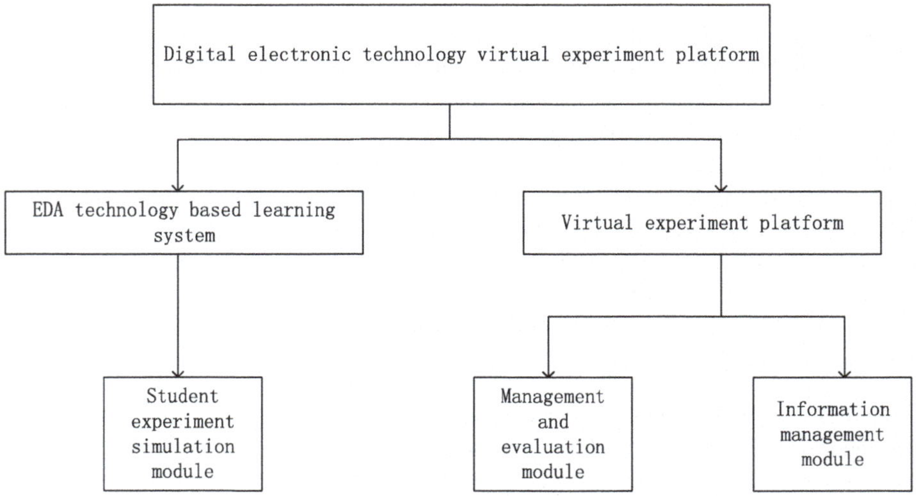

Fig. 2. Virtual experiment platform constructed on EDA technology

experiment system includes two parts, the system and the virtual laboratory. The developing and construction are done with the software Quartusll and Matlab etc. The learning system supports the simulation experiments for the students, while the virtual laboratory is for the developer to do information management, evaluation management and teacher management. The above functions construct a complete virtual experiment teaching system and the structure is shown as Fig. 2.

4.2 Functions of the Modules

Constructing the virtual experiment system is very complicated. To ensure the operation quality and efficiency, the system shall be equipped with suitable network structure. Because the virtual experiment system is developed on the campus network and the scope of application is small. In addition, the system shall be very interactive with real-time responses. To meet the requirements above, this design selects the method of C/S to realize rich interactive effects at the client. According to real experiment teaching process, the design, execution and evaluation of digital electronic experiment, and the characteristics of computer platform, the whole virtual experiment teaching system is divided into three modules, experiment simulation, management and evaluation.

Platform Information Management Module. This module is the reception desk of the virtual experiment teaching system as well as the demonstration part for teaching and management modules. The experiment platform can display if the teaching management works well. This module has the functions of registration, log-on, experiment information management and fault treatment and its key task is managing daily experiment information, such as registration and log-on of students, experiment item downloading, and fault maintenance done by the management etc. Users have to get registered and verify their identity. When doing the registration, users have to fill in their registration information correctly. After the system reviewed the registered information, it will be stored in the database automatically. If the users need to enter the virtual experiment system, they shall enter the correct accounts and passwords. If the account and the passwords are wrong, the system will shift to the interface for re-logon and the experiments can be done on the virtual experiment platform only after the verification is successful.

Basic Learning Module. This module is composed of instrument and theory learning, EDA tool learning and hardware programming learning etc. Among these, EDA learning includes some excellent simulation tools, DSP, QuartusII and Protel etc. It provides good learning and simulation process for digital circuit theory and digital circuit design. Through learning the tools mentioned above, students can improve their abilities of circuit design effectively. As is known to all, the success of virtual experiment system lies in the factors of teaching resources, new technology application and case construction etc. The case construction is the most important factor. When setting up the general teaching plan, new theory and technology shall be considered, the theoretical level and acceptance ability of the students at different stages shall also be considered to improve their learning interest and enthusiasm. Therefore, basic learning module provides complete digital design cases for learners, such as traffic lights control system, data collection system, and camera monitor system etc. This is good for students to know the digital electronic experiment system and to enhance their designing ability.

Student Experiment Simulation Module. This module is composed of several submodules, obtaining information, basic learning, starting and saving virtual experiment and sending experiment results etc. Through virtual laboratory, students obtain the experiment task and related information. After basic learning, they select required EDA tool to do virtual experiment. When the experiment is done, they save the results, such as schematic diagram and program codes etc., and upload their experiment procedures and results for their teacher to check. The module structure is shown as Fig. 3.

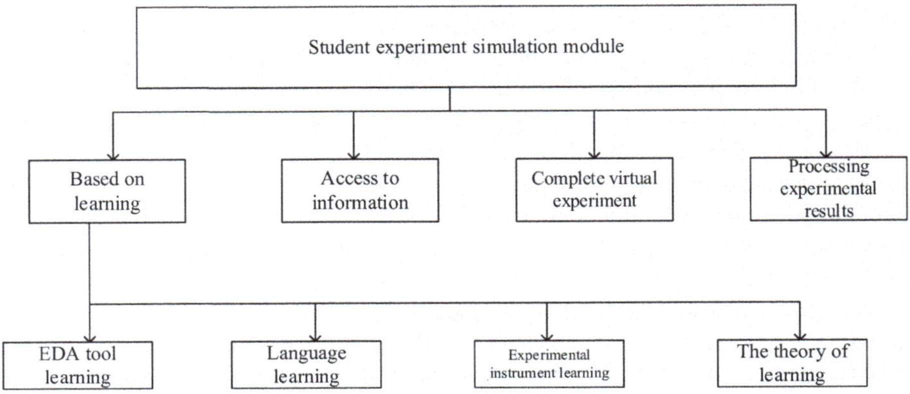

Fig. 3. Main functions of experiment simulation module

Teaching Management and Evaluation. The functions of this module include releasing experiment contents, obtaining experiment items, reviewing experiment items and managing student information etc., as shown in Fig. 4. The teacher displays the experiment contents on the virtual experiment platform according to the teaching task for the students to do corresponding experiments. When the students fulfil the experiments, the teacher gets the uploaded information and gives responses to the students with the review results.

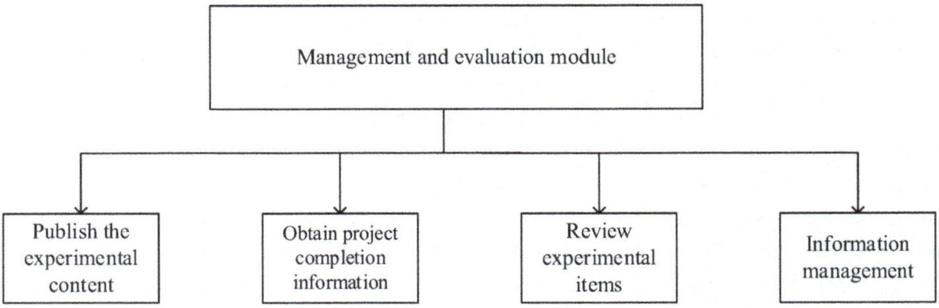

Fig. 4. The structure of teaching management and evaluation module

5 Conclusion

To summarize, virtual digital electronic experiment system is a new mode for experiment teaching. It can provide a humanized, practical and open experimental teaching environment for students and exert positive influence on the improvements of digital electronic experiment teaching. Based on EDA technology, this study analyzes the advantages of EDA technology in digital electronic experiment teaching and puts forward the virtual experiment system and its main function modules constructed with EDA technology in hope of providing some references to digital electronic experiment teaching.

Acknowledgements. This work was supported by the China Heilongjiang Province Philosophy and Society Project Planning (Grant No. 18EDC217), HIT Teaching Methods and Examination Methods Reform Project (Grant No. XJKGG2018006), China Ministry of Education Industry-University Cooperation around Teaching Project (Grant No. 201801145015, 201801244004, 201801005002).

References

1. Synopsys: Library Compiler User Guide. Synopsys, Inc. (2016)
2. Masanori, M., Nair, R.: Power Integrity for Nanoscale Integrated Systems. McGraw-Hill, New York (2014)
3. Jing, Z., Xinguang, L.: Multisim based schematic design and simulation. Comput. Simul. **22** (5), 109–110 (2005)
4. Xiong, F.: Digital Modulation Technique. Artech House Inc., London (2000)
5. Anthes, G.: HTML5 leads a web revolution. Commun. ACM **55**(7), 16–17 (2012)
6. Wang, L., Chang, Y., Cheng, K.: Electronic Design Automation: Synthesis, Verification, and Test, 1st edn. Morgan Kaufmann, Burlington (2009)
7. Shoufan, A., Lu, Z., Huss, S.A.: A web-based visualization and animation platform for digital logic design. IEEE Trans. Learn. Technol. **8**(2), 225–239 (2015)
8. Li, S.S., Liu, J.H., Quan, C.B.: Exploration in circuit logic experiment teaching for computer specialty. Exp. Sci. Technol. **14**(2), 115–118 (2016)
9. Wang, Z.Y., et al.: Research on the training of Computer Majors' ability and system curriculum system. Comput. Educ. **189**(9), 1–6 (2013)
10. Johnson, B.: Control, analysis, and design of distributed inverter systems. Dissertations & Theses – Gradworks (2013)

Thinking on the C Language Teaching Method for the Major of Agricultural Mechanization Engineering

Xiaoqiang Wu[1] and Ruican Hao[2(✉)]

[1] College of Mechanician Engineering,
Inner Mongolia University for the Nationalities, Tongliao, China
[2] Beijing Polytechnic, No. 9 Liangshuihe First Street, Yizhuang, Beijing, China
haoruican@163.com

Abstract. As the entry-level subject in computer science, the C language programming is a very important course that have been opened in various majors in the university. But the short period for the theoretical and practical study and the abstraction of the C language make it a very difficult course for the students who are major in Agricultural Mechanization Engineering. According to the interaction with the students who are major in Agricultural Mechanization Engineering in Inner Mongolia University for the Nationalities, some teaching methods suitable for the students were obtained, and the teaching practice was carried out in class. The main teaching method is progressive catechesis to inspire the students gradually. By solving the problem of side to mobilize the students' interest on learning the C language. Once the students' enthusiasm and the sense of achievement were motivated, the teaching effect could be improved greatly.

Keywords: Agricultural machinery major · C language teaching · Teaching practice teaching

1 Introduction

The C language has many advantages, such as the rich functions, good expression ability, flexible and convenient application, wide application range, high efficiency, good portability and so on. It has both the advantages of high-level language and many characteristics of low-level language [1]. Since the C language has so many advantages, the C language program design has been set as a basic compulsory course in the College of Mechanician Engineering in Inner Mongolia University for the Nationalities. Take the major of Agricultural Mechanization Engineering as an example, the period for theoretical study is 30 h and for practical study is 16 h. As the entry-level subject in program design, the C language course is opened in every major in the College of Mechanician Engineering. By studying this course, the students could learn how the computer works and lay the foundation for learning the other kinds of programming languages. The mechanical and electric are not independent from each other. For the mechanical majors, some control courses are included and the students need to learn how to control the devices through programming. So it is very important for

G. Sun et al. (Eds.): eLEOT 2019, LNICST 299, pp. 210–215, 2019.
https://doi.org/10.1007/978-3-030-35095-6_24

students to learn C language well. But for the beginners, the C language is too abstract with a lot of knowledge to be understood and recited. Those objective causes weaken the students' learning enthusiasm greatly. Meanwhile, the short period for the students in Agricultural Mechanization Engineering major makes it impossible for the teachers to explain the knowledge points in details. Therefore, by mastering the students' learning psychology and improving the teaching skills to mobilize the learning enthusiasm are the keys to improve the teaching effect [2].

2 To Clear the Importance of the C Language and Mobilize the Enthusiasm of the Students

At For the Agricultural Mechanization Engineering major, after finishing the C language program design course, there are another two programming courses in the follow-up classes. But for the students, the one year interval may result in the forgetting of the C language. For the students who are major in Agricultural Mechanization Engineering, they do not know the real purpose of the C language course. They think that programming is useless for them. Under this psychological effect, as well as the abstraction and a lot of knowledge point need to recite, most of the students abandon the study of this course directly. All the causes mentioned above make the C language course has a higher rate of failing during the final exam. To change this bad situation in the C language course, the first thing is to make the students understand the importance of learning the C language. And the enthusiasm of learning the C language can be mobilized by understanding the usefulness of this course.

In order to make the students realize the importance of the C language, the topic of employment which mostly concerned by the students was used. The total number of newly graduated students was over 7 millions and the problem of employment has always been a hot topic every year. In the process of employment, the certificates have always been the important stepping-stones to a good job. In addition to the Certificates IV and VI in English, the Computer Certificate II also has a higher gold content. Once the crisis sense of the students was awaken by the problem of employment, the enthusiasm of learning the C language could be aroused, too. Through the combination of the C language course and the national computer grade examination, the students' attention on the C language was attracted greatly.

3 The Existing Problems

There were some problems still after the students' attention was attracted by the C language course. To achieve a good teaching effect, all the existing problems should be solved. The outstanding problems in the teaching process are as follows.

3.1 The Teaching Method of Repeating What the Book Says Leads to the Students' Lower Learning Enthusiasm

Previously, the popular teaching method for C language course was to repeat what the book says with the help of the multimedia slides. The evaluation criteria of teachers' teaching were mainly by the smooth explanation and no error but without taking the teaching effect into account. Therefore, the teachers were skillful and spoke fluently on the C language class. But actually, the students learned a little about the C language knowledge point and there were still a big gap between the theoretical knowledge and the practical application. If the situation continues in this way, the students soon lost their interests about the course. Both sides of the teaching would find it difficult to put forward the teaching process without a good foundation and the overall learning efficiency would be further affected.

3.2 The Low Combining Degree Between Theory and Practice Leads to the Unsatisfaction of the Computer Practice

In the traditional teaching process, most of the computer practices were about the conversion problems from the mathematical formula to the computer program based on the single knowledge point. The aim of this kind of problem was to reinforce the single knowledge instead of combining the previous knowledge point. And they were helpless for the students to solve the comprehensive problems. Meanwhile, the questions aimed at the programming grammar were boring and weakened the students' learning enthusiasm greatly.

3.3 The Lacking of the Effective Interaction Between the Students and Teachers Makes It Difficult to Master the Students' Actual Learning Situation

In the previous teaching process, the communication between teachers and students was limited in class and homework. However, due to the restrictions such as the study period, the teaching content and the student number, the communication during the class was in small-range and superficial, which could not truly reflect the overall learning situation. In addition, it took a certain amount of time for the teachers to correct the homework. So the communication through the homework was useless for the teachers to master the real-time learning situation. All the factors mentioned above made it difficult for the teachers to make targeted adjustments about their teaching method.

In the traditional teaching mode, the theory divorced from the practice in a certain degree which affected the teaching results. The teachers should find the suitable solutions according to the practical problems to improve the teaching effects.

4 The Teaching Method of Progressive Catechesis to Inspire the Students Gradually

4.1 Classroom Teaching

Teaching according to the textbook says could only transfer the knowledge to the students but could not lead the students to understand and master them. Therefore, an effective teaching method which combined the heuristic and examples should be proposed to attract and motivate the students to learn. The following contents could be contained in the classroom teaching.

For some programs, if the rules could be summarized easily, the students should be inspired to do by themselves. Before explaining the examples, let the students to summarize the rules after observing the computational results of the program. This could effectively deep the students' understanding of the knowledge point and further stimulate the students' learning interest. For example, when explaining the 'if-else' function, the following program could be run firstly.

```
#include <stdio.h>
int main()
{
char c;
printf("Input a character:");
c=getchar();
if(c<32)
printf("This is a control character\n");
else if(c>='0'&&c<='9')
printf("This is a digit\n");
else if(c>='A'&&c<='Z')
printf("This is a capital letter\n");
else if(c>='a'&&c<='z')
printf("This is a small letter\n");
else
printf("This is an other character\n");
return 0;
}
```

When running the program, to enter a different value for the variable x and observe the output value of the variable y. By the single-step debugging method, the students could summarize the functional characteristics of the "if-else" function. Through this way, the knowledge point could be explained vividly.

There was no feeling of difficulty for the students by using of the progressive catechesis teaching method to inspire the students gradually. For example, when explaining the loop structure, the question was to output an asterisk pattern of five lines and five columns. For the students who just learned the "printf" function, their first response was to use the "printf" function five times and the question cold be settled easily. But if the question was slighted modified and the output was changed into outputting an asterisk pattern of ten lines and five columns, their answer would to use the “printf” function ten times. If the question was modified into outputting the asterisk pattern of two hundred lines and five columns, should the “printf” function be used for two hundred times to settle the question? Was there a more concise answer? At this moment, the concept of loop structure was proposed and the question could be settled by a program in three lines. Through a thinking process like this, the students’ impression of the loop structure would be more profound.

The flexible using of textbook examples in class could also be very effective. By making small transformations on the basis of examples, gradually deepening the difficulty, the curiosity of the students could be mobilized and drive the students to think and to deep the understanding of the knowledge points. The question about selecting the bigger number in two numbers was a classic example in the C language. It was very easy and could be settled by comparing one time. But if the question was modified as to select the biggest number in three numbers, the students could answer the question by comparing two times. The teaching result by explaining a knowledge point after the students’ own thinking was much better than explain it directly.

In addition, in the teaching practice, it was found that the students’ attention could be attracted easily when the teacher made mistakes during the demonstration process. According to this phenomenon, the mistakes could be added intentionally to improve the students’ attention and enthusiasm. By the explaining of the mistakes, the students’ recognition of the common mistakes was deepen.

The TurboC2.0 in Chinese version was used as the experimental software. Since the error notification was in Chinese, the students could change the grammar mistake according to the notification. But the TurboC2.0 was based on the DOS operating system, it was very inconvenient without the mouse and copy/paste operation. To begin with, most of the mistakes were concentrated on the input and the grammar. After the students were familiar with the software and the structure of the program, the software was changed into Visual C++ 6.0. Meanwhile, the excursion would focus on the logical capability instead of the input and the grammar by improving the difficulty of the examples.

4.2 Humanistic Care

During the improvement of the teaching method, most teachers were more concentrated on the visible things like the contents of the courses, the teaching methods rather than the emotion. But actually, the teaching process could be influenced by the emotion enormously since the students were not the machine. Once the students started to get bored when they saw the teacher, even if a teacher has high level of teaching skills, it couldn’t be applied to improve teaching quality. So, it was important to deal the relationship well to create a good atmosphere to guarantee the smooth development of the teaching process. There were many ways to promote the relations between students and teachers, such as the encouragement after a correct answer or the help in the times of difficulty as well as by remembering the students’ names. The teachers should treat the students as their friends and solve the problems from the students’ standpoint to let the students feel the teachers’ mind.

4.3 Improving the Quality of Teachers

The "student oriented" teaching method put forward higher requirements for teachers. On the one hand, the time and resources were needed to guarantee the teacher could stand at the students' standpoint to stimulate the students' interest in learning and improve their learning efficiency. On the other hand, the teachers need to teach in accordance with the clearly defined syllabus and plans to ensure the smooth implementation of the teaching process. The exploration still needed to balance the two aspects above to achieve the optimal result. For the new students in the new semester, their ability and the way of thinking were quite different from the previous students. So the teaching method should be changed according to the matter of fact to achieve the teaching goals. And it was a high requirement for the teachers' personal ability. It was said that "If you want to give a bowl of water to a student, a teacher needs a bucket of water first". It was not only that the teachers should have enough knowledge about the knowledge of the courses they were teaching, but also have relevant knowledge of the professional field of the students. Only in this way could the actual application be brought into the classroom, which makes the teaching come from practice and serves practice.

5 Conclusion

The time for theoretical and practical study in C language course is little for the students who are major in Agricultural Mechanization Engineering. But they could also learn it well with the help of the flexible teaching method to mobilize their study enthusiasm and to lay a foundation for them to pass the computer grade test. With the fast development of the society, the teaching method should also keep pace with the time by inspecting and learning from the other teachers to improve the teaching skills to drive the students' learning enthusiasm.

Acknowledgment. This article thanks Inner Mongolia University for Teaching Reform Project: Based on the CDIOM model of undergraduate engineering mechanical engineering (YB2017034); Science and Technology Innovation Guide Project of the Inner Mongolia Autonomous Region KCBJ2018028 Supported By Program for Young Talents of Science and Technology in Universities of Inner Mongolia Autonomous Region 'NJYT-19-B15'.

References

1. Jin, L., Liu, Y.: Some experiences in the teaching of C language. J. Sci. Technol. Inf. **5**, 53–54 (2012)
2. Wang, C., Liu, D.: Discussion on the reform of C language teaching for non computer major. J. Sci. Technol. Inf. **23**, 527–528 (2009)
3. Tan, H.Q.: The programming of C language. Tsinghua University Press, Beijing (2010)
4. Yang, C.X.: C language program design experiment guidance and answers. China Railway Press, Beijing (2005)
5. Tang, G.MS.: The programming of C language. Tsinghua university press, Beijing (2009)
6. Zou, X.C.: C language program design training course. Southwestern Normal University press, Chongqing (2008)

Application of Artificial Intelligence in Wireless Sensor Network Training Teaching

Fei Hu(✉), Heng Tang, Wanshun Chen, and Jian Cheng

Wuhu Institute of Technology, Wuhu 241006, China
540999537@qq.com, 195952801@qq.com,
858708130@qq.com, 19321686@qq.com

Abstract. As an important part of the teaching activities of science and engineering, combining artificial intelligence technology, face detection, biopsy detection, text and voice recognition technology are applied to the practical teaching, and presented in different ways in the pre-class supervision, in-class assessment and after-class evaluation stages, so as to make the practical teaching more automated and intelligent. APP also gets good feedback in the application stage.

Keywords: Artificial intelligence · Training teaching · Internet of Things

1 Sketch

As an important part of Applied Technology Teaching of Internet of Things in Higher Vocational colleges, practical teaching aims to internalize knowledge in theoretical classroom into skill points through students' hands-on practice. Its goal is to consolidate and strengthen existing skills, digest and absorb new skills points. In the new period, it advocates "learning by doing" in practical teaching of Higher Vocational colleges, especially in the competence competition of teachers in Higher Vocational Colleges in 2018, It clearly puts forward the concept of learning by doing in practice teaching [1], which requires students to do as much as possible in practice class, and more information-based means to assist students in learning.

Taking the core course of Internet of Things 《Wireless Sensor Network Technology and Application》 as an example, this paper elaborates on introducing artificial intelligence technology into practical teaching, forming a three-dimensional "learning by doing" system with supervision before class, assessment in class and evaluation after class.

2 Supervision Before Class

Due to the limitation of the environment, the demonstration of practice operation in class can not be accurately understood by every student, and the details can not be clearly demonstrated, which are all painful points difficult to solve in traditional practice teaching [2]. It also causes long training time, but the effect is not good. Artificial Intelligence changes the mode of teachers' demonstration once and students'

G. Sun et al. (Eds.): eLEOT 2019, LNICST 299, pp. 216–220, 2019.
https://doi.org/10.1007/978-3-030-35095-6_25

demonstration once in traditional practice teaching, and records the key steps of teachers' operation into short videos, which are play backed the operation details. Publishing preview tasks before class requires students to watch short videos. In view of the poor autonomy of higher vocational students in learning and the phenomenon of brushing classes, we use Baidu artificial intelligence platform's "biopsy + face verification" technology to supervise students' learning. When there are non-self-watching or no one watching, the videos will automatically withdraw, and the data will be recorded in the background. According to the frequency and effect of students watching videos, the pre-class evaluation is carried out.

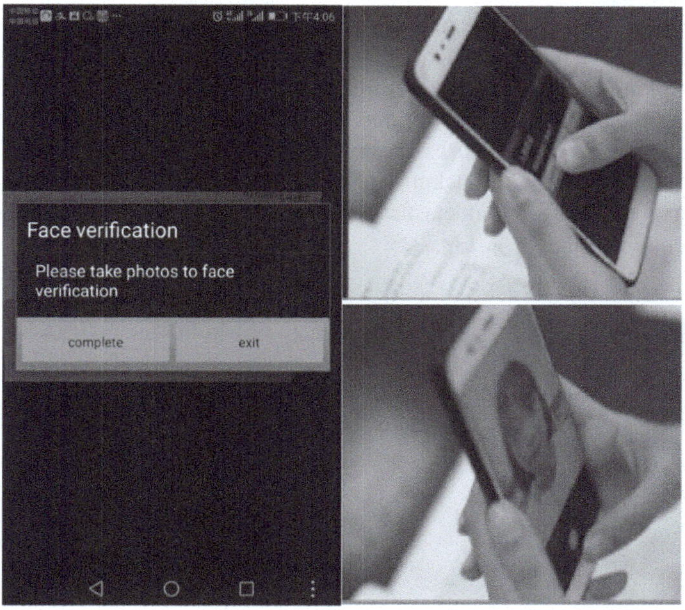

Fig. 1. Face verification and result recording effect map

Taking the practical training link of 《Basic Installation and Debugging of Wireless Sensor Networks》 (excerpted from the second section of Chapter 4) as an example, [3] Before class, the key skill points are the installation and wiring of electrical parts, the generation and debugging of firmware, and the operation links of these contents are recorded into short videos for students to watch before class. The key skill points that are the installation and wiring of electrical parts, the generation and debugging of firmware, are recorded for students to watch before class.

3 Assessment in Class

The practical training class is the stage of students' practice, and also an important moment for students to internalize skills. In order to achieve the goal of internalized skills, we need to make full preparations before class and closely integrate with orderly practical operation in class. In the process of practical classroom teaching, grouping is usually carried out due to the limitation of the number of experimental equipment, so real-time feedback and participation of students are very important.

In order to solve the problem of untimely feedback in class, taking the "firmware generation and debugging" part as an example, students need to establish an understanding of the meaning of firmware parameters before class, set and operate firmware parameters in the training class, and download and debug firmware. The key to solving the problem is to give the assessment and evaluation of the practical process in time. In traditional training teaching, it is very difficult for teachers to guide and evaluate each group at the same time. This paper adopts the image recognition technology of Baidu artificial intelligence platform to extract parameters and modify the keywords of the page and compare them with background data. According to the similarity level, the teachers can give timely reminders according to the errors. The keywords extracted from the picture are shown in Fig. 2.

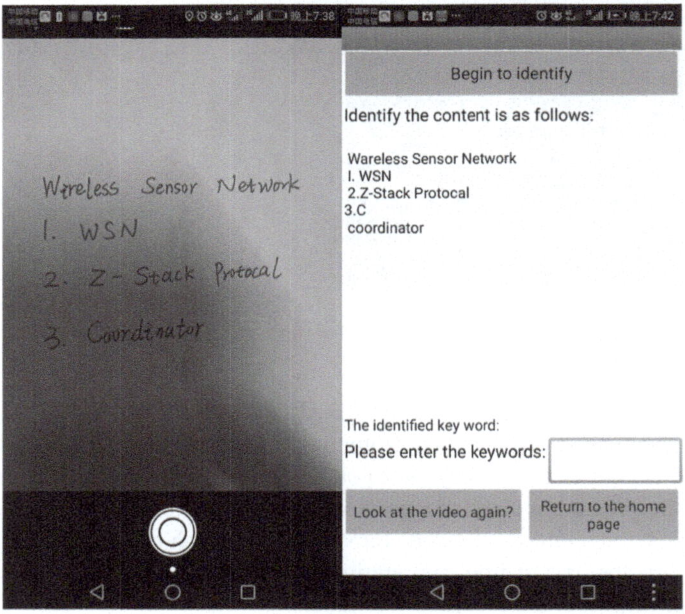

Fig. 2. The results of image recognition

In order to solve the problem of students' participation and fully mobilize their enthusiasm, a camera is installed on the experimental platform, and the image is collected once every 30 s. According to the face recognition technology of artificial intelligence platform [4], the information of the operator in the front desk is obtained. According to this information, the classmates who are not in front of the experimental platform for a long time are reminded. The installation position of the camera and the marking of the image recognition result are shown in Fig. 3.

Fig. 3. Camera on the experimental platform and face recognition record

4 Evaluation After Class

It is necessary to review the content of practical training course in time after class and expand the extension of practical training content so as to let students know the useful place of learning. In view of this goal, On the one hand, breakthrough game in APP are set up to review the training content, and students are required to complete the corresponding game, mainly including the operation process in the training practice and the specific application scenario of the training content, which are used to motivate students by the scoring system. On the other hand, the scene is selected from the school-enterprise cooperation, and VR video related to the training content is produced for students to watch. Then the students are asked to submit the related pictures and voices in the form of casual shooting and recording after class, and score them according to the results of picture and speech recognition.

5 Conclusion

Integrating information technology and artificial intelligence technology into vocational education is the future development direction of vocational education [5]. In this paper, Baidu artificial intelligence platform technology is used to penetrate into all aspects of wireless sensor network training and teaching, which plays a very good role in mobilizing students' learning enthusiasm and stimulating learning motivation. The key technologies used in each aspect are shown in Fig. 4.

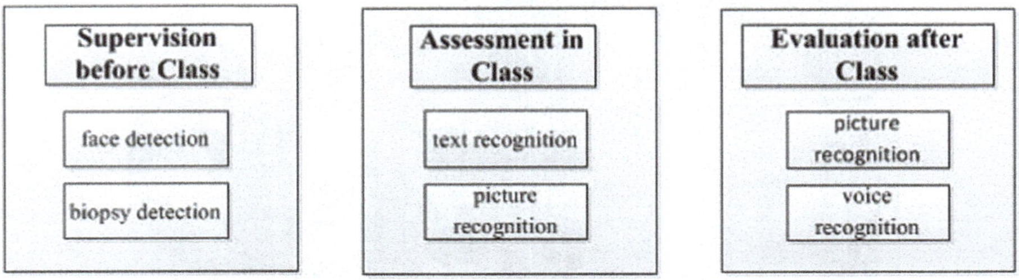

Fig. 4. Artificial intelligence technology applied in "Learning by Doing" APP

Introducing artificial intelligence technology into the training process can make higher vocational students experience more fun about hands-on. Timely evaluation can make students have a clear understanding of their abilities. At the same time, teachers can be freed from the repetitive and miscellaneous supervision and evaluation work and concentrate more energy on the construction of curriculum content, which is of great benefit to both students and teachers.

Acknowledgment. This work was supported by the research on high school provincial quality engineering project of Anhuigrant No. 2015mooc109, No. 2016ckjh224, No. 2017mooc368, No. 2017zhkt466 and No. 2017sjjd041, and University-level key projects grant No. Wzyzrzd201702.

References

1. Minmin Jiang, F.: Exploration of the relationship between teaching and competition based on information technology– based on the national vocational college information teaching competition. Industr. Inf. Technol. Educ. **10**, 73–78 (2018)
2. Haihong Chen, F.: Analysis on the reform strategy of practical training for computer major in higher vocational colleges. Education. Modernization **4**(31), 216–217 (2017)
3. Xie, J.F., Renda Deng, S.: Wireless Sensor Network Technology and Application of Internet of Things (Zigbee Edition). Posts and Telecommunications Press, Beijing (2016)
4. Huanzheng Yang, F., Guohua Yang, S., Ling Xu, T.: Research on face, speech and object recognition system based on Baidu AI and STM32. J. Hunan Post Telecommun. Coll. **17**(04), 28–30 (2018)
5. Zhe Wang, F.: Experience from competition of information-based instructional design–research on building intelligent classroom. China New Telecommun. **20**(09), 196 (2018)

Best Practices and Teaching/Educational Models

Scientific Interpretation of the Connotative Development of Higher Vocational Colleges in Yunnan in the New Era

Aihua Wen[1], Chao Ye[2], and Jingjing Li[3](✉)

[1] School of Arts and Sciences, Yunnan Jiaotong College, Kunming, Yunnan, China
[2] Yunnan Physical Science and Sports Professional College, Human Resources Office, Kunming, Yunnan, China
[3] Higher Education and Regional Development Research Institute, Yunnan Normal University, Kunming, Yunnan, China
242107349@qq.com

Abstract. Yunnan higher vocational education, which is an important component of Yunnan higher education, has a good development momentum. However, it is also facing severe challenges in education quality and difficulties of meeting social needs of talent cultivation. In the face of the new era, only connotative development model can enable Yunnan higher vocational education to adapt to the economy and social demands. This research empirically analyzes the layout, type, specialty and hierarchy of 40 higher vocational colleges in Yunnan, and systematically diagnoses its existing problems in the process of development on the basis of the research results. The research focuses on scientific interpretation of college connotative development, which contains type function, professional characteristics and hierarchical structure in Yunnan higher vocational colleges in the new era. Finally, it proposes applicable measures to promote the connotative development of Yunnan higher vocational colleges in the new era from three dimensions of government, school and society.

Keywords: Yunnan higher vocational colleges · Connotative development · Structural optimization · Scientific interpretation

1 An Overview of the Connotative Development of Higher Vocational Colleges in the New Era

1.1 A Subsection Sample

Since the implementation of the reform and opening-up policy, Vocational education provides powerful talents and intellectual support for China's economic and social development, and it is also the most direct and closely related type of education with social and economic development. As China enters the development stage of the new era, industrial upgrading and economic structure continue to accelerate and adjust, the demand for technical and technical personnel in all walks of life is becoming more and

G. Sun et al. (Eds.): eLEOT 2019, LNICST 299, pp. 223–237, 2019.
https://doi.org/10.1007/978-3-030-35095-6_26

more urgent, and the important role of vocational education is becoming more and more prominent.

As an important part of higher education, higher vocational education has advanced towards the process of popularization with the implementation of enrollment expansion policies in recent years. Higher vocational colleges also face severe challenges in education quality. The current extensional development of higher vocational colleges is difficult to meet the needs of talent cultivation, higher vocational education and social development in the new era. What is needed in the new era is the new type of education from quantity to quality. Higher vocational colleges, which are the carriers of higher vocational education, play a key role in safeguarding and improving the quality of education. Therefore, to take education quality as the core, it is necessary to take the connotative development path, which is not only the rational choice for the development of higher vocational colleges, but also the realistic basis for the sustainable development of higher vocational colleges.

After the 21st century, higher education institutions across the country have developed rapidly due to enrollment expansion, as have Yunnan Higher Vocational Education. Up to now, the overall development momentum of higher vocational education in Yunnan is good, mainly reflected in the expansion of the scale, the improvement of the structure, the renewal of the concept and the improvement of benefits. However, rapid development will intensify the expansion of college scale, which will lead to the imbalance of the structure of higher vocational colleges in Yunnan. The fundamental solution to the problem is to reform and adjust the educational and teaching structure of higher vocational colleges in Yunnan, and gradually take the road of connotative development, and finally achieve higher level of adaptation to social development in Yunnan higher vocational colleges. This is the choice and demand for the connotative development of higher vocational colleges in Yunnan.

2 The Structure Setting and Scientific Interpretation of Higher Vocational Colleges in Yunnan

2.1 The Layout Structure and Scientific Interpretation of Yunnan Higher Vocational Colleges

The layout structure of higher vocational colleges in Yunnan is mainly represented by the number of higher vocational colleges and the number of students, which is reflected in the spatial distribution of the higher vocational colleges and the spatial distribution of students and their relationship. Generally speaking, the layout structure of higher vocational colleges, regardless of the number of schools or the number of students, is consistent with and compatible with the development strategy of the local economy, society and culture.

Amount of Higher Vocational Colleges in Various Provinces of Yunnan Province
Generally speaking, the distribution of higher education areas in Yunnan Province is based on the level of local economic development. According to the actual situation of Yunnan Province, we have divided the higher education areas of Yunnan Province into three major areas: core area, abdomen area and remote area. As Table 1 shows, as of 2018, there are 40 higher vocational colleges in Yunnan Province, and relatively the most is Kunming City, the capital city of Yunnan Province, reaching 24, accounting for 60% of the province's higher vocational colleges. There are relatively few state cities, and there are at most two of the five prefectures, one of the five prefectures, and one of the four prefectures. This also fully demonstrates the strength of the development of the provincial capitals, and other higher education institutions, especially in the remote areas, are even less.

Table 1. List of the number of higher vocational colleges in various provinces of Yunnan

	Prefecture	Quantity	Percentage of higher vocational colleges in the region (%)
Core Area	Kunming	24	60
	Yuxi	1	2.5
Abdominal Region	Qujing	2	5
	Baoshan	1	2.5
	Dali	2	5
	Lijiang	1	2.5
	Dehong	2	5
	Cuxiong	2	5
	Xishuangbanna	1	2.5
	Honghe	2	5
Remote Area	Wenshan	1	2.5
	Lincang	0	0
	Zhaotong	1	2.5
	Puer	0	0
	Nujiang	0	0
	Diqing	0	0

The Scale of Students in Various Higher Vocational Colleges in Yunnan Province
Due to the number of states in Yunnan higher vocational colleges, it is also possible to conclude that the number of students is also proportional to the number of schools, which is clearly reflected in Table 2. More than 65% of the students are concentrated in Kunming and Yuxi, which are the core areas of Yunnan. As can be seen from the table, the number of people in the remote areas is less than 15,000. The development of its higher vocational colleges and the number of students are consistent with their level of social and economic development.

Table 2. List of the amount of students in higher vocational colleges in various regions of Yunnan

	Prefecture	Quantity	Percentage of the province (%)
Core Area	Kunming	222863	66.88
	Yuxi	5000	0.15
Abdominal Region	Qujing	12251	3.68
	Baoshan	11000	3.30
	Dali	7500	2.25
	Lijiang	6473	1.94
	Dehong	16381	4.92
	Cuxiong	19159	5.75
	Xishuangbanna	8813	2.64
	Honghe	10800	3.24
Remote Rrea	Wenshan	8463	2.54
	Lincang	0	0
	Zhaotong	4549	1.37
	Puer	0	0
	Nujiang	0	0
	Diqing	0	0
Total		333252	100

Analysis and Interpretation

The number of higher vocational colleges in Yunnan only reflects a feature and an indicator of the layout structure of higher vocational colleges. It is not enough to consider this factor, and it is not scientific enough. Therefore, we must conduct a comparative analysis with the entire higher education institutions in Yunnan. See Table 3 below for details.

Table 3. Comparison of the amount of universities higher vocational colleges in Yunnan

	Prefecture	Number of institutions of higher education	Number of higher vocational colleges	Gap
Core Area	Kunming	45	24	21
	Yuxi	2	1	1
Abdominal region	Qujing	3	2	1
	Baoshan	2	1	1
	Dali	4	2	2
	Lijiang	1	1	0
	Dehong	2	2	0
	Cuxiong	3	2	1
	Xishuangbanna	1	1	0
	Honghe	3	2	1

(*continued*)

Table 3. (*continued*)

	Prefecture	Number of institutions of higher education	Number of higher vocational colleges	Gap
Remote area	Wenshan	2	1	1
	Lincang	1	0	1
	Zhaotong	2	1	1
	Puer	1	0	1
	Nujiang	0	0	0
	Diqing	0	0	0
Total		72	40	32

From Table 3, we can see that there are 40 higher vocational colleges out of a total number of 72 universities in Yunnan, and higher vocational colleges account for more than half of the number of universities in Yunnan. It can be concluded that the importance and vigorous development of higher vocational colleges in Yunnan in current society. Of course, its level of development is similar to that of other regions. College development in the core area is superior to the abdomen, especially far superior to the remote areas, in terms of quantity and students. For the layout above, Yunnan higher vocational colleges are already in the forefront of development.

Table 4. List of development of higher vocational colleges in Yunnan

No.	Name of vocational college	Actual Area (mu)	Planned area (mu)	Gap (mu)
1	Kunming Metallurgy College	1244.43	2000	−755
2	Yunnan JiaoTong College	677.32	1100	−422
3	Yunnan Vocational Institute of Energy Technology	503	700	−197
4	Yunnan Vocational College of Mechanical & Electrical Technology	623	900	−277
5	Yunnan Land and Resources Vocational College	1155	1000	+155
6	Yunnan National Defense Industry Vocational and Technical College	900	500	+400
7	Kunming Vocational and Technical College of Industry	1114.9	1100	+15
8	Dehong Normal College	1130	600	+530
9	Lijiang Teachers College	1148.02	700	+448
10	Yunnan Vocational and Technical College of Agriculture	1058	600	+458
11	Yunnan Vocational College of Culture & Art	150	300	−150
12	Yunnan Vocational College of Judicial Police	350	300	+50
13	Qujing Medical College	367	600	−233
14	Yunnan Tin Vocation Technical College	634.21	400	+235

(*continued*)

Table 4. (*continued*)

No.	Name of vocational college	Actual Area (mu)	Planned area (mu)	Gap (mu)
15	Yunnan College of Tourism Vocation	216	900	−684
16	Yuxi Agriculture Vocation-Technical College	300	500	−200
17	Xishuangbanna Vocational and Technical Institute	200	900	−700
18	Chuxiong Medical and Pharmaceutical College	452.6	500	−47
19	Honghe Health Vocational College	624	800	−176
20	Baoshan College of traditional Chinese Medicine	544	1100	−556
21	Yunnan Forestry Technological College	944.5	1100	−155
22	Yunnan Sports Vocational College	320	500	−180
23	Dehong Vocational College	800	1200	−400
24	Dali Vocational and Technical College of Agriculture and Forestry	213.68	500	−286
25	Yunnan Finance and Economics Vocational College	253	600	−347
26	KunmingRailway Vocational Technical College	158.88	400	−241
27	Health Vocational School	275.66	500	−224
28	Dali Nursing Vocational College	462	400	+62
29	Yunnan Water Resources and Hydropower Vocational College	700	700	0
30	Yunnan Vocational College of Science and Technology Information	880	600	+280
31	Yunnan Business Vocational College	698.21	500	+199
32	Yunnan Modern Professional Technical College	1305	1500	−195
33	Yunnan Sanxin Vocational and Technical College	1725	900	+825
34	KunMing Health Vocational College	1278	2800	−1522
35	Yunnan City Construction of Career Academy	150	1000	−850
36	Yunnan Vocational College of Foreign Economic and Trade	1062	1500	−438
37	Yunnan Xinxing Occupations Institute	380	2200	−1820
38	Kunming Professional College of Arts	143.35	800	−656
39	Yunnan College of Foreign Affairs & Foreign Language	393.58	600	−206
40	Yunnan Engineering Vocational College	309	1200	−891

In terms of site area, Yunnan higher vocational colleges are far less than other universities in Yunnan. Due to the expansion of enrollment and the encouragement of independent enrollment policies in higher vocational colleges, according to the regular practice, there are 100 mu of school area for every 1,000 students. Many high vocational colleges have large students number but less land area. This will limit students' teaching, logistics, accommodation and so on. This is also the problem that is being solved currently by major vocational colleges. Many higher vocational colleges are relocating and are in the process of building new campuses.

The layout structure of Yunnan higher vocational colleges depends on the regional economic development and social reality of Yunnan. The key point is the development concept, discipline construction, professional development of various higher vocational colleges, and the structure of the faculty and other aspects of the development of indicators at all levels.

2.2 The Type Structure and Scientific Interpretation of Higher Vocational Colleges in Yunnan

Generally speaking, the type structure of colleges and universities is divided into different types and structures according to different forms of learning. Here we mainly analyze the two types of school types and subject types.

Types of Higher Vocational Colleges in Yunnan
As can be seen from Table 5, there are 40 higher vocational colleges in Yunnan, including 29 public higher vocational colleges, accounting for 72.5% of the province's higher vocational colleges, and 11 private higher vocational colleges, accounting for 27.5% of the province's high vocational colleges. Private higher vocational colleges are still less than half of public higher vocational colleges. In the current reality in Yunnan, public colleges are generally much more than private colleges.

Table 5. List of types of higher vocational colleges in Yunnan

Types of college	Quantity	Percentage (%)
Public Higher Vocational Colleges	29	72.5
Private Higher Vocational Colleges	11	27.5
Total	40	100

The Types of Disciplines in Various Higher Vocational Colleges in Yunnan
From Table 6, it is found that there are 14 science and engineering vocational colleges in Yunnan, accounting for 35% of the higher vocational colleges in the province. Secondly, there are 8 medical schools, accounting for 20% of the higher vocational colleges in the region. In addition, there are 4 agricultural agriculture and forestry colleges, 3 financial and accounting colleges, 2 normal and art colleges, and 1 in politics, law, sports and language.

Table 6. List of subject types in various higher vocational colleges in Yunnan

Subject type	Quantity	Percentage (%)
Science and Engineering	14	35
Normal Education	2	5
Agricultural Agriculture and Forestry	4	10
Art	2	5
Medicine and Health	8	20
Law	1	2.5
Financial Accounting	3	7.5
Sports	1	2.5
Language	1	2.5
Miscellaneous	4	10
Total	40	100

Analysis and Interpretation

From the analysis of the previous situation, it is known that Yunnan's higher vocational colleges have a good momentum of development, especially in a fast rapid. There are a large number of higher vocational colleges, whether they are public or private, and the competition, exchanges and cooperation among them are becoming more and more obvious. For Yunnan higher education, higher vocational education is indispensable, and it plays an important role in the contribution of talent cultivation in Yunnan.

For the discipline orientation of Yunnan higher vocational colleges, it also has strong professionalism and distinctive brand. Each higher vocational college is specialized and targeted according to social needs and its own reality. The subject profession has basically covered and grasped the key points of the current society, or it is more in line with the provincial conditions and reality of Yunnan.

2.3 The Professional Structure and Scientific Interpretation of Higher Vocational Colleges in Yunnan

The professional structure is a very important part of the structure of higher vocational education. It not only reflects the division of disciplines, but also reflects the division of labor in social occupations. It also reflects the contribution of a local higher vocational education to the regional social and economic development. For any college, professional structure is the core to the analysis of educational structure.

As can be seen from Table 7, there are a total of 283 faculties in 40 higher vocational colleges in Yunnan, with 1,234 major settings, but only 27 national-level majors that concentrated in less than 10 public higher vocational colleges. Among them, there are 162 provincial-level majors, and the province has only four provincial-level majors. Among the higher vocational colleges, the off-campus and on-campus training bases are the highlights, with 1910 and 1434 respectively; while the national-level quality courses and provincial-level quality courses are also lack, 26 and 185 respectively.

Table 7. List of professional structure of various higher vocational colleges in Yunnan

No.	Vocational college name	Amount of							
		Department	Number of majors	Number of national-level majors	Number of provincial-level majors	Off-campus training bases	Campus training bases on	National-level quality course	Provincial-level quality course
1	Kunming Metallurgy College	16	78	8	13	363	28	14	21
2	Yunnan JiaoTong College	14	52	3	4	60	99	9	15
3	Yunnan Vocational Institute of Energy Technology	7	34	3	3	46	53	0	6
4	Yunnan Vocational College of Mechanical & Electrical Technology	6	34	4	11	32	28	0	13
5	Yunnan Land and Resources Vocational College	13	44	0	8	26	36	0	14
6	Yunnan National Defense Industry Vocational and Technical College	7	25	0	6	31	42	0	2
7	Kunming Vocational and Technical College of Industry	6	58	2	10	28	33	0	10
8	Dehong Normal College	11	54	1	4	36	31	0	4
9	Lijiang Teachers College	9	40	0	7	21	26	1	7
10	Yunnan Vocational and Technical College of Agriculture	7	47	0	4	100	80	0	10
11	Yunnan Vocational College of Culture & Art	4	18	2	6	32	97	2	6
12	Yunnan Vocational College of Judicial Police	4	14	0	3	20	13	0	5
13	Qujing Medical College	7	12	3	4	22	16	0	7
14	Yunnan Tin Vocation Technical College	4	21	0	5	41	36	0	4
15	Yunnan College of Tourism Vocation	7	30	0	4	52	13	0	4

(*continued*)

Table 7. (*continued*)

No.	Vocational college name	Amount of							
		Department	Number of majors	Number of national-level majors	Number of provincial-level majors	Off-campus training bases	Campus training bases on	National-level quality course	Provincial-level quality course
16	Yuxi Agriculture Vocation-Technical College	6	38	0	5	54	48	0	3
17	Xishuangbanna Vocational and Technical Institute	8	24	0	2	34	21	0	6
18	Chuxiong medical and pharmaceutical College	8	19	0	3	75	139	0	1
19	Honghe Health Vocational College	4	15	0	1	27	20	0	0
20	Baoshan College of traditional Chinese Medicine	6	23	0	3	76	18	0	5
21	Yunnan Forestry Technological College	6	39	0	10	57	82	0	15
22	Yunnan Sports Vocational College	13	18	0	4	28	13	0	6
23	Dehong Vocational College	8	28	1	14	45	28	0	0
24	Dali Vocational and Technical College of Agriculture and Forestry	6	23	0	6	27	23	0	4
25	Yunnan Finance and Economics Vocational College	4	5	0	3	21	16	0	2
26	Kunming Railway Vocational Technical College	5	6	0	2	11	15	0	2
27	Health Vocational School	3	7	0	3	31	24	0	4
28	Dali Nursing Vocational College	5	26	0	2	54	32	0	2
29	Yunnan Water Resources and Hydropower Vocational College	4	14	0	3	44	25	0	2
30	Yunnan Vocational College of Science and Technology Information	14	28	0	4	45	18	0	3
31	Yunnan Business Vocational College	4	27	0	2	31	26	0	0

(*continued*)

Table 7. (*continued*)

No.	Vocational college name	Amount of							
		Department	Number of majors	Number of national-level majors	Number of provincial-level majors	Off-campus training bases	Campus training bases on	National-level quality course	Provincial-level quality course
32	Yunnan Modern Professional Technical College	9	36	0	0	36	28	0	0
33	Yunnan Sanxin Vocational and Technical College	5	37	0	0	41	34	0	0
34	Kunming Health Vocational College	10	39	0	0	32	27	0	0
35	Yunnan City Construction of Career Academy	5	46	0	0	82	45	0	0
36	Yunnan Vocational College of Foreign Economic and Trade	6	45	0	3	52	36	0	2
37	Yunnan Xinxing Occupations Institute	3	29	0	0	21	18	0	0
38	Kunming Professional College of Arts	6	28	0	0	26	21	0	0
39	Yunnan College of Foreign Affairs & Foreign Language	7	32	0	0	32	25	0	0
40	Yunnan Engineering Vocational College	6	41	0	0	18	21	0	0
Total		283	1234	27	162	1910	1434	26	185

The development of higher vocational colleges in Yunnan should be based on their own ideas, the use of advanced concepts and the integration of production and education, to form and develop majors that with distinctive brand and high employment rate. Among the faculties, we must also create a group of professional leaders and teaching backbones with solid basic theories and outstanding teaching and practicing abilities. A batch of practical training bases or workshops that integrate teaching, training, vocational skills appraisal and technology research and development functions should also be constructed. We should also cooperate to develop a group of courses that embody the combination of enterprise and study, and combine engineering and learning characteristics to create a prominent professional group supported by key construction majors and other related majors, and improve the social and economic development of higher vocational colleges in Yunnan, Southwest China and even the whole country.

2.4 The Hierarchical Structure and Scientific Interpretation of Higher Vocational Colleges in Yunnan

The educational hierarchy generally refers to a form of structure in which education is interconnected, coordinated and connected. The most important indicator that can reflect the hierarchical structure of higher vocational education is the student's hierarchical structure related to both certification and program. Generally, higher vocational colleges mainly have three levels, technical secondary school, five-year college and secondary school. Their enrollment, number of students in school and graduates and their relationship can reflect the ability of a region or a higher vocational college of training talents. Therefore, it is necessary to combine this issue with the current policy implementation and evaluation of Yunnan higher vocational colleges to fully analyze and study its hierarchical structure.

As can be seen from Table 8 above, 40 higher vocational colleges in Yunnan have three-year colleges which are the main body, including 29 public higher vocational colleges and 11 private higher vocational colleges. In terms of five-year colleges, there are 36 higher vocational colleges in the region, including 25 public colleges and 11 private colleges. In terms of secondary schools, there are only 10 in the region, including 6 public and 4 private.

Table 8. The hierarchical structure of higher vocational colleges in Yunnan

	Three-year college	Five-year college	Secondary school
Public Higher Vocational Colleges	29	25	6
Private Higher Vocational Colleges	11	11	4
Total	40	36	10

It is found from Table 9 that although there are 40 higher vocational colleges in Yunnan, there are only 3 national demonstration higher vocational colleges, namely Yunnan Jiaotong College, Kunming Metallurgy College and Yunnan Vocational College of Mechanical and Electrical Technology, and All three of them are private. There are 9 national modern apprenticeship pilot units, all of which are private. There are 13 high-quality vocational colleges in Yunnan, including 11 public colleges and 2 private colleges. There are 18 provincial-level demonstration higher vocational colleges, including 15 public colleges and 3 private colleges. These evaluations and reputations are relatively high at the national or provincial level.

Table 9. The hierarchical structure of higher vocational colleges in Yunnan

Project	Number of public higher vocational colleges	Number of private higher vocational colleges	Total
National Model Higher Vocational Colleges	3	0	3
National Modern Apprenticeship Pilot Unit	9	0	9
Construction Unit of High Quality Vocational Colleges in Yunnan	11	2	13
Provincial Demonstration Higher Vocational Colleges	15	3	18

In the development of higher vocational education, Yunnan higher vocational colleges still adhere to the rules and regulations of higher vocational education development and the corresponding institutional structure. At the same time, it can be seen that higher vocational colleges are mainly three-year colleges, and at the same time five years is developing. The junior colleges will gradually enter the secondary school. At the national level and the provincial level, in order to improve the development level of higher vocational colleges, it is highlighted that to establish national modern apprenticeship pilot units, high-quality vocational colleges, provincial-level demonstration higher vocational colleges. To achieve leading in all aspects of higher vocational colleges, it is required to have a good construction environment, and breakthroughs in talent mode, experimental training base, teacher team construction, curriculum system and teaching content, etc. As long as it does not violate the law of education development and the education system, it can cultivate useful hands-on talents and skilled talents in society. This is the ultimate goal and purpose of higher vocational colleges.

3 New Measures to Promote the Connotative Development of Higher Vocational Colleges in Yunnan in the New Era

3.1 The Government Level Connotation and Realization Path of the Development of Higher Vocational Colleges in Yunnan

The connotative development of higher vocational colleges in Yunnan is inseparable from the government's policy support and guidance, mainly the competent departments and education departments of the state, Yunnan provincial government and various higher vocational colleges. At present, the "Professional Education Law of the People's Republic of China", "Decision of the State Council on Accelerating the Development of Modern Vocational Education", "Action Plan for the Innovation and Development of Higher Vocational Education", and "Opinions on Improving the Teaching Quality of Higher Vocational Education" have been issued. "Notice of the State Council on

Printing and Distributing the Implementation Plan for the Reform of the National Vocational Education", "The Outline of the Medium and Long-Term Education Reform and Development Plan of Yunnan Province", and "Implementation Measures for the Innovative Development of Higher Vocational Education in Yunnan Province". The competent departments of vocational colleges are supervised, managed and developed in strict accordance with the requirements of the State and Yunnan Provincial Government.

In view of the characteristics of the development of higher vocational colleges, talents and social needs, as a government department is necessary to control the quality of education and the efficiency of running colleges, mainly reflected in the macro-control of professional settings, the construction of information platforms and inputs of specific fund. The macro-regulation of professional settings requires the higher vocational colleges to consider the needs of the market and their own development, but it also requires the government to provide appropriate guidance. Many vocational colleges now have misunderstandings in professional settings, which have certain blindness, arbitrariness, utilitarianism and similarity. Under this circumstances, the government should guide the higher vocational colleges to clarify the connotation of the majors, to set up and adjust the professional structure according to law, and to conduct professional management in a standardized and scientific manner. For the information platform, the government and other relevant departments must not only rebuild, but also manage, dynamically manage the information of the network platform information, and ensure the accuracy and timeliness of the information. The government should pay attention to the contact with schools and industry associations and other related institutions, obtain enrollment information and employment information from colleges, and talent demands from industry associations. For school-enterprise cooperation, the government can invest a certain amount of special funds to maintain the operation of school-enterprise cooperation, and through a certain period of time, explore an effective model that can not only cultivate the professional quality of students, but also generate income for enterprises.

3.2 The College Level Connotation and Implementation Path of the Development of Higher Vocational Colleges in Yunnan

The main body of the connotative development of higher vocational colleges in Yunnan are the higher vocational colleges themselves. The higher vocational colleges in Yunnan have distinct characteristics. All higher vocational colleges should conduct self-analysis and reflection on the actual situation, find out the problems that affect the quality of personnel training internally and improve them, so as to achieve intensive development.

According to the contents of the current implementation plan of vocational education reform, it mainly needs the transformation and development of education concept, major setting, school-enterprise cooperation mode, characteristic brand and teacher strength. Educational Professional settings should be based on industry-side structural development trends and social needs. A school-enterprise cooperation model that is suitable for students' professional growth and employment should be Explored. Specialized branding construction and professional settings should be carried out.

The construction of teachers should be Strengthened, especially the pre-service and post-employment education of skills-based teachers. So as to improve the quality of teaching.

3.3 The Social Level Connotation and Realization Path of the Development of Higher Vocational Colleges in Yunnan

Regardless of any society or any industry, the whole society is a weather vane. This social vane is constantly changing with the changes of the times, economic development and culture. As a higher vocational college, it is also necessary to make appropriate and reasonable changes in the changes of social wind vane. Otherwise, higher vocational colleges will fall into the predicament and challenges of development.

The development of higher vocational colleges requires bridges and cooperation between industry and enterprises, mainly in the aspects of industry associations, enterprise participation, training system and quality control. Industry associations: As a bridge, college-enterprise cooperation should make full use of the role of various industry associations. College-enterprise cooperation should give full play to the role of industry associations. Enterprises must actively and effectively participate in the construction of distinctive brands and majors in higher vocational colleges. The deepening of college-enterprise cooperation is mainly reflected in the practice base of training, and it is necessary for colleges and enterprises to improve the practical practice system. The improvement of social satisfaction is entirely in cultivating the quality of talents, and it is necessary for colleges and enterprises to jointly monitor the quality of talents.

References

1. Yuan, G., Jia, D.: Exploration of the Connotation Development of Colleges and Universities. Higher Education Press, Beijing (2012)
2. Wang, Z.: Exploring the Practice of Connotation Construction in Higher Vocational Colleges. Southwest Jiaotong University Press, Chengdu (2013)
3. Shan, M.: Research on the Connotation Construction of Colleges and Universities——Intensive. Synergistic and Dynamic Mechanism Innovation. Shanghai University Press, Shanghai (2017)
4. Shen, J.: Practical research on CIPP evaluation mode of professional construction in vocational colleges. Doctoral thesis of Southwest University (2016)
5. Wang, Z.: A school-based study on the connotative development of higher vocational education from the perspective of education modernization monitoring. China Adult Educ. **1**, 50–52 (2019)

The Combination of the Downward Shift of the Teaching Focus and the Sublimation of the Teaching Objectives

Wen Wang[1] and Danyang Li[2(✉)]

[1] Wen Wang's High School Teaching Studio, Kunming, Yunnan, China
[2] Foreign Language School, Yunnan Normal University, Kunming, Yunnan, China
2274313674@qq.com

Abstract. Current English class in China has gained great achievement, but there are still many problems in it such as the wrong emphasis of teaching focus and incomplete teaching objectives. In current English class, the teaching focus do not care about the personalized individuals' development, which lead to negative results of English teaching. Shifting the teaching focus down to the actual learning condition of every students can guaranty the learning quality of students in English class and change students' learning attitude for English to a positive direction. On the other hand, teaching objectives, now, are the language knowledge including vocabularies, grammar and so on, but they neglect the morality education which is significant to individuals and society. So the paper mainly focuses on the functions of the downward shift of the teaching focus, the sublimation of the teaching objectives and the combination of these two, and how to combine the downward shift of the teaching focus and the sublimation of the teaching objectives in English classes of senior high schools. First, the current problems of the teaching focuses and teaching objectives of English classes in senior high school are pointed out and proposed corresponding ways to solve these problems. Second, the view of the combination of the downward shift of the teaching focus and the sublimation of the teaching objectives is proposed including the benefits of implementing the view and the way to do it.

Keywords: English class · Senior high school · The downward shift of the teaching focus · The sublimation of the teaching objectives

1 Background of the Study

Since the founding of the New China in 1949, Chinese education has gained great achievements. However, facing rapid development of technology around the world and innovation of educational concepts and technology, the ministry of education proposed that educational reform should continue being deepened, and promote quality education in an all-round way. During the process of promoting new curriculum, English course of senior high schools not only has the function of accomplishing the content of text books, imparting language knowledge to students and making students' English level reach the standard of college entrance examination, but also effects on the

G. Sun et al. (Eds.): eLEOT 2019, LNICST 299, pp. 238–243, 2019.
https://doi.org/10.1007/978-3-030-35095-6_27

nurturing objectives which are demanded by new curriculum, the improvement of students' core competence and shaping students in all-round development into builders and successors of China.

However, in recent observation and research of English classes in senior high schools, we often found that it seems hard for teachers to shift the focus of teaching language knowledge down to personalized individuals, which neglects the effectiveness of students' learning in class, at the same time, it is difficult for teachers to sublimate the teaching goal of moral education to the teaching atmosphere of the whole class, which neglects to nurture students' global competence required by 21st century. In the English teaching of senior high schools, teachers neither can abandon nurturing students' basic language knowledge and skills nor neglect to build students' thinking quality and cultural character. How to combine downward shift of teaching focus in English class with the sublimation of teaching objectives is the content that English teachers and related educators need to explore and practice in the implementation of curriculum reform, and it is also the significance of the curriculum reform.

2 The Downward Shift of the Teaching Focus Means Focus on the True Performance of Individual Students in English Class

In English teaching of senior high schools, teachers often fail to implement the "the shift of teaching focus". "Student-centered" means that teachers should pay attention to the students' "learning." If the student does not study effectively in class, the reason is that the student does not listen to the class, not talk about, read, write, watch, translate or think about the teaching content nor to ask or answer any questions about the content. Teachers have to think about: How to test whether a class is successful, or not? There is only one standard that is whether students control the knowledge, or not. Then how do teachers know that whether students control the knowledge, or not? As far as English classes are concerned, teachers can use a variety of English activities to let students to listen to the class, to speak, to read and to write English. As Sato Manabu mentioned in his *"The Quiet Revolution"*, teachers and students need to create a communication in the class based on mutual listening. In the book, Mr. Lin, the leading character in the book, holds the view that to judge whether your work is good or not, the only way you can use is that look at the facial expressions of each student in the classroom, their attitudes of learning, and see if they continue to learn.

How to do it? First, the English instruction used by a teacher in teaching need to be clear and simple, so that the concept of English learning activities can be implemented in class, fully mobilizing students' eyes, ears, mouth, hands, heart and brain into the learning. For example, when a teacher asks a student to divide the textual text in the textbook into three paragraphs, it is not necessary to use the sentence that students can't comprehend easily like "Please divide the passage into 3 parts", but the basic expression like "Please cut the passage in to 3 parts". Thus, teachers can effectively communicate with students in class, guarantying the quality of English learning effectively and imparting language knowledge including English pronunciation, vocabulary, grammar, and language skills such as listening, speaking, reading, writing, reading and translating to personalized individuals of students.

Second, teachers can create an effectively learning atmosphere, however it is only based on the establishment of a harmonious teacher-student relationship. A harmonious teacher-student relationship helps to create a harmonious class's atmosphere, which requires teachers to make positive efforts subjectively. Teachers should be the intimate people of students, to understand their psychological characteristics, to care about their learning, physical and mental health, to understand their difficulties in learning English, to respect the students' ideas, and to be adept at spurring them. For example, when a student's mood is low, the teacher can help the student to dispel the smog of the soul by simply saying "I like your big smile".

In addition, only teachers respect the actual cognitive level of students, they could ensure that students learn effectively. In the actual teaching process, the knowledge content provided by teachers and teaching materials may not be experienced by students. Therefore teachers should respect students' actual cognitive level to adjust the progress and difficulty of teaching in time, so that the effectiveness of knowledge learning can be guaranteed. For example, as teaching the unit whose theme is *Travelling Abroad*, teachers have to realize the fact that senior high school students may not have the experience in traveling abroad. In this case, teachers can display photos of their overseas travels to students, or graft relevant English expressions to some tourist attractions that students are familiar with.

At the same time, it is also essential to stimulate students' interest in learning and to maintain effective and subjective learning. To make students learn well and to make learning become interesting, as a teacher, it is necessary to fully explore the interesting factors of the teaching materials, so that students are interested in English class and change their negative attitude for English learning. For example, in the teaching process of the unit *First Aid*, teachers can encourage students to play a lively short English sitcom. Only liveliness can attract the attention of students; only vividness fits the psychological characteristics of students, so that they could feel the joy of learning.

3 The Sublimation of Teaching Objectives Means Explore the Important Role of Educating People in Teaching Content

Students not only should pay attention to the learning process and methods while developing basic knowledge and basic skills, but also develop emotional attitudes and values, and finally achieve the improvement of language ability, learning ability, thinking quality and cultural character. *China Student Development Core competence* proposes that education should be based on the nurture of "all-round development", which can be divided into three aspects: cultural foundation, independent development, and social participation. The comprehensive performance is six qualities which are humanistic, scientific, learning, healthy living, responsibility, practice and innovation, and they could be specifically refined into 18 bases such as national identity and so on. In 2017, the General Office of the CPC Central Committee and the General Office of the State Council issued *Opinions on Implementing the Inheritance and Development of Chinese Excellent Traditional Cultural*, which mainly talked about: culture is the blood of the nation and the spiritual home of people, cultural self-confidence is more basic and more deep, more lasting power, and the unique concept, wisdom, tolerance, and the charm of Chinese culture will add the confidence and pride of the Chinese people and the Chinese nation.

So, firstly, teachers need to set high-level teaching objectives before teaching, and can not only focus on teaching the knowledge points presented by the teaching materials. For example, before teaching the unit *Nelson Mandela*, teachers should design the teaching objectives for the students' thinking quality and cultural character after designing the teaching objectives for language knowledge and learning ability. The class can be designed like this. Let the students analyze what quality makes Mandela become a great person through analysis and inference. It is good for students to form a unique way of thinking and thinking ability. They can also learn to think and solve problems from different aspects. And through learning the life and history of former South African President Mandela, students are able to understand the emotional attitudes and values of other ethnic groups, and form their own emotional attitudes and values through the analysis and induction of the quality of great men.

Secondly, teachers should encourage students to tell Chinese stories in English. For example, teachers can integrate the content of traditional Chinese culture elements such as Chung Teung Festival into the unit *Festivals around the World* to guide students to show respect and filial respect to the old, or Dragon Boat Festival which reflects the great love and spirit of Chinese poet Qu Yuan for his motherland also can be integrated into the theme to guide students to think deeply about life and personality.

In addition, teachers should be good at using the textbook, the carrier of teaching content, to make secondary exploration and sublimation of its educational goal in educating people to achieve different effects although using the same textbook. For example, when teaching the unit *Friendship*, the teacher not only let the students control the vocabularies that describes personality characteristics, but also can add these words into the vocabulary table such as "responsible", "humorous", "patient", "generous", "honest" and "diligent". Let students discuss which words can describe the qualities that their ideal friends must possess, then ask students to discuss which words can describe the quality that are not available for themselves, and finally reflect on how to correct their shortcomings.

At the same time, teachers should actively develop curriculum resources that can achieve educational goal in educating people to form a unique school-based curriculum. For example, teachers often ignore the elements of "emotion" and "culture" in daily teaching, and these factors precisely are the points of English college entrance examination in recent years. Such topics as "Chopsticks Culture", "Visit Panda", "credit management" and "importance of environmental protection" are all presented in the papers of English college entrance examination. If students lack contact with these topics in English learning process, they will lose points in the college entrance examination. Based on this, teachers need to search for texts that have relevant topics on the Internet and adapt them to form school-based textbooks.

4 The Downward Shift of the Teaching Focus Does not Contradict the Sublimation of Teaching Objectives

"After being properly educated, people can become a person." According to the principle that education adapts to nature, in the "Great Teaching Theory", Comenius said that "to compare the psychology of people coming to the world to a seed or a grain of rice is very legitimate." The educational goals proposed by Comenius have three levels: "study," "morality," and "belief." China's educational goals also range from "two bases" to "three-dimensional goals", and finally to "six competences" in the reform and development. Both of them reflect a profound understanding of the nature of education. Only after the scientific educational goals are clarified, the teaching activities of the schools have a direction, and the professional work of teachers has a soul.

We could imitate this great educator to compare the educated young children to the saplings that have been germinated by education. When he reaches the first level of educational goal, he can grow long branches, so that people can recognize that he is a tree (an educated person), but this tree has no leaves, flowers or fruits, and the bare branches make his life not full, lacking vitality. Just like Comenius said: "the vines that have not been cultivated well can't produce good grapes". Young children who have not reached the second-level educational goal will not be able to produce green leaves, beautiful flowers or tasty fruits on the branches. According to the third-level educational goal, the "root" of person who receives education should be deeply rooted in culture and faith, which is similar to "belief" called by Comenius. Only after the educated person has the "belief", the people would evaluate him as a tree that stands tall (a well-educated, ideal, ethical, cultural, and disciplined person).

Therefore, every educator should bear in mind that the fundamental task of education in China should be "moral education". A tree with long branches, green leaves, beautiful flowers and tasty fruits will make people recognize immediately even in a long distance because he is a precious tree (a well-educated person), and people can't help running to him enjoying the cool under its shade. But if the tree does not have a deep root in the ground, people can only describe him just as "beautiful", and when a strong wind blows, he will be swept away.

If the students do not learn, do not speak, talk, read, write, translate, think, ask anything about English, the basic knowledge and skills that students have learned will not be improved, the process and methods of learning will not be practiced, emotional attitudes and values will not be developed, and core competence will be impossible to be achieved. However, if teachers can promote the teaching goal on this basis, promoting "teaching" by "educating people", let the class be full of cultural atmosphere, and irrigate the "roots" of students' growth, thus students will have the motivation to learn, and ultimately achieve the development of language ability, learning ability, thinking quality and cultural character. Therefore, actually, teachers play a role as a bridge for the downward shift of the teaching focus and the sublimation of the teaching objectives in English classes of senior high schools. Teachers should fully effect on teaching language knowledge, learning skills, learning process, learning method, right emotion, positive value, profound culture, the sublime belief, and nurturing students as true "people", comprehensive "people", rooted "people". Teachers not only need to ensure that the selected teaching steps, teaching methods, and others are based on the actual condition of the individual students, but also need to ensure that the designed teaching content, teaching objectives and others are consistent with the overall cultural beliefs of the human being.

All in all, in the teaching process, English teachers of senior high schools should pay attention to the students' reactions at any time, such as a student's eye contact, an action, a frown, a grin, and so on to adjust their teaching plan in time according to the student's reaction. They also need to start from the actual English level of students to stimulate students' interest in learning, and when students' attention is not concentrated on class, they would give some time to students to relax rather than continuing the class. Last but not least, when students do not understand the problem, they are not recommended to talk about another problem. In the process of teaching design, teachers should break the barriers of traditional English class and teaching materials, opening up the culture and belief space of teachers and students, and rooting the cultural self-confidence of our country in the hearts of student, and open up the ideas of nurturing the quality of students to develop students' multiple intelligence and to pay attention to the overall development of students, and they also should promote the comprehensiveness of teaching, focusing on nurturing students' global competence in the 21st century as well as pay high attention to the development of students' emotions, attitudes, values and core competence. By doing a good job of these two aspects, we can achieve the goal of shifting the focus of teaching in English class of senior high schools and sublimating the teaching objectives.

References

1. Comenius: Great Didactic. Educational Science Press, Beijing (2014)
2. China Student Development Core competence Research Group: Chinese students develop core competence. J. Chin. Soc. Educ. **10**(10), 1–3 (2016)
3. Formulated by Ministry of Education of the People's Republic of China: Full-Time Compulsory Education of Ordinary High School: English Course Standards. Beijing Normal University Press, Beijing (2001)
4. Ministry of Education of the People's Republic of China formulated: Full-Time Compulsory Education of Ordinary High School English: Curriculum Standards (2017 edition). People's education Press, Beijing (2018)
5. People's Education Press - Institute curriculum materials: Experimental Textbook of Curriculum Standards for Senior High School. People's Education Press, Beijing (2007)
6. Sato, M.: The Quiet Revolution - The Classroom Changes, the School Will Change. Educational Science Press, Beijing (2014)
7. The General Office of the CCCPC, The General Office of the State Council: Views on Implementing the Inheritance and Development Project of Chinese Excellent Traditional Culture. Beijing Normal University Press, Beijing (2017)

Toward a Virtual Vocational Guidance Model

Gustavo Santana[1(✉)], Karina Mendoza[2], Michellc Zambrano[2], Carlos Chancay[2], and Jaime Meza[2]

[1] Universidad de La Habana, Havana, Cuba
gusansar@hotmail.com
[2] Universidad Técnica de Manabí (UTM), Portoviejo 130105, Ecuador
luzdelia_7@hotmail.com,
{mdzambrano, cchancay}@utm.edu.ec,
jaimemezal@gmail.com

Abstract. Selecting the best profession from the antic until today have been looking for new ways in order to improve the methods for advising to the people interesting in continuing their formation in higher education. Several efforts have been develop from the education field, and now with Information and Communication Technologies (ICT) tools support. However, nowadays-integral solutions in order to correct this issue are scare explored. This paper presents the advance in the research in order to create a Virtual vocational guidance model that allows advising in real time to people interesting in get a professional degree. Action research design approach has been applied in order to get interactive information from higher education applicant and improve prototype and model by each interaction. Early outcomes have shown increase the number of student that access to higher education. Outcomes allow us show a list of recommendation in order to find ways for applied ICT tools as support for effectiveness vocational guidance.

Keywords: Virtual education · Vocational systems · Higher education

1 Introduction

The scientific-technical development, the everyday advances in the working market, as well as the Information and Communication Technologies (ICT) impact of in the different spheres of life, require an adequate professional training of citizens able to assume the changes imposed by the socio-historical moment in which they live and respond to the challenges that the accelerated socio-political and economic transformations generate.

The educational institutions must have educational strategies that allow the student the responsibility of becoming aware or decisions that are not acquired with temporary solutions or casual practices. The adequate incorporation of ICTs in education does not reside so much in the technology itself but in the human being that guides it [1].

[2] attributes to L.S. Vygotsky "… the choice of profession is not simply the choice of one or another professional activity, but that is a determined path of life, the search for a specific place in the social process of production. In this area, the role played by Vocational Guidance (VG) in the choice of a career acquires great significance in response to what society requires.

G. Sun et al. (Eds.): eLEOT 2019, LNICST 299, pp. 244–252, 2019.
https://doi.org/10.1007/978-3-030-35095-6_28

Ecuador is currently in search of quality assurance of professionals who graduate from Higher Education Institutions (HEI), with solid foundations in their training and above all based on a true vocation in their profession, which is evidence in their regulations that have been created since 2012, however despite the efforts made by the authorities of higher education, there have been contrary effects to those expected with these institutions, so according to Technical University of Manabí, a decrease of 15% of the net enrollment in relation to the historical (50%) has been generated. Some factors identified with this decrease are related to the economic and material factors that vocational guidance processes require. In this sense, multiples [3, 4], agree that the use of Information and Communication Technologies (ICT) allow a range of resources and possibilities for the achievement of new communicative realities and educational, playing an important role in our society and in the world of Professional Vocational Guidance.

The evidenced conditions ratify the opportunity that ICT offer in the solution of those problems, therefore, this research explores the effectiveness of the use of a Virtual Vocational Guidance System for young people who aspire to enter the careers developed by the UTM-Ecuador.

This article first examines the state of the art and the socio-pedagogical conditions that support the analysis of VG, and the integration of Information and Communication Technologies (ICT), then the process of designing the Virtual Vocational Guidance model is presented, where the methodological requirements for its implementation are described; and finishing, some previous results that allow to establish a list of recommendations to be considered by higher education institutions in Ecuador in order to improve the vocational guidance process for applicants to Higher Education.

The remainder of this document is structured as follows. Section 2 explains the theoretical background. Section 3 describes the methodological approach based on action research approach. Section 4 shows the prototype design and preliminary outcomes obtained with its delivering. Finally, Sect. 5 details conclusions and proposes future work.

2 Theoretical Background

2.1 Vocational Guidance, ICT and Virtual Environments

The Vocational Orientation began in 1908 in Boston, United States, in its origins had great acceptance by its beneficiaries as it directly contributed to the generation of a motivated workforce.

Fitch J., cited in Maura [5] defined Vocational Guidance as: "The individual assistance process for the selection of an occupation, preparation for it, initiation and development in it."; at the same time economic theories emerged, which, contrary to random positions, see the subjects outside of what they aspire for themselves. The occupational definition is determined by the rise that occupations acquire in society.

The person chooses his occupation only in dependence on his economic and power advantages. According to [11], this is a cause of demotivation because the individual is not aware of the profile of his occupation. In this sense, the Vocational Guidance was determined as a process of help for the choice and professional development, but this value was limited to the moment of the choice of a profession. In addition to these orientations many other authors have configured similar concepts. The currents analyzed by the authors at the level of the world and of Latin America today have evolved towards the use of ICTs as a way to improve the efficiency of Vocational Guidance processes.

Moodle is one of the tools of Virtual Learning Environments (VLE) with greater acceptance in the world. VLE s are considered to be characterized by expanding access to education, promoting collaborative learning and group work, promoting active learning, creating learning communities because they are focus on student and make fulfilled the function of the teaching-learning process more fluency. Therefore, any proposal that uses virtual learning environments must take into account the characteristics and demands of technological platforms [6], where the student can already learn "on their own" in these, to acquire the knowledge and the respective skills, committed to a greater responsibility in the learning outcome, what energizes the VLE as a solution for the improvement of the Vocational Guidance processes, since the way in which they are created and used depends of the role that universities, organizations, families and the socio-cultural environment assign to technology in education, so that they can be considered as communities of human interrelations, artifacts, or technological systems that hold their stakeholders together for the objective that arises the virtual environment.

2.2 Philosophical, Sociological and Psychopedagogical Foundations of Professional Vocational Guidance in Virtual Environments

The Vocational Guidance (VG) is analyzed from understanding the complexity of the nature of human motivation, and its regulatory function in the decision-making process in relation to a profession has been studied from functionalist, psychoanalytic and humanist conceptions, since this is based on the recognition of the dialectical unity between the subjective, active nature of the psyche and its historical-social determination, which conditions any assumed position. In this context, it is worth what was mentioned by [7], who maintains that the principle that man is formed for life, starts from recognizing all the formative actions from school to the social coexistence that they have in the preparation for a profession.

Several authors agree on the process of reflection of vocational counselors, before this several questions arise in the guiding process: (a) the educational purposes; (b) the objectives to be achieved; (c) the selected contents; (d) methodological strategies; (e) the social relations between the actors of the guidance process; and (f) the evaluation criteria of the learning with the intervention. In order to cover these questions, VG programs must contribute to the development of the student's natural potential, in a climate of cooperation, acceptance, cordiality and empathy [8].

The VG over time has been influenced by philosophical, sociological, psychopedagogical and technological foundations, towards an effective vocational guidance, which contributes to the design of a system that integrates the school-family-community relationship from virtual environments; This VG must guarantee the security to the subjects that aspire to enter the University and their permanence in the university work.

2.3 University Direction Towards a Virtual Professional Vocational Guidance Model

Over the years, trends in Vocational Guidance (VG) have focused on individual interventions with a reactive and therapeutic nature, focused on the resolution of specific problems and taking little interest of the context, however at present the approach to Vocational Guidance has been changed and is conceived as a permanent process that takes place throughout life, from the social point of view, economic and social goals are drawn up with the aim of labor, and the educational institution from the educational point of view, it is set goals of retention of their students in the educational system and more comprehensive training of young people. In this sense, [9] refers to four principles to be taken into account.

- Principle of Prevention: VG has a proactive character, that is, it must anticipate and anticipate the problems.
- Principle of development: VG must be a continuous process aimed at the integral development of the person accompanying him throughout his life to reach his maximum potential.
- Principle of social intervention: also called ecological, refers to how the context of the subject should address the guiding action. According to this principle, all guiding interventions must consider the environmental and contextual conditions of the person, as they influence their decision making and personal development.
- Principle of personal empowerment: the guiding action should be aimed at modifying the structures and systems that impede the development of the less favored in their context of both economic and cognitive relationships.

These postulates undoubtedly affect the process of developing a VG. It should be noted that the practice of the VG in Ecuador is a great challenge, since Ecuador is a scenario of cultural diversity, with heterogeneous characteristics of the actors in different cultural contexts; therefore, the effective VG must be sectorized based on the context of complexity, recognizing that it is not pertinent to apply standardized and unified solutions, but to generate an approach that respects and recognizes individual differences such as, for example, cultural heritage and traditional professions within families that are transmitted over several generations in certain regions of the Coast, Sierra and Amazonia and that give young people a sense of identity and continuity.

Among the Professional Vocational Guidance models that develop basic skills for vocational or professional training in a context of high cultural diversity such as Ecuador, it is necessary to work on the following aspects:

- Deep self-knowledge of the individual and cultural identity (Who am I?)
- Be aware of other cultures (Who are the others?)
- The needed skills to build a career in a context of cultural diversity (Benett 1993) (What competencies are necessary?)
- Be aware of social demands in the current context and the real possibilities of personal fulfillment. (What is needed and how is achieved?)

The cultural aspects and the emergence of ICT through the VLE, ratify the challenge and changes of approach that should be applied in the VG processes that allow to generate the permanence of the students in the university cycle and cover the demands that the market labor requires.

Virtual Vocational Guidance is a process of helping the individual mediated by virtual environments in which the student is inclined to learn to know himself, the work market and the educational possibilities in the educational institution, with which he identifies his aptitudes, competences, motivations and interests for its determination by a profession for life, through the advice and approach to the process of search and analysis of information about the educational and work offer in the inclusive environment that allows to make the decision on a responsible future and with total autonomy to start and continue a life project and professional development from the personal and sociocultural insertion context.

The integration of the models exposed in this section ratifies the opportunity of a Virtual Vocational Guidance model that affects decision-making for the responsible self-determination of the subjects, of their professional career as an expression of the interaction and integration of the socio-cultural, educational, psychopedagogical, guidelines, training and technological (Fig. 1). The elements presented in Fig. 1, are the theoretical components that motivate the design of the Virtual Vocational Guidance model in virtual environments that is detailed in section III (System Design).

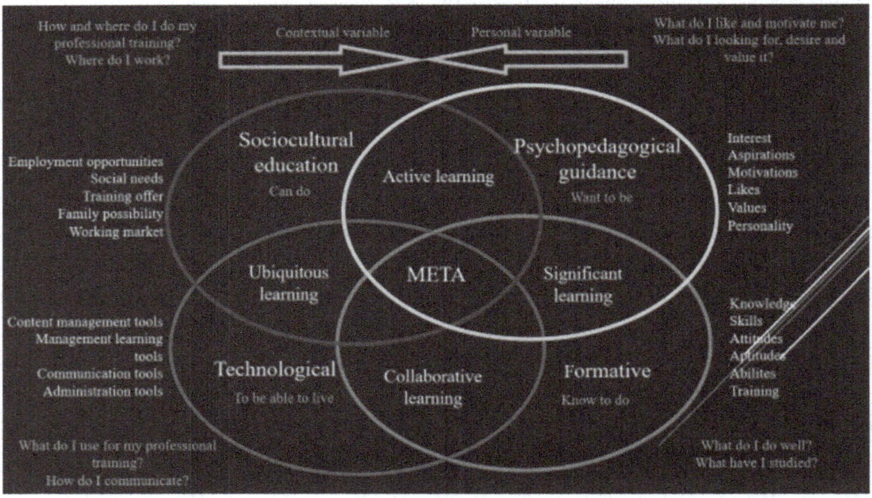

Fig. 1. Factors that influence the decision making of the subjects in their professional career. Source: Authors

3 Methodology

This section explains the methodological approach of the research carried out and presents the Virtual Vocational Guidance System at Technical University of Manabí, consisting of a set of premises, principles that support the characteristics of the system, its structure organized by levels, dimensions stages and actions for the design.

The applied research approach is action-research, this approach is the core of information systems. The applied approach conceptualizes the research process as if it contained inseparable and inherently intertwined activities to construct the IT artifact, put it into practice in the institution and evaluate it simultaneously [10].

4 Virtual Guidance Model Virtual Prototype and Outcomes

The prototype presented to date has undergone two iterations since August 2016. It implements the components presented in Fig. 1, in several sections that allowed application of the theoretical underpinnings in the technological solution, the sections in mention are summarized in the following paragraph.

4.1 Prototype Design

Section # 1 - Home Page. Shows a welcome message and the components and tools that the system has, as well as the "Alma Mater" location, taking advantage of the Google Maps resource.

Section # 2 - About Us. On this page the student can visualize and attest to the work done by the vocational counselors through photographs of past training sessions, in the same way he can know in greater detail about the objective or the reason to be of this area.

Section # 3 - Leveling.

3.1. Areas
In this sub-section are the academic areas available at the Technical University of Manabi, the student, by selecting an area, can access to more detailed information and thus know in a better way the specialty or major he wishes to study.

3.2. Series: My Route
In this sub-section the student will find countless videos, which include a route on vocational guidance, which will help him to develop strengths and generate vocational guidance projects.

3.3. Be a Bachelor
In this sub section the student will find resources that will help him to take the exam of "Being a Bachelor"; the available tools are the following:

- Simulator
- Instructions
- Android application

Section # 4 - Counseling

4.1. Guidance
In this sub-section the student can review the professional profiles of the vocational counselors of the Technical University of Manabí, in the same way he will know in greater detail about the work experience, the degrees he has and different courses that guarantee the quality of teaching of each counselor.

4.2. Vocational Choice
In this sub-section the student will be able to access information that will allow him to make strategic decisions and choose the career he is looking for, here he will have the opportunity to follow the proposed conceptual process for an adequate VG.

- Self-knowledge
- Knowledge of the environment
- Decision making
- Vocational Project

4.3. Vocational Guidance Test
In this sub section the student will have the opportunity to perform a variety of tests that will evaluate his skills and qualities; the tests he will find are the following:

- Emotional Intelligence Skills Test
- Self-esteem Test
- Interests and Aptitudes Test
- Integrator Test

Section # 5 - Contact Us
On this page the student can have a real time communication with the vocational counselors, in such a way, it will be able to clear up his doubts and clarify any type of concern.

Section # 6 - Virtual Classroom
This section leads to a link to the UTM platform where it is intended to replicate and give the guidelines proposed by the National Secretariat of Higher Education, regarding the processes of admission to universities, their academic proposals and to be able to reach to the awareness that the student can choose his career responsibly and comfortable with it.

You can visualize the schedule with dates, in relation to the process of admission to higher education institutions in Ecuador; it will serve in the guide so that the students postulate to a quota responsibly and can continue their university studies.

4.2 Prototype Testing

The first applied artifact was made based on a template according to the structure of the website of the Technical University of Manabí. In this first iteration, 300 users, both students and interested people accessed it and followed all the phases of the model implemented in the templates. At the end of the process of use, users were invited to fill out a questionnaire to evaluate the platform, both related to conceptual design and navigability. The results of this piloting allowed to show an average level of acceptance and several suggestions that allowed to enrich the system and adjust the applied instruments.

The second iteration, the staff of the technology department of the UTM agreed to implement the system in the web portal of the university leaving behind access until the end of the design. To test this second prototype, random invitations were made to 1000 users, of which 45% responded to the invitation. It should be noted the multiplier effect that this type of initiatives has had in the UTM, where in the current semester there are 3,600 face-to-face students and 3,200 virtual students who have requested access to a leveling course, these indicators show that the number of beneficiaries has doubled this year.

5 Conclusions

The results presented in this article are preliminary, since they are part of a research in progress, however, the model and the results obtained show a positive effect reflected in the number of aspirants to university leveling.

Several reflections emerge from the theoretical study of Vocational Guidance (VG), we believe that these reflections should be the starting point for Higher Education institutions in Ecuador to expand the VG in Virtual Learning Environments (VLE).

- The VG is a continuous process of helping the subject to develop his cognitive and motivational potentials that allow him to consciously choose a profession and commit to the quality of his training during the study of it, where all the educational agents participate in the orientation actions (teachers, school psychologists, pedagogues, parents, representatives of the community).
- The VG is done not with the isolated individual (attended in an office) but with the individual belonging to a group (school, institutional, community), through a preventive and non-therapeutic process that ceases to be a process of help to the student who spontaneously requests it because it manifests a conflictive situation regarding the professional choice, to become a prevention process in which one works for the development of the potentialities of the student with the objective of preparing them for the realization of a responsible professional choice.
- The student must be considered an active entity in the VG to the extent that he participates in making professional decisions based on a complex process of reflection and reconstruction of his personal possibilities and the possibilities offered by the medium in which develops for the study of one or another profession.
- The VG is a complex process of training and systematic development of the subject's motivation for a profession, where the reasons and the need must coincide.
- The VG with the ICT, has to be conceived on the basis of a scientific foundation that contributes to the design of new learning spaces, these ones could be used for the development of new learning based on the occupation to be chosen by the subjects.

In future researches we are working on measure the impact of VG in the number of graduates students.

Acknowledgments. The authors wish to thank the Technical University of Manabí for the support and access to the experimental spaces that have enabled the scientific motivations to be put into practice.

References

1. Alvárez Quiroz, G.B.: Percepciones de los docentes rurales con respecto a las tecnologías de la información y comunicación en sus prácticas pedagógicas (Master's thesis) (2016)
2. Rodríguez, R.: El efecto de la orientación vocacional en la elección de carrera. Recuperado de (2016). http://pepsic.bvsalud.org/scielo.php?script=sci_arttext&pid=S1665-7527200800-0100004
3. Cabero, J.: Impacto de las nuevas tecnologías de la información y la comunicación en las organizaciones educativas. En Lorenzo, M., et al. (eds.) Enfoques en la organización y dirección de instituciones educativas formales y no formales, pp. 197–206. Grupo Editorial Universitario, Granada (1998)
4. Lorenzo, M., et al.: enfoques en la organizacion y direccion de instituciones educa. Granada: grupo editorial Universitario(1998)
5. Maura, V.G.: La Orientación Profesional desde la perspectiva histórico-cultural del desarrollo humano. Revista Cubana de Psicología **20**(3), 260–268 (2003). http://pepsic.bvsalud.org/pdf/rcp/v20n3/12.pdf
6. Vidal, W.L., Ledo, C., Pardo, M.E.: Papel o rol de los profesores en el Entorno Virtual de Enseñanza Aprendizaje (EVEA). Revista Pedagógica Maestro y Sociedad **12**(4), 92–100 (2015)
7. Alvarez de Sayas, C.M.: La Escuela en la vida, p. 487. ALSIE Consultores Pedagógicos S.R.L. Décima Edición, Pág (2016)
8. Calonge Cole, S.: Fundamentos contextuales de la orientación educativa. INVESTIGACIÓN Y POSTGRADO **19**(1), 145–170 (2004). Recuperado de http://revistas.upel.edu.ve/index.php/revinpost/article/view/1466/613
9. Navarro, L.: Análisis de las páginas WEB de orientación vocacional de las comunidades autónomas y su relación con la acreditación de las competencias profesionales (Tesis de maestría). Universidad de Valladolid (2014). Recuperado de https://uvadoc.uva.es/bitstream/10324/4504/1/TFM-G277.pdf
10. Sein, M.K., Henfridsson, O., Purao, S., Rossi, M., Lindgren, R.: Action design research. MIS Q. (35: 1), 37–56 (2011)
11. Clark, H.F.: The influence of economic forces upon education. Teachers College Rec. **32**(4) (1931)

Teaching Practice Exploration of Economic Mathematics Course of Economic Management Major Under the Background of "New Engineering"

Fengxia Li[1(✉)] and Zeguang Lu[2]

[1] Department of Information Engineering, Heilongjiang International University, Harbin 150025, China
lifengxiavip@126.com
[2] National Academy of Guo Ding Institute of Data Sciences, Beijing 100190, China

Abstract. This paper mainly starts from the following four points to explore the solutions to some problems in the teaching process of economic mathematics 2, which is, from updating the teaching concept, integrating the teaching content to hierarchical teaching method, and adopting the project-driven mode and Massive Open Online Course teaching mode.

Keywords: Integrating the teaching content · Project-driven · Hierarchical teaching

1 Introduction

Economic mathematics is a compulsory course for the student management major; all the majors would enroll both liberal arts students and science students. Students, based on their applications, were divided into different classes [1, 2]. As the students came from different places, there are large differences between their admission scores [3]. Students with good math scores and bad math scores are intermingled, which bring about test to economic mathematics course of teaching content, as well as teaching method and so on. How to handle the relationship between the teaching task and teaching effect becomes the core problem of the practicing of teaching [4, 5]. This paper mainly starts from the following four points to explore the solutions to some problems in the teaching process of economic mathematics 2, which is, from updating the teaching concept, integrating the teaching content to hierarchical teaching method, and adopting the project-driven mode and Massive Open Online Course teaching mode.

2 Renew the Teaching Philosophy

2.1 Design Typical Cases Based on Major Features

The description of the cases should take into account the major characteristics of students, aiming to guide students to understand the relationship between economic

G. Sun et al. (Eds.): eLEOT 2019, LNICST 299, pp. 253–259, 2019.
https://doi.org/10.1007/978-3-030-35095-6_29

mathematics course and subsequent courses, and cultivate students' ability to observe, analyze and solve problems from the perspective of mathematics. For example, when explaining determinants, the value of the second-order determinant represents the area of the parallelogram in the two-dimensional space constructed by two column vectors, and the value of the third-order determinant represents the volume product of the parallelepiped in the three-dimensional space constructed by three column vectors [6].

In the explanation of a matrix, the case of gray scale image can be taken into as an example, which by itself, is a matrix, and every element in the matrix is a data between 0 and 255; Or, the computer screen could also be taken as an example, the three basic colors of the computer screen, red, green and blue, are composed of three 1024 * 768 (or 1024 * 1024, etc.) matrix.

In the explanation of the system of linear equations, begin with mathematical modeling instance, and then, followed with the concept of general linear equations, introduces the general system of linear equations solution (gauss elimination method, the augmented matrix method), give a judgment theorem of solutions of linear equations, the theory of the structure of a solution, and finally, aiming at the students doubt of how to solve the question of multiple equation, to properly introduce Seidel iteration method suitable for computer operation, Jacobi iteration method and the approximate numerical calculation method.

2.2 Pay Attention to the Introduction of the Application of Knowledge

In the linear algebra part of Economic mathematics 2, a great deal of concepts are involved, and many of them are abstract concepts, making it necessary to introduce the theoretical knowledge, properly cited the linear algebra associated mathematician historical background, interesting story, the main contribution and present situation of the development of the theory, for example, kramer, Laplace, Gloria, Tianjin horse racing, the game theory, etc., to help students, in a relaxed environment, in the meantime of understanding the context of knowledge and understanding the concept, broaden the students' knowledge, improve the math attainments.

2.3 Add a Practice Link to the Theory

In economic mathematics 2, the most time consuming and energy consuming parts are the complex calculation of higher-order determinant, higher-order matrix operation, and the solving of a linear equation group. The combination of modern technology and mathematical software in the teaching process, the additional link of the practice to theories could, on one hand, lay a good foundation for students to apply the software in engineering, information and other fields for calculation and simulation in the future, and on the other hand, make the students feel useful in learning, strengthen students' application consciousness, cultivate students' practical ability, deepen students' grasp and understanding of knowledge, and enhance students' interest in learning.

3 The Integration of the Teaching Content

Most of the compilation of mathematics textbooks tends to focus on the integrity of the theory itself, and the order of knowledge cohesion and other factors. Therefore, I suggest adding an introduction class before and an extension class after explaining the theoretical content. For example, in the first class at the beginning of the term, the teacher reintegrate the teaching materials and told the students what the course contains, its main contents, core methods and applications, so that the students get a fully understand to the course from a macro perspective and the once scattered teaching materials are integrated.

3.1 Add of the Introduction Section

In the introduction section of the Economic mathematics 2, several problems are supposed to be solved: what to tell, in what way to tell, and how to tell. (1) Clearly define the main content and core methods of the course, in the meanwhile, highlight the practical problems that linear algebra is going to solve. It is a must that the examples selected are closely related to the majors of students. For example, students majoring in economics and management can cite the benefit matrix and input-output model in the assignment problem of production and management. (2) The teaching method is demonstrated by multimedia courseware, accurately calculated by EXCEL and MATLAB software, and online learning by Blackboard online teaching platform. (3) In the course of explanation, typical examples are explained in simple terms, and after the point is given, let the students complete it, like cast away a brick in order to get a gem, setting up suspense, paving the way for the follow-up course content, so as to stimulate students' interest in learning.

3.2 Add the Extension Course

Before the end of the course, it becomes necessary to give the expanded course, which is supposed to give some guidance to students in depth and breadth of the course, and to arise some representative practical issues related to the linear algebra course.

The introduction course, in a macro perspective, has given to the course some of the "preview" of the content and methods. The expanded course is the corresponding to the introduction course in its content; also it is the extension and continuation to the course content.

Course teaching inevitably involves teaching content, teaching mode and other issues, in the fourth part of this paper, the teaching mode will be explained, and the following is only a simple statement of the teaching content.

3.3 Integrate the Teaching Contents and Optimize the Curriculum System

The Combination of Required Knowledge Points and Optional Knowledge Points. In teaching, it is necessary to grasp the internal relationship between knowledge points, combine the requirements of obligatory knowledge points and the requirements of optional knowledge points, to optimize the course system, to grasp the core issues, and to refine and select the teaching content. The obligatory knowledge points are determinant calculation, matrix and its operation, elementary transformation of matrix and how to solve general linear equations. The optional knowledge points are cramer's rule, structure of solution of linear equations, similar matrix and quadratic form, linear space and linear transformation.

The Combination of Detailed and Roughed. While arranging the teaching content, those detailed should be combined with the roughed, and those primary content be clearly separated with the secondary content. For example, in solving the inverse matrix, the emphasis is on teaching of the primary line transformation method and the companion matrix method should be taken as a secondary method, students only need to master the composition of the companion matrix and its important equation. In finding the rank of matrix, the primary line transformation method is what should be taught mainly, rather than the method of highest order non-zero sub expression given by the definition. Matrix block method focuses on higher-order matrix multiplication, block diagonal matrix, and matrix addition, multiplication, transpose and other operations only considered as to be understood.

Change the Sequence if it is Proper. If it is proper, try to integrate linear algebra teaching content, change the order according to the order of the matrix, matrix elementary transformation, and linear equations, determinant. For example, taking matrix theory as the main line, the calculation of second-order and third-order determinants is interspersed into inverse matrix theory, and matrix equations, linear equations and linear relations of vector groups are solved mainly by using the primary transformation method of matrices.

4 The Adoption of the Leveled Teaching Method

In the teaching process, each teaching class is composed of two administrative classes with a total number of 52–72 students. The students' math scores are different, some are low, and some are high, uneven and different. Compared with students' mathematical foundations, the teaching objectives set by the syllabus are fixed. Taking this into considered in the process of teaching, the teacher could of course use the flexible and varied teaching methods, teaching design, teaching content set in the introduction, examples and exercises, problem sets, however, the breadth of content should not be too great, and as to the depth, in consideration of the level of most of the students, the only thing to do is to keep it at low and medium level, and even by doing so, for a bottom student, the content would sounds just like language from another galaxy. On the other hand, for students with good foundation and high qualification, it is not enough for their mind to absorb, like a person not having enough to eat and always in starving; this is, in all the majors of our school of economic management, a very popular phenomena.

The college mathematics course for students majoring in economics and management has a total class time of 96 class hours, which is divided into two semesters. When the number of class hours remains the same and the teaching scope remains the same, multi-level teaching can be implemented for students with large numbers and the same major. For example, there are about 500 students in the department of economics and management of the class of 2018, and 180 students in 6 classes of financial management, which is a large number. At the same time, due to different major mathematics curriculum should be separated on the class, the leveled teaching for financial management specialty is possible, formulated professional university mathematics teaching outline, teaching outline should include other similar professional knowledge teaching outline, the depth and breadth should be distinguished on the consideration of the basis of various levels of students, added with the university mathematics course and the subsequent financial management majored course system. Then revise the corresponding teaching calendar, teaching process design, assessment method, effectiveness analysis and other links involved in the teaching process, so that each link serves each other and complement each other. It is shown in Table 1.

Table 1. The proportion stratification

Before stratification	Grade of achievement	90–100	80–89	70–79	60–69	<60
	Number of people	56	63	39	52	31
	The proportion	23.24%	26.14%	16.18%	21.58%	12.86%
After leveling	Grade of achievement	90–100	80–89	70–79	60–69	<60
	Number of people	60	69	47	42	23
	The proportion	24.90%	28.63%	19.50%	17.43%	9.54%

5 Adopt the Project-Driven and Massive Open Online Course Combined Teaching Mode

5.1 Project-Driven Teaching Mode

Using the characteristics of economic mathematics 2 teaching content and knowledge being progressed layer by layer and being linked to each other, a problem could be raised to influence a class and produce a special lecture, combined with a practical case, the teaching content could be consolidated and small problems in real life could be solved.

For example, the contents of linear equations group are closely related to the primary and high school binary equations group. From the concept of equations to the writing method, from the elimination method of binary equations group to the elimination method of linear equations group, although there are differences and the applicable range is quite different, the ideas and methods are the same.

5.2 The Teaching Model of Massive Open Online Course Collaborated

MOOCs are a challenge to higher education today. With the continuous update of MOOC resources, students are expecting the change of traditional teaching mode, so it is imperative to reform the teaching mode of linear algebra course into MOOC collaborated.

Traditional Classroom and Learning Based on Massive Open Online Course. In a traditional classroom, the whole teaching progress and transfer of knowledge are controlled by teachers through face-to-face explanation to complete the teaching tasks and objectives. MOOC teaching provides rich digital teaching resources and flexible teaching space, which is conducive to students' independent inquiry oriented learning, thus cultivating their self-control ability and exploration and innovation ability. Traditional classroom teaching and MOOC teaching have their own advantages and disadvantages, while the mixed teaching mode combining offline and online under the highly developed information resource environment combines the two and achieves complementary advantages.

Three Steps of a Class, Before, on and After. But for financial management major, other majors, because of the small number of students and the major itself being scattered, are difficult to implement leveled teaching, so, other teaching methods can be adopted. For example, for students with a general foundation, they can arrange the preview content before class, give key guidance in class, consolidate and review after class. For students who have a good foundation and are able to learn, the combination of pre-class online MOOC learning, in-class key guidance and after-class tutoring and Q&A is adopted. The following is a brief statement on the details of the teaching design in the three links before, on and after class.

Before class, students are required to prepare for the class by logging on their mobile phones, and teachers are supposed to make good teaching design in advance, and upload MOOC courses, learning guiding courses to software. Before class, students in preview, should be equipped with necessary learning guiding courses, and the learning guiding courses should give enough priority to the introduction of detailed stuff and covering all knowledge points, also it should include basic exercises together with all the answers, as it is designed to be a class preview, and to help students to complete their autonomous learning, and eventually, to guide students to watch the video with the problem. Students, if encountered with problems in their learning process, could always communicate with teachers at any time via the platform. Therefore, teachers could collect and sort out the difficult problems of students before class, as the focus of detailed classroom teaching.

In the guidance class, teachers explain the general problems and key contents of students, so that students can deepen their understanding of the knowledge in this section.

After class answering questions section is the stage for students to expand their knowledge. Combined with the guidance in class and discussion in study, the teacher gives students online assignments, which can be submitted by students online. For the application of knowledge points, teachers propose research directions for students, and provide learning resources, so that students continue to deepen learning and expand knowledge. Teachers can also guide students to conduct mathematical modeling training and apply mathematical knowledge to solve practical problems. Offline learning provides students with a broader horizon.

5.3 Reasonable Application of Rain Classroom Software

Due to the uneven foundation of students' mathematics, and the substantial reduction of college mathematics class, many contents in the class cannot be fully explained. Reasonable use of rain classroom software can achieve effective and fast management of students, such as the quick collection of pre-class preview results before class, detailed explanation of students' common problems in class, and answering questions and doubts after class, so that many problems encountered by students in daily study can be solved in time. Teachers can upload courseware, exercises and thinking questions corresponding to the content of class to the rain classroom, and students can review and consolidate independently, which makes up for the lack of class hours and the problems of different learning levels. The use of rain classroom can realize the sharing of problems and methods, enabling students to put forward problems encountered in the learning process, both teachers and students can provide solutions, which are conducive to strengthening the communication between teachers and students, students and students, and stimulate students' enthusiasm for learning.

Under New Engineering background, the university mathematics teaching should not only focus on 90 min of class, what should be done is that, it should further care students about how to learn after class, how to do, and what difficulties they have. Only by always thinking about what the students are requiring and thinking, could the teachers find out the most urgent question the students are running into, fundamentally solve all the various upcoming new problems in teaching, and finally, improve the learning efficiency and make the learning effective.

Acknowledgement. This work was supported in part by school projects of Heilongjiang International University of YN2017-11 and by National Education Innovation Science Research Planning Project (CMAS180506).

References

1. Nie, C.: Preliminary study on the reform of higher mathematics stratification teaching in higher engineering colleges under the construction of "New Engineering". J. Hunan Inst. Eng. (2018)
2. Zhang, X.: The application of hybrid teaching based on online learning in higher mathematics. J. Shandong Inst. Commer. Technol. (2018)
3. Xiang, M.: Research on the reconstruction reform of the public applied higher mathematics curriculum system in local applied high-level universities. Gao Shili Sci. J. **15**, 12–18 (2019)
4. Zhou, W.: Research on higher mathematics teaching reform under the background of "Internet". J. Shandong Inst. Commer. Technol. (2018)
5. Yang, H.: An analysis of the reform of higher mathematics teaching in independent colleges. Modern Commun. **23**, 45–50 (2018)
6. Cao, H.: Based on the teaching of "Advanced Mathematics" under the background of "New Engineering". J. Qingdao Univ. Sci. Technol. (Nat. Sci. Ed.) **8**, 89–93 (2018)

An Empirical Research on English Learning Strategies of Li Nationality College Students

Dan Ren(✉), Wei Wang, and Yuan Yao

Sanya Aviation and Tourism College, Sanya 572000, Hainan, China
340459345@qq.com, dick_1980@126.com,
graceyao1021@163.com

Abstract. English learning strategy is one of the decisive factors for learners' English achievements. In order to know Li nationality college students' present condition of using English learning strategies, a questionnaire survey has been conducted from three perspectives including metacognitive strategy, cognitive strategy, affective/social strategy. On the basis of an empirical research upon the results through SPSS, it has come to the conclusion: the level of affective/social strategy of Li nationality college students is a little bit higher than that of their cognitive strategy and metacognitive strategy; cognitive strategy has a significant positive influence on both affective/social strategy and metacognitive strategy, and affective/social strategy has a significant positive influence on metacognitive strategy. Meanwhile, affective/social strategy plays as a partial intermediation between cognitive strategy and metacognitive strategy.

Keywords: English learning strategy · Li nationality college students · Empirical research

1 Introduction

Learning strategies is a term referring to the processes, rules, actions, skills and control methods that are consciously deployed by learners to help them to learn effectively [1, 2]. It can either be implicit rules, or explicit operation program or steps. Learners can obtain and accumulate learning strategies through practice in English learning. At present, Oxford's study on English learning strategies has the greatest influence. In his study, language learning strategies are classified as two types: direct strategies and indirect strategies, and the former include memory strategy, cognitive strategy, metacognitive strategy and compensation strategy, while the latter mainly include affective strategy and social strategy [3, 4]. Most of the researchers think that English learners' achievement is closely related to the efficiency and frequency of using learning strategies [5–9].

Li nationality is not only the indigenous people but also the minority with the largest population in Hainan island. Its special culture is a crucial resource for Chinese cultural tourism, attracting numerous tourists from home and abroad every year. In order to popularize Li culture and promote the development and protection of Li cultural tourism, a group of talents who are quite familiar with the Li culture and can use Li language, Chinese and English proficiently are badly in need. Then, Li nationality college

G. Sun et al. (Eds.): eLEOT 2019, LNICST 299, pp. 260–269, 2019.
https://doi.org/10.1007/978-3-030-35095-6_30

students exactly become the "pyramid" for the reserve of talents who can meet the needs above [10].

In China, the study on English learning strategies is marked with a late start. Most of the current studies focus on the whole group of college students, with almost none being conducted for Li nationality students on an ad hoc basis. Meanwhile, most of them are subjective analyses or description statistics based on frequency or percentage statistics [11], and uncertainty still remains in their conclusions. In this research, a questionnaire based on both direct and indirect English learning strategies is conducted on Li nationality students, and after a strict statistic analysis of the results, it aims to summarize the features of Li nationality college students on using English learning strategies, thus to provide some advice for them to use these strategies effectively.

2 Research Methods and Process

2.1 Research Participants, Methods and Contents

Based on English learning strategies, a sampling questionnaire survey is conducted on Li nationality college students in Sanya. The questionnaire is delivered to students through the platform of wenjuan.com, and SPSS is used to analyze the results. 144 questionnaires have been gathered, with 143 valid.

In the 143 participants, there are 76 females, accounting for 53.1%. 77 participants are freshmen and 49 participants are sophomores, accounting for 88.1% in total. Through the frequency analysis of demographic variables, the result is shown in Table 1.

Table 1. Frequency Statistics (N = 143)

Variables	Attribute	Frequency	Percentage (%)
Gender	male	67	46.9
	female	76	53.1
Grade	freshman	49	34.3
	sophomore	77	53.8
	junior	16	11.2
	senior	1	0.7

The learning strategies mentioned in the questionnaire mainly include memory strategy, cognitive strategy, metacognitive strategy, affective strategy, social strategy and compensation strategy. The questionnaire adopts Likert Scale, and the format of each item is as follows: "strongly agree", "agree", "neither agree nor disagree", "disagree", "strongly disagree", with each option respectively scoring 5 points, 4 points, 3 points, 2 points, 1 point, with 3-point the critical value. High score represents high level and consciousness of using strategies, and vice verse.

2.2 Empirical Analysis Procedure

Validity Test
In order to test the questionnaire structure, factor analysis is conducted on 47 items. Before factor analysis, it is necessary to check whether the KMO value is greater than 0.7, thus to check whether Bartlett's test reaches significant or not. As it is shown in Table 2, KMO value is 0.935, greater than 0.7, while the value of Bartlett's test is 6778.558, and its significance level is lower than 0.001, suggesting that this sample is fit for factor analysis.

Table 2. Check list of KMO and Bartlett in the first factor analysis

KMO		0.935
Bartlett's test	Approximate chi-square	6778.558
	df	1081
	Sig.	0.000

By using PCA(Principal Component Analysis), factor analysis is conducted on the 47 items, and the analysis result is listed in a table, including extractive factors, factor loading, accumulated variance contribution rate, etc.

Table 3. Contribution rate of each factor in the first factor analysis

Factor	Characteristic root	Accumulated contribution rate (%)
1	6.244	13.285
2	5.873	25.78
3	5.13	36.695
4	4.541	46.356
5	4.443	55.809
6	4.378	65.124
7	3.978	73.589

As shown in Table 3, when extracting 7 factors whose characteristic roots are greater than 1, the accumulated variance contribution rate reaches 73.589%. The Rotated component matrix is shown in Table 4. The maximum factor loading value for Item 15, 20, 23, 28, 36, 42, 44, 46 and 47 are all below 0.5, so these nine items should be removed. As two high factor loading values (above 0.5) simultaneously exist in Item 5 and 49, these two items should also be removed. Factor analysis will be used again on the items after removing the unqualified.

Table 4. Rotated component matrix of the first factor analysis

Item No.	Factor 1	Factor 2	Factor 3	Factor 4	Factor 5	Factor 6	Factor 7
31	**0.768**	0.229	0.245	0.105	0.104	0.117	0.261
32	**0.71**	0.239	0.219	0.179	0.298	0.178	0.243
34	**0.636**	0.234	0.447	0.231	0.086	0.02	0.262
33	**0.623**	0.129	0.281	0.253	0.333	0.289	0.156
30	**0.594**	0.301	0.222	0.313	0.205	0.247	0.106
37	**0.534**	0.281	0.054	0.434	0.312	0.281	0.086
40	**0.53**	0.126	0.244	0.329	0.431	0.133	0.272
50	**0.513**	0.23	0.209	0.255	0.388	0.268	0.208
44	**0.496**	0.314	0.154	0.187	0.496	0.186	0.22
36	**0.418**	0.174	0.036	0.388	0.409	0.248	0.311
12	0.164	**0.8**	0.223	0.123	0.003	0.045	0.237
13	0.142	**0.655**	0.114	0.218	0.188	0.319	0.281
9	0.282	**0.654**	0.019	0.164	0.104	0.339	0.267
18	0.166	**0.607**	0.263	0.198	0.264	0.35	0.175
17	0.075	**0.597**	0.241	0.239	0.323	0.427	0.051
5	0.241	**0.567**	0.186	0.097	0.179	0.059	**0.523**
4	0.288	**0.542**	0.386	0.127	0.187	0.121	0.166
16	0.177	**0.536**	0.462	0.074	0.426	0.054	−0.048
15	0.318	**0.432**	0.421	0.276	0.103	0.271	0.073
28	0.264	**0.431**	0.336	0.291	0.308	0.328	0.124
27	0.189	0.205	**0.698**	0.105	0.305	0.191	0.152
14	0.213	0.358	**0.65**	0.164	−0.053	−0.019	0.311
24	0.45	0.271	**0.579**	0.101	0.177	0.344	0.129
29	0.268	0.035	**0.573**	0.105	0.32	0.196	0.419
22	0.371	0.251	**0.561**	0.037	0.311	0.234	0.265
25	−0.054	0.183	**0.507**	0.489	0.191	0.406	0.119
20	0.31	0.217	**0.469**	0.059	0.289	0.265	0.417
35	0.171	0.128	0.102	**0.833**	−0.045	0.09	0.212
38	0.263	0.269	0.039	**0.74**	0.298	0.252	−0.053
39	0.221	0.166	0.296	**0.6**	0.351	0.05	0.136
41	0.265	0.305	0.068	**0.526**	0.395	0.232	0.082
42	0.376	0.017	0.178	**0.483**	0.378	0.381	0.271
47	0.275	0.082	0.301	**0.422**	0.41	0.363	0.333
45	0.296	0.196	0.193	0.16	**0.686**	0.286	0.321
43	0.197	0.27	0.307	0.229	**0.642**	0.028	0.043
48	0.254	0.05	0.425	0.248	**0.539**	0.096	0.359
46	0.328	0.23	0.082	0.403	**0.447**	0.355	0.266
26	0.176	0.251	0.248	0.286	0.176	**0.662**	0.196
10	0.231	0.394	0.006	0.12	0.148	**0.632**	0.354
49	**0.504**	0.126	0.19	0.302	0.109	**0.536**	0.193

(*continued*)

Table 4. (*continued*)

Item No.	Factor 1	Factor 2	Factor 3	Factor 4	Factor 5	Factor 6	Factor 7
21	0.346	0.353	0.352	0.148	−0.018	**0.526**	0.314
19	0.313	0.361	0.318	0.17	0.231	**0.524**	0.209
23	0.21	0.385	0.384	0.347	0.162	**0.444**	−0.104
11	0.224	0.228	0.419	0.142	0.165	0.202	**0.625**
8	0.265	0.283	0.249	0.116	0.182	0.341	**0.622**
6	0.243	0.377	0.231	0.197	0.163	0.166	**0.6**
7	0.382	0.378	0.125	0.178	0.183	0.184	**0.538**

Before doing the next factor analysis, unqualified items should be removed. Unqualified items refer to the items whose maximum factor loading value is lower than 0.5, and the factor loading value of many factors are simultaneously above 0.5. Factor analysis is conducted again after removing the unqualified items. The final questionnaire structure is formed when doing the seventh factor analysis. As shown in Table 5, when doing the seventh factor analysis, the KMO value is 0.943, greater than 0.7, and the value of Bartlett's test is 10216.411, with its significance level lower than 0.001, so the sample is fit for factor analysis.

Table 5. Check list of KMO and Bartlett in the seventh factor analysis

KMO		0.926
Bartlett's test	Approximate chi-square	2380.205
	df	210
	Sig.	0.000

Table 6. Contribution rate of each factor in the seventh factor analysis

Factor	Characteristic root	Accumulated contribution rate (%)
1	5.766	27.456
2	5.113	51.801
3	3.386	67.925

As shown in Table 6, when extracting 3 factors whose characteristic roots are greater than 1, the accumulated variance contribution rate reaches 67.925%. The Rotated component matrix is shown in Table 7. The three factors are renamed as follows: Factor 1 is renamed as "metacognitive strategy", including item 29, 30, 31, 32, 33, 34, 40, 48, 50; Factor 2 is renamed as "cognitive strategy", including item 4, 10, 13, 16, 17, 18, 21 and 26; Factor 3 is renamed as "affective/social strategy", including item 35, 38, 39 and 41. All the maximum factor loading values of these items are above 0.5, and high load only exists in one factor, suggesting that the construct validity is good.

Table 7. Rotated component matrix of the seventh factor analysis

Item No.	Factor 1	Factor 2	Factor 3
31	0.816		
32	0.776		
34	0.765		
33	0.748		
40	0.72		
29	0.7		
48	0.645		
30	0.628		
50	0.613		
17		0.8	
18		0.774	
13		0.737	
10		0.712	
21		0.682	
26		0.639	
4		0.607	
16		0.572	
38			0.828
35			0.768
39			0.704
41			0.669

Reliability Test

Reliability test is respectively conducted on cognitive strategy, affective/social strategy and metacognitive strategy, and Table 8 reports the results. According to the result, Cronbach's α coefficient will not rise no matter which item is removed, suggesting that all these items can be kept. The Cronbach's α coefficient of cognitive strategy, affective/social strategy, metacognitive strategy are respectively 0.914, 0.862, 0.942, all above 0.7, suggesting that the result of reliability test is good.

Table 8. Result of Reliability Test

Variables	Item No.	Cronbach's α coefficient after deleting this item	Cronbach's α coefficient of the variable
Cognitive Strategy	4	0.907	0.914
	10	0.905	
	13	0.901	
	16	0.912	
	17	0.897	
	18	0.897	
	21	0.901	
	26	0.904	

(*continued*)

Table 8. (*continued*)

Variables	Item No.	Cronbach's α coefficient after deleting this item	Cronbach's α coefficient of the variable
Affective/Social Strategy	35	0.862	0.862
	38	0.778	
	39	0.822	
	41	0.832	
Metacognitive Strategy	29	0.939	0.942
	30	0.935	
	31	0.934	
	32	0.93	
	33	0.931	
	34	0.935	
	40	0.933	
	48	0.939	
	50	0.935	

Correlation Analysis

Description statistics and correlation analysis are used to analyse cognitive strategy, affective/social strategy, metacognitive strategy, and Table 9 reports the results. This scale is a 5-point scale, with 3 point a mid-value. According to the result of description statistics, the average value of affective/social strategy is above 3, suggesting that the participants get a relatively high score in affective/social strategy; the average value of both cognitive strategy and metacognitive strategy are all below 3, suggesting that the participants get a relatively low score in these two strategies. According to the result of correlation analysis, among the three variables including cognitive strategy, affective/social strategy, metacognitive strategy, positive correlation exists between each two variables ($p < 0.001$).

Table 9. Description statistics and correlation analysis

	Cognitive strategy	Affective/Social strategy	Metacognitive strategy
Cognitive strategy	1		
Affective/Social strategy	0.655***	1	
Metacognitive strategy	0.756***	0.683***	1
Mean value (M)	2.858	3.136	2.750
Standard deviation (SD)	0.898	0.947	0.887

Note: *stands for $p < 0.05$,**stands for $p < 0.01$,***stands for $p < 0.001$

Mesomeric Effect Model

Structural equation model is built to test the mesomeric effect of affective/social strategy between cognitive strategy and metacognitive strategy. [12] Because there are too many constitute indexes of cognitive strategy and metacognitive strategy, items are packed in order to simplify the model and improve the degree of model fitting. The items of cognitive strategy is packed in 4 packages(X1 ~ X4), and the items of metacognitive strategy is packed in 3 packages(Y1 ~ Y3). As shown by the model modified index (MI), there is a high correlation between X1 and X2, so correlation is set on the residual to modify the model, and the final structural equation model is obtained as it is shown in Fig. 1.

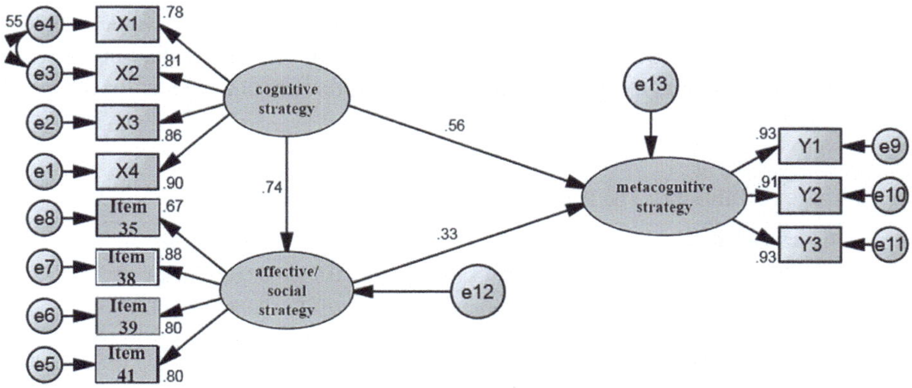

Fig. 1. Diagrammatic figure of mesomeric effect

The main fit index of each item in this structural equation model is shown in Table 10. X2/df = 1.824 < 3, RMSEA = 0.076 < 0.08, RMR = 0.044 < 0.05, GFI = 0.916 > 0.9, NFI = 0.948 > 0.9, RFI = 0.928 > 0.9, IFI = 0.976 > 0.9, TLI = 0.966 > 0.9, CFI = 0.975 > 0.9, all of them are inside the fitting range, suggesting that this structural equation model is acceptable.

Table 10. Global fitting result of structural equation model

Model fitting index	Critical value	Research model	Fitting judgement
X^2/df	<3	1.824	Yes
RMSEA	<0.08	0.076	Yes
RMR	<0.05	0.044	Yes
GFI	>0.9	0.916	Yes
NFI	>0.9	0.948	Yes
RFI	>0.9	0.928	Yes
IFI	>0.9	0.976	Yes
TLI	>0.9	0.966	Yes
CFI	>0.9	0.975	Yes

Table 11 reports the path coefficients of this structural equation model. As it is shown in the result, cognitive strategy has a significant positive influence on affective/social strategy ($\beta = 0.737$, $t = 8.329$, $p < 0.001$), and it also has a significant positive influence on metacognitive strategy ($\beta = 0.332$, $t = 3.421$, $p < 0.001$); and affective/social strategy has a significant positive influence on metacognitive strategy ($\beta = 0.561$, $t = 5.729$, $p < 0.001$).

In order to test the indirect effect of cognitive strategy on metacognitive strategy with affective/social strategy as a mediating variable, after using bootstrap method to sample for 2000 times, the indirect effect value is 0.245, while the confidence interval is [0.075, 0.511], except 0, suggesting that the indirect effect is significant and positive. The direct effect is the effect of cognitive strategy on affective/social strategy in the model, and its value is 0.561, suggesting that the direct effect is significant and positive. Gross effect refers to the sum of direct effect and indirect effect, and its value is 0.806, positive. Thus, affective/social strategy plays as a partial intermediation between cognitive strategy and metacognitive strategy, and indirect effect accounts for 30.4% of the gross effect.

Table 11. The Path coefficient of structural equation model

Influence path	β	S.E.	C.R.	P
cognitive strategy → affective/social strategy	0.737	0.087	8.329	***
affective/social strategy → metacognitive strategy	0.332	0.097	3.421	***
cognitive strategy → metacognitive strategy	0.561	0.096	5.729	***

3 Conclusion

Through the empirical analysis, it is easy to know that Li nationality college students do not use English learning strategies so often. When using English learning strategies, the frequency of using affective/social strategy is a little bit higher than that of using cognitive strategy and metacognitive strategy. Also, cognitive strategy has a significant positive influence on both affective/social strategy and metacognitive strategy, and affective/social strategy has a significant positive influence on metacognitive strategy. Meanwhile, affective/social strategy plays as a partial intermediation between cognitive strategy and metacognitive strategy.

To a large extent, English learning strategy is one of the decisive factors for learners' English achievement. In order to improve learners' English ability, firstly, college English teachers should introduce more English learning strategies to Li nationality students [13], and intensify their cognitive strategy. Secondly, both teachers and students should attach more importance to the training and cultivation of Li students' autonomous learning ability [14, 15], and students should practice metacognitive strategy persistently. Thirdly, teachers should provide more encouragement and support for Li students, and bring affective/social strategy into full play. Li students are kind and optimistic, and they are keen on questioning and communicating with their classmates and teachers [16, 17], so teachers should make full use of this advantage, thus to improve their frequency of using affective/social strategy as well as their oral English ability. Last but not least, colleges should create a good information environment for students, and provide necessary courses for Li students to improve their ability in using network resources, as in the future English learning, information technology and network resource will bring great convenience for English learners [18].

References

1. Liu, D.: Learning strategy. J. Subject Educ. 1, 34–36 + 43 (1997)
2. Sun, G., Li, S., Chen, T., et al.: Active Learning Method for Chinese Spam Filtering. Int. J. Performability Eng. **13**(4), 511–518 (2017)
3. Hsiao, T.Y., Oxford, R.L.: Comparing theories of language learning strategies: a confirmatory factor analysis. Modern Lang. J. **86**(3), 368–383 (2002)
4. Oxford, R.: Language Learning Strategies. What Every Teacher Should Know. Newbury House, New York (1990)
5. Wen, Q.: The difference on learning methods between successful and unsuccessful English learners. Foreign Lang. Teach. Res. **3**, 61–66 (1995)
6. Liu, Z., Yuan, F., Xu, B.: Research on the relationship between TEM4 Scores of high group and low group and learning strategies. Foreign Lang. Lit. **2**, 112–117 (2005)
7. Liu, Y.: A study of difference of english-learning strategy. Theory Pract. English **24**(3), 50–52 (2004)
8. Wang, J.: A research on english learning strategies of college students in the bilingual teaching environment. J. Inner Mongolia Normal Univ. Educ. Sci. **27**(3), 123–126 (2014)
9. Zhang, M.: A research on college students' English learning strategy under the teaching mode of content. HeiNongJiang Educ. (High. Educ. Res. Appraisal **6**, 43–45 (2019)
10. Li, M., Wang, L.: An empirical study of the present use of Li language and countermeasures. J. Hannan Univ. Humanit. Soc. Sci. **28**(4), 20–24 (2010)
11. Zhang, R., Kang, X., Peng, W., Liu, D.: A study on college students' English learning strategy characteristics and development trend. Psychol. Dev. Educ. **3**, 94–99 (2008)
12. Sun, G., Lang, F., Xue, Y.: Chinese chunking method based on conditional random fields and semantic classes. J. Harbin Inst. Technol. **43**(7), 135–139 (2011)
13. Du, X.: Exploration of English learning strategies for Li nationality students in Hainan Province. J. Jiangxi Vocat. Tech. Coll. Electricity **32**(1), 12–14 (2019)
14. Xiao, H.: Research on status Quo of Non-English major's autonomous learning ability in vocational college and its promotion strategies. ZheJiang GongShang Univ. **32**(1), 36–39 (2019)
15. Wang, L.: A research on the influence factors of higher vocational college students' autonomous learning ability. J. Jiangxi Vocat. Tech. Coll. Electricity **32**(1), 36–39 (2019)
16. Zhu, X., Li, S.: On the influence of emotional factors on English learning in Hainan Li Zu areas. J. Qiongzhou Univ. **18**(3), 61 (2011)
17. Chen, H.: On the transfer of Li minority culture and psychology to English learning. J. Beijing Inst. Technol. (Soc. Soc. Ed) **8**(2), 88–91 (2006)
18. Chen, L., Zhu, Q., Liu, X.: Research on higher vocational English teaching reform from the perspective of cultivation of professional English ability. J. Civil Aviat. Flight Univ. China **29**(6), 25–30 (2018)

Higher Vocational Computer Course Reformation Based on Integration of Industry and Teaching

Yi-Nan Chen[1(✉)], Yuan Yao[1], Xia Liu[1], and Ming-Rui Chen[2]

[1] Sanya Aviation and Tourism College, Sanya 572000, Hainan, China
305780161@qq.com, graceyao1021@163.com,
paolo_lx@qq.com
[2] Hainan University, Haikou 570208, Hainan, China
1607885098@qq.com

Abstract. This paper puts forward the curricular reformation on computer course in higher vocational colleges in accordance with the analysis of the issues existing in the current computer course teaching. In light of the modern concept of vocational curriculum development, the aspects of teaching mode, teaching methods, teachers' abilities and evaluation system should be adjusted to integrate the industry with the vocational teaching process.

Keywords: Integration of industry and vocational teaching · Computer course · Curricular reform · O2O hybrid teaching mode · TPACK

1 Introduction

It is of great significance to deepen the integration of industry and teaching and to promote the cooperation between schools and enterprises as the basic institutional arrangement for the national education reform and the development of human resources according to the report of the 19th CPC National Congress by Xi Jinping, the chairman of China [1]. It is obligatory to improve the quality of teaching in an all-round way under the new educational situation and to promote the supply-side structural reform of human resources [2]. The integration of industry and teaching and the cooperation of schools and enterprises are the most significant parts of the current vocational education policy, which guide and create opportunities for the development of higher vocational education. Under the background of the integration of industry and teaching, keeping up with the pace of the times and promoting the teaching reform of computer courses in higher colleges is an issue worth studying and thinking deeply about.

2 Status of College Computer Course

College computer course is a basic course with the function of general education, which is open to freshmen in colleges. With the popularization of computer, there are some one-sided viewpoints such as "it is enough to know how to use computer",

G. Sun et al. (Eds.): eLEOT 2019, LNICST 299, pp. 270–277, 2019.
https://doi.org/10.1007/978-3-030-35095-6_31

"computer is just for designing programs" and "computer course is to explain the use of software" for a long time. The popularity of these viewpoints has caused a great impact on the computer course teaching in colleges. The teaching hours of computer course are compressed in the professional training plan, and the teaching resources of computer course are not adequately allocated. Along with this, the college computer course becomes an optional course. Students are satisfied with the basic operation of computer, the use of daily-used software and the basic programming language.

In the rapid development of information age, the significance of college computer course should not be ignored, but should be strengthened. It is not only the necessary knowledge and skills but also the necessary means for modern college students to adapt themselves to survive in the society. It is an essential link in the cultivation of college students' comprehensive quality and innovative talents. The importance of college computer course is self-evident, but there are still some problems in teaching the course.

2.1 Student Levels

Nowadays, computers have been applied to all industries [3, 4], with the application of the Internet in full swing. Students growing up in such an era are a generation of digital natives who can receive information and vision more quickly than in old times. They prefer graphic thinking, interactive learning communication mode, and a variety of digital tools.

The students in higher vocational colleges are recruited mainly from high schools, single entrance examination and independent enrollment. Among them, the students graduating from high schools belong to the third round of enrollment, while most students with good cultural foundation have entered better universities or colleges through the first or second round. Those who enter through single entrance examination and independent enrollment also have a relatively low cultural level in high schools. Limited by the source of students, the learning levels of students in higher vocational colleges are uneven and their foundation is relatively weak [5, 6]. Take computer skills for example, a small number of students have reached high computer levels or participated in computer competitions in high schools. There is also a minority of students who have never been exposed to computers, which is completely zero basis. The common situation is that students who have already come into contact with computers mainly engage in recreational activities, but their ability to apply computers is poor. In college computer classes, the students with basic knowledge of computer could not concentrate in class for having a certain understanding of the teaching content; the starters can neither respond to the teacher nor keep up with the computer operation. Therefore, the teaching turns out as a failure since the students have no idea what is happening in the class.

2.2 Teaching Mode

Different enterprises also need the talents with varied abilities. The traditional teaching mode during the teaching process of college computer course is still continued till present to train the students in a batch way, in a teacher-centered classroom. Teacher is regarded as the master of knowledge, on the contrary, student is purely the knowledge receiver. Teacher carries on the infusion-type teaching mode and student passively listens to the class. The teaching pattern which ignores students' initiative of study tends to be cliche, dull and boring. Lacking of interaction between teachers and students, the two parties not sparing enthusiasm in class leads to an unfavorable attendance [7–9].

2.3 Teaching Method and Teaching Content

Many teachers use the traditional teaching method, that is, multimedia courseware, to teach when giving college computer classes. Teaching combined with practical demonstration and operation emphasizes on teacher explaining the key points respectively to students. Because the operation points involved in college computer course are individual, students cannot connect these themselves to the process of learning, it is difficult to attract students' attention to achieve a better learning effect. In addition, most of the time the school formulates the talent training plan without comprehensive investigation of enterprises' demands for talents. Copying the teaching content of other colleges results in the disconnection between teaching and application, and students trained in this way is barely even up to meet the employment standard of enterprises and cannot be qualified for work.

2.4 Teacher's Work Ability

At present, the number of "double-qualified" teachers in higher vocational colleges is small, and most of the full-time teachers are the ones that start teaching directly after graduation. Lacking of working experiences in the enterprise, teachers do not understand the specific post requirements in the enterprise. At the same time, most of the teachers at certain professional level pay more attention to the literal knowledge of this major, not acknowledging TPACK (Technological Pedagogical Content Knowledge) [10, 11], the integrated technology on the subject or still staying in the preliminary phase of learning the mixed teaching mode named O2O.

2.5 Assessment System

The form of final computer examination is generally adopted after the teaching of college computer course. The questions of the test are selected randomly from the item bank. Students are supposed to answer them on the computer. The two parts of the class performance and the final computer test result are combined as the final evaluation results. However, there is no quantified standard for class performance. This kind of examination neglects to cultivate students' ability of calculating thinking of using computer to analyze and solve problems, so it is impossible to adequately evaluate students' comprehensive ability of using computer.

3 Research and Exploration on the Reformation of College Computer Course

3.1 Exploring Interactive Teaching and Cultivating the Sense of Teamwork

In order to solve the problem of uneven computer basis, interactive teaching is explored to cultivate the sense of teamwork. The specific operation of the unit is as follows: first of all, during the military training period of freshmen, a questionnaire survey and a mapping test of computer basic level are organized to better understand the situation of students. Secondly, groups which 4 students are divided into will sit in fixed seats according to the arranged plan in the computer classroom. Students with good and bad foundation will be staggered in the same group, after the mid-term test, the seats are about to be adjusted according to the students levels at the present stage. In this way, it can ensure that students with poor foundation can not only seek advice from teachers, but also ask for help from the students in the group during the daily learning process. This will help to cultivate students' sense of teamwork. At the same time, the introduction of inter-group competition mechanism is to stimulate the learning enthusiasm of students. Finally, in the teaching process, in the practice link students are asked to practice on stage with the explanations from the teacher demonstration. For one thing, it promotes the students' ability of expressing and learning; for another, the teacher is no longer the teacher in a traditional way, and the students pay more attention to the class. The learning results will be improved by teacher summarizing the demonstration link of the students, strengthening the error-prone points and the difficult points in the form of interaction between teachers and students.

3.2 O2O Hybrid Teaching Mode

The integration of industry and teaching should focus on the cultivation of talents and pay attention to the growth of students. In order to break the traditional teacher-centered and classroom-centered teaching mode, we should take the students as the center and the teachers as the leading force by adopting the O2O hybrid teaching mode which combines offline teaching with online teaching [12–14].

The teaching of computer course should make full use of computer network. Teachers should arrange study tasks ahead of time through uploading multimedia courseware, small videos in course website and posting in WeChat account. Students should make use of piecemeal time to prepare for the class in advance. It is feasible to improve students' initiative and efficiency of learning during the process of classroom teaching, group discussion, virtual experiment exercises, induction and summary. After class the teacher arranges the expansion tasks, guides the students to carry on the individualized and independent inquiry study; students can learn by themselves online after class through the micro classes, MOOC [15] and complete the after-school expansion tasks. Taking our college as example, we use the course website, WeChat account, simulative software, and the combination of Lan Moyun classes. Students participate and learn much more positively. In the aspect of curricular reform, we can combine schools and schools, integrate high quality teachers, and build excellent free online courses to make up for the lack of offline education and teaching resources.

With the help of the O2O hybrid teaching mode, online learning and teaching can provide students with a large number of high-quality learning resources. The interaction between teachers and students has been greatly enhanced, not only in class, but also online to discuss and study problems. The cooperation with teachers can arouse the enthusiasm and initiative in learning, and at the same time, teachers can play a supervisory role, which can effectively ensure the completion of teaching goals, as shown in Fig. 1.

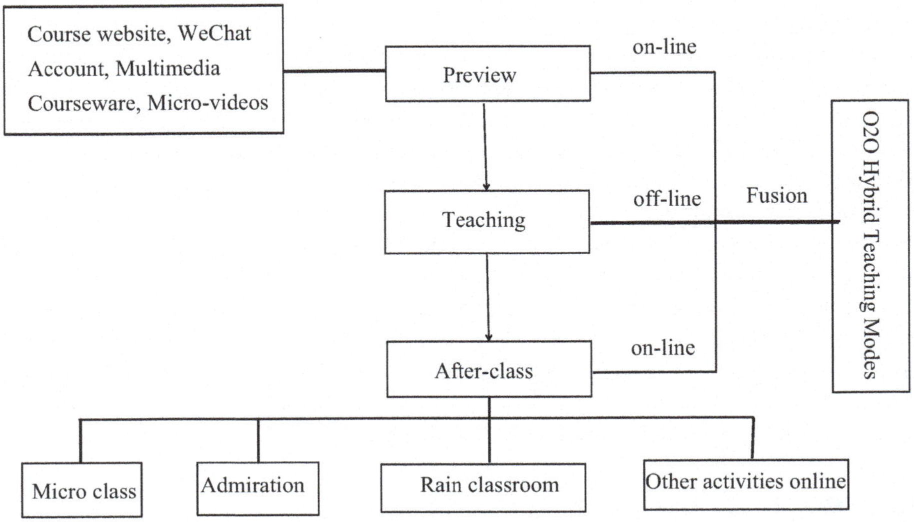

Fig. 1. O2O hybrid teaching modes

3.3 Diversity of Teaching Methods and Refinement of Teaching Contents

In the rapid-developing Internet era, university computer teachers can not only use multimedia courseware to teach, but to try to use a variety of teaching methods, the integration of information-based and traditional teaching methods. At the same time, in the teaching process, we should base on the needs of the enterprises, industrial chain, after investigating the requirements of the enterprises to realize the connection between the curriculum content and the professional standard. The teaching contents should be refined and individualized, so as to provide students with different knowledge, from focusing on course learning to emphasizing the ability, and cultivate talents with high quality and sustainable competitive ability [16].

For example, the production training project of "Voice of Spark" of Sanya Aviation and Tourism College needs to input the data into the spreadsheet quickly. The major of finance needs to use a large number of functions of the spreadsheet, and it emphasizes on Excel when teaching knowledge points. The flight log should be written in the flight crew post, and the maintenance log should be written in the cabin post of aviation electric mechanical maintenance major, and the software Word is the main focus. When students participate in the innovation and entrepreneurship competition, it involves the standardized production of project plans and the beautification of the effects of demonstrating PPT. The college has set up relevant public limited courses, such as advanced Word operation, advanced PPT operation, etc. It can improve students' practical ability of computer application.

Schools can also introduce intelligent teaching platform. After collecting a large number of data, artificial intelligence will analyze the data for students to develop personalized learning content through online activities to collect students' learning information [17, 18]. On the basis of the teacher's teaching content, it can provide different learning contents as a supplement according to the students' learning progress and the degree of mastering knowledge, which can be used for students' independent learning after class, so that students can either consolidate the foundation from scratch, or learn more knowledge on a better basis, improving the learning efficiency.

At the same time, the method of virtual experiment can be used to refine students' practical ability. In the traditional college computer classroom, students' practical ability is difficult to be fully or effectively cultivated, but under the virtual experiment condition, we can create the real learning situation related to the current learning content. Through virtual experiments we can solve problems, complete tasks and have multidimensional interaction, so that students can learn and use the combination of knowledge and practice. It is also possible to visualize the dull and abstract knowledge and display it directly in a simple and clear way to solve the monotonous problem of teaching form and to improve the students' interest in learning.

3.4 Double-Qualified Teachers and Teachers' TPACK Ability

The construction of teaching staff is the key to the construction of curriculum and the improvement of teaching quality. Teachers play a leading role in the teaching process, and the level of teachers directly determines the quality of teaching. Schools can combine teachers and teacher training to create a dual-qualified faculty team [19, 20]. Full-time teachers and teachers working for local enterprises constitute a mixed team of teachers, in which they can promote with assistance and learn from each other. We send full-time teachers to enterprises to take part in training and studying during the holidays. For example, our college sends teachers to aviation, hotels, logistics and other enterprises in turn for training during the holidays, so as to innovate in practice and solve the practical problems in the production activities of enterprises, as well as understand the orientation of talent trends. Training young teachers through participation in expert lectures, academic conferences at home and abroad, competition training and other activities, college make great efforts on teachers' teaching and scientific research, innovative practice and other comprehensive ability.

In addition, TPACK is a kind of new knowledge that teachers should possess. Only when teachers change their educational concepts, adapt to the rules of information technology development and enhance the ability of information-based teaching, can they better adopt the O2O hybrid teaching model which combines online and offline.

3.5 Application Ability and Pluralistic Evaluation

Examination is an important link in the teaching process to check whether the teaching goal is completed or not. It is necessary to construct the whole process and multiplex computer ability evaluation system [21, 22] with the application ability examination as the core, so as to urge the students to attach importance to self-learning in their spare time to cultivate students' serious attitude, independent thinking, problem-solving and independent innovation ability. The suggested ratios of the process factors are as follows: 10 points of pre-class preparation, 40 points of examination (including 20 points of test and 20 points of final examination), 40 points of virtual experiment and 10 points of homework. In this way, teachers can evaluate the whole learning process of students through their courseware, video viewing, chapter test, final examination, experiment task completion, homework and so on. This reflects students' understanding of knowledge points more truthfully and raises their levels of ability to apply the knowledge to solve problems.

4 Conclusion

In the new era, with the development of vocational education, the supply-side structural reform of human resources cannot be separated from the integration of industry and teaching and the cooperation of schools and enterprises, which also brings opportunities and challenges to the reform of college computer education. Interactive teaching in the college computer teaching cultivates the consciousness of team cooperation, takes the student as the foundation and starts the O2O mixed teaching pattern by merging the information-based teaching method and the traditional one. It is a bold innovation and attempt to connect the teaching content with the professional standard, which builds the double-qualified teaching staff, enhances the teachers' TPACK ability with attention to the application ability. It constructs the whole process and builds a pluralistic evaluation system not only conducive to the development and perfection of university computer curriculum, but also to the cultivation of students' comprehensive and practical abilities, which meets the requirements of modern economic and social development for skilled talents.

References

1. Chen, C.: The problems to be solved urgently in deepening the cooperation between schools and enterprises in the integration of industry and education 2018 speech at the meeting of the expert committee of the Chinese Vocational Education Society abstract. Chin. Vocat. Tech. Educ. **13**, 5–6 (2018)
2. Xi, D.: Industry contribution under the cooperation of industry and education integration in the new era. Chin. Vocat. Tech. Educ. **16**, 32–40 (2018)
3. Sun, G., Lang, F., Xue, Y.: Chinese chunking method based on conditional random fields and semantic classes. J. Harbin Inst. Technol. **43**(7), 135–139 (2011)
4. Sun, G., Lang, F., Yang, M.: Traffic measurement system based on hybrid methods. Electr. Mach. Control **15**(6), 91–96 (2011)

5. Tang, K., Du, G.: Thinking and exploring on the teaching of the course of College computer Foundation under the mode of "Internet". Asia Pac. Educ. **01**, 101–102 (2016)
6. Li, H., Tuo, M., Zhang, H.: A preliminary study of layered teaching of computer basic courses. Comput. Eng. Sci. **38**(s1), 262–264 (2016)
7. Wang, J., Huang, L., Sun, J., et al.: A study on the teaching reform of the course of "College computer Foundation" in the era of "Internet". J. LanZhou Inst. Educ. **34**(04), 107–108 (2018)
8. Xie, P., Zhang, H.: Computational thinking-oriented teaching reform and practice on university computer basic courses. Comput. Eng. Sci. **38**(S1), 245–247 (2016)
9. An, L., Zhao, Y.: Study on college teaching reform based on basic computer courses. Comput. Eng. Sci. **36**(S2), 179–181 (2014)
10. Wang, L.: Internet education: TPACK vocational education under the concept O2O a probe into the reform of teaching mode. Comput. Educ. **08**, 61–66 (2017)
11. Zhang, Z., Zhang, H., Wang, Y.: Research on the factors affecting the development of pre-service teachers' TPACK. Mod. Educ. Technol. **26**(01), 46–52 (2016)
12. Jing, J., He, H., Wang, Z., et al.: O2O application principles of teaching mode in college computer major teaching. Comput. Educ. **02**, 85–89 (2016)
13. Yang, W., Liu, M.: Research on the model and application of multi-mixed teaching oriented by computational thinking. China Educ. Technol. **04**, 129–136 (2017)
14. Lu, X., Tian, M., Li, Q.: Mixed experimental teaching mode for college computer based on micro-class and rain classroom. Exp. Technol. Manage. **35**(06), 203–206 (2018)
15. Wang, X., Wang, F., Peibin: The construction of the intelligent teaching mode based on the rain class. Comput. Educ. **04**, 139–142 (2018)
16. Xu, X., Li, L., Zhan, D., et al.: A new perspective of new engineering: an agile teaching system for sustainable competitiveness. China Univ. Teach. **10**, 44–49 (2018)
17. Zhou, J., Wang, X.: Research on the teaching model of information technology in artificial intelligence era. Comput. Educ. **12**, 109–112 (2017)
18. Yuan, F., Nie, Y.: Research on the bases and teaching support services of ubiquitous learning in the smart era. Mod. Educ. Technol. **29**(05), 26–32 (2019)
19. Han, C.: Research on the construction of computer science and technology in the background of the integration of production and education. Knowl. Econ. **19**, 175–176 (2018)
20. Zhu, L.: Path for cultivating teachers with "Dual-Qualification" and "Double-Competency" in local colleges and universities in the transitional period. Acad. Explor. **12**, 149–152 (2016)
21. Liu, X., Chen, M.: Introduction of computational thinking to the teaching of computer basic courses in higher vocational colleges. Comput. Educ. **5**, 39–43 (2013)
22. Fang, X.: Construction of an evaluation system for computer courses in practical teaching. Comput. Eng. Sci. **38**(S1), 108–111 (2016)

An Empirical Analysis of Public English Teachers in Higher Vocational Colleges

Wei Wang(✉), Yuan Yao, and Dan Ren

Sanya Aviation and Tourism College, Sanya, Hainan 572000, China
dick_1980@126.com

Abstract. This paper seeks to investigate the current state of Public English teachers in the higher vocational colleges in Hainan Province through the questionnaire inquiring information on the main information-based teaching means adopted, professional quality, job saturation and job satisfaction. Taken as a whole, the results suggest that the professional quality and job satisfaction of the tested group are high while job saturation is at an intermediate level, and those three elements are not necessarily related according to the descriptive statistics and regression analysis. The strategies derived from the analysis elaborate the advice from multiple perspectives including three aspects of society, school and teacher.

Keywords: Public English teachers · Professional quality · Job saturation · Job satisfaction

1 Introduction

Along with the concept of lifelong learning and sustainable development, the societyhas put forward higher requirements for talents. Higher vocational education takes the all-round development and quality improvement of vocational talents as a new viewpoint of curriculum design. Hainan Provincial Government issued a notice on supporting Hainan to comprehensively raise the foreign language proficiency and calling vigorously for cultivating cross-culture awareness of the citizens. As an important branch of the teaching work to cultivate international language level, Public English teachers in higher vocational colleges can project their own teaching abilities, innovative spirit and professional accomplishment into every link of teaching. Therefore, the construction of Public English teaching staff in higher vocational colleges is particularly crucial, while the benign development of teachers is an strong guarantee to promote and upgrade the social adaptability and globalized thinking of talents.

The domestic researches on the construction of teaching staff in higher vocational education are mainly carried out from the following aspects: structure of teaching staff, academic ability of teachers, job satisfaction, professional development of teachers, job burnout, etc. At present, there are few researches merely digging on the present situation of Public English teachers. Foreign studies on public teaching staff are rare due to two prime factors. One reason is that the teachers engaged in higher vocational education in developed countries and regions are basically "double-qualified" teachers with practical experience in related industries. The teachers of higher vocational

G. Sun et al. (Eds.): eLEOT 2019, LNICST 299, pp. 278–286, 2019.
https://doi.org/10.1007/978-3-030-35095-6_32

education are stapled with the following characteristics: being selected through strict recruitment requirements, getting generous salaries and reaching high profession level; moreover, these countries and regions do not offer similar public courses at higher vocational level as in China. More attention is paid to teachers' practical ability and continuing education there than at home, so the researches abroad mainly focus on the employment, guarantee, and assessment systems, as well as the turnover mechanism of teaching staff.

Public English teachers in higher vocational colleges in Hainan Province are taken as the study object in this paper. The number of teachers, knowledge structure, age, educational level, part-time or full-time, the teaching situation, and the scientific research situation are all taken into consideration. In order to find out the shortcomings in promoting the Public English teachers and establish the process of training for teachers through scientific orientation, so as to standardize the management system of teachers, this paper analyzes the current situation of Public English teachers in higher vocational colleges in Hainan by SPSS and illustrates the relationship among professional accomplishment, job saturation and job satisfaction of the teachers. The innovative thoughts of the "double-qualified" teachers, optimization of the teaching staff structure, overall improvement of teachers' quality and level will all contribute to the development of higher vocational education.

2 Research Design

2.1 Research Object

The research object, randomly chosen from the Public English teachers in Hainan higher vocational colleges, takes the multidimensional differences, such as demonstration, typicality, and so on into account. The frequency statistics of demographic variables are given, and the results are shown in Table 1. Female teachers have accounted for more than 80% of the total number of teachers, most of whom are aged between 31 and 40 years old. They have mainly gained master degrees, as their professional title was mainly lecturer, and the proportion of teachers with dual qualities achieves up to 67.5%. All but one of them are full-time teachers. The workloads of teachers, including the amount of scientific research and class periods, are all above the requirements of the colleges. Only fewer than 10% of the teachers have never used information-based teaching means. However, most teachers hold the opinion that the opportunities of fatter salary, promotion and further training are fewer than those for the professional teachers.

Table 1. Frequency statistics (N = 59)

Variable	Attribute	Frequency	Percentage (%)
Gender	Male	11	18.6
	Female	48	81.4
Age	Under 30	6	10.2
	From 31 to 40	39	66.1
	From 41 to 50	7	11.9
	From 51 to 60	7	11.9
Academic qualification	Undergraduate	24	40.7
	Postgraduate	35	59.3
Academic degree	Bachelor	19	32.2
	Master	40	67.8
Profession title	Associate professor	9	15.3
	Lecturer	35	59.3
	Assistant	8	13.6
	Not getting any title yet	7	11.9
Full-time teacher	Yes	58	98.3
	No	1	1.7
"Double-qualified" Teacher	Yes	27	67.5
	No	13	32.5
Number of published papers in the last three years	None	12	20.3
	1 to 3	37	62.7
	4 to 5	8	13.6
	Above 5	2	3.4
Number of hosted educational or scientific researches in the last three years	None	44	74.6
	1 to 2	14	23.7
	Above 4	1	1.7
Number of attended educational or scientific researches in the last three years	None	18	30.5
	1 to 2	34	57.6
	3 to 4	5	8.5
	Above 4	2	3.4
Teaching class periods in the latest year on average	Under 8	2	3.4
	8 to 12	21	35.6
	13 to 16	19	32.2
	Above 16	17	28.8
Used information-based teaching means	Sometimes	54	91.5
	Never	5	8.5
Opportunities of higher salary, promotion and training	Relatively Few	48	81.4
	Same as the professional teachers	11	18.6

2.2 Research Methodology

With the aid of Hainan Province Education Science Planning Project "Present Situation Demonstration Research of Hainan Higher Vocational College Teachers", this research applies the self-designed questionnaire based on the related questionnaires of the other members in the research group. The questionnaires were distributed to the higher vocational colleges according to the number and locations of colleges of the cities and counties in Hainan. With certain representativeness, the samples of investigation were comparatively comprehensive. The questionnaire includes three factors: teachers professional quality, job saturation and job satisfaction. 59 valid questionnaires out of 63 were completed. The effective rate was 93.65%. SPSS software was used to describe the data, correlation regression and reliability and validity analysis.

2.3 Validity and Reliability

This part is to analyze the professional quality, job saturation and job satisfaction of higher vocational Public English teachers. The results of factor analysis for the first round are shown in Tables 2 and 3. The variance of single factor explanation for all variables is less than 50%. From the factor loading point of view, the factor loading values of professional quality 3, professional quality 4, professional quality 6, job saturation 1, work saturation 5, job saturation 6, job satisfaction 1, job satisfaction 5 are lower than 0.5. Therefore, these will be eliminated and then be analyzed again.

Table 2. Factor analysis results of the first round

Variable	KMO value	Bartlett sphericity test			Characteristic root test	Corrected model (%)
		Approximate chi-square test	df	p		
Professional Quality	0.638	61.866	15	0.000	2.192	36.531
Job Saturation	0.426	56.338	15	0.000	1.972	32.874
Job Satisfaction	0.495	43.314	10	0.000	1.908	38.156

Table 3. Factor loading of the first-round factor analysis

Index	Factor loading	Index	Factor loading	Index	Factor loading
Professional Quality 2	0.871	Job Saturation 2	0.88	Job Satisfaction 3	0.801
Professional Quality 1	0.804	Job Saturation 3	0.784	Job Satisfaction 4	0.783
Professional Quality 5	0.694	Job Saturation 4	0.506	Job Satisfaction 2	0.576
Professional Quality 4	0.382	Job Saturation 5	0.447	Job Satisfaction 1	0.468
Professional Quality 6	−0.319	Job Saturation 6	−0.291	Job Satisfaction 5	0.319
Professional Quality 3	0.24	Job Saturation 1	−0.207		

The final factor analysis results are shown in Tables 4 and 5. Table 4 shows that the KMO values of professional quality, job saturation and job satisfaction are all above 0.5, and the Bartlett globality test reaches a significant level of 0.001, which indicates that the sample can be used for factor analysis. The number of factors whose characteristic root is greater than 1 is obviously 1, and the explanatory variance of each factor is more than 50%. The factor loading of each index is above 0.5, which indicates that the single factor structure of professional quality, job saturation and job satisfaction is available, that is, the structure validity is feasible.

Table 4. Factor analysis results of the last round

Variable	KMO value	Bartlett sphericity test			Characteristic root test	Corrected model (%)
		Approximate chi-square test	df	p		
Professional quality	0.626	43.814	3	0.000	1.978	65.920
Job saturation	0.550	32.935	3	0.000	1.808	60.273
Job satisfaction	0.508	33.900	3	0.000	1.770	58.991

Table 5. Factor loading of the last-round factor analysis

Index	Factor loading	Index	Factor loading	Index	Factor loading
Professional quality 2	0.88	Job Saturation 2	0.883	Job Satisfaction 3	0.896
Professional quality 1	0.842	Job Saturation 3	0.788	Job Satisfaction 4	0.799
Professional quality 5	0.704	Job Saturation 4	0.639	Job Satisfaction 2	0.572

The reliability of professional quality, job saturation and job satisfaction were tested. The results are shown in Table 6. Table 6 shows that the Cronbach's α coefficients of professional quality, job saturation and job satisfaction were all above 0.6, which indicates that the reliability has passed the test.

Table 6. Reliability test result

Variable	Cronbach's α coefficient	Indicator
Career quality	0.726	3
Job saturation	0.658	3
Job satisfaction	0.640	3

3 Research Statistics and Analysis

3.1 Analysis of Current Status of the Public English Teachers

The descriptive statistics of the current status of the faculty are shown in Table 7. All themes in this section are 5 points, with 3 as the median. It can be seen that the number of English teachers in the Public English class is less than that of the current public curriculum teaching and research, and the number of teachers aged 30 to 45 years is on the high side. The working environment of teachers and the policies for the current process of publishing the topic papers are relatively poor. The training frequency of teachers further training, the salary and welfare are lower. It is much more difficult to apply for projects related to public courses. Public English teachers tend to be dissatisfied with the present incentive rewards and measures for the publication of education-reform and scientific papers.

Table 7. Descriptive statistics of the present situation of public courses teachers

Theme	1 means	5 means	Average	Standard deviation
Number of the public teaching staff	Least	Most	2.93	0.868
Working conditions	Worst	Best	2.95	0.57
Frequency of the further professional training	Lowest	Highest	2.27	0.806
Wage and benefits	Lowest	Highest	2.42	0.747
Number of the ones aged from 30 to 45	Least	Most	3.58	0.792
Present teaching and research funds for public courses	Least	Most	2.25	0.733
Difficulty in applying for subjects related to public courses	Most difficult	Easiest	2.36	0.76
Policies of current publication of papers	Worst	Best	2.59	0.812
Incentive measures on the publication of the educational and teaching papers	Worst	Best	2.68	0.6
Rewards on the publication of scientific papers	Worst	Best	2.64	0.609

3.2 Analysis of Main Information-Based Teaching Means

The frequency statistics of information-based teaching means in the form of multiple-choice questions in the questionnaire are shown in Table 8. Among the 54 samples that have used the main information-based teaching methods, blended teaching method is the most popular one among the Public English course. 40.70% and 38.90% of the teachers respectively chose online and offline teaching and micro-class as their options of teaching means. Only a small number of English teachers adopted the unconventional means of flipped classroom, MOOC and SPOC during teaching, accounting for 11.10% and 3.70% respectively.

Table 8. Frequency statistics of the multiple choices questions (N = 54)

Variable	Attribute	Frequency	Percentage
Main information-based teaching methods	MOOC	6	11.10%
	SPOC	2	3.70%
	Micro class	21	38.90%
	Flipped classroom	14	25.90%
	Online and offline teaching	22	40.70%
	Blended teaching	41	75.90%

3.3 Analysis of Professional Quality, Job Saturation and Job Satisfaction

Descriptive statistics and correlation analysis of professional quality, job saturation and job satisfaction are given in Table 9. The results of descriptive statistics show that the average values of professional quality and job satisfaction are above 3, which indicates that the professional quality and job satisfaction are both high. The mean value of work saturation is lower than 3, but it is extremely close to 3. It can be considered that the working saturation of the tested population is at the middle level. The results of correlation analysis showed that there was no significant correlation between the two variables in the three variables of professional quality, job saturation and job satisfaction ($p > 0.05$).

Table 9. Descriptive statistics and related analysis

	Professional quality	Job saturation	Job satisfaction
Professional quality	1		
Job saturation	0.176	1	
Job satisfaction	0.119	0.254	1
Mean value	3.627	2.949	3.062
Standard deviation	0.476	0.615	0.586

Regression analysis was used to explore the effect of professional quality on job satisfaction. The results are shown in Table 10. The results of Table 10 showed that the regression equation was not significant ($F = 0.819$, $R2 = 0.014$, $p > 0.05$), and there was no significant effect of professional quality on job satisfaction ($\beta = 0.119$, $t = 0.905$, $p > 0.05$).

The results of the effect of job saturation on job satisfaction investigated by regression analysis are shown in Table 11. It showed that the regression equation was not significant ($F = 3.915$, $R2 = 0.064$, $p > 0.05$), and there was no significant effect of job saturation on job satisfaction ($\beta = 0.254$, $t = 1.979$, $p > 0.05$).

Table 10. Regression analysis of career quality and teachers job satisfaction

	Non-standardized coefficient B	Standard error	Standardized coefficient β	t	p
Constant	2.531	0.592		4.276	0.000
Professional quality	0.146	0.162	0.119	0.905	0.369
R2	0.014				
F	0.819				

Table 11. Regression analysis between job saturation and job satisfaction

	Non-standardized coefficient B	Standard error	Standardized coefficient β	t	p
Constant	2.351	0.367		6.402	0.000
Job saturation	0.241	0.122	0.254	1.979	0.053
R2	0.064				
F	3.915				

4 Conclusion

According to the results of empirical analysis, both professional quality and job saturation have no significant effects on job satisfaction of Public English teachers. However, the teachers have less funds for public teaching and research, when the working environment and the policies for the applying for the projects and publishing the papers are poor. It is suggested that the following factors from the objective and subjective views should be capable to improve the academic setting for Public English teachers.

Social enterprises can provide practical opportunities for Public English teachers. Taking Hainan Province for instance, tourism, culture, catering, commerce and other public service industries can admit higher vocational public English teachers into enterprises in a planned way to carry out varied levels of the vocational on-the-job training and help to bring about the regular cooperation between schools and enterprises in the field of specialized English training. At the practice, teachers have the windows to see the present situation and the future trend of the profession, so as to promote English teaching in higher vocational colleges. Government should guide the enterprises to set up the platform between the imported, reserved English talents and local English teachers to achieve free communication.

Higher vocational colleges should get started from the professional characteristics of Public English teachers in line with their own professional strengths and research direction, and set training goals and overall planning to construct the teaching staff. By creating excellent environment for publishing papers, applying for projects on Public English and formulating certain incentive mechanism which encourages teachers to improve the overall scientific research ability, colleges may increase the opportunities for teachers to gain further training in schools, provinces, countries and even the whole world. In the light of local social resources, colleges ought to impel the cooperation between schools and enterprises and formulate the standards of "double-qualified" English teachers. Meanwhile, the improvement of the salary leaves teachers no worries in livings.

The Public English teachers in higher vocational colleges should combine the characteristics of both social and regional development to strengthen their own vocational skills and adapt to the changes of the times through lifelong learning. Obtaining the qualification of "double teachers" and stepping up with the curriculum reform are also required to meet the construction of the International Free Trade Area. Given the advantages of the higher vocational colleges, the talents should take the responsibility of serving the society through taking the initiative to take on the training work of English in the off-campus industries. The combination of the English knowledge itself with practical experience in the practice of enterprises would contribute to improving the service industry.

References

1. Shao, J., Xu, Z.: Solutions to the demands, problems of constructing the higher vocational teaching team under the modern vocational education system. China High. Educ. Res. **3**, 100–103 (2016)
2. Yang, Y.: A study on the path of diversified construction and cooperative innovation of teachers in higher vocational college. Res. High. Educ. Eng. **2**, 163–166 (2016)
3. Zhou, L., Chen, X.: Investigation and analysis of vocational teachers' job burnout: a case study of beijing agricultural vocational college. Chinese Vocat. Tech. Educ. **27**, 51–56 (2017)
4. Sun, G., Song, Z., Liu, J., et al.: Feature selection method based on maximum information coefficient and approximate markov blanket. Zidonghua Xuebao/acta Automatica Sinica **43** (5), 795–805 (2009)
5. Gao, Z.: Correlation analysis of professional identity and professional development of higher vocational teachers. Educ. Vocat. **19**, 87–93 (2018)
6. Wu, D.: A study on the academic training mechanism of higher vocational teachers in the construction of "double First-class". Heilongjiang Sci. **8**, 36–37 (2018)
7. Sun, G., Lang, F., Yang, M.: Traffic measurement system based on hybrid methods. Electr. Mach. Control **15**(6), 91–96 (2011)
8. Tang, J.: Development of the college English teachers' professional learning communities scale: with Jiaoyanshi as an example. Foreign Lang. Res. **3**, 86–93 (2019)

An Empirical Research on the Status Quo of Ideological and Political Teachers in Higher Vocational Colleges in Hainan Province

Zhipeng Ou(✉), Dan Ren, and Yuan-hui Li

Sanya Aviation and Tourism College, Sanya 572000, Hainan, China
hainanozp@126.com, 340459345@qq.com, 576735855@qq.com

Abstract. In order to build a high-quality team of teachers in vocational higher education institutions, deeply understand, and investigate the current situation of ideological and political teachers in vocational higher education institutions of Hainan Province, a questionnaire survey has been conducted from four aspects including the satisfaction of teaching and scientific research, professional quality, work saturation and teacher's job satisfaction. On the basis of an empirical research upon the results through SPSS, it has come to the conclusion: the professional quality of ideological and political teachers cannot significantly influence the satisfaction of teaching and scientific research; Job saturation can positively influence teaching and research satisfaction; teaching and research satisfaction can positively influence teachers' job satisfaction. Vocational higher education institutions should attach great importance to teachers' development needs and respond to them, formulate policies to support teachers' professional development, their promotion of professional title and further training, and improve the quality and level of teachers.

Keywords: Higher vocational colleges · Ideological and political courses · Teacher · Empirical research

1 Introduction

As a significant part of higher education, higher vocational education aims to cultivate high-skilled talents for the first-line positions of production, construction, management and service. The talent cultivation quality in higher vocational college is not only related to the existence and development of a school, but also influences the social and economic development of a country. It has become an instant historical mission for higher vocational education to speed up the cultivation of high-quality and high-skilled talents. Strengthening the construction of teaching staff is not only a special requirement for higher vocational education, but also an inevitable demand for the times as well as the social and economic development. "Some Advice on Deepening the Educational Reform in Vocational Education and Improving the Quality of Talent Cultivation (exposure draft)" conducted by Ministry of Education has clearly mentioned "Reinforce and improve the teaching of basic socializing courses. Strengthen the cultural and basic education while guaranteeing the cultivation quality of students' technical skills. On the basis of teaching programme (curriculum standards) issued by

G. Sun et al. (Eds.): eLEOT 2019, LNICST 299, pp. 287–296, 2019.
https://doi.org/10.1007/978-3-030-35095-6_33

Ministry of Education, vocational schools should provide abundant, complete and first-class basic socializing courses for students, including moral education, Chinese, mathematics, English, history, sports and health, art, basics and professional theories of computer application." Thus, the status of ideological and political course in higher vocational colleges has been intensified by the state. Thus, the construction of teaching staff for ideological and political course is especially important, and the professional development of teaching staff for basic socializing courses is the key to improve the teaching quality and cultivate talents' social adaptation ability in higher vocational education.

At present, the systematic study on teaching staff construction of ideological and political course in higher education institutions is far from many, and these researches are mainly conducted from the following aspects, including the structure of teaching staff [1, 2], teachers' academic competence [3, 4], teachers' basic quality [4], job satisfaction [5–8], professional development [9–11], job burnout [12, 13], etc. A questionnaire survey was conducted on ideological and political teachers in higher vocational colleges in Haikou, Sanya and Qionghai, in order to know the current situation of these teachers in Hainan higher vocational colleges.

2 Statistic Analysis of Data Description

Through the frequency analysis of demographic variables, a conclusion has been drawn as shown in Table 1. Among the 51 test samples, there are 39 females, accounting for 60%. 27 participants are aging 31 to 40, accounting for 52.9%. About 27 participants have postgraduate education background, accounting for 52.9%; 31 participants have master's degree, accounting for 60.8%. 24 teachers get lectureship as professional qualification, accounting for 47.1%. 47 participants are full-time teachers, accounting for 92.2%; 7 participants are double-professionally-titled teachers, accounting for 13.7%. In the recent three years, 23 participants published 1–3 papers, accounting for 45.1%; 22 participants are not the leading researcher of any teaching and scientific projects, accounting for 43.1%; 25 participants hosted 1 or 2 research projects, accounting for 49%; 23 teachers participate in 1 or 2 research projects, accounting for 45.1%. In the recent year, the average weekly class hours for 24 participants are between 8 and 12, accounting for 47.1%. 49 participants adopt information-based teaching, accounting for 96.1%; 19 participants think it is difficult for ideological and political teachers to get a raise in liberal wages and benefits, as well as get promotion, training and learning opportunities, accounting for 37.7%; while 30 participants think they are treated almost the same as teachers of other courses in these aspects.

The frequency statistics of multiple choices are shown in Table 2. Among the 49 samples adopting information-based teaching, the main information-based teaching method used in class is mixed teaching method, about 40.20% of the teachers choosing this option, followed by on-line and off-line teaching, about 24.10% of the teachers choosing this option. The rest options are also chosen by some teachers. Thus, the teaching methods used by ideological and political teachers in Hainan Province have transformed from traditional to information-based and diversified. The information-based teaching methods are also diversified.

Table 1. Frequency statistics (N = 51)

Variables	Attribute	Frequency	Percentage (%)
Gender	male	12	23.5
	female	39	76.5
Age	below 30	8	15.7
	31–40	27	52.9
	41–50	13	25.5
	51–60	2	3.9
	Above 60	1	2
Education background	undergraduate	17	33.3
	postgraduate	27	52.9
	Doctor	7	13.7
Degree	bachelor	13	25.5
	master	31	60.8
	doctor	7	13.7
Professional qualifications	professor	5	9.8
	associate professor	11	21.6
	lecturer	24	47.1
	teaching assistant	6	11.8
	no qualification	5	9.8
Full-time teacher	yes	47	92.2
	no	4	7.8
Double-professionally-titled teacher	yes	7	13.7
	no	44	86.3
Number of papers published in recent 3 years	none	5	9.8
	1–3	23	45.1
	4–5	11	21.6
	>5	12	23.5
Number of teaching and scientific research projects presided in recent 3 years	none	22	43.1
	1–2	25	49
	3–4	2	3.9
	above 4	2	3.9
Number of teaching and scientific research projects participated in recent 3 years	none	13	25.5
	1–2	23	45.1
	3–4	8	15.7
	above 4	7	13.7
Average weekly teaching hours in the recent year	below 8 h	11	21.6
	8–12 h	24	47.1
	13–16 h	11	21.6
	above 16 h	5	9.8
Using information-based teaching	yes	49	96.1
	no	2	3.9

(*continued*)

Table 1. (*continued*)

Variables	Attribute	Frequency	Percentage (%)
Liberal wages and benefits, opportunities for promotion, training and further-study	relatively difficult	19	37.3
	average	30	58.8
	relatively easy	2	3.9

Table 2. Frequency statistics of multiple choices (N = 49)

Variables	Attribute	Frequency	Percentage
Main information-based teaching method	MOOC	13	14.90%
	SPOC	2	2.30%
	Micro-lecture	5	5.70%
	Flipped class	11	12.60%
	On-line and off-line teaching	21	24.10%
	Mixed teaching	35	40.20%

The description statistics of the current situation of teaching staff is shown in Table 3. All the items are rated on a 5-point format, with 3 points the median. As shown in the table, the number of teachers and the teaching and scientific research funds for ideological and political course are relatively in short supply; teachers aging 30 to 45 are relatively in large quantity; the working environment for ideological and political teachers is relatively good, but the policy environment for them to publish a paper is not so satisfactory; the further-study and training opportunities for ideological and political teachers are relatively few, and the salary and social benefits are relatively low; the possibility for teachers to apply for research project related to ideological and political courses is relatively low; teachers are not satisfied with the reward system for publishing a researching paper, no matter it is a paper related to educational reform or scientific research.

Table 3. Description statistics of the current situations of ideological and political teachers

Items	Option for 1 point	Option for 5 points	Average	Standard deviation
Number of teachers	Very few	Very many	2.670	0.739
Working environment	Very bad	Very good	3.180	0.740
Frequency of further-study	Very low	Very high	2.840	0.644

(*continued*)

Table 3. (*continued*)

Items	Option for 1 point	Option for 5 points	Average	Standard deviation
Salary and social benefits	Very low	Very high	2.750	0.659
Number of teacher aging 30 to 45	Very few	Very many	3.490	0.857
Expenditure for teaching and scientific research of ideological and political course	Very little	Very much	2.880	0.765
Difficulty in applying for a research project related to ideological and political course	Very difficult	Very easy	2.530	0.784
Policy environment to publish a paper	Very bad	Very good	2.550	0.808
Reward system for publishing a paper related to educational reform	Very unsatisfied	Very satisfied	2.710	0.855
Reward system for publishing a paper related to scientific research	Very unsatisfied	Very satisfied	2.800	0.800

3 Reliability and Validity Test

Factor analysis [14] is used to respectively analyse teaching and scientific research satisfaction, professional quality, working saturation, and teachers' job satisfaction. By using single factor test, Tables 4 and 5 report the first factor analysis results of each variable. Only the explained variance of teachers' job satisfaction reaches 66.375%, while that of the rest variables is less than 50%. The factor loading value for teaching and scientific research satisfaction 4, professional quality 6, working saturation 1 are all less than 0.5. So, these items are excluded and factor analysis is used on the rest items again. In the second factor analysis, professional quality 3 and 4 are also excluded due to their low explained variance.

Table 4. Result of the first factor analysis

Variables	KMO value	Bartlett sphericity test			Characteristic root	Explained variance (%)
		Approximate chi-square	df	p		
Teaching and scientific research satisfaction	0.757	56.348	15	0.000	2.553	42.554
Professional quality	0.639	72.812	15	0.000	2.525	45.084
Working saturation	0.756	79.448	15	0.000	2.859	47.653
Job satisfaction	0.818	117.842	10	0.000	3.319	66.375

Table 5. Factor loading of first factor analysis

Index	Factor loading	Index	Factor loading	Index	Factor loading	Index	Factor loading
Teaching and scientific research satisfaction 3	0.775	Professional quality 2	0.828	Working saturation 2	0.792	Teachers' job satisfaction 5	0.865
Teaching and scientific research satisfaction 2	0.75	Professional quality 4	0.813	Working saturation 4	0.775	Teachers' job satisfaction 4	0.816
Teaching and scientific research satisfaction 1	0.75	Professional quality 1	0.715	Working saturation 5	0.772	Teachers' job satisfaction 2	0.815
Teaching and scientific research satisfaction 6	0.665	Professional quality 5	0.569	Working saturation 3	0.72	Teachers' job satisfaction 3	0.811
Teaching and scientific research satisfaction 5	0.62	Professional quality 3	0.513	Working saturation 6	0.718	Teachers' job satisfaction 1	0.764
Teaching and scientific research satisfaction 4	0.025	Professional quality 6	0.282	Working saturation1	0.044		

Tables 6 and 7 report the final results of factor analysis, and none index of teachers' job satisfaction isn't excluded. As shown in Table 6, the KMO value of teaching and scientific research satisfaction, professional quality, working saturation and teachers' job satisfaction are all above 0.6, and Bartlett sphericity test reaches 0.001, suggesting factor analysis can be used on these samples. The number of factors with the characteristic root above 1 is 1, and the explained variance of each single factor are all above 50%. As for factor loading, each index is above 0.5, suggesting that the single factor structure of teaching and scientific research satisfaction, professional quality, working saturation and teachers' job satisfaction is good, that is, the construct validity is good.

Table 6. Result of the final factor analysis

Variables	KMO value	Bartlett sphericity test			Characteristic root	Explained variance (%)
		Approximate chi-square	df	p		
Teaching and scientific research satisfaction	0.780	53.759	10	0.000	2.553	51.057
Professional quality	0.654	50.617	3	0.000	2.127	70.888
Working saturation	0.786	76.241	10	0.000	2.858	57.159
Job satisfaction	0.818	117.842	10	0.000	3.319	66.375

Reliability test is used on teaching and scientific research satisfaction, professional quality, working saturation and teachers' job satisfaction, and Table 8 reports the result. As shown in Table 8, the Cronbach's α coefficient of teaching and scientific research satisfaction, professional quality, working saturation and teachers' job satisfaction are all above 0.7, suggesting good reliability.

Table 7. Factor loading of final factor analysis

Index	Factor loading	Index	Factor loading	Index	Factor loading	Index	Factor loading
Teaching and scientific research satisfaction 3	0.776	Professional quality 2	0.896	Working saturation 6	0.795	Teachers' job satisfaction 3	0.865
Teaching and scientific research satisfaction 6	0.75	Professional quality 1	0.872	Working saturation 3	0.775	Teachers' job satisfaction 4	0.816
Teaching and scientific research satisfaction 5	0.748	Professional quality 5	0.75	Working saturation 2	0.772	Teachers' job satisfaction 2	0.815
Teaching and scientific research satisfaction 2	0.665			Working saturation 4	0.718	Teachers' job satisfaction 1	0.811
Teaching and scientific research satisfaction 1	0.621			Working saturation 5	0.718	Teachers' job satisfaction 5	0.764

Table 8. Results of reliability and validity test

Variables	Cronbach's α coefficient	Index number
Teaching and scientific research satisfaction	0.757	5
Professional quality	0.794	3
Working saturation	0.811	5
Job satisfaction	0.870	5

4 Correlation Analysis

Description statistics and correlation analysis are used to analyse the four variables including teaching and scientific research satisfaction, professional quality, working saturation and teachers' job satisfaction, and Table 9 reports the result. The result of description statistics shows that the average value of each variable is above 3, suggesting that the participants' teaching and scientific research satisfaction, professional quality, and job satisfaction are relatively high. The average value of working saturation is a little bit lower but quite close to 3, suggesting that the working saturation of the participants is in medium level. The result of correlation analysis shows that in the four variables, there are obvious correlation between each two variables.

Table 9. Description statistics and correlation analysis

	Teaching and scientific research satisfaction	Professional quality	Working saturation	Job satisfaction
Teaching and scientific research satisfaction	1			
Professional quality	0.549***	1		
Working saturation	0.579***	0.451**	1	
Job satisfaction	0.743***	0.639***	0.765***	1
Mean value (M)	3.012	3.399	2.984	3.031
Standard deviation (SD)	0.563	0.640	0.623	0.608

Note: * stands for $p < 0.05$, **stands for $p < 0.01$, ***stands for $p < 0.001$.

5 Regression Analysis

Regression analysis [15] is used to explore the influence of professional quality on teaching and scientific research satisfaction, and the result is shown in Table 10. As shown in Table 10, the regression equation is significant (F = 21.160, adjusted R2 = 0.287, $p < 0.001$), suggesting that professional quality has a significant positive influence on teaching and scientific research satisfaction ($\beta = 0.549$, $t = 4.6$, $p < 0.001$).

Table 10. Regression analysis of professional quality to teaching and scientific research satisfaction

	Nonstandard coefficient B	Standard error (S.E.)	Standard coefficient β	t	p
(constant quantity)	1.367	0.364		3.76***	0.000
Professional quality	0.484	0.105	0.549	4.6***	0.000
R^2	0.302				
Adjusted R^2	0.287				
F	21.160***				

Regression analysis is used to explore the influence of working saturation on teaching and scientific research satisfaction, and the result is shown in Table 11. As shown in Table 11, the regression equation is significant (F = 24.725, adjusted R2 = 0.322, $p < 0.001$), suggesting that working saturation has a significant positive influence on teaching and scientific research satisfaction ($\beta = 0.579$, $t = 4.972$, $p < 0.001$).

Table 11. Regression analysis of working saturation to teaching and scientific research satisfaction

	Nonstandard coefficient B	Standard error (S.E.)	Standard coefficient β	t	p
(constant quantity)	1.45	0.321		4.519***	0.000
Working saturation	0.523	0.105	0.579	4.972***	0.000
R^2	0.335				
Adjusted R^2	0.322				
F	24.725***				

Regression analysis is used to explore the influence of teaching and scientific research satisfaction on teachers' job satisfaction, and the result is shown in Table 12. As shown in Table 12, the regression equation is significant ($F = 60.506$, adjusted $R2 = 0.543$, $p < 0.001$), suggesting that teaching and scientific research satisfaction has a significant positive influence on teachers' job satisfaction ($\beta = 0.743$, $t = 7.779$, $p < 0.001$).

Table 12. Regression analysis of teaching and scientific research satisfaction to teachers' job satisfaction

	Nonstandard coefficient B	Standard error (S.E.)	Standard coefficient β	t	p
(constant quantity)	0.614	0.316		1.942	0.058
Teaching and Scientific Research Satisfaction	0.803	0.103	0.743	7.779***	0.000
R^2	0.553				
Adjusted R^2	0.543				
F	60.506***				

6 Conclusion

Through the empirical analysis of questionnaire, it is obvious that personal profession quality of ideological and political teachers in higher vocational colleges in Hainan province can not significantly influence their teaching and scientific research satisfaction, and their working saturation has a significant positive influence on their teaching and scientific research satisfaction; and the latter can directly influence their job satisfaction. As a special teaching group, ideological and political teachers take up a certain proportion in the whole teaching group of higher vocational education, and their working conditions including their professional quality, teaching and scientific research satisfaction, job satisfaction and job burnout have a great influence on the development of higher vocational colleges. Therefore, it is necessary for higher vocational colleges to clearly know the special function of training for vocational education teachers. They should reply to teachers' requirements, perfect the content and process design of teaching staff training. They should create good working environment, provide more training and further-study opportunities for ideological and political teachers, and better the rules and regulations of teaching and scientific research as well as formulate policies beneficial to their development. Usually, ideological and political teachers in higher vocational colleges have a strong desire for promotion, and their teaching and scientific research satisfaction not only influences their job satisfaction, but also influences their professional career development and job burnout. It is also crucial on the construction and development of a high-quality teaching group.

References

1. Chenwei, Y., Zong, S., Hui, B.: Strengthening the construction of teaching staff for basic socializing courses in order to adapt to higher education development—a research report on the construction of teaching staff for basic socializing courses in liaoning higher education institutions. Liaoning Educ. Res. **04**, 29–31 (2002)
2. Yuqin, L.: A survey on the current situation of teaching staff for basic socializing courses in sichuan higher education institutions and the research of its countermeasures. Acad. J. Sichuan Normal Univ. (Soc. Sci.) **30**(1), 59–65 (2003)
3. Xuemei, L.: An reflection on academic development and teaching competence of teachers in guangxi higher vocational colleges. Educ. Vocat. **10**, 83–86 (2017)
4. Murong, G.: The current difficulty and realization route of developing young teachers' teaching and academic competence in higher education institutions. Contemp. Sci. Educ. **11**, 65–68 (2018)
5. Qin, W.: Quality requirements of teachers in basic socializing courses in vocational-technique schools. China Adult Educ. **24**, 79–80 (2012)
6. Hongxia, M., Liu, Y.: The construction of teaching staff for basic courses in higher vocational colleges from the perspective of constructivism. Educ. Vocat. **12**, 72–73 (2013)
7. Beini, L.: An Theoretical and Empirical Research on Teachers' Working Hours in Higher Education Institutions. Capital University of Economics and Business, Peking (2014)
8. Jingyi, M., Simiao, L., Tingna, S.: Acceleration or obstruction: an empirical research of the influence of a school organization structure on teachers' job satisfaction. Contemp. Educ. Manag. **12**, 79–84 (2018)
9. Jinpei, L., Jianhui, L.: The influence of college teachers' scientific research pressure on scientific research performance—the intermediary and regulating effect of job satisfaction and emotional intelligence. J. Fujian Normal Univ. (Philos. Soc. Sci.) **06**, 72–78 (2018)
10. Ying, T.: The professional development of basic courses teachers in higher vocational colleges from the perspective of NYP model. Educ. Vocat. **10**, 85–86 (2013)
11. Shenghui, Z., Shasha, N., Shiwei, R.: An reflection of teachers' professional development in private higher education institution from the perspective of ecology of education. J. Zhejiang Shuren Univ. (Hum. Soc. Sci.) **19**(01), 20–24 (2019)
12. Yinchen, H.: A Research on the Hardship of the Demonstration Construction of Teaching Staff in Higher Vocational Colleges—Take College D in Shanghai As an Example. East China Normal University, Shanghai (2014)
13. Haiju, J.: A diagnosis of teachers' job burnout of basic socializing courses in Jiangsu. J. Nanjing Univ. Posts Telecommun. (Soc. Sci.) **13**(4), 104–108 (2011)
14. Sun, G., Song, Z., Liu, J., et al.: Feature selection method based on maximum information coefficient and approximate markov blanket. Zidonghua Xuebao/acta Automatica Sinica **43**(5), 795–805 (2009)
15. Sun, G., Qi, H.: Spam filtering based on online ranking logistic regression. J. Tsinghua Univ. **53**(5), 734–740 (2013)

The Application of Heuristic Teaching Method in Explaining the Asterisk Triangles Pattern in C Language

Xiaoqiang Wu[1], Ruican Hao[2](✉), and Hongfang Cheng[3]

[1] College of Mechanician Engineering, Inner Mongolia University for the Nationalities, Tongliao, China
[2] Beijing Polytechnic, No. 9 Liangshuihe First Street, Yizhuang, Beijing, China
haoruican@163.com
[3] Wuhu Institute of Technology, Wuhu, Anhui, China

Abstract. The C language is a programming language which has both the characteristics of the low-level and high-level. The C language program design course has been set up in every major of the College of Mechanical Engineering at the Inner Mongolia University of Nationalities. However, as a non computer major student, when studying the knowledge of loop structure, the complexity and abstraction of the knowledge point and the various multiple loop structures are difficult to learn. But as the most common and basic knowledge point, it must be mastered skillfully. In this paper, the pattern of a isosceles right triangle composed of asterisks was used as an example. By using the loop structure to output the pattern, the students were inspired and learned how to find ways to solve the similar problems. The actual teaching practice achieved good results which proved the effectiveness of the teaching case.

Keywords: Program design · Triangle · Graphical method · Heuristic teaching

1 Introduction

The C language is an important basic lesson of general knowledge. The basic goal of this course is to make the students master the skills of using a computer programming language to write the algorithms to solve problems as well as to develop the ability to analyze problems. After the lesson, the students can effectively use the computer to solve the problems in the professional field, and to lay a good foundation for the follow-up study and work. As an object oriented general programming language with the characteristics of high execution efficiency, function reconfigurability and the portability, the C language program design course has been set up in every major of the College of Mechanical Engineering at the Inner Mongolia University of Nationalities.

The loop structure is a very important basic knowledge point in the C language, and almost used in every program. So to learn the loop structure well is very important in the C language course. According to the 8 years of teaching experience of C language, most of the students were not good at the knowledge of the loop structure. The way of reciting the programs was not effective to learn the knowledge. When the loop program was slightly modified during the examination, the students would give an irrelevant answer.

G. Sun et al. (Eds.): eLEOT 2019, LNICST 299, pp. 297–302, 2019.
https://doi.org/10.1007/978-3-030-35095-6_34

The theoretical teaching time is 16 h and the practical time is 32 h of the C language program design course in the mechanical manufacturing and automation major. According to the previous teaching experience, the teaching result was relatively general by explaining the examples according to the textbook directly when learning the loop structure knowledge point in C language.

Most of the students responded that they could not understand well in this way. So the teaching method should be improved when explaining the loop structure knowledge point. In this paper, the patterns of the triangles composed of asterisks were used as examples. By using the loop structure to output the pattern, the teaching method of progressive catechesis to inspire the students gradually was proposed.

Before explaining the loop structure knowledge point, the students were asked to output the pattern in Fig. 1 through programming by themselves. Because they have just learned the "print()" function, the first reaction in everyone print mind was to use the "print()" function to solve the problem. And the program is as follows:

```
Int main()
{
printf("    *    ");
printf("   ***   ");
printf("  *****  ");
printf(" ******* ");
printf("*********");
}
```

Fig. 1. A asterisk pattern of 5 lines and 5 columns

If the question was slightly modified as to output an asterisk pattern of 200 lines and 10 columns, most of the students would think of using the "print()" function 200 times continuously to solve this problem. Was there a simpler method to solve it? And then the loop structure knowledge point was introduced and the program is as follows. Obviously, the using of the loop structure made the program much concise and can achieve the same function as the sequential statement in 200 lines.

```
int main()
{
Int i=1;
While(i<=200)
{
printf("**********");
i++;
}
}
```

Fig. 2. The right triangle pattern

In the hybrid teaching platform to modify homework, some of the typical problems that exist in students to organize, check each student's progress and learning status.

Through this example, the concept of loop statement was introduced and left a deep impression in the students' mind after the careful thinking. To output the asterisk pattern of 5 lines and 5 columns was the simplest and most basic loop structure question. Based on this question, a new question was raised to output a right triangle pattern composed by the asterisks of 5 lines and 5 columns as shown in Fig. 2. For beginners who just learned the loop structure, they may feel very difficult since they could find the breakthrough to solve the problem. The textbook gives the answer directly without the solving process in details which is helpless to the students. For this kind of questions, the routine teaching method of teaching examples directly should be changed by the progressive catechesis to inspire the students gradually.

But how to use the progressive catechesis to solve this kind of problems? By observing the Fig. 2, it could be find that there was a law on the number of the asterisks in each line. Then the question was transformed into finding the law of the asterisks' number in each line with the line number. The question could be answered easily once the law was figured out. By observing the Fig. 2, it could be found that the number of the asterisks in each line was similar to the line number. In other words, there was an asterisk in the first line and two asterisks in the second line and so on. The relationship between the asterisks' number in each line with the line number is shown in Table 1.

Table 1. The relationship between the asterisks' number and the line number

The line number	The asterisks' number in each line
i	j
1	1
2	2
3	3
4	4
5	5
The relation ship	I=j

The program was written quickly after the relationship was figured out. The program is as follows:

```
Int main()
{
Int i=1,j=1;
for(i=1;i<=5;i++)
for(j=1;j<=i;j++)
printf("*");
}
******
*****
****
**
*
```

After answering the two questions above, the students have developed a deep understanding about the loop structure. In order to enable the students to master the knowledge point skillfully, a new question was proposed to output the pattern in Fig. 3 based on the previous questions. The new question was quite similar to the last one and after the relationship between the asterisks' number and the line number was found out, the question could be settled by the loop structure easily. The relationship between the asterisks' number in each line with the line number is shown in Table 2.

Table 2. The relationship between the asterisks' number and the line number

The line number	The asterisks' number in each line
i	j
1	5
2	4
3	3
4	2
5	1
The relation ship	J=5;j>=I;j−−

The program was very simple once the relationship was figured out. The program is as follows:

```
Int main()
{
Int i=1,j=1;
for(i=1;i<=5;i++)
for(j=5;j>=I;j--)
printf("*");
}
```

The question was complicated again to use the loop structure to output the pattern in Fig. 1. It was still a loop structure of 7 lines and 7 columns but contained the extra loop sentences to output the spaces. The letters i, j and k were used to indicate the times of the three loop structures. The sign i denotes the line loop; the sign j denotes the space output loop; the k denotes the asterisks' loop numbers. The question could be settled by inspiring the students to find out the internal relationships between these three variables. By decomposing this question, it could be found that the line loop was very simple and its loop number was directly related to the output line number. The internal loop were the space output loop and the asterisk output loop which were directly related to the line loop, too (Table 3).

Table 3. The relationship between the asterisks' number and the line number

The line number	The space number in each line	The asterisks' number in each line
i	J	k
1	6	1
2	5	3
3	4	5
4	3	7
5	2	9
6	1	11
7	0	13
The relation ship		J=7;j>=I;j−−

2 Course Evaluation

The traditional teaching model evaluates students' learning only in the final exams. As a result, many students do not usually study at the end of the exams. They take a comprehensive assault before the final exams, and their participation in learning is not high enough to deal with the exams. In a blended teaching model, evaluating a student's learning can actually achieve procedural evaluation. In the evaluation of the dimension is not limited to the final grade in the class and the final exam scores, but also the completion of each knowledge point in the teaching task, the completion of each experiment, the whole dimension of the students' learning evaluation. Evaluation of quantitative methods shown in Table 1, the assessment criteria shown in Table 2.

3 End

For this question, once the relationship between the space number and the line number and the relationship between the asterisks' number and the line number were clear, it could be settled by nesting the space loop and the asterisk loop into the line loop. The relationship between the line loop and the space loop was (j=7;j>=0;j-i;) and the relationship between the line loop and the asterisk loop was (k=2*i-1;k<=13;j++). Through the decomposement process of the question, the students could study the loop structure knowledge point from shadow to deep and could leave a deep impression about the loop structure. The same question could be settled easily by the students and proved that the progressive catechesis teaching method was much better than just explaining the example according to the textbook.

Acknowledgment. This work was supported by Science and Technology Innovation Guide Project of the Inner Mongolia Autonomous Region KCBJ2018028, Inner Mongolia University for Nationalities of Educational teaching research topics YB2017034.

References

1. Jin, L.F.: Some experiences in the teaching of C language. Sci. Technol. Inf. **5**(8), 53–54 (2012)
2. Tan, H.H.: The Programming of C Language. Tsinghua University Press, Beijing (2010)
3. Yang, C.X.: C Language Program Design Experiment Guidance and Answers. China Railway Press, Beijing (2005)
4. Tang, G.M.: The Programming of C Language. Tsinghua University Press, Beijing (2009)
5. Zou, X.C.: C Language Program Design Training Course. Southwestern Normal University Press

An Empirical Study on the Correlation Among Language Attitude, Ethnic Identity, Learning Burnout and English Achievements of Achang Ethnic Minority Students in Trilingual Context

Yi-Chuan Yuan, Jing-jing He(✉), and Yuan Yuan

Foreign Language School, Yunnan Normal University, Kunming 650500, Yunnan, China
408233827@qq.com

Abstract. This study, from three aspects, language attitudes, ethnic identity, learning burnout, investigated Achang middle school students' English learning situation, aiming to survey the relationship between the three variables and English achievement. It adopted the Likert questionnaire, and 317 middle school students from Jiubao Achang Township Middle School and Nang Song Achang Township Middle School, Lianghe County were investigated. The collected data were processed by SPSS 20.0 with the programs such as descriptive statistical analysis, correlation analysis, and regression analysis. Finally, the following conclusion was reached: (1) In spite of the trilingual environment, Achang middle school students keep contact with and communicate daily with other ethnic groups, especially the Han nationality, and they still attach great importance to their own ethnic language; Achang middle school students are far more fluent in Chinese than their mother tongue. The English scores of the Achang students are not ideal, of which the girls are obviously stronger than the boys in English study; (2) The subjects' language attitude is average and ethnic identity is relatively strong, and the study burnout is not very serious. Therefore, the overall situation is relatively optimistic; (3) The students' language attitude and learning English achievement are significantly and positively correlated, but the correlational strength is weak; learning burnout and English achievement are significantly, moderately and negatively correlated; the students' ethnic identity is not correlated with English learning. Among the three variables, the contribution rate of learning burnout to the predicted learning achievement is 17.9%.

Keywords: Achang middle school students · Language attitude · Ethnic identity · Learning Burnout

1 Background of the Study

English education in China emerged after 1979 under a mixed circumstance of the ending of the Cultural Revolution, the adopting of the Open Door Policy, and the establishment of strong diplomatic ties with the United States. Teaching English as a

G. Sun et al. (Eds.): eLEOT 2019, LNICST 299, pp. 303–315, 2019.
https://doi.org/10.1007/978-3-030-35095-6_35

foreign language refers to teaching the English language to students with different first language. English, which is one of the three basic subjects in middle school, may face a weakening in future college entrance examination. Still, English is of great significance in our country's foreign language teaching. In China, most of schoolchildren begin to have their first English lesson in third grade in primary school, but, of course, situations in different areas vary. In Yunnan, Chinese was not only taught as a second language but used as instruction language throughout the academic years. At the same time, English was also introduced into secondary schools in those areas as a regular and compulsory subject in the same way in the centralized Han Chinese educational system [1]. In the two schools we investigated, students did learn English in their primary school, but it produced very little effect for English is not a vital part of the entrance examination of junior middle school. Because of the less critical function in the entrance to a higher grade, English as a subject was not taken seriously. And from the questionnaires we received, English proficiency of these students is quite limited. Therefore, improving the teaching quality and perfecting the educational system are clearly something which needs to be fixed. Li pointed out that the authorities should endeavor to vigorously coordinate language planning in foreign language education and international spread of Chinese in the context of English globalization [2]. In the areas inhabited by ethnic minorities, the ethnic languages are used by children at home, both Mandarin Chinese and their own language in community, and at school, they need to study and practice their third language, English. So English teaching in the region inhabited by ethnic minority is different from that of other places. Under the circumstance of trilingualism, they have their own characteristics and patterns in terms of language learning. There is no doubt that EFL in ethnic minority area is very important in light of China's development of economy, culture, education and national defense [3].

These topics had attracted scholars' attention for several decades and the academic results of each topic are quite abundant in respective disciplines. But there are quite few related studies on the combination of these three topics, let alone their relationships with English achievements under the circumstances of learning English as a third language. In addition, no previous studies related to Achang ethnic minority students have been found. This is an exploratory research that took Achang ethnic minorities as subjects in history. On the whole, lack of core documents is one of the issues that should not be overlooked. Middle school students are a group of people with the most active thoughts, the strong thirst for knowledge as well as the incomplete view of life, whose identification to their own culture and nationality to some extent represents the tendency of the whole community's ethnic identity.

Quite a group of scholars focused on empirical study on these topics, and some scholars tried to clarify the current situation and some of them were devoted to find a solution to the obstacles we encountered in foreign language teaching in Yunnan or ethnic minority regions. On one hand, those references gave me the hints that these three topics are all worth studying and there is no existence of the studies aiming at the foreign language learning of Achang ethnic minorities. On the other hand, the study of the relationships among the four factors: language attitude, ethnic identity, learning burnout and English learning, is pretty enlightening for English discipline. Meanwhile, it can enrich present empirical study and will be helpful for future study for English pedagogy in the middle school, helping the teachers to handle the issues arose by

English teaching as well as the students to adjust their learning conditions. To sum up, it is a unique and exploratory topic that is worthy of investigation.

2 Research Methodology

2.1 Research Questions

The present study specifically asks the following two questions:

(1) What are their statements on language attitude, ethnic identity and learning burnout?
(2) Is Achang ethnic minority students' English achievement related to language attitude, ethnic identity and learning burnout?

2.2 Setting of Subjects

The Achang, one of the 56 ethnic groups officially recognized by the People's Republic of China. The Achang people number about thirty hundreds [4], mainly distributing in Yunnan province, especially in Dehong Autonomous Prefecture. Most of them live in three ethnic townships named Husa Achang Township in Longchuan County, Jiubao Achang Township and Nangsong Achang Township in Lianghe County. The Achang speak a Burmish (Burmese-related) language called Achang and it is the important language tool during their daily life, but there is no indigenous writing system to accompany it. Chinese characters are often used instead. Many Achang ethnic minorities also speak the Tai Lü language, mainly to make commercial transaction with Dai people and many of them are also capable of speaking Palaung language (the ethnic language of De'ang nationality) for living together with De'ang community. According to the research of Dai [5], there are about 30 thousands Achang ethnic minority people living in the west-south of China. And 90% of them live in Lianghe County and Longchuan County. In the past, feudalism was dominant economic form in the areas in which the Achangs lived and farming was the main way for them to earn a living. Two years after liberation, an Achang autonomous district was established in Longchuan County, and then three more Achang autonomous districts in counties of Luxi and Lianghe. Later, local industries built up from nothing, are centered in Lianghe. Still, economy in Achang regions lags far behind other Han areas, so does the education. Lianghe County is close to Tengchong, a tourist city that is famous for hot spring and local snacks, and it also bring some chances to develop for Lianghe County. With the increasing political, commercial and cultural communications between Han and Achang nationality, Mandarin and the variety of Kunming dialect are widely used in some Achang townships. As Dai presented, Achang ethnic minorities living in Lianghe County have been heavily affected by Han Chinese and mandarin, they are losing their ability of first language, unlike other regions such as Longchuan town and Luxi town, are in a very steady state of the Achang ethnic language use [4]. Most of them are capable of speaking a variety of Yunan dialect, which is belong to the category of Mandarin. In a word, people living are Lianghe is going through a language transaction. Some of the Achangs living in Lianghe town have already finished the transfer and Chinese are used by them as a daily language while others are still in a language transitional process that from the ethnic language to Mandarin. This special situation of language use transfer is the reason why we chose Nangsong and Jiubao Achang townships as subjects in this research.

2.3 Instruments

Three Likert scales were adopted in this dissertation:

Language Attitude Scale. It adopted from previous studies [6, 7] and includes four parts: attitude towards ethnic minority identity scale; attitude to foreign languages and cultures scale; attitude towards learning English scale; attitude towards speakers of English scale.

Ethnic Identity Scale. Qin's revised Likert Scale for Ethnic Identity [8], based essentially on the Multigroup Ethnic Identity Measure designed by Phinney [9].

Ethnic Identity Scale. It can be divided into four parts, the first one is Cognition which refers to comprehending his own ethnic identity and ethnic knowledge; the second dimension is Evaluation which refers to the positive appraisal of his own ethnic identity as well as the importance of it; and next in this order is Emotion, it is a kind of sense of belonging and attachment, indicating the individual regards himself as a part of his nationality; Behavior, as the last one, including some typical behaviors and behavior tendencies acted by individual to defend his ethnic identity and ethnic culture.

Learning Burnout Scale. Hu and Dai's Questionnaire of High School Student's Burnout [10] includes 4 factors: emotional exhaustion; reduced learning efficacy; alienation to teacher; and physical exhaustion.

English Achievement. The latest English final term examination score and their self-evaluation on English verbal fluency. The self-evaluation on verbal fluency scale is employed to measure their own appraisal of the verbal fluency of Mandarin, Ethnic language and English and it is divided into four groups: fluent, average, poor and unable to speak any.

As shown in Table 1, the reliability of Learning Burnout Scale is good, and Ethnic Identity variable is also considered to be pretty high, but Language Attitude is not so favorable.

Table 1. Reliability analysis of three scales.

Scale	N of Items	Cronbach's Alpha
Language attitude	17	0.591
Ethnic identity	23	0.773
Learning burnout	21	0.903

The respondents will specify their level of agreement or disagreement (1–5) on the questionnaire. Specifically, number 1–5 respectively represents strong disagreement, disagreement, neutral, agreement and strong agreement.

2.4 Sample and Sampling

The investigation was carried out in 2 Achang ethnic minority townships in Lianghe County, Dehong Autonomous Prefecture, i.e. Nangsong and Jiubao Ethnic Minority Townships. As we mentioned in the previous chapter, the reason why we chose Achang as the survey sample is the absence of related researches that took Achang ethnic minorities as subjects, and it is special period of language transition is very worth studying. I went to the only two local junior high schools in the two townships: Jiubao Middle School and Nangsong Middle School. Jiubao Middle School is near the county seat while Nangsong Middle School is located on the top of a little hill that is relatively far away from the county seat. It's not so convenient for students in Nangsong Middle School to go home after school, so it offers accommodations for the students. There were three steps to collect the data for the present study. The Achang ethnic minority students were gathered in a room and finished the questionnaires with the help of the principal and the English teachers in the school. The representative sampling method was adopted in the research, and out of the returned questionnaire forms 317 copies were completed. The following three tables illustrate the sample: 166 boys and 151 girls were included in the survey. Among these 317 Achang students, 52.4% are boys while 47.6% are girls. And 172 students come from Nangsong Township while 145 from Jiubao Township. There are 107 seventh grade students, 90 eighth grade students and 120 ninth grade students (see Table 2).

Table 2. Demographics.

		N	Percent %
Sex	Male	166	52.4
	Female	151	47.6
School	Nangsong	172	54.3
	Jiubao	145	45.7
Grade	Seven	107	33.8
	Eight	90	28.4
	Nine	120	37.9
Total		317	100

2.5 Treatment of Data

Statistical Package for Social Sciences 20.0 (SPSS 20.0) was employed in our data analysis. Reliability analysis of three scales was used to make sure the overall consistency of the measure and the high reliability proves that the measures can produce similar results under consistent conditions. Descriptive analysis was conducted to analyze the mean value and standard deviation of the items, factors and variables.

Pearson correlation was adopted to measure the correlations between English achievements and three other variables. Stepwise regression was used to identify the predictors of English achievements. Mediation analysis was carried out to find out the mediating effect among the variables.

3 Results and Discussion

3.1 Descriptive Analysis of Factors and Items in Each Variable

For the purpose of a better understanding of the integral situation of the three measurements in terms of each variable, the descriptive statistics of the three measurements will be presented first. We can summarize the general attitude of students from the mean value of each item or all items, and the SD value can offer us the differences in distribution of students' statements.

Descriptive Analysis of Four Factors of Language Attitude. According to Table 3, most of the Achang middle school students are willing to learn English. On the whole, it can be concluded that these ethnic minority students do have a relatively positive language attitude and it has a lot to do with the unique code-mixing phenomenon in their daily life as well as the specific stage of social development. The conclusion is similar with that of Rahimi and Hassani's case study [11] on Iranian high school students' English learning attitude that Iranian students had positive attitude towards it in general. In addition, He, Li and Wang [12] did a case study on Bai ethnic minorities in the Shalang Township of Kunming City, and most of the Bai ethnic minorities can fluently speak their Bai dialect as well as Kunming dialect. They speak Bai dialect within their own community while speaking Kunming dialect with other ethnic groups. Moreover, Bai people speak highly of Mandarin and English, recognizing the vital role in their children's future.

Table 3. Descriptive statistics of four factors in language attitude.

Factor	N	Mean	SD
Attitude towards ethnic minority identity factor	317	3.75	0.565
Attitude to foreign languages and cultures factor	317	3.66	0.669
Attitude towards learning English factor	317	3.37	0.761
Attitude towards speakers of English factor	317	2.69	0.629
Total	317	3.37	0.446

Descriptive Analysis of Factors of Ethnic Identity. It can be observed in Table 4 that the ethnic identity of these Achang ethnic minority students is generally positive for the mean value is 3.72. All the means of four factors fell in between 3.65 to 3.82. The factors of Cognition and Behavior scored slightly lower than other factors, but in general, the variances are small. According to the data in Table 4, some items in Ethnic Identity Variable achieved scores lower than 3, such as items 11, 13, 14. And among them, item 11 is a question that needs to be counted in a reverse way, indicating that children are not sure that they know their ethnic culture so well. As is mentioned before, this region is going through a special period of language transition because of the increasing intimate communication with the Han people. The intimate communication with Han people, the frequent use of Mandarin and the contacts with the Han culture all have had a great influence on the ethnic minority students to explore their own ethnic culture. These Achang middle school students are exactly the generation that is heavily impacted. Therefore, that is why bilingual education in ethnic minority regions has attracted so much attention. As for item 13, the score 2.95 indicates that students barely feel the disturbance when they are far from their community, that is to say, they are apt to adapt to the life in places far away from home. Item 14, with a score of 2.82, shows the neutral attitude about the positive influence on their identity as an ethnic minority. According to item 1 and item 23 (reversed question), students are pretty sure about their identity of ethnic minority and care about the future of their ethnic group. Gan and Wang [13] conducted a similar research on Wa ethnic minority students' ethnic identity. His questionnaire is also based on Phinney's MEIM and divided into four factors: cognition, evaluation, emotion and behavior. Similarly, they made a conclusion that Wa middle school students' ethnic identity is generally positive and the factor of Behavior scored the lowest in mean score among the four factors.

Table 4. Descriptive statistics of four factors of ethnic identity.

Factor	N	Mean	SD
Cognition (1, 3, 6, 11, 20)	317	3.65	0.514
Evaluation (2, 4, 5, 7, 12, 14)	317	3.73	0.547
Emotion (8, 10, 13, 15, 19, 23)	317	3.82	0.464
Behavior (9, 16, 17, 18, 21, 22)	317	3.69	0.486
Total	317	3.72	0.386

Descriptive Analysis of Factors of Ethnic Identity, It can be referred from Table 5 that the degree of Achang ethnic minority students' English learning burnout is not too serious. Yang [14] did a research on the third language learning burnout with Wa ethnic minority students as subjects and found that the burnout syndrome was frequently seen among the third language learners in the ethnic bilingual context and the third language learners in such context appeared to be more likely to be faced with burnout with the increase of grades or learning years. Nevertheless, the results of this research and Yang's study show that these ethnic minority students did face English learning burnout.

Table 5. Descriptive statistics of 4 factors of English learning burnout variable.

Factor	N	Mean	SD
Emotional exhaustion (2, 3, 6, 7, 8, 10, 11, 18)	317	2.41	0.824
Reduced learning efficacy (1, 12, 13, 15, 21)	317	2.70	0.740
Alienation to teacher (5, 14, 16, 17)	317	2.31	0.761
Physical exhaustion (4, 9, 19, 20)	317	2.64	0.731
Total	317	2.52	0.594

However, it also illustrates in Table 5 that the students' reduced learning efficacy and physical exhaustion respectively scored 2.70 and 2.64, which is higher than other two factors. So these two factors that belong to the middle group may give the clue that these two issues need to be paid more attention to for educators during English teaching, and the two burnout factors of this group may be caused by many factors like unprofessional third language teacher, limited teaching resources, poor elementary education qualities as well as a short time of English learning. On the whole, the scenario of Achang ethnic minority students' English learning burnout is not too bad.

To sum up, the descriptive statistical mean scores of the three variables are 3.37 for language attitude, 3.72 for national identity and 2.52 for learning burnout. This means that Achang students have positive language attitude, strong ethnic identity and weak English learning burnout.

3.2 Correlations Between English Achievement and Language Attitude, Ethnic Identity and Learning Burnout

The two schools in which we conducted the investigation are located in the poor area of Yunnan Province, where the educational conditions are very weak. English is not taken into the junior school entrance examination, that is to say, the students did not learn much English in their primary school. Therefore, the 7th grade students did not have the entrance exam results of English. This is why we did not take 7th grade students as samples in this part. The sample we analyzed here includes 201 8th and 9th grades Achang ethnic minority students and their latest English final examination score as we explained before. We can measure the degree of correlation by the p value, short for Sig (2-tailed) value. In general, when the p value is lower than 0.05, it indicates the correlations between the subjects, and according to the Rule of Stars, there are other standards 0.01 and 0.001, which indicate more significant correlation [15].

Table 6 shows that the Pearson values of each variable is 0.334, 0.060, −0.428 while the p values are 0.000, 0.401, 0.000, which indicates that students' English achievement have weak and significant positive correlations with Language Attitude as well as the significant but weak negative correlations with Learning Burnout, but no significant correlations with Ethnic Identity.

Table 6. Correlations between three variables and English achievements.

		Language attitude	Ethnic identity	Learning burnout
English achievement	Pearson correlation	0.334[b]	0.060	−0.428[b]
	Sig. (2-tailed)	0.000	0.401	0.000
	N	201	201	201

[a]Correlation is significant at 0.05 level (2-tailed)
[b]Correlation is significant at the 0.01 level (2-tailed).

3.3 Stepwise Regression of the Variables

Table 7 shows that the first variable entered is English Learning Burnout, which explains 17.9% of the total variability of English achievements. Then the Language Attitude increases 2.2% to the variability of dependent variable. On the whole, these two independent variables – Learning Burnout and Language Attitude – contributed 20.1% to the variance in the English grade. Obviously, learning burnout has a greater influence on the acquisition of English. Therefore, maintaining a good physical and mental condition and then forming a good study habit are the priorities for English learning. Besides, a positive attitude to English is also essential.

Table 7. Stepwise regression model summary of English achievement on language attitude and learning burnout.

Model	R	R square	Adjusted R square	Std. error of the estimate
1	0.428[a]	0.183	0.179	0.814
2	0.457[b]	0.209	0.201	0.803

[a]Predictors: (Constant), Learning Burnout
[b]Predictors: (Constant), Learning Burnout, Language Attitude

3.4 The Correlations and Mediation Effects Analysis Among the 4 Variables

Table 8 reveals the correlations among the three independent variables: Language Attitude, Ethnic Identity and Learning Burnout. It can be referred from the data that Language Attitude and Ethnic Identity are significantly and weakly correlated for the Pearson value is 0.283 and the p value is 0.000. Meanwhile, Language Attitude is proved to be significantly, moderately but negatively correlated with Learning Burnout as the Pearson value and p value respectively are −0.201 and 0.003. As for the Ethnic Identity and Learning Burnout, there are significant but weak and negative correlations between these two variables. In summary, these three independent variables do have some correlations with each other. The situation of students' language attitude, ethnic identity and learning burnout may have various influences on each other in their study.

Table 8. Correlations among the three independent variables.

		Language attitude	Ethnic identity	Learning burnout
Language attitude	Pearson correlation	1	0.283[a]	−0.447[a]
	Sig. (2-tailed)		0.000	0.000
	N	210	210	210
Ethnic identity	Pearson correlation	0.283[a]	1	−0.201[a]
	Sig. (2-tailed)	0.000		0.003
	N	210	210	210
Learning burnout	Pearson correlation	−0.447[a]	−0.201[a]	1
	Sig. (2-tailed)	0.000	0.003	
	N	210	210	210

[a]Correlation is significant at the 0.01 level (2-tailed).

It has been proved that there are some correlations between Language Attitude, Ethnic Identity and Learning Burnout. To find out the relationships among the three independent variables, the mediation analysis was conducted. According to the former correlation and regression analysis, the independent variable Ethnic Identity can be excluded for having no relation with English Achievements. In this Mediation Analysis, Language Attitude is set to be the x while the English Achievements is the Y, and take the Learning Burnout as the M, the mediate. The Learning Burnout plays the role of an intermediary or conciliator between persons or sides [16].

According to Table 9, after three steps, we can make a conclusion that the model works successfully and the percentage of the mediation effect is $(-0.348 \times -0.447)/0.180 = 86.42\%$. Language Attitude not only can directly influence English Achievements, but also can make an impact on English Achievements through Learning Burnout with 86.42% forces. So these two aspects are of great importance in the teaching of English in ethnic minority areas.

Table 9. The mediation analysis of language attitude

	Standardized equation	SE	t	F	R square	Adjusted R square	Sig.
First step	Y = 0.334x	0.129	5.003	25.031	0.112	0.107	0.000
Second step	M = −0.447x	0.083	−7.200	51.838	0.200	0.196	0.000
Third step	Y = 0.180x	0.136	2.547	26.162	0.209	0.201	0.012
	Y = −0.348m	0.101	−4.935				0.000

4 Conclusion

4.1 Main Findings

Achang Middle School Students' Statements on Language Attitude, Ethnic Identity and Learning Burnout. In this research, Language Attitude Scale contains four factors: Attitude towards Ethnic Minority Identity, Attitude to Foreign Languages and Cultures, Attitude towards Learning English and Attitude towards Speakers of English. Subjects showed generally positive attitude to the former three factors except Attitude towards Speakers of English. The ethnic minority students are pretty proud of their own identity as one of the Achang people and have realized how important Achang ethnic minority language and culture are in the Chinese culture, showing that they still have pretty strong sense of belonging to their nationality after the increasing communication with the Han people. Although they were not able to master English, they expressed interest in English learning. It demonstrates that these Achang ethnic minority students are increasingly aware of how vital English is as a language tool in their future development even though they are just adolescents who are going through the period of forming the outlook of life and the view of the world. The development of local economy and social life, the variation of government policies and national education policy as well as the prevalence of learning English made them realize that English is becoming a necessity of a better life.

The subjects' ethnic identity was divided into four factors based on Phinney's MEIM. The score of Emotion factor stands out among the four factors, indicating their feeling as one part of the nationality and the sense of belonging and attachment. However, Cognition factor scored the lowest among the four factors. It may illustrate the inadequate education about their own nationality and ethnic knowledge. In general, Achang ethnic minority students have a relatively strong identity for their own nationality.

What is noticeable in the four factors of English learning burnout are students' reduced learning efficacy and physical exhaustion, whose mean value is higher than other two factors. It may be connected to the unsatisfied exam grades as well as the linguistic obstacles brought by complex using of the three languages. Physical Exhaustion factor got a low score which may state the present condition of students' educational overburden that the mastering of the three languages is a great challenge for these adolescents. To sum up, these Achang ethnic minority students' English learning burnout is not too serious.

The Correlations Between Achang Ethnic Minority Students' Language Attitude, Ethnic Identity, Learning Burnout and English Achievements. It is proved that Achang ethnic minority students' English achievement did have some correlations with their language attitude and English learning burnout. Subjects' attitude to foreign languages and cultures as well as attitude to learning English in Language Attitude variable is significantly and positively but weakly correlated with their English Achievement. As for the four factors of English Learning Burnout, the Emotional Exhaustion is significantly and negatively related to students' achievement in English while Reduced Learning Efficacy, Alienation to Teacher and Physical Exhaustion have significant and negative but weak correlations with English achievement. On the whole, Learning Burnout is the most important predictor variable that can explain 17.9% of the total variability of students' English achievement, and then the Language Attitude increases 2.2%. The result indicates that the students' mental health is an important aspect to be paid more attention to. These Achang ethnic minority students are adolescents who are in the period of forming the view of value and the outlook of the world, and this period is important to help them to become a grown-up. In this period, they are sensitive to find out the new things in their life, meanwhile, curious about all surrounding them. This characteristic made them eager to learn but easy to be distracted. Focusing on the change of students' emotions and teaching them to maintain a good learning state is conducive to assist them to achieve better results in English learning. What's more, boosting the students' confidence, establishing the good relationship with students, implementing high quality education can relieve the students' overburden and pressure and help them making progress in language acquisition and exams in school.

4.2 Implications of This Research

This research has confirmed the English learning motivation theories through the analysis of the data collected from Achang ethnic minority middle school students. It shows their relatively positive language attitude, pretty high degree of ethnic identity and moderate English learning burnout. The possible implications are of great significance to the English teaching in the context of trilingualism in ethnic minority areas, and the main implications are presented as follows.

This research takes Achang ethnic minority middle school students as subjects, which provides the unique variety of ethnic minority middle student samples in the researches on language attitude, ethnic identity and learning burnout in the context of trilingualism, and which also enriches the universality and feasibility of these motivational theories in ethnic minority areas in China. At the same time, it offers some quantitative evidence for future theoretical researches on these topics. This thesis has confirmed that Achang ethnic minority middle school students' ethnic identity is not significantly correlated with their English achievement, which does not agree with some other scholars' conclusions. It is an issue that remains to be further investigated.

Through the presentation of Achang ethnic minority middle school students' statements on language attitude, ethnic identity and learning burnout, English teachers can get to know more about ethnic minority students' learning situation. The discussion of the correlations among language attitude, ethnic identity, learning burnout and English achievement can provide educators with some advises to cope with the difficulties confronted by student' bad language attitude, weak ethnic identity and serious learning burnout during their teaching, and it also offers some suggestions to the policy makers to develop an appropriate local education policy. It is supposed to create more chances for those ethnic minority students to access to foreign language and culture as well as a change from the teaching styles with intense pressure to the comfortable and efficient teaching mode. Moreover, the analysis and discussion of the differences of the three variables in terms of grades, genders and schools can offer the educators some implications for specific teaching plans for various types of students. Language attitude variable in regression analysis is proved to be effective to predict English achievement. Learning Burnout, the most prominent predictor variable shows the significant but negative correlations with students' English achievement, which reminds teachers that they must pay more attention to the students' burnout of English learning and try to create a relaxing and enjoyable learning environment for students.

References

1. Yuan, Y.C.: An empirical study on minority students' English learning attitude and motivation. Foreign Language Education Press, Shanghai (2007)
2. Li, W.W.: Language planning in the context of globalization – a review of language policy and planning: language policy and globalization. Lang. Strategy Res. **5**, 89–96 (2017)
3. Dai, Q.X.: Current situation and evolution of Achang language use. Commercial Press, Beijing (2008)
4. Dai, Q.X.: Twenty years of "endangered language fever". J. Yunnan Normal Univ. (Philos. Soc. Sci. Edn.) **4**, 1–6 (2012)
5. Gardner, R.C., Lambert, W.: Attitudes and Motivation in Second Language Learning. Newbury House, Rowley (1972)
6. Dörnyei, Z.: The social psychology of the language learner: individual differences in second language acquisition. Lawrence Erlraum Associates, Mahwah, NJ (2005)
7. Qin, X.R.: National identity and development of Chinese adolescents aged 11 to 20. Central China Normal University, Wuhan (2005)
8. Phinney, J.S.: Ethnic identity in adolescents and adults: review of research. Psychol. Bull. **108**, 499–514 (1990)
9. Hu, Q., Dai, C.L.: Research on the structure of learning burnout in middle school students. Psychol. Sci. **1**, 162–164 (2007)
10. Rahimi, M., Hassani, M.: Attitude towards EFL textbooks as a predictor of attitude towards learning English as a foreign language. Procedia - Soc. Behav. Sci. **31**, 66–72 (2012)
11. He, L., Li, Q.Y., Wang, X.: Language harmony in a harmonious society: a study of language use, language relations and language attitudes in multi-ethnic areas in Yunnan Province: a case study of the Salang Bai nationality township in kunming. J. Southwest Univ. Nationalities **3**, 27–30 (2010)
12. Gan, K.P., Wang, Q.: Research on ethnic identity psychology of middle school students from ethnic minorities. Guizhou Ethnic Studies **3**, 185–191 (2012)
13. Yang, S.: Research on the influence of English education on the ethnic identity of contemporary college students in China under the background of globalization. Surv. Res. **17**, 125–128 (2014)
14. Qiu, H.Z.: Quantitative research and statistical analysis – analysis of SPSS (PASW) data analysis examples. Chongqing University Press, Chongqing (2013)

A Study of Correlation Between Self-efficacy, Language Anxiety, Metacognitive Strategies and English Achievements of Achang Ethnic Minority Junior High School Students in the Trilingual Background

Yuan Yuan, Xiao Xie(✉), and Yi-chuan Yuan

Foreign Language School, Yunnan Normal University,
Kunming 650500, Yunnan, China
yuanyuanuni@163.com, 747919496@qq.com,
yycyunnan@163.com,

Abstract. This study used the empirical quantitative method to investigate the correlation between self-efficacy, language anxiety, metacognitive strategies and English achievement of 317 Achang ethnic students from Nangsong Ethnic Minority Junior High School and Jiubao Achang Ethnic Minority Junior High School in the trilingual background in Lianghe County of Yunnan province, China. The data was measured with descriptive analysis, Pearson correlation and regression analysis with SPSS21.0. The conclusion was drawn as following:

1. Most of Achang middle school students speak Achang language, more than half of the students speak Mandarin, no one speak English fluently, and there are more than half of the students failed to pass the final English exam. The Achang ethnic students sometimes have self-efficacy and foreign language anxiety, and sometimes use metacognitive learning strategies in English learning;
2. There is a significant positive correlation between English achievement and self-efficacy and metacognitive strategies, but foreign language anxiety is significantly and negatively correlated with English achievements;
3. The predictor which influences the students' English achievement is self-efficacy.

Keywords: Achang ethnic students · Self-efficacy · Foreign language anxiety · Metacognitive strategies

1 Background of the Study

China is a unified country with 56 nationalities including Han nationality and 55 minority nationalities. Yunnan is a multicultural province, located in the southwest part of China, bordered by Vietnam, Laos and Burma, with 25 ethnic minorities which make up a very low proportion of Chinese population. It has been difficult to overcome the

G. Sun et al. (Eds.): eLEOT 2019, LNICST 299, pp. 316–326, 2019.
https://doi.org/10.1007/978-3-030-35095-6_36

barriers of geographical isolation and overall poor economic conditions, and so education in most parts of the ethnic minority areas in China is relatively weak. With special small population, Achang ethnic minority is one of 56 ethnic groups in China, belonging to cross-border minority, distributing in Yunnan province and Guizhou province [1], but it is mainly distributed in Dehong Autonomous Prefecture in Yunnan province, including Husa Achang township in Longchuan County, Nangsong Achang township and Jiubao Achang township in Lianghe County, and their language is Achang language belonging to Tibeto-Burman group of Sino Tibetan languages [2], but there is no written language. Achang language is closely related to Zaiwa language and Burmese, then Yi language, including three dialects: Longchuan dialect, Luxi dialect and Lianghe dialect [3]. Historically, as for multiple reasons, Achang ancestors migrated frequently and interlaced with other nationalities for a long time in a large region, therefore, their language has been permeated with others, absorbing other words from other languages for daily use, which has made Achang language complex [3]. According to Xie [4], the Achang language is well preserved in Longchuan County and Luxi County where language vitality is strong, while it is a different situation in Lianghe where some villages have turned to use Chinese. Present use of Achang language has assumed some serious declining features, and the phenomenon of language transfer is prominent [3], which means the Achang language is greatly affected by Mandarin and most of Achang ethnic minorities use Mandarin in most of social and daily life.

The phenomenon of bilingualism is a common scenario in many ethnic minority areas, which is the change of language use function after the accumulation of language contact to a certain degree. In China, students have to complete the compulsory education from 7 years old to 16, thus in ethnic minority areas, ethnic students may live in the situation of multilingualism, and they not only learn Mandarin Chinese but English along with the use of their mother tongue in daily communication, which has made teaching English in ethnic areas become complicated. This thesis has chosen Lianghe Achang ethnic minority students as research subjects to study their English learning in the trilingual background.

Lianghe County is located in the southwest end of the Hengduan Mountains in the west of Yunnan Province, belonging to Dehong Autonomous Prefecture. It is bordered with Tengchong County in the northeast, Longling County in the southeast, Luxi and Longchuan County in the north, and Yingjiang County in the west. Zhedao, the County seat, is about 690 km from Kunming the capital of Yunnan province and about 114 km from the prefecture capital, Mangshi [5]. The Achang ethnic minority in Lianghe County mainly lives in Jiubao Achang Township and Nangsong Achang Township; besides, they also live in administrative villages including Wanzhong, Menglai, and Manghui etc. According to the latest statistics (2010), the total population of Achang nationality in Linghe is 12708, about 7.9% of the whole County's population [3]. Two middle schools have been investigated in Lianghe County including Nangsong Achang Minority Junior High School and Jiubao Achang Minority Junior High School.

Therefore, a comprehensive study is necessary, and a focus on ethnic minority students is more meaningful in China whereas study on this area is a little deficient, and so a further research is needed.

As the research of language learning theory has gradually developed and advanced, which has inspired many researchers to place emphasis on the characteristics of language learners. The term self-efficacy was firstly proposed by Bandura in 1977. Foreign language anxiety scale was developed by Horwitz, Horwitz, and Cope [6]. As an affective factor, anxiety is crucial for language learning. From 1980s, there are plenty of studies on foreign language anxiety both home and abroad. Metacognitive strategies are an indispensable part in language learning strategies, which play a critical role in language learning. To a great extent, whether achieving success in language learning depends on the use of metacognitive strategies [7]. As the study of SLA has expanded and developed significantly in the past 40–45 years [8], there have been numerous studies about the characteristics of the language learner both home and abroad.

But there is a lack of ethnic minority studies concerned, therefore, what do exactly the Achang minority students come to know about their third language–English? What is the relationship among self-efficacy, foreign language anxiety, metacognitive strategies and English achievements? Additionally, how to improve English achievements of Achang minority students is also a focus of this research.

2 Research Methodology

2.1 Sampling and Samples

This study employed the convenience sampling method. Students from Nangsong Achang ethnic minority Junior High School and Jiubao Achang ethnic minority Junior High School are the research subjects. Nangsong Achang ethnic minority Junior High School is one of the three townships of Achang nationality in China, which is located in the northeast of Lianghe County, about 10 km from the County seat. Jiubao Achang ethnic minority Junior High School also is one of the three townships of Achang nationality in China, which lies in the outskirts of the County seat. Employing the representative sample method to extract the sample, the author of this thesis investigated 172 students of Nangsong Achang ethnic minority Junior High School including 87 males and 85 females, including 55 students in grade seven, 49 students in grade eight, and 68 students in grade nine. And 145 students of Jiubao Achang ethnic minority Junior High School participated in the probe, including 79 males and 66 females, 52 students in grade seven, 41 students in grade eight, and 52 students in grade nine. All of them are Achang ethnic minorities. All students started to learn English from grade seven because Lianghe County is a remote place with a weak education background.

2.2 Instruments

The instrument used in this study is a questionnaire consisting of self-efficacy scale, foreign language classroom anxiety scale and metacognitive strategies scale. The questionnaire of this study has two parts. The first part is the basic information and complementary questions for Achang ethnic minority students, and in this part, students' scores were taken from their last term final examination of which the total score is 120. As investigated, Achang ethnic minority students study English from grade 7, therefore, this study has offered self-evaluated language proficiency from fluent to knowing nothing. There were a total of 51 question items in the second part of the questionnaire. The subjects were asked to give response to the questionnaire based on a 5-point Likert scale, ranging from "strongly disagree" to "strongly agree".

Table 1. The Alpha-Coefficient of the Questionnaire

	Self-efficacy	LA	Meta-cognitive strategies
Cronbach Alpha	0.739	0.822	0.91

The questionnaire demonstrates internal reliability (see Table 1) and validity (see Table 4.2). The Cronbach's alpha value of self-efficacy scale is 0.739, indicating the moderate internal consistency. And both Language Classroom Anxiety and Metacognitive Strategies have high internal consistency of which Cronbach's alpha values are 0.822 and 0.910 respectively.

2.3 Data of Treatment

The 317 effective questionnaires sheets were collected. SPSS 21.0 (Statistical Product and Service Solutions) was used to analyze the quantitative data. The procedures of data treatment were as the followings: (1) testing the Alpha-Coefficient of the three scales; (2) using Descriptive Analysis to measure variables' and question items' Mean Value and Std. Deviation; (3) adopting Pearson Correlation Coefficient to analyze the relationship between the factors and English achievements; (4) conducting Linear Stepwise Regression to predicate the factors affecting the English achievements.

3 Discussion and Analysis

3.1 Descriptive Analysis of Overall Situation of Self-efficacy, Language Anxiety and Metacognitive Strategies

Table 2. Descriptive statistics of the overall situation of three variables

	N	Minimum	Maximum	Mean	Std. Deviation
Self-efficacy	317	1	5	3.19	0.626
Language Anxiety	317	1	4	3.02	0.417
Metacognitive Strategies	317	1	5	3.28	0.768

As is shown in Table 2, the mean of self-efficacy is 3.19, which suggests that the participants are sometimes confident in English learning. And the Std. Deviation is 0.626 which means the students' answers for the self-efficacy question are relatively centralized. Similar to the study of Tuo, Yang and He [9] on Xinjiang ethnic minority students, the result of self-efficacy in this study implies that most students have the moderate sense of self-efficacy when learning English. In the present study, the mean of language classroom anxiety is 3.02 around the medium point, and the Std. Deviation is 0.417 indicating that many students feel anxiety in English study. However, the level of language classroom anxiety is lower than that of Tibetan students [10], but is similar to that of Han, Naxi and Yi students [11]. This occurred due to the fact that Achang language has presented a declining feature [3] for being strongly influenced by Mandarin Chinese, all the Achang ethnic students speak Mandarin Chinese, so that Achang ethnic minority students learn English with Mandarin as inter-language more easily than Tibetan students, and have lower foreign language classroom anxiety relatively. The mean value of metacognitive strategies is 3.28 which is above the medium point, and the Std. Deviation is 0.768, which means these students sometimes chose to use metacognitive strategies. Consistent with the results of learning strategies playing an important role in second/foreign language learning [12, 13], the result of this study shows that Achang ethnic minority students tend to use metacognitive strategies as a kind of learning strategies when learning English, but inconsistently.

Table 3. Descriptive Statistics of Self-efficacy Factors

	N	Minimum	Maximum	Mean	Std. Deviation
Self-confidence for English achievements	317	1	5	3.10	0.750
Self-confidence for learning tasks	317	1	5	3.29	0.647

3.1.1 The Descriptive Statistics of the Two Factors of Self-efficacy

Table 4. Descriptive Statistics of four factors of language anxiety

	N	Minimum	Maximum	Mean	Std. Deviation
Language learning anxiety	317	2	4	3.06	0.447
Classroom nervousness	317	1	4	2.89	0.533
Communication apprehension	317	1	4	3.04	0.455
Fear of questioning	317	1	5	3.11	0.649

As is shown in the Table 3, the mean of self-confidence for English achievements and self-confidence for learning tasks is 3.10 and 3.29 respectively. The Std. Deviation of self-confidence for English achievements is 0.750, and self-confidence for learning tasks is 0.647. Both have low Std. Deviation indicating that most students have similar answers as sometimes they have confidence in English learning. Compared with the study of Zhang and Yu [14], Achang ethnic minority students have lower self-efficacy in English study than college students. The reason may be that they have lower mastery experience, vicarious experience, social persuasion, and physiological states [15] than college students, which suggests middle school students have lower self-confidence for English achievements and self-confidence for learning tasks in English study.

3.1.2 The Descriptive Statistics of the Four Factors of Language Anxiety

Table 5. Descriptive statistics of three factors of metacognitive strategies

	N	Minimum	Maximum	Mean	Std. Deviation
Metacognitive learning plan	317	1	5	3.16	0.919
Metacognitive self-monitoring	317	1	5	3.39	0.817
Metacognitive regulation	317	1	5	3.3	0.783

It can be seen from the Table 4 that the average value of the four factors of the language anxiety is 3.06, 2.89, 3.04 and 3.11 accordingly. From this table, the mean value of language learning anxiety is 3.06, and the Std. Deviation is 0.447, indicating that most of students sometimes have language learning anxiety. Classroom nervousness scores the lowest level of the four factors with 2.89 slightly below the medium point 3, and the Std. Deviation is 0.533, suggesting that most of the students sometimes think they are nervous in English class. And this is corresponded with the answer of item 17 (see Table 5.5). The fear of questioning is ranked the highest level with 3.11, and the Std. Deviation is 0.649, which implies that most students are sometimes unlikely to answer questions in English class. This agrees with the answer of item 3 (see Table 4). The results are different from the study of Chinese college students [16] in which the communication apprehension is in the first place, whereas in this study fear of questioning gets the highest score among the four factors of foreign language anxiety. By contrast, when being questioned, middle school students will have higher anxiety as they have little knowledge of English at the beginning.

3.1.3 The Descriptive Statistics of the Four Factors of Metacognitive Strategies

As is shown in Table 5, the mean value of these three factors is 3.16, 3.39 and 3.3 respectively. The highest mean is metacognitive self-monitoring scoring 3.39 with the Std. Deviation 0.817, which implies that students tend to use metacognitive self-monitoring in English learning, with the corresponding answer item 10 (see Table 5.9). Then it is followed by factor of metacognitive regulation which scores 3.3 and its Std. Deviation is 0.783. The last is metacognitive learning plan scoring 3.16 with its Std. Deviation 0.919. Compared with the former two factors, metacognitive learning plan is less used in English study by Achang ethnic students, which is similar to the study of Xu [17] which reveals that metacognitive learning plan is the least used strategies by both ethnic minority and the mainstream Han ethnic students.

3.2 The Pearson Correlation Results of English Achievements and the Three Variables

Table 6. Pearson Correlation results between English achievements and three variables

		Self-efficacy	LA	Metacognitive strategies
English achievements	Pearson Correlation	.389**	−.256**	.341**
	Sig. (2-tailed)	.000	.000	.000
	N	201	201	201

**. Correlation is significant at the 0.01 level (2-tailed).

It can be seen that there is a weakly positive correlation between English achievements and self-efficacy ($r = 0.389$, $p < 0.01$) indicating that the higher the level of self-efficacy, the higher English scores students get; a weakly negative correlation between English achievements and foreign language classroom ($r = -0.256$, $p < 0.01$), revealing that the higher the level of anxiety, the lower scores students achieve; a weakly positive correlation between English achievements and metacognitive strategies ($r = 0.341$, $p < 0.01$), purporting that students use more metacognitive strategies, and their English scores will be higher. The result of the relationship between English achievements and self-efficacy is similar to the study of Tuoya et al. [21] whose research subjects are Xingjiang ethnic minority students. As for foreign language anxiety, the result of this study is consistent with those of previous studies [6, 18, 19]. The result of the relationship between English achievements and metacognitive strategies of Achang ethnic minority students is different from that of the study by Zhou and Xie [20] which proves that the no relationship is found between metacognitive strategies and English achievements of ethnic minority students in Yunnan province. The reason may be that Achang ethnic students from the remote place are good at using metacognitive strategies to learn English well. Therefore, they can find a way to get higher education in cities (Table 6).

3.3 The Stepwise Regression Results of English Achievements and the Three Variables

Through the stepwise liner regression analysis, Table 7 provides the results of predicating the main variables affecting English achievements.

Table 7. Stepwise regression model summary of English achievement on the three variables

Model	R	R Square	Adjusted R Square	Std. Error of the Estimate
1	.389[a]	0.151	0.147	0.829

a. Predictors: (Constant), Self-efficacy

According to the Table 7, only one optimal independent variable entering the model is self-efficacy. Self-efficacy can explain 15.1% variance of English achievements and it still has 14.7% explanation after the adjusted R square. The reason why this phenomenon appears may be that self-efficacy, foreign language anxiety and metacognitive strategies are correlated with each other as dependent variables, therefore, foreign language anxiety and metacognitive strategies are lost in the regression analysis.

3.4 The Mediation Effect of English Achievements and the Three Variables

Table 8. The mediation effect of English achievements

	Standardized Equation	SE	t	F
First step	$Y = 0.366X_1$	0.105	4.502**	17.809**
Second step	$M = 0.622X_1$	0.065	11.462**	131.383**
Third step	$Y = 0.289X_1$	0.107	3.481**	19.911**
	0.162M	0.092	1.948*	

*. Correlation is significant at the 0.05 level (2-tailed).
**. Correlation is significant at the 0.01 level (3-tailed).

In order to discuss the further relationship among self-efficacy, foreign language anxiety, metacognitive strategies and English achievements, this research has chosen mediation effects' model. Through the regression analysis, the results can be seen from Table 8 and Fig. 1. The self-efficacy can predicate English achievements, and indirectly affect English achievements through metacognitive strategies, but foreign language anxiety cannot predicate English achievements as it cannot be enter the model (see Table 8). The metacognitive strategies operate as a mediate role between self-efficacy and English achievements. Through the further analysis, compared with the direct predication of self-efficacy, the explanation of English achievements through self-efficacy to metacognitive strategies is relatively weak ($0.162 \times 0.622 < 0.289$), which means the direct effects are more powerful to predicate English achievements than the indirect way. Actually, teachers need to consider both self-efficacy and the relationship between self-efficacy and metacognitive strategies to improve students' English achievements even though the mediation effects are weak.

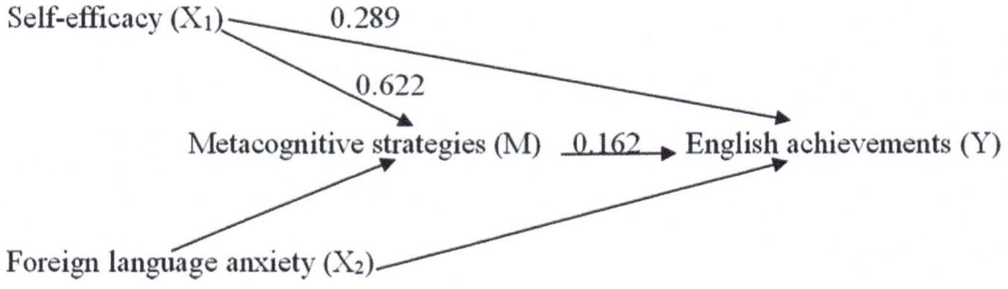

Fig. 1. The mediation effects

Figure 1 is the path way analysis of mediation effects. X1 stands for self-efficacy, X2 refers to foreign language anxiety, M represents metacognitive strategies, and Y is equal to English achievements.

4 Conclusion

4.1 Main Findings

The descriptive results of self-efficacy, foreign language anxiety and metacognitive strategies are around the midpoint, implying that Achang ethnic minority students sometimes have self-efficacy and foreign language anxiety, and use the metacognitive strategies in English study. In view of the first question, the overall situation of Achang minority junior high school students related to self-efficacy indicates that Achang minority students have a little confidence when learning English. And they have the moderate degree of anxiety in English study. They have used more metacognitive strategies than the other two variables.

As for the second question, the self-efficacy, metacognitive strategies and English achievement are positively but weakly related, while the correlation between foreign language anxiety and English achievement is negative. Through the correlation analysis, self-confidence for learning tasks, classroom nervousness and metacognitive regulation show the significant and weak correlation with English achievements. With the response to the third question, the stepwise regression results indicate the main predicator of English achievements is self-efficacy. The results also suggest that self-confidence for learning tasks; classroom nervousness and metacognitive regulation have the significant and weak correlation with English achievements.

4.2 Implications

From the analysis of the relationship among self-efficacy, foreign language anxiety, metacognitive strategies and English achievements in the trilingual background, the results indicate that the higher self-efficacy students have more frequently metacognitive strategies they use and lower anxiety they have in English learning, they will have greater achievements. Teachers need to provide students with the best possible conditions for learning. Because Achang ethnic students learn English in the trilingual background, their education should be in accordance with their learning characteristics.

In the first place, as Achang ethnic students sometimes have self-efficacy which is significantly positively related to their English achievements, teachers can help Achang ethnic students experience the success in English learning so as to improve students' confidence. In addition, English teachers should assist students in carrying out appropriate learning tasks, because both too difficult and too easy learning tasks are unlikely to review the students' authentic English level. Otherwise, students will lose their confidence in English learning. Moreover, the special language background and geographical locations make Achang ethnic students' English learning more difficult and complicated.

Secondly, teachers should guide students to alleviate their language anxiety, especially the classroom nervousness. As investigated in this study, classroom nervousness is significantly and negatively related with English achievements of Achang ethnic students. Therefore, the set-up of a harmonious classroom environment is vital to students. On the one hand, teachers can encourage students to speak out their difficulties and anxiety, and then help students to overcome them. On the other hand, this study shows that some Achang ethnic students think they will feel frightened when they don't understand what the teacher say in English. Therefore, teachers can organize classroom activities concerning the comparison of the Achang culture with Western culture, which will be good for students to understand English. So Achang ethnic students will feel less anxiety when they understand in English study.

Lastly, the Achang students sometimes use metacognitive strategies, meaning that they occasionally select the key points of their studies, make language plan, regulate language process, and evaluate the effect of learning. As a result, it is necessary for the students to enhance the use of metacognitive strategies. As a kind of mediator, metacognitive strategies play a non-ignorable role. Thus, instructors should teach their students how to use metacognitive strategies, and especially guiding them to make a reasonable language learning plan, regulate and monitor their learning process.

References

1. Li, S., Tan, F.: Inheritance and prospect: review of the research on Achang culture in China for ten years. J. Tongren Univ. **17**(1), 134–143 (2015)
2. Dai, Q.: Questions on Linguistic Theories and Methods. Central University for Nationalities Press, Beijing (2012)
3. Dai, Q.: Current Situation and Evolution of Achang Language Use. Commercial Press, Beijing (2008)
4. Xie, H.: Exploration on Achang language decay in lianghe river. In: The 3rd International Symposium on the Protection of Endangered Language Heritage in Yunnan, China, Yuxi, Yunnan, China, 01 January 2010
5. Lianghe County Chronicles Compilation Committee of Lianghe County, Yunnan Province. Yunnan People's Publishing House, Kunming (2011)
6. Horwitz, E.K., Horwitz, M.B., Cope, J.: Foreign language classroom anxiety. Mod. Lang. J. **70**(2), 125–132 (1986)
7. O'Malley, J.M., Chamot, A.U.: Learning Strategies in Second Language Acquisition. Cambridge University Press, Cambridge (1990)
8. Gass, S.M., Selinker, L.: Second Language Acquisition: An Introductory Course. Taylor & Francis, New York (2008)
9. Toya, Y.J., He, Y.: Research on English learning self-efficacy of Xinjiang minority preparatory students.. J. Beijing University of Posts and Telecommunications (Soc. Sci. Ed.), **10**(5), 67–71 (2008)
10. Gong, J., Gao, X.: Study on English learning anxiety of ethnic minority college students – a case study of Tibetan college students. Guizhou ethnic studies **29**(4), 166–171 (2009)
11. Yang, H., Yu, P., Fu, J.: Survey on English learning anxiety of middle school students of han, naxi and yi nationalities. Chinese J. Mental Health **18**(3), 205–206 (2004)

12. Rubin, J.: Learner strategies: theoretical assumptions, research history and typology. In: Wenden, A., Rubin, L. (eds.) Learner Strategies in Language Learning. Prentice Hall, Englewood Cliffs, N. J. (1987)
13. Oxford, R.L.: Language Learning Strategies: What Every Teacher Should Know. Newbury House Publisher, New York (1990)
14. Zhang, S., Yu, W.: Research and analysis of college freshmen's self-efficacy in English learning. Educ. Res. Exp. (5), 93–96 (2010)
15. Bandura, A.: Self-Efficacy: The Exercise of Control. Freeman, New York (1997)
16. Wang, C.: Test report of foreign language anxiety scale in college students. Psychol. Sci. **26** (2), 281–284 (2003)
17. Xu, S.: Comparative analysis of English vocabulary learning strategies between minority and han students. Foreign Lang. Teach. **32**(4), 57–60 (2011)
18. Yuan, Y., Holliday, L., Shang, Y., Yuan, K., Huang, W.: Empirical study on the relationship between English learning motivation and English performance of minority students in Yunnan. J. Yunnan Normal University (Philosophy Soc. Sci. Ed.) **41**(1), 81–88 (2009)
19. Yu, W., Kaiqi, S., Xiang, Y.: Relationship between emotional intelligence, foreign language learning anxiety and English learning performance. Modern Foreign Lang. **38**(5), 656–730 (2015)
20. Zhou, L., Xie, L.: On the correlation between English learning strategies and scores of minority junior middle school students. J. Chuxiong Normal Univ. **28**(7), 98–108 (2013)

Assessment and Learning Analytics

Construction of Scientific Evaluation System for Connotative Development of Higher Vocational Colleges in Yunnan in the New Era

Chao Ye[1(✉)], Aihua Wen[2], and Liusheng Liu[3]

[1] Human Resources Office, Yunnan Physical Science and Sports Professional College, Kunming, Yunnan, China
242107349@qq.com
[2] School of Arts and Sciences, Yunnan Jiaotong College, Kunming, Yunnan, China
[3] Higher Education and Regional Development Research Institute, Yunnan Normal University, Kunming, Yunnan, China

Abstract. The evaluation of the development of higher vocational colleges is the key to promoting the intensive development of higher vocational colleges. It can not only enable higher vocational colleges to form a relatively unified, systematic, scientific understanding on what is connotative development, how to operate and evaluate connotative development., but also help vocational colleges to recognize the level of their own connotative development and the development of regional higher vocational colleges. Through the current setting of the intensive development research platform of Yunnan higher vocational colleges, focusing on the basic principles and methods of evaluation indicators, under the preliminary construction of the scientific evaluation index of the intensive development of Yunnan higher vocational colleges, this study scientifically construct the scientific evaluation index system and the dynamic response plan for the intensive development of higher vocational colleges in Yunnan.

Keywords: Yunnan higher vocational colleges · Connotative development · Scientific evaluation system · Construction

1 Current Research Status and Problems of Development Evaluation of Higher Vocational Colleges in Yunnan

Higher vocational education is part of the most crucial part of our higher education. With the implementation of the enrollment expansion policy in recent years, higher vocational education has moved toward the process of popularization. As show in Table 1, between 2013 and 2017, the number of higher vocational colleges in Yunnan increased from 38 to 45. The enrollment increased from 40,800 to 98,900, an increase of 58.71%, and the number of students in the school increased from 11 million to 29.2 million, an increase of 62.35%. Up to now, the overall development momentum of higher vocational education in Yunnan is good, mainly reflected in the expansion of the scale, the improvement of the structure, the renewal of the concept and the improvement of benefits.

G. Sun et al. (Eds.): eLEOT 2019, LNICST 299, pp. 329–337, 2019.
https://doi.org/10.1007/978-3-030-35095-6_37

Table 1. Preliminary construction of the evaluation system of connotative development indicators in higher vocational colleges in Yunnan

Year	Number of higher vocational colleges	Entrants	Enrolment
2013	38	40845	109953
2014	37	72186	197833
2015	38	79621	228621
2016	41	79321	255335
2017	45	98919	292023

However, rapid development will intensify the expansion of college scale, which will lead to the imbalance of the structure of higher vocational colleges in Yunnan. To solve this problem, the key is to reform and adjust the education and teaching structure of higher vocational colleges in Yunnan, gradually take the road of connotative development, and finally make Yunnan higher vocational colleges more adapt to social development, which is also the rational choice and objective demand for the connotative development of higher vocational colleges in Yunnan.

There are many problems in the development of higher vocational colleges, such as utilitarianism, surface layering and formalization. However, the evaluation of higher vocational colleges lacks operational, reliable and scientific standards and methods. At the same time, rather than processes, there are more focus on results, quantitative research is also more popular than qualitative research. The scientific evaluation of the development of higher vocational colleges is the key to promote higher vocational colleges to develop orderly. It can not only enable higher vocational colleges to form a relatively unified, systematic, scientific understanding on what is connotative development, how to operate and evaluate connotative development, but also help vocational colleges to recognize the level their own connotative development and the development of regional higher vocational colleges. Therefore, the construction of the evaluation system of the connotative development of higher vocational colleges has important theoretical and practical significance.

2 The Setting of the Research Platform of Connotative Development in Higher Vocational Colleges in Yunnan

In order to make higher vocational colleges sustainably and healthily developing, the regional government plays the role as senior designer in top-level construction, and it can fully coordinate the relationship among the various elements of higher vocational education. The government should first coordinate the various higher vocational colleges in the region, formulate the professional layout of the higher vocational colleges, and provide matching high-level talents for the economic development of Yunnan, so as to promote the professional placement and enrollment scale of Yunnan higher vocational colleges. Secondly, the government should adopt legislation to establish a vocational education guarantee mechanism that can promote government-academic-industry cooperation, and to clarify the responsibility of enterprises in participating in vocational education. Thirdly, the government should combine the professional layout of the higher vocational colleges and the current number of enrollment in Yunnan, and focus on supporting the professions that meet the needs of the talents in the labor market, and adapt appropriately regulation to form a special running model of Yunnan higher vocational colleges. Finally, the government should systematically sort out the disadvantage majors in the vocational colleges and provide corresponding funds and supporting policies, which is more conducive to the rational development of higher vocational colleges.

3 Construction of Scientific Evaluation Indicators of Connotative Development in Yunnan Higher Vocational Colleges

3.1 The Basic Principles and Methods of Index Construction

The basic principles for constructing scientific evaluation indicators for the in-depth development of higher vocational colleges in Yunnan include directional principles, scientific principles, feasibility principles, the combination of systemic and importance principles, and the principle of combining commonality and individuality. The principle of directional is to evaluate the purpose of the connotative development of higher vocational colleges, mainly reflected in the development of students' individuality and the improvement of the quality of school education. The scientific principle is the evaluation index system and its process is scientific and effective, and the scientific methods, methods and means are scientific theory and factual basis. The feasibility principle is feasible and operable, which is reflected in the fact that it is built on the international perspective and the actual foundation of the intensive development of higher vocational colleges. Considering the different level of connotative development of higher vocational colleges in different regions and schools. The principle of combining systematicness and importance is to reflect the characteristics of the college and the specific professional curriculum on the basis of comprehensive consideration. The combination of commonality and individuality is to comprehensively consider the essence and particularity of the intensive development of higher vocational colleges.

The basic methods for constructing the scientific evaluation index of connotative development in Yunnan higher vocational colleges are top-down, bottom-up, top-down and bottom-up integration. From top to bottom, the researchers propose preliminary indicators and frameworks based on the results of the research, and then thoroughly seek comments and suggestions from experts and relevant parties to revise and improve them. For the bottom-up, researchers extensively seek the opinions and suggestions of experts and relevant parties, then summarize the index system of the connotative development of higher vocational colleges. Top-down and bottom-up integration, while conducting theoretical research, extensively solicits opinions and suggestions from experts and relevant parties.

3.2 Preliminary Construction of Scientific Evaluation Index for Connotative Development of Higher Vocational Colleges in Yunnan

Based on the research of the connotative development of higher vocational colleges, the evaluation index system of connotative development of higher vocational colleges is preliminarily constructed. The index system mainly includes four aspects: cultural construction, curriculum setting, organizational characteristics management and quality improvement. Each large aspect contains 15 dimensions of the indicator system. The table below shows details (Table 2):

Table 2. Preliminary construction of the evaluation system of connotative development indicators in higher vocational colleges in Yunnan

NO.	Dimension	Dimension connotation	Indicator system
1	Cultural construction	The internal values, external style and brand temperament of the college	1.1 The development direction of featured products (such as reading, technology, calligraphy, etc.)
			1.2 Internal values (such as school mission, vision, goals, etc.)
			1.3 Teacher-student quality culture, behavior (such as activities, behavioral norms, relationships)
			1.4 Cultural representation (such as logo, cultural facilities, campus environment)
2	Curriculum setting	The characteristics of the curriculum, and its consistency with the school culture construction	2.1 Curriculum orientation
			2.2 Curriculum development (including curriculum resources, textbook development, etc.)
			2.3 Curriculum implementation (including corresponding teaching objectives, method reform)
			2.4 Course evaluation
3	Organizational management	The guarantee effect of school organization characteristic management on development	3.1 Faculty (especially teachers in advantage fields)
			3.2 President leadership (especially in the process of connotative development of the college)
			3.3 Mechanism construction (such as curriculum evaluation, student evaluation, teacher evaluation mechanism, etc.)
			3.4 Resource support (such as funding, facilities, professional, administrative support)

(*continued*)

Table 2. (*continued*)

NO.	Dimension	Dimension connotation	Indicator system
4	Quality improvement	The Effect and Influence of the Connotative Development of Higher Vocational Colleges on the Quality of School Running	4.1 Student Development (The impact of connotative development of higher vocational colleges on students)
			4.2 Teacher Development (The influence of connotative development of higher vocational colleges on teachers)
			4.3 College development (the impact of the connotative development of higher vocational colleges on colleges)

3.3 Scientific Evaluation Index of Connotative Development in Higher Vocational Colleges in Yunnan

Based on the research on the connotative development of higher vocational colleges, combined with the preliminary construction of the evaluation index system of the intensive development of higher vocational colleges in Yunnan, the process of connotative development of Yunnan higher vocational colleges contains three links: concept, practice and effect. The concept is the philosophy and goal of school-running. The practice is the curriculum setting and organizational characteristics management. The effect is the development of students, teachers and the college. Each major aspect contains 20 dimensions of the indicator system. Check the table below for details (Table 3):

Table 3. Scientific evaluation indexes of connotative development of higher vocational colleges in yunnan province

No.	Dimension	Content	Indicator	Indicator connotation
1	The degree of internal and external adaptability of the college's characteristic brand	Does the matching of core values and goals lead the development of the college's characteristic brands?	1.1 Schooling philosophy	1.1.1 The college's educational philosophy and core values are in line with the its actual needs and traditions 1.1.2 Schooling philosophy reflects the college's characteristics, brand and core values, and has personality, stability and inheritance
			1.2 Target direction	1.2.1 The college has distinct characteristics and reflects real needs and traditional history 1.2.2 Individualized educational goals and development goals 1.2.3 The goal is in line with the society's requirements for talent and actual needs of students
2	The consistency of the development of college's characteristic brand practice and concept	Mainly reflected in the consistency of the curriculum, school values and goals	2.1 Curriculum	2.1.1 The school sets the characteristic curriculum according to the goal and direction of the development of the characteristic brand, so that the educational goal can be completed

(*continued*)

Table 3. (*continued*)

No.	Dimension	Content	Indicator	Indicator connotation
				2.1.2 Characteristic curriculum reflects the college's values and students' abilities, interests and actual needs 2.1.3 Focusing on the completion of the characteristic goal and reflecting the values of the college during teaching progress 2.1.4 Exploring unique teaching models and forming unique teaching styles
			2.2 Organizational management	2.2.1 Presidents and teachers perform their duties to promote the completion of the school's target direction; 2.2.2 Course evaluation, student evaluation, and teacher evaluation are oriented to the school's values and goals; 2.2.3 College environment culture, construction and activities reflect the values, school philosophy and goal orientation
3	The quality of the college's characteristic practice	The impact of college development on students, teachers, and colleges	3.1 Student development	3.1.1 Students agree and like the characteristics of the college; 3.1.2 The development of college characteristics has enabled students to have certain interests and specialties, which promoted the development of students' core literacy and enhanced their interest in learning
			3.2 Teacher development	3.2.1 Teachers agree with the college characteristics; 3.2.2 The development of college characteristics enhances the teachers' cohesiveness and self-confidence, which enhances the teachers' curriculum executive force and improves their teaching philosophy and teaching methods
			3.3 College development	3.3.1 Parents are satisfied with the characteristics and effects of the college 3.3.2 The implementation of the course is recognized and praised by students and peers; 3.3.3 Through the development of featured brands, the overall quality of schooling has been significantly improved; 3.3.4 The college's characteristic culture is transformed into a common value criterion and behavioral method for teachers and students

4 Formulating the Dynamic Response Plan for the Connotative Development of Higher Vocational Colleges in Yunnan

4.1 For the Establishment of the Evaluation System, It Is Necessary to Improve the Legal System Timely and Effectively

The establishment of the evaluation system requires the government to correctly position its functions and status during the progress. The characteristics of higher vocational education require social evaluation as the leading factor in formulating the evaluation system. The government must guide all sectors of society to participate in the evaluation through various laws and regulations, and truly establish an evaluation system suitable for the development of local higher vocational education. Higher vocational colleges themselves must put increasing quality in a prominent position while expanding their scale.

In the system design of the social evaluation system of higher vocational colleges, innovation and continuous optimization should be carried out from the cultural level and the institutional level. In the systematic design progress, it should reflect the scientific nature, and enhances the quality and competitiveness of the national vocational talents. Establishing an evaluation system of restraint, incentive and competition can promote the connotation construction of higher vocational colleges, restrain bad behaviors, and promote the optimization construction of social evaluation system in higher vocational colleges.

4.2 The Government Should Decentralize, and the Industry Should Take the Initiative to Evaluate

The government should change its position as a guide, give the evaluation leading power to the society, and give industrial enterprises and social intermediary organizations the responsibility to participate in higher vocational evaluation. At the same time, taking advantage of foreign experience to improve the higher vocational evaluation system, Government departments should also hand over power to social organizations to implement social evaluation of higher vocational colleges and stimulate diversified evaluation. The evaluation agencies should extensively absorb third-party evaluations of enterprises, industry organizations, educational research institutions, and other social forces to implement the quality of education.

Government regulation should reduce its direct jurisdiction, support higher vocational evaluation to promote communication and management services, and rely on industry associations to achieve its management and service functions over higher vocational colleges. The new assessment mechanism should enable students to assess teachers, teachers to assess students, industry and students to assess each other.

4.3 The Improvement the Evaluation Index System and Innovation of Evaluation Methods

At present, the index system for evaluation of higher vocational colleges is not perfect, and the evaluation index system should be further improved. The evaluation system should reflect professionalism, regularity and forward-looking. First of all, we should study the evaluation index system in depth and improve the quality of evaluation. Secondly, we should pay attention to the social satisfaction and social service quality to adapt to the development of higher vocational characteristics in the evaluation, and increase the proportion of advantage majors in the weight of evaluation indicators. The evaluation content should increase the evaluation of students' knowledge and skills, and the evaluation method should reflect the scientific nature of the data. Finally, the feedback mechanism should be timely and effective.

In the new era, the evaluation of vocational colleges should adopts a combination of quantitative evaluation and qualitative evaluation, and adopts new methods such as Internet+, big data, and cloud computing. Data mining should be conducted on the evaluation results to obtain deep-seated influencing factors. It is necessary to integrate resources and obtain information according to needs, thereby reducing resource costs such as manpower and financial resources. At last, in order to achieve the improvement and optimization of education quality, it is important to improve the scientificity of the evaluation results and the rapid conversion of the results data.

4.4 Emphasizing the Construction of the Expert Team and the Dynamics of the Management Mechanism

To overcome the negative role of the mindset of evaluators, the differences of the evaluation of general higher education and higher vocational education should be distinguished, and the particularity of higher vocational education should be highlighted. Only in this way can the evaluation results of higher vocational education be more credible and authoritative, so that the evaluation of higher vocational education can adapt to the new changes and new situations that are constantly developing in current society. As a highly professional higher vocational education assessment activity, the diversity of experts and evaluating forms is critical. It is necessary to continuously improve the evaluation level so that the assessment is more international and scientific.

4.5 The Establishment of an Effective Monitoring Mechanism and to Ensure the Fairness of the Evaluation Process

The supervision mechanism is required by any system. Reasonable supervision can constrain the behavior of the evaluation subject, guarantee the quality of the evaluation subject, ensure the evaluation results are fair and accurate, and thus obtain good evaluation benefits. Therefore, the number of evaluation subjects in the evaluation of higher vocational colleges is increasing. These departments produce assessment reports and innovative assessment methods at different levels through continuous, dynamic, and scientific data collection and analysis.

It is not only the requirements of the times, but also the urgent desire of current society to integrate education fairness and transparency into the performance appraisal system of higher vocational education and to improve the fair and transparent system of higher vocational education. In order to ensure the fairness and transparency of higher vocational rankings, an open punishment mechanism, feedback mechanism and management mechanism are needed. Higher vocational colleges should make adjustments, according to their own limitations, to enhance their own connotation construction, improve their own competitiveness, and strengthen their service functions. In this way, the influence and competitiveness of higher vocational education can be continuously improved, so that the long-term development of higher vocational education can be realized.

References

Yan, Z. (ed.): Characteristic Schools: The Connotation Breakthrough of Education Development. Chongqing Publishing House, Chongqing (2010)

Wang, Z.: Exploring the Practice of Connotation Construction in Higher Vocational Colleges. Southwest Jiaotong University Press, Chengdu (2013)

Yang, J., et al.: Research on the Construction of Connotation Construction and Evaluation System in Higher Vocational College. Higher Education Press, Beijing (2018)

Fan, Y.: Research on the evaluation model of school characteristics development. Doctoral thesis of Southwest University (2017)

Song, Y.: Research on Service Quality Evaluation of Higher Vocational Education. Ph.D. Thesis of Tianjin University (2008)

Zhu, B.: Research on the rationality of curriculum structure in higher vocational colleges. Master's thesis of Hunan University of Science and Technology (2015)

Ning, Y.: The construction of evaluation criteria for the connotation development of schools—Based on the field research of three schools. Master's thesis of Zhejiang Normal University (2009)

Huang, Y.: Research on the social evaluation system of higher vocational colleges in China. Master's thesis of Hubei University of Technology (2017)

Gu, Y., Liu, G.: Research on the evaluation index of the intensive development of higher vocational colleges under the background of quality school construction. Jiangsu Sci. Technol. Inf. (2018)

Zhou, X., Wang, Z., Wang, Q.: Research on the evaluation index of connotative development of higher vocational education in China. Vocational Education Forum, Journal (2017)

Dong, G., Yang, L., Zhang, Q.: Construction of the quality evaluation system of connotative development in higher vocational college. High. Educ, Res. (2013)

Zhou, X., Wang, Z.: Analysis of key elements and characteristics of connotative development evaluation of higher vocational education. Vocat. Educ. Forum (2016)

Zhou, J., Chen, Z.: Connotative development of higher vocational education: basic elements, main characteristics and realization way. Heilongjiang Res. Higher Educ. (2018)

Wu, Z., Sun, X., Zhao, M.: Countermeasure research and practice of connotative development strategies of higher vocational education under perspective of educational ecology. Heilongjiang Res. High. Educ. (2018)

Wang, Z.: A school-based study on the connotative development of higher vocational education from the perspective of education modernization monitoring. China Adult Educ. (2019)

A Study on the Ways to Improve the Quality of Talent Cultivation in Higher Vocational Colleges-Take Sanya Aviation and Tourism College as an Example

Xiaoli Wang(✉), Chunting Ma, and Xia Liu

Civil Aviation School, Sanya Aviation and Tourism College,
Sanya, Hainan, China
49592041@qq.com

Abstract. It is crucial for higher vocational colleges to analyze precisely the problems to be solved under the background of strengthening the integration of industry and education, to explore effectively the ways and approaches to improve the quality of talent training and to cultivate the talents that are suitable and qualified for the society. In the further study of Opinions on Strengthening the Integration of Industry and Education and Measures for Promoting the University-Enterprise Cooperation to in Vocational schools, on the basis of the state policies and documents, combined with the operation mode of large enterprises running schools and school-enterprise integration, on the premise of practicing and summarizing a number of deep school-enterprise cooperation projects, our school reconstructs the way of talent cultivation in higher vocational colleges from six aspects: top-level design, resource optimization, team construction, curriculum reform, cultural integration and mode innovation.

Keywords: Talent cultivation · Ways and approaches · Integration of Industry and Education

1 Background of the Study

Since the launch of these documents such as Opinions on Strengthening the Integration of Industry and Education [1] and Measures for Promoting the University-Enterprise Cooperation to in Vocational schools [2], the state has promoted the integration of industry and education and school-enterprise cooperation into the basic system implementation of national education reform and human resource development, aiming to gradually solve the main contradiction between talent training and industrial development and advance the implementation of school-enterprise collaborative education. Therefore, it is significantly important for every vocational college to study and analyze the practical problems affecting the cooperation between industry and education, school and enterprise in depth, and search for ways and methods to accelerate the speed and improve the quality of education.

G. Sun et al. (Eds.): eLEOT 2019, LNICST 299, pp. 338–346, 2019.
https://doi.org/10.1007/978-3-030-35095-6_38

2 The Urgent Problems to Be Solved Under the Background of Strengthening the Integration of Industry and Education

2.1 The Dislocation Between Industry and Education

There is a common phenomenon that it is difficult for enterprises to recruit and graduates to hunt jobs. The reasons are as follows:

First, higher vocational education is divorced from economic development. Advanced economic development should be matched with higher vocational education in order to promote and improve each other. At present, policies and regulations of higher vocational education and economic development in China are disjointed from execution strength, specialty setting is disjointed from industrial structure, talent training is disjointed from post demand, and faculty is disjointed from technical skill demand, which leads to the inconsistency between the short talent supply and the strong talent demand [3].

Second, professional transformation lags behind economic transformation. China is standing in a critical crossroad of economic and social transformation, and the technical talents cultivated by schools will finally return to the workplace. However, the students jointly cultivated by the school's professional setting, teaching mode, teaching content, teaching staff and other factors cannot satisfy the need of the economic transformation, resulting in the current situation that the reform of the school's talent cultivation is not responsive to the economic transformation and is disconnected from the accelerated transformation [4].

Third, the student employment is divorced from the enterprise recruitment. Companies want to recruit students who have formal employee quality, ethics, culture, values and skills. While most of the students are lack of reasonable thinking and orientation and long-term career planning life, tending to pay attention to the immediate interests. It shows that high expectations and low qualifications affect employment and at the same time lead to the phenomenon of poor school enrollment and employment [5].

2.2 The Dislocation Between School and Enterprise

School-enterprise cooperation has not really touched the interests and needs of enterprises, and the present situation of cooperation is still "two parties, but only one is enthusiastic", that is, the enterprise and the school are two parties, the school is enthusiastic and the enterprise is indifferent. It is mainly reflected in the following three aspects:

First, there is a disconnect between school and corporate interests. In the process of school-enterprise cooperation, enterprises have to provide the school with front-line production equipment and human resources to guarantee the teaching activities of the school, which is bound to directly affect the production efficiency of the enterprise, which deviates from the philosophy of the enterprise that takes profit as the and maximization of interests as the goal.

Second, there is a disconnect between school and corporate culture. Campus culture and enterprise culture, student quality and professional quality, professional knowledge and post ability, student character and professional ethics are different in the training environment, process and method. The school emphasizes the process of training, but the enterprise focuses on the results of training.

Third, there is a disconnect between school and corporate information. The training of technical talents of schools is not carried out simultaneously with the demand of enterprises. The school lacks sufficient understanding of the level, type, and structure of all kinds of talents required by the enterprise, resulting in that the students cultivated by the school cannot meet the requirements of the enterprise.

3 Exploring Ways to Improve the Quality of Talent Training Under the Background of Strengthening the Integration of Industry and Education

3.1 The School-Enterprise Cooperation to Improve the Top-Level Design

The enterprise-running school is a part of the enterprise and the skilled and technical talents needed by the enterprise come from the school. Therefore, the school and the enterprise build a relationship of complementing and promoting each other and growing together. HNA's executives have always attached great importance to the development of our school. Over the years, they have given great support to our school in terms of policy support, institutional innovation, investment in teaching funds, construction of training bases, training of faculty, as well as professional construction and curriculum development. In this way, both the school and the enterprise can fully share material resources, information resources and human resources, and realize maximum benefits on the basis of optimized allocation of resources [6, 7]. Based on the above, the school has promoted the group to set up a professional construction and development committee to carry out special cooperation. At the same time, the group specially formulated the Notice on the Selection of Excellent Personnel to Serve as Part-time Teachers in SATC (Sanya Aviation and Tourism College), which strengthened the complement of "double-qualified teachers" in the school. The Notice on Supporting student work of SATC is formulated to guarantee the students' internship and employment. The Notice on Accelerating and Supporting the Development of SATC has been formulated to ensure that the school is equipped with the latest technical data and training equipment used in enterprises. The implementation and perfection of the above system completely realize the sharing of all kinds of information based on technical standards, employment needs, site facilities and industry permits during the school training stage, and realize the seamless docking between personnel training standards and enterprise employment needs in the training results [8, 9].

3.2 Overall Planning and Coordination to Optimize and Share Both School and Enterprise Resources

At present, the focus of vocational colleges has shifted to the cultivation of students' abilities, so the position of vocational skills is more prominent. However, the school needs the support and guarantee of up-date equipment and technology for the cultivation of exquisite technical skills. But the enterprise strive to achieve immediate employment without training links. In order to solve the above situation, the school and enterprise complement each other with resources superiority, has realized the school enterprise resources superiority complementary, that is, enterprises provide the latest production technology and equipment, schools provide personnel and venues. The significance lies in that, on the one hand, through direct contact with posts and on-site experience of key links and key elements in the production process, students are encouraged to apply theories to practice and deepen what they have learned, which shortens the internship and on-job cycle and saves the cost of practical training and internship for the school. On the other hand, the enterprise entrusts the college to cultivate all kinds of highly skilled talents by taking advantage of the college's sites and teaching staff, which is time-saving, labor-saving and practical [10]. Based on the above considerations, civil aviation call lines of HNA Sales Company was introduced into our campus, HNA Lufthansa Aircraft Maintenance Company was introduced to our school, 147 training equipment for special skills and crew simulation training equipment were purchased, two Xian Y-7 aircraft and five Donier 328 Jet aircraft were allocated from various aviation sectors by HNA Group and the 360° and 120° panoramic navigation simulators were purchased. All of the above facilities are used for students' training and practice. By constructing the real production situation and the highly simulated virtual learning situation, the docking of the real production environment was realized, which laid a solid foundation for cultivating high-quality students.

3.3 Mutual Training and Sharing, Strengthening the Construction of Double-Qualified Teachers Team

When it comes to the importance of the faculty, Chen Baosheng, Minister of Education, pointed out that teachers are the most fundamental and significant part of education. The characteristics and emphasis of faculty construction in higher vocational colleges are double-qualified teachers who can not only complete the enterprise's post teaching but also complete the classroom theoretical knowledge teaching. In the training process, the teachers should pay special attention to school-enterprise combination. Considering the advantages of our school, the construction and training of this team are mainly carried out from the following five aspects: first, education concept construction. The School-Enterprise Joint Construction Committee was established to analyze and discuss specific cases through organizing school-enterprise cooperation discussion days, so as to improve the theoretical level; second, capacity building for scientific research and innovation. Our school has issued various policies and documents, such as Award Method for Scientific Research Achievement in SATC, to encourage teachers to take the initiative to do scientific research. We have set up special teams for teaching, research, application, innovation and entrepreneurship, which are composed of teaching, scientific research, technical and professional backbones; third, practical capacity building. By means of joint construction and cooperation projects and teachers' temporary post training in enterprises, teachers participating in special construction are required to make a daily record of their learning and students' learning. Each of the teachers who take part in the temporary training shall be trained no less than one month per year, and provide the learning content and results in the enterprises; fourth, training capacity building. The school has sent teachers to participate in the training of China Air Transport Sales Agent, IATA, Civil Aviation Dangerous Goods, Civil Aviation Safety Inspector and these teachers have obtained the corresponding qualifications. Teachers who have obtained training qualifications regularly go to enterprises around the country for staff training and teachers' and students' training at school.

3.4 Measures to Deepen the Reform of the Curriculum

In recent years, in order to improve the quality of talent training and effectively serve the needs of HNA Group and Hainan local economic development, our school pays special attention to the reform of course content and teaching method in the process of talent training. First, our school introduced industry standards and promoted curriculum reform. The school and the enterprise jointly completed the formulation of three national standards, namely The Civil Aviation Transportation Professional Standard of Field Work, The Aviation Services Professional Standard of Field Work and The Air Cabin Professional Practical Teaching Facilities Construction Standard. Our standards accurately match the direction and specifications of talent training and have been used for reference by other similar institutions. Second, the teaching method of situation teaching realizes the transformation of teaching scenes into actual workplaces. For example, the aviation electron-mechanical equipment maintenance major in the school adopts the work order system in the course of class to achieve seamless docking with the actual work process of the enterprise. Third, our school built an open resource base. The online quality courses jointly developed and put into use by the school and the enterprise include Air Crew and Diet Nutrition and Health. The Air Crew major has been selected into the national teaching resource base, and the Air Transport Geography is under construction. Fourth, the joint undertaking of vocational skill competitions not only strengthens inter-school communication, but also builds a platform for students to improve their technical skills. By organizing and participating in various skill competitions, students can not only develop the spirit of solidarity and cooperation, but also improve their skills. At present, our school has formed a stable platform for national, provincial, municipal and school skill competitions. Students majoring in aircraft mechanical and electrical equipment maintenance have won the second prize and the third prize for many times in the National Aircraft Engine Dis-assembly, Debugging and Maintenance Competition and have won the first prize in the Pan-Pearl River Delta Computer Works Competition. Through participating in the competition, craftsman spirit of perseverance and excellence is inculcated into students in daily teaching and training.

3.5 Cultural Integration and Construction of Adaptive Value System

3.5.1 Shaping Excellent Corporate Culture

Corporate culture is a combination of the value idea, the enterprise system, the work environment and the historical tradition in the long-term production process, the value idea, the enterprise system, the work environment and the combination of historical tradition. It is formed through long-term accumulation, it is a kind of spiritual civilization and material civilization that represents enterprise image and characteristics.

It is the ideological guidance of the enterprise operation, the speaker of the brand, and an important lever to promote the development of enterprises. Planning for the Construction of a Modern Vocational Education System (2014–2020) clearly proposes that vocational education should carry forward the excellent national culture and modern industrial civilization, and inherit and pass down the fine traditions of virtue first, pursuit of skills and emphasis on inheritance of national craft culture [11]. Therefore, excellent enterprise talents should not only master excellent professional technology and skills, but also highly identify with professional qualities such as attitude, responsibility and integrity. Our school implements the unique cultural system (based on integrity, innovation-oriented, sincere dedication, strong implementation, and brave moral responsibility) of HNA throughout the process of training. The culture of integrity, innovation, dedication, execution and responsibility is integrated into students' life daily life by means of inviting enterprise experts to give lectures, analyzing outstanding enterprise cases and organizing various team activities.

3.5.2 Building a Quality Campus Culture

Like the saying goes "Who keeps company with the wolf will learn to howl", campus culture has a direct impact on what kind of talents are cultivated. Therefore, it should be highly valued. In the process of the construction of campus culture, we should not only have the standard academic atmosphere, but also have the healthy and upward cultural atmosphere. Campus culture should be integrated into the characteristics of the industry and the professional spirit. Our school construct campus culture mainly through activities of regularly carrying out the study day of teachers' ethics and morality, holding symposiums, giving lectures to by enterprise experts, setting up psychological guidance classes, and carrying out popular science day, science and technology festival, vocational skills y festival, campus space day and other activities science and by the establishment of various types of associations, model aircraft association, the implementation of the campus department uniform day and other ways. The purpose is to let the students accept the edification, cultivate professional ethics and professional character imperceptibly.

3.5.3 Observing Professional Ethics

Industry spirit is a group concept combining industry characteristics and professional consciousness, and also it is an important embodiment of enterprise culture. Schools focus on the spirit of "Love and excel at what you do" in the process of training. For example, students majoring in civil aviation transportation should have the civil aviation spirit of "loyalty and responsibility, rigorous and scientific professional spirit, solidarity and cooperation work style, professional ethics of dedication"; students majoring in aviation mechanical and electrical equipment maintenance are equipped with the spirit of "concentration, research, professionalism, rigorousness, exactness and earnestness" [12].

3.6 Mode Innovation, Carrying Out "In-Advance" Training

3.6.1 Developing Productive Cognitive Practice Programs

According to the Regulations on the Administration of Student Internship in Vocational Schools (No. 3 [2016] issued by the Ministry of Education and other four departments), the internship program for post cognition is developed combining professional knowledge with major national political activities. For example, the security check major of our school has been undertaking the security check task of BFA (Boao Forum for Asia) for 11 consecutive years since 2008. The students not only improve their security check skills, but also enhances their safety awareness and political consciousness through participation. At the same time, in order to transfer the practical training class to the first-line enterprises, our school cooperated with Phoenix Airport to carry out the explosion-proof productive internship project at the entrance of the airport for the security major. The integration of real roles and scenes enables teachers and students to have double identities in the process of completing the project, that is, teachers are teachers/employees and students are students/employees. This teaching activity not only enables students to quickly master professional knowledge and skills, but also rapidly improves students' comprehensive vocational ability.

3.6.2 Constructing Productive Training and Practice Base on Campus

Under the background of strengthening the integration of industry and education, the school introduced the customer service hotline of HNA Sales Company and built a productive internship and training base. On the basis of the school-enterprise jointly formulating talent training program, sharing teachers and management, the on-job training and on-job talent cultivation of students are realized. The specific process is classroom teaching, centralized training, alternative-duty internship, following-on-duty internship and in-post internship. Through this method, while completing the professional theoretical knowledge, students are trained in advance with the knowledge content of the post. Thus, the win-win situation of the school and the enterprise is realized.

3.6.3 Developing a Comprehensive Practical Training Project Integrating Production and Teaching

Based on the regional development characteristics and combining with the needs of Sanya hotel industry, intercontinental hotel elite class was established. Therefore, the classroom and research and development location are moved to the hotel for on-site teaching, practical training and research and development. In the process of training, teaching, production and research and development are integrated; teaching, management, operation and service are integrated; teaching, practical training, cognition, on-the-job training and in-post training are integrated. This kind of teaching method enables students to work independently in each hotel when they graduate from school, realizing the seamless docking between the teaching process and the production process.

3.6.4 Carrying Out Pilot Reforms of Apprenticeships

Under the guidance of the Opinions on the Pilot work of Modern Apprenticeship issued by the Ministry of Education in 2014, our aircraft electrical and mechanical equipment maintenance major hotel management major respectively work with HNA Lufthansa Technology Training Company and Intercontinental Hotel Group to carry out the pilot reform of apprenticeship, which was rated as the pilot major of apprenticeship by the Ministry of Education. At the same time, our school, together with the major airlines of HNA Group and China Southern Airlines, jointly implements the modern apprentice training for flight attendants. On the basis of the admission plan, training plan and order agreement jointly formulated by the university and the enterprise, we adopt the training mode of recruiting employees upon admission and being on duty upon entrance, so that students can take into account the dual identity of student/apprentice.

The reform of personnel training mode aimed at deepening the integration of industry and education and introducing enterprises into the school has been carried out gradually and has achieved certain results. The achievements of the reform have been reported for many times by mainstream media such as China Education Daily, People's Daily and China Civil Aviation Daily. According to the survey data, the average income of our graduates ranked first in Hainan province and 23rd among the top 100 vocational colleges in China. Under the premise of national policy documents, various regions and colleges and universities have also introduced supporting policies. It is believed that the reform of deepening the training mode of industry-education integration will be gradually advanced and deepened. At the same time, we also hope that our efforts and exploration in the reform of talent training mode can provide reference for other similar institutions.

References

1. Several Opinions on Strengthening the Integration of Industry and Education, document from the General Office of the State Council, no. 95 (2017)
2. Measures for Promoting School-Enterprise Cooperation in Vocational Schools, document from six departments including the Ministry of Education, no. 1 (2018)
3. Cao, Z.-J., Yang, K.-K., Wang, H.-J.: The problems and countermeasures of the system construction of industry and education in vocational education. Educ. Teach. Res. **32**(6), 12–19+124 (2018)
4. Luo, M.-Y.: Research on the Realization Mechanism of Industry-Education Integration in Higher Vocational Colleges. Zhejiang University of Technology (2017)
5. Hu, Y.-Y.: Analysis on the dilemma and countermeasures of industry-education integration in higher vocational colleges. Think Tank **20**, 132+135 (2019)
6. Lu, Z.-Z., Cui, Y.-T.: Current situation, problems and prospects of modern apprenticeship research in China. Educ. Career **20**, 45–51 (2018)
7. Wu, X.-R.: Research on the construction mechanism and path of vocational college based on integration of industry and education. China Vocat. Tech. Educ. **29**, 5–11 (2018)
8. Lian, Z.-Z., Ge, B., Zhang, H.-Y.: Research and practice of dual-element cultivation mode of industry-education integration in higher vocational college. J. Changzhou Inst. Inf. Technol. **18**(03), 11–14 (2019)

9. Cai, L.-W.: Construction of practice base for higher vocational colleges based on in-depth integration of industry and education. Educ. Occup. **22**, 110–112 (2018)
10. Kong, F.-C.: Discussion on ways and means of sharing school-enterprise cooperative education resources. J. Yantai Vocat. Coll. **2**, 1–3 (2007)
11. Zhai, L.-X., Chen, X.: Research and practice on the cultivation of students' professional quality in vocational colleges. China Vocat. Tech. Educ. **11**, 92–96 (2018)
12. Yang, H.-T.: Research on the cultivation path of civil aviation craftsman spirit under the background of integration of school and enterprise. China High. Educ. **15**, 73–75 (2018)

The Strength and the Correlation Between English Learning Attitudes and Professional Development Needs of Secondary-School English Teachers in Multilingual Areas of China

Wei Zhong, Danyang Li(✉), and Yuanbing Duan

Yunnan Normal University, Kunming 650510, Yunnan, China
2274313674@qq.com

Abstract. This paper explores the professional development needs of secondary school English teachers from multilingual areas in Yunnan, P. R. China, in particular, the strength of their language learning attitudes and in-service training motivation, the correlations between their language learning attitudes and in-service training motivation, and their difficulties and solutions in English teaching. The data analysis indicates three major findings: (1) attitudes to English contribute most to the motivation to participate in in-service training; (2) attitudes to English speakers have considerable effect on the motivation in relation to professional advancement and cognitive interest; (3) instrumental attitudes to English lead to particular practical needs in teaching training.

Keywords: Language learning attitudes · Professional development needs · Secondary-school English teachers · Multilingual areas

1 Background of the Study

As an essential part of teacher professional development, teacher education, in terms of both pre-service and in-service training, has gradually drawn more and more attention from scholars and the public in China. Influenced by the concepts of lifelong education, different levels of government issued policies and projects have been promoted to enhance the quality of primary and secondary school teachers' education [1]. In the summer of 2010, Ministry of Education (MoE) and Ministry of Finance (MoF) co-issued the National Primary and Secondary Teacher Training Plan (hereinafter National Training Plan, NTP). At the beginning, NTP included two projects, "Primary and Secondary Teacher Training Modeling Project (2010–2012)" and "Primary and Secondary Leading Teacher Training Project in Central and Western Rural Areas of China". The central government thought highly of the function of NTP. In the first part of the "Announcement on implementing National Primary and Secondary Teacher Training Plan by Ministry of Education and Ministry of Finance" [2], it clearly stated the purposes of this national program:

G. Sun et al. (Eds.): eLEOT 2019, LNICST 299, pp. 347–367, 2019.
https://doi.org/10.1007/978-3-030-35095-6_39

> "Primary and secondary school teacher training is local government's duties and responsibilities, and it should be implemented mainly by local authorities. Central government's implementation of "National Training Plan" (NTP) is aiming at playing a role for demonstrating, "offering fuel in a snowy winter" and promoting reform. Through implementing the NTP, a batch of "seed" teachers will be trained so as to fulfill their backbone function in carrying forward education for all-round development and teacher training. NTP will develop high quality teacher training resources, innovate teacher training modes and methods, for the sake of carry a nation-wide primary and secondary teacher training into a new stage. NTP focuses on supporting rural teacher training in central and western areas, guiding and encouraging local government, improving teacher training system and intensifying rural teacher training, in order to significantly improve rural teachers' quality. NTP will foster teacher education reform, and push forward tertiary teacher colleges and universities serving the basic education". (author's translation)

As claimed at the beginning of this official document, teacher training is part of "local government's duties and responsibilities", and central government's guidance should be merely understood as "playing the role for demonstrating" which can be taken as providing the model of teacher training. More ironically, the Chinese idiom "offering fuel in a snowy winter", showing good intention, was originally emphasized in parentheses in this official document. The use of parentheses leads to ambiguous meanings. For one part it can be deemed as emphasizing the original good intention. For the other, it can be interpreted as expressing the view that teacher-training programs run by the local government in the past years were so weak in proficiency that central government was not satisfied with its consequence and the serious educational inequity between urban and rural areas. Whether this is a criticism of local government's act of omission from central government, or central government really wants to grant this reward to central and western areas, it could not be denied that

> "implementing the 'National Training Plan' is an important action for improving primary and secondary teachers' quality, especially rural teachers' quality. It has significance in fostering equal development of compulsory education, promoting basic education reform and improving education quality" ([2] author's translation).

In this official document, not only the purposes of initiating the NTP are stated, but also the main problems of teacher professional development in rural China are pointed out, the shortage of financial support, lack of well-directed and systematic guidance, and insufficient academic resources [3–6]. Financial constraint has been consistently argued as one of the major reasons of the poor performance of rural education. According to studies [3, 6–8], the gap of educational expenditure between urban and rural cities is addressed as an important reflection of educational inequity. Teacher quality, however, is addressed as the "chief criminal" for low efficiency in rural areas. Insufficient full time teachers and unqualified teachers are two reasons for students' poor academic achievements in entrance examinations [3–5, 9]. Nevertheless, as the saying goes, "the world does not hate for no reason", and this unsatisfactory situation is the result of a series of integrated causes which can be traced from the divergence between policy and practice [10, 11].

As trainers and curriculum developers in NTP hosted by one teacher's university in Yunnan, the researchers witnessed both the problems and improvements of the Program from 2010 to 2018. Since the training in 2010, the weaknesses in teaching and learning English were revealed among these trainees through the classroom discussions. Their strong mother tongue accent merges into their Chinglish (Chinese English); their poor English vocabulary results in the "dumb English" phenomenon; and the lack of confidence and necessary disciplinary knowledge lead to teaching English through Mandarin; they cherished the opportunities of the training but were reluctant to make efforts in the training and/or changes in their teaching after they returning to the workplace [12]. Thus, it has become of our first concern to research about their English learning attitudes and motivation to participate in teacher training programs. Meanwhile, their difficulties as qualified English teachers in rural and ethnic minority areas of China were the concerns as well. For instance, would it be more difficult for them to teach English to ethnic minority students? Would ethnic minority teachers have more difficulty in teaching English?

2 Key Concepts of the Study

2.1 Motivation and Adults' Education Participation

Talking about adults' learning motivation theory, it is inevitable to mention Abraham Maslow's Hierarchy of Human Needs Theory, not only for it has been one of the most widely discussed theories of motivation, but also in that it activated studies and researches on learning motivation theories. The basic Hierarchy of Human Needs Theory indicated that human beings had desires influencing their behaviour; only unsatisfied needs would affect behaviour, but satisfied needs could not. Since needs were of various kinds, Maslow grouped them into five categories. Then the needs were arranged in order of their importance, from the basic to the complex, namely, physiological, safety and security, love, self-esteem, and self-actualization. The person advances to the next level of needs only after the lower level need is greatly satisfied. The further the progress up the hierarchy, the more individuality, humanity and psychological health a person will develop.

Building on Maslow's theory and force-field analysis of Lewin, Miller provided the motivational force theory [13]. From the work of Maslow, Miller hypothesized that adults from lower socio-economic classes would participate education for job-related and basic skill reasons, whereas participants from higher social classes would seek education to satisfy achievement and self-realization needs. Moreover, Cross presumed a tendency that "members of the lower social classes will be interested primarily in education that meets survival needs, mostly job training and basic adult education, while the upper social classes will have fulfilled those needs and will seek education that leads to achievement and self-realization" [14]. This tendency was related to one's place in the life cycle as well: younger people would be more interested than older people in achieving economic security [15]. If these presumptions were correct, teachers with lower level of income would be more interested in participating in training for getting higher economic security. However, in-service training is part of teacher professional development; economic security might be one reason for participation but there are other factors, such as working environment, and recognition for achievement.

Herzberg's "satisfiers-dissatisfiers" theory of motivation concluded that some factors (i.e., pay, working condition, supervision, interpersonal relationships, company policy, and administration) could cause employees' dissatisfaction, but even when the conditions complained about were corrected, they contributed very little to job satisfaction. Conversely, while the presence of other factors (i.e., achievement, recognition for achievement, intrinsic interest in the work, responsibility, and advancement) produced satisfaction, their absence caused very little dissatisfaction. That is to say, changing economic related factors has little effect on employees' satisfaction in their work, but their self-realization is the main factor of their job satisfaction. Regarding teachers, low income might cause them to be unsatisfied with the teaching career; nevertheless, the "satisfiers-dissatisfiers" theory suggests that in specific conditions, professional development needs outweigh economic security needs.

Talking about the five kinds of needs discussed in Maslow's hierarchy, there is a tendency for low-level ones (physiological, safety and security) to be external oriented and high-level ones (love, self-esteem, and self-actualization) to be internal oriented. Hence, considering Herzberg's "satisfiers-dissatisfiers" theory, Maslow's hierarchy can be put in another way that when external needs are satisfied, people tend to pay more attention to internal ones. Teachers' motivation in in-service training or professional development, in this case, is more related to internal needs. To study this kind of needs, the focus should be on the relationship between learners' internal psychological factors and the external environment in which the learning appeared. Houle's typology [16] and Boshier's congruence model [17–19] presented a social cognitive viewpoint for this research to test secondary school teachers' in-service training motivation.

In examining adults' motivations to learn, Houle conducted a very influential study. Through a study of 22 adult learners, he was able to identify three distinct groups of learners in terms of their motivation to learn. (1) Goal-oriented learners use learning to achieve very specific objectives, such as learning how to deal with stress or planning for retirement. They tend to be practical in outlook, turning to any readily available source for the information and instruction they need. (2) Activity-oriented learners value the activity itself. They pursue learning in order to escape boredom or to make social contacts. (3) Learning-oriented learners value learning for its own sake; they see learning as a way of staying mentally alert and tend to learn throughout most of their lives.

Following Houle typology, from 1971 to 1991, Roger Boshier made efforts in developing the Education Participation Scale (EPS) on account of his congruence model. Boshier believed that motivation for learning was a function of the interaction between internal psychological factors and external environmental factors. The discrepancy between participants' (students') self-concept and other aspects of the educational environment will directly result in the participation or dropout of adult education. Based on his test, Boshier found out that students with high incongruence scores are significantly more likely to drop out than other people are [14]. Hence, according to Boshier, it is important to provide suitable educational environments for students. At the same time, Boshier suggested that self-esteem of the individual [19], a kind of high-level need in Maslow's hierarchy, was important for educational participation. Those who evaluated themselves negatively were less likely to experience congruence with the educational environment.

As lifelong learners in their professional life, teachers will be continuously confronting various in-service training programs. As far as Boshier's congruence model is concerned, learners' motivations or orientations in participating in all kinds of training were deeply interrelated to their educational environment. Consequently, the strength of their motivation would be the basic and key factor to the final efficiency of the training program. In my study, Boshier's EPS was used to test trainees' educational participation strength and the results would in turn reveal the characteristic of the self-initiated motivational orientations of English teachers in ethnic minority areas of China.

2.2 Attitudes in Language Learning

Kiesler et al. Indicated [20] that Thurstone pioneered the study of attitudes and made a great number of findings. Thurstone [21] defined attitude as the intensity of positive or negative affect for or against a psychological object, and a psychological object was any symbol, person, phrase, slogan, or idea towards which people can differ as regards positive or negative effect. Thurstone theorized that the opinion about an object was not the same as the concept of the attitudes to an object; in that an opinion was simply a display of an attitude, and that opinion could be employed to detect the underlying attitudinal predisposition. On the one hand, opinion was viewed as the expression of an overt belief about an affective reaction; alternatively, attitude consisted of an affective reaction [20, 22, 23].

According to Baker [23], attitude was a hypothetical construct utilized to expound the orientation and persistence of human behaviour. Attitude can be used to predict behaviour but it is invisible and cannot be measured directly. Therefore, attitude is a relatively constant system of evaluative processes toward an object based on what individuals have learned in previous settings. Even though attitudes are relatively constant in individuals, attitudes have been learned. Because attitudes are learned, they may be changed through learning process [20].

Referring to second language learning (SLL), Ellis states that

> (L)earners manifest different attitudes toward (1) the target language, (2) target language speakers, (3) the target-language culture, (4) the social value of learning the L2, (5) particular uses of the target language, and (6) themselves as members of their own culture [24].

These attitudes to language are likely to reflect the particular social settings in which learners find themselves. Teachers used to be learners and their attitudes had an impact on the level of their language learning, which ultimately might influence their language teaching methods and professional development as well. In this research, Ellis' six dimensions of language learning attitudes for the following reasons were adopted.

3 Methodology

3.1 Sampling

The sampling of this study is nonprobability in nature, which means the probability of selecting a subject is unknown [25]. Quantitative study was proposed to investigate the trainees who participated in the "Primary and Secondary Schools Leading Teacher

Training Project in Central and Western Rural Areas of China" (one of the two projects in NTP) at one teacher's university in Yunnan from 2012 to 2014. However, it was impossible for the researcher, within the constraints of time and finance, to collect information from all the teachers trained in the whole. It was a convenience and purposive sampling approach on the basis of the demographic variables regarding teaching subject (English and non-English), ethnicity (ethnic minority and Han people), location of working place (ethnic minority areas), roles in NTP (trainers, trainees and program director), and their proximity to the researcher. The investigation was carried out in three schools of the university, the School of Foreign Languages and Literature, the School of Mathematics and Science, and the School of Chinese Literature. These three schools were responsible for the training of English, Chinese and Mathematics teachers respectively in the NTP. It was proposed that 200 questionnaires would be distributed to 100 English teachers and 100 Non-English teachers.

3.2 Questionnaire Distribution and Collection

Questionnaire sheets were distributed four times when the NTP was taken in 2012 and 2013. About 60 answered questionnaire sheets were collected from two classes at their classrooms immediately after they finished the classes in 2012. As for others, the trainees took the questionnaire sheets back to the dormitory and returned the answered sheets the following day or the day after to their monitors. About 50 were distributed in 2012, and about 100 in 2013. Approximately 200 questionnaire sheets were distributed, and 190 were returned, among which 4 sheets were not fully answered; thus the valid answered sheets were 186.

3.3 Measurement

Questionnaire. The whole questionnaire is given in Chinese to avoid the misunderstanding of the meaning. The questionnaire distributed contains four parts, with sections on personal information, language learning attitudes, teacher efficacy, and education participation. Except for the personal information, the other three parts of the questionnaire are adopted from social cognitive psychology and social linguistic theories [17–20, 24, 26–29].

Personal Information. Personal information contains seven kinds of demographic information, namely gender, age, teaching year, teaching subject, professional title, ethnicity, and mother tongue. For the convenience of data imputing, multiple questions are given in each kind.

Attitudes Towards Languages Learning. Referring to second language learning (SLL), Ellis states that

> "(L)earners manifest different attitudes toward (1) the target language, (2) target language speakers, (3) the target-language culture, (4) the social value of learning the L2, (5) particular uses of the target language, and (6) themselves as members of their own culture." [24].

Gardner and Lambert [30] proposed "if individuals had a strong interest in another language community, or if they had an open appreciation and interest in other languages groups in general, this could make them more open to learning in a second language" [28]. In his socio-psychological model of second language learning [26–28], same as Ellis, Gardner pointed out the importance of interest in foreign languages (not limited to target language but foreign languages in general) and attitudes toward the target group (target language speakers and target language culture). They are also in accordance with the instrumental orientation (social value and particular use) of language learning. However, Gardner emphasized the significance of integrating into target culture by pointing out that individuals who are high in integrative orientation are "willing and able to take on features of another language group as part of their own behavioral repertoire" [28]. Gardner also stated that high integrative orientation doesn't mean individuals are willing to become a member of the target language culture, because orientation does not equal to identification in his theory. For Gardner, high integrativeness just means students are more open to the foreign culture and willing to do things with features of another language group, such as communicate in other language. He explained that if individuals have strong awareness to their own ethnicity, their integrative orientation is low; if their sense of ethnicity is weak, their integrative orientation is high. The discrepancy here is it is difficult to separate the definition of "integrative orientation" from "identification". According to social psychology study, cognition, evaluation and conation are three major correlated dimensions or representations of social identity. Identification is greatly represented through the sense of ethnicity, or cognition to the ethnic group or social group. Gardner's integrativeness can be viewed as conation aspect of social identity. If a person has strong sense of ethnicity, in Gardner's theory, he would have low integrativeness; however, in social identity theories, strong sense of ethnicity means strong social identity to the ethnic group or social group. Thus, if one person has strong social identity to his own ethnic group, he has weak social identity to other groups, which indicates integrativeness actually has close relationship to identification. Hence, Ellis' "attitudes to themselves as members of their own culture" and Gardner's "integrative orientation" are two opposite but correlated aspects of social identity. One is cognition to personal ethnic group, and the other is conation to target language ethnic group (Table 1).

The Attitude/Motivation Test Battery (AMTB) developed by Gardner [26] to access various individual difference variables is based on socio-psychological model. The problem with AMTB is that it not only includes attitudes but also behaviour. Gardner [26–28] believed that highly motivated individuals not only have high attitudes but also study and use the language in their daily life as a manifestation of their motivation. However, Gardner's AMTB mixed attitude/motivation and motivated behaviour, which makes it harder to "decide the exact nature of the underlying learner trait that the instrument targets" [31]. In this research, emphasis is on individuals' attitude to target language they are willing to learn, not their actual behaviour in learning the language. Hence, researchers chose five attitudes that mentioned by Ellis' attitudinal theory and Gardner's socio-educational model to explore the language attitudes of secondary school teachers.

20 items based on five attitudes (attitude to target language, attitude to target language speakers, attitude to target language culture, attitudes to the social value of

Table 1. Attitudinal dimensions comparison between Gardner and Ellis

Gardner's AMTB		Ellis
Integrativeness	Interest in target language	The target language
	Attitudes toward the target group	Target language speakers
		The target language culture
	Integrative orientation	/
	/	Themselves as members of their own culture
	Interest in foreign languages in general	/
Motivation	Attitudes towards language learning	/
	Motivation intensity	/
	Desire to learn the language	/
Attitudes towards language learning environment	Teacher	/
	Classroom	/
Instrumentality	Instrumental orientation	The social value of learning the L2
		Particular uses of the target language

learning the L2, and attitudes to the particular uses of the target languages) are designed to test teachers' attitudes towards three languages, Chinese, English and ethnic minority languages. For those whose L1 is Chinese, English and ethnic minority languages are considered as target languages. This group of teachers represents a large amount of the total proportion; however, most of them may not learn minority languages in their whole life. Correspondingly, for those participants whose L1 is ethnic minority language, Chinese and English are the target languages.

Education Participation Scale (EPS). The original EPS was published in 1971 by Boshier with 48 items and a 9-point scale, which contained 8 subscales. As time goes by, EPS has been modified for several times, from EPS (F-form) [17] into EPS (A-form) [19], and to EPS (Chinese) [32], which includes 42 EPS items with 6 items for each factor arrayed on the same 4-point scale as the English version. However, factor analysis indicated that EPS (Chinese) and EPS (English) have many differences, e.g. factor loading for certain items are quite low in Chinese samples. Moreover, some items have repeated or overlapped meaning, e.g. make friend and make new friends. Also, some items are aiming at all the population which is not suitable for teachers, e.g. items in Communication Improvement are about improving language ability, but not in relation to a specific language. Hence, to modify EPS (Chinese) for testing teachers is necessary. In this research, researchers focused on Chinese characters relating more to teachers, especially English teachers. Researchers kept items which have high factor loading both in EPS (English) and EPS (Chinese). At the same time, researchers mingled some items which have similar meaning in Chinese concepts. The researchers also specified all the items in Communication Improvement into improving English ability. Meanwhile, considering the NTP was an in-service training program which did not provide degree or certificate for participants, the training did not have the function of "educational preparation" in EPS. Hence, modified EPS (Chinese Teachers) contained 24 EPS items from 6 factors arrayed on the 4-point scale (from "no influence" to "much influence").

3.4 Data Analysis Methods

Questionnaire Data Analysis. The collected questionnaire data were analyzed by non-parametric analysis aided by SPSS 20.0.

Descriptive Analysis. Boxplot (known as box-and-whisker diagram) is a non-parametric way of graphically depicting groups of numerical data through the smallest observation (sample minimum), lower quartile (25th percentile), median, upper quartile (75th percentile), and the largest observation (sample maximum).

Correlation Analysis. Spearman's rho analysis or Spearman's rank correlation coefficient is a nonparametric measure of statistical dependence between two variables. It assesses how well the relationship between two variables can be described using a monotonic or function. If there are no repeated data values, a perfect Spearman correlation of +1 or −1 occurs when each of the variables is a perfect monotone function of the other. It is often named after Charles Spearman and often denoted by the Greek letter ρ (rho) or as r_s.

Difference Analysis. Two-sample Mann-Whitney Test, Wilcoxon Signed Rank Test and Kruskal-Wallis Test are used for comparison between differences.

Exploratory Factor Analysis (EFA). Exploratory factor analysis (EFA) is aiming at identifying the underlying relationships between measured variables (Norris & Lecavalier 2010) and maximizing the amount of variance explained based on the data (Suhr 2006). EFA allows the researcher having no hypotheses on the number of factors, and items or variables each factor will comprise. EFA is used to test the factor structures of language learning attitudes and modified EPS (Chinese Teachers) in this study.

4 Findings

4.1 General Profiles of the Subjects

As shown in Table 2, 126 female and 59 males are reported. 41.3% of the subjects are aged from 21 to 30, 39.2% are 31 to 40 years old, and 17.7% are over 40 years. 47.3% of the subjects have been teaching over 10 years. Only 10 of the participants have been teaching over 20 years, which doesn't reach the requirement of minimum samples of group difference. 78.5% are English teachers and the other 21% are non-English teachers. As mentioned at the Background section, teaching multiple-subjects is one of the facts that teachers are facing in rural or ethnic minority areas due to the shortage of teachers. Hence, though all subjects were chosen from the three schools, teachers who used to teach English would be assigned to join Chinese training, or vice versa, which is one difficulty of teacher in-service training in rural areas of Yunnan.

Table 2. Demographic analysis of gender

		Gender				Total	
		Female		Male			
		N	%	N	%	N	%
Age	21–30	60	32.2	17	9.1	77	41.3
	31–40	49	26.3	24	12.9	73	39.2
	41–50	16	8.6	17	9.1	33	17.7
Total		125	67.1	58	31.1	183**	98.2
Professional title	Advanced level	6	3.2	5	2.7	11	5.9
	Intermediate level	79	42.5	41	22.0	120	64.9
	Primary level	33	17.7	13	7.0	46	24.7
Total		118	63.4	59	31.7	177***	95.1
Teaching subjects	English	105	56.5	41	22.0	146	78.5
	Non-English	21	11.3	18	9.7	39	21.0
Total		126	67.8	59	31.7	185*	99.5
Teaching years	Less than 5 years	44	23.7	9	4.8	53	28.5
	6–10 years	32	17.2	12	6.5	44	23.7
	11–20 years	50	26.9	38	19.7	88	41.9
	Over 20 years	5	2.7	5	2.7	10	5.4
Total		126	68.2	59	31.8	185*	99.5

*missing value = 1; **missing value = 2; ***missing value = 8

Talking about professional title, primary level teachers (24.7%) and intermediate level teachers (64.9%) are the main constituent part. Owing to few samples of advanced-level subjects, group difference analysis of professional level will be conducted only between primary-level and intermediate-level. For the same reason, group difference analysis of teaching years will be conducted only within three groups, namely less than 5 years, 6 to 10 years and 11 to 20 years.

4.2 Language Learning Attitudes

20 items of five attitudinal dimensions, (1) attitude to target language, (2) attitude to target language speaker, (3) attitude to target language culture, (4) attitude to particular use of the language, (5) attitude to social value of target language are designed to test teachers' attitudes towards their second language (L2) or third language (L3). Owing to the fact that some subjects' mother tongue is not Chinese, subjects are asked to choose their attitudes to language learning from the following categories: Chinese, English,

and minority language. Subjects were asked to choose any language which fit the description, such as "I want to learn_ because it represents a civilized culture" (Item 12). Hence, for those Chinese is their L2, they can choose Chinese and/or English; for whose mother tongue is Chinese, they can choose English and/or ethnic minority languages. Each choice of the language is scored 1 and 0 for not chosen. If two languages are chosen, both are scored 1 respectively. If none of the language fits the description, subjects can leave it blank and the data are scored 0 in all categories.

Reliability Test and Exploratory Factor Analysis. Since English is not the mother tongue for all subjects, scores in English are used in the reliability test and exploratory factor analysis (EFA) to test the structure and pattern of the items. With 20 items, Cronbach's alpha is 0.854 and Guttman Split-Half Coefficient is 0.762 (refer to Table 3). Reliability test shows that the items have high internal consistency, which is suitable for factor analysis.

Table 3. Reliability statistics of language learning attitudes.

Cronbach's alpha	.854	N of Items	20
Cronbach's alpha	Part 1	Value	.769
		N of Items	10[a]
	Part 2	Value	.776
		N of Items	10[b]
	Total N of Items		20
Correlation between forms			.621
Spearman-Brown Coefficient	Equal length		.766
	Unequal length		.766
Guttman Split-Half Coefficient			.762

Principal Component Analysis and Varimax with Kaiser Normalization are used in exploratory factor analysis. KMO is 0.856 and Bartlett's test also shows that data are significant for factor analysis (refer to Table 4). Using Eigenvalues over 1 method, 5 factors were extracted, and the total variance explained was 55.345. Considering Cronbach's Alpha if Item Deleted, Communalities and the explanation of each factor, 4 items were deleted.

Table 4. KMO and Bartlett's test.

Kaiser-Meyer-Olkin measure of sampling adequacy		.856
Bartlett's test of sphericity	Approx. Chi-Square	1051.917
	df	190
	Sig.	.000

The final Teachers' Language Attitudinal Dimension (TLAD) contains 16 items (refer to Table 5), and the total variance explained was 59.799. Five dimensions of the attitudes are (1) attitudes to target language culture (AC), (2) attitudes to target language speaker (AS), (3) attitudes to target language (AL), (4) attitudes to social value of target language (SV), and (5) attitudes to particular use of target language (PU).

Table 5. Teachers' language attitudinal dimensions (TLAD).

Items		Factors				
		AC	AS	AL	SV	PU
12	I want to learn___because it represents a civilized culture	X				
9	I want to learn___because it represents a great culture	X				
2	I want to learn___because its culture has long history	X				
10	I want to learn___because it represents the culture I favour	X				
6	I want to learn___because people who speak it are knowledgeable		X			
7	I want to learn___because people who speak it have great fortune and in high status		X			
8	I want to learn___because people who speak it are respectable		X			
1	I want to learn___because I want to study it			X		
4	I want to learn___because I like it			X		
3	I want to learn___because it is beautiful			X		
15	I want to learn___because it can let me communicate with people from different cultures				X	
20	I want to learn___because it can satisfy some of my personal needs				X	
16	I want to learn___because it can make me knowledgeable				X	
19	I want to learn___because my leaders arranged it					X
17	I want to learn___because it can help me deal with my work better					X
18	I want to learn___because it can help me improve my teaching proficiency					X

① X indicates the item is loaded in that factor. AC = attitudes to target culture; AS = attitudes to target language speaker; AL = attitudes to target language; SV = attitudes to social value of learning the target language; PU = attitudes to particular use of target language.
② The order of the items are based on the rotated component loading of each item in the factor in from high to low.

Distribution and Strength of English Learning Attitude. Guttman scaling is used to test the strength of attitudinal dimensions. Guttman scaling allows researchers to simply see a series of subjects' responses which belong to the same dimension in a simple "K+1" scales (K is the number of questions). By scoring each answer 1 (correct answer) or 0 (wrong answer) and then summing up all answers in the same dimension can get the general results for this category. Consequently, it becomes easier for comparative discussion when many possibilities exist.

General English Learning Attitude (GELA). Skewness value ($-1 < -0.566 < 1$) indicates a normal distribution of general English learning attitude (GELA). Median value ($0.2110 > 0$) shows that in average participants have positive attitudes to English learning (refer to Table 6). However, the distribution of data shows that many participants have negative attitudes (Z score < 0) (refer to Fig. 1). Detailed analyses on five English learning attitudinal dimensions will reveal more findings.

Table 6. Descriptive Analysis of GELA.

				Percentile			
Z score of GELA	Median	Range	Skewness	25th	50th	75th	N
	.2110	4.2417	−.566	−.5844	.2110	.7412	186

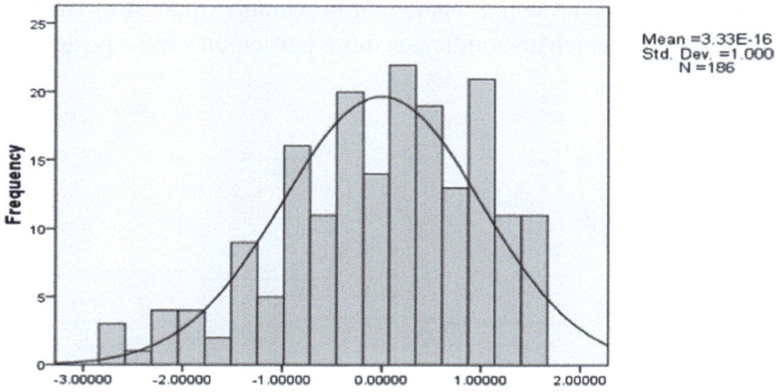

Fig. 1. Histogram of GELA

Five English Learning Attitudinal Dimensions. Descriptive analyses of five attitudinal dimensions imply more obvious differences. Skewness value suggest that attitudes to social value and English (SVE) and attitudes to particular use of English (PUE) have left-skewed distribution, while the other three have normal distribution (refer to Table 7). As mentioned before, left-skewed distribution shows most participants have positive attitudes. Boxplot graph will imply more findings.

Table 7. Descriptive analysis of five English learning attitudinal dimensions.

		ZAEC	ZAES	ZAEL	ZSVE	ZPUE	N
Median		−.4433	.0254	.0980	.6275	.7440	186
Skewness		.321	−.639	−.401	−1.561	−1.273	
Range		2.8678	2.8370	2.8777	3.3347	3.0982	
Percentiles	25	−1.1602	−.9203	−.8612	−.4841	−.2887	
	50	−.4433	.0254	.0980	.6275	.7440	
	75	.9906	.9711	1.0572	.6275	.7440	

Z = Z score; AEC = attitudes to English culture; AES = attitudes to English speaker; AEL = attitudes to English language; SVE = attitudes to social value of English; PUE = attitudes to particular use of English

Boxplot of five English learning attitudinal dimensions (refer to Fig. 2) suggests the following findings. Firstly, in general, most participants have negative attitudes to learning English because of its splendid culture (AEC) (Median = −0.4433 < 0, refer to Item 2, 9, 10, and 12 in Table 6) but positive attitudes to the other four dimensions. Secondly, the minimum value in AEC is the same as the 25th percentile value, which indicates 25% of participants have similar negative attitude to English culture. Thirdly, the maximum values in attitudes to English speaker (AES) and attitudes to English language (AEL) are the same as their 75th percentile values, which implies 25% of participants have similar positive attitude to AES and AEL. Fourthly, though there is single case at low score, the median value and maximum value of the majority are the same in SVE and PUE, which also indicates more participants have positive attitudes to SVE and PUE.

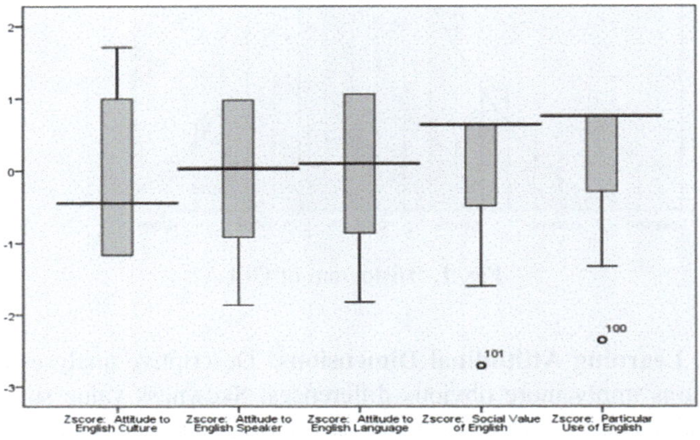

Fig. 2. Boxplot of five English learning attitudinal dimensions.

Spearman Correlation Analysis of English Learning Attitudes. Spearman's rho analysis (refer to Table 8) shows that the five dimensions of attitudes all have significant positive correlation to general attitudes to English learning. However, among the five, attitudes to English culture (r_s = .773) and attitudes to English language (r_s = .725) are more related to the general attitudes to English learning. This indicates that either positive or negative attitudes towards English culture and/or English language will increase or decrease their general attitudes towards English learning.

Table 8. Spearman correlation analysis of English learning attitudes.

Spearman's rho	GELA	AEC	AES	AEL	SVE	PUE	Number of cases
	r_s	.773**	.687**	.725**	.601**	.561**	186
	Sig. (2-tailed)	.000	.000	.000	.000	.000	

**Correlation is significant at the 0.01 level (2-tailed).
AEC = attitudes to English culture; AES = attitudes to English speaker; AEL = attitudes to English language; SVE = attitudes to social value of English; PUE = attitudes to particular use of English; GELA = general English learning attitudes

4.3 Education Participation Motivation.

24 items of modified EPS (Chinese) are adopted from Boshier et al.'s EPS (Chinese) [32] and contain only six subscales of the original seven. The six factors are Communication Improvement, Social Contact, Cognitive Interest, Professional Advancement, Social Stimulation and Family Togetherness. A four-point Likert scaling is used in correspondence with CTSE for further analysis. Items were coded so no influence = 1, little influence = 2, moderate influence = 3, and much influence = 4. Because each of the six factors contains 4 items, a minimum scale score is 4 (suggesting low influence) and maximum scale score is 16 (suggesting high influence).

Reliability Analysis. EPS (Chinese Teachers) data were secured from 186 subjects participated in the National Training Plan. Reliability analysis (refer to Table 9) shows that the 24 items of modified EPS (Chinese Teachers) have high internal consistency (Cronbach's alpha = 0.859). Five of the six sub-scales have Cronbach's alpha over 0.60, but the Cronbach's alpha of Professional Advancement is 0.588.

Table 9. Reliability test of EPS (Chinese Teachers)

	EPS (Chinese Teachers)	CIm	SC	CIn	PA	SS	FT
Cronbach's Alpha	.859	.899	.801	.736	.588	.640	.768
N of items	24	4	4	4	4	4	4

CIm = communication improvement; SC = social contact; CIn = cognitive interest; PA = professional advancement; SS = social stimulation; FT = family togetherness

Strength of EPS. Because each of the six factors contains 4 items, a minimum scale score for each factor is 4 (suggesting low influence) and maximum scale score is 16 (suggesting high influence). Mean value of the six factors is computed to show the general strength of educational participation. Main focus of this study is on English teachers, so data used for the following studies are 146 English teacher subjects. Generally speaking, subjects have weak educational participation strength (Mean = 9.6923). Subjects are strongly motivated by communication improvement (Mean = 13.25), cognitive interest (Mean = 12.95) and professional advancement (Mean = 11.65). However, they are weakly motivated by social contact (Mean =7.25), family togetherness (Mean = 6.67) and social stimulation (Mean = 6.39). Of the six motivational orientations, subjects are comparatively highly motivated by cognitive interest (Mean = 12.95), same as samples in Shanghai and Vancouver [32]. Distribution of social stimulation shows a right-skewed tendency, indicating most subjects are low motivated by social stimulation in their educational motivation in NTP (refer to Table 10).

Table 10. Descriptive analysis of EPS strength

	N	Mean	SD	Skewness		Spearman's rho
				Statistics	SD	
General EPS	146	9.6923	1.50496	.259	.201	/
Communication improvement	146	13.25	2.316	−.797	.201	.592**
Social contact	146	7.25	2.720	.822	.201	.604**
Cognitive interest	146	12.95	2.293	−.601	.201	.615**
Professional advancement	146	11.65	2.166	−.026	.201	.729**
Social stimulation	146	6.39	2.226	1.132	.201	.507**
Family togetherness	146	6.67	2.508	.897	.201	.599**
Valid N (listwise)	146					

**p < .01

Spearman's rho coefficient test shows that Professional Advancement has the strongest correlation to the general EPS (r_s = .729, p < .01). Cognitive interest (r_s = .615 p < .01) and social contact (r_s = .604, p < .01) have significant high correlation to the general EPS. Social Stimulation has the weakest correlation to general EPS (r_s = .507, p < .01).

4.4 Correlations Between English Learning Attitudes ELA and EPS

Studies in second language acquisition (SLA) have gradually accepted that attitudes play an important role in forming individual's English learning motivation [24, 26, 28, 33]. English learning motivation is theoretically constructed on the general learning motivation theories, which means English teachers' English learning attitudes, which influence English learning motivation, will consequently affect their in-service training motivation. However, to what extent and in what ways can English learning attitudes make the influence? Correlation matrix between ELA and EPS can provide a general view of their relationships.

Spearman's rho analysis (refer to Table 11) shows that in the primary level general English learning attitudes do not have significant correlation with general educational participation strength, but general English learning attitudes have stronger positive relationship to communication improvement (r_s = .204, p < .05) and cognitive interest r_s = .204, p < .05).

Table 11. Correlation between English learning attitudes and EPS.

		GEPS	CIm	SC	CIn	PA	SS	FT
GELA	Correlation coefficient	.110	.204*	−.002	.204*	.112	−.046	−.026
	Sig (2-tailed)	.187	.013	.983	.013	.179	.581	.759
AEC	Correlation coefficient	.025	.135	−.037	.108	−.059	−.021	−.030
	Sig (2-tailed)	.763	.105	.661	.195	482	.802	.723
AES	Correlation coefficient	.083	.145	−.013	.176*	.186*	−.090	−.075
	Sig (2-tailed)	.317	.081	.878	.034	.024	.278	.367
AEL	Correlation coefficient	.286**	.278**	.156	.290**	.265**	.027	.095
	Sig (2-tailed)	.000	.001	.060	.000	.001	.749	.254
SVE	Correlation coefficient	−.014	.043	−.180*	.155	.090	−.108	−.032
	Sig (2-tailed)	.863	.610	.030	.062	.281	.195	.704
PUE	Correlation coefficient	.003	.026	.024	−.075	−.065	.006	.026
	Sig (2-tailed)	.972	.756	.772	.370	.435	.939	.758
N	146							

GELA = general English learning attitudes, AEC = attitudes to English culture, AES = attitudes to English speaker, AEL = attitudes to English language, SVE = attitudes to social value of English, PUE = attitudes to particular use of English, GEPS = general educational participation strength, CIm = Communication Improvement, SC=Social Contact, CIn = Cognitive Interest, PA = Professional Advancement; SS=Social Stimulation; FT = Family Togetherness; GEPS = General EPS. *p < .05(2-tailed), ** p < .01(2-tailed)

Considering the secondary level, some dimensions of English learning attitudes can influence English teachers' educational participation strength to some extent. First of all, among the five dimensions of English learning attitudes, attitudes to English language (AEL) is the most important factor that determine English teachers' in-service training motivation (r_s = .286, p < .01). Meanwhile, it positively affects teachers' communication improvement needs (r_s =.278, p < .01), cognitive interests needs (r_s = .290, p < .01), and professional advancement needs (r_s = .265, p < .01). Attitudes to English speaker (AES) is another factor that has positive influence to professional advancement needs (r_s = .186, p < .05). Social value of English (SVE), on the other hand, has significant negative relationship to social contact (SC) needs (r_s = −.180, p < .05).

It is likely that learning English cannot bring English teachers stronger motivation for social needs. Table 11 indicates that English learning attitudes have negative relationship with social contact, social stimulation and family togetherness needs. Attitudes to English culture, attitudes to English speaker, and social value of English all contribute to these negative influences.

5 Conclusion

In conclusion, through literature review and profound interview, researchers found out three major results.

5.1 Attitudes to English Language Contribute Most to the Motivation on in-Service Training

Some studies claim that attitude consists of an affective reaction. Attitude to the social value of a target language is a determinate cause for subjects' general desire for learning that language. Baker even proposed that attitude could be used to expound upon the orientation and predict the persistence of human behaviour [23]. In this investigation, attitudes to English language learning contribute most to the motivation in teacher training programs, particularly in three orientations of education participation, namely cognitive interests, communication improvement, and professional advancement.

The reasons for this might be related to the measurement used for testing teachers' education motivation being modified in relation to some distinctive needs of English teachers, such as four items in communication improvement. In the mean time, the three items (Item 1, 3, 4, refer to Table 5) chosen to test language-learning attitudes indicate strong individual affection towards the target language. Moreover, teachers' motivation in cognitive interests, communication improvement, and professional advancement were highly correlated to the general strength of education participation; thus like a chain reaction, direct connection to any one would affect its influence on others. In addition, this result implies the tendency that increasing individuals' feeling about the target language would probably stimulate them more to participate in the in-service training program.

5.2 Attitudes to English Speaker Have Considerable Effect on the Motivation in Professional Advancement and Cognitive Interests

Gardner's socio-psychological model of second language learning suggested that a positive relationship exists between learners' motivation in learning a language and their interests in the target language community, in other words their attitudes to English speakers and English culture. Data indicated that the correlation between subjects' feelings bout English speaker and their motivational orientation regarding professional advancement and cognitive interest were insignificant (refer to Table 11), though data suggested that subjects have similar weak attitudes to English speaker and English culture.

Possible reasons would be that three items used to test attitudes to English speakers might in fact demonstrate some requirements of Chinese *Shi De* (teaching ethics), the commanding element of the professional teacher in the Chinese concept. "Knowledgeable", "great fortune and high status" and "respectable" (Item 6, 7, and 8 respectively, refer to Table 5) have been necessary characteristics of a professional teacher characterized by Confucian sages. Although teachers' current financial conditions were not particularly sound, they seem to be longing for the ideal position of intellectuals. Thus, their feelings towards English speakers that are "knowledgeable", "(having) great fortune and high status" and "respectable" correlated to their needs in cognitive interests and professional advancement; in other words, in the process of pursuing professional development, their beliefs about professional teachers are unintentionally revealed through their attitudes to English speakers.

5.3 Instrumental Attitudes to English Lead to Pragmatic Needs in Teacher Training

As stated before, studies show that in foreign language learning contexts, instrumental motivation would be stronger rather than integrative one due to the exposure of learners to the target language community being very limited. Data suggest that subjects have considerably strong attitudes to the social value and particular use of English, which are instrumental-oriented attitudes in nature. Moreover, their attitudes to the social value of English have significant negative correlation to the social contact orientation of training motivation ($r_s = -.180$, $p < .05$), which implies that the stronger instrumental attitudes to English they hold, the weaker their desire to participate in the training for interpersonal connections. In addition, similar to their attitudes to the social value of English, attitude to English culture presents negative correlation to social contact and social stimulation orientations of in-service training as well.

The reasons would be, firstly, the training was happening in a Chinese context, thus interpersonal connection would merely be with Chinese people rather than English speakers. In this circumstance, the attitude to social value of English had little connection to their desire for communicating with Chinese people. For the same reason, their attitudes to English culture present a similar tendency to their motivation in interpersonal connections through in-service training.

References

1. Wang, S.N.: Gaoxiao waiyu jiaoshi geren jiaoxue xiaoneng gan jiqi jiaoling tedian yanjiu. J. Chifeng Univ. (6), 97–98 (2009)
2. MoE & MoF. Jiaoyubu caizhengbu guanyu shishi zhongxiaoxue jiaoshi guojiaji peixun jihua de tongzhi (Announcement on implementing National Primary and Secondary Teacher Training Plan by Ministry of Education and Ministry of Finance, (Document No. Teacher (2010) 4)). From Zhongguo Zhengfu Wang: http://www.gov.cn/zwgk/2010-06/30/content_1642031. Accessed 13 Feb 2013
3. Wang, D.: The new curriculum and the urban-rural literacy gap. Chin. Educ. Soc. **44**(6), 87–101 (2011)
4. Wang, J.Y., Li, Y.: Research on the teaching quality of compulsory education in China's west rural schools. Front. Educ. China **4**(1), 66–93 (2009)
5. Zhang, T.S., Deng, Y.C., Yang, R.Y., Zuo, X.M., Chu, Z.H., Li, X.J.: Balanced development of compulsory education: cornerstone of education equity. Front. Educ. China **2**(4), 469–493 (2007)

6. Zhu, H.H.: Zhongxue Yingyu Jiaoshi Jiaoxue Xiaoneng Gan Diaocha Yanjiu. J. Bais Engl. Educ. **8**(4), 23–28 (2006)
7. Bao, C.Y.: Policies for compulsory education disparity between urban and rural areas in China. Front. Educ. China **1**, 40–55 (2006)
8. Wang, J.Y., Zhao, Z.C.: Basic education curriculum reform in rural China: achievements, problems, and solutions. Chin. Educ. Soc. **44**(6), 36–46 (2011)
9. Zeng, X.D.: Jiaoshi lanpishu: Zhongguo zhongxiaoxue jiaoshi fazhan baogao (Blue Book of Teacher: Annual Report on the Teachers in China 2012). Social Science and Academic Press, Beijing (2012)
10. Feng, A.W.: English in China: convergence and divergence in policy and practice. AILA Rev. **22**, 85–102 (2009)
11. Feng, A.W. (ed.): English Language Education across Greater China. Multilingual Matter Ltd., Clevedon (2011)
12. Zhong, W.: Personal Report on NTP in 2011. Yunnan Normal University, School of Foreign Languages and Literature, Kunming (2011)
13. Miller, H.L.: Participation of adults in education: a force-field analysis. http://eric.ed.gov/ERICWebPortal/recordDetail?accno=ED011996. Accessed 15 May 2018
14. Cross, K.P.: Adults as Learners: Increasing Participation and Facilitating Learning, p. 121. Jossey-Bass Inc., California (1988)
15. Merriam, S.B., Caffarella, R.S.: Learning in Adulthood: A Comprehensive Guide. Jossey-Bass Publishers, San Fransisco (1999)
16. Houle, C.O.: The Inquiring Mind. University of Wisconsin Press, Madison (1961)
17. Boshier, R.: Factor analysts at large: a critical review of the motivational orientation literature. Adult Educ. **27**(1), 24–27 (1976)
18. Boshier, R.: Motivational orientations re-visited: life-space motives and the education participations scale. Adult Educ. **27**(2), 89–115 (1977)
19. Boshier, R.: Psychometric properties of the alternative form of the education participation scale. Adult Educ. Q. **41**(3), 150–167 (1991)
20. Yuan, Y.C.: Attitude and motivation for english learning of ethnic minority students in China. Shanghai Foreign Language Education Press, Shanghai (2007)
21. Lemon, N.: Attitudes and Their Measurement. B.T. Batsford Ltd., London (1973)
22. Summers, G.F.: Attitude Measurement, 2nd edn. Rand Mc Nally, Chicago (1969)
23. Baker, C.: Attitudes and Language. Multilingual Matters Ltd., Adelaide (1992)
24. Ellis, R.: The Study of Second Language Acquisition, p. 198. Oxford University Press, Oxford (1994)
25. Charles, C.M., Mertler, C.A.: Introduction to Educational Research. Foreign Language Teaching and Research Press, Beijing (2004)
26. Gardner, R.C.: Social Psychology and Second Language Learning: The Role of Attitudes and Motivation. Edward Arnold, London (1985)
27. Gardner, R.C.: Correlation, causation, motivation, and second language acquisition. Can. Psychol. **41**, 10–24 (2000)
28. Gardner, R.C.: The socio-educational model of second language acquisition: a research paradigm. Eurosla Yearb. **6**, 237–260 (2006)
29. Zhong, W., Li, P.: Teacher working motivation, self-efficacy, and their correlation: Modification of WPI and TSES. Yunnan Normal University, Kunming (2010)
30. Gardner, R.C., Lambert, W.E.: Attitudes and Motivation in Second Language Learning. Newbury House, Rowley (1972)

31. Huang, S.C.: Assessing motivation and learning strategies using the motivated strategies for learning questionnaire in a foreign language learning context. Soc. Behav. Pers. **36**(4), 529–534 (2008)
32. Boshier, R., Huang, Y., Song, L.: Market socialism meets the lost generation: motivational orientations of adult learners in Shanghai. Adult Educ. Q. **56**(3), 201–222 (2006)
33. Dörnyei, Z., Clément, R.: Motivational characteristics of learning different target languages: Results of a nationwide survey. In: Dörnyei, Z., Schmidt, R. (eds.) Motivation and Second Language Acquisition, pp. 399–432. University of Hawaii at Manoa, Second Language Teaching and Curriculum Center, Honolulu (2001)

The Practice of Content-Based Academic English Instruction Among Graduate Students of Non-English Major

Qingling Wang, Hong Duan(✉), and Xiangxing Wan

School of Foreign Languages and Literature,
Yunnan Normal University, Kuming 650500, Yunnan, China
beyoungdh@163.com

Abstract. English is a compulsory course for all graduate students in China. In the highest stage of education, students have strong demands of using English as a tool in their academic study and research. Based on theories of content-based instruction and English for academic purpose, the author puts forward a model of content-based academic English instruction which is summarized as "literature study + academic corpus building + classroom presentation and discussion + paper review writing". In this model, students as the center of the English classroom are required to carry out a series of tasks to study academically specialized knowledge independently and cooperatively. In such a classroom, graduate students use English as a tool to study literature and to do research in their academic fields through which their motivation is stimulated, their research ability is cultivated, and their English competence is developed. The examination and evaluation approaches are also suggested in this article.

Keywords: Content-based instruction · Academic English · Graduate students

1 Background

Graduate education in colleges and universities is the main source for high-level professionals in China, and graduate students, as advanced learners, will become experts and key talents in various professional fields after graduation. In order to cultivate them in adaptation to the requirements of the globalized world and to help them seize the opportunity for future jobs and researches, English education is the compulsory course for all graduate students in China. Then for all graduate English instructors, how to teach and what to teach, are problems they must face. In graduate education, English course should aim at improving student ability of using English in academic research and international academic communication. Then English academic content of specialized fields can be used as materials of the class, and teaching students to learn them should be an approach for training qualified talents in the globalized world.

However, there are a variety of problems in English instruction for graduate students. (1) Most of the English class is based on texts irrelevant to students' needs and focuses on the explanation of English words and grammatical structures they have learned through secondary and undergraduate English classrooms. Such methods of

G. Sun et al. (Eds.): eLEOT 2019, LNICST 299, pp. 368–376, 2019.
https://doi.org/10.1007/978-3-030-35095-6_40

instruction deviate from the essence of language as a communicative tool. Moreover, the teaching materials are far from meeting the needs of graduate students for English. In graduate programs, students' demand for English has changed from learning language skills to the use of English in their academic study. In the university setting, they are frequently required to use English in academic study and research in their specialized fields.

CAI [1–3] pointed out that language learning is more of the learning of meaning than of the structure. Although the pattern of a language is necessary, after mastering certain rules and vocabulary, and after reaching a certain level, it is necessary to improve language ability through knowledge learning. Hence, English learning based on academic content is necessary in university settings. Shu [4] believes that in China, the priority of English instruction should serve for the global communication. In graduate phase, students should use English as a tool to learn subject matter, to cultivate their academic capacity and communication skills. English is not to learn to communicate, but should learn in communication. Liu [5] points out that in senior grades of college, English learning should shift from skill learning to content learning, and content should be used to attract students so that they could acquire language in such a learning process.

The ultimate goal of English learning is to acquire more knowledge through the language and to conduct international cooperation and communication. In the elementary and secondary phases of English learning, language skill courses can improve students' English and lay a foundation for their future use of English. However, in postgraduate education, English instruction should center on the content, namely, the discipline-based academic materials. In this way, students can acquire more English and cultivate cross-cultural communicative competence in the process of learning subject knowledge and improving academic ability by using English as a tool.

2 Concepts of Content - Based Instruction and English for Academic Purpose

Content Based Instruction (CBI) refers to the teaching of the content or materials of a field in the target language, enabling students to acquire the language while learning specialized knowledge [6] CBI believes that language and content are interdependent. Language is the carrier of content, and content reflects the specific application of language. Learners acquire language while learning content, and the improvement of language ability makes it easier for them to learn subject knowledge carried by target language [7]. This teaching concept advocates the teaching of a second language or foreign language by means of subject content, which is effective, authentic and combines the learning of language and content [8]. CBI language course is strongly discipline-oriented. It combines language learning with subject matter study, which shifts the focus from language itself from the subject matter of a discipline [9]. This teaching concept can not only improves students' language ability, but also cultivates their academic capacity. CBI emphasizes the learning of subject content, the authenticity of language materials, the novelty of information and the needs of students. Language teaching under this concept improves students' English ability on the premise of fully meeting their learning needs and stimulating their learning enthusiasm. In this process, students learn professional knowledge, understand the latest information of the subject, and cultivate academic ability

English for Academic Purpose (EAP), a branch of English for Specific Purposes (ESP), was originally put forward by Tim Johns in 1974 [10]. It advocates that in university setting, English teaching should train students to use the language in academic study or research, and to make academic exchange [11]. An EAP program focuses instruction on skills required to perform an academic study in English context in specialized subject areas. Such English course is based on learners' specific academic goals and needs. EAP teachers not only enable students to learn English, but also help them to construct their subject knowledge system and grasp subject cultural background in English. EAP teaching mode is highly promoted in college English teaching to cultivate research-oriented, high-level international talents [12]. In most cases, EAP courses employ content-based instruction, using academic materials from the students' degree subjects. Such courses may be desirable to help students develop language skills and academic capability

Both CBI and EAP emphasize the use of English as a tool to help students learn professional knowledge for cultivating students' academic ability and professional quality, encouraging them to use English for international academic exchanges. In the process, students' English competence is improved. In addition, in CBI and EAP classroom, teachers and students focuses on academic content, then the language becomes a tool indispensable in learning subject content and doing research. In such a classroom, the roles of students and teachers have changed dramatically. Instead of being passive language learners, the students become active language users, who use English to learn specialized academic knowledge to do researches required by the program or by their advisors. In such a model, teachers are the guides and supervisors of students' active learning process, in which they organize the class, motivate and guide students, control steps of the teaching and learning, learn with students the academic materials in different fields. CBI and EAP teaching can take many forms, including classroom teaching, topic discussion, supervision and inspection, individual counseling, professional literature reading, report, and paper writing [13].

3 Design and Procedures of the Content-Based Academic English Instruction

3.1 Teaching Design

Academic English instruction is faced with questions as what to choose as teaching materials (content) and how to conduct the teaching. Graduate students are very specialized in their fields of study, and even in same major, they may choose different research directions or focuses. However, as far as academic English are concerned, it is impossible for English instructors (whose majors are mostly linguistics or literature) to teach the content of different fields, especially those of science and engineering, which is beyond their reach. The successful practices (models) abroad in academic English course are taken by two instructors, one for the subject content and the other for language teaching. In such modes, the two instructors cooperate with and complement each other. One is responsible for instructing academic knowledge and the other for language skills. However, the university the author teaches does not have conditions for such a model. Moreover, as a common required course, one English teaching class is often composed of graduate students from multiple discipline directions, so it is hard to conduct academic English instruction with unified materials or contents in students need. Therefore, based on the concept and theory of CBI and EAP, we decide to use academic materials of students' research fields prepared by graduate students themselves after consulting with their advisors, and the English class is conducted in the way of students' independent study with supervision from the English instructors. In teaching process, which is more suitable to be referred as independent and collaborative learning process of students, English instructors mainly help students in their understanding and use of English, as well as the general approach in academic learning, such as how to read literature, how to write literature review, and how to prepare for an academic presentation, etc.

In each class, students are divided into several groups according to their majors and research focuses. Each group is required to determine a list of English academic articles in their specialized research fields for them to study in the semester. Then they are required to study one article each week and to carry out series of tasks. The design can be summarized as "literature reading + corpus building + class presentation and discussion + paper review writing".

The teaching design of academic English for one school hour can be illustrated as follows. The instructor requires students to study one academic article each week and to complete the following tasks individually or in groups. (1) Students are required to find out the research topic, research purpose, theoretical basis, research methods or experimental steps, research results and conclusions and research creativities or innovations, etc. of the research paper. (2) They are required to build an academic corpus in which they need to collect and sort out the English specialized academic terms, expressions and typical academic sentence patterns involved in the literature they read. (3) They need to make PPT for class presentation. The instructor selects 4–5 groups each week to present the research articles they study in class. The presentation lasts for no more than 8 min each. Then the class will discuss around the presentation and the article. (4) Finally the instructor requires the students to write a review of about 300 words in English based on the article they have read and to submit it to the teacher along with the corpus they have made. As English language instructors, they mostly make judgements on the logic, the structure and the language use of the review.

In this teaching design, the content of students' learning fully conforms to their research directions and demands of their advisors, which also meets requirements for the degree. In the process of learning specialized academic literature, students can improve their English communicative competence and academic research ability. While studying the academic papers, students construct academic knowledge in their specialized fields and learn the procedures, methods and theories of academic research. Corpus building aims to guide students to accumulate professional English academic terms, expressions, and to understand English academic discourse. Class presentation and discussion can cultivate the ability of graduate students to participate in international academic conferences and to make international academic communication. Paper review is to train students in writing academic papers in English through which they can fully study and internalize the English academic materials. This teaching design uses task-based teaching method, focusing on students' independent as well as cooperative learning. The instructor is responsible for organizing each step of the teaching, making judgments and guidance to the language use and the way to do academic research. In this process, the English teacher can learn the specialized knowledge together with students and participating in classroom discussions. Such a teaching design can effectively avoid the dilemma that language instructors cannot conduct academic English teaching because they do not understand the professional knowledge of various disciplines. In addition, this mode makes English classroom a place of learning specialized knowledge for graduate students. It not only improves students' language skills, but also encourages them to use English as a tool for academic learning and research.

3.2 Teaching Procedures

The procedures of the "academic English" teaching model can be summarized as the following 4 steps in which 7 tasks should be carried out (see diagram 1):

Step 1(task 1). Determining the materials to study. In the first weeks of the class, students are required to work in groups (groups are divided by majors, mostly students of the same advisor are divided into one group) to determine the English academic articles to study in a semester in consultation with their advisors and professors in their research fields.

Step 2. Assigning the pre-class tasks. The language teacher assigns students to read one academic article one week in advance, and to complete the following tasks in group cooperation and independent learning:

Task 2. To answer questions. What is the research focus of this literature? What is the purpose of this study? What problems does the study aim to solve? What is the theoretical basis of the research? What research methods or experimental steps did the study use? What results and conclusions did the study come to? What are the creativities or innovations of the research?

Task 3. To build academic corpus. Students are required to sort out specialized English terms/words/expression and typical English academic sentence patterns in the literature in order to establish an English-Chinese academic corpus.

Task 4. To make PPT for class presentation. Students are required to work in groups to make PPT for presentation in class.

Step 3. Conducting classroom activities.

Task 5. To make class report. Group representatives or all members of the group shall make presentation in the class on the research article they have studied in the form of PPT, and they also need to display the corpus they accumulate on academic words, terms and sentence patterns in the article. The presentation of each group should last no more than 8 min.

Task 6. To do class discussion. After the class report, a class discussion is conducted. Other students of the class ask questions around the topic of the research article. The teacher joins in the discussion and comments on the class report and class discussion of the students and points out the language problems of the students in the PPT.

Step 4 (task 7). Writing paper review. This is also the seventh task of this teaching model. Each student should independently write a review of 300 words in English based on the research article they have read and submit it to the instructor. The instructor judges the review mainly based on the logic, writing structure and language use. The instructor is not necessarily familiar with the students' majors and research fields, he/she gives general comments on the language use and research methodology.

From Fig. 1, we can see the teaching is conducted through various tasks in which students develop their language skills of reading, writing, speaking and listening by studying the academic materials they need in their graduate programs. In the process, teachers encourage students to learn academic content through both independent and cooperative learning. While students are learning the specialized academic knowledge, they acquire language communication ability. In the meanwhile, they also improve their self-learning ability and cultivate the capability to cooperate and communicate with others. In such an academic content-based classroom, students are active knowledge constructors and motivated learners rather than passive receivers. This model encourages them to learn from others, including instructors and classmates. By communicating with excellent students, they gradually improve their language skills and learn more knowledge. In this positive learning environment, students reflect on the knowledge they learn, speculate on the relationship between new knowledge and existing knowledge, and constantly deepen their understanding of the academic content. For example, in academic English learning, students learn theoretical knowledge, research methods, basic steps of scientific research, and the latest international academic trends of their majors through studying English literature. In this way, their academic ability is improved and their academic horizons are broadened. In this process, their English language ability has been developed, which in turn further helps them to learn more professional and academic knowledge. In this learning process students need to cooperate with other students, in which they need help from others, and they also need to help others, which fully embodies the experiential and constructivist learning theories, that is, learning is a process of experience and construction, at the same time, it is social activities involving interactions with others and the environment.

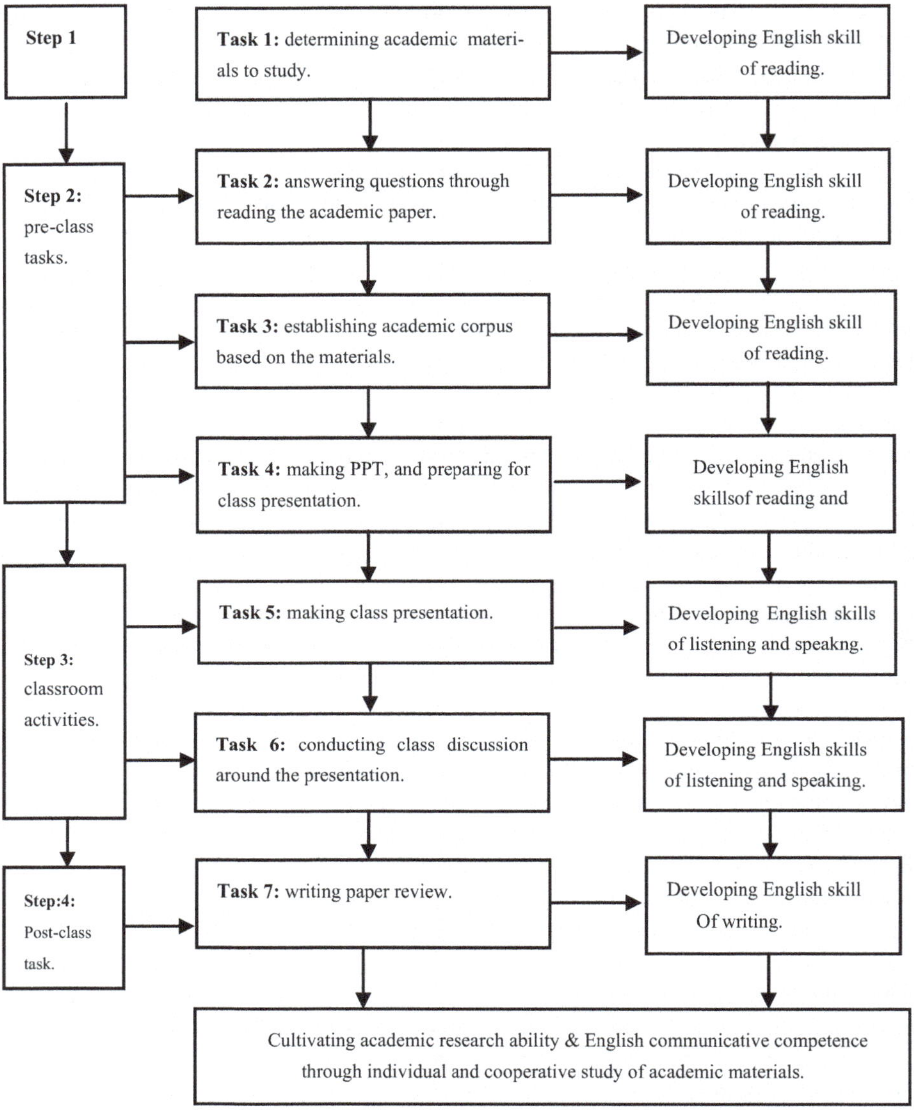

Fig. 1. Procedures of academic English course

4 Design of Examination and Evaluation

Content-based academic English teaching model differs dramatically from the teaching of general English which focuses on language skills. Content-based academic English teaching model cultivates and improves students' English language ability by learning academic content in their research fields. Students acquire English language and develop academic competence through content learning. In this model, language becomes a tool to learn academic knowledge.

Then how to test students in such a model? What should the test focus on, academic contents or language skills? How should the instructors evaluate the learning process of students to make assessments? We hold that the goal of academic English teaching is to train students to use English for academic research and international academic exchanges. And to examine students' academic English in the form of literature review writing is a way to comprehensively examine and judge students' ability to use English for literature reading, paper writing and academic research. In this model, students learning process is as important as the final submission because this mode of teaching is student-centered. In instruction, students need to complete the tasks required by teachers through independent learning and cooperative learning. In class, they frequently need to make presentations, to participate in discussions. Only by controlling every step of teaching and learning well and by conducting quantitative evaluation on students' performance, can teachers make this teaching mode effective.

As a result, we establish the following examination and evaluation system. (1) English academic ability examination. Students are required to write a standard literature review in English on a certain topic of their research fields with no less than 2000 words. (2) Process evaluation. In the whole teaching process, instructors quantitatively evaluate students' class attendance, paper review writing, and classroom performance including class discussion, class presentation, academic corpus they made. (3) Students' final scores are composed of two parts: the final literature review accounts for 50%, and process evaluations account for 50%.

Such a test design adequately embodies the ultimate goal of academic English teaching and learning. English literature review writing can comprehensively examine students' capability in using English for academic research. Process evaluations are vital for the success of this student-centered model. In this model, most of the tasks are carried out by students individually or collaboratively, while the instructor is only a classroom controller, an evaluator and coordinator of the student's learning process.

5 Conclusion

This content-based academic English instruction practice develops the model of "literature study + academic corpus building + classroom presentation and discussion + paper review writing". In such a student-center classroom, learning is done independently and cooperatively. In this model, students are exposed to a large amount of input in a natural language environment through academic study. Moreover, unlike the teacher-centered classroom, where students are in a passive position, content-based academic English class makes students the center of the classroom activities, in which they deeply involve in learning materials in combination with their academic research with a series of tasks. Finally, it provides students with various opportunities to use English as a tool to do research and academic study. In a word, in such a mode of learning, English is acquired through doing academic study and research.

Content-based academic English instruction is in line with the practical needs of graduate students and the goal of graduate student cultivation. This model enables students to improve their English language competence by learning specialized academic knowledge. In this way, their international communication ability and academic vision are improved. This practice solves the challenge that graduate English instructors face in implementing academic English teaching due to limitations in specialized knowledge, and it provides an approach of academic English instruction for master and doctoral students.

References

1. Cai, J.G.: Specialization and Contextualization is the Way to Solve the Major Contradiction of Foreign Language Education in Colleges and Universities in China in the New Era – Review and Reflection on Foreign Language Education in Colleges and Universities in China at the 40th anniversary of Reform and Opening up. J. Zhejiang Foreign Lang. Univ. **2** (2018)
2. Cai, J.G.: Theoretical basis and significance of specialized academic English teaching in Chinese Colleges and Universities. Foreign Lang. Audio-visual Teach. **2** (2018)
3. Cai, J.G.: English teaching in disciplines under the framework of CBI theory. Foreign Lang. Teach. **5** (2011)
4. Shu, D.F., Chen, S.Y.: The Road to Success in College English Teaching: a Survey of the "discipline -oriented" English Teaching Model in the University of Nottingham Ningbo. Shanghai Foreign Language Education Press, Shanghai (2010)
5. Liu, R.Q.: Using content teaching to drive language teaching. In: The Third Annual Meeting of the Chinese Educational Linguistics Research Association and the Academic Seminar on "New Model Of Foreign Language Teaching Based On Disciplines", Xi'an (2012)
6. Snow, M., Brinton, D.: Content-based Classroom. Longman, New York (1997)
7. Stoller, F.: Content-based instruction: perspectives on curriculum planning. Ann. Rev. Appl. Linguist. **24**(2004), 261–283 (2004)
8. Stoller, F.: Promoting the acquisition of knowledge in a content-based course. In: Crandall, J., Kaufman, D. (eds.) Content-based instruction in higher education settings, pp. 109–124, VA: TESOL, Alexandria (2002)
9. Stryker, B., Leaver, L.: Content-based instruction: Some lessons and implications. In: Stryker, B., Leaver, L. (eds.) Content-Based Instruction in Foreign Language Education: Models and Methods, pp. 282–310. Georgetown University Press, Washington, D.C. (1997)
10. Jordon, R.: English for Academic Purpose. Cambridge University Press, Cambridge (2002)
11. Flowerdew, J., Peacock, M.: Research Perspectives on English for Academic Purposes. Cambridge University Press, Cambridge (2001)
12. Graddol, D.: The Future of English? British Council, London (1997)
13. Hyland, K.: English for Academic Purpose—An Advanced Research Book. Routledge Taylor & Francis Group, London and New York (2006)

A Study of Intercategorial Polysemy Teaching Based on Conceptual Blending Theory in Senior High Schools

Hong Duan[1], Qingling Wang[1(✉)], and Lihua Xia[2]

[1] School of Foreign Languages and Literature, Yunnan Normal University, Kunming 650500, China
2316207767@qq.com

[2] Experimental Junior Middle School of Suzhou Hi-Tech & New District, Suzhou 215010, China

Abstract. This thesis adopts Conceptual Blending Theory into intercategorial polysemy teaching in senior high school, so as to test the effectiveness of the new teaching method based on CBT. The findings of this thesis are demonstrated as follows. Firstly, after two months instruction, the mean score of posttest 1 in the EC is 10.93% higher than that of the CC and the value of Sig. is 0.017. It suggests compared with the traditional method, the new polysemy teaching approach based on CBT is effective in polysemy teaching. Secondly, two weeks later, the mean score of posttest 2 in the EC is 36.28% higher than that of the CC and the value of Sig. is 0.000. It supports the idea that the new polysemy teaching approach is more beneficial to students' long-term retention. Thirdly, a month later, the mean score of posttest 3 in the EC is 6.29% higher than that of the CC and the value of Sig. is 0.030. It means that in comparison with the traditional method, the new polysemy teaching approach can improve students' independent learning capability. Furthermore, the paired-sample test value of Sig. in the EC is 0.032 while the paired- sample test value of Sig. in the CC is 0.539. It gives evidence that the new polysemy teaching approach makes a big difference to the experimental class while the conventional teaching method doesn't have the same effect on the control class.

Keywords: Conceptual blending theory · Polysemy teaching · Senior high schools

1 Introduction

Polysemy is the characteristic of a single word which has two or more distinct but related senses. It is a common phenomenon in natural language. Within the vast array of new cognitive linguistics of polysemy construction, most of the researchers analyzed polysemy from their spatial structures based on image schema theory (Talmy 1988). The networks were frequently applied to terms such as on, above, below, outside, to the right (left) of, across, and into for spatial relations and motions (Chen and Xu 2009). Whilst some were keen on the meaning extension mechanism of polysemy in terms of metaphor, metonymy and prototypical categorization (Lakoff 1987; Goossens 1990;

G. Sun et al. (Eds.): eLEOT 2019, LNICST 299, pp. 377–390, 2019.
https://doi.org/10.1007/978-3-030-35095-6_41

Verspoor 1998; Langacker 1999; Boers 2000; Liang 2002; Csabi 2004; Xu and Huang 2006; Liao 2009; Liu 2010; Kuang 2010; Guo 2012). All these researches accelerate the analyses of polysemy, especially monocategorial lexical polysemy, in different angles, and some of them suggest effective ways to help students learn polysemy better. As opposed to these linguistic theories, Conceptual Blending Theory (CBT for short) emphasizes the on-line processes of meaning construction (Fauconnier 1985, 1997; Fauconnier and Turner 1996, 1998a, 1998b, 2002), which lead to better understanding of polysemy. Within the paradigm, Zawada (2007) did a research on intercategorial lexical polysemy on CBT, as a supplement to former monocategorial lexical polysemy research. But up to now, there has been no empirical research on polysemy teaching from the perspective of CBT in senior high school. This research is aimed at the effective intercategorial polysemy teaching based on CBT in middle school.

2 Methodology

2.1 Research Questions

This study aims at testing the effect of application of conceptual blending to English polysemy teaching and learning process. To be specific, the purposes of this experiment are to answer the following questions:

(1) What is the current situation of students' English polysemy learning?
(2) What effects does the CBT-based polysemy teaching method have on students' understanding of different senses of polysemous words?
(3) What effects does the CBT-based polysemy teaching method have on students' long-term retention of polysemy?
(4) How much can the CBT-based polysemy teaching method improve students' ability of independent polysemy learning?

2.2 Research Subjects

There are 72 students involved in the experiment. All of them come from two classes in Grade one from Tangyang Senior High School where the author works as the English teacher of two classes. All the subjects are interested in the experiment and they volunteer to provide real information during the experiment. First, the two classes receive a test. It turns out that they are at the similar level of using polysemous words they have learned. So Class 1 made up of 36 students is chosen as the experimental class (EC); while Class 2 consisting of 36 students is treated as the control class (CC) to participate in a contrastive and empirical study. After that, the author will teach these two classes using the same materials and textbooks. However, the subjects of each class are exposed to different ways of polysemy teaching and learning. The experiment will last for three and a half months.

2.3 Instruments

In the study, we comb students' books from Module 1 to 8 in middle school in Jiangsu province, then sorts out 88 polysemous words that are used as intercategorial polysemy, which covers seven elements, namely locatives, instruments, results, occupations, human relations, animal's characteristics and emotions. The main instruments which help to put the experiment plan into practice are composed of a questionnaire and four times of polysemy tests. A questionnaire is used at the beginning of the term to get a general information and make the researcher know the subjects' capability of polysemous words better. Four times of polysemy tests are carried out step by step. A pretest, followed by three posttests on different purposes, is conducted in both classes. However, polysemy teaching, as part of daily teaching activities, differs in two classes.

2.3.1 Questionnaire

The questionnaire is scheduled to conduct at the beginning of the term. The purpose of the questionnaire is to get the information about students' attitudes towards polysemous words, as well as their strategies on studying polysemous words. Its theoretical basis is the O'Malley and Chamot's (1990) classification of learning strategy. The questionnaire consists of the instructions and 12 questions indicating the participants' attitudes towards polysemy, self-learning strategies and memorizing strategies. The participants are told to finish the Five Point Likert Scale. "5" represents the complete agreement. "4" means usual agreement. "3" stands for uncertainty. "2" refers to usual disagreement. "1" has the meaning of complete disagreement. The participants are supposed to choose only one answer which can represent the real situation.

2.3.2 Tests

The polysemy tests in the whole experiment are made up of one pretest and three posttests. Each test contains 10 target polysemous words. There are two criteria to select the target words. One is that 10 words in each test are selected from the students' book in Grade One. The other one ensures that there are at least three different senses of each target words students are required to master during the middle school period. Each test will give the target word first, followed by the core senses of the word. Then several sentences containing the target words will be presented. Subjects are required to match these sentences with the correct meaning of the target word provided above. Each time of the correct match will guarantee them one score. Each test will be finished in 40 min. Subjects are required to finish them alone, with no discussion between classmates and no additional instruments, such as the dictionaries.

2.4 Procedures

The whole procedures could be divided into six steps. In brief, a questionnaire was scheduled to conduct at the beginning of the term. Then a pretest was conducted before teaching activities. In the next step, different teaching activities were undertaken, with a new approach under the guidance of CBT in the experimental class but a traditional way in control class. After two months, posttest 1 was conducted to verify the effectiveness of the new approach on understanding polysemy. Two weeks later, posttest 2 was carried out without any warning to test the students' acquisition of the same polysemous words which had been tested in posttest 1 and long-term retention of those words. Posttest 3 was performed a month later to test whether subjects could guess the polysemous words independently even though these words hadn't been taught in class.

Step 1: Questionnaire
The questionnaire was conducted at the beginning of the term. The purpose of the questionnaire was to get the information about students' attitudes towards polysemous words, as well as their strategies on studying polysemous words. The questionnaire was applied to all the students in Grade one including experimental class and control class on September 3. The teachers were in each class to read the instructions of the questionnaire to make students understand that there was no standard answer to each question and what they needed to do was give the honest answer. Students could consult the teacher whenever they came across with questions. The questionnaire was finished in 15 min. The aim of the whole experiment was to make it clear what the situation of vocabulary learning was at present and to check the necessity of finding an effective way to teach polysemy to middle school students.

Step 2: Pretest
The pretest was carried out the next week. The author selected the target polysemous words, each of which was presented with four or five different senses and the sentences corresponding to each senses. The aim of this test was to evaluate subjects' capability of understanding polysemy according to the background information obtained from the context of the sentences, and to test whether there was significant difference in this capability between the experimental class and the control class. The participants looked anxious when they first saw this kind of test. To relieve their anxiety, the author told them that it was a test to check their present level of polysemy, the results of which was collected for teaching adjustments and had nothing to do with the evaluation of their daily performance or final grades. The pretest was finished within 40 min.

Step 3: Teaching Activities
After the pretest, the new approach to teaching polysemy which was based on CBT was adopted in the experimental class. At first, the author introduced some basic knowledge CBT to the students, including the types of blending and how the blending took place when people used polysemy of a word to express different situation. It aimed to arouse their cognitive mechanisms to learn polysemy better. The author explained numerous samples to the students with drawings to make the theory visible and understandable, such as the polysemous words "limit", "failure", "comfort", "loss" and so on. The majority of the examples were adopted from the eighth version of the Oxford Advanced Learners' English-Chinese Dictionary. This dictionary played an important role in the whole experiment. It functioned as the a reference to select polysemous words as well as to illustrate the connections among different senses.

The students in the control class were taught about the senses of those words one by one in a traditional way. In this case, there was no need to guide students how to figure out exactly the relationship between the senses, or to tell why there was such a development of the polysemy.

Step 4: Posttest 1

Students were exposed to different approaches to dealing with polysemy for two months. Then posttest 1 was concluded to test whether the approach adopted in EC had positive effects on students' capability of polysemy. The layout of posttest 1 was the same as that of the pretest. The words were adopted from different units of students' book. They had already been taught, but the author taught them in different ways on purpose. The test lasted for 40 min under the supervision of the author.

Step 5: Posttest 2

After posttest 1, the author explained the target words together to the students in different classes in different ways. After the test paper review class, the author reminded students of referring to the test paper in their favorite ways at their spare time. There was no advance warning of the next test to be given.

Two weeks later, posttest 2 was conducted on schedule in both classes. The test was designed the same as the posttest 1. They shared the same target words. The author made slight changes of the sentences to make them look new and different, but actually they provided the same context. Posttest 2 was designed to check whether this new polysemy teaching approach had great effects on students' long-term retention of polysemy.

Step 6: Posttest 3

The posttest 3 was conducted a month later to check whether the new polysemy teaching approach improved students' ability of independent polysemy learning. Therefore, the target words in posttest 3 were not taught in advance to the students. All subjects were expected to finish the test with their polysemy capability they had developed this term.

2.5 Data Collection

Five parts of the data require collecting in the whole experiment to guarantee the follow-up analyses. Generally speaking, they are about a questionnaire, a pretest and three posttests. The SPSS software is widely used in this kind of thesis. "Independent-samples t-test", "paired-samples t-test" and "frequency test" of the data are scientific angles to calculate relevant data. These steps are fundamental to the experiment and giving convincing evidence to evaluate the experiment. In addition, some related figures and tables are required to be finished by Excel.

3 Results and Discussion

3.1 Results and Analyses of the Questionnaire

140 questionnaires were sent out to students in Grade One in Tangyang Senior High School. All the results of 120 valid questionnaires were input into SPSS 17.0. The questionnaire is a Five Point Likert Scale. The scores from five to one stand for students' response to the situation from complete agreement to complete disagreement. Mean scores and frequencies are calculated to illustrate the students' attitudes towards polysemy, self-learning strategies and memorizing strategies. The following tables

exhibit the scores of each strategy. If the score gets higher than 4 points, the item is regarded as the highly common phenomenon.

The first three questions make up the part to test students' attitudes towards polysemy. The results below respectively show that students have awareness of the high percentage of polysemy existing in English vocabulary (Table 1).

Table 1. Frequency chart (Q1–3)

	Q1	Q2	Q3
N Valid	120	120	120
Missing	0	0	0
Median	3.90	3.90	3.32
Mode	4.00	4.00	3.00
Sum	4	4	3

At the same time, they feel confused when using polysemy. About 19% of the students would rather skip it, while half of the students would find ways to overcome it, as is shown in Fig. 1. In a word, the figure shows the importance of teaching polysemy and students' curiosity on effective ways to learn polysemy.

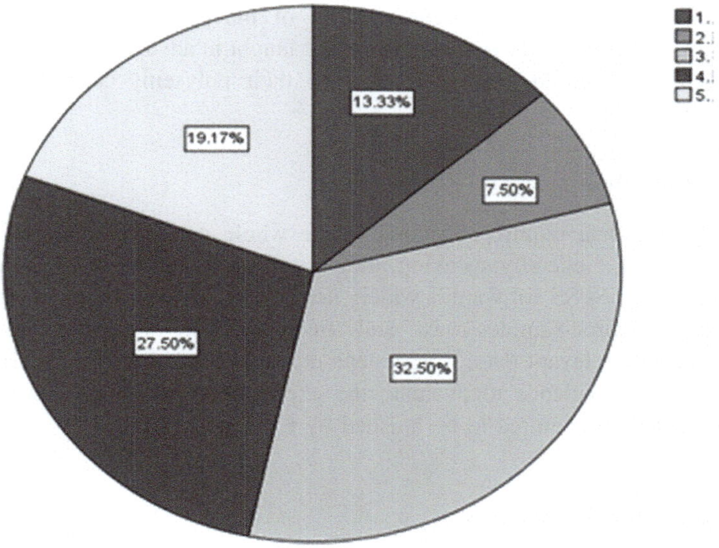

Fig. 1. Frequency chart (Q3)

Students' self-learning strategies are made up of Q 4, 5, 7 and 8. The Figure below indicates that compared with discussing with classmates, referring to the dictionary, finding meaning connection and guessing from the context are their self-learning strategies. But through Q6, they declare that they have the awareness of the interrelations among different senses of a word, but they never perceive the underlying rules, which leads to the inaccuracy of understanding, as is shown by Q9 (Table 2).

Table 2. Frequency chart (Q4–9)

	Q4	Q5	Q6	Q7	Q8	Q9
N Valid	120	120	120	120	120	120
Missing	0	0	0	0	0	0
Media	3.11	3.58	3.81	3.56	3.65	3.74
Mode	3.00	4.00	4.00	4.00	4.00	4.00
Sum	3	4	4	4	4	4

Students' memorizing strategies are shown in Table 3. The media and mode value of Q11 indicates that understanding polysemy in sentences is likely to be their better choices.

Table 3. Frequency chart (Q10–12)

	Q10	Q11	Q12
N Valid	120	120	120
Missing	0	0	0
Media	3.9	3.67	3.53
Mode	4.00	4.00	4.00
Sum	4	4	4

The data of Q10 reveal that more than one third of the students are unwilling to list various meanings, then memorize them by rote. More than half of the students think it unnecessary to recite all the senses at a time, which indicates by the data of Q12. The results are vividly shown in the following two figures (Figs. 2 and 3).

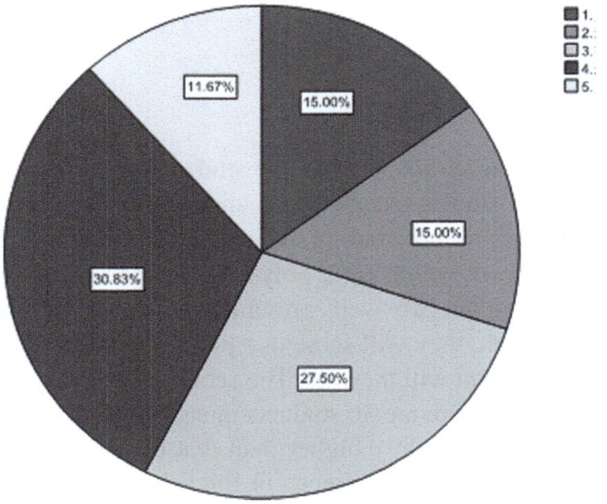

Fig. 2. Frequency chart (Q10)

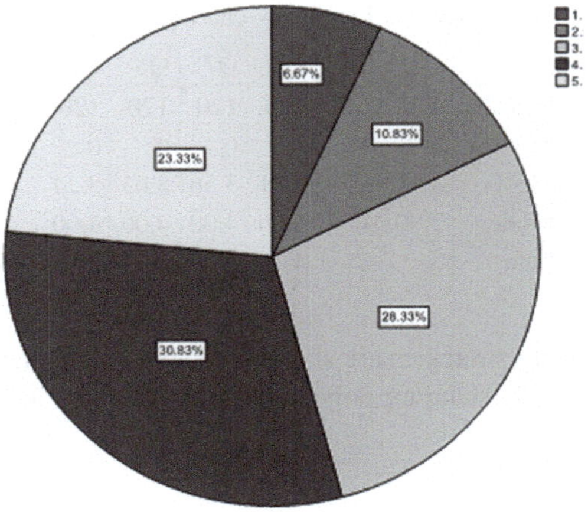

Fig. 3. Frequency chart (Q12)

As is indicated above, students feel confused about polysemy learning. An evident contradiction can be sensed that students want to learn polysemy well but they are lacking in skills. The majority of students have found polysemy common in English and they are fully aware of the importance of polysemy learning. They also acknowledged that they had much difficulty in understanding various senses. On the other hand, they considered memorizing the senses of words by rote as the ineffective way in their learning and they agreed that there exist relations between the senses though they can't make it clear. An agreement can be reached from the analyses in this part that it is high time to explore a new approach to teaching polysemy. The author believes the conceptual blending approach is likely to be a better way to deal with the tough situation. The new approach attracts students' attention on the relations of the meaning and presents clearly how the related meanings are developed in different sentences.

3.2 The Pretest of the EC and CC

The pretest was designed to check whether the students in the experimental class and the control class had the similar capability of understanding polysemy based on the context obtained from the sentences before the whole experiment. 10 target words were listed on the pretest paper, of which eight polysemous words were presented with five different senses and the other two were presented with four different senses. If the students make a right match, they will score one point. On the contrary, if the students make a wrong match, no point will they get. The scores sum up to 48 in total (Table 6).

The Table 4 shows that there are 36 students in each class taking part in the pretest. The mean score in class 2 is slightly higher than that of class 1, which indicates that class two has a little bit individual difference in English proficiency, but it is not quite obvious.

Table 4. Group statistics of the pretest scores

Class		N	Mean	Std. Deviation	Std. Error Mean
pre	EC	36	25.14	6.165	1.028
	CC	36	25.64	6.298	1.050

Only descriptive statistics are not enough. Further proof is provided by independent samples t-test. The first value of sig. in "Levene's test for equality of variances" is 0.825. According to the software, if the value is higher than 0.05, the equal variances are assumed. So the next step is to read the data from the "equal variances assumed". As is shown in the Table 5, the value of Sig. (2-tailed) reaches 0.735, which is greatly higher than 0.05, and reaching 1.00. It can be concluded that there is little difference between the pretest scores of class 1 and class 2. That is to say, there was no significant difference in the polysemy ability they had developed until that moment. Now that subjects in class 1 and class 2 are regarded at the similar level of inferring different senses according to context provided by each sentences, class 1 can be reasonably appointed to be the experimental class (EC), while class 2 will be regarded as the control class (CC) out of question.

Table 5. Independent samples test of the pretest scores

	Levene's Test for Equality of Variances		t-test for Equality of Means						
								95% Confidence Interval of the Difference	
	F	Sig.	t	df	Sig. (2-tailed)	Mean Difference	Std. Error Difference	Lower	Upper
pre									
Equal variances assumed	.050	.825	−.340	70	.735	−.500	1.469	−3.430	2.430
Equal variances not assumed			−.340	69.968	.735	−.500	1.469	−3.430	2.430

3.3 The Tests During the Experiment

3.3.1 The Effectiveness of the New Teaching Approach

The posttest 1 was conducted after the teaching activities for two months. 10 target words were listed on the pretest paper, of which eight polysemous words were presented with five different senses and the other two were presented with four different senses. If the students make a right match, they will get one point of the scores. On the contrary, if the students make a wrong match, no point will they get. The scores sum up to 48 in total.

Table 6. Group statistics of posttest 1

Class		N	Mean	Std. Deviation	Std. Error Mean
post 1	EC	36	28.81	6.541	1.090
	CC	36	23.56	5.321	0 887

It is quite evident that the mean score of the experiment class is much higher than the control class after two months' teaching with different methods. The value of Sig. (2-tailed) is 0.000, which is lower than 0.05. It indicates that significant changes have taken place in the scores of the experimental class after the teaching activities. It strongly proves that the teaching activities conducted in the experimental class have a positive effect on the students' learning (Table 7).

Table 7. Independent samples test of posttest 1

	Levene's Test for Equality of Variances		t-test for Equality of Means						
								95% Confidence Interval of the Difference	
	F	Sig.	t	df	Sig. (2-tailed)	Mean Difference	Std. Error Difference	Lower	Upper
post 1									
Equal variances assumed	2.732	.028	3.736	70	.000	5.250	1.405	2.447	8.053
Equal variances not assumed			3.736	67.213	.000	5.250	1.405	2.447	8.055

The following step is to make the data comparison between the pretest and the posttest 1 in the experimental class (EC) and the control class (CC). It is clearly shown that the value of Sig. (2-tailed) in the EC is 0.017, which is much lower than 0.05, indicating significance improvement due to the new teaching method, while the value of Sig. (2-tailed) in the CC is 0.14, suggesting no significant disparity during these two months' study (Table 8).

Table 8. Paired-samples test post-test 1

		Paired Differences					t	df	Sig. (2-tailed)
		Mean	Std. Deviation	Std. Deviation	95% Confidence Interval of the Difference				
					Lower	Upper			
EC	pre-post1	−3.667	8.796	1.466	−6.643	−.690	−2.501	35	.017
CC	pre-postl	2.083	8.275	1.379	−.717	4.883	1.511	35	.140

3.3.2 Students' Long-Term Retention of Polysemy

The posttest 2 was conducted two weeks after the posttest 1 evaluation and explanation with different methods. Students in both the EC and the CC are not required to recite the polysemy of the target word, and they were not informed of the test in advance. The posttest 2 was designed the same as the posttest 1. They shared the same target words. The author made slight changes of the sentences to make them look new and different, but actually they provided the same context. As is clearly shown that the mean score of the posttest 2 in the EC is much higher than the mean score in the CC (Table 9).

Table 9. Group statistics of posttest 2

Class		N	Mean	Std. Deviation	Std. Error Mean
post 2	EC	36	37.61	7.736	1.289
	CC	36	26.31	5.440	0.907

The value of sig. (2-tailed) is 0.000, which is even lower than 0.001. The result indicates there is significant difference in the scores of two classes in the long-term retention. Because the new method of commenting the test paper in the EC is based on CBT, it strengthens students' understanding of target words intensively and enhances their long-term retention of target words. The scores of the experimental class are especially remarkable, compared with those of the control class (Table 10).

Table 10. Independent samples test of posttest 2

	Levene's Test for Equality of Variances		t-test for Equality of Means						
								95% Confidence Interval of the Difference	
	F	Sig.	t	df	Sig. (2-tailed)	Mean Difference	Std. Error Difference	Lower	Upper
post 2									
Equal variances assumed	3.891	.049	7.173	70	.000	11.306	1.576	8.162	14.455
Equal variances not assumed			7.173	62.812	.000	−11.306	1.576	8.156	14.449

3.3.3 Students' Ability of Independent Polysemy Learning

A month later, posttest 3 was conducted without any advance warning to students in both classes. The target words in this test were not mentioned or given special explanation of in daily teaching process these days. The aim of the test is to check whether the new polysemy teaching approach can improve students' ability of independent polysemy learning. As is clearly shown in the below table, the mean score of the posttest 3 in the EC is higher than that of the CC. Students in the EC are likely to develop high-level polysemy-learning ability (Table 11).

Table 11. Group statistics of posttest 3

Class		N	Mean	Std. Deviation	Std. Error Mean
post 3	EC	36	28.42	6.082	1.014
	CC	36	25.53	4.902	0.817

At the same time, the value of sig. (2-tailed) is 0.030, which is even lower than 0.05. The result definitely suggests that students' ability of independent polysemy learning differs greatly. This kind of ability is what a learner needs to obtain during the process of learning. Posttest 3 indicates CBT can not only promote students' understanding of polysemy but also benefit their independent learning capacity of polysemy (Table 12).

Table 12. Independent samples test of posttest 3

	Levene's Test for Equality of Variances		t–test for Equality of Means						
								95% Confidence Interval of the Difference	
	F	Sig.	t	df	Sig. (2-tailed)	Mean Difference	Std. Error Difference	Lower	Upper
post 3									
Equal variances assumed	4.020	.049	2.219	70	.030	2.889	1.302	.292	5.486
Equal variances not assumed			2.219	66.975	.030	2.889	1.302	.290	5.488

To get more evidence, the author designed a "paired sample t-test" of the pretest and posttest 3. As is clearly shown in the following table, the value of sig. (2-tailed) is 0.032, which is even lower than 0.05. The result definitely suggests that there exists a large amount of difference between the level of the students in the EC at the beginning of the term and their level now. On the contrary, students in the CC don't achieve that change. The Table 13 indicates that three and a half months' teaching of polysemy with different methods gives rise to great discrepancy between the experimental class and the control class. The student in the EC improved a lot and there is significant difference from their level at the beginning of this term. The traditional teaching didn't make a big difference to the students in the CC.

Table 13. Paired-samples test of posttest 3

		Paired Differences					t	df	Sig. (2-tailed)
		Mean	Std. Deviation	Std. Error Mean	95% Confidence Interval of the Difference				
					Lower	Upper			
EC	pre-post 3	−3.139	8.435	1.406	−5.993	−.285	−2.233	35	.032
CC	pre-post 3	.806	7.789	1.298	−1.830	3.441	.620	35	.539

4 Conclusion

What the thesis concerns is to research whether the new teaching approach based on CBT has positive effects on polysemy teaching and acquisition in senior high school. Summing up the above results, a large number of students have found polysemy learning important but challenging in their study. The experiment was conducted in two classes of the similar polysemy learning level taught by the author. The experimental class was instructed with the new polysemy teaching approach while the control class was guided by the conventional teaching method. The data were collected mainly from four times of polysemous words tests and then SPSS 17.0 software was used to make horizontal and vertical comparative analyses of these tests. Compared with the traditional method, the new polysemy teaching approach based on CBT is effective in polysemy teaching. Moreover, the new polysemy teaching approach is more beneficial to students' long-term retention. Finally, in comparison with the traditional method, the new polysemy teaching approach can improve students' independent learning capability.

References

Boers, F.: Metaphor awareness and vocabulary retention. Appl. Linguist. **21**(4), 553–571 (2000)

Chen, X.X., Xu, Y.: The effects of the image-schema theory on the acquisition of the polysemous prepositions: on, over and above. Foreign Lang. Teach. **9**, 18–23 (2009)

Csabi, S.A.: A Cognitive linguistic view of polysemy in Englilsh and its implications for teaching [A]. In: Achard, M., Niemeier, S. (eds.) Cognitive Linguistics, Language Acquisition, and Pedagogy. Mouton de Gruyter, Berlin (2004)

Fauconnier, G., Turner, M.: Blending as central process of grammar [A]. In: Goldberg, A.E. (ed.) Conceptual Structure, Discourse, and Language. Center for the Study of Language and Information, Stanford (1996)

Fauconnier, G., Turner, M.: Conceptual integration networks. Cogn. Sci. **22**, 133–187 (1998a)

Fauconnier, G., Turner, M.: Principles of conceptual integration. Discourse Cogn. **37**(6), 269–283 (1998b)

Fauconnier, G., Turner, M.: The Way We Think: Conceptual Blending and the Mind's Hidden Complexities. Basic Books, New York (2002)

Fauconnier, G.: Mapping in Thought and Language. Cambridge University Press, Cambridge (1997)

Fauconnier, G.: Mental Spaces. The MIT Press, Cambridge (1985)

Goossens, L.: Metaphtonymy. The interaction of metaphor and metonymy in expressions for linguistic action. Cogn. Linguist. **1**(3), 323–342 (1990)

Guo, X.X.: Implications of prototype theory for vocabulary teaching in high schools. J. Basic English Educ. **2**, 64–70 (2012)

Kuang, F.T.: A Categorization-Based Vocabulary Instruction for English Majors in China. Southwest University, Chongqing (2010)

Lakoff, G.: Women, Fire, and Dangerous Things: What Categories Revealed About the Mind. The University of Chicago Press, Chicago (1987)

Langacker, R.W.: Grammar and Conceptualization. Mouton de Gruyter, Berlin (1999)

Liang, X.B.: The enlightenment of cognitive linguistics on English vocabulary teaching. Foreign Lang. Teach. **2**, 35–39 (2002)

Liao, G.R.: The simulation, properties and special features of word concept frame. Foreign Lang. Teach. **5**, 21–23 (2009)

Sun, G., Song, Z., Liu, J., et al.: Feature selection method based on maximum information coefficient and approximate Markov blanket. Zidonghua Xuebao/acta Automatica Sinica **43**(5), 795–8051 (2009)

Liu, Y.: Metaphor and Vocabulary Teaching. Southwest University, Chongqing (2010)

O'Malley, J., Chamot, A.: Learning Strategies in Second Language Acquisition. Cambridge University Press, Cambridge (1990)

Talmy, L.: Force dynamics in language and cognition [J]. Cogn. Sci. **12**(1), 49–100 (1988)

Verspoor, M.: Cognitive exploration of language and linguistic. John Benjamins Publishing Company, Amsterdam/Philadelphia (1998)

Xu, Z.S., Huang, G.F.: On the formation & teaching method of English polysemy from prototype theory. J. Xihua Univ. (Philos. Soc. Sci.) **25**(4), 100–102 (2006)

Zawada, B.: Conceptual integration and intercategorial polysemy. Lang. Matters **38**(1), 150–175 (2007)

Sun, G., Lang, F., Xue, Y.: Chinese chunking method based on conditional random fields and semantic classes. J. Harbin Inst. Technol. **43**(7), 135–139 (2011)

Study on Open Educational Resources Construction in Colleges and Universities in the Information Age

Liming Zhang[1(✉)] and Zeguang Lu[2]

[1] Jilin International Studies University, Changchun 130117, China
zhanglm574@sina.com
[2] National Academy of Guo Ding Institute of Data Sciences, Beijing 100190, China

Abstract. Nowadays, informatization has changed our work method and way of thinking as well as our educational mode. In future, education will break free from the constraints of time and space inevitably, and developed into the vast network world. Presently, the education informatization has basically completed its initial stage and application stage. Next it will adopt the development principle of "in-depth integration of information technology and education and teaching", guided by "application-driven" and "mechanism innovation", to enter the era of education information integration and innovation. Institutions of higher learning, as a concentration of high-level educational resources, whose popular and open digital education resources is a great guarantee for realizing new education in the intelligent era.

Keywords: Education resources · Open · Colleges and universities

1 Introduction

Digital learning is the product of the development of education informationization. Since the concept of digital learning was introduced for the first time in 2000, digital learning has been recognized globally as an important learning method with the rapid development of information technology. Digital education resources are the basis of digital learning, so its quality directly affects the effect of digital learning. The open and popular digital education resources (hereinafter referred to as "big resources") is the guarantee for digital learning to achieve that everyone have right to learn and can learn anywhere and anytime.

2 Social Background of Construction of Big Resources

Today, as digital learning grows, its resource construction has gradually become a core factor affecting digital learning. For this, countries' study on the construction of educational resources has continued to go deep with network information.

G. Sun et al. (Eds.): eLEOT 2019, LNICST 299, pp. 391–398, 2019.
https://doi.org/10.1007/978-3-030-35095-6_42

The American Department of Education has always attached great importance to the construction and application of open educational resources. At the beginning of this century, about 90% of public colleges and universities in the United States provided distance education courses of electronic media. In 2012, MOOC began to grow rapidly in the American top universities and quickly spread around the world. Course suppliers, represented by Coursera, Udacity and edX, cooperate with famous universities around the world to provide high-quality online courses to learners from all over the world.

Since the late 1990s, UK has paid special attention to the construction of digital learning resources. And its "community learning network" established is the main method for the development of community education in the UK currently. In the *European 2020 Strategy*, curriculum resources reform is proposed. Education fields and business circles develop school-enterprise cooperation by creating "Knowledge Alliance', and jointly develop high-quality curriculum resources with high practicality to solve the practical problems of lack of innovative skills for learners.

Japan is a world leader in the construction of education informatization. The *i-Japan Strategy 2015* emphasizes that, to promote rapid changes in teaching methods and innovation in teaching models, more digital teaching resources should be developed and the utilization of teaching resources in public institutions should continue to be expanded. MOOC of Japan has made new progress in content form after experiencing a transition from university-led to multi-subject, promoting the effective use and diffusion of public education resources.

China's educational informationization started late. With the development of informatization education, *the Ministry of Education's Opinions on Strengthening the Application and Management of Online Open Courses in Colleges and Universities* is issued in 2015. It points out the direction for building an open online curriculum system with Chinese characteristics, and deeply promotes the construction and popularization of open curriculum resources. At the second summit of "Internet plus Education" in 2017, the education informatization of next stage was proposed, and efforts should be made to realize the transformation from the development, application and service of special education resources to that of big resources.

3 The Popularization Transformation of Special Education Resources in Universities

In order to better adapt to the changes in the new era, education informatization should shift from the development, application and service of educational resources to that of big resources; shift from improving the application ability of information technology to improving the information literacy of teachers and students; and shift from the development of integration to that of innovation [1]. Among them, the development, application and service of educational resources are the basis for the development of educational informationization. Big resources can not only support the new educational model based on information technology, provide rich educational resources for the open learning environment, and build an intelligent platform that can be learned everywhere and anytime; but also it can also develop an Internet-based information education service model and integrate educational resources. In the era of "Internet plus" today, rich online resources has promoted the development of various online services, so every learner, whether or not he is at school, can find a learning service and learning resource suitable for himself on the Internet as long as he is willing to learn, to achieve the needs of learning for all and lifelong learning that everyone can learn and learn at any time.

Education resources are an important basis of carrying out educational activities. Its quality is related to whether education can be carried out normally and orderly, and its form affects the performance of educational form. In a long time, the printed-type educational resources represented by textbooks have formed people's deep-rooted educational form, That is, formal education represented by schools. In the information age, digital education resources have got rid of the constraints of printed-type educational resources like textbooks in quantity and space, and become an opportunity of the transformation of new-type education.

Traditional education resources have obvious special-purpose. The vast majority of education resources constructed is centered on teaching materials and oriented to specific students, and has strong relevance and dependence, especially for education resources in colleges and universities. Higher education is different from compulsory education. It's flexible training mode and professional characteristics make universities choose teaching materials more independently. Different universities have different focuses for the same course, so the materials they selected will also be different. This will result that the digital resources of a school building for a course cannot be used by other schools or even students of other majors.

A major feature of education informatization in the new era is to change special education resources to big resources, making the special resources of education become popular and open, and providing a guarantee for individualized learning and lifelong learning. With the continuous integration and innovation of disciplines, the knowledge in class is no longer attached to only one textbook. Interdisciplinary teaching resources have become an important carrier of teaching content. In addition, the development of emerging artificial intelligence, blockchain, virtual reality and other technologies has made digital education resources no longer just the form that everyone sees now. Dynamic educational resources with intelligent interaction will become the main form of educational resources in the information age.

4 The Planning of the Construction of Education Big Resources in Colleges and Universities

With the development of information technology, it will become the trend of education development to build an education system of networking, digitalizing, personality and lifelong and to build a learning-type society of "everyone learns and can learn everywhere and at any time" [2]. The realization of this kind of society cannot leave the support of a large number of high-quality digital education resources. The digital education resources built currently mainly include online courseware, cases, online courses, media materials, test databases, literatures, questions and answers, resource index and others, as shown in Fig. 1.

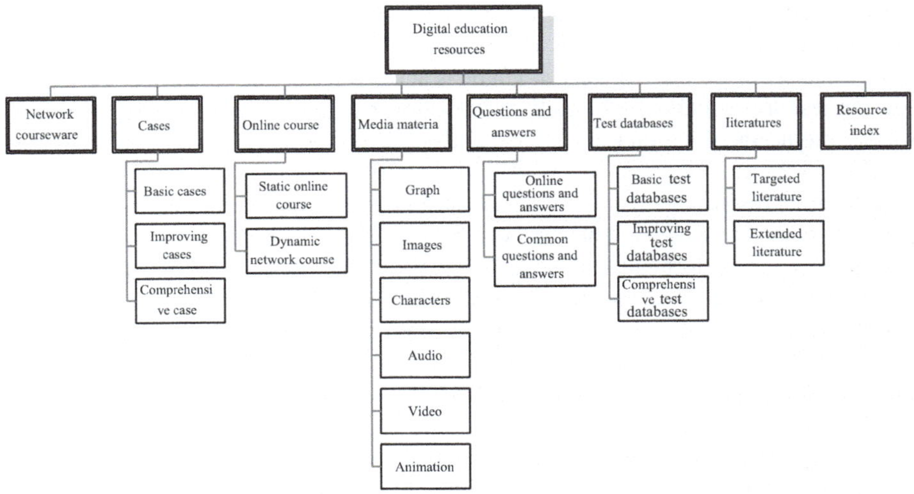

Fig. 1. Forms of digital education resource

Colleges and universities are the primary productive force of science and technology and the first resource to provide professionals, open majors covering all fields required in social production, and own the hardware and software conditions to build high-quality educational resources. With the transformation of higher education from elite education to popular education, the educational resources of application-type colleges and universities have already been equipped with the basis of transforming to popular educational resources. The open popular digital education resource needs to meet the needs of people in different levels and with different needs, and needs to coordinate all parties to avoid causing chaos that each acts (in) his own way. The big resources in the era of education informationization can be divided into two parts: basic resources and specialized professional resources.

Basic knowledge is the basis for people to recognize things and learn professional knowledge, such as Marxist political economics, advanced mathematics, university foreign languages, university physics, etc. Basic resources, characterized by less knowledgeability and changibility, can organize authoritative organizations to conduct unified development and construction, and use them as the basic resources of professional learning, to avoid low-level and repetitive construction of departments and universities at all levels.

The specialized professional resource, based on the basic resources and the professional development and the needs of social development, is cutting-edge resources, and also is the focus of popularity of the special education resources in colleges and universities. Colleges and universities should fully play their advantages in professional, science and research, resources, equipment and others, prioritize to construct scarce education resources, so that the digital education resources constructed should be free from the influence of restrictive factors such as teaching materials to solve practical problems in a targeted manner, meanwhile they should also have relative independence as much as possible, so as to provide resource support for online open courses, flipping classrooms and other new-type education methods.

In the information age, the construction of education resources should not only consider whether it conforms to the student-centered learning theory, but also examines the depth and breadth of the constructors' professional knowledge to check whether they own rich teaching experience and other qualifications, and whether they have related hardware equipment and so on. In addition, it also needs to ensure the richness of educational resources, and provides a variety of supporting materials such as media materials, literature, cases, etc., to help learners learn and understand better. However, if all these tasks are undertaken independently by the colleges and universities, their pressures are obviously increased, so multiple construction modes flexibly can be adopted to attract multiple forces, gather the power and the wisdom of the people, and build more high-quality education resources, to benefit more learners.

5 Construct Educational Resources and Build Ecological Environment

The construction of high-quality education resource requires a good ecological environment. The ecosystem of constructing education big resources in colleges and universities includes the educators, developers, users, supervisors, and operators of colleges and universities, as well as factors that affect their construction of open education resources, such as metadata standards, supervision mechanisms, operation mechanisms, safeguard mechanisms and so on. Only these factors are interconnected, interdependent and interacting can the ecosystem constructed be more powerful, more valuable and more meaningful.

5.1 Metadata Standard

In the information age, the metadata standard for the education big resources of colleges and universities is the basis for effectively describing big resources and realizing resource sharing and exchange. The attribute of the resource is labeled according to the metadata standard, which can make it be reused in different learning systems, and make it easier for learners to quickly retrieve, and serve as a basis for learners to screen resources. At present, the relatively complete educational metadata standard is IEEE LOM, and many countries have established localized educational metadata standards based on it. LOM divides learning objects into nine categories, with each containing several elements, in which element sets of educational category and technical category [3] are shown in Tables 1 and 2.

Table 1. Learning object metadata element set of education category

Category	Elements
Educational	Interactive level
	Semantic density
	Intended end user role
	Context
	Typical age range
	Difficulty
	Typical learning time
	Description
	Language
	Interactive type
	Learning resource type

Table 2. Learning object metadata element set of technical category

Category	Elements	Child element
Technical	Format	
	Size	
	Location	
	Requirement	Type
		Name
		Minimum version
		Maximum version
	Installation remarks	
	Other platform requirements	
	Duration	

5.2 Supervision Mechanism

The supervision mechanism is a mechanism to ensure that the education big resource construction of colleges and universities can be carried out orderly and normatively. It is a strategy and method implemented to ensure the construction of high-quality education resources. The educational resources will ultimately serve the popular education situation and learning situation in the era of education informationization. If there is no a good supervision mechanism, it will lead to the redundant construction of resources, and will appear the excessive construction of low-level education resources and the relative lack of high-level education resources. If we neglect the educational needs under the new situation to build resources blindly, it will inevitably make the content and form of the resources constructed unable to meet the requirements of the learners, and eventually lead the resources constructed to be abandoned. At the same time, if the evaluation and opinions of the resources in the process of resources use are not feedback to the resource builders, the excellent resources will not be promoted and spread, and the old resources will not be improved and updated in time.

The education information age is a new era that advocates diversification, individualization and lifelong learning. It requires resource builders to build new-type resources that are rich, diverse, safe, highly utilized, and adapt to the information-based teaching model according to the development of era. Resource users and third-party managers can participate in the construction of resources, which is undoubtedly a strong support for the innovative application of educational resources.

5.3 Operation Mechanism

At present, the development of digital educational resources is mainly based on the independent construction of college teachers, and a small part of the resources are constructed by inter-university or enterprise outsourcing. Since resources construction task is heavy, and it also is influenced by professional content, information technology and hardware conditions, the resources constructed can only be applied and practiced in a small scope. To build high-quality digital education resources that can develop for a long time, we must first integrate the latest developments of the industry with the latest technologies while adopting multiple operation mechanisms.

In the university, policy encouragement and economic encouragement are adopted to encourage teachers of colleges and universities to continuously accumulate, refine and update education resources around the field of their own professional characteristics, and continue to develop digital education resource construction. In the inter-university, the mode of co-construction and co-sharing is adopted to realize the inter-university collaborative construction, to form the complementary advantages of different university disciplines. Outside the university, the university-enterprise cooperation and service outsourcing are used to attract online learning service enterprises and resource development enterprises to participate in the construction of education big resources of colleges and universities.

In this way, in addition that some front-end featured disciplines need professional teachers to grasp the form and content of resource construction in person, for teaching resources which are used widely and frequently, such as public courses and professional foundations, school-enterprise cooperation and service outsourcing can be adopted to make enterprises become the main body of resources construction and in charge of development and cooperation. Experts in colleges and universities participate in the construction of curriculum resources as a course consultant.

5.4 Protection Mechanism

A large number of high-quality digital education resources support the new networking and digitalizing learning method, while they also bring great challenges for resource builders in the aspect of intellectual property right. The openness and sharing of the Internet makes it easy for people to access resources on the network. We should promptly adopt protection technology of digital intellectual property right, formulate relevant laws and regulations, and appeal people to strengthen the protection awareness of intellectual property right, to ensure that resource on the network is respected and protected. We should strengthen the supervision of resource construction and application market, crack down on illegal misappropriation of digital resources, and purify the environment for the construction and application of high-quality resources.

In education information age, high-quality education resources are indispensable, especially those of colleges and universities. Colleges and universities, as the origin of the dissemination of high-level education content, whose education big resources structed can greatly improve the quality of online learning. Every educator and educational resource builder in colleges and universities should participate in the practice of educational informatization to accelerate the construction of open educational resources in universities.

References

1. Lei, C.: Education informationization from 1.0 to 2.0. http://www.edu.cn/xxh/focus/li_lun_yj/201803/t20180303_1587698.shtml. Accessed 03 Mar 2018
2. Congratulatory letter from Xi Jinping to the International Education Informatization Conference. http://www.xinhuanet.com/politics/201505/23/c_1115383959.htm. 23 May 2015
3. Draft Standard for Learning Object Metadata. http://www.doc88.com/p-7894440895025.html. Accessed 09 Oct 2015
4. The 42nd Statistical Report on Internet Development in China. http://www.cac.gov.cn/2018-08/20/c_1123296882.htm. Accessed 20 Aug 2018
5. Wang, Z.: Core essentials and implementation suggestions of education informatization 2.0. Distance Educ. China 5–8 (2017)
6. Yang, Z., Wu, D., Xu, D.: Education informatization 2.0: the key historical transition of information technology transformation education in the new era. Educ. Res. 16–22 (2018)
7. Song, G., Zhao, F., Man, L.: Research on the ecological construction of open resources in university libraries. Libr. Inf. 70–74 (2016)
8. Sun, M., Gao, J., Ma, Y., Hai, J.: The construction and application of open education resources in distance education. West. China Qual. Educ. 129 (2019)
9. Cui, L., Chen, T., Quan, G., Wang, M.: Construction of practical education resources and sharing. China Educ. Technol. Equip. 39–45 (2018)
10. Yang, H., Wang, H.: Study on evaluation index system of open education micro-curricular resources construction. J. Yunnan Open Univ. 6–11(2018)

A Survey on the Internship Status of Students Majoring in Civil Aviation-Take Sanya Aviation and Tourism College as an Example

Xiao-li Wang(✉), Chao Li, Wei-wei Fan, and Xia Liu

Sanya Aviation and Tourism College, Sanya 572000, Hainan, China
49592041@qq.com, 55734322@qq.com,
108771777@qq.com, 13258514@qq.com

Abstract. The post practice of students in higher vocational colleges has become an important issue concerned by the government, society, schools and practice units. In order to strengthen the management of students' post practice and ensure the effect of students' practice, this paper takes students majoring in civil aviation at Sanya Aviation and Tourism College as research objects, and conducts a survey from four aspects: the students' basic situation, the school training situation, the students' concern about the internship and the students' satisfaction with the internship unit. After summarizing the results, this paper analyzes the factors and reasons that affect students' internship, and finally attaches importance to planning and layout, and strengthens guidance and supervision. Measures are explored to ensure the accurate connection with the industry, improve the course setting, broaden the scope of practice, innovate the practice mode and protect the rights and interests of students.

Keywords: Integration of enterprises with vocational schools and universities · Post practice · Status research

At present, China's aviation industry has ushered in the peak of development. However, compared with other enterprises, aviation enterprises are still unbalanced in regional distribution and relatively small in number. As a high-tech intensive industry, the aviation industry has high requirements on the quality of front-line technical staff. Some posts need to go through strict training and get corresponding certificates before they can take up posts. Due to the particularity and rigor of relevant posts, there are relatively few professional counterpart internship units and post. Job intensity also makes some posts lack of qualified personnel, resulting in the demand and supply can not be effectively linked. In order to further understand the current situation of vocational civil aviation students' in-post internship, effectively promote employment, and provide basis for the adjustment and implementation of talent training program, provide guidance for improvement of internship management efficiency, the school has deepened the integration of industry and education, and explored and implemented several cooperative projects in school-enterprise cooperation to promote student training according to the *Guidelines of the General Office of the State Council on Deepening the Integration of Industry and Education* issued by the State Council no. 95 (2017), the relevant contents of the R*egulations on the Management of Students' Internship in*

G. Sun et al. (Eds.): eLEOT 2019, LNICST 299, pp. 399–410, 2019.
https://doi.org/10.1007/978-3-030-35095-6_43

Vocational Schools jointly issued by the Ministry of Education and five other departments. In this paper, the questionnaire is designed from the three aspects of the school's cultivation status of students, students' concerns and satisfaction with the internship unit. Through the survey, we get to know the problems existing in the internship process and seek appropriate solutions. In this survey, 310 students of grade 2016 were given questionnaires in the form of questionnaire star. A total of 298 questionnaires were collected, with a recovery rate of 95.8%, among which 297 questionnaires were valid, with an effective recovery rate of 99.7%.

1 Research on Post Practice Status and Statistics

1.1 Basic Information of the Students

According to the research needs, the collected questionnaires were summarized, screened and counted. Among them, male students account for 49.49%, while female students account for 50.51%. 75.42% of the students are over 20 years old, and 24.58% are between 18 and 20 years old. Due to the difference in the number of majors, the number of collected questionnaires is also in direct proportion to the number of majors. More than 80% of the internship units are airlines, airports and ticket agencies across the country.

1.2 School Training

This paper studies the training situation of the school mainly from four aspects: training time before the internship, the situation of the counterpart internship, the adaption of the skills learned in school to the position, and the importance of the courses through the analysis of the internship experience. The results shows: 37.37% of them receive training for one week before they start work and what they are trained is not business knowledge, but corporate culture and management system; 39.73% of them receive training for one month before they start work and the training focuses on the update of business and enterprise management system and culture; 22.9% of them receive training for three months before they start work and the span of major and internship is large (as shown in Fig. 1). Only 37.37% of the internship posts are completely related to the major they have learned, while 28.28% are basically related to the major studied (as shown in Fig. 2). 31.31% of them can fully adapt the knowledge and skills learned in school to the needs of internship positions, while 39.39% of them can basically adapt what they learn in school to the needs of internship positions (as shown in Fig. 3). According to the experience of in-post internship, it is believed that the school can adjust the courses and proportion. 70.03% of them think that the professional practice courses should be increased, 47.81% of them believe that professional theory courses should be increased, and 43.77% of them advocate that basic theory courses should be increased, 21.21% of them feel that non adjustment should be made (as shown in Fig. 4). The above data show that the theoretical course, practical course, in-post internship, knowledge system are closely connected with the internship posts and can basically meet the needs of enterprises and employers. However, with the development and reform of the civil aviation industry, the application of modern information technology equipment exerts great impact on the civil aviation professional, which has accelerated the updating of the teaching content, management system and school-enterprise cooperation mode of each major in civil aviation.

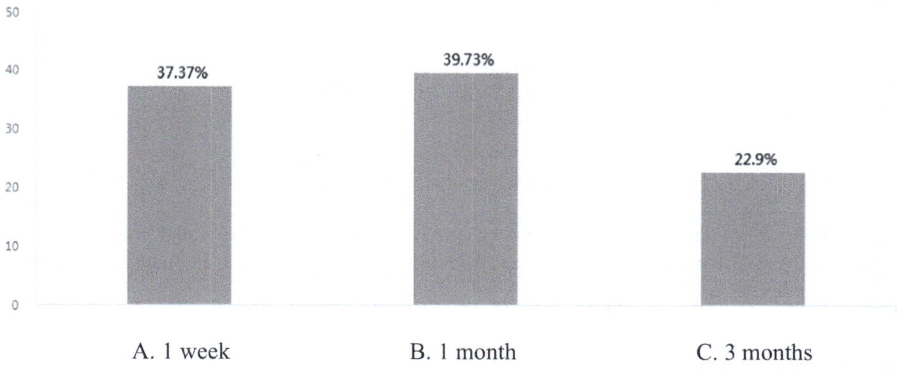

Fig. 1. Note: Pre-job training time of the internship unit

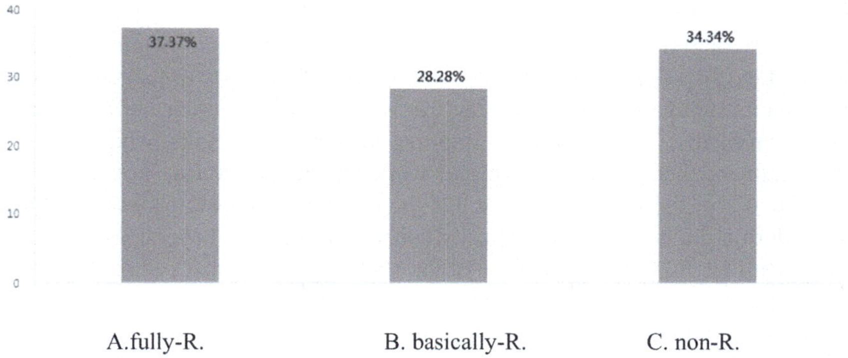

Fig. 2. Note: R. for related

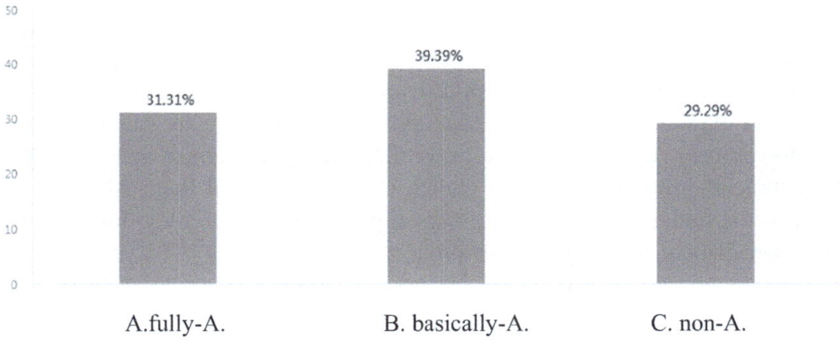

Fig. 3. Note: A. for adapted

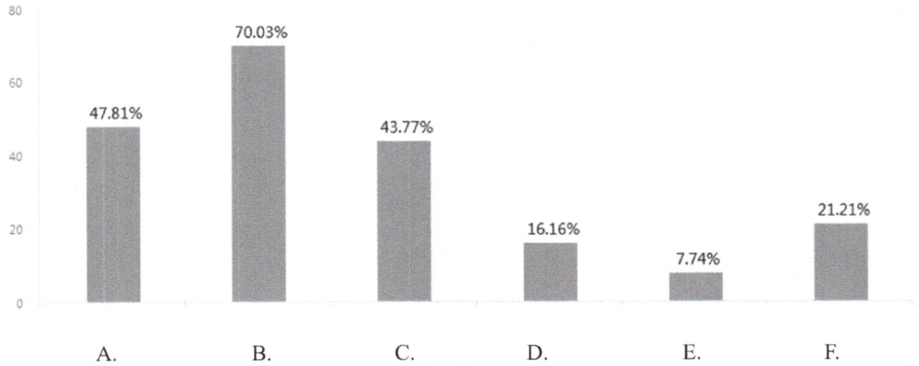

Fig. 4. Note: A. increase professional theory courses, B. increase professional practice courses, C. increase basic theory courses, D. reduce professional theory courses, E. reduce professional practice courses, F. no change.

1.3 Student Concerns

This paper studies the issues that students are concerned about during the internship from five aspects. Firstly, according to the survey data, during the internship, 43.77% of the students paid the most attention to the issue of prospect for personal development, and 18.18% of them paid the most attention to the issue of employment (as shown in Fig. 5); secondly, during the internship, 75.76% of the students want to improve their communication skills, 75.76% want to improve their ability to analyze and solve problems, 73.06% want to improve their practical skills, while only a few want to improve their ability to live and work independently (as shown in Fig. 6); thirdly, 75.76% of the students believe that the improvement of knowledge and ability acquired during the internship is basically consistent with and beyond the expectation (as shown in Fig. 7); fourthly, 62.97% of the students believe that personal ability and working atmosphere are the most important factors affecting the effect of internship and communication with classmates and supervisors is less important (as shown in Fig. 8); fifthly, during the internship, 67% of the students have signed contracts with the internship units, and the rest of the students have found other employment units or are still hesitating (as shown in Fig. 9). The data results show that students have new understanding and requirements for the internship units, and pay more attention to the self-development of interpersonal communication skills, the ability to analyze and solve problems and practical skills. Students have improved their abilities and gained more than expected during the internship. Even under the background that internship units are short of employees and want to retain employees, there are still some students who do not want to sign contracts. It shows that under the premise that students have certain technical skills, the space for choice is expanding, but there is still a certain deviation in the understanding of the internship process, which overlooks the importance of management in the internship process.

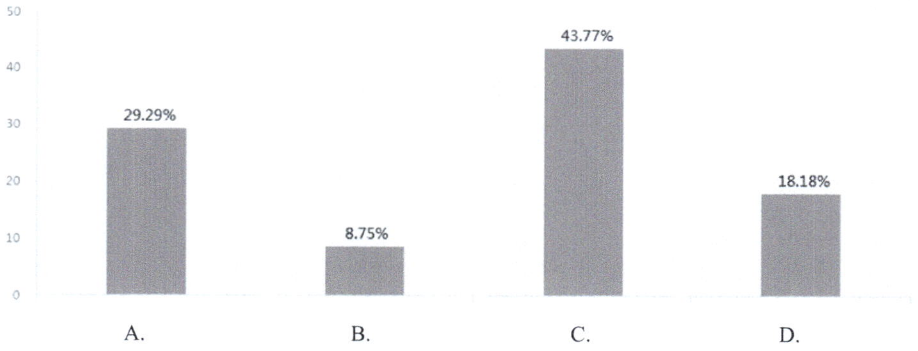

Fig. 5. Note: A. benefits, B. skills upgrading, C. personal development, D. employment

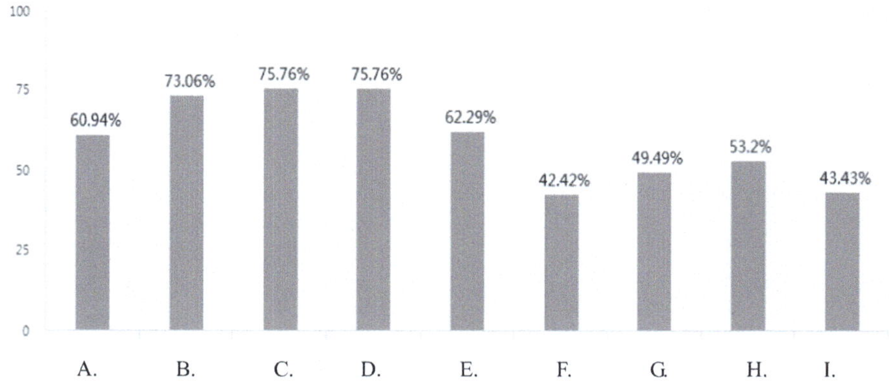

Fig. 6. Note: A. professional knowledge, B. practical skills, C. communication skills, D. ability to analyze and solve problems, E. teamwork, F. self-supplied ability, G. self-discipline, H. code of conduct, I. respect for the elderly and discipline awareness

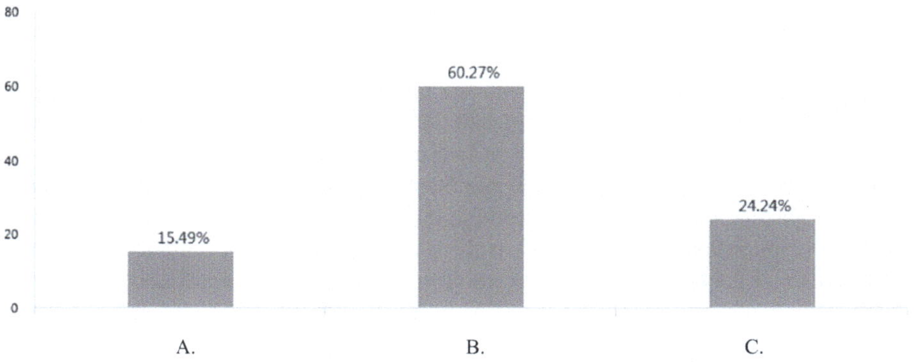

Fig. 7. Note: A. beyond expectation, B. consistent with expectation, C. below expectation

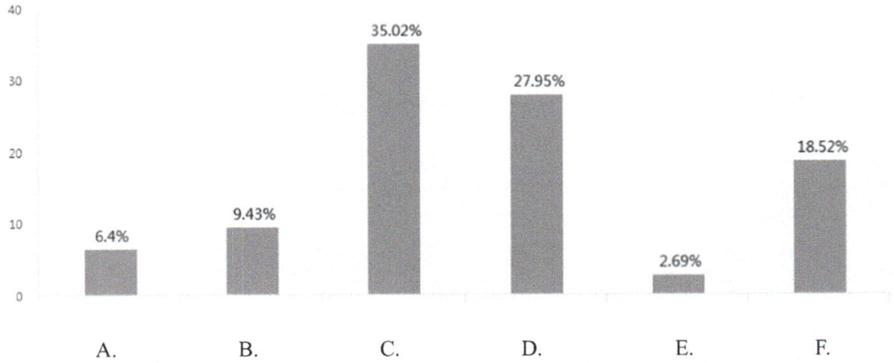

Fig. 8. Note: A. school supervision, B. professional level of instructors, C. personal ability, D. working atmosphere, E. communication with classmates and teachers, F. the richness of internship content

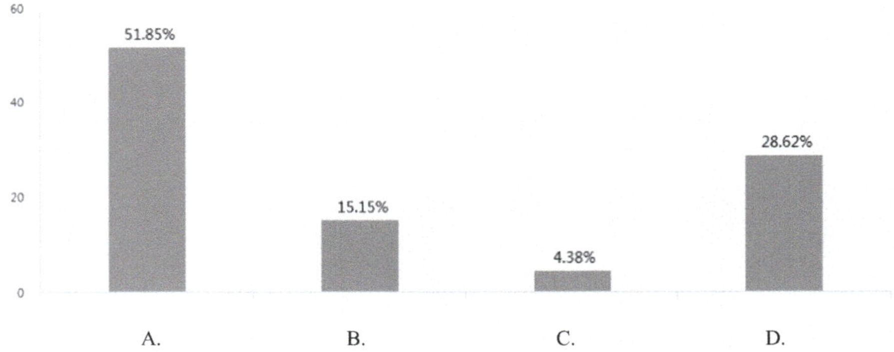

Fig. 9. Note: A. intention to sign, B. have signed, C. have signed with other units, D. no intention to sign

1.4 Students' Satisfaction with Internship Units

The degree of students' satisfaction with the internship units is the foundation for the further cooperation between the college and the enterprise. The survey data shows that: in terms of internship benefits, 80.48% of interns get a salary between 1000–3500, only 9.76% of them get a salary above 3500 and most of them are satisfied with their salaries (as shown in Fig. 10); in terms of incentive mechanism, 20.88% of students are often rewarded or punished, while 58.92% of them are occasionally rewarded or punished, but all of them acknowledge both incentive mechanism and reward and punishment system (as shown in Fig. 11); in terms of training, more than 84% of students often take part in various training organized by the company regarding professional ability improvement, rules and regulations, corporate culture, etc. (as shown in Fig. 12); more than 80% of the students are satisfied with the accommodation conditions provided by the internship units, medical care for on-duty injury, work environment, interpersonal relationship among colleagues, and cooperation among colleagues (as shown in Fig. 13). Some students quit their jobs in the middle of the internship. The main reasons for the demission are listed in the order from high to low, including returning to their hometown for development, salary and welfare issues, wanting to change careers and industries, high work requirements, great pressure, and being unable adapt to the management system and culture of the company. Data prove that the benefits, work environment and management system in civil aviation related enterprises and units are relatively complete and suitable for students. Selection and requirements, but the work pressure, work intensity, work requirements and distance from home for civil aviation enterprises are the factors that many students finally choose to leave civil aviation enterprises. The work pressure, work intensity, work requirements and distance from home of civil aviation enterprises are the factors that result in many students finally choosing to quit.

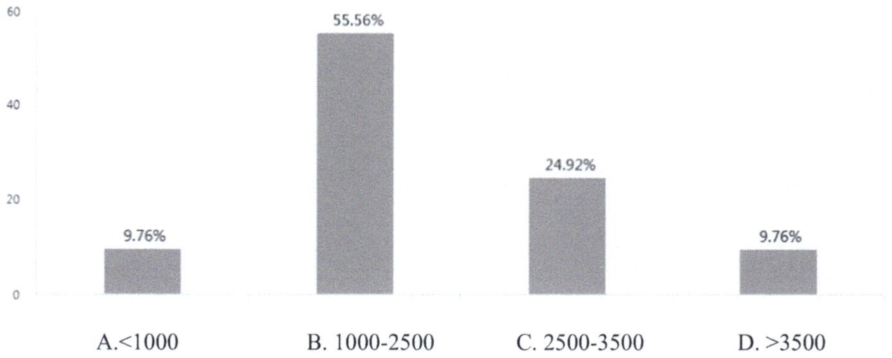

Fig. 10. Note: Intern salary

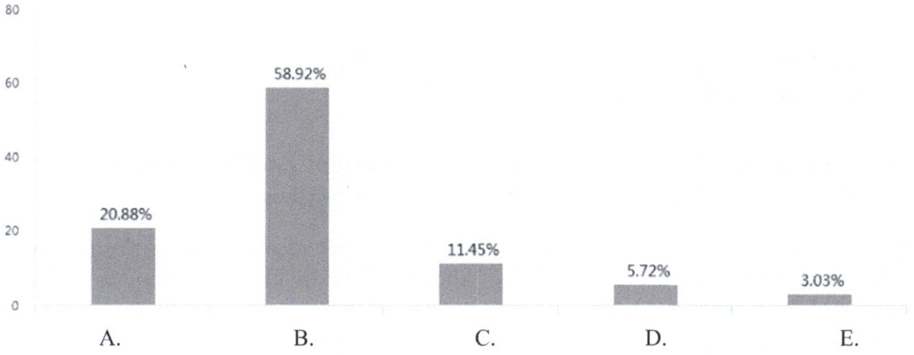

Fig. 11. Note: A. usually, B. occasionally, C. uncertain, D. none, E. none at all

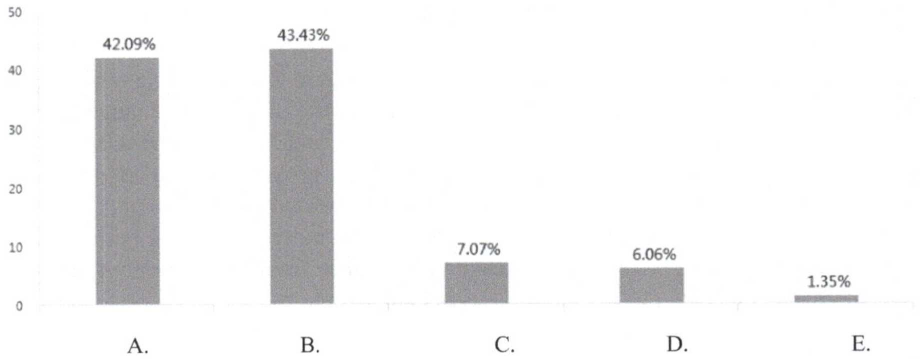

Fig. 12. Note: A. usually, B. occasionally, C. uncertain, D. none, E. none at all

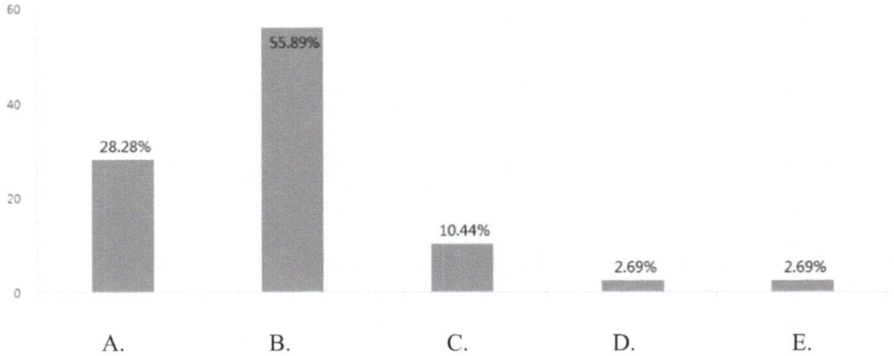

Fig. 13. Note: A. very satisfied, B. basically satisfied, C. uncertain, D. dissatisfied, E. very dissatisfied

2 Analysis of the Factors and Reasons that Affect the Post Practice of Students [2–4]

2.1 The Origin of Students Is One of the Important Factors Affecting the Choice of Internship and Employment Location

Although students are satisfied with the conditions provided by the internship units, there are still 34.34% mismatch interns. After the investigation and analysis of these students, it is not that the enterprise does not provide positions, but that these students would rather choose an internship in a different professional position in their hometown, rather than leave their hometown to work in an airline or airport. And due to the decentralization of civil aviation enterprises, it is difficult to arrange a large number of students to intern or be employed in a province or region. The origin of students is a very important factor affecting the internship and employment.

2.2 Students' Attention to Internship Units Has Shifted from Integration of Internship and Employment to Seeking Development Prospect and Ability Improvement

With the reform of educational system and mechanism, the improvement of the comprehensive quality of talents required by employers and the influence of new technological revolution, students' internship and employment concepts have also undergone great changes. Students no longer only focus on the employment after the internship, but to seek all kinds of units that are conducive to their own quality cultivation, professional and technical ability improvement and communication ability enhancement. These enterprises have the sense of teamwork, strong competitiveness and good development prospects, thus students can lay the foundation for future career choice.

2.3 During the Internship, Students Pay More Attention to the Guidance and Management of Enterprises Rather Than that of Schools

In terms of professional layout, curricula, ability improvement, quality cultivation, measures guarantee, management system and atmosphere building, the school has completed the work under the comprehensive factors of national policies, regional economic development characteristics and the school's own advantages. In the process of internship, students' learning mode and learning place have changed, but learning content and learning result assessment still belong to the scope of school teaching plan. But after entering the internship, some students have reversed the priority of supervision and put too much emphasis on the important role played by enterprises, while they have one-sided and radical understanding of the schools' supervision, and some students even refuse to cooperate with the schools' management.

3 Measures to Improve the Practical Effect of Students' Post Practice Work

3.1 Attach Importance to Planning and Layout, Strengthen Guidance and Supervision [5–7]

With comprehensive consideration of the development trend of civil aviation industry, school advantages, student source characteristics, professional composition and other elements, the school, colleges and departments distribute internship positions accurately and efficiently. The school ensures that students can learn, make achievements and make use of what they have learned while avoiding wasting high-quality internship resources and affecting the production of enterprises. In terms of student guidance and supervision, before the internship, it can be carried out by selecting internship units, setting internship standards, formulating internship plans and signing internship agreements; during the internship, it can be carried out by filling in the internship log (weekly), tracking and instructing records of the instructor, training records of the interns, tracking and interviewing of the school and other methods; after the internship, the university and the enterprise should jointly carry out strict assessment on students' internship results. At the same time, the school also introduced the "engineering cloud" internship management platform to timely track the students' internship through the mobile phone app. It is just to ensure the internship is carried out orderly and effectively.

3.2 Connect with the Industry Precisely, Improve the Curriculum and Broaden the Innovative Internship Modes [8, 9]

All majors should precisely meet the needs of industries and enterprises in terms of curriculum setting. The curriculum system inside and outside the university should be improved through the setting of training content system, teaching content system, teaching condition guarantee system, management system and evaluation system. Considering the monotony of internship mode, the school has carried out various internship modes in the spirit of serving regional economic development and meeting industrial needs through the integration of production and teaching, such as post cognition internship, on-campus simulation internship, on-campus production internship, staged production support internship, post training, post following and in-post internship, through the integration project of production and teaching. For example, our school has maintained close cooperation with the Bureau of Hainan Public Security Guard since 2008. The school sends students majoring in security check to protect Boao Forum for Asia Annual Conference every year. The students' excellent performance has been well received by the leaders of the Public Security Department and people from all walks of life. The college also undertakes the security check and explosion protection task at the entrance of Sanya Phoenix Airport and developed it into a productive cognition internship project.

3.3 The University and the Enterprise Make Concerted Efforts to Improve the Protection of the Rights and Interests of Students

According to the "Measures for Promoting School-Enterprise Cooperation in Vocational Schools" [10, 11], school-enterprise cooperation is a kind of win-win cooperation, and internship is also one of the common projects of school-enterprise cooperation, so the protection of the rights and interests of internship students has become the premise and foundation of cooperation. The school should undertake detailed regulation and restriction to the content such as the internship pay, board and lodging, on-duty injury and medical insurance, job intensity, the guidance of professional ability to the students during practice. Before the internship, the university and the enterprise should reach an agreement on the above aspects. When signing the internship agreement, the school may take the following aspects into consideration. For example, the units that accept students' in-post internship should reasonably determine the interns' pay by referring to the payment standard of the same position and the workload, work intensity, work time and other factors and it shall not be lower than 80% of the salary standard of the same post during the probation period; schools and internship units shall not charge students for internship deposits, commissions on internship income, management fees or other forms of internship expenses, and shall not detain students' ID cards; internship units should abide by the national regulations on working hours, rest and vacation; and other arrangements that are inconsistent with the internship.

It is found that internship can help students acquire practical work skills, problem-solving skills, interpersonal skills and post adaptability, which has a significant positive impact on employment ability [12, 13]. In order to effectively improve the effect of on-post internship, we can enhance the depth of school-enterprise cooperation through the school-enterprise co-construction of major, school-enterprise co-construction of courses, and school-enterprise co-management of students. The breadth of school-enterprise cooperation can be enhanced through the cooperation of related and similar professional positions. Through the whole process and stages of school education, the time span can be extended [14], so as to ensure the organization, management, assessment, safety and rights and interests during the internship, and lay a foundation for effective internship and employment.

Fund Project. This paper is the phased achievement of the 2018 Hainan Educational Science Planning Project "Research and Practice on Talent Training Mode by Deepening the Integration of Industry and Education and Introducing Enterprises into School" (project code: QJY20181068).

References

1. Huang, Y.: Legislative thinking on student internship management in vocational schools. Vocat. Tech. Educ. **30** (2016)
2. Ma, L.: Confusion and management path analysis of in-post internship. Vocat. Educ. BBS **8**, 7–10 (2013)
3. Hou, J.: Construction of evaluation mechanism for students' in-post internship in higher vocational college. Vocat. Techn. Educ. **29**, 62–65 (2014)
4. Cheng, Y.: Research and practice of "Wuhua" based enterprise internship management. China Vocat. Tech. Educ. **11**, 81–86 (2019)
5. Han, X., Gong, X.: Investigation on the current situation of students' in-post internship in vocational colleges: a case study of Zhejiang Province. Vocat. Educ. Newsl. **11**, 29–31 (2014)
6. Wang, D.: Research on school-enterprise cooperation mechanism based on the "double 11" activity: taking the cooperation between school A and enterprise B as an example. Oper. Manag. **8**, 155–157 (2018)
7. Zhou, C.: Reflection and connotation expansion of combining work with study. China Vocat. Techn. Educ. **6**, 22–25 (2014)
8. Dai, Y.: Research on vocational employment guidance course teaching practice in post practice. Acad. Theory **8** (2017)
9. Sun, J.: Research report on the current situation of students' management of in-post internship in higher vocational colleges-taking a higher vocational college in Tianjin as the research object. Tianjin Normal University of Vocational Technology (2017)

10. Notice of the Ministry of Education and Other Five Departments on the Issuance of "Measures for Promoting School-Enterprise Cooperation in Vocational Schools", no. 1 (2018)
11. Sun, G., Lang, F., Yang, M.: Traffic measurement system based on hybrid methods. Electric Mach. Control **15**(6), 91–96 (2011)
12. Chen, X.: An empirical study on the current situation of students' practice in vocational schools. Educ. Dev. Res. **38**(01), 52–60 (2018)
13. Sun, G., Li, X., Hou, X., et al.: GPU-accelerated support vector machines for traffic classification. Int. J. Perform. Eng. **14**(5), 1088–1098 (2018)
14. Zhu, C.: Path analysis of vocational college students' employability improvement from the perspective of school-enterprise cooperation. Hebei Vocat. Educ. **2**(06), 100–104 (2018)

Application of SPOC Model in Training Craftsman Spirit of High-Skilled Talents

Yong Wang(✉), Wanshun Chen, and Hongfang Cheng

College of Information Engineering,
Wuhu Institute of Technology, Wuhu, China
1075738542@qq.com, 858708130@qq.com, 403242688@qq.com

Abstract. "Craftsman Spirit" is a necessary professional accomplishment for high-skilled talents. Polytechnic colleges should integrate the cultivation of craftsman spirit into daily teaching. In order to overcome student 's deficiency including the lack of learning motivation, a weak foundation as well as the lack of self-management ability, we established SPOC resource platform and introduce SPOC model into the cultivation of craftsman spirit. Besides, an index system was established to evaluate the effectiveness of the teaching model.

Keywords: Craftsman spirit · SPOC · Project-based teaching

1 Introduction

"Craftsman Spirit" is the precious spiritual wealth condensed by the tillers and toilers in the process of working and culture succession. Craftsman spirit is a kind of reverence for professional skills, a kind of devotion for work, a kind of spirit of striving for excellence and unremitting efforts in products and service, as well as a kind of persistence in doing a good job throughout one's life [1, 2]. Nowadays, the great craftsmen are also the important builders of socialist modernization, although technology development alters from day to day. The burden they shoulder is even related to the success or failure of the country. In order to meet the requirements of new technology, new industry and new model, the great craftsmen must master a large amount of knowledge, accumulate experience year after year, and hone exquisite skills to solve practical engineering problems. In the new era, the great craftsmen must have self-learning ability so as to keep pace with the times, constantly introduce new technologies, new concepts and new models into their work, make breakthroughs in their positions and promote the progress and development of the industry. In the Process of realizing the strategy of made-in-China 2025, it is an important mission of polytechnic colleges to integrate the cultivation of craftsman spirit into daily teaching and cultivate high-skilled talents. However, at present, the students in polytechnic colleges have weak foundation, weak self-learning ability, and they are short of good self-management ability. Many of them pay no attention to classes and even are addicted to mobile phones, so that it is necessary to adopt a new teaching mode to improve students' learning motivation.

G. Sun et al. (Eds.): eLEOT 2019, LNICST 299, pp. 411–416, 2019.
https://doi.org/10.1007/978-3-030-35095-6_44

Small Private Online Course (SPOC) was presented in 2013 by professor Armando Fox of University of California, Berkeley. This model emphasizes the construction of teaching resources while focusing on improving students' participation. As a result, SPOC model is introduced into curriculum teaching. It is an open online course for specific and small-scale groups. It can integrate the advantages of traditional face-to-face teaching and modern online learning with information technology, which mixes online and offline teaching. If the resource platform is efficiently established and perform effectively, it can effectively improve students' participation in learning, activate class atmosphere and improve students' self-learning ability [3, 4].

2 The Establishment of Resource Platform

First of all, our college divides talents into three types based on the model of talent training, in order to overcome polytechnic college students' deficiency including the lack of learning motivation, a weak foundation and so on. The three types are professionally technical type, technical management type and technical service type. Our main idea is that let students with different personalities and interests find their own development path. Therefore, the assessment of the course is no longer simply based on their examination results. Secondly, by setting the core curriculum Data Structure as an experimental course, we show more concern for craftsman spirit in the design of teaching objectives of traditional culture courses. We can design teaching objectives according to the characteristics of course so as to excavate the knowledge which can reflect the craftsman spirit. As a result, with the immersion of craftsman spirit, our students can feel the charm of traditional culture and the importance of craftsman ship, whether theoretical or experiential teaching situation.

The implementation effect of SPOC model largely depends on the richness and effectiveness of teaching resources. We subdivide projects related to core curriculums into several tasks. Then each task is implemented to specific knowledge points. After the knowledge points reorganized, we make tutorial videos and give test questions to students through mobile client. We are committed to building a SPOC resource platform, which comes from projects, is applied to projects and is jointly instructed. With the help of virtual simulation training platform, school-enterprise cooperation, regular guidance of enterprise engineers and other superior resources, the efficient and rigorous working attitude and the atmosphere of strictly obeying industry regulations are introduced into the daily teaching of schools, in order to forming rich soil for cultivating craftsman spirit.

Relying on the cloud platform of vocational education, to improve teaching effect, we establish a set of learning model consisted of pre-class guidance, classroom teaching and after-class research. Figure 1 illustrates the learning model. Taking students of grade 14 and 15 as study subjects, this model is tested (See Fig. 1).

Through pre-class guidance, students can preliminarily obtain knowledge points while teachers can learn about students' learning situation. The emphasis of classroom teaching is on the analysis of important and difficult points. After-class research is mainly to consolidate and strengthen the knowledge learned and the application of it in the second classroom composed of skills competitions and scientific and technological

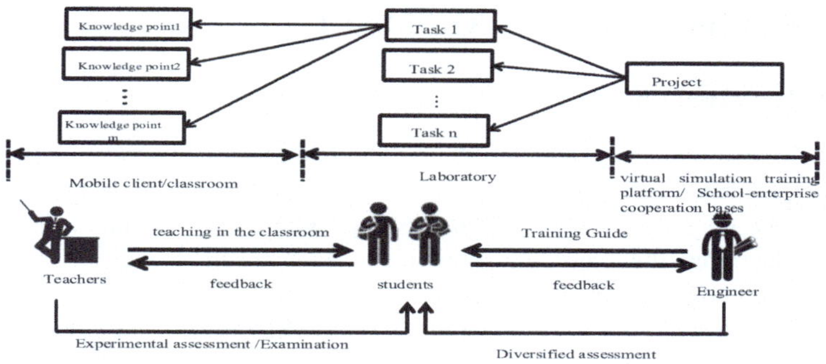

Fig. 1. Teaching resources construction of SPOC model

activities. As long as students find their own shortcomings and deficiencies in the second classroom, they will go back to the first classroom for more knowledge. A virtuous cycle forms (See Fig. 2).

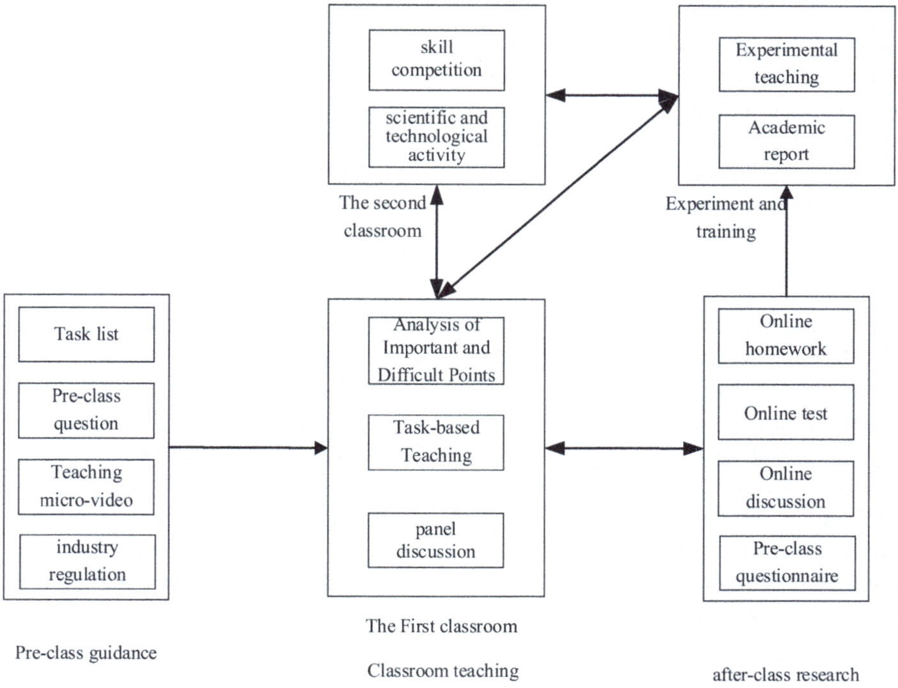

Fig. 2. Teaching resources construction of SPOC model learning model based on SPOC

3 The Implementation of SPOC Model

3.1 Pre-class Guidance

The weak foundation and poor self-management ability of students in polytechnic colleges always lead to their failure in traditional education. Their confidence is often insufficient, and they are afraid of learning. Many students have a mind to learn, but in the way of learning, they lose the motivation. As a result, a vicious circle forms. Therefore, promoting learning motivation and adopting a step-by-step teaching model become two major measures to be taken urgently. In order to enhance students' interest in learning, through pre-class micro-videos, students can understand the application and significance of knowledge points in industry. In the process of students' understanding of industry knowledge, they realize that work regulations must be strictly obeyed. In the experiment or work, a miss is as good as a mile. Over time, students will be awed by the basic knowledge and operant skills, which is also the basis and prerequisite for the formation of craftsmanship spirit. Students will stimulate their internal learning motivation after they understand the application prospects of the knowledge they have learned. At the end of the micro-video, the knowledge points of the next course will be condensed into corresponding questions for students. Guiding students to complete a small task through a few simple questions may be another form, so that students can complete the preview with tasks or purposes. Due to the otherness of students, different students have different cultural foundations and they meet different problems in their study. Students send the problems to teachers through mobile app while teachers can give targeted answers in the course of teaching. Both of them can get twice the result with half the effort.

3.2 Teaching in the Classroom

In the traditional teaching model, teachers teach and students learn. This model usually leads to either a dull classroom atmosphere or a condition that lots of students play mobile phones. The SPOC model adopts the model of students' learning first, teachers' teaching later, and the classroom teaching mode is also diversified. In the SPOC model, students are selected randomly to show their results of preview on their own initiative. The types of results are diverse, such as understanding of principles, written programs, produced works and so on. Every student has the opportunity to participate in the speech, which provides students internal motivation. Besides, it also promotes students' ability of communication and cooperation. Because there are unilateral and deficient opinions in students' report inevitably, teachers can point out and correct them. As a result, the class atmosphere is enlivened and students' participation is improved.

3.3 After-Class Research

In order to enable students to apply what they have learned and master their skills, we mainly make efforts in the following three aspects.

(1) **Organize Interest Groups Related to Courses.** Excellent teachers are arranged to organize students to carry out science and technology activities and lectures

related to the curriculum, as well as to answer questions for students. The students who are capable of learning more have an opportunity to participate in teachers' teaching and research projects to promote themselves with specific problems in engineering practice. Various forms of group activities have a good effect on consolidating students' basic knowledge and practical skills.

(2) **Focus on Skill Competitions**. The skill competition is a way for students to accumulate knowledge and develop skills. It is also an important means to cultivate students' craftsman ship. Teachers should play a leading and demonstrating role in skill competitions. With the influence of teachers' diligence and skillful learning, students must study assiduously and keep on carving.

(3) **Play a Promoting Pole in School-Enterprise Cooperation.** Effective development of school-enterprise cooperation can realize a good situation of mutual benefit and win-win results. It is a typical case of the school-enterprise cooperation base of instrument research and testing established by our institute and Jiangsu Xintongda Co, Ltd. We provide offices for enterprises while enterprises organize excellent engineers to train our students during winter and summer vacation and the weekends. Students got excellent grades can directly enter the enterprise after graduation. after training, students understand that whether the instrument function is correct and reliable is directly related to the safety of drivers and the great interests of enterprises. Students also learn how to develop and test instrument meticulously, which promotes the cultivation of students' craftsman spirit, their ability to transfer knowledge, and volitional quality.

4 The Evaluation of SPOC Model for Cultivating Craftsman Spirit

In order to evaluate the cultivation of students' craftsman spirit, this paper takes the students from the computer application major of Wuhu Vocational and Technical College as the research objects, and establishes an index system to evaluate the craftsman spirit of them. We take 14 grade students as the control group and 15 grade

Table 1. The index system of evaluating craftsman spirit

Craftsman spirit	Index	Weights	Methods to evaluate
	Self-confidence	15%	Issue questionnaires
	Knowledge reserved	25%	Take average score of final exam
	Compliance with industry regulations	10%	Train students in electricians for two hours, and then experimental equipment is provided to enable them to complete relevant wiring tasks. At last, evaluate students' performance
	Vocational skills	25%	
	learning ability	25%	Introduce self-learning task in graduation design, and inspect students' learning situation in final replay

students as the sample group of SPOC teaching model. The weights and implemented methods of the index system are shown in Table 1.

Through comparative experiments, the scores of students in grade 14 are 71.26, while those in grade 15 who are implemented SPOC model are 76.18. Students in grade 15 are obviously better than those in grade 14.

5 Conclusions

The cultivation of "craftsman spirit" begins at school and is achieved at enterprises. As the main force of training high-skilled talents for the future, polytechnic colleges should integrate craftsman spirit into daily teaching. Taking basic knowledge, industry regulations, experimental teaching and skill competitions as carriers, students' "ingenuity" can be cultivated from daily life bit by bit. By adopting SPOC model and improving the construction of corresponding platforms, two shortcomings of weak foundation and insufficient learning motivation of polytechnic college students can be overcame to a certain extent. Thus, students build up confidence, acquire knowledge, obtain certain skills, and lay the foundation for entering society, after three years of colleges.

Acknowledgement. This work was supported by the research on high school provincial quality engineering project of Anhui grant No. 2016ckjh224, No. 2017mooc368 and No. 2017sjjd041, and University-level key projects grant No. Wzyzrzd201702.

References

1. Quan, Y.: Research on the cultivation practice of vocational education talents based on the spirit of craftsman. Educ. Mod. **5**(47), 24–25 (2018)
2. Cui, W., Yan, H., Chen, J., et al.: Cultivating ways of "craftsmanship spirit for college students in vocational education. Vocat. Technol. **18**(2), 29–32 (2018)
3. Xie, Y., Ma, J., Dai, R.: Research on curriculum training model based on SPOC for personalized learning. Chin. Vocat. Tech. Educ. (02), 93–96 (2019)
4. Wang, Y.: The influence of the development of SPOC in the post-MOOC era on modern vocational education. Econ. Trade Pract. (17), 311 (2018)

An Empirical Study on the Effect of Information-Based Teaching of Ideological and Political Courses in Higher Vocational Colleges Based on Moso Teach

Min Li[1(✉)], Jie Yang[2(✉)], and Yuan-hui Li[1]

[1] Sanya Aviation and Tourism College, Sanya, Hainan 572000, China
44391522@qq.com, Seprina77@126.com
[2] Hainan Tropical Ocean University, Sanya, Hainan 572000, China
576735855@qq.com

Abstract. Using modern information technology to assist the reform of ideological and political course teaching has become a hotspot and a difficulty needing to be addressed immediately in ideological and political education. In order to further understand the effect of ideological and political education via information teaching platform in higher vocational colleges, the author takes Sanya Aviation and Tourism College as the research object, adopts questionnaire survey method, and makes an empirical analysis with SPASS software. The results show that Moso Teach plays a positive role in teaching management, teacher-student interaction, student assessment etc. The report also points out some problems in the process of teaching with Moso Teach, which leads us to the direction of future reform.

Keywords: Moso teach · Higher vocational colleges · Ideological and political courses · Information-based teaching

1 Introduction

Nowadays, information technology has a wide and far-reaching impact on people's learning, work and life. The integration and innovation of information technology and education has generated many new educational models. Moso Teach is such a teaching software based on Internet. It has two versions of mobile terminals, IOS and Android. It can be accessed directly by computer or mobile phone APP. Moso Teach has the characteristics of "small and smart". And its platform has multiple functions such as signing in, sharing teaching resources, sending notifications, leaving assigning tasks, voting, questionnaire survey, testing. This application is very easy to download and operate, thus is very popular among teachers and students in many Higher Vocational colleges.

What is the effect of using Moso Teach in ideological and political course? What are the advantages and disadvantages? What problems should we pay attention to while using it? Taking the practice of applying Moso Teach in ideological and political courses in Sanya Aviation and Tourism College as an example, this paper makes an

G. Sun et al. (Eds.): eLEOT 2019, LNICST 299, pp. 417–428, 2019.
https://doi.org/10.1007/978-3-030-35095-6_45

in-depth analysis with the help of questionnaires and data analysis, with a view to providing suggestions and references for similar colleges to carry out the information-based teaching reform of ideological and political courses.

2 Research Objects and Research Methods

This research was conducted in Sanya Aviation and Tourism College with questionnaire. Since the first half year of 2017, Sanya Aviation and Tourism College has used Moso Teach Platform to carry out the teaching reform of ideological and political courses. After two years of construction, it has gradually established Moso Teach Courses of "ideological and moral cultivation and basic law education", "Introduction to Mao Zedong Thought and the Theoretical System of Socialism with Chinese Characteristics". At present, all students of 2017 and 2018 are studying ideological and political course on this platform.

Empirical analysis method was adopted in this survey. The samples cover five secondary schools, including School of Civil Aviation Transport, School of International Tourism, School of Flight Attendants, School of Mechanical and Electrical Engineering and School of Maritime Transport. All together, we give out and collect 403 questionnaires.

3 Empirical Analysis

3.1 Description of Statistics

We analyze the frequency of the demographic variables and get the result in Table 1. Among 403 tested samples there are 203 females, taking up 50.4% of the total amount; there are 402 freshmen students, taking up 99.8% of the total amount; and the tested students are mainly from School of Civil Aviation Transportation and School of Flight Attendants, the numbers of these students are 132 and 172 respectively taking up 75.5% together. Their Knowledge about Moso Teach can mainly be divided as familiar and generally familiar, the numbers of these students are 194 and 122 respectively, taking up 78.4% all together. 325 students often use "Moso Teach" in ideological and political course, taking up 80.6% of all the tested students. Students' favorite studying methods are "teachers upload instructional resources on Moso Teach platform, then students study them after class" and "teachers combine face-to-face teaching and Moso Teach on-line learning", 176 and 193 students like these two studying methods respectively, taking up 91.6% together. As for their attitudes towards teaching ideological and political course with Moso Teach, 251 students "totally accept it and think it is helpful for classroom teaching", then 141 students "can accept it but still hold doubts about its defects", all those students take up 97.3% of the total amount. And the numbers of students who think that the general effects of using Moso Teach are very good and relatively good are 178 and 162 respectively, taking up 84.4% of all the tested samples.

Table 1. Frequency statistics (N = 403)

Variables	Attribute	Frequency	Percentage (%)
gender	male	200	49.6
	female	203	50.4
age	freshman	402	99.8
	sophomore	1	0.2
Schools or departments	School of Civil Aviation Transportation	132	32.8
	School of International Tourism	53	13.2
	School of Flight Attendants	172	42.7
	School of Mechanical and Electrical Engineering	33	8.2
	School of Maritime Transport	13	3.2
familiar of Moso Teach	very familiar	79	19.6
	familiar	194	48.1
	general familiar	122	30.3
	not familiar	5	1.2
	not heard of	3	0.7
Frequency of using Moso Teach in ideological and political class	often	325	80.6
	occasionally	75	18.6
	rarely	2	0.5
	never	1	0.2
Favorite learning methods	teachers upload instructional resources on Moso Teach platform, then students study them after class	176	43.7
	teachers combine face-to-face teaching and Moso Teach on-line learning	193	47.9
	face-to-face teaching without Moso Teach APP	34	8.4
Attitudes to teaching ideological and political course with Moso Teach	totally accept and think it is helpful for classroom teaching	251	62.3
	can accept but still hold doubts about its defects	141	35
	can't accept, prefer traditional teaching method	8	2
	can't accept at all	3	0.7
General effect of using Moso Teach platform	very good	178	44.2
	relatively good	162	40.2
	just so so □	54	13.4
	not good □	5	1.2
	very bad	4	1

Table 2 shows the frequency statistics of multiple-choice questions. Among 403 samples, more than half students used the functions of "sign-in", "assignment/group task", "test", "check, download teaching resources" and "Q&A/discussion" in Moso Teach APP during the study of ideological and political course; less than half students used the functions of "vote/questionnaire", "brainstorm" and "send notification"; and only very few students used "send gift card" and "others" functions.

Table 2. Frequency statistics of multiple-choice questions (N = 403)

Variables	Attribute	Frequency	Percentage
Functions used in Moso Teach software during the study of ideological and political course	sign-in	394	97.80%
	check, download teaching resources	244	60.50%
	send notification	128	31.80%
	assignment/group task	325	80.60%
	vote/questionnaire	184	45.70%
	brainstorm	148	36.70%
	Q&A/discussion	214	53.10%
	test	258	64.00%
	send gift card	38	9.40%
	others	5	1.20%

3.2 Validity Test

We conduct exploratory factor analysis on 22 questions to explore the questionnaire structure. Before the exploratory factor analysis, we need to check whether the KMO value is above 0.7 and whether Bartlett sphericity test reaches significance. According to Table 3, the KMO value is 0.943, which is above 0.7, and the Bartlett sphericity test value is 10216.411, whose significance level is less than 0.001. Therefore, this sample is fit for factor analysis.

Table 3. Test list of KMO and Bartlett

KMO		0.943
Bartlett sphericity test	approximate chi-square	10216.411
	df	231
	Sig.	0.000

Principal component analysis is used to do factor analysis on 22 questions and the analysis result is made into list, including: the extracted factors, factor load capacity, eigenvalue and cumulative variance contributing rate etc.

Table 4. Contributing rate of factors

Factors	Eigenvalue	Cumulative contributing rate(%)
1	6.662	30.283
2	5.364	54.663
3	5.166	78.146

From Table 4 we can see the cumulative contributing rate of those three factors whose eigenvalue are above 1 has achieved 78.146%. The rotated component matrix is as shown in Table 5. The three factors are renamed: factor 1 is named as "advantage", which includes 8 questions; factor 2 is named as "effect evaluation", which includes 6 questions and factor 3 is named as "problem", which includes 8 questions. The maximum factor loads of all the questions are all above 0.5, and the maximum load exists only on one factor, which means the structure validity is good.

Table 5. Rotated component matrix

Question	Factor 1	Factor 2	Factor 3
advantage 8	0.882		
advantage 2	0.872		
advantage 5	0.871		
advantage 1	0.86		
advantage 4	0.849		
advantage 7	0.845		
advantage 3	0.816		
advantage 6	0.787		
effect evaluation 3		0.883	
effect evaluation 4		0.878	
effect evaluation 5		0.876	
effect evaluation 6		0.866	
effect evaluation 2		0.863	
effect evaluation 1		0.847	
problem 5			0.873
problem 2			0.866
problem 8			0.852
problem 7			0.824
problem 3			0.814
problem 6			0.798
problem 1			0.706
problem 4			0.632

3.3 Reliability Test

We run reliability test on all studied variables and get the result as shown in Table 6. The result shows that Cronbach's α coefficient lowers as we delete any question, which means all the question items could be kept. The Cronbach's α coefficients of "advantage", "problem" and "effect evaluation" are 0.969, 0.919 and 0.976 respectively, all above 0.7, which reflects that the result of reliability test is good.

Table 6. Reliability test table

Studied variable	Item	Deleted Cronbach's α coefficient	Cronbach's α coefficient of studied variable
advantage	advantage 1	0.964	0.969
	advantage 2	0.962	
	advantage 3	0.966	
	advantage 4	0.966	
	advantage 5	0.963	
	advantage 6	0.967	
	advantage 7	0.962	
	advantage 8	0.964	
problem	problem 1	0.915	0.919
	problem 2	0.901	
	problem 3	0.907	
	problem 4	0.922	
	problem 5	0.901	
	problem 6	0.909	
	problem 7	0.906	
	problem 8	0.903	
effect evaluation	effect evaluation 1	0.974	0.976
	effect evaluation 2	0.971	
	effect evaluation 3	0.971	
	effect evaluation 4	0.973	
	effect evaluation 5	0.97	
	effect evaluation 6	0.971	

3.4 Correlation Analysis

We did descriptive statistics and correlation analysis on "advantage", "problem" and "effect evaluation". The result is shown in Table 7. The maximum score is 5, while 3 as the mid-value. The descriptive statistics shows that the mean values of "advantage", "problem" and "effect evaluation" all exceed 3, which means the scores of "advantage", "problem" and "effect evaluation" from the tested objects are relatively high. The result of correlation analysis reflects that among the three variables of "advantage", "problem" and "effect evaluation", each two variables show significant positive correlation ($p < 0.05$).

Table 7. Descriptive statistics and correlation analysis

	Advantage	Problem	Effect evaluation
advantage	1		
problem	0.141**	1	
effect evaluation	0.684***	0.113*	1
mean M	4.435	3.427	4.297
standard deviation SD	0.599	0.942	0.680

Note: * stands for p < 0.05, **stands for p < 0.01, ***stands for p < 0.001

3.5 Mediating Effect Model

We build structural equation model to examine the mediating effect of "advantage" between "problem" and "effect evaluation". We find the MI modification indexes of "advantage 2" and "advantage 3", "advantage 6" and "advantage 7", "problem 5" and "problem 6" and "effect evaluation 5" and "effect evaluation 6" are relatively high, thus we set correlation for their residuals to adjust the model and the final structural equation model is as follows:

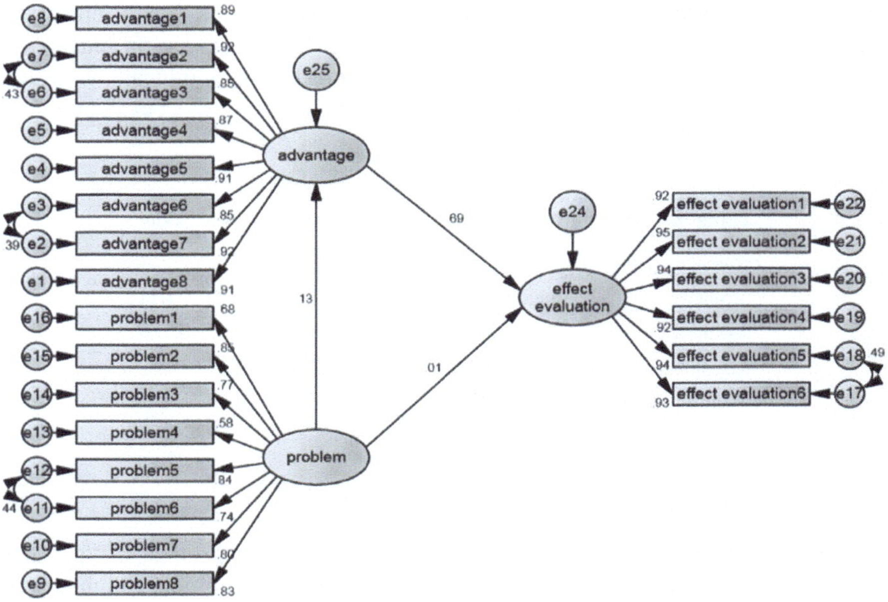

The major fit indexes of this structural equation model are shown in Table 8, $X^2/df = 2.931 < 3$, RMSEA = 0.069 < 0.08, RMR = 0.041 < 0.05, NFI = 0.943 > 0.9, RFI = 0.935 > 0.9, IFI = 0.962 > 0.9, TLI = 0.956 > 0.9, CFI = 0.962 > 0.9, which are all in the range of fitting, thus the structural equation model is proved acceptable.

Table 8. The fitting result of the structural equation model

The fit index of the model	Critical value	Studied model	Fitting result
X^2/df	<3	2.931	fitting
RMSEA	<0.08	0.069	fitting
RMR	<0.05	0.041	fitting
NFI	>0.9	0.943	fitting
RFI	>0.9	0.935	fitting
IFI	>0.9	0.962	fitting
TLI	>0.9	0.956	fitting
CFI	>0.9	0.962	fitting

Table 9 shows the path coefficients of the structural equation model. According to the result, "problem" has significantly positive influence on "advantage" ($\beta = 0.074$, $t = 2.539$, $p < 0.05$), "problem" has no significant influence on "effect evaluation" ($\beta = 0.008$, $t = 0.307$, $p > 0.05$), and "advantage" has significantly positive influence on "effect influence" ($\beta = 0.859$, $t = 16.035$, $p < 0.001$).

In order to examine the indirect effect "problem" has on "effect evaluation" via "advantage", we adopted bootstrap and leant after 2,000 extraction the indirect effect is 0.092, and the confidence interval is [0.024, 0.164], excluding 0, which reflects significant indirect effect. The direct effect that is the effect "problem" has on "advantage" does not reach significance, which means the direct effect is not significant. Therefore, "advantage" exerts full mediating effect between "problem" and "effect evaluation", the indirect effect is 0.092 and positive.

Table 9. The path coefficients of the structural equation model

Influence path	β	S.E.	C.R.	P
"problem" → "advantage"	0.134	0.029	2.539	0.011
"problem" → "effect evaluation"	0.012	0.027	0.307	0.759
"advantage" → "effect evaluation"	0.691	0.054	16.035	***

Note: *** stands for $p < 0.001$

3.6 Moderating Effect Model

We build structural equation model to examine the moderating effect of "problem" between "advantage" and "effect evaluation". In order to avoid multiple collinearity, all the questions put into the model have already been standardized. According to the principle of "big with big, small with small", the 8 standardized questions of "advantage" times the 8 standardized questions of "problem" one by one, then we get 8 constitutional question items of interactive items (i.e. int1 ~ int8). We find the MI modification indexes of "advantage 2" and "advantage 3", "advantage 6" and "advantage 7", "problem 3" and "problem 4", "problem 5" and "problem 6", "problem 7" and "problem 8", "int 1" and "int 6" and "effect evaluation 5" and "effect evaluation 6" are relatively high, thus we set correlation for their residuals to adjust the model and the final structural equation model is as follows:

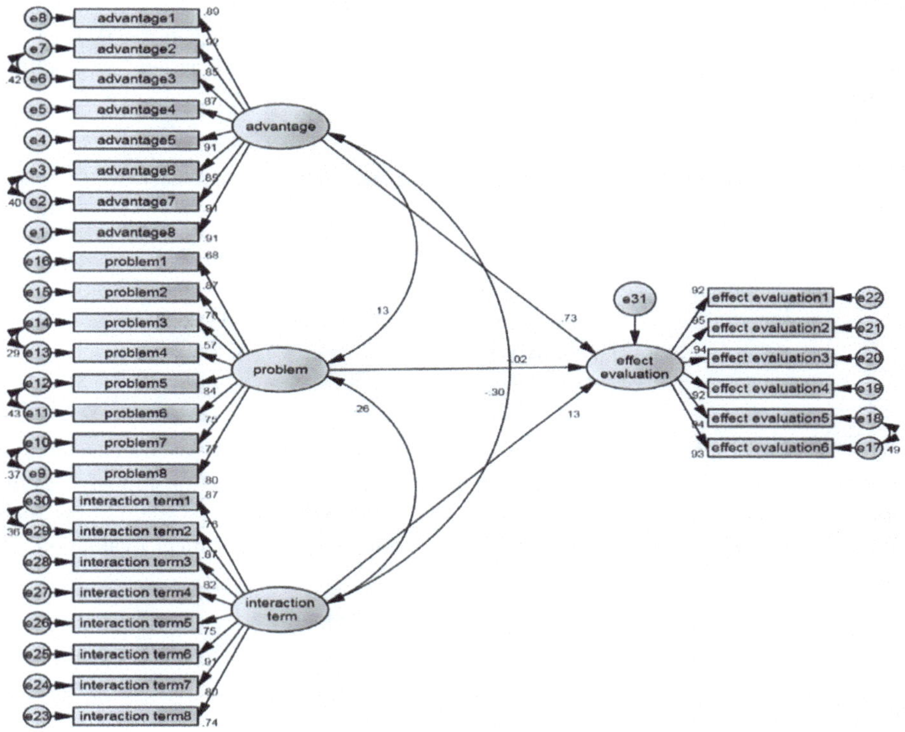

The major fit indexes of this structural equation model are shown as in Table 10, X2/df = 2.928 < 3, RMSEA = 0.069 < 0.08, RMR = 0.055, NFI = 0.916 > 0.9, RFI = 0.907 > 0.9, IFI = 0.943 > 0.9, TLI = 0.937 > 0.9, CFI = 0.943 > 0.9, except RMR is a bit higher, other indexes are all within the range of fitting, so the structural equation model is acceptable.

Table 10. The fitting result of the structural equation model

The fit index of the model	Critical value	Studied model	Fitting result
X^2/df	<3	2.928	fitting
RMSEA	<0.08	0.069	fitting
RMR	<0.05	0.055	not fitting
NFI	>0.9	0.916	fitting
RFI	>0.9	0.907	fitting
IFI	>0.9	0.943	fitting
TLI	>0.9	0.937	fitting
CFI	>0.9	0.943	fitting

Table 11 shows the path coefficients of the structural equation model. According to the result, "advantage" has significantly positive influence on "effect evaluation" ($\beta = 0.744$, $t = 15.958$, $p < 0.001$), "problem" has no significant influence on "effect evaluation" ($\beta = -0.022$, $t = -0.46$, $p > 0.05$), and the interactive items have significantly positive influence on "effect influence" ($\beta = 0.129$, $t = 2.911$, $p < 0.01$), which shows conformed positive moderation of "problem" between "advantage" and "effect evaluation".

Table 11. The path coefficients of the structural equation model

Influence path	β	S.E.	C.R.	P
"advantage" → "effect evaluation"	0.744	0.047	15.958	***
"problem" → "effect evaluation"	−0.022	0.048	−0.46	0.646
interactions → "effect evaluation"	0.129	0.044	2.911	0.004

Note: *** stands for $p < 0.001$

Below is the interaction chart of the moderating effect, from which we can see that when the "problem" gets low scores, the positive correlation relationship of "advantage" and "effect evaluation" is relatively flat, while when the "problem" gets high scores, the positive correlation relationship of "advantage" and "effect evaluation" is relatively steep.

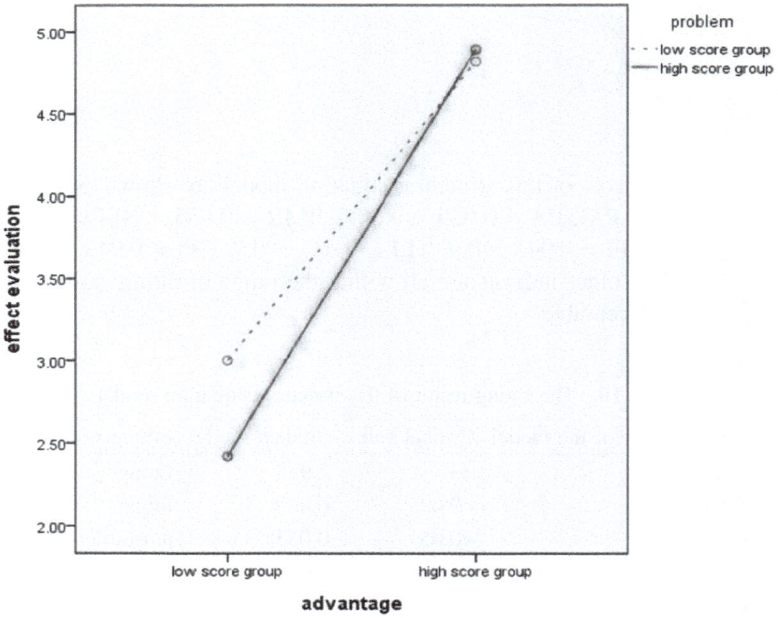

4 Conclusion and Suggestions

The results show that the problems in using Moso teach have significantly positive influence on the platform's advantages, but have no significant influence on the teaching effect evaluation. The advantages of Moso teach have significantly positive influence on the teaching effect evaluation of ideological and political course; its advantages play a full mediating effect between the problems and effect evaluation, while problems exert positive moderating function between the advantages and effect evaluation.

To conclude, Moso teach has remarkable advantages in improving class management efficiency, strengthening the interaction and communication between teachers and students, and it's quite helpful in the assessment and evaluation of students in ideological and political teaching. However, some functions of the platform still have been underutilized because of teachers' and students' insufficient understanding of the teaching media and ability of using it. In addition to the teaching environment and the technology itself, the integration level of information technology and ideological and political course can also be affected by teachers' teaching concept, innovative ideas and technology application capability as well as students' understanding and mastering of the teaching media. There is still plenty of room for both teachers and students to improve their media literacy. Besides, there are still some problems need to be solved, such as how to reduce the negative influences of the platform in order to give better play to the role of Moso teach in students' independent learning and in-depth learning and how to better combine the qualitative evaluation with the descriptive evaluation. All of these still require our further and specific study and they are also the directions for future exploration and reform of ideological and political course.

Fund Project. Sanya Aviation & Tourism College Subject on "Research on Ideological and Political Education Mode Innovation in Higher Vocational Colleges under New Media Environment" (XY201806).

References

Li, L.: Research on the deep integration of information technology and ideological and political education. Shanghai university, Shanghai, pp. 49–57 (2017)

Luo, H., Zuo, M., Anthony, R.: Empirical study on the effect of student mutual evaluation of large-scale open online learning. Open Educ. Res. **2**, 75–83 (2017)

Li, J., Chen, G.: Integration and development of ideological and political theory course and new media and new technology in universities: achievements, problems and solutions. J. Soc. Sci. Shanxi Univ. **6**, 42–45 (2017)

Ye, Z.: Teaching process management of ideological and political theory courses under the mobile Internet environment – a case study of MOSO Teach course platform. J. Guangxi Normal Univ. Nationalities **5**, 131–133 (2017)

Xie, L.: Analysis on the wisdom class of ideological and political theory course in higher vocational colleges in the Internet + era – a case study of MOSO Teach. J. Guangdong Inst. Water Resour. Electric Power **3**, 52–57 (2017)

Sun, G., Song, Z., Liu, J., et al.: Feature selection method based on maximum information coefficient and approximate Markov blanket. Zidonghua Xuebao/acta Automatica Sinica **5**, 795–805 (2009)

Sun, G., Lang, F., Xue, Y.: Chinese chunking method based on conditional random fields and semantic classes. J. Harbin Inst. Technol. **7**, 135–139 (2011)

Application and Practice of APT Teaching Model in Teaching Metals and Heat Treatment

Huayang Zhao(✉), Li Li, and Guangyu Liu

College of Mechanical Engineering, Inner Mongolia University for Nationalities, Tongliao, Inner Mongolia, China
Zhaohy9198@163.com

Abstract. The combination of information technology and modern university classroom has become a trend in higher education reform. In this study, APT teaching model is applied to metallurgy and heat treatment courses which is difficult for student to study, advocating "the main learning" information technology teaching philosophy. Taking "Iron and carbon phase diagram" in "Metallography and Heat Treatment" as an example, this paper designs and implements teaching activities based on the APT teaching model, and uses the experimental research method to compare the teaching effects of the APT teaching mode under the traditional and informational environments. The results show that the teaching mode of APT in the information environment has promoted students' interest in the study of metallurgy and heat treatment courses, and their achievements have obviously improved, but also increased the students' learning load.

Keywords: APT teaching model · Metallography and heat treatment · Teaching reform · Multimedia

1 Introduction

Learning how to learn and becoming a lifelong learner is a major mission for education in the 21st century. In the framework of 21st century learning ability proposed by 21st Century Skill Alliance, learners are required to possess the innovative ability, critical thinking and problem solving ability, communication and cooperation ability, self-orientation and individual adaptability needed in the information age. China promulgated the "national long-term education reform and Development Planning (2010–2020) "also emphasizes the importance of promoting the formation of individualized learning methods and mobilizing students to participate actively and autonomously in their studies [1]. In order to cultivate students' learning abilities in the 21st century, autonomous learning, cooperative research and research learning become the three new learning methods in current education reform. However, the traditional classroom teaching methods and conditions can not meet the needs of new learning methods [2–5].

Metallography and heat treatment is a compulsory major course in materials engineering. In material forming and control engineering professional training program of our school, the course schedule involves 48 h (including 10 h), mainly describes the structure and properties of metal materials, the organization and performance control of

G. Sun et al. (Eds.): eLEOT 2019, LNICST 299, pp. 429–438, 2019.
https://doi.org/10.1007/978-3-030-35095-6_46

metal materials, steel heat treatment principle and technology and metal materials, etc. This course is a combination course of theory and experiment, informative and comprehensive and practice. Meanwhile, this course is a course to guide students to enter the field of specialization, training students with the ability to apply own innovative ability, which plays a crucial role in the training of personnel in the aspect of materials. In the past, students encountered many problems when they were studying. For example, many new concepts and abstractions were difficult to understand, their knowledge of knowledge was disorderly, and their systematicness and logic were not strong and difficult to remember [6–8] Leading to the beginning of the course can keep up with the majority of students in the course of the beginning of learning difficulties, after the end of the course some students still do not know the main content of this course. Part of the reason are the nature of the course, mainly because students did not pre-learn, did not master the learning methods for this course, there is no self-learning ability; another reason is that teachers did not improve teaching methods according to the characteristics of this course and the status quo of student learning at present. There are teaching methods to improve, teacher-centered classroom teaching only emphasizes the imparting of knowledge, while ignoring the students' ability to accept, and always place the students in a passive position, thus losing their interest in learning the course.

With the rapid development of information technology, it has provided conditions for the development of new learning methods. Promote the "Four Changes" of Teaching Reform in Metallography and Heat Treatment Course through Informatization: ① Transformation from predominance of teaching to learning-oriented ② transformation from a combination of general education to general education and professional education ③ From To classroom teaching mainly to the class, combination of extracurricular ④ From the results of evaluation mainly to the combination of results and process, the heart process evaluation. Effective teaching of information technology support is inseparable from the integration of a variety of factors, such as teaching methods, teaching content, teaching evaluation, technical tools. Teaching methods play an important role in teaching activities.

Teaching evaluation and classroom teaching activities are an indivisible organic whole [9]. A single result evaluation can not feedback the teaching process information, and it is difficult for teachers to monitor the dynamic changes of students in the teaching process. Teachers need to use a combination of procedural and evaluation of the results of a wide range of evaluation tools to fully examine the learning process of students for the regulation and improvement of classroom teaching. Fareed found that using instant evaluation methods such as Clicker interactive tools can enhance the interaction between teachers and students to facilitate the timely adjustment of teaching activities [10] TPACK theoretical framework proposed by Koegler and Mishra, emphasize the pedagogy, technology and disciplines The important role of content in the effective integration of information technology and teaching [11]. As early as 1998, Black & William pointed out that evaluation can effectively support learning, actively involve students in the evaluation process, and make students learn more actively. Focus on immediate assessment of classroom teachers can cultivate and stimulate student learning enthusiasm and self-confidence.

Thus, technology, teaching method and evaluation are three indispensable elements in teaching. Classroom teaching evaluation is an important part of classroom teaching and is based on quantitative or qualitative description of value judgments. The scientific evaluation system is an important guarantee to achieve the goal of the course. Teaching methods play an important role in the process of teaching activities, but also are key factors affecting the teaching quality.

2 APT Teaching Model Based on Evaluation

Learning activities based on ability cultivation in the 21st century are important components in cultivating students' ability of critical thinking and problem solving, effective communication, collaboration and innovation. Students who become qualified in the 21st century are currently educated major mission. Effective teaching in the information environment can not be separated from the depth integration of evaluation, teaching methods and information technology. As shown in Fig. 1, APT teaching model highlights the importance of teaching evaluation [12–15], advocating information-based teaching students under the environment, the openness of teaching space.

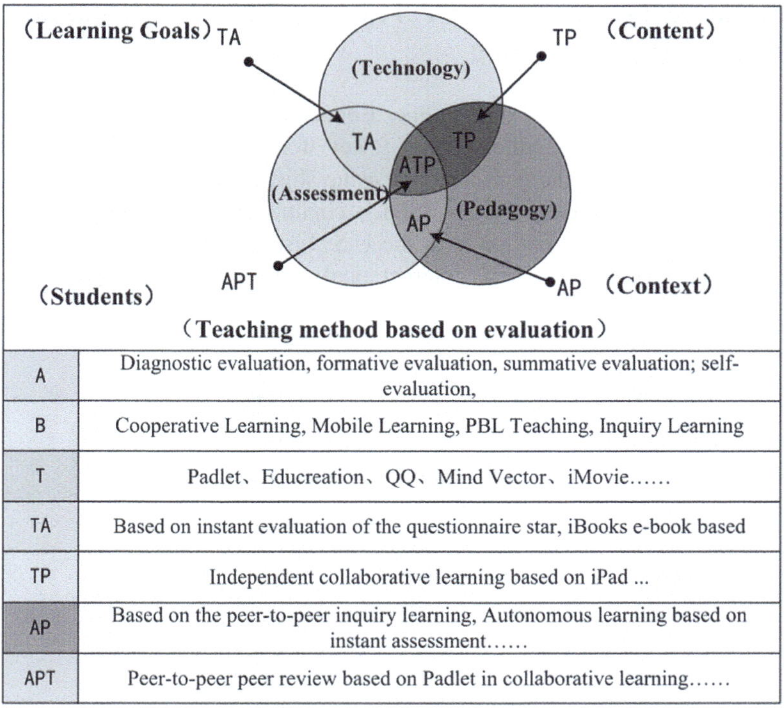

A	Diagnostic evaluation, formative evaluation, summative evaluation; self-evaluation,
B	Cooperative Learning, Mobile Learning, PBL Teaching, Inquiry Learning
T	Padlet、Educreation、QQ、Mind Vector、iMovie......
TA	Based on instant evaluation of the questionnaire star, iBooks e-book based
TP	Independent collaborative learning based on iPad ...
AP	Based on the peer-to-peer inquiry learning, Autonomous learning based on instant assessment......
APT	Peer-to-peer peer review based on Padlet in collaborative learning......

Fig. 1. ATP teaching model

As shown in Fig. 1, the model advocates the design of a scientific and multi-dimensional evaluation system based on in-depth analysis of the characteristics of learners and the content of teaching contents. It not only pays great attention to summative evaluation but also pays more attention to procedural evaluation. After the evaluation, the comprehensive use of tests, gage, teacher observation, learning contract, real-time evaluation, electronic portfolio, peer assessment and other evaluation tools; Meanwhile, a variety of teaching should be carried out under the information environment, including task-driven Type teaching, research teaching, connected teaching, guided teaching, game teaching, role play, collaborative learning and other teaching methods; make full use of a variety of hardware and software tools, such as whiteboard, electronic double board, iPad and other hardware Environment, and forums, concept maps, office tools, e-mail and APP software. Through the scientific and reasonable integration of evaluation methods, teaching methods and technical tools, students are transformed into independent, cooperative, inquiry and ubiquitous learning styles to create Efficient classroom teaching, students' knowledge acquisition, sharing, construction, innovation ability, promotion Health innovation and cooperation and active learning ability.

3 Innovative Teaching of APT Teaching Model to Promote Students' Deep Learning

《2017 New Media Alliance China Higher Education Technology Outlook: Horizon Project Regional Report》 predicts one of 9 key trends in China's higher education technology adoption over the next five years: the shift from higher education to deep learning. The Deep Learning Project (SDL), conducted by the William and Flora Hewlett Foundation in cooperation with the U.S. Institute, divides deep learning into three dimensions: cognitive area, interpersonal field personal and personal area (Table 1).

Table 1. The alpha-coefficient of the questionnaire.

Cognitive area	Master core discipline knowledge
	Critical thinking and complex problem solving
Interpersonal field	Teamwork
	Communicate effectively
Personal area	Learn to learn
	Learn perseverance

Deep learning, as opposed to surface learning, aims to develop students' higher-order thinking skills and to guide students to finish the changes from surface learning such as memorization, understanding and application to deep cognitive process, such as analysis, evaluation and creation, etc. And train students critical thinking, innovative ability, problem solving ability, improve students' interest and motivation, investment, etc., and promote students' learning in the field of cognitive, ability and emotional attitude, As shown in Fig. 2.

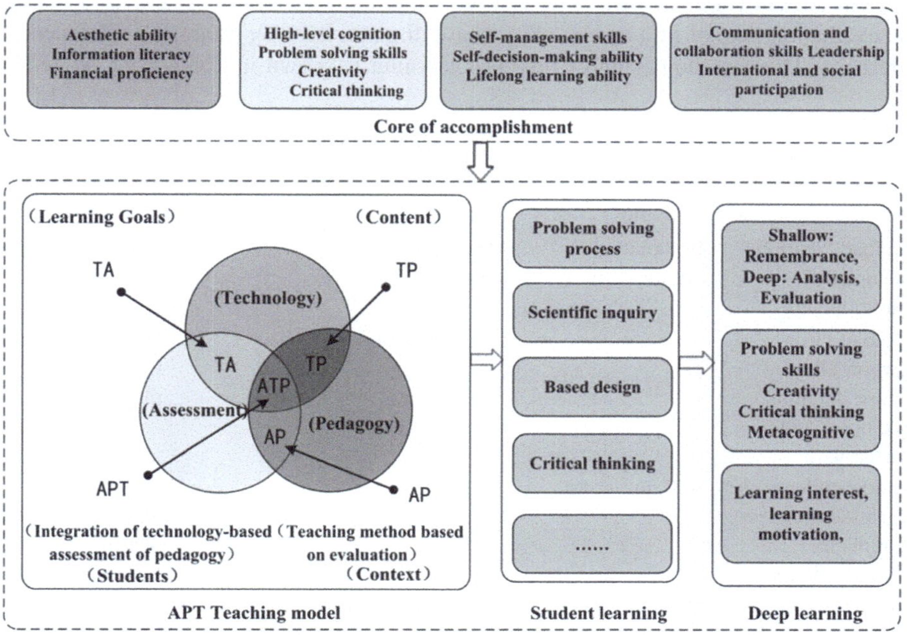

Fig. 2. APT promote student learning in depth model

4 Application of ATP Teaching Model in Metallography and Heat Treatment Courses

Based on "Questionnaire Star", Knowledge Construction Worksheet, "Micro-aided Teaching" Learning Platform and Clicker Feedback Tool, taken the phase diagram of "iron and carbon alloy phase diagram" in the course of "Metals and Heat Treatment" for example, the teaching process consists of three parts: Pre-class learning, classroom teaching and after-school reflection, teaching design.

4.1 Study Before Class

Pre-lesson learning begins with the analysis of learner characteristics. Teachers use the Questionnaire star to upload a questionnaire and analyze basic knowledge of the students, available knowledge, motivation, learning style and so on. According to the characteristics of students' study and the contents of this chapter, teachers design the pre-course list of "Iron-carbon alloy phase diagram" together with learning resources and upload them to the "Micro-teaching and Learning" platform resource section. Students prepare and submit homework according to the pre- Students preview the situation, at the same time, teachers guide students to ask questions through the forum of platform and collect prevalent teaching problems. Before class, middle school students choose research topics in the form of small groups, put forward their research goals and problems, and finally write research programs. In this process, teachers through the network platform and the learning groups are closely linked, and upload the evaluation plan of iron carbon alloy phase diagram learning program for learners to reference. The specific design of pre-class learning is shown in Table 2.

Table 2. Learning design before class

Teacher activities	Student Activities	Evaluation method	Teaching method	Technical tools
Upload "learning status quo" questionnaire	Complete the questionnaire	Questionnaire analysis		"Questionnaire Star"
Upload "iron carbon alloy phase diagram" pre-order and materials		Job evaluation		"Micro-teaching aid" platform
Guide students in discussion forums to preview doubts	Ask questions	Forum interaction		"Micro-teaching aid" platform
Instruct various groups to choose research tasks, design iron carbon phase diagram research programs, and upload evaluation rules	In the group as a unit, the design method of iron and carbon-phase drawing method, analysis of iron-carbon alloy crystallization process		Research teaching, Cooperative learning	"Micro-teaching aid" platform

(1) Study guide

① Project Title: Iron-carbon alloy phase diagram.
② Achieve the goal: complete the task of "independent learning task list" to master the iron carbon alloy phase diagram by watching the teaching video, reading teaching materials, analysis of given learning materials, Learning Methods and Recommendations:
③ Learning method and suggestion: Learn iron carbon alloy phase diagram based on three basic phase diagrams; It is suggested that the basic phase and phase diagrams of iron-carbon alloys be understood in connection with allotropic transformation.
④ Classroom learning form notice: a, analysis of the typical iron-carbon alloy crystallization process in the group; communicate painting techniques of Iron carbon alloy phase diagram with each other in the group. b, class promotion

job (paint iron carbon alloy phase diagram without any reference). c, by consulting the literature data, each group summed up the application of a carbon-carbon alloy in the class exchange.

(2) Learning tasks: answer the following questions

① What are the basic iron-carbon alloy phase?
② What are the basic organization of iron-carbon alloy? What is the relationship with the basic phase?
③ How to build Iron-carbon alloy phase diagram? How many steps?
④ What is the relationship between allotropic transformation of pure iron and the basic phase of iron-carbon alloy?

(3) Confusion and advice: This content is filled out by the students after their own study.
Learning resources include textbooks, reference books, essays, video resources, teaching video which is the focus of learning resources. Teaching video production process includes analysis of teaching objects and capabilities, finishing courseware, pictures, audio, video files and production of the script, marked each segment of the video presentation, production and distribution of video, according to the views and suggestions of students to modify the teaching video.

4.2 Classroom Teaching

APT teaching model advocates a student-centered teaching of this class starting from the teaching, and gradually into the teaching content. The teacher presents the learner with the problems in the preview in the order of the teaching contents. The students discuss and answer the questions. The teacher determines the next teaching activity based on the answer. After the explanation of the problem is completed, the teacher throws different kinds of practical engineering application cases to guide the students to respond. Finally, the teacher organizes the students to report the work done in the pre-class study (reflected in the work of knowledge construction) as a group and organize the students to evaluate each other. Evaluation and promotion are advocated in this teaching.

4.3 Reflections After Class

After class teaching, teachers guide students to self-reflection, and write a reflection report submitted to the "micro-teaching aid" platform. Finally, based on student electronic files, the group reported the situation and student testing, teachers analyze the teaching effectiveness and reflect classroom teaching.

5 Application of ATP Teaching Model in Metallography and Heat Treatment Courses

(1) Under the teaching environment based on APT teaching model, there is a significant difference between students' academic performance and the traditional multimedia classroom. Before the beginning of the class teaching, in order to

ensure that students in the control and experimental groups had the same level of competency, teachers conducted a pretest of students in both classes. After the implementation of the teaching, teachers once again post-test students to compare the two grades of students' academic performance changes. And through the independent sample T test in SPSS, the two classes were analyzed whether there are significant differences before and after the test results, the specific results are shown in Table 3.

Table 3. Comparison of the results of the study

Variable	Group	Student class	Sample size	Average value	Standard deviation	t値
Front side	Test group	Material 1 class	58	7.51	1.61	1.52
	Control group	Material 2 classes	55	7.92	1.97	
Back side	Test group	Material 1 class	58	8.71	1.34	3.11
	Control group	Material 2 classes	55	7.87	1.96	

As shown in Table 3, in the front-test sectin, the average scores of students in experimental group and control group were 7.51 and 7.92 respectively, and the standard deviations were 1.61 and 1.97. The P-value of significance test of two independent samples was greater than 0.05, indicating that there are no significant differences between classes. In the post-test section, the average scores of students in experimental group and control group were 8.71 and 7.87 respectively, the standard deviations were 1.34 and 1.96. The significant P-value of T test in independent samples was less than 0.01, indicating that there were significant differences between the two classes, And the average score of experimental group are higher than the control group and the degree of dispersion is lower than that of the control group. That is, the learning effect of the experimental group is obviously better than that of the control group.

(2) The experimental group had higher cognitive load than the control group, and the appropriate cognitive load was beneficial to the improvement of students' academic performance.

Cognitive load is related to the way in which human beings solve their learning goals through their cognitive framework during the learning process. The cognitive load is measured from the two dimensions of mental stress and mental effort. The mental stress is related to the cognitive load caused by the amount of information presented to the students at the same time. Teaching based on APT may have an impact on students'cognitive load, However, a larger cognitive load is conducive to improving students' academic performance to a certain extent.

6 Research Conclusions and Discussion

Applying the teaching model of APT to the teaching of metallurgy and heat treatment under the mobile environment, this paper designs a teaching mode based on the teaching model of "Iron and Carbon" and compares the classroom teaching results by experimental teaching method with based on the APT Teaching model of classroom teaching results, the conclusions are as follows:

(1) Students in the mobile environment based on the APT teaching model have better academic performance than traditional multimedia environments. The comparison between pre-test and post-test shows that the average of pretest scores of experimental group (based on APT teaching model in mobile environment) is slightly lower than that of control group, and the standard deviation is slightly higher than that of control group. By the independent sample T test, There is no significant difference between the two groups and the level between two groups can be considered equivalent; by analyzing the test results found that the independent sample T test significant probability of less than 0.01, indicating significant differences between the two groups, and the experimental group was significantly better than the control group.

(2) The cognitive load of students based on APT teaching model in mobile environment is higher than that of traditional multimedia environment, but in a certain range, higher cognitive load is beneficial to the improvement of students' academic performance.

The research is still in the exploratory stage. There are still some problems in the teaching process of teachers under the APT environment, such as technical operation, classroom time control and teaching activities organization. The questionnaire data did not achieve the expected results. The practice of research has a preliminary validation of the "evaluation to promote learning" effectiveness. In the future teaching, how to further improve the integration of teaching evaluation, teaching methods and information technology, integrate the application of diverse teaching resources, and really return the class to the students still need further exploration and reflection.

Acknowledgment. This work is supported by Education and teaching research subject of Inner Mongolia university for nationalities (YB2019013, ZDA2019006, YB2019043).

References

1. Jiehui, H., Zhongjie, W.: MOOC-based college English flip classroom teaching model. Foreign Lang. Teach. **6**, 40–45 (2014)
2. Eberlein, E., Keller, U.: Hyperbolic distributions in finance. Bernoulli **1**(3), 281–299 (1995)
3. Fan, W.: Large-scale open network courses based on relevanceism (MOOC) and its learning support. J. Distance Educ. **30**(3), 31–36 (2012)
4. Wang, Y., Zhang, J., Zhang B.: Analysis and revelation of typical project characteristics of large-scale open network courses (MOOC). J. Distance Educ. (4), 67–75 (2013)

5. Liu, S., Pan, Z., Song, H.: Digital image watermarking method based on DCT and fractal encoding. IET Image Process. **11**(10), 815–821 (2017)
6. Liu, S., Pan, Z., Cheng, X.: A novel fast fractal image compression method based on distance clustering in high dimensional sphere surface. Fractals **25**(4), 1740004 (2017)
7. Liu, S.: Special issue on advanced fractal computing theorem and application. Fractals, 25(4) (2017)
8. Pan, Z., Liu, S., Fu, W.: A review of visual moving target tracking. Multimedia Tools Appl. **76**(16), 16989–17018 (2017)
9. Liu, S., Lu, M., Liu, G.: A novel distance metric: generalized relative entropy. Entropy **19** (6), 269 (2017)
10. Liu, S., Fu, W., He, L., et al.: Distribution of primary additional errors in fractal encoding method. Multimedia Tools Appl. **76**(4), 5787–5802 (2017)
11. Liu, S., Pan, Z., Fu, W., et al.: Fractal generation method based on asymptote family of generalized Mandelbrot set and its application. J. Nonlinear Sci. Appl. **10**(3), 1148–1161 (2017)
12. Liu, S., Cheng, X., Fu, W., et al.: Numeric characteristics of generalized M-set with its asymptote. Appl. Math. Comput. **243**, 767–774 (2014)
13. Liu, S., Cheng, X., Lan, C.: Fractal property of generalized M-set with rational number exponent. Appl. Math. Comput. **220**, 668–675 (2013)
14. Liu, S., Fu, W., Deng, H., et al.: Distributional Fractal Creating Algorithm in Parallel Environment. Int. J. Distrib. Sensor Networks (2013). https://doi.org/10.1155/2013/281707. SCI
15. Liu, S., Fu, W., Zhao, W.: A novel fusion method by static and moving facial capture. Math. Prob. Eng. (2013). https://doi.org/10.1155/2013/503924

Author Index

The manufacturer's authorised representative in the EU is Springer Nature Customer Service Centre GmbH, Europaplatz 3, 69115 Heidelberg, Germany. If you have any concerns regarding our products, please contact ProductSafety@springernature.com

Printed and bound by CPI Group (UK) Ltd, Croydon, CR0 4YY
30/09/2026
02225597-0019